Hellenistic Culture and Society

General Editors: Anthony W. Bulloch, Erich S. Gruen, A. A. Long, and Andrew F. Stewart

The Cynics

The Cynics

The Cynic Movement in Antiquity and Its Legacy

Edited by **R. Bracht Branham**
and **Marie-Odile Goulet-Cazé**

University of California Press
Berkeley / Los Angeles / London

University of California Press
Berkeley and Los Angeles, Calif.

University of California Press, Ltd.
London, England

© 1996 by
The Regents of the University of California

Library of Congress Cataloging-in-publication Data

The Cynics : the cynic movement in antiquity and
its legacy / edited
by R. Bracht Branham and Marie-Odile Goulet-Cazé.
     p.   cm. — (Hellenistic culture and society ; 23)
  Includes bibliographical references and index.
  ISBN 0-520-20449-2 (alk. paper)
  ISBN 0-520-21645-8 (pbk.: alk. paper)
   1. Cynics (Greek philosophy) I. Branham, Robert
Bracht.
II. Goulet-Cazé, Marie-Odile. II. Series.
B508.C94 1997
183'.4—dc20   96-20375
                                            CIP

Printed in the United States of America
9 8 7 6 5 4 3 2

Contents

Chaque siècle, et le nôtre surtout, auraient besoin d'un Diogène; mais la difficulté est de trouver des hommes qui aient le courage de l'être, et des hommes qui aient le courage de le souffrir.

—D'Alembert, *Essai sur la sociéte des gens de lettres* (1759)

Der moderne Diogenes. —Bevor man den Menschen sucht, muss man die Laterne gefunden haben. —Wird es die Laterne des Cynikers sein müssen?

—Nietzsche, *Menschliches, Allzumenschliches* 2.2.18 (1880)

Cynicism is merely the art of seeing things as they are instead of as they ought to be. —Oscar Wilde, *Sebastian Melmoth* (1904)

Acknowledgments

First and foremost, we wish to thank our contributors for making this collection possible. Second, we would like to thank those who read and commented on particular contributions, namely, Brad Inwood, Tony Long, Walter Reed, and David Sedley. Finally, we want to acknowledge the vital support given this project by the Centre National de la Recherche Scientifique, Emory University, and the Stanford Humanities Center.

Introduction

Cynicism was arguably the most original and influential branch of the Socratic tradition in antiquity, but not until D. R. Dudley's *A History of Cynicism from Diogenes to the Sixth Century A.D.* (London 1937) did the literary and philosophical significance of the Cynics begin to be acknowledged by modern scholars. Curiously, until about 1975, Cynicism still remained in the shadows, apparently condemned to marginalization outside the canonical philosophical schools. Since that time, however, there have been many studies of the subject,[1] and today Cynicism is finally being taken seriously as a philosophical and cultural movement of lasting interest. Léonce Paquet's French translation of

The editors are thankful to Michael Chase for translating those sections of the introduction originally written by M.-O. Goulet-Cazé in French.

1. We shall cite here, in chronological order, a few titles that may illustrate the breadth of the revival of Cynic studies in the last twenty years: Léonce Paquet, *Les cyniques grecs: Fragments et témoignages* (Montreal 1975; 2d ed. 1988; abridged ed. in the collection Livre de Poche [Paris 1992]); J. F. Kindstrand, *Bion of Borysthenes* (Uppsala 1976); E. N. O'Neil, *Teles the Cynic Teacher* (Missoula 1976); Margarethe Billerbeck, *Epiktet: Vom Kynismus* (Leiden 1978) and *Der Kyniker Demetrius* (Leiden 1979); Heinrich Niehues-Pröbsting, *Der Kynismus des Diogenes und der Begriff des Zynismus* (Munich 1979); Peter Sloterdijk, *Kritik der zynischen Vernunft* (Frankfurt 1983); G. Giannantoni, *Socraticorum Reliquiae,* 4 vols. (Naples 1983–85); T. Flynn, "Foucault as Parrhesiast: His Last Course at the Collège de France (1984)," in *Final Foucault,* ed. J. Bernauer and D. Rasmussen (Cambridge, Mass., 1988); M.-O. Goulet-Cazé, *L'ascèse cynique: Un commentaire de Diogène Laërce VI 70–71* (Paris 1986); J. Hammerstaedt, *Die Orakelkritik des Kynikers Oenomaos* (Frankfurt 1988); R. Bracht Branham, *Unruly Eloquence: Lucian and the Comedy of Traditions* (Cambridge, Mass., 1989); M. Onfray, *Cynismes* (Paris 1989); G. Giannantoni, *Socratis et Socraticorum Reliquiae,* Elenchos 18 (Naples 1990); A. Brancacci, *Oikeios logos: La filosofia del linguaggio di Antistene,* Elenchos 20 (Naples 1990); M. Billerbeck, *Die Kyniker in der modernen Forschung* (Amsterdam 1992); P. Marshall, *Demanding the Impossible: A History of Anarchism* (London 1992); J. Relihan, *Ancient Menippean Satire* (Baltimore 1993).

the major fragments—recently reprinted in the popular collection Livre de Poche—and the comprehensive edition of the ancient texts by Gabriele Giannantoni (1983–85; 2d ed. 1990) have made all the relevant evidence available. The fact that an international colloquium entitled "Ancient Cynicism and Its Influence" could be held in Paris in July 1991 testifies to the increasing interest that Cynic philosophy has aroused in recent years.[2] The present work also shares in this revival of interest for Diogenes and his followers and illustrates once again the fascination that the "Dogs" have continued to exert.

The title we have chosen—*The Cynics: The Cynic Movement in Antiquity and Its Legacy*—indicates the nature and breadth of our project. Our purpose is, on the one hand, to investigate ancient Cynic philosophy and literature in all its aspects, and, on the other, to sketch the main lines of its impact on Western culture from classical antiquity to the present, focusing on the domains of literary production and of ethical reflection. To be sure, the figure of Diogenes, with his staff, knapsack, and tattered cloak, may seem remote from us. Yet the Cynic movement not only lasted for almost a millennium in antiquity, but also generated a remarkable range of literary forms that would outlive classical culture. Menippean satire is probably the most familiar Cynic genre, but in antiquity Cynics were known for innovating forms of parody, satire, dialogue, diatribe, and aphorism. Yet, as Heinrich Niehues-Pröbsting and Daniel Kinney demonstrate so persuasively in their contributions to this volume, Cynicism was also a central philosophical concern for thinkers as different as the Renaissance Humanists, Wieland, Rousseau, Diderot, and Nietzsche—although, as we shall see, the distinction between Cynicism's literary and philosophical significance is often difficult to maintain.

The nature of the "movement" and its longevity call for some explanation. Cynicism was not a "school": Cynic philosophers did not give classes in a specific place, nor do we find among them any scholars succeeding each other at the head of an institution. Their philosophy was less a matter of classes or lectures than of mimesis—the imitation in action of exemplary figures. In other words, what we have here is best understood not as a school, but as a philosophical and even a cultural movement that, albeit highly diversified, remained faithful to Diogenes' example—to his way of life and philosophical principles as these were interpreted over the centuries. It is thus easy to understand that there are significant differences between Diogenes himself, whose target and audience was the highly cultured society of late classical Greece (in the fourth century B.C.), and those bands of Cynics who roamed the streets of Alexandria or Constantinople in the time of the Roman empire claiming him as their pa-

2. *Le cynisme ancien et ses prolongements: Actes du Colloque international du C.N.R.S.,* ed. M.-O. Goulet-Cazé and R. Goulet (Paris 1993). Several of the papers read at this conference have been turned into contributions to the present volume: namely those of Billerbeck, Branham, Goulet-Cazé, Griffin, Moles, and Niehues-Pröbsting. We thank the Presses Universitaires de France (Paris), which kindly granted permission to publish them.

tron and model. Modes of behavior and perceptions of problems necessarily evolved, as a function of differing contexts, in the six centuries separating the age of Diogenes from that of the emperor Julian (A.D. 332–61).

One of the advantages of a collection is that, unlike a monograph, it can—and should—embrace divergent perspectives. The diversity of the contributions to this collection is a deliberate response to the variegated character of "Cynicism" as it has emerged over time. To approach such a motley set of traditions with a single point of view or methodology would be to deny its variety and thereby to impoverish it; while the collection is generally arranged chronologically—Greek, Roman, Renaissance, modern—we open not with the question of origins, but with a salvo of synoptic examinations of the most influential figures and concepts of the movement; these serve in turn as leit-motifs for the entire collection—such as the significance of Diogenes and Crates for moral philosophy (Long), the radical Cynic critique of religion (Goulet-Cazé), and the central Cynic concepts of freedom (Branham) and cosmopolitanism (Moles). Once the nature of the movement has been sketched, we turn to consider possible precedents for Cynic ideology in classical and archaic Greek culture with comparative studies of proto-Cynic forms of discourse (Romm) and of the legendary "Cynic sage," Anacharsis of Scythia (Martin). When we then turn to consider a central figure of the third century B.C., the Cynicizing Stoic, Aristo of Chios (Porter), we are already involved in assessing the reception of Cynicism, a process that inevitably concerns us from the outset, given our sources, but that moves into the foreground of our account in the rest of the collection.

We approach the reception, or "legacy," of Cynicism as a long, discontinuous, and centrifugal cultural process, not as a series of autonomous thinkers engaged in a timeless conversation. Some of the most important aspects of the Roman reception of this very Greek tradition are addressed in the areas of philosophy (Billerbeck), education (Krueger), and Roman society (Griffin). We next explore the complex literary and philosophical transformations of Cynicism in the Christianized culture of the Renaissance (Matton, Relihan, Kinney), and the modern reevaluation of Cynicism that begins in the Enlightenment of the eighteenth century and persists into the present in the work of Niehues-Pröbsting (q.v. in this volume), Sloterdijk, Foucault, and others, a reevaluation to which we hope to contribute. We conclude our survey of the Cynics and their legacy with an illustrated essay on the visual representation of Cynics in antiquity and the Renaissance (Clay).

The central problem encountered by our contributors is that of evidence. The most influential works of Cynic literature—which had once been abundant—have disappeared, and we are left with only meager fragments cited by intermediaries, who, moreover, are sometimes hostile to the Cynics they cite: this is the case, for instance, with the Epicurean Philodemus (in the first century B.C.) and with some of the Church Fathers. Further, these fragments are not always easy to interpret, as is shown by a passage on law in Diogenes Laertius (6.72) that has already provoked extensive discussion.[3] Consequently, we must be extremely wary in deciphering certain passages that, at first sight, we have no particular reason to suspect, but that, nevertheless, may be misleading, deliberately or otherwise. This may be the case for several traditions reported in Book 6 of Diogenes Laertius, *Lives and Opinions of Famous Philosophers* (of the first half of the third century A.D.),[4] which, by positing the succession Socrates–Antisthenes–Diogenes–Crates–Zeno, attributed to Stoicism a Socratic pedigree by way of Cynicism. It is not impossible that, behind these texts, we can glimpse a thesis formulated after the fact, either by Stoics anxious for Socratic legitimacy or by authors of *Successions* in search of unambiguous lines of affiliation.

Consequently, the Cynics are known today not by their literary works, but by "sayings" (*apophthegmata* or *chreiai*) transmitted in ancient collections (*gnōmologia*) that were later drawn on by such authors as Diogenes Laertius. This fact alone justifies a cautious approach, since nothing guarantees the historicity of the tradition; indeed, some "sayings" are reported in more than one form or are attributed to more than one philosopher: at the most, we are justified in considering them to be part of the ancient dialogue provoked by the Dogs.

History of the Movement

Let us begin by recalling the origin of the word "Cynic"—literally, "Doglike." There are two competing etymologies. According to one, the word comes from the gymnasium where Antisthenes used to teach: that of the Cynosarges, dedicated to Heracles (who was to become a legendary proto-Cynic).[5] Exactly what the name "Cynosarges" means is itself far from clear: Is it "White [or "Quick"] Dog" or "Dog's Meat"? It is easy to imagine that such an etymology (making Antisthenes the first "dog") could have been fabricated after the fact, by analogy with the Stoa or the Academy, both of which are named after the places in Athens where their founders taught. The second etymology is far more plausible: it goes back to a joke that compared Diogenes (or Antisthenes) to a dog, presumably because his mode of life seemed doglike—that is, "Cynic." Accordingly, the Cynics were renowned not only for being frank and direct (e.g., for "barking" and "wagging their tails"), or for

---

3. See, for example, M. Schofield, *The Stoic Idea of the City* (Cambridge 1991), appendixes.

4. Cf. M.-O. Goulet-Cazé, "Le livre VI de Diogène Laërce: Analyse de sa structure et réflexions méthodologiques," *ANRW* 2.36.6 (Berlin 1992) 3880–4048.

5. The Cynosarges was reserved for νόθοι (the offspring of illegitimate unions). On this gymnasium, see the archaeological study by M.-F. Billot, "Antisthène et le Cynosarges dans l'Athènes des Vᵉ et IVᵉ siècles," in Goulet-Cazé and Goulet (above, n. 2) 69–116; ead., "Le Cynosarges: Histoire, mythes et archéologie," in *Dictionnaire des philosophes antiques,* ed. R. Goulet, vol. 2, *Babélyca d'Argos à Dyscolius* (Paris 1994) 917–66.

their skill at distinguishing between friends and enemies (in their case, those capable of philosophizing vs. those who were not), but, above all, for their way of living in public like dogs, "shamelessly indifferent" to the most entrenched social norms. Their deliberate rejection of shame, the cornerstone of traditional Greek morality, authorized them to engage in modes of life that scandalized their society but that they regarded as "natural." Their radical idea of freedom— "to use any place for any purpose" (Diogenes Laertius 6.22)—made the insulting canine epithet so appropriate to our philosophers that they defiantly claimed it as a metaphor for their novel philosophical stance.[6] Or so the story goes.

It is both convenient and historically accurate to distinguish two phases of the movement: (1) early Cynicism (of the fourth to third century B.C.), and (2) its reception in the Roman empire (from the first century A.D. to late antiquity). These two great currents were separated by what our evidence suggests was a decline of Cynicism during the second and first centuries B.C.[7] The first of these two phases took place in Greece, whereas the second had as its background the great cities of the Roman empire: Rome, Alexandria, and Constantinople. The first was based on a radically individualistic philosophy advocated by charismatic spokesmen, whereas the second, though not lacking in memorable personalities—one thinks, for example, of Demetrius, Demonax, or Peregrinus Proteus—evolved toward a collective philosophical praxis that gradually made Cynicism the preeminent popular philosophy of the Roman empire.

Why Did Cynicism First Appear in Greece in the Fourth (or Fifth) Century B.C. and Reappear at the Beginning of the Roman Empire?

At the beginning of the Hellenistic period (ca. 323–31 B.C.), Greek society enjoyed the refinements and luxury of a highly developed civilization, yet social inequalities were always widespread. It is often asserted, and with some justification, that with the decline of the polis (or city-state) as the comprehensive center of social life, each individual felt compelled to secure his own happiness in a world in which it was not uncommon to be sent into exile, taken prisoner by pirates, or sold into slavery, according to the whims of Fortune (*Tukhē*). From this point of view, Cynicism was intended as a response to this quest for happiness, by which the Greeks of this uncertain time were almost obsessed. Consequently, it offered Hellenistic society a systematic moral practice (*tekhnē*) capable of guiding the individual toward happiness and delivering him from anguish.

Of course, such an account does not "explain" why Cynicism arose when it

---

6. The most common way to designate a Cynic philosopher in Greek is simply the word "dog" (*kuōn*).

7. For more details on the fate of Cynicism in the second and first centuries B.C., see M.-O. Goulet-Cazé, "Le cynisme à l'époque impériale," *ANRW* 2.36.4 (Berlin 1990) 2723–24, and below note 34.

did, since a similar line of reasoning could be invoked to "explain" the emergence in the fourth century B.C. of other philosophies that sought to define the sufficient conditions of human happiness, such as Stoicism or Epicureanism (or the philosophy of Plato or Aristotle, for that matter). The reasons why a new ideology emerges in a particular time and place and becomes influential are complex and obscure. We offer this account as the conventional one, in lieu of a more persuasive alternative.[8] A complete account would have to consider many other factors—demographic, social, and cultural—beyond the scope of this introduction. It would also need to consider that the Cynics themselves were agents of the historic changes of the fourth century, as we can see in the essay by Goulet-Cazé on religion and the early Cynics in this volume.

It is no less difficult to explain the revival of Cynicism in the early Roman empire. In this society, *gravitas* still had a meaning; Cynic cosmopolitanism, as reconstructed in John Moles's contribution, did not readily cohere with the imperial assumptions of an ancient empire, and the extreme asceticism and subversive antics of our philosophers shocked more than a few Roman plutocrats. But in the midst of its prosperity the teeming metropolis of Rome offered its ruling elites wealth and luxury on such a scale that, as in late classical Athens, there was a calling for moralists and satirists who would denounce such excesses. It is not surprising, then, that the Cynics' exhortations to return to an original simplicity and to a state of nature prior to all civilization found attentive audiences at Rome.

If, moreover, Cynicism is today attracting a lively interest once again, and a writer like Sloterdijk meets with phenomenal success when he calls upon his contemporaries to abandon modern "cynicism" (*Zynismus*) in order to return to ancient "Cynicism" (*Kynismus*),[9] is it not because our sophisticated civilization, invaded by gadgets and enslaved to appearances, craves to learn all over again the meaning of such terms as "happiness," "simplicity," "freedom," and "autonomy"?

The Early Cynics

Throughout antiquity Antisthenes (ca. 445–after 366 B.C.) was considered the founder of Cynicism. The son of an Athenian also named Antisthenes and of a Thracian woman, he first studied rhetoric under the great rhetorician Gorgias (D.L. 6.1–2) and became a rhetor himself before turning into an assiduous companion of Socrates; thanks to Plato,[10] moreover, we know that he was one of the few followers present at Socrates' death. Antisthenes was also the author

---

8. For criticisms of the "crisis" view of Hellenistic philosophy, see A.A. Long, "Hellenistic Ethics and Philosophical Power," in *Hellenistic History and Culture,* ed. P. Green (Berkeley and Los Angeles 1993) 140; *Hellenistic Philosophy* (Berkeley and Los Angeles 1986) 2–4.

9. P. Sloterdijk, *Kritik der zynischen Vernunft* (Frankfurt 1983).

10. Plato, *Phaedo* 59b (= V A 20 G.).

of an extensive literary oeuvre. Diogenes Laertius quotes an impressive catalogue of his works, which contains more than seventy titles divided into ten "tomes." Unlike later Cynics, Antisthenes wrote on rhetoric and logic,[11] as well as on ethical, political, and literary topics.

Whether or not he was the first to be called "the Dog," [12] it is probably more accurate to see Antisthenes as an important forerunner of the movement (rather than a founder) whose teachings, whether conveyed personally, by oral tradition, or by his writings, provided Diogenes' practice with some basis in theory. Particularly relevant would be his beliefs that virtue "is a matter of deeds and does not need lots of discourses and learning" and that it is sufficient for happiness "since happiness requires nothing else except the strength of a Socrates." [13] If, as many believe, Xenophon follows Antisthenes in his representation of Socrates, then Antisthenes must have laid particular stress on Socrates' "self-mastery" (*egkrateia*). In his *Symposium* (4.34–44), Xenophon represents Antisthenes as discounting the importance of wealth for happiness and actually praising poverty, which certainly resonates with Cynicism. Diogenes Laertius (6.15) says that Antisthenes provided the model for Crates' "self-mastery" and Diogenes' "imperturbability" (*apatheia*), which he learned by imitating Socrates (6.2; V A 12 G.), thereby inaugurating the Cynic way of life.

Whatever his relationship to Antisthenes, Diogenes of Sinope (ca. 412/403–324/321 B.C.) was the paradigmatic Cynic of antiquity. While Diogenes was a historical figure, he quickly became a literary character—probably in his own lost works; certainly in those of others. Hence, his life, lost writings, and oral teachings are intertwined in a tradition of at least two strands: a biographical strand, transmitted by Diogenes Laertius's *Lives and Opinions of Famous Philosophers,* that is itself a collage of literary and oral traditions about the Cynic, the historicity of which is always problematic; and the more overtly literary representation of Diogenes by writers of the empire such as Lucian and Dio Chrysostom. "Diogenes" is, therefore, always already in the process of reception.[14] We lack the kind of extensive contemporary evidence for him that we have, for example, for Socrates in Plato and Xenophon.

Critical assessment of the biographical tradition is more than usually important in Diogenes' case, since his thought is transmitted to us primarily in the form of pointed anecdotes and aphorisms about his life. According to Diogenes Laertius,[15] Diogenes was the son of the banker Hicesias and was exiled from Sinope (on the southern coast of the Black Sea) for defacing the city's coins.

---

11. Antisthenes was the first to define the λόγος; he held that there was only one predicate for each subject, which allowed the formulation only of judgments of identity and excluded all attributive judgments. He also upheld the impossibility of contradiction and even of uttering falsehoods.

12. See Appendix B, "Who Was the First Dog?"

13. D.L. 6.11: V A 134 G.

14. As Niehues-Pröbsting observes (above, n. 1: 17).

15. D.L. 6.20–21: V B 2 G.

"Defacing the currency"—the reason for the philosopher's exile—was to become a central metaphor for Diogenes' philosophical activity: driving out the counterfeit coin of conventional wisdom to make room for the authentic Cynic life. Surprisingly, numismatic evidence discovered in this century appears to confirm the story of Diogenes' exile, but that may be the only trustworthy part of the biography. The tradition (in Diogenes Laertius) also claims that (1) Diogenes studied with Antisthenes;[16] (2) that he discovered his vocation ("defacing the currency") by consulting an oracle;[17] and (3) that he was sold into slavery and spent the rest of his life as a private tutor to his master's children.[18] The first claim may be chronologically impossible (and may have been fabricated by Stoics eager to give their school a Socratic pedigree via the Cynics). The second claim is suspiciously reminiscent of similar stories told of Socrates and of Zeno of Citium, the founder of Stoicism. The third is incompatible with the tradition that Diogenes grew old spending his summers in Corinth and his winters in Athens living in his pithos, a large wine jar (Dio Chrysostom, *Or.* 6.1–3). In all probability, both the second and third claims are based on literary works by or about Diogenes that were later treated biographically. This kind of "evidence" is characteristic of the tradition. There are three versions, for example, of how Diogenes died, reflecting both hostile and sympathetic views of the philosopher (D.L. 6.76–79).

Similarly, there are several conflicting versions of Diogenes' literary activity in Diogenes Laertius. Two Hellenistic authorities, Satyrus and Sosicrates, reportedly deny that Diogenes left anything in writing. Nevertheless, Diogenes Laertius records two lists of works attributed to him. The first consists of thirteen dialogues (including a *Republic*), some epistles, and seven tragedies. A second list, transmitted by Sotion and probably of Stoic origin, consists of twelve dialogues (eight of which are absent from the first list), some letters, and sayings (*chreiai*). The second list, therefore, implicitly denies the authenticity of Diogenes' *Republic* and of his tragedies.[19]

But the confused state of the evidence need not prevent us from evaluating Diogenes' philosophical significance, since that significance was as much a product of the manifold traditions purporting to represent him as it was of the facts of his life, of which we know few. The central ideas of Diogenes' Cynicism are: (1) nature provides an ethical norm observable in animals and inferable by cross-cultural comparisons; (2) since contemporary Greek society (and

---

16. D.L. 6.21: V B 19 G.
17. D.L. 6.20: V B 2 G.
18. D.L. 6.30–32, 74: V B 70–80 G.
19. For a persuasive analysis of what Diogenes' "tragedies" would have been like, see K. Döring, " 'Spielereien, mit verdecktem Ernst vermischt': Unterhaltsame Formen literarischer Wissensvermittlung bei Diogenes von Sinope und den frühen Kynikern," in *Vermittlung und Tradierung von Wissen in der griechischen Kultur,* ed. W. Kullmann and J. Althof (Tübingen 1993) 337–52.

by implication any existing society) is at odds with nature, its most fundamental values (e.g., in religion, politics, ethics, etc.) are not only false but counterproductive; (3) human beings can realize their nature and, hence, their happiness only by engaging in a rigorous discipline (*askēsis*) of corporeal training and exemplary acts meant to prepare them for the actual conditions of human life—all the ills that mortal flesh is heir to; (4) the goal of Cynic "discipline" (*askēsis*) is to promote the central attributes of a happy life, freedom and self-sufficiency (*autarkeia*); (5) while Cynic freedom is "negative" in Isaiah Berlin's sense—"freedom from" rather than "freedom to" [20]—it is also active, as expressed in the metaphor of "defacing" tradition (by parody and satire) and in provocative acts of free speech meant to subvert existing authorities (e.g., Plato, Alexander the Great, et al.).

All these points find support in the anecdotes about Diogenes, but in summary form the daring, paradoxical quality of his experiment and the singular sense of humor that informs it are lost.[21] Diogenes' unconditional pursuit of happiness led him to challenge the most fundamental ideas and taboos of Greek civilization and to valorize nature as a greater source of moral insight than custom or the existing philosophical schools. While it is often said that Diogenes advocated "life according to nature," this formula, as we shall see, raises as many questions as it answers.[22]

Plato's famous characterization of Diogenes as "Socrates gone mad" (D.L. 6.43) encapsulates some of the most important questions posed by the Cynic tradition: In what respects is Cynicism continuous with the Socratic tradition of moral philosophy, and in what respects is it a reaction against that tradition's distinctive intellectualism and attachment to the classical polis? The image of a "mad Socrates" calling us "back to nature" and seeking to redefine what it means to be human without an appeal to religion captures both the originality and the deeply ambiguous character of Cynicism, qualities that gave it and its founders (particularly Diogenes and Menippus) a rich literary and philosophical life after antiquity.

The most influential Cynic in antiquity after Diogenes was Crates of Thebes (ca. 368/365–288/285 B.C.),[23] a wealthy landowner, and therefore at the opposite end of the social spectrum from a poor exile like Diogenes. (He was the brother of the Megarian philosopher Pasicles, a student of Euclid of Megara.)

---

20. I. Berlin, "Two Concepts of Liberty," in *Four Essays on Liberty* (Oxford 1979) 131.

21. It is often suggested that Diogenes (and the Cynic tradition generally) are lacking in arguments, but this is clearly untrue: the tradition abounds in inductive and deductive arguments in rhetorical form, i.e., in examples and enthymemes.

22. See Branham's essay in this volume.

23. In addition to Crates, tradition mentions the names of several of Diogenes' disciples: Onesicritus of Aegina and his two sons, Androsthenes and Philiscus; and a second Onesicritus (of Aegina or Astypalaea) who was helmsman of Alexander's ship during the latter's expedition to India. Others included Monimus of Syracuse; Menander, nicknamed "Oakwood"; Hegesias, nicknamed "Dog Collar"; the statesman Phocion "the Good"; and Stilpo of Megara.

He was a hunchback, and several anecdotes refer to his comic appearance (D.L. 6.91). He married Hipparchia of Maronea, who (along with her brother Metrocles) became a practicing Cynic and, as such, the most famous female philosopher of antiquity. Their Cynic marriage (*kunogamia*), based only on mutual consent, was consistent with Diogenes' views but radically at odds with Greek custom.[24] The tradition holds that Hipparchia adopted the simple Cynic garb of Diogenes—a rough cloak (without a chiton), knapsack, and staff—and lived on equal terms with her husband, attending events usually reserved for men and successfully defending her decision to pursue philosophy instead of weaving.[25] Crates and Hipparchia were also notorious for living and sleeping together in public places, Cynically indifferent to shame and public opinion.[26] It was Crates who described the fruits of philosophy as "a quart of beans and to care for naught." [27]

However Crates came to know Diogenes, his life was a remarkable application of the Cynic's principles. He clearly regarded himself as a follower, calling himself a "fellow citizen of Diogenes." [28] There are several (probably fictitious) accounts of how Crates became a Cynic, which revolve around the remarkable fact that he evidently sold all his possessions and gave the proceeds to his fellow citizens, thereby embracing poverty, as had Diogenes (D.L. 6.87). Crates died in old age and was buried in Boeotia. In contrast to Diogenes with his combative style and acerbic tongue, Crates was remembered as a benevolent figure and, thanks to his role as arbiter of family quarrels, actually revered as a household deity at Athens.[29] But his fragments are clearly informed by a satiric (or seriocomic) perspective: "He used to say that we should study philosophy until we see in generals nothing but donkey drivers" (D.L. 6.82).

Crates was one of the most influential literary figures of the fourth century, and his writings did much to disseminate Cynic ideology and establish parody as a distinctly Cynic mode of "defacing" tradition. His oeuvre is notable both for its originality and for its variety. We know he composed "tragedies," elegies, epistles, and parodies such as his poem in hexameters entitled *Pēra* (Knapsack), a hymn to Frugality, a *Praise of the Lentil,* and an *Ephēmerides* (Diary).

In addition to his wife Hipparchia and his brother Pasicles, Crates' pupils include his brother-in-law Metrocles, who was probably the first to collect and publish Cynic "sayings" (*chreiai*), and Monimus of Syracuse, whose

24. D.L. 6.72: V B 353 G.
25. D.L. 6.98: V I 1 G. The idea that "virtue" (*aretē*) is essentially the same for men and women goes back to Plato's *Meno* and *Republic* as well as to Antisthenes (D.L. 6.12).
26. Cf. V H 20–25 G.
27. D.L. 6.86: V H 83 G.
28. He is also said to be the pupil of Bryson of Achaea (D.L. 6.85) and of Stilpo (Seneca, *Ep.* 1.10).
29. Apuleius, *Florida* 22: V H 18 G.

"trifles [*paignia*] blended with covert seriousness" were early examples of the "seriocomic" style—a hallmark of Cynic literature associated particularly with Crates and his followers.[30]

Menippus (of the first half of the third century B.C.) is the most famous Cynic of antiquity after Antisthenes, Diogenes, and Crates. He is said to have been a pupil of Crates. The unreliable biographical tradition depicts him as a Phoenician slave who acquired his freedom by begging or usury and hanged himself when his business failed. Be that as it may, Menippus is among the most influential of Hellenistic authors. He is the only Cynic expressly called *spoudogeloios* ("seriocomic") in antiquity (Strabo 16.2.29, C 759), and, as the name indicates, he is credited with the invention of Menippean satire, a form that parodied both myth and philosophy. Diogenes Laertius attributes thirteen books to Menippus, including a *Necyia.* The imitations and adaptions of his work by Varro (116–26 B.C.) and Lucian (in the *Icaromenippus,* the *Menippus,* and the *Dialogues of the Dead*) gave Menippean forms a long and influential afterlife in antiquity and the Renaissance, making Cynicism one of the primary sources of satiric literature in Europe. "Menippus" also became a literary character in his own right, particularly popular with Renaissance neo-Latin authors (see Relihan in this volume).

Bion of Borysthenes (ca. 335–245 B.C.) also played an important role in early Cynicism, especially in the domain of literature. Tradition holds that he was sold into slavery as a boy but was bought by a rhetorician and received a rhetorical education. Later, he evidently received an eclectic education in philosophy at Athens: he studied with the Academics (Xenocrates and Crates), with the Cynics, the Cyrenaics, and finally, the Peripatetics. Bion probably originated the literary form of the diatribe—an argumentative monologue with imagined interlocutors that was an important model for satirists and essayists of the empire. Because Bion's Cynicism seems less radical and more opportunistic than that of Diogenes, it has sometimes been characterized as a "hedonizing Cynicism."[31] References in Horace and other writers suggest an eclectic thinker with remarkable literary talents, as do his witty fragments.

In this context it is worth mentioning Teles (*fl.* ca. 235 B.C.), a teacher and moralist who quotes extensively from such philosophers as Diogenes, Crates, Metrocles, Stilpo, and Bion, his favorite authority and model. The surviving excerpts of his *Diatribes*—seven fragments transmitted by Stobaeus (of the fifth century A.D.), who quotes them from the epitome of a certain Theodo-

---

30. See Demetrius, *De Elocutione* 170: V H 66 G.

31. So G. A. Gerhard, "Zur Legende vom Kyniker Diogenes," *Archiv für Religionswissenschaft* 15 (1912) 388–408. Contrast Kindstrand in *Bion of Borysthenes* (66–67), who maintains that the original Cynicism was influenced by the eudaemonist asceticism of Socrates, and that Bion did not, therefore, inaugurate a new form of Cynicism, since it was already present at the beginning.

rus—are the earliest examples we possess of the influential tradition of the Cynic diatribe.

In the works of Cercidas of Megalopolis (ca. 290–220 B.C.)—the last important early Cynic—Cynicism takes a surprising political turn. Cercidas was unusual for a Cynic in being a soldier, politician, and lawmaker as well as a poet. He is best known for his *Meliambi* (written in the Doric dialect), in which he uses a lyric form to mount a serious Cynic critique of contemporary politics.[32]

Here we have given only a brief overview of the early Cynics, concentrating upon a few important figures. There were others, but for us they are little more than names.[33] Also noteworthy in this context are early Stoics whose thought developed out of a dialogue with Cynicism, including the school's founder, Zeno of Citium (ca. 332–261 B.C.), who was converted to Cynicism by Crates before developing his own system, and his influential pupil Aristo of Chios (see Porter in this volume). We hope this brief survey will at least serve the purpose of underlining the crucial importance of the literary activity of the early Cynics and suggest the sources of the influence and authority they came to exert. Today, unfortunately, the fragments of their lost works can give us only a tantalizing glimpse of what this literature was really like.

The Reception of Cynicism in the Roman Empire

Whatever the causes of its apparent decline between Cercidas (ca. 290–220 B.C.) and Demetrius (of the first century A.D.),[34] when Cynicism reemerges

---

32. The biographical tradition never gathers together all of Cercidas's functions into one notice, with the exception of the late source Stephanus of Byzantium (sixth century A.D.). The belief that Cercidas was a Cynic poet, however, is based on papyrological evidence (a subscription in *POxy.* 1082, discovered in 1906: Κερκίδα κυνὸς μελιάμβοι). Cercidas's involvement in political life does not, to be sure, harmonize very well with the antipolitical attitude generally adopted by the Cynics. Nevertheless, the themes of the meliambs that have come down contain nothing that contradicts the hypothesis of a Cynic Cercidas. For reservations on this point, see J.L. López Cruces, *Les Méliambes de Cercidas de Mégalopolis: Politique et tradition littéraire* (Amsterdam 1995), esp. 52–63. Two collections of poetry are attributed to Cercidas: the *Iambs,* only one verse of which is preserved, and the *Meliambs.* Cercidas may also be the author of a *Moral Anthology,* if two texts written in iambs and transmitted by three papyri of the second century are really by him.

33. See Appendix A, "A Comprehensive Catalogue of Known Cynic Philosophers."

34. This apparent decline may represent the state of our evidence rather than historical fact. J. Moles, "*Honestius Quam Ambitiosus:* An Exploration of the Cynic's Attitude to Moral Corruption in His Fellow Men," *JHS* 103 (1983) 103–23, argues persuasively that Cynicism did in fact continue to exist in the last two centuries B.C. (p. 122). For the reception of Cynicism in the empire, see M. Billerbeck, "La réception du cynisme à Rome," *L'Antiquité Classique* 51 (1982) 151–73; M.-O. Goulet-Cazé, "Le cynisme à l'époque impériale," *ANRW* 2.36.4 (Berlin 1990) 2720–2833. For Demetrius, see Moles (as above); J.F. Kindstrand, "Demetrius the Cynic," *Philologus* 124 (1980) 83–98; M. Billerbeck, *Der Kyniker Demetrius: Ein Beitrag zur Geschichte der frühkaiserzeitlichen Popularphilosophie,* Philosophia Antiqua 36 (Leiden 1979).

in the Roman empire, it has changed, as has the world. In a series of confrontations under Nero, Vespasian, and Domitian, Roman aristocrats with republican sympathies were put to death, and the philosophers associated with them—both Stoics and Cynics—were banished from Rome. The best-known Cynic of this period, Demetrius, a friend and hero of the philosopher Seneca, is a conspicuous example of Cynic involvement in the "philosophical opposition" to the emperor. He is said by Tacitus (*Ann.* 16.34–35) to have been present at the suicide of one of Nero's most esteemed and influential opponents, Thrasea Paetus. Demetrius was evidently driven from Rome by Nero and returned under Galba only to be banished to an island by Vespasian, whereafter he is not heard of again (Dio Cassius 65.13).[35] We also hear of Cynics' getting flogged and beheaded under Vespasian (for publicly criticizing the proposed marriage of the emperor's son Titus to the Jewish princess Berenice: D.C. 65.15).[36] The final attempts to suppress the philosophical opposition were undertaken by Domitian and again resulted in a general expulsion of philosophers from Rome; moreover, the Roman authors (Arulenus Rusticus, Herrenius Senecio) of hagiographic accounts of Stoic martyrs (Thrasea Paetus, Helvidius Priscus) were put to death, and their books were publicly burned.

The story of the "philosophical opposition" in Rome provides a dramatic illustration of some of the defining features of Cynicism's reception in the empire:[37] (1) the Roman cultural context in which Cynics are ambiguously associated with, and sometimes ideologically conflated with, their more respectable descendants, the Stoics;[38] (2) the imperial political context in which the price of engaging in Cynic *parrhēsia* ("free speech") may be flogging, exile, or beheading; (3) and, most significant, the striking ambivalence of the ruling elites toward philosophers generally and Cynics in particular, an ambivalence profound enough to provoke both hagiographic eulogies and book burnings.

The emergence of Cynicism as a potent political ideology—opposed to hereditary monarchy—in the first century A.D. is highly significant but potentially misleading: most Cynics lived not in Rome or the West, but in the Greek-speaking cities of the East, from Athens to Alexandria. Most were not politically active but busily engaged living the Cynic way of life—begging their daily bread and bearing witness to Diogenes' example. Socially their

---

35. *Pace* Philostratus; see Kindstrand (above, n. 34) 89.

36. See Griffin's essay in this volume.

37. Cf. D.R. Dudley, *A History of Cynicism from Diogenes to the Sixth Century* A.D. (London 1937) 135: "Opposition to the principle of hereditary monarchy may well have been a feature of Stoic-Cynic propaganda, and as Rostovtseff points out, philosophy made a truce with the monarchy when the principle of adoption was observed, as it was from Nerva to Marcus Aurelius." For the "philosophical opposition," see Dudley, chap. 7.

38. Commenting on Mucianus's criticism of the Stoics that evidently led to Vespasian's expulsion of philosophers (reported at D.C. 65.13), Dudley observes: "The passage is interesting as showing how at this period Stoic and Cynic philosophers were practically indistinguishable, alike in their rationale and their propaganda" (137).

status had been extremely mixed from the beginning, but as a rule they were not the associates of men of wealth and power such as Seneca the Younger.[39]

While all this is true, the Cynic role in the philosophic opposition is worth recalling, not only because it shows how seriously some philosophers and Cynic (or Stoic) teachings were taken in certain contexts, but also because it illustrates the range of activities that we are referring to here as "reception"— from idealization of the tradition (see Billerbeck in this volume) to selective reinterpretation and appropriation (see Griffin and Krueger), to satiric denunciation (e.g., by Lucian) and overt suppression (e.g., by Nero, Vespasian, et al.). It is also worth stressing that the "reception" of the Cynics does not begin as we turn our attention to the Roman period; the identities of the founders of Cynicism, presented above, are almost entirely constructed from imperial sources, particularly our primary source, Diogenes Laertius's *Lives and Opinions of Famous Philosophers,* which is itself "a compilation of compilations." [40] We cannot readily contrast the original Dogs (of the fourth and third centuries B.C.) with later Roman representations, since our own representations are themselves based almost entirely on sources from the Roman period, written over five hundred years after the events related. The study of Cynicism— unlike, say, that of Platonism—is inseparable from the study of its reception.[41]

Accordingly, our contributors focus on some of the most important aspects of this convoluted process that we call the reception of Cynicism, a process distinguished both by its breadth in time and space, and by the intensity of the controversy it excited, and not only at Rome. But the controversy was not over contemporary Cynic literature. In fact, one of the central paradoxes of Cynicism's reception in the empire is that the influence of Cynic ideology reached its apogee (in the second century A.D.) when very little in the way of original Cynic literature was being produced by practicing Cynics. Our most important sources (other than Diogenes Laertius) are sophists such as Lucian and Dio Chrysostom,[42] who make extensive use of Cynic personae, and Stoic moralists such as Seneca and Epictetus, who are concerned to reconcile Cynicism with the mainstream of (Socratic and Stoic) moral philosophy in the empire. The most prominent Cynics of the second century A.D., Peregrinus and Demonax, are known not as writers but as teachers and practicing Cynics and would be all but forgotten if Lucian had not satirized the former (in *On the Death of*

---

39. See Goulet-Cazé (above, n. 34) 2731–46.

40. See Goulet-Cazé (above, n. 4) 3976–77.

41. For example, many of the stories told about Diogenes by Diogenes Laertius as if they reported actual events illustrating the practice of Cynicism may be lifted from literary works— dialogues, parodies, satires—by or about the early Cynics. See Niehues-Pröbsting (above, n. 1) 27.

42. It is often difficult to categorize the eclectic writers of the empire. This is symptomatic of their postclassical cultural context. Dio Chrysostom is clearly interested in both Stoicism and Cynicism, and may have made particular use of the works of Antisthenes. For his self-presentation as a Cynic at certain stages in his career, see J. Moles, "The Career and Conversion of Dio Chrysostom," *JHS* 98 (1978) 79–100.

Peregrinus) as memorably as he eulogized the latter (in *The Life of Demonax*). Oenomaus of Gadara (of the second century A.D.) is the only Cynic of the empire known to us by his written work, *Charlatans Unmasked,* a lively if not particularly original attack on the veracity of oracles that survives because it is quoted by Eusebius (in Books 5 and 6 of the *Praeparatio Evangelica*) but does not seem to have made a great impression on Oenomaus's contemporaries.[43] Neither Diogenes Laertius nor Lucian mentions him. His other works, including "tragedies" that scandalized the pious emperor Julian (*Or.* 7.210d–211a), are lost.

All we have of Cynic literature from the empire to set beside Oenomaus are the *Cynic Epistles,* a collection of fictitious letters attributed to the early Cynics and other sages.[44] The authors of the letters are unknown, and their dates of composition may vary considerably (from the third century B.C. to the second century A.D.). The epistles (written in Koine) offer a valuable survey of the topoi and anecdotes that must have informed many a "diatribe,"[45] the term conventionally used to describe the oral performances of the Cynic street preachers that are so often remarked on by our sources. These oral performances were probably the primary means by which Cynic teachings were disseminated among the general populace. The *Cynic Epistles* confirm the impression that Cynic literary production in the empire is no longer marked by the innovative parodies and polemics of the classical period and now serves primarily to propagate Cynicism as a popular ideology and collective moral praxis.

It is precisely the collective, popular, and practical form that Cynicism takes in the empire that explains the controversy surrounding its reception from the time of Nero to that of Julian, and the curious ambivalence of our principal sources (e.g., Lucian, Dio Chrysostom [ca. A.D. 40–ca. 111], Epictetus [ca. A.D. 55–ca. 135], and Julian), who typically admire the Cynics of old—known, perhaps, from the lost Cynic classics[46]—almost as much as they despise the mass of contemporary Cynics.[47] This habitual contrast between the

43. For Oenomaus, see Goulet-Cazé (above, n. 34) 2802–3; J. Hammerstaedt, *Die Orakelkritik des Kynikers Oenomaus,* Beiträge zur Klassischen Philologie 188 (Frankfurt 1988); "Der Kyniker Oenomaus von Gadara," *ANRW* 2.36.4 (Berlin 1990) 2834–65.

44. The letters are attributed to Anacharsis, Crates, Diogenes, Heraclitus, Socrates, and the Socratics. See A. J. Malherbe, *The Cynic Epistles: A Study Edition* (Missoula 1977); Eike Müseler, *Die Kynikerbriefe,* 2 vols. (Paderborn 1994). Stoic and other philosophical influences limit the value of the *Epistles* as evidence for Cynic ideology.

45. For bibliography, see Goulet-Cazé (above, n. 34) 2804 n. 538.

46. Some works by the early Cynics were undoubtedly available in the empire, but it is often difficult to tell when an author is drawing directly on them or on the extensive secondary literature that grew up around the Cynics. See Goulet-Cazé (above, n. 34) 2724–27. It is significant that Demetrius (*De Eloc.* 259) can speak (with reference to Crates) of a *kunikos tropos* ("Cynic style"), which suggests a well-known body of texts.

47. See Epictetus 3.22.50, 4.8.5; Dio Chrysostom 32.9, 34.2; Julian 7, 9. Lucian's most vitriolic attacks on the Cynics are *The Runaways* and *On the Death of Peregrinus.*

contemporary and the classical, the real and the ideal, should not be dismissed as a mere commonplace. The persistence of this twofold response over several centuries is highly significant: our sources are registering the single most significant fact about the fate of Cynicism in the empire, namely, that the movement split along the lines of class, wealth, and education—the very social distinctions Cynicism sought to annul. So we now find a popular ideology and way of life, on the one hand, and a highly literate tradition of ethical reflection and satire, on the other. All our sources are affiliated to varying degrees with the latter; most practicing Cynics, some of whom were literate, were part of the former.

Cynicism was unique among classical intellectual traditions in becoming something like a "mass movement." [48] While it is impossible to quantify exactly, we can identify over eighty ancient Cynics; [49] and if our sources are any indication, the sight of Cynics begging and preaching was not an uncommon one in the cities of the East. This popularization of a classical tradition provoked anxiety and outrage among the cultured elites, all the more so if they considered themselves to be the authentic spokesmen for this particular tradition, as did Lucian, Dio Chrysostom, Epictetus, and Julian. But the appeal of Cynic ideology was too contagious to contain and control, as we see if we consider how disparate were the positions, both social and intellectual, of those who took a serious interest in it: Philo Judaeus, [50] the early Christians, Roman aristocrats (see Griffin in this volume), satirists, Greek sophists, imperial educators and moralists, the Church Fathers (see Krueger in this volume), a pious emperor (see Billerbeck in this volume), and the urban poor, both free and slaves [51]—all these parties had an opinion on the meaning and uses of Cynicism, an opinion shaped by their own social and intellectual trajectories. For that very reason we should resist the temptation to reduce these many individual acts of reception to a single structure or pattern. What we see taking place in the empire is an argument over a "legacy": Who are the legitimate heirs? What is the ultimate value of the tradition—literary, social, ethical, political? And, not least, who is entitled to speak with the authority of Diogenes?

The careers of Lucian and Peregrinus offer themselves as allegories for the conflicting tendencies within the Cynic movement of the empire—the tendency toward "literary Cynicism," on the one hand, and toward collective praxis, on the other. Like other imperial interpreters, they took what they needed from the tradition and in so doing tended to remake it in their own image. For Lucian, Cynic literature was a liberating example of innovation and subversion within the classical tradition. The Cynic classics (and Cynic ide-

---

48. Its missionary character, however, bears comparison with that of Epicureanism. Cf. N. W. De Witt, *Epicurus and His Philosophy* (Minneapolis 1954).

49. See Appendix A, "A Comprehensive Catalogue of Known Cynic Philosophers."

50. See Dudley (above, n. 37) 186–87.

51. E.g., Lucian, *The Runaways* 17.

ology) gave him nothing less than a license to write satire on all things Greek, which now, of course, included Cynics and Cynicism itself. When he was attacked for his hilarious caricature *Philosophers for Sale!*, in which the founding fathers of Greek philosophy, including Diogenes, are auctioned off as slaves, it is a comic-Cynic mask (*Parrhēsiadēs*) he dons to defend his literary principles.[52] His many works using Cynic personae (e.g., Diogenes, Antisthenes, Crates, Menippus, et al.) or indebted to Cynic traditions of parody and satire (e.g., *Philosophers for Sale!*, *Zeus the Tragic Actor*, *Dialogues of the Dead*) give us the liveliest images we have of what the Cynic classics might have been like, and are the primary means whereby Cynic traditions became part of European literature. In his *Demonax*, Lucian even shows a serious interest in constructing a contemporary ethical model from Cynic (and Socratic) traditions.[53] Yet for all his undeniable affinities with Cynicism, Lucian is scathingly satiric toward contemporary Cynics (other than Demonax), precisely because they offend his sense of the tradition's true center of gravity—in the practice of satire (*parrhēsia*) and an individualist, not a collectivist, ethic.[54] While other contemporary observers saw in Peregrinus a serious philosopher,[55] Lucian can see in him only a fake who is hijacking Cynic traditions for reasons of self-aggrandizement and fame—pointedly un-Cynic motives. And, in a characteristically Lucianic twist, he is not even a good fake: to imitate Heracles' fiery death is an absurd way to perpetuate the tradition, a comically inept attempt at mimesis: Heracles' tragic death was forced on him; Peregrinus's immolation is freely chosen (*Peregrinus* 25), announced four years ahead of time, and performed at the Olympic Games (A.D. 165)![56] By pushing Cynicism in

---

52. For an analysis, see Branham (above, n. 1) 28–38.

53. For an analysis of the *Demonax*, see Goulet-Cazé (above, n. 34) 2763–64; Branham (above, n. 1) 57–63.

54. Niehues-Pröbsting (above, n. 1: 211–13) usefully distinguishes three strands in Lucian's Cynicism: (1) a tendency toward idealization in the *Demonax* and *The Cynic;* (2) the satiric critique of contemporary practicing Cynics in *On the Death of Peregrinus* and *The Runaways;* and, most important, (3) the use of Cynic voices and personae in his satire—e.g., *Zeus Refuted, The Downward Journey, Dialogues of the Dead*, etc. In general this is correct, but one could argue that *The Cynic* is a paradoxical encomium and its hyperbolic praise of the traditional Cynic garb is ironically intended. For *The Cynic*, see R. Bracht Branham, "Utopian Laughter: Lucian and Thomas More," *Moreana* 86 (1985) 23–43; for the authenticity of *The Cynic*, see Branham (above, n. 1) 237 n. 4.

55. See Aulus Gellius, *Attic Nights* 12.11, cited by Goulet-Cazé (above, n. 34) 2766.

56. While suicide in some contexts is genuinely Cynic, Peregrinus's showy suicide is a travesty of the Cynic attachment to life, even under the most adverse conditions. We should remember the story told of Antisthenes (D.L. 6.18) and Nietzsche's comment (discussed by Niehues-Pröbsting [above, n. 1] 147): "When the ailing Antisthenes cried out, 'Who will release me from these pains?' Diogenes replied, 'This,' showing him a dagger. Antisthenes responded: 'I said from my pains, not from life.'" Nietzsche commented apropos of this anecdote (cited by Niehues-Pröbsting 147): "Eine ganz tiefsinnige Äusserung. . . . Es ist ersichtlich, dass der Cyniker am Leben hängt, mehr als die andern Philosophen: 'der kürzeste Weg zum Glück' ist so viel als, 'Lust am Leben an sich' und volle Anspruchslosigkeit in Bezug auf alle andern Güter" (*Philologica* 2.196).

the direction of a religious cult,[57] by turning it into another myth, Peregrinus's career inevitably appears to Lucian as a profound betrayal of the original Cynic impulse to "deface" the idols of the tribe. *On the Death of Peregrinus* is not only about the ambitious Cynic:[58] it is a case study in how and why such ambitions get turned into myth and cult. Fame was a subject of particular interest to Lucian, who had invested so much energy in the creation of his own authority as a satirist, not least by means of a series of Cynic masks and voices. Peregrinus's theatrical imitation of Heracles thus struck him as an illegitimate appropriation of the tradition he had cultivated: if successful, it would turn Cynicism into just another cult; and, indeed, that is always what it is in danger of becoming merely in virtue of reproducing itself over time, a process that entails imitation and easily lapses into mere conformity to a type.[59]

The Afterlife of Cynicism

While Cynicism as such disappears with classical antiquity, Cynicism as an ideological force and literary tradition has had a remarkable afterlife, and its consequences for Western culture are only beginning to be understood. Four contributors to this volume (Matton, Relihan, Kinney, and Niehues-Pröbsting) pioneer an attempt to map some of the uncharted terrain of Cynicism's postclassical reception from the medieval to the modern period. As we have already seen in the Roman empire, the reception of Cynicism was not the exclusive concern of professional philosophers but entered into literary, religious, political, and moral discourse generally. In fact, the most potent expression of Cynicism's vitality in the early modern and the modern world is arguably not in the domain of philosophy per se, but in a literary tradition of satiric (or seriocomic) fantasy and dialogue that runs from Lucianic works such as Erasmus's *Praise of Folly,* More's *Utopia,* and Rabelais's *Gargantua and Pantagruel* through Ben Jonson's satiric comedies to Swift's *Gulliver's Travels* and Diderot's *Rameau's Nephew* (see Niehues-Pröbsting).[60] Yet one of the striking features of Cynicism as an ideology throughout its postclassical history is how very provocative the Cynic model remained even when its original practitioners had become literary figures safely relegated to a legendary pagan past. Whether we

57. Dudley (above, n. 37: 179–81) argues that Peregrinus may have succeeded in establishing a cult.

58. For an excellent analysis, see Niehues-Pröbsting (above, n. 1) 195–213; cf. Branham (above, n. 1) chap. 4.

59. This is precisely the point of *The Cynic*'s ironic praise of the Cynic uniform—its reduction of philosophy to the most literal form of imitation.

60. In addition to the contributions of Relihan, Kinney, and Niehues-Pröbsting in this volume, see Niehues-Pröbsting (above, n. 1) 214–43; Branham (above, n. 54); M. Bakhtin, *Rabelais and His World,* trans. H. Iswolsky (Bloomington 1984) chap. 2; M. A. Screech, *Rabelais* (Ithaca 1979) 441; D. Duncan, *Ben Jonson and the Lucianic Tradition* (Cambridge 1979); C. Robinson, *Lucian and His Influence in Europe* (Chapel Hill 1979); R. E. Compean, "Swift and the Lucianic Tradition" (Ph.D. diss., University of California, Davis, 1976).

consider the response of medieval Christians (in the West: Matton), the Humanists of the Renaissance (Kinney, Relihan) or the *philosophes* of eighteenth-century France (Niehues-Pröbsting), we find that the Cynic model of a naturally free and autonomous self exerts a powerful attraction that can be as difficult to resist as it is to domesticate. The ambivalence of the Roman response to Cynicism proved proleptic.

Thus Cynicism remained a vital source of oppositional discourse throughout its history, which consists of a continual process of reevaluation beginning with the Christians, as one dominant culture after another attempts to "house-break" the Dogs. Contact between Cynics and Christians probably dates from the earliest stages of Christianity. It has been argued that the Cynics provided an important pagan model for early Christian communities.[61] Be that as it may, the two movements were closely associated in the minds of their sharpest critics, such as Lucian (in the *Peregrinus*), Aelius Aristides (*Or.* 46), and the emperor Julian (*Or.* 7.224); and there were Cynics, such as Peregrinus and Maximus Hero (of the fourth century A.D.), who evidently converted to Christianity for a time. Indeed, Lucian goes so far as to attribute the authorship of "many" Christian books to Peregrinus, probably as a way of subverting both the Cynic and his Christian audience; for the Christians themselves are represented as gullible fools who worship a "crucified sophist" and require no rational basis for their beliefs (*Peregrinus* 11–13). The common ground shared by Cynics and Christians was presumably the practice of an ascetic way of life, but the end of Cynic "asceticism" (*askēsis*)—happiness—is unambiguously immanent and secular; and as Augustine was clearly aware, the Cynic rejection of shame flies in the face of the most basic Christian doctrine.[62] Yet the ostensible resemblance of Cynic to Christian virtue—particularly the embracing of poverty and asceticism of some kind—inevitably excited the admiration of many Christians: Dante would place Diogenes among the greatest philosophers in the first circle of Hell, the Limbo reserved for the unbaptized yet virtuous.[63] And as Matton shows in his contribution to this volume, both the medieval encyclopedic tradition and medieval humanism as represented, for example, by John of Wales (ca. 1220/1230–ca. 1285) and Jacques Legrand (ca. 1365–1415) evince a surprising sympathy for Cynic traditions as they attempt to reconcile pagan and Christian forms of wisdom.

The delicate medieval balancing act that permitted selective appropriation of Cynic ideology within a traditional Christian framework was destabilized by two factors: (1) the renaissance of classical culture fostered by humanists in the fifteenth and early sixteenth centuries brought into circulation previously inaccessible Cynic and Lucianic texts (including our principal source, Dioge-

61. See F. G. Downing, *Cynics and Christian Origins* (Edinburgh 1992); Goulet-Cazé (above, n. 34) 2788–99.

62. *City of God* 14.20; see Krueger's contribution to this volume.

63. See Matton's contribution to this volume.

nes Laertius's Book 6) that would prove combustible in the polemicizing contexts of the Reformation; (2) inspired by their expanded knowledge of the relevant traditions, humanists writing in Latin, such as Erasmus and More, as well as vernacular authors from Rabelais to Montaigne,[64] enter into the literary and philosophical perspectives disclosed by Cynicism with such imagination and evident glee that a conservative Christian backlash was engendered. The experimental "Christianization" of Cynicism by humanists is answered by a thoroughgoing demonization of the Dogs in the seventeenth century, as the Cynics are condemned as the source of contemporary heresies such as those associated with the "Society of the Poor" (or Beghards and Turlupins).[65] Although there were still defenders ready to answer these often ahistorical attacks, the Counter-Reformation polemic against the Cynics was ferocious, and the Dogs were not systematically rehabilitated until they became part of the discourse of the Enlightenment in eighteenth-century France and Germany.

In his contribution to this volume, "The Modern Reception of Cynicism," Heinrich Niehues-Pröbsting brings our story up to the present, arguing that neither the ideology of the Enlightenment nor the risks it ran can be understood historically without reference to the role played by Cynicism in the self-definition of such influential figures as Wieland, Rousseau, Diderot, and Nietzsche. His analysis is rich in its implications for the origins of both post-Christian and post-Enlightenment concepts of the self.[66] He concludes his study with a telling critique of what is currently the most influential account of the relation of ancient Cynicism to modern cynicism, Peter Sloterdijk's *Critique of Cynical Reason.*

There were many important topics that we would have liked to explore in this collection but could not, including (1) the Byzantine and Arabic receptions of Cynicism,[67] (2) the vernacular reception in the Renaissance (by Rabelais or Montaigne),[68] (3) the encounter of Michel Foucault and the Cynics.[69] Much remains to be done. Of course, all our discussions assume some identifiable

---

64. See R. Esclapez, "Montaigne et les philosophes cyniques," *Bulletin de la Société des Amis de Montaigne* 5–6 (1986) 59–76; A. Comte-Sponville, "Montaigne cynique? (Valeur et vérité dans les *Essais*)," *Revue Internationale de Philosophie* 46, no. 181 (1992), 234–79.

65. See Matton's contribution to this volume.

66. Yet the Cynics are strangely absent from C. Taylor's fine study *Sources of the Self: The Making of Modern Identity* (Cambridge, Mass., 1989); cf. also *The Ethics of Authenticity* (Cambridge, Mass., 1991).

67. For the Arabic reception, see D. Gutas, "Sayings by Diogenes Preserved in Arabic," in Goulet-Cazé and Goulet (above, n. 2) 475–519. For the Byzantine reception, see D. Krueger, *Symeon the Holy Fool: Leontius's "Life" and the Late Antique City* (Berkeley and Los Angeles 1995).

68. See Esclapez and Comte-Sponville (above, n. 64), and n. 60 above. There were also lively vernacular traditions in Spain (Menippean satires of the sixteenth century) and Italy. See, for example, *Il cane di Diogene*, a prose satire by F.F. Frugoni (ca. 1620–86), in which the author "impersonates" Diogenes' dog. Each chapter is called a "bark," *latrato.*

69. While Foucault did not live to publish his late work on the Cynics, see Flynn's account (above, n. 1).

idea or set of concepts to which the term "Cynicism" refers; but the problem of identifying Cynicism—whether as a practical ascetic morality for the have-nots, as a universal ethical model of freedom and autonomy, or as a cultural practice devoted to "defacing" the false values of the dominant culture—is one of the central concerns of this volume, to which we now turn.

Was Cynicism a Philosophy?

It may seem strange to ask such a question since the Cynics presented themselves as philosophers. We cannot avoid asking it, however, for since antiquity many have denied them the status of philosophers.[70]

It must be admitted, moreover, that the Cynics furnished their opponents with a great many arguments. They had no school, in the institutional sense of the term, and they did not hesitate to make stinging criticisms of the philosophical praxis of their contemporaries. Above all, they made no secret of their intention to "deface the currency," not only in the areas of social intercourse, religion, politics, and ethics, but also in philosophy. As a matter of fact, they distrusted words and demanded action instead; they rejected the very idea of culture as traditionally conceived and conducted their philosophical praxis more as a mode of life than as an intellectual discipline.

The Reproaches Formulated by the Cynics' Adversaries

While the Cynics' status as a philosophical school was always problematic—as the anecdotal tradition shows clearly enough—the fact that there were also formal critiques of the school's status at least from the time of Hippobotus (of the second century B.C.) suggests that "Cynicism" had to be taken seriously by Hellenistic philosophers.[71] In any event, there were three principal criticisms leveled against "Cynicism" as a philosophical school.

The absence of dogmata.   The movement was reproached with not having philosophical *dogmata* ("a principled set of beliefs"). In antiquity, there were two competing conceptions of a "school of philosophy" (*hairesis*),[72] both of them Skeptic in tone. We find the echoes of them in Diogenes Laertius (1.20)

---

70. See M.-O. Goulet-Cazé, "Le cynisme est-il une philosophie?" in *Contre Platon*, vol. 1, *Le platonisme dévoilé*, ed. M. Dixsaut (Paris 1993), 273–313.

71. Hippobotus was the author of a work entitled Περὶ Αἱρέσεων and another entitled Τῶν Φιλοσόφων Ἀναγραφή. According to D.L. 1.19, he refused, in his Περὶ Αἱρέσεων, to range the Cynic school, not unlike the Eleatic and Dialectical schools, within the αἱρέσεις. Hippobotus's date is controversial; the editor of his fragments places his *floruit* in the first half of the second century B.C. Cf. M. Gigante, "Frammenti di Ippoboto: Contributo alla storia della storiografia filosofica," in *Omaggio a Piero Treves*, ed. A. Mastrocinque (Padua 1983) 151–93.

72. For the concept of *hairesis*, see Long (above, n. 8) 138–40.

and in Sextus Empiricus.[73] One of these defines a "school" (*hairesis*) as the "adherence to several beliefs, apparently coherent with one another,"[74] "belief" being defined as an "assent given to something that is uncertain."[75] The other views a "school" (*hairesis*) as a form of "conduct that is apparently based on a philosophical principle that indicates how it is possible to appear to live correctly."[76]

By excluding the Cynic school, Hippobotus shows that he considered the presence of a systematic form of speculation—a set of beliefs or hypotheses—to be a necessary condition for a tradition to lay claim to the title "school" (*hairesis*). For critics like Hippobotus, if Cynicism does not present a systematic ensemble of beliefs, it is merely a "way of life."[77]

The absence of an "end" or "philosophical goal" (telos). The second criticism was that Cynicism lacked an "end" (*telos*).[78] To be sure, we do possess ancient evidence on the Cynic *telos*,[79] but it cannot be attributed to Antisthenes or Diogenes. It was not until philosophical schools began to be characterized according to the "sovereign good" at which they aimed (following Aristotle) that later authors, who wished to consider Cynicism a genuine "school," formulated a particular *telos* for it. According to the definition given by Diogenes Laertius (6.104), "the 'end' [of Cynicism] consists in living in accordance with virtue." It has been suggested that this formulation probably originates with the Stoic Apollodorus of Seleucia,[80] to whom we also owe the famous definition of Cynicism as a "shortcut to virtue."[81] In attributing to Cynicism its

73. Sextus Empiricus, *Pyrrhonian Hypotyposes* 1.16–17.

74. πρόσκλισιν δόγμασι πολλοῖς ἀκολουθίαν ἔχουσι πρὸς ἄλληλά τε καὶ φαινόμενα.

75. δόγμα τινὶ ἀδήλῳ συγκατάθεσιν.

76. τὴν λόγῳ τινὶ κατὰ τὸ φαινόμενον ἀκολουθοῦσαν ἀγωγήν, ἐκείνου τοῦ λόγου ὡς ἔστιν ὀρθῶς δοκεῖν ζῆν ὑποδεικνύοντος. The text we have quoted of the two definitions is that of Sextus, since he presents them in more developed form than does Diogenes Laertius.

77. The formula ἔνστασις τοῦ βίου ("way of life") is used by D.L. 6.103. To be sure, the latter does not attribute it expressly to Hippobotus; he merely says: "We maintain that Cynic philosophy is a school of thought and not, as some believe, a way of life." Inasmuch as he explains in 1.19–20 that Hippobotus excluded the Cynic school from the list of αἱρέσεις, it is likely that Diogenes Laertius ranges Hippobotus among those who consider cynicism a mere way of life.

78. Beginning with Aristotle's *Nicomachean Ethics* (cf. Book 1 *ad init.*), it became customary to go through an enumeration of the various ends and especially the ultimate end, or *telos*. One sovereign good was then attributed to each philosophical school so that they could be placed in relation to one another.

79. Thus Clement of Alexandria, *Strom.* 2.21, 130, 7; vol. 2, p. 184, 18 Stählin ("Antisthenes says that *atuphia* is the goal of life"); Julian, *Or.* 9.8.188b–c ("The goal of the life of Antisthenes, Diogenes, and Crates, and their end, was, in my view, knowledge of oneself, contempt for vain opinions, and also the pursuit of the truth . . . with all the strength of their intelligence"); 12.192a ("The goal proposed by Cynicism is apathy, which is equivalent to becoming God"); and 13.193d ("The goal and the end proposed by Cynic philosophy, as, moreover, by all philosophy, is happiness; now, this happiness consists in living in conformity with nature, not according to the opinions of the crowd").

80. Goulet-Cazé (above, n. 4) 3941–49.

81. D.L. 7.121.

own particular end, Apollodorus was trying to support his belief in a genealogy (Socrates–Antisthenes–Diogenes–Crates–Zeno of Citium) that linked the Cynics and Stoics directly to Socrates. This construction was vital to Apollodorus's claim that Cynicism should be recognized as a full-fledged philosophical "school" (*hairesis*).

Others, however—and not only Hippobotus—denied that Cynicism had its own *telos*. We find an echo of this position in a passage from Varro's *De Philosophia* in which Cynicism is reduced to a simple "style of life" (*habitus* or *consuetudo*) compatible with any philosophical school, whatever its *telos*.[82]

The rejection of all intellectual culture (paideia).   In order to do philosophy, the Cynics refused to take the route of intellectual culture (although this did not prevent them from being cultivated). They therefore neglected the traditional disciplines, such as music, geometry, and astronomy, which they judged to be useless and unnecessary.[83] In their view, such theoretical pursuits distract humankind from its proper study—the human being (*anthrōpos*).

This attitude was often criticized in antiquity. Galen reproached the Cynics with shunning everything that had to do with logic and transformed the characterization of Cynicism as a "shortcut to virtue" into a "shortcut to conceit."[84] Similarly, Lucian speaks of a "shortcut to notoriety."[85] Apuleius, for his part, was scathing in his contempt for those "brutish, filthy and uncultivated people," who "by speaking badly and living likewise" were corrupting philosophy.[86]

Clearly, Cynic philosophy had a dubious reputation in antiquity, and critics did not hesitate to denigrate it and even to deny its status as a philosophy. When the emperor Julian speaks about it, he feels obliged to add that "it is not the most vile and discredited form of philosophy, but the rival of the most estimable forms";[87] when Eunapius (in the fourth century A.D.) evokes the Cynic Carneades, he feels it necessary to add: "He was by no means obscure among the Cynics, if we are to take Cynicism into consideration."[88]

What Philosophy Did the Cynics Claim as Their Own?

The Cynics were undaunted by the criticisms showered upon them from all sides: they declared themselves, unequivocally, to be philosophers and chal-

---

82. The passage is cited by Augustine, *City of God* 19.1.2–3.

83. Cf. D.L. 6.73.

84. Galen, *De Peccatorum Dignotione* 3.12–13; p. 48, 23–49, 10 de Boer (= vol. 5, p. 71 Kühn).

85. Lucian, *Vitarum Auctio* 11. *Doxa* here is clearly pejorative.

86. Apuleius, *Florida* 7.10–13.

87. Julian, *Or.* 9, *Against the Uneducated Cynics,* 2, 182c.

88. Eunapius, *Lives of the Philosophers and Sophists,* 2.1, 5; p. 3, 11–12 Giangrande.

lenged all others to the title. Their conception of philosophy, however, turns out to be highly idiosyncratic, since they defined it by the act of "defacing."

"Defacing the currency." As represented by tradition, Diogenes' aim was to demonstrate by his own example the superiority of nature to custom, and he spent his whole life trying to "deface" the false values of the dominant culture. In every area of human activity, this "defacing" led the Cynics to adopt scandalous positions.

To take an example from politics: the Cynics appeared at a time when, even though the traditional polis was beginning to be shaken to its foundations by the conquests of the young Alexander, many were not yet ready to abandon their traditional roles in civil and political life. And yet Diogenes preached "cosmopolitanism," declaring himself "without a city" (*a-polis*), "without a home" (*a-oikos*),[89] and "citizen of the universe" (*kosmopolitēs*).[90] Until now, such cosmopolitanism has been considered essentially negative—a rejection of all existing states—but Moles's contribution to the present work has launched the debate once again. Be that as it may, Diogenes urged people to abstain from all political engagement that, like family or social obligations, might constitute an obstacle to individual freedom.

Cynic "defacing" was just as radical in religious matters.[91] In the first place, they stood the traditional hierarchy of beings on its head: the series animal–man–god was transformed into man–animal–god. For man, as a being of desire and anguish, animal and god constituted, respectively, the concrete and the theoretical model of self-sufficiency and indifference, and consequently of happiness. This does not mean, however, that the Cynics were pious. They had no interest in religious questions, and considered god as a mere theoretical reference point. In general, one can say that their attitude toward religion was skeptical or agnostic: they preferred not to pronounce judgment upon questions that transcended their understanding. Although they viewed man as confronted by an irrational world, constrained to bend to the whims of Fortune, they refused to live in constant fear of the gods and the punishments of Hades. This, moreover, is why they envied animals, which they considered happy for lacking any idea of a god who can reward and punish. Such viewpoints, combined with scathing criticisms of anthropomorphism, the Mysteries, prayer, the interpretation of dreams, ritual purifications, and other religious institutions, ran directly against traditional religious ideology.

Diogenes also "defaced" philosophy, not only because he criticized such contemporary philosophers as Plato, Euclid, or Aristippus and rejected all sys-

---

89. Cf. D.L. 6.38 (= V B 263 G.).
90. Cf. ibid. 6.63 (= V B 355 G.).
91. See Goulet-Cazé's contribution to this volume.

tems, preferring to demonstrate his beliefs by his actions, but also because he asserted that philosophy is not within our grasp, and that all we can do is pretend.[92] How like Diogenes it was to disown his "defacing" loud and clear! Just as Socrates had urged, philosophy was no longer to be reserved for a social or intellectual elite: everyone could philosophize. It is thus not surprising that, under the Roman empire, Cynicism became the popular philosophy of antiquity.

Armed with the metaphor of "defacing" that he himself had chosen, Diogenes was prepared for every act of "shamelessness," and accepted his role as one who scandalizes society.

Ethical choice leading to practical philosophy.   The Cynics, following in the footsteps of Socrates, adopted a strongly ethical orientation. Even if we are appropriately skeptical of the characterization of them by Diogenes Laertius (according to which they rejected the logical and the physical topoi of philosophy),[93] it remains true that their entire philosophical attitude was inseparable from the field of ethics. For the Cynics, what mattered was to live well in order to be happy. When Diogenes was asked what was the profit he derived from philosophy, he replied: "This, if nothing else—to be prepared for every kind of luck," [94] or "To be rich even without an obol to my name." [95] The point of Cynicism is, among other things, to demonstrate that we are so constituted by nature that happiness is possible under the most adverse conditions. Whoever practices it lives a life close to nature. Cynics broke away from the intellectualist model of philosophy and privileged the existential experience of the sage.

In order to obtain happiness, Diogenes and his successors insisted on the importance of acts as opposed to words. Ironically in view of their extensive literary activities, their slogan could have been: "good living instead of good talking." We ought not to be surprised, therefore, if the forms of speech they became known for bore little resemblance to traditional philosophical discourse. The Cynics' discourse was caustic and aggressive; it backed the interlocutor into a corner until he was forced to put himself in question. This is why wordplay, biting sarcasm, and merciless witticisms are characteristic of their own methods and of the way they were represented by others.

92. D.L. 6.64 (= V B 364 G.).

93. Cf. Goulet-Cazé (above, n. 70) 291–92. The conclusions of the global demonstration carried out by P. Hadot, "Les divisions des parties de la philosophie dans l'antiquité," *Museum Helveticum* 15 (1979) 201–33, may be applied to D.L. 6.103. We are therefore justified in supposing that it was after the fact that some Stoics—perhaps more specifically Apollodorus of Seleucia—gave to the conception that the Cynics had of philosophy, which was certainly unitary, a formulation that brought into play the three parts of philosophy that they themselves distinguished.

94. D.L. 6.63 (= V B 360 G.).

95. *Gnomologium Vaticanum* 743, no. 182, p. 74 Sternbach (= V B 361 G.).

Cynic Discipline

Cynicism defined itself—or rather, was defined[96]—as "a shortcut to virtue" as opposed to the long road, which passed through laborious textual study and the acquisition of theoretical knowledge. But this "shortcut" was arduous and difficult, for it required the application of a demanding method: *askēsis* ("exercise," "practice," "training," "discipline").[97]

Understood in the Cynic sense of the term, *askēsis* was intended as a preventive method. Every day, the Cynic trains the self physically in the arts of endurance; the daily exercise of the will causes fear to dissipate, since the practicing Cynic is constantly fortifying the self against unforeseen misfortunes.

The concept of "discipline" (*askēsis*), borrowed from the vocabulary of athletics, was not used by the Cynics only in a metaphorical sense. Like the athlete's, the philosopher's "discipline" (*askēsis*) was wholly concrete. The only difference resided in the *telos* of his training: while the athlete trained his body with a view to victory in the stadium, the Cynic trained it in order to strengthen his will and to ensure his capacity for endurance.

Cynic training (*askēsis*) is in preparation for a contest, and the agonist must be sure not to miss the point of his struggles. Diogenes warned against any useless suffering demanded by social custom, family, business, or politics as not worth the candle: "He would praise those who were about to marry but did not, those who were about to set sail but did not, those who were about to engage in politics but did not, those who were about to raise children but did not, those who were about to live at court but did not" (D.L. 6.29). Instead of such vain pursuits, Diogenes trained himself to fight against such existential adversaries as exile, poverty, hunger, and death. For him, this was the only battle worth winning. Whereas civilized existence represents these trials (*ponoi*) as evils, the Cynic sought to endure them precisely by refusing to consider them evil. In order to acquire this state of mind, the Cynics exhorted themselves and others to practice a life in accordance with nature (*kata phusin*). Someone "trained" to drink water, sleep on the ground, eat and dress simply, and put up with the heat or cold of the seasons will know how to respond with serenity when Fortune attacks. The law of Cynic *askēsis* was simple: it consisted of living in poverty and satisfying only one's natural needs—"the tuition-free way to learn philosophy."[98] In this way, the Cynic sought freedom from emotional turmoil (*apatheia*) and independence from the outside world. In Diogenes' Cynicism, there is no self-denial for its own sake or in the service of a transcendent goal. While it is true that much that made

96. Cf. Goulet-Cazé (above, n. 4) 3941–49. This definition can hardly be due to the first Cynics; it must rather be attributed to the Stoics and more specifically to Apollodorus of Seleucia.

97. D.L. 70–71 conserves an extract from a work by Diogenes in which the philosopher presents his conception of *askēsis*. For an analysis of this passage, see Goulet-Cazé (above, n. 1).

98. Stobaeus 4.2, 32, 19 (= V B 223 G.).

Diogenes influential in antiquity is lost if we characterize his Cynicism solely as a practical morality, the practical element was, nevertheless, fundamental to his appeal.

Diogenes liked to proclaim himself [99]

> Without a city, without a home, bereft of fatherland,
> A beggar and a vagabond, living from day to day.

The tangible signs of his "discipline" (*askēsis*) were the accoutrements the philosopher carried with him: his knapsack containing everything he possessed, his walking staff, and his short, coarse cloak, his only clothing in winter or summer, which he also used as a blanket. The Cynic, missionary and "doctor" of souls,[100] headed out on the road to spread his message. The therapy he recommended was highly unusual: it was based, in the first instance, on frankness and freedom of speech (*parrhēsia*), which often led to withering retorts and reprimands, and on laughter—fearless laughter that shook the interlocutor and forced him to react. Finally, it was based upon provocation, particularly in the form of "shamelessness," which Diogenes used not as an end in itself, but as a pedagogical instrument intended—here again—to shock his interlocutors out of their complacency. Diogenes' practice sought to make others become aware of the incoherencies of civilized life when compared with "natural life" and to make them abandon their false shame. These were the indispensable preliminaries to any pretensions to practice philosophy.

99. D.L. 6.38 (= V B 263 G.).

100. For the philosophical application of this metaphor in other Hellenistic schools, see M. Nussbaum, *The Therapy of Desire: Theory and Practice in Hellenistic Ethics* (Princeton 1994).

The Socratic Tradition:
Diogenes, Crates, and Hellenistic Ethics

A. A. Long

Of all the routes by which Socrates' philosophy was transmitted to the Hellenistic world, that followed by the Cynics was the most startling and, in certain respects, the most influential. The Cynic Crates was the first teacher at Athens of Zeno of Citium, the founder of Stoicism. Crates is described in the biographical tradition as "a man like the Socrates of Xenophon's *Memorabilia*" (D.L. 7.2–3). The early Stoics can be assumed to have readily propagated such stories, determined as they were to connect their founder with Socrates.[1] Hence they publicized the philosophical succession Socrates, Antisthenes, Diogenes, Crates, Zeno. In the Stoic canon of saints and quasi sages, Socrates and Diogenes form a ubiquitous duo.[2]

A shorter version of this paper will appear as part of the chapter "The Socratic Legacy" in the forthcoming *Cambridge History of Hellenistic Philosophy,* ed. J. Barnes, J. Mansfeld, and M. Schofield. I am grateful to these scholars for their comments on an earlier version. For the leisure to write this paper I gratefully acknowledge a fellowship awarded to me by the John Simon Guggenheim Memorial Foundation.

1. Cf. my article "Socrates in Hellenistic Philosophy," *CQ* 38 (1988) 150–71 (reprinted in my book *Stoic Studies* [Cambridge 1996] 1–33), esp. pp. 151–54, 161–62. Some later Stoics, especially the Pergamene librarian Athenodorus, tried to play down the Cynic influences on early Stoicism, to avoid contaminating the founders of the Stoa with Cynic shamelessness. These contrasting attitudes toward the Cynics have left their mark on D.L.'s life of Zeno: cf. J. Mansfeld, "Diogenes Laertius on Stoic Philosophy," *Elenchos* 7 (1986) 297–351; and D. Hahm, "Diogenes Laertius VII: On the Stoics," *ANRW* 2.36.6 (Berlin 1992) 4088–4105.

2. Cf. Epictetus 2.16.35, 2.3.24, 3.21.19 (which adds Zeno), 3.22.63 (Antisthenes, Diogenes, Crates), 3.24.40, 3.24.60–71, 3.26.23, 4.1.152–69, 4.7.29, 4.9.6, 4.11.21–22. Epictetus's treatment of Diogenes, and of Cynicism, is undisguisedly idealized. Hence his attempt to sift out the genuine Cynic from the charlatan trappings of the calling cannot be retrojected onto the historical Diogenes. Nonetheless, Epictetus's long discourse on Cynicism (3.22, well commented on by M. Billerbeck, *Epiktet: Vom Kynismus* [Leiden 1978]) is important in showing how much common ground a late Stoic could find between Cynic sayings or actions and his own philosophy.

In contrast with the Stoics, Epicurus specifically denied that the wise man would "practice Cynicism" (D.L. 10.119). Yet the principles an Epicurean should adopt concerning satisfaction of desires, attitudes to society, self-sufficiency, and freedom have much in common with Cynic precepts; this affinity is most clearly seen in the satirical tone of Epicurean maxims, many of which call attention to the vanity of conventional human motivations (cf. Epicurus, *KD* 15, 21, 29; *Gnom. Vat.* 21, 25, 33, 46, 65). Cynic tendencies are still more evident in our accounts of the philosophies of two of Epicurus's rivals, the Cyrenaics Theodorus and Hegesias.[3] There are also pronounced Cynic elements in Timon's Pyrrhonean critique of the philosophical tradition.[4] Whether their official acknowledgment of the Cynics was positive or negative, the new Hellenistic schools recognized that Cynicism was an ethical movement that anticipated and adumbrated some of their own leading concerns.

An informed appreciation of this point is rendered difficult for many reasons. First, our reliable evidence for the earliest Cynics is sparse and difficult to evaluate. Second, it would be false to the nature of the Cynic movement to abstract a *purely* theoretical set of notions from the Cynics' deliberately bizarre styles of behavior and literary expression. Third, Cynic principles of action, to the extent that they can be formally stated, are likely to appear jejune when considered alongside the more sophisticated ethics of Stoics and Epicureans. In view of such difficulties, one may be tempted to agree with Hegel that "there is nothing particular to say of the Cynics, for they possess but little philosophy, and they did not bring what they had into a scientific system."[5]

The temptation should be resisted. Cynicism is of philosophical interest in its own right. Nietzsche firmly grasped this point.[6] The current willingness of philosophers to take Nietzsche seriously is good news for the ancient Cynics. But even if they were relevant to the history of philosophy only for their influence on the major Hellenistic schools, that would make the Cynic contribution a significant one. In much livelier language than I use here, they can be seen to have advocated the following propositions:

1. Happiness is living in agreement with nature.
2. Happiness is something available to any person willing to engage in sufficient physical and mental training.

3. Hegesias: external conditions, including resources and status, have no bearing upon pleasure (D.L. 2.94). Theodorus: citizenship of the world, worthlessness of popular morality, public sexual behavior by the wise man (D.L. 2.99).

4. Timon's Cynic leanings have been explored in detail: cf. my article "Timon of Phlius: Pyrrhonist and Satirist," *PCPhS*, n.s. 24 (1978) 68–91; F. Decleva Caizzi, "Τῦφος: Contributo alla storia di un concetto," *Sandalion* 3 (1980) 53–66; A. Brancacci, "La filosofia di Pirrone e le sue relazioni con il cinismo," in G. Giannantoni, ed., *Lo scetticismo antico* (Rome 1981) 213–42.

5. See *Lectures on the History of Philosophy,* trans. E.S. Haldane and F.H. Simson (repr. London 1983), vol. I, p. 479.

6. Cf. H. Niehues-Pröbsting, *Der Kynismus des Diogenes und der Begriff des Zynismus* (Munich 1979).

3. The essence of happiness is self-mastery, which manifests itself in the ability to live happily under even highly adverse circumstances.

4. Self-mastery is equivalent to, or entails, a virtuous character.

5. The happy person, as so conceived, is the only person who is truly wise, kingly, and free.

6. Things conventionally deemed necessary for happiness, such as wealth, fame, and political power, have no value in nature.

7. Prime impediments to happiness are false judgments of value, together with the emotional disturbances and vicious character that arise from these false judgments.

Collectively, these propositions constitute the account of eudaimonism that had paramount appeal in Hellenistic philosophy.[7] An adherent of Epicurus or a Pyrrhonean skeptic, unlike a Stoic, would not accept all of them. But there was no disagreement on the connections drawn between happiness and self-mastery, training, rejection of mere convention as a foundation for values, and virtuous character. Hellenistic philosophers shared a general interest in completely internalizing happiness; their project was to make happiness depend essentially on the agent's moral character and beliefs, and thus to minimize or discount its dependence on external contingencies. (The Epicurean, as well as the Stoic wise man, is happy on the rack—a thought Aristotle found outrageous: *EN* 7.14, 1153b19.) If the primary credit for this conception of happiness belongs to Socrates,[8] it was the Cynics, probably under the influence of Antisthenes' Socratic writings, who were its most vivid representatives at the beginning of the Hellenistic period.

For the purpose of this study, the Socratic tradition includes only the early years of Cynicism, which are the time when the movement was encountered by the founders of the leading Hellenistic schools. Accounts of Diogenes and Cynicism by writers living under the Roman empire—Epictetus, Lucian, Dio Chrysostom, Julian—are highly idiosyncratic; they also reflect philosophical and social developments that make them of dubious *historical* value for interpreting Hellenistic philosophy. Fortunately, Diogenes Laertius wrote a life of the Cynic Diogenes rich in material that has a good chance of being authentic or at least true to the spirit of Diogenes' discourse, even though parts of it are contaminated by Stoicism to a degree that is often difficult to deter-

---

7. For further exploration of this point, cf. my articles "Stoic Eudaimonism" in *Proceedings of the Boston Area Colloquium in Ancient Philosophy*, ed. J. Cleary and D.C. Shartin, vol. 4 (Lanham 1989), pp. 77–101 (reprinted in my book cited in n. 1 above, 179–201); and "Hellenistic Ethics and Philosophical Power," in Peter Green, ed., *Hellenistic History and Culture* (Berkeley and Los Angeles 1993) 138–56.

8. Cf. Glaucon's challenge to Plato's Socrates to prove that a just man, even one consistently vilified as a criminal and subjected to every possible privation and torture, will be happier than the unjust: *Rep.* 2.360e–362c.

mine.[9] That text is the principal source I will use here for reconstructing early Cynic thought.[10]

Diogenes Laertius's anecdotal style is generally an impediment to philosophical informativeness. In the case of the Cynic Diogenes, however, anecdote and aphorism should be construed as the essential vehicles of his thought. He was not the kind of philosopher to found a school with a curriculum, a regular meeting place, and an acknowledged successor. To have done these things would have defeated his radical enterprise of defacing the currency. Nonetheless, it would be mistaken to interpret Diogenes as anything other than a philosopher in a recognizably Greek tradition—a walking and talking philosopher, as we might say. In his style of discourse, he shares features with earlier critics of conventional ethics, especially Xenophanes, Heraclitus, and above all Socrates in some of his representations.[11] At the same time, however, Diogenes' voice is utterly distinctive, and designedly so. He sought publicity, and it is hardly fanciful to conjecture that he regarded biographical narrative concerning himself as appropriate material for philosophical reflection. His lifestyle, in other words, is best interpreted not as a spontaneous enactment of his convictions, but as a studied attempt to construct a life that would breed just the kind of anecdotal tradition Diogenes Laertius records. Diogenes intended not only to shake his immediate audience out of complacency but to go down in history as a dog whose bark would echo in the stories posterity would tell about him. This point seems to have been missed in modern scholarship. To the ancient Greeks, with their interest in memorializing themselves, it was probably self-evident. In any case, our Diogenes is part and parcel of the anecdotal tradition. We should allow it to provoke thought not simply about his doctrines but also about his conception of the philosopher's role as a model for life.

Antisthenes and Diogenes

Who were the Cynics? The earliest surviving reference comes from Aristotle's *Rhetoric* (3.10, 1411a25). Speaking of metaphor, Aristotle says: "Cephisodotus [a sculptor] called the triremes decorated mills, and the Dog called the

---

9. For the Cynic presence in Diogenes Laertius's life of Zeno, cf. Mansfeld (above, n. 1) 317–51; and for Stoic influence on the representation of Diogenes, see M.-O. Goulet-Cazé, *L'ascèse cynique: Un commentaire de Diogène Laërce VI 70–71* (Paris 1986).

10. In this I side with K. von Fritz, *Quellenuntersuchungen zur Leben und Philosophie des Diogenes von Sinope,* Philologus Suppl. 18 (Leipzig 1926), and D. R. Dudley, *A History of Cynicism from Diogenes to the Sixth Century* A.D. (London 1937), against R. Höistad, *Cynic Hero and Cynic King* (Uppsala 1948), whose reconstructions of Diogenes' philosophy are heavily dependent on the Roman Cynics, especially Dio.

11. The resonance between the recorded discourse of Socrates and Diogenes is too marked to be illustrated extensively here. Characteristic instances include each philosopher's choice of a startling sobriquet—Socrates' self-descriptions as gadfly or midwife; Diogenes' as hunting dog (D.L. 6.33) or scout (*kataskopos,* D.L. 6.43), a title that Epictetus elaborates on at length (3.22.23–5)—and their common attack on inconsistency or mental disharmony and neglecting practice for vacuous theorizing (cf. Xen. *Mem.* 1.1.11–15, D.L. 6.27–28).

taverns of Attica [Spartan] messes." [12] "The Dog"—that is, the Cynic—almost certainly refers here to one particular person, Diogenes of Sinope. Aristotle, in other words, knew of only one Cynic—the original one. He speaks several times of Antisthenes or "the Antistheneans" but never connects them with Diogenes or with Cynics. [13] Quite possibly Diogenes arrived in Athens after the death of Antisthenes (see the appendix to this essay). The master-pupil relation between them and the treatment of Antisthenes as a founder of Cynicism are almost certainly an ancient biographical fabrication. [14]

Even so, Antisthenes' writings and his interpretation of Socrates were probably the most potent influences on Diogenes' philosophical development. In a passage from Xenophon's *Symposium* (4.34–44), Antisthenes defends the claim that, although he is penniless, he prides himself on his wealth. True wealth and poverty, he argues, are possessed in people's souls. He observes persons who are conventionally wealthy yet pathologically unsatisfied by their possessions. As for himself, he has sufficient to satisfy all his basic bodily needs, and, since he is not choosy, he can always find some willing woman if he wants sex. For enjoyment, instead of buying expensive things, he draws on his soul's resources. Anticipating Epicurus (cf. *Ep. Men.* 130–31), he says that it is more pleasurable to satisfy his appetite when genuinely hungry or thirsty than when not in need. Such frugality promotes honesty and contentment.

We would do Antisthenes a grave injustice by complaining about the banality of these sentiments. They are banal only from the perspective of a much later tradition saturated with such homely maxims. In its historical context, his praise of poverty is revolutionary. It also fits well with two theses elsewhere attributed to him: "Virtue pertains to actions and does not need copious theories [*logoi*] or lessons" and "Virtue is sufficient for happiness, since virtue needs nothing in addition to Socratic strength" (D.L. 6.11). The most emphasized characteristic of Socrates in Xenophon's writings is *enkrateia*, self-mastery, where self includes body and mind. [15] It is highly probable that Xenophon was principally influenced here by Antisthenes. [16]

---

12. Diogenes appears to be saying that the Athenian equivalent to what the Spartans called military messes ($\phi\iota\delta\iota\tau\iota\alpha$), where their soldier-citizens dined in common, was the taverns where Athenians gourmandized and got drunk together.

13. Unlike Aristotle, apparently, Theophrastus was sufficiently interested in Diogenes to write τῶν Διογένους συναγωγή (D.L. 5.43). This probably refers not to a collection of Diogenes' writings but to a collection of his sayings; as such it may be hypothesized as a primary source of the anecdotal material. What this amounted to can be inferred from D.L. 6.22, where Theophrastus's dialogue *The Megarian* is cited for a story of how Diogenes discovered resourcefulness by watching the activities of a mouse.

14. This is now widely recognized (see G. Giannantoni, *Socratis et Socraticorum Reliquiae* vol. 4 [Naples 1990], pp. 223–33), though some scholars (e.g., Höistad) still accept the master-pupil relationship. According to Sosicrates, an ancient author of philosophical "Successions," the first figure to adopt a Cynic lifestyle was Diodorus of Aspendus (D.L. 6.13).

15. Cf. *Mem.* 1.2.1 and my discussion of self-mastery in "Hellenistic Ethics and Philosophical Power" (see n. 7 above).

16. As the supposed founder of Cynicism according to the doxographical tradition, Antisthenes is credited with basically the same ethical doctrines as Cynics viewed from a Stoic perspective

Whatever may have been Diogenes' relation to Antisthenes, it is impossible not to read the anecdotal material (nearly all that survives of his philosophy) as evidence of a consistent attempt to play the role of Socrates gone mad (as Plato is said to have called him: D.L. 6.54), or to take Antisthenes' recommended frugality and self-sufficiency to extremes. The stories are too familiar to need more than brief exemplification here—masturbating in public, living in a wine jar, sleeping in temples or temple precincts, walking on snow barefoot, trying to eat raw meat.[17] However, most of the anecdotes are concerned not with what Diogenes did but with what he said. Like Socrates, he was above all a great talker and discussant. The philosophical significance of Diogenes consists in his efforts to deface the currency, as the Cynic slogan puts it.[18] To understand what this involved, it will be best to start from a selection of his reputed sayings.

Asked where one might see good men in Greece, he said: "Men nowhere, but boys in Sparta" (D.L. 6.27). When captured and put up for sale, he was asked what he knew how to do, and answered, "Rule over men"; and he told the herald to announce, "Does anyone want to buy a master for himself?" (D.L. 6.29). Seeing temple officials arresting someone who had stolen a bowl belonging to the treasurers, he said: "The big thieves are arresting the little thief" (D.L. 6.45). Asked which beast has the worst bite, he said: "Of wild ones, the sycophant, and of tame ones the flatterer" (D.L. 6.51). Asked why gold is pale, he said: "Because it has many people plotting against it" (ibid.).

These aphorisms—merely a representative selection—have at least three things in common: black humor, paradox or surprise, and ethical seriousness. They accept the ordinary connotations of words—for example, the manliness of men, the authoritativeness of a master, the impropriety of theft—and insist that their conventional denotations are misapplied or need to be inverted. A genuine man must be harder and better-trained than a Spartan warrior; a genuine master must be someone who has total command over himself and the moral authority to tell others how they should behave; theft can apply to state officials no less than to common criminals. These aphorisms present a powerful

---

(cf. D.L. 6.10–13 with 6.103–5). There must be some oversimplification here, probably at Antisthenes' expense. All we can say for certain is that the early Stoics found Antisthenes and Diogenes sufficiently close to their own ethical viewpoint to welcome them as links for connecting themselves with Socrates.

17. In *CR* 38 (1988) 163, reviewing Goulet-Cazé's *L'ascèse cynique,* Mansfeld writes: "If Diogenes wanted to train for total independence, then why e.g. make a habit of masturbating in the market-place (D.L. 6.69) rather than in private? He was an actor, constantly needing a public." Mansfeld, who wishes to contest Diogenes' moral seriousness, fails to mention that this anecdote is coupled with Diogenes' saying: "I wish it were possible to get rid of hunger by rubbing the belly." Diogenes' independence is not at stake. To be sure, he is an exhibitionist, but one who uses his own behavior as a way of commenting on human nature's possibilities and limitations. The sober Chrysippus cited the whole anecdote about Diogenes with approval; cf. Plutarch, *St. Rep.* 1044b.

18. παραχαράττειν τὸ νόμισμα: cf. D.L. 6.20, 71; and for examples of the expression in later Cynicism, cf. Giannantoni, *Socr. Rel.* vol. 2, V B 8–10.

challenge to unreflective views on the relation between language and ethical judgment.

We shall probably never know whether Diogenes or his father actually defaced the currency of Sinope, as the biographical tradition maintains (D.L. 6.20–21). It does seem certain, however, that the story was in circulation during his residence at Athens and that, so far from denying it, he supported its diffusion. As the slogan of his own lifestyle and discourse, defacing the currency, that is, trying to put bad money out of circulation, perfectly exemplifies the features just noted in his aphorisms. Diogenes Laertius, our source, took the point with this comment on the Cynic's discourse and behavior (6.71): "He really defaced the currency, giving to matters of convention nothing of the weight that he granted to matters that accord with nature."

It is customary to relate Diogenes' practice to the fifth-century sophistic fashion of pitting convention (*nomos*) against nature (*phusis*). Undoubtedly, his insistence that nature's prescriptions should be preferred to those of conventional norms has a formal resemblance to the use of this antithesis by the sophist Antiphon and by Callicles in Plato's *Gorgias*. But there is a striking difference between Diogenes' perception of what this comes to and sophistic arguments about the superiority of natural justice to conventional morality. Antiphon and Callicles both argue that conventional morality is an *unnatural* constraint on the rights of a person to pursue his own advantage without concern for the interests of other people. Thus, according to Callicles, natural justice licenses a powerful man to dominate his fellow citizens and indulge his appetites without any restraint (Plato, *Gorg.* 491e–492c). Diogenes, on the evidence of the anecdotal material, derives a very different moral message from his polarization of nature and convention. Someone who follows the guidance of nature, as Diogenes understands it, will have no interest in Callicles' ideal of freedom—acquiring the power and resources to give free rein to every appetite—he limits his desires to those that his nature prescribes. On examination it turns out that these desires (for sustenance, shelter, sex, company) can be satisfied by only a minimum of readily available provisions. Far from requiring the Cynic to pursue his interests at other people's expense, all that nature requires of him is that he cultivate the resourcefulness to become totally adaptable to fortune.

There is a second important difference between Diogenes' use of the nature/convention distinction and that of the sophists. For the latter, the conventions or norms antithetical to nature are the ethical principles of popular morality—justice, moderation (*sōphrosunē*), and so forth, as these are found in the Greek literary and educational tradition. Such principles, of course, were an easy target for philosophical criticism, grounded as they were in usage or ideology rather than systematic thought. Nonetheless, they could be and regularly were invoked as sanctions against unethical conduct such as theft, adultery, and profligacy, which Callicles' natural justice licenses. The anecdotes and aphorisms of Diogenes exhibit his caustic criticism of robbers, adulterers, and profligates.

In other words, Diogenes did not attack the general principles of Greek popular morality. Rather, the target of his attack on convention was largely its hypocrisy and inconsistency. He saw the same conventional norms being invoked both to proscribe unethical conduct and to condone it, and conventional practice sanctioning what conventional precept prohibited.

Diogenes' appeal to nature, then, should not be construed as a critique of all the ethical principles that *nomos* customarily sanctioned. He appears to have regarded much conduct that was conventionally unjust as *naturally* so. The conventions he sought to dislodge by his discourse and the example of his own behavior were ones that he regarded as mere irrational prejudice and as inimical to the satisfaction of natural needs. He accepted the sobriquet "dog" (*kuōn*) as a symbol of his own shamelessness (*anaideia*). The opposite quality, *aidōs*, was hallowed in tradition as a necessary mark of civilized life. As such, it served as a sanction both against antisocial conduct in the strong ethical sense, and as the grounds of modesty in daily life. In the latter sense, *aidōs* covered manners rather than morals—the socially acceptable behavior of men and women in matters of dress, styles of eating, conversing, making love, and so on.

It is clear that Cynic shamelessness, as publicized by Diogenes, concerns contempt for *aidōs* mainly in this second sense. He is explicitly said to have reproached various people for behaving unethically in the first sense with the words, "Are you not ashamed . . . ?" (D.L. 6.65). The positive counterpart of Cynic shamelessness is summed up in the catchword "freedom of speech" (*parrhēsia*). Having reduced all norms to which he must attend to those of nature, Diogenes finds himself liberated from bourgeois inhibitions and social practices. Being merely conventional, mere matters of local practice, these do not spring from human nature, as is evident from the great variety of different people's customs (D.L. 6.73). Equipped with a rough cloak, a wallet, and a stick (the beggar's standard accoutrements), the Cynic adopts a lifestyle that symbolizes his independence from the nonmoral values that enslave the majority of people.

Triumphing, as he claimed to do, over all adversities (as conventionally conceived: D.L. 6.38), Diogenes had the precedent of Antisthenes for his notion that the Cynic is the moral equivalent of Heracles, slayer of monsters.[19] The Cynic's equivalent to the labors of Heracles is the effort he expends in training himself to reject all values not sanctioned by nature and to become ready for all contingencies (cf. D.L. 6.68). Because he alone of men has command over himself, the Cynic is the only king, properly speaking.[20] In this

19. For Antisthenes' and Cynic sanctification of Heracles, see Höistad (above, n. 10) 22–73; and for Diogenes' own comparison of his lifestyle to Heracles', D.L. 6.71. Some Stoics interpreted the mythical Heracles as an allusion to cosmic tension: *SVF* 1.514.

20. For this tradition and its background, see Höistad (above, n. 10) *passim*. Once again, the Stoics followed suit; cf. *SVF* 3.617. Even if the encounters between Diogenes and Alexander the

much-repeated claim (as in other Cynic uses of language), we may observe another legacy of the nature/convention antithesis, and a further aspect of Diogenes' profession of defacing the currency.

Are names natural or conventional? And in what does the correctness of names consist? Debate on these issues had been a dominant occupation of philosophers since the later years of the fifth century. Defenders of the naturalist option argued that there is, or should be, a connection between names and things such that names denominate their nominata in virtue of affinity or shared properties. Antisthenes should probably be counted in the camp of the naturalists; he denied the possibility of contradiction on the ground that only one account, the proper *logos,* could strictly be applied to any one thing.[21] A proper account—which was also the only possible account—was one that revealed the essence of the thing. The Stoic Epictetus, in reference to Antisthenes, asks who wrote that the investigation of names is the beginning of education (1.17.10).[22]

These snippets suggest another aspect of Antisthenes' influence on Diogenes. Some of Diogenes' linguistic practice shows him turning names that are primarily descriptive into words that only pertain to those who *merit* the description. Non-Cynic "rulers" do not actually qualify as rulers. There are no Athenian or even Spartan *men.* In other cases, he substitutes a new name for the conventional one: "He used to call demagogues 'menials of the mob,' and their crowns 'foliage of fame'" (D.L. 6.41). These hyperbolical procedures should be interpreted as an integral part of Diogenes' philosophy. His defacing of the currency included an attempt to stimulate reflection by reforming the language. In rejecting the standard denotations of certain terms and in renaming certain things, he indicated the gulf between current ethical discourse and what he took to be the natural meaning of terms. The Stoics followed his reformist lead.[23]

Though simple and minimalist in its needs, the Cynic life is alleged to de-

---

Great are spurious, they became the favorite Cynic illustration of the superiority of ethical to political kingship.

21. For details and discussion, see W.K.C. Guthrie, *A History of Greek Philosophy,* vol. 3 (Cambridge 1969), pp. 209–17.

22. The catalogue of Antisthenes' writings credits him with a work in five books *On Education or Names* and another book *On the Use of Names:* D.L. 6.17.

23. Stoic reform of ethical language is more radical and formalized than anything attributed to the Cynics. In order to make their point that only the morally good is good, the Stoics allocated conventional goods such as health and wealth to the category of indifferent things (*adiaphora*), subdividing this category into things that are preferred, dispreferred, and unequivocally indifferent; cf. A.A. Long and D. Sedley, *The Hellenistic Philosophers* (Cambridge 1987), section 58. The direct influence of Cynicism on Stoicism is more evident in the Stoic practice of treating their wise man as the only bearer of such predicates as "free," "king," etc. Both philosophies could invoke the precedent of Socrates; cf. Xen. *Mem.* 1.1.16, where Socrates authorizes "slavish" as the characteristic of people who are ignorant of morality; and Plato, *Gorg.* 521d, where Socrates claims to be perhaps the only Athenian expert in politics.

mand constant training and exertion from its practitioner. This requirement offers perhaps the most promising explanation of the connections Diogenes seems to have intuited between nature, happiness, virtue, rationality, self-mastery, and internal and external freedom. Discussion of this point depends largely on the following passage from the biography by Diogenes Laertius (6.70–71):

> He [*sc.* Diogenes] used to say that training is of two kinds, mental and bodily. The latter refers to the acquisition in continuous exercise of mental impressions [*phantasiai*] that provide easy access to virtuous deeds. The one kind of training is incomplete without the other, since good condition and strength are included no less in the appropriate things that concern the mind than in those that concern the body. He used to provide evidence of the fact that from exercise virtue is easily acquired. Thus in the case of manual and other crafts we observe craftsmen achieving extraordinary dexterity by practice; similarly we observe the extent to which flutists and athletes excel in their respective fields by continuous exertion. We realize that if they had transferred their training to the mind as well, they would not have toiled unprofitably and unproductively.
>
> He used to say that nothing at all in life can succeed without training, and that training can prevail over anything. Therefore instead of useless toils people should choose ones that are natural and thus live happily, whereas in fact they are unhappy as a result of folly. In fact the actual despising of pleasure is thoroughly pleasurable when it has become habitual. Just as those accustomed to live pleasurably find it disagreeable to pass to the opposite, so those whose training has been the converse derive more pleasure from despising actual pleasures.

Although some of the language and thought of this passage are probably anachronistic, so far as Diogenes himself is concerned, its main tenor coheres with the anecdotal evidence and with what seems plausible in a philosopher whose principal antecedents were Socratic.[24] It is Socrates who pioneered the usage of craft analogies in moral philosophy. There is also ample evidence in Xenophon and Plato that Socrates would have sympathized with Diogenes' remarks on pleasure and the causal links between bodily and mental training. The passage also tallies well with the kind of education Diogenes is said to have given the sons of Xeniades (D.L. 6.30): sufficient physical training to promote a good condition as distinct from athletic bodies, memorizing litera-

---

24. Dudley (above, n. 10: 216–20) and Höistad (above, n. 10: 38–47) seem to me successful in showing that this passage (as distinct from its subsequent paragraph, section 72) is not *heavily* contaminated with Stoicism, as von Fritz (above, n. 10: 58) maintained. The one term that is almost certainly a Stoic infiltrator (*pace* Dudley and Höistad) is "mental impressions" ($\phi\alpha\nu\tau\alpha\sigma\acute{\iota}\alpha\iota$). I am not convinced that the twofold training with which the passage starts is an importation from Roman Stoicism, as Goulet-Cazé (above, n. 9: 210–13) insists. Plato's Socrates makes such training essential to the citizens of his ideal state; cf. *Rep.* 3.403c–412b. By contrast, we hear virtually nothing about physical training in our reliable sources for Stoic theory.

ture, the habit of looking after themselves without servants, contentment with a minimum diet, plain and simple dress.

If Diogenes is now beginning to sound too much like a Victorian high-school principle, a quick reminder of his public masturbation and omophagy will rapidly dispel the impression. What we need to focus on is the unity of reason and purpose underlying his radical exhibitionism. The passages just cited entitle us to credit him with a unitary philosophy, unsystematic in formulation though this doubtless was. That body and soul are mutually related and affect each other's good or bad condition is a thought that has ample Socratic backing. Yet the emphasis on bodily hardiness is distinctively Cynic. It obviously fits the notion that one will be happier the less dependent one is on external circumstances, but apparently more is involved: a good physical condition helps to promote a steady flow of "mental impressions that provide easy access to virtuous deeds." What could this mean?

If Diogenes had a theory (as distinct from an unarticulated concept) of virtue, it is not revealed in our record. Yet the Stoics would not have endorsed much of Cynicism if the Cynic life in accordance with nature was seriously at odds with their own ethics. Indeed, the Stoic Apollodorus (of the second century B.C.) described Cynicism as a shortcut to virtue—that is, virtue as the Stoics themselves understood it.[25] Perhaps this memorable expression can help. Cynicism presumably gets you to virtue quickly because, if you can actually live the Cynic life—if you can master your passions, restrict your needs and interests solely to what your rational nature requires, treat no contingencies as capable of disturbing your strength of mind—you have acquired or come close to acquiring a virtuous character, as the Stoics conceived of this. And you have done so without spending years of study in logic, physics, and ethics.

Accordingly, if by "virtuous deeds" Diogenes meant actions that stem from a character fortified in the ways just mentioned, it would not be absurd to suppose that a hardy physical condition is conducive to the formation of such a character. The Cynic has trained himself to be utterly indifferent to what he eats or drinks, where he sleeps, how he satisfies his sexual desires, and so forth; and thanks to his frugality he presumably enjoys excellent health. Consequently, it is reasonable to think that his bodily condition frees him from many of the fears and desires that disturb people of less robust condition and from many of the characteristic motives for unethical behavior. It would be absurd,

---

25. D.L. 7.121. The expression has been interestingly examined by V. Emeljanow, "A Note on the Cynic Shortcut to Happiness," *Mnemosyne* 18 (1965) 184–86. He refers to Ps.-Diogenes, *Ep.* 30, in which two routes to happiness are set out, and compared with alternative ascents to an acropolis—the one long, smooth, and easy; the other short and difficult. To attempt the latter, the Cynic route, it is necessary to be well trained and to exchange city wear for the Cynic's garb. The shortcut is explained in Ps.-Crates' *Ep.* 13 as security, health, and freedom, and in *Ep.* 21 as practice through daily deeds as distinct from the route via discourses. See also Goulet-Cazé (above, n. 9) 22–24 n. 22.

of course, to suppose that a robust physique entails a virtuous character, but Diogenes is not said to have made this claim. His doctrine is that good physical condition promotes states of mind that facilitate virtuous deeds—*mens sana in corpore sano.*

More problematic, it may seem, is the relation supposed to obtain between training and living in accordance with nature. These customarily form a contrasting pair in Greek thought. Training involves deliberate practice (*askēsis*), the shaping of what may (or may not) be "naturally" given. Probably the best rejoinder available to Diogenes would invoke animal behavior, which became a favorite Cynic device for illustrating the superiority of the natural to the conventional. The notion that humans have something to learn from animals does not imply, as has been supposed, that Diogenes wished to reduce human nature to that of beasts.[26] Against this interpretation, it is sufficient to invoke his maxim Reason or a Hangman's Rope (D.L. 6.24). Diogenes' ethical theory and practice only make sense on the assumption that human nature is rational, and that reason can and should be deployed to remove the impediments of irrational convention. At the same time, he evidently insisted that human beings *are* animals, and as such share many properties with beasts. Civilized and conventional humanity, he probably reasoned, has lost sight of this fact. Animals, living in their natural way, fend effectively for their needs and have no needs that they cannot fulfill. They are trained by nature, as it were. But human nature, under current living conditions, is not equipped without training to live a comparably satisfying life. Human nature, which is essentially rational, demands rigorous training in order to attain the self-sufficiency that is the appropriate condition of every animal.

Leaving speculation aside, interpretation of Diogenes should resist the frequent representation of him as, to cite George Boas, "the most extreme cultural primitivist." [27] According to Boas, Diogenes and the Cynics "apparently had no interest in appraising contemporary life," had a program whose logical consequences included renunciation "of all social life [and schooling] whatsoever" and "roaming about in solitude," were in "revolt against the intellect," and "attributed to our primordial ancestors only those forms of behavior which were not based on learning." The best testimony for Diogenes and his immediate influence tells a completely different story. What has been said already is sufficient to refute Boas's remarks on the appraisal of contemporary life and revolt against the intellect. Nor, in evidence known to me, does Diogenes appeal to the behavior of our primitive ancestors. As to Boas's remarks about social life, they justify a longer rejoinder.

Even if none of Diogenes' reported anecdotes and aphorisms were authen-

26. This is the view of Niehues-Pröbsting in *Der Kynismus des Diogenes* (above, n. 6).

27. I refer to Boas's article "Primitivism," in *Dictionary of the History of Ideas,* ed. P.H. Wiener, vol. 3 (New York 1973), p. 585.

tic, it strains credulity to suppose that they falsify the general impression that his life created. In those anecdotes and aphorisms Diogenes is no more portrayed as a solitary figure uninterested in social life than is Socrates. Nor is Diogenes said to have attacked community life as such or recommended a brutish and solitary existence, though in anecdotes he described himself as a wandering beggar without city, home, or country (cf. D.L. 6.38). He appears to have been a well-educated man who enjoyed argument with other philosophers, and earned the respect of many citizens. His way-out lifestyle had a philosophical purpose, as his contemporaries seem to have realized. In addition, he is credited with the composition of a large number of writings. Some of these were almost certainly genuine, especially his *Republic,* a work cited by several Stoic philosophers.[28] Although he attacked convention (*nomos*), his agenda was not the abandonment of all forms of social organization but a radical critique of the Greek polis. The writings of his follower Crates (see below) offer confirmation of this.[29]

If "cultural primitivism" fits some aspects of Diogenes' philosophy, it is too limited a category to characterize his ethics in general and his style of discourse. The same holds good for Höistad's influential assessment—"pure ethical individualism."[30] If this is taken to signify complete self-centeredness and lack of interest in society, the record, as has been seen, speaks otherwise. Diogenes claimed to offer a route to happiness, the prime constituents of which were freedom and self-sufficiency. His free and self-sufficient man needs nothing that he cannot easily procure, and thus prefigures the Stoic and Epicurean sages. However, self-sufficiency, as I have interpreted it above, does not entail Diogenes' contempt for what they or a Socrates would regard as ethical principles. Rather, it guarantees observance of them, since the Cynic has no interest in procuring his own advantage at other people's expense. The Cynic is conventionally antisocial in his contempt for what he takes to be irrational conven-

28. The key text concerning the authenticity of Diogenes' *Republic* is Philodemus, *De Stoicis* cols. 13–10 = Giannantoni, *Socr. Rel.* vol. 2, V B 126. Philodemus (cf. the edition of Philodemus's text by T. Dorandi, "Filodemo, Gli Stoici (P Herc. 155 3 339)," *Cron Erc* 12 [1982] 91–133) indicates that the doubts of some of his contemporaries (first century B.C.) should be resolved by the catalogues of Diogenes' works and by allusions to the book by the Stoics Cleanthes, Chrysippus, and Antipater. Evidently, then, such a work existed as early as the third century. Later Stoics who were embarrassed by Zeno's *Republic* probably took the lead in denying the authenticity of his Cynic model; cf. Mansfeld (above, n. 1) 348–51; M. Schofield, *The Stoic Idea of the City* (Cambridge 1991) 9–10. See also, on Diogenes' literary activity, Goulet-Cazé (above, n. 9) 85–90.

29. Criticism of Greek xenophobia is the theme of the first two *Letters of Anacharsis,* ascribed to a Scythian prince of the sixth century. This fabricated correspondence, consisting of ten short letters that develop standard Cynic themes, has been dated by its language and style to 300–250 B.C. by F.H. Reuters, *Die Briefe des Anacharsis* (Berlin 1963).

30. Höistad (above, n. 10) does not clarify what he means by ethical individualism, but he applies this and suchlike expressions to the Cynics repeatedly: cf. pp. 33, 37, 47, 50, 92. Cf. also Schofield, (above, n. 28) 52: "The values in terms of which they [the Cynics] conduct their argument are solely individual, not communal."

tions. Nothing, however, suggests that he is required by his principles to opt out of all forms of cooperative life.

Crates and the Cynic Ethical Tradition

Diogenes probably had no pupils in the sense of persons he trained to be his official followers. But whether through personal contact, hearsay, or writing, he succeeded in establishing his own lifestyle as an ethical practice that others could imitate. Those who did so, like Crates of Thebes, were consequently called Cynics. We have names and brief details concerning several other Cynics from the last decades of the fourth century B.C., but Crates is the only one of these who merits attention as a creative philosopher.[31] In the last years of the fourth century B.C., the influence of Cynicism, or at least of its ethical principles, was much more widely diffused than would be apparent from a tally of all those called Cynics in the ancient sources. Because Cynicism was not a formal school with a codified body of doctrine, some of its characteristic precepts and attitudes could be readily appropriated by philosophers of other persuasions, as I noted at the beginning of this study. Two philosophers who manifest this diffused influenced are the Megarian Stilpo and Menedemus of Eretria, said to have been once called "dog" by his fellow countrymen (D.L. 2.140).[32] With the flowering of Stoicism and Epicureanism in the next generation, Cynicism ceased to offer an ethical option powerful enough to withstand the more complex attractions of these rival philosophers, who reinterpreted and incorporated its most effective contributions to ethics. Ousted from the mainstream of Hellenistic philosophy, Cynicism degenerated into popular moralizing, satirical commonplaces, and charlatan street preaching.

At the time of Crates' maturity (ca. 325 B.C.), these developments could not be foreseen. However he came to know of Cynicism, his life and surviving writings are remarkably consonant with Diogenes' ethical principles as reconstructed above. The chief difference between Crates and Diogenes lies in their external circumstances. Diogenes may well have suffered exile and slavery; he vaunted his indifference to his misfortunes (D.L. 6.38), which no doubt contributed to his appeal. Crates was a citizen of Thebes and a wealthy landowner. We are entitled to doubt the nice story that he turned to philosophy after seeing

---

31. Of the others, who are usefully discussed by Dudley (above, n. 10), the most interesting was probably Onesicritus, a soldier and historian rather than a philosopher. As a member of Alexander's campaigns, he recorded his experience of Indian sages, whom he interpreted as excellent practitioners of Cynicism; see the excellent study by T.S. Brown, *Onesicritus* (Berkeley and Los Angeles 1949); and also M.-O. Goulet-Cazé, "Une liste de disciples de Cratès le cynique en Diogène Laërce 6, 95," *Hermes* 114 (1986) 247–52.

32. In the biographical tradition Stilpo is linked to Crates both as pupil and as teacher! Cf. the testimonies collected by K. Döring, *Die Megariker* (Amsterdam 1972) 46–53. He is also said to have been a teacher whom Zeno the Stoic heard after he left Crates (D.L. 7.1). The minimum that such testimonies show is a perceived congruity between Cynic, Megarian, and Stoic philosophy.

the beggar King Telephus in a tragedy (D.L. 6.87), but the story probably has its basis in a remarkable fact: Crates sold his lands and gave away the proceeds to his fellow citizens![33]

If Crates' renunciation of wealth was a deliberate assumption of Cynic poverty, his practice in regard to sex was no less radical. The second thing for which he is renowned was his relationship with his wife Hipparchia. In the face of all Greek convention, but in line with the views of Diogenes, the relationship of Crates and Hipparchia was apparently based on nothing except mutual consent (D.L. 6.96), which fits the doctrine on marriage attributed to Diogenes (D.L. 6.72). Flouting parental approval and the normal criteria of wealth and status, Hipparchia is said to have fallen in love with Crates and his life and discourses. Allowing all due weight to biographical embellishment, we must acknowledge that their relationship was sufficiently remarkable to become notorious. Apuleius and Christian scandalmongers give prurient accounts of public sexual intercourse between Crates and Hipparchia.[34] More interesting, and probably closer to truth, is the tradition that Hipparchia was a wholly liberated woman who shared Crates' interests and did not differ in her public behavior from her husband. On the conventional view of a Greek woman's proper place, that will have counted as a shocking example of sexual exhibitionism.

We do not need to speculate on the historicity of stories about Crates' offering his daughter on a month's trial marriage or initiating his son into sex by taking him to a brothel (D.L. 6.89, 93). Cynicism would be mere pretense if it were not fulfilled by radical practice. Criticism of convention in regard to wealth and sex had been among Diogenes' prime targets. The Stoic Zeno's respect for Crates and the *Memoirs of Crates* (D.L. 7.4) that he wrote are reason enough to believe that Crates consistently acted upon his Cynic principles even if the biographical tradition involves some fabrication.[35]

Crates' life, then, should be regarded as a contribution to Hellenistic ethics, just like that of Diogenes. There is a tendency, in the current study of Greek ethics, to ignore biography, on the grounds that the philosophical historian should restrict attention to the formal analysis of moral concepts. In the case of philosophers in the Socratic tradition, life and thought are too closely related for such restriction to be defensible. Greek ethical philosophy is supposed to tell you how to be happy and how you should live in order to be happy. The

33. For the various accounts of this, cf. Giannantoni, *Socr. Rel.* vol. 2, V H, pp. 4–17.

34. Cf. Giannantoni, *Socr. Rel.* vol. 2, V H 24–25. Cynic views on sexual morality are well discussed by J. Rist, *Stoic Philosophy* (Cambridge 1969) 56–62. Schofield (above, n. 28: 45 n. 39) attractively speculates that the marriage of Crates and Hipparchia influenced Zeno's doctrines on love and sex in his *Republic*.

35. The Cynic imprint on early Stoic literary activity is very strong: books of *chreiai* are attributed to Aristo (D.L. 7.163), Persaeus (D.L. 7.36), and Cleanthes (D.L. 7.175). Other Cynic-sounding titles include *Memorabilia on Vain Opinion* (Aristo; D.L. 7.163), *On Training* (Herillus; D.L. 7.166), a work in two books with the same title for Dionysius of Heraclea (D.L. 7.167), and much else besides.

presumption is that the philosopher is as interested in happiness as his audience, and that the reasons he can give them for living in a certain kind of way are reasons that he himself finds sufficiently convincing to act upon. If Diogenes and Crates, or for that matter, Pyrrho, Zeno, Arcesilaus, and Epicurus, did not live lives that were broadly consistent with their official thought, their philosophy would be completely discredited.

Crates publicized his Cynicism by writing satirical verse. The surviving lines, in a variety of meters, include parody of archaic poetry. This device can be interpreted as one of Crates' contributions to defacing the currency, and was directly imitated by the Pyrrhonist Timon.[36] In a famous hymn to the Muses, the Athenian statesman Solon had prayed that he might enjoy prosperity and a good reputation from all men. Crates (fr. 1 Diehl; Giannantoni, *Soc. Rel.* vol. 2, V H 84) substitutes "constant fodder for my belly." Where Solon wished that he be "sweet to my friends and bitter to my foes," Crates writes: "helpful, not sweet, to my friends." Instead of desiring, as Solon had done, "justly acquired possessions," Crates likens these to the wealth of a beetle or an ant; he asks simply for "a share in justice and wealth that is harmless, easy to transport, easy to acquire, and valuable for virtue."

The opening of his most famous poem (fr. 6 Diehl; Giannantoni, *Socr. Rel.* vol. 2, V H 70) begins by parodying the Homeric description of Crete (*Od.* 19.172–73):

There is a city Pera [punning on the word for the beggar's wallet] in the midst of wine-dark mist [punning on the Cynic catchword *tuphos,* meaning the trumpery of conventional values] fair and fertile, thoroughly squalid, possessing nothing, into which no fool sails, no parasite or lecher who delights in a whore's backside; but it bears thyme and garlic, figs, and loaves, which are no cause for its inhabitants to war with one another, nor do they take up arms for profit or for fame.

The other verses are equally direct in their message, for instance:

Deposit ten minas for the cook, a drachma for the doctor, five talents for the flatterer, smoke for the counselor, a talent for the whore, three obols for the philosopher.[37]

(fr. 13 Diehl; Giannantoni, *Socr. Rel.* vol. 2,
V H 78)

Hunger puts an end to lust; if not, time does; but if you can't use these, a rope.

(fr. 14 Diehl; Giannantoni, *Socr. Rel.* vol. 2,
V H 79)

36. For examples of Timon's parodies, cf. my "Timon of Phlius" (n. 4 above) 75–6.

37. Count 6 obols to the drachma, and 100 drachmas to the mina. As a unit of weight, the talent cannot be given a precise monetary equivalent. It should be taken here as appreciably more valuable than 10 minas.

I don't have one country as my refuge, nor a single roof, but every land has a city
and house ready to entertain me.

(fr. 15 Diehl; Giannantoni, *Socr. Rel.* vol. 2,

V H 80)

Crates stamped his mark on the Cynic tradition not just through poetry but
also through records of his remarks. Many of these set the scene for what later
became stock Cynic themes—the indifference of exile, the necessity, for happiness, of freedom from passion. One surviving item has more theoretical
interest.

Crates argued that a happy life cannot be based upon a preponderance of
pleasures.[38] He sought to prove this by running through all stages of life from
infancy to old age. "At every stage, one who reflects will find pains are considerably more numerous than pleasures." As formulated, this argument is
scarcely a searching attack on hedonism. Crates may have developed it more
subtly than it is transmitted. In any case, he probably had a philosophical target
in view as well as, perhaps, a popular conception of happiness. If so, the best
candidate is the Cyrenaic hedonism of Aristippus Senior and Junior, both of
whom had identified the supreme good with the pleasure of the moment. That
an attack like Crates' went home is virtually proved by the odd attempts of
the later Cyrenaics to modify their hedonism. One of them, Hegesias, even
denied the possibility of happiness, on grounds similar to those found in
Crates' refutation of hedonism, and nominated absence of pain as the ethical
goal (D.L. 2.94–95). It was left to Epicurus to disarm the force of Crates'
criticism by identifying the ethical goal and limit of pleasure with absence of
pain (*Ep. Men.* 128, 131). Thus he could agree that pleasurable sensations, as
construed by the Cyrenaics, might not predominate over pains, without conceding that tranquillity (freedom from pain in body and mind) was similarly
at risk.

Crates emerges as a Cynic who remained faithful to Diogenes' ethical principles. By disseminating those principles in attractive and satirical verse, he
probably did as much as anyone to make Cynicism familiar to an audience far
wider than that of other philosophers. Hence the Cynic became a characteristic
figure of Hellenistic culture, contributing to literature and appearing in it as a
topos. If the simplicity and extremity of Cynicism were its undoing, so far as
creative philosophy is concerned, they also help to account for its significance
in Hellenistic ethics. The Cynics had succeeded in showing that many conventional values were vulnerable to critical scrutiny. They had liberated happiness from its customary dependence on external circumstances and dramatized the capacity of reason to discover an autonomy that could ground living

---

38. Teles, pp. 38–39 Hense = Giannantoni, *Socr. Rel.* vol. 2, V H 44.

well exclusively in its own resources. Thus they transmitted to Hellenistic philosophy the notion of the sage or superman, answerable to no one but himself, and unaffected by the passions that trouble less fortified characters. These were radical contributions to Greek ethics, and capable of being fruitfully developed quite independently of the Cynic's way-out lifestyle and hyperbolical discourse.

Appendix:
Chronology of Antisthenes, Diogenes, and Crates

Antisthenes appears to have been at least fifteen years older than Plato (b. 427). He is said to have fought at Tanagra (D.L. 6.1), which probably refers to the battle of 426 (Thuc. 3.91), and was still alive perhaps in 366 or at least in 371 (cf. Giannantoni, *Socr. Rel.* 4.199). Hence his life approximately spanned the period 445–365. Diogenes is reputed to have died at eighty or close to ninety on June 13, 323 (D.L. 6.76, 79), the same day as Alexander the Great. If the coincidence is improbable, the chronology seems satisfactory as an approximation. As some forty years younger than Antisthenes, Diogenes could have had close contact with him, but it is quite possible they never met. In *Transactions of the International Numismatic Congress (1936)*, ed. J. Allan et al. (London 1938), 121, C. T. Seltman drew attention to the existence of defaced coins from Sinope dating from the period 350–340, and to the existence of other coins from around this period that bear the name of the official who issued them, Hicesias. This is the name of Diogenes' father. According to the biographical tradition (D.L. 6.20–21), Hicesias was the financier in charge of Sinope's currency; he or Diogenes himself defaced the currency, and Diogenes was sent into exile or fled of his own accord. If Seltman is right, the currency was defaced not for criminal reasons but in order to put bad money out of circulation. However that may be, the numismatic evidence offers remarkable corroboration to the biography. (See further Dudley [above, n. 10] 54–55; Giannantoni, *Socr. Rel.* 4.423–33; Höistad [above, n. 10] 10–12, who tries to discredit it; and H. Bannert, "Numismatisches zu Biographie und Lehre des Hundes Diogenes," *Litterae Numismaticae Vindobonenses* 1 [1979] 49–63.) It is not, of course, impossible that Diogenes visited Greece and Antisthenes before the currency episode, and then returned to Sinope. (According to the *Chronicon Paschale* [Giannantoni, *Soc. Rel.* vol. 2, V B 2], Diogenes was already famous by the year 362.) But if the numismatic evidence and associated dating carry weight, events in Sinope probably preceded and helped to influence Diogenes' decision to deface the currency in the Cynic sense; in which case Diogenes will have been in his fifties when he first came to Greece; and not only will Antisthenes have been dead, but possibly also Plato, with whom the biographical tradition associates him.

Crates' *floruit* is assigned to 328–325 (D.L. 6.87). He appears to have lived to a ripe old age, which is in keeping with his having taught the Stoic Zeno in the last years of the century (D.L. 7.1–3). Though Thebans by origin, Crates and Hipparchia probably lived in Athens for much of their lives. Crates may have encountered Diogenes there, but it should not be taken for granted that they ever met. He is naturally called Diogenes' pupil, but is also described as the pupil of Bryson the Achaean (D.L. 6.85) and of Stilpo (Seneca, *Ep.* 1.10).

Religion and the Early Cynics

M.-O. Goulet-Cazé

The idea of taking a fresh look at the religion of the early Cynics first came to me when I realized how widely divergent were the interpretations of their religious attitudes proposed by scholars hitherto, and how completely lacking those interpretations have been in any rigorously systematic approach to the problem. Zeller spoke of *Aufklärung* (enlightenment).[1] Bernays wrote of adherents of "the purest deist sect" of antiquity.[2] Gomperz explained that the monotheism of the Cynics introduced a divinity that was "an utterly colorless abstraction, comparable with the First Cause of the English deists."[3] Guthrie referred to the pantheism of Antisthenes.[4] Rahn went so far as to entitle one of his articles "Die Frömmigkeit der Kyniker" (The Piety of the Cynics).[5] And that list takes no account of the reputation for atheism with which certain classical authors saw fit to grace Diogenes of Sinope or Bion of Borysthenes. Such diversity of views cried out for closer examination.

In tackling such an issue, two major pitfalls must be avoided. The first one consists in projecting onto the religious attitudes of the Cynics our modern ideas concerning religion. The temptation to do so is particularly strong be-

My thanks to Helena Caine-Suarez, who kindly undertook to translate my article into English.

1. E. Zeller, *Die Philosophie der Griechen in ihrer geschichtlichen Entwicklung*, 4th ed. (Leipzig 1889), 2.1.328.
2. J. Bernays, *Lucian und die Kyniker* (Berlin 1879) 31.
3. T. Gomperz, *Les penseurs de la Grèce: Histoire de la philosophie antique*, 2d ed. (Paris 1908), 170 (French translation of *Griechische Denker: Eine Geschichte der antiken Philosophie*, [Leipzig 1902] 2.134).
4. W.K.C. Guthrie, *A History of Greek Philosophy* 3 (Cambridge 1969) 249 and n. 2.
5. H.Rahn, "Die Frömmigkeit der Kyniker," *Paideuma* 7 (1959–61 [1960]) 280–92.

cause the primary sources are so few in number and it is difficult to take account of them without adopting an interpretation that is in fact highly subjective—the more so since, with the exception of Antisthenes, the Cynics did not develop any consistent theory on the subject of religion. Furthermore, the anecdotes and apophthegms that have come down to us are often contradictory, and the question of their authenticity is a controversial one. To try to understand such texts, we have to put them back into the historical and religious context from which they arose and in which they took shape.

The second pitfall is one common to any study of ancient Cynicism. We must not place any reliance on the ancient sources until we have done our best to evaluate as carefully and as critically as possible their historical value. Some ancient authors are hostile: the Epicureans,[6] for instance, took against the Cynics. Conversely, Epictetus and Julian had a tendency to idealize them and to turn them into models of piety.[7] These contradictory attitudes make it necessary, above all, to read the evidence on the religious attitude of the Cynics in the light of the underlying ideas that were essential to their philosophy.

To begin with, let us look briefly at the religious climate that fostered the first generations of Cynics, from the fourth to the third centuries B.C.[8]

The Religious Climate at the End of the Classical Period and at the Beginning of the Hellenistic Age

The end of the classical period and the beginning of the Hellenistic age saw new attitudes develop toward the gods and religion.[9] The criticisms voiced and the objections raised are far from being hewn from a single block. We must be able to distinguish a whole range of positions, from questioning based on simple common sense to outright professions of atheism.

Educated people generally, and more particularly philosophers, showed themselves increasingly critical of religion in all its traditional forms. They were opposed alike to anthropomorphism and to the various myths, whose immorality was widely denounced, as well as to religious practices that were essentially ritualistic and to prayers that were blatantly and shockingly self-interested. In certain circles receptive to this type of criticism, impiety took on

6. The best-known passage occurs in Book 2 of Epicurus's Περὶ Βίων (D.L. 10.119 = fr. 14 Usener; 10 Arrighetti²): οὐδὲ κυνιεῖν [sc. τὸν σοφόν] . . . , οὐδὲ πτωχεύσειν. For later anti-Cynic polemic, see M. Gigante, "Cinismo e epicureismo," in Le cynisme ancien et ses prolongements: Actes du Colloque international du C.N.R.S., ed. M.-O. Goulet-Cazé and R. Goulet (Paris 1993), 169–75.

7. See, e.g., M.-O. Goulet-Cazé, "Le cynisme à l'époque impériale," ANRW 2.36.4 (Berlin 1990) 2773–81.

8. The religion of the Hellenistic period has stirred a large number of scholars to put pen to paper. I will mention here only the classic study of M.P. Nilsson, Geschichte der griechischen Religion, vol. 2, Die hellenistische und römische Zeit, 3d ed. (Munich 1974).

9. In La révélation d'Hermès Trismégiste, vol. 2, Le dieu cosmique (Paris 1949; repr. 1981) 153–95, A.J. Festugière has a chapter well worth reading on what he calls "the spirit of the age."

practical forms: the Mysteries are parodied, or the herms mutilated. In other circles, criticism of traditional religion brought about a whole process of reflection leading to a bitter skepticism. Injustice (it was felt) is at work in the world. The plethora of evils that weigh upon mankind is a sign of the gods' inefficiency or, at least, of their massive indifference. And recognition of this indifference leads to the expression of radical doubts over the very foundations of religious belief. Such skepticism may lead to real intellectual pessimism when people turn to meditate on the behavior of the entity that will end up acquiring the full status of divinity: *Tukhē,* or Fortune. Yet others go so far as to question the very existence of the gods, and can be considered as atheists in the full sense of the word.

As far as the philosophers who do not renounce transcendence are concerned, they bring about a sort of displacement of the divine, whereby they end up adopting a peculiarly individualistic and highly intellectualized form of religion. So it is with Plato and his Ideas, united by the One that is also the Good. So it is with Aristotle and his Prime Mover. So it is with the Stoics and their Logos, this latter at one and the same time both Destiny and Providence. In all cases, the gap widens between popular religion, faithful to a religious practice founded on ritual, and the bold theorizing of a significant number of intellectuals.

The Simultaneous Progress of Superstition and Impiety

Popular faith remains lively enough, but gets locked into rites that are linked with what we tend to think of as superstition. We must, however, understand this word in its old sense, which is to say, the perpetual fear of divine individuals.[10] A great deal could be said about tablets inscribed with curses and on the description of magic rituals. But this is not the place for detailed discussion of such subjects. Instead, I will quote just three examples that bring out the force of superstitious belief.

First, one of Diogenes' apophthegms, as reported by Diogenes Laertius: "When someone who was much given over to superstition said to him, 'With a single punch, I shall smash your head open,' Diogenes replied, 'And I shall make you tremble by sneezing to my left.'"[11] A second apophthegm is reported by Clement of Alexandria.[12] Here Diogenes makes fun of the inscrip-

---

10. See A.J. Festugière, *Épicure et ses dieux* (Paris 1946; repr. 1968) 73–76. Festugière reminds us of the definition given by Theophrastus (*Characters* 16): "δεισιδαιμονία would seem to be a feeling of constant terror (δειλία) in the face of divine power."

11. D.L. 6.48 = fr. V B 346 in G. Giannantoni, *Socratis et Socraticorum Reliquiae* 2 (Naples 1990). Sneezing was taken to be an omen (*Anth. Pal.* 11.268, 375), and sneezing to the left was an unlucky omen.

12. Clement of Alexandria, *Strom.* 7.4.25.5–26.1 Stählin (cf. D.L. 6.39 and 50) = V B 347 G. See also Ps.-Diog. *Ep.* 36 to Timomachus (pp. 249–51 Hercher = V B 566 G.). Cf. Nilsson (above, n. 8) 189 and n. 5.

tions that were often to be found on the walls of houses and were believed to have a magical and apotropaic value. For example, when he reads on the house of a dubious individual, "Heracles of the great victories lives here; may no evil enter," he remarks, with perfidious naivety, "But how ever will the master of the house get in?"

The third example concerns the death at Chalcis in the middle of the third century of the Cynic philosopher Bion of Borysthenes, as reported by Diogenes Laertius.[13] His whole life long, Bion had criticized superstition and in particular the amulets that old women used to wear around their necks. And yet, when he was about to die and felt that his condition was hopeless, he supposedly allowed himself to be persuaded to wear just such a thing. It is true that the historical value of this report is generally considered to be dubious. Nonetheless, it confirms the importance of superstitious practices in daily life.

We may also remember that Menander wrote a comedy entitled *The Superstitious Man,* and that Chapter 16 of Theophrastus's *Characters,* written around 319 B.C., dealt with the same type of character.[14]

Throughout the Hellenistic age, religion easily shades off into superstition. Certain rituals are ascribed a magical value. On all sides, people resort to omens, to divination, and to sacrifices. Religion becomes a refuge from the uncertainties of life and from the fear of the world that lies beyond the grave.

The irrational side of these practices naturally aroused a strongly adverse reaction among educated people, to such a point that we are obliged to distinguish between popular religion and the religion of the philosophers. This intellectual backlash allows us to understand how the radical reevaluation of traditional religion by the Cynics became possible, and equally how it is that their religious ideas were not always as revolutionary as they might at first sight appear.

---

13. D.L. 4.54.

14. In this chapter, Theophrastus offers several concrete examples of the superstitions of the δεισιδαίμων. If a weasel runs across the road, the superstitious man will go no farther until he has either seen another person or thrown three pebbles across the path taken by the animal. If a sack of flour has been nibbled at by a mouse, he consults the diviner to find out what he should do. And if the diviner tells him to go to the cobbler to get a patch put on the sack, then he ignores the advice and offers an expiatory sacrifice on leaving. If on a journey he hears an owl screech, he gives a start and does not go on his way again until he has uttered the words "Athena is stronger." Several centuries later, Plutarch wrote a treatise Περὶ Δεισιδαιμονίας, wherein he took up the habitual themes of the Epicurean school, which was extremely hostile to all forms of superstition. Cf. Festugière (above, n. 10) 78–80. Some scholars, notably W. Abernetty, "De Plutarchi Qui Fertur de Superstitione Libello" (diss. Königsberg 1911) 89ff., followed by H. Erbse, "Plutarchs Schrift Περὶ Δεισιδαιμονίας," *Hermes* 80 (1952) 299–300, have suggested as a possible source a work by Bion on the same subject, written under the influence of Theophrastus and of Menander. Others disagree; see J.F. Kindstrand, *Bion of Borysthenes: A Collection of the Fragments with Introduction and Commentary* (Uppsala 1976) 235.

The Reaction of the Intellectuals[15]

The Presocratic philosophers.   From the sixth century onwards, the Presocratic philosophers had brought their critical acumen to bear upon the practice and theory of traditional religion.[16] Xenophanes, in his *On Nature,*[17] had already demolished polytheism and eased the way toward a monotheistic concept of divinity. He claimed that "God is one, greatest among gods and men, in no way like mortals either in body or in mind."[18] By expressing himself in this way, Xenophanes does not deny the plurality of the gods, though he does affirm the supremacy of one god over all others. He does also imply that this god is of a superior and transcendent nature. This is in itself a revolutionary idea. On the other hand, Xenophanes also criticizes the anthropomorphic vision of divinity that lent to the gods the voice, the body, and even the clothes of human beings,[19] as well as assigning to them such dubious acts as theft, adultery, and deceit, habitual exploits of the gods in the works of Homer and Hesiod.[20] Such opinions go a great deal farther than simple criticism, since they lead toward a new type of piety. Thus it is that Xenophanes, in all likelihood shocked by the self-interested prayers of his contemporaries, wanted the gods praised through pious myths and pure language, and thought that the only demand addressed to them should be for the strength to practice justice.[21] These views, very advanced for their time, influenced later generations of philosophers, and most noticeably Antisthenes.[22]

Tradition ascribes to Heraclitus—possibly erroneously—a book entitled *On Nature,* of which the third part was supposedly of a theological nature.[23] In

---

15. See D. Babut, *La religion des philosophes grecs de Thalès aux stoïciens* (Paris 1974).

16. See, e.g., W. Jaeger, *Die Theologie der frühen griechischen Denker* (Stuttgart 1953).

17. The existence of a work by Xenophanes bearing this title has aroused considerable controversy. It has been vigorously defended by K. Deichgräber; cf. Guthrie (above, n. 4) vol. 1 (Cambridge 1967), p. 366 n. 1.

18. Fr. 23 Diels-Kranz, with Guthrie's translation (above, n. 17) 1.374.

19. Fr. 14 D.-K. Cf. Guthrie (above, n. 4) 1.373–75.

20. Frr. 11, 12 D.-K.

21. Fr. 1.13–16 D.-K.

22. Cf. G. A. Gerhard, *Phoinix von Kolophon: Texte und Untersuchungen* (Leipzig 1909) 178 n. 6, who explains that the Cynics saw in Xenophanes one of their own "beliebten alten Gewährsmänner."

23. Cf. D.L. 9.5: Τὸ δὲ φερόμενον αὐτοῦ βιβλίον ἐστὶ μὲν ἀπὸ τοῦ συνέχοντος Περὶ φύσεως, διῄρηται δ' εἰς τρεῖς λόγους, εἴς τε τὸν περὶ τοῦ παντὸς καὶ πολιτικὸν καὶ θεολογικόν. See G. S. Kirk, *Heraclitus: The Cosmic Fragments* (Cambridge 1954) 7, who explains that the rigid division of the work into three parts, physical, political, and theological, as presented by Diogenes Laertius, could not come from Heraclitus himself and that, as K. Deichgräber remarked ("Bemerkungen zu Diogenes' Bericht über Heraklit," *Philologus* 93 [1938–39] 19), it coincides, even if the order is not exactly the same, with the last three of the subdivisions that Cleanthes distinguished in philosophy, which were as follows: dialectics, rhetoric, ethics, politics, physics, and theology. The division made by Diogenes Laertius could, therefore, be of Stoic origin. As far as the book mentioned is concerned, Kirk suggests that, rather than being a true work in its

this work or elsewhere, Heraclitus criticized initiation into the Mysteries, which he considered impious,[24] as well as prayers and sacrifices, which he found irrational. For example, a person who has spilled the blood of another believes he will be purified by staining himself with the blood of sacrifice. As Heraclitus says, it is as if someone who has walked through mud were to try to clean himself with mud.[25]

We see the same desire to purify religion in Empedocles. Empedocles claims that it is impossible for us to win over the divine to our own ways and to our own purposes, and that it is impossible for us to assimilate the divine to things human by attributing to it human forms and by claiming to reach it with our eyes or with our hands.[26]

By these very brief allusions to Presocratic philosophers, I have hoped to show how the ground was well prepared for the outbursts—the "barkings"— of the Cynics. The same preparatory work was done by the sophists, some of whom went so far as to question the very existence of the gods.

The sophists.   Fifth-century religious debates center on Protagoras's *On the Gods.* A striking extract from the introduction has been preserved by Diogenes Laertius[27] and by Eusebius, who tells us in his *Praeparatio Evangelica* that the opinion upheld by Protagoras in this passage was atheistic.[28] We know that because of this passage the sophist found himself banished and his works burned in the agora.[29] Here are the famous sentences taken from the introduction: "Concerning the gods I am unable to discover whether they exist or not, or what they look like. For there are many hindrances to knowledge: the obscurity of the subject and the shortness of human life." A crucial step is taken here, for this is a clear statement of agnosticism.

Prodicus goes even further than Protagoras, in daring to state outright that the gods arose and took shape in men's imagination when these were faced with the spectacle of nature: "The sun, the moon, the rivers, the springs, and in short all that is useful to our daily life, were all thought by the ancients to be gods because of the benefit they reaped from them, in the same way that the Egyptians thought the Nile was a god."[30] Sextus, who mentions the passage, comments: "It is for this reason that we saw Demeter in bread, Dionysus in wine,

---

own right, it might be a later compilation. There are a fair number of fragments that seem to be isolated γνῶμαι. Originally, these could have been sayings of the philosopher that were collected together after the death of the master.

24. 22 B 14 D.-K.
25. 22 B 5 D.-K.
26. 31 B 133 D.-K.
27. D.L. 9.51 (= 80 B 4 D.-K.).
28. Eusebius, *Praeparatio Evangelica* 14.3.7 (= 80 B 4 D.-K.).
29. D.L. 9.52 (= 80 A 1 D.-K.).
30. 84 B 5 D.-K.

Poseidon in water, Hephaistus in fire, and so on for everything that is useful."
Seen from this point of view, the gods are but the result of a sanctification of
those things that people deemed necessary to their existence.

I will allow myself a final reference. It concerns Critias, who was both a
sophist and a disciple of Socrates. Critias was believed to have taken part in
the mutilation of the herms in 415, and as a result he was brought before the
boulē and the *ekklēsia* on an accusation of impiety.[31] It is true that he had in
fact written a satyric drama entitled *Sisyphus,* a long fragment of which has
come down to us through Sextus.[32] For Sisyphus, and therefore for Critias, men
at the dawn of time led a life that was *ataktos,* without order, *thēriōdēs,* on the
level of wild animals, and subject to the rule of the strongest. The good were
not rewarded, nor the evil punished. To palliate the disadvantages of such a
condition, people decided to make laws. As a result, evildoers, who until then
had acted in broad daylight, were obliged to act in secret. At this point, some
wise soul invented the fear of the gods to frighten those who acted, spoke, or
even thought in secret. This was the person who introduced divinity among
men, and this was the reason for his doing so.[33]

This text is crucial. Written as part of a satyric drama, it proves that the idea
of the gods as purely the result of human imagination and of human conventions was able to reach a wide public.[34]

The circle of Socrates.   Since Critias was also a disciple of Socrates, we
learn with surprise that, even within the circle of Socrates—himself respectful
of the religious practices of the city [35]—such bold ideas in respect to traditional

31. Cf. Andocides 1.47. See O. Aurenche, *Les groupes d'Alcibiade, de Léogoras et de
Teucros: Remarques sur la vie politique athénienne en 415 av. J.-C.* (Paris 1974) 69–70.

32. 88 B 25 D.-K. Recently A. Dihle, "Das Satyrspiel *Sisyphos*," *Hermes* 105 (1977) 28–42,
suggested that this work should be attributed to Euripides rather than to Critias.

33. Cf. Guthrie (above, n. 4) 3.243–44; H. Ley, *Geschichte der Aufklärung und des Atheismus*
(Berlin 1966) 1.275–77.

34. Euripides must be taken account of among the sophists because he was very close to them
and the Cynics apparently knew his tragedies well. In some passages of his plays we come across
quite revolutionary ideas. Thus at line 800 of *Hecuba,* we read: "It is custom that makes us believe
in the gods," νόμῳ γὰρ τοὺς θεοὺς ἡγούμεθα. Cf. Guthrie (above, n. 4) 3.231–32; see also the
quotation from *Bellerophon* (*TGrF* 445 n. 286) translated by Festugière (above, n. 9) 2.162. On
Euripides, see also W. Fahr, Θεοὺς Νομίζειν: *Zum Problem der Anfänge des Atheismus bei den
Griechen,* Spudasmata 26 (Hildesheim 1969), 50–69.

35. Cf. Xenophon, *Mem.* 1.4.15–18: Socrates maintains, as against Aristodemus, that divination and marvels are messages from the gods, that divine intelligence disposes everything as it
wishes, that it deals with all things at the same time, and that the eye of god sees everything at
once and understands everything. Socrates bids his disciples to commit no impiety, since no action
escapes the notice of the gods. See also *Mem.* 1.3, where Xenophon outlines the religious position
of Socrates, who believed that on such matters men should obey the law of the state, ask the gods
for good things without specifying them, and make offerings in accordance with their income,
because what pleases the gods most is a pious offering, not a rich one. In all circumstances the
word of the gods should be obeyed, even if that means being thought ill of by men.

practices were on offer. This is confirmed by what we know of the religious ideas of one of Socrates' most fervent disciples, Aristodemus the Dwarf, as they are put forward in Chapter 1 of Xenophon's *Memorabilia*. Aristodemus upheld a position in many ways similar to that of the Cynics, daring to declare that he did not sacrifice to the gods, did not pray, and did not practice divination. Such an attitude on his part did not spring from any contempt for the divine. He simply thought that the divine was too great to require his services.[36]

One can easily see how atheism in the sense we understand it today was able to develop in such a climate. In antiquity the word *atheos* had in fact two meanings. First, it meant "impious" and designated all who did not respect the state religion or who wanted to introduce into it any innovation. From this point of view Protagoras, Aristodemus, and Socrates were all *atheoi*. The word had also its modern sense, however, describing those who deny the existence of the gods.[37] Thus notorious atheists like the fifth-century poet Diagoras of Melos and the fourth/third-century Cyrenaic philosopher Theodorus, later the teacher of Bion of Borysthenes,[38] were both declared atheists.

As the *Historia Philosopha* of Pseudo-Galen tells us,[39] Diagoras and Theodorus held in common the fact that they dared maintain *mē einai theous,* that the gods do not exist.[40] Society did not take the matter lightly. Diagoras, who had in addition divulged the Mysteries, was obliged to flee with a price on his head,[41] and, without the intervention of Demetrius of Phalerum, Theodorus would have been forced to appear before the Areopagus to answer for his impious ideas.[42]

As a result of this there gradually developed a considerable climate of skepticism and atheism in both the ancient and modern meanings of those words, as is proved by the growing numbers of trials for impiety.[43] It was a time that

36. Ibid. 1.4.2, 10.

37. The expression θεοῖς ἐχθρός is a synonym of ἄθεος. On the other hand, it seems that the two substantives ἀθεότης and ἀθεΐα were used interchangeably to designate (1) the attitude of the impious man who does not attend the sanctuaries, neglects ritual, and thus shows his disregard for the traditional gods, or in other words ἀσέβεια pushed to its extreme (cf. Philo of Alexandria, *De Ebrietate* 18; Julian, *Against the Cynics* 17.199b); (2) the same attitude, but in the name of another faith (Julian, *Misopogon* 363a–b; *Ep.* 84.429b; Dio Cassius 57.14); and (3) the fact of not believing in the existence of the gods (cf. Plutarch, *De Superstitione* 2.165b–c; Sallust, *De Dis et Mundo* 18).

38. The fragments left by these two well-known atheists have been collected by M. Winiarczyk in *Diagorae Melii et Theodori Cyrenaei Reliquiae* (Leipzig 1981).

39. Diagoras T 52 = Theodorus T 38 in Winiarczyk, ibid. 17.

40. In his *De Natura Deorum* 1.1–2 (Diagoras T 40 = Theodorus T 29), Cicero underlines the difference that separates them from a Protagoras. While Protagoras voiced doubts about the existence of the gods, Diagoras of Melos and Theodorus of Cyrene claimed that there was absolutely no god, *nullus esse omnino.*

41. Diagoras T 6B, T 7, 17.

42. Theodorus T 3.

43. See E. Derenne, *Les procès d'impiété intentés aux philosophes à Athènes au Vᵉ et au IVᵉ siècles avant J.-C.,* Bibliothèque de la Faculté de Philosophie et Lettres de l'Université de Liège 45 (Liège 1930); G. Marasco, "I processi d'empietà nella democrazia ateniese," *Atene e Roma* 21 (1976) 113–31.

saw simultaneously a progression of superstition among the weak-minded and a progression of atheism among the strong-minded.

New Developments on the Divine Scene in the Hellenistic Age

Since I cannot here paint a detailed picture of the religion of the Hellenistic age, nor enter into details of historical context and background, I will simply mention two important new elements that appeared at that time on the religious scene.

The cult of Tukhē.   *Tukhē,* or Fortune, who brings about all sorts of reversals,[44] played an important role in the worldview of the Cynics. Her cult saw a rapid expansion in the Hellenistic world,[45] at a time when people had a great facility for personalizing abstractions and for creating cults around them: *Dēmokratia, Homonoia, Eirērē,* to name but a few. Many towns erected temples to *Tukhē:* Megalopolis, Argos, Elis, Hermione, Antioch—where the *Tukhē* built by Seleucus I has remained particularly famous—and Athens, which in 335 started construction of a temple to *Agathē Tukhē.* And yet the truth is that the preponderant role played by *Tukhē* points to an absence of true religion. As Nilsson says,[46] it is a sort of *Ersatz,* which draws its strength more from symbolism and allegory than from any feelings that are genuinely religious.

From the poets of the New Comedy, such as Philemon, Menander, or Diphilus, from a historian such as Polybius, from orators such as Demosthenes, and of course from philosophers who set about writing books entitled *On Fortune,*[47] we are familiar with the characteristics of an entity that, from being a simple abstraction, gradually succeeded in occupying an important place in the world of religion. *Tukhē* is *kuria,* that is to say, the mistress of the world.[48] She is jealous,[49] blind, perverse,[50] paradoxical, capricious, irrational. In other words, she does nothing *kata logon,* according to the rule of reason. Furthermore, she has an unpleasant character, which is both impersonal and unpredictable. When Philemon invokes her, he speaks of *to automaton* (the accidental),[51] while Menander speaks of *ta prospiptonta* (what happens).[52] Men complain that she

---

44. Cf. Menander fr. 590 Kock: ὦ μεταβολαῖς χαίρουσα παντοίαις τύχη.

45. The earliest trace that we can find of the cult of Fortune is at Thebes, at the beginning of the fourth century (cf. Pausanias 9.16.1: a temple had been dedicated to her in the city, where there could be seen a statue of the goddess with the child Plutus, the god of riches, in her arms. Plutus was later replaced by the horn of plenty, the specific attribute of Τύχη). On this cult, see Nilsson (above, n. 8) 2.200–210.

46. Ibid. 207.

47. E.g., Aristippus, Sphaerus, and Demetrius of Phalerum.

48. Cf. Demosthenes 18.194: οὔτε τῆς τύχης κύριος ἦν, ἀλλ᾽ ἐκείνη τῶν πάντων.

49. Cf. Plutarch, *Consolatio ad Apollonium* 6.105b.

50. Cf. Menander fr. 417 Kock.

51. Philemon fr. 137 Kock; cf. Menander fr. 275 Kock.

52. Menander fr. 51 Kock, where the aorist participle τὰ προσπεσόντα is used.

plays with them,[53] laughs at them.[54] This is why the schools of philosophy set themselves the task of raising man above the level of such a being and of rendering him impervious to her attacks. And this is why the early Cynics fought her with mockery and attempted to make themselves totally impervious to the blows she inflicted upon them: "When Diogenes fell once more into misfortune, he said: 'Really, Fortune, you do well to stand up to me in as virile a way as possible'; in such a situation he was able to go off humming to himself." [55] The philosopher added to his contempt a sort of audacity, which was a mixture of ebullience in victory and of plain impudence: "Diogenes used to say that he thought he saw Fortune hurling herself at him and saying [here he takes the opportunity to quote Homer, *Il.* 8.299]: 'I cannot reach this mad dog with my darts.' " [56] Similar attitudes are found in his disciple Crates.[57] Facing the slings of Fortune, Crates cried out: "Bravo, Fortune, you teach me what is right. See how easily I am reduced to the threadbare cloak of the philosophers!" And the same attitude is found in Metrocles, the brother of Hipparchia.[58] Far from seeing her as a divinity properly so called, the early Cynics held Fortune in contempt, refused to take her seriously, and interpreted her blows as an incitement to moral effort.[59] Nonetheless, from Bion of Borysthenes onwards (ca. 335– 245 B.C.), their attitude changed significantly. They tried to accept whatever she sent them, considering her the *khorēgos* of the great human comedy, the leader who attributes to each his role on the stage of life and whom therefore we must obey.[60]

The Oriental gods.   Gods imported from the Orient played an important role in the Hellenistic world. I will note just two of them, since they appear in Cynic documents: Cybele, the Great Mother, who is mentioned in two apophthegms attributed to Antisthenes,[61] and the Egyptian god Serapis, who is spoken of by Diogenes, though probably anachronistically, since his cult seems to have been introduced into the Greek world by Ptolemy I. Serapis was a combination of Osiris, the husband of Isis, and of Apis, the sacred bull of

53. Cf. *Anth. Pal.* 9.49.

54. Philemon fr. 110 Kock. In a fragment of Diphilus (fr. 107 Kock), we learn that where she sends one blessing she sends three misfortunes at the same time.

55. Stobaeus 4.44.71 = fr. V B 351 G.

56. Stobaeus 2.8.21 = fr. V B 148 G.

57. Fr. V H 8 G.

58. Fr. V L 3 G.

59. The attitude of the Stoics on this matter is similar. For example, Persaeus, *SVF* 1.449: ὁ σοφὸς ὑπὸ τῆς τύχης ἀήττητός ἐστι καὶ ἀδούλωτος καὶ ἀκέραιος καὶ ἀπαθής.

60. Cf. Teles, *Diatribe* 6, p. 52 Hense. Bion puts the point thus: ἡ τύχη ὥσπερ ποιήτριά τις οὖσα παντοδαπὰ ποιεῖ πρόσωπα, ναυαγοῦ, πτωχοῦ, φυγάδος, ἐνδόξου, ἀδόξου.

61. Fr. V A 2 G.: "To whoever said to him, 'Your mother is Phrygian,' he replied, 'So is the mother of the gods.' " Also fr. V A 182 G.: "Antisthenes was right when he said to the priests of the Great Mother whom he saw begging: 'I do not feed the Mother of the Gods; the gods feed her.' "

Memphis. He was represented with Cerberus, the dog of the underworld, at his side. And he was said to have come from Sinope to Alexandria. These two details perhaps explain the anecdote in which Diogenes, on hearing that Alexander had made himself an object of worship in the guise of Dionysus, suggested that he in turn should be worshipped as Serapis.[62] Such a suggestion was obviously intended to ridicule both the pretensions of Alexander and the obsequiousness of the Athenians.

The increased importance of the oracles and the Mysteries.   Alongside these two new developments should be noted the increased importance of the oracles and the Mysteries.[63] Apollo uttered oracles at Delphi, Delos, Didyma (near Miletus), and Clarus (near Ephesus). It was the oracle of Delphi (or perhaps of Delos) that led Diogenes to deface the currency.[64] An increasing importance was also enjoyed by the Mysteries, which offered initiates guarantees for their life after death. The Mysteries became an extremely widespread institution in the Hellenistic age. There were Orphic Mysteries, Mysteries of Demeter and of Kore at Eleusis, Mysteries of Dionysus, of Isis and Osiris in Egypt, Mysteries of Attis in Phrygia, of Adonis in Syria, and of the Cabiri in Samothrace. Antisthenes at one point wanted to be initiated into the Orphic Mysteries, but the process of the initiation came to an abrupt end, as we shall see. Diogenes did not refrain from lampooning the Mysteries of Demeter and of Kore at Eleusis.

The attitude of the Cynics on questions of religion is thus explained by the context of the Hellenistic age against which they reacted. We need, however, to appreciate that the criticisms they brought against religion were in themselves no more revolutionary than those of the philosophers already quoted. Insofar as the Cynics were original, we need to look elsewhere for their originality.

The Criticism Formulated
by the Ancient Cynics on Religious Questions
Limited Interest in Religious Issues

When we survey the list of titles of the works of the early Cynics, we notice immediately that there are very few dealing with religious subjects, almost as though religion was something that did not really interest these philosophers.

---

62. D.L. 6.63; cf. J. Servais, "Alexandre-Dionysus et Diogène-Sérapis. À propos de Diogènes Laërce VI 63," *L'Antiquité Classique* 28 (1959) 98–106. Servais suggests that the witty remark attributed to Diogenes may have been invented in the first quarter of the third century, at the time of the two first Lagids.

63. Cf. Nilsson (above, n. 8) 2.90–113.

64. D.L. 6.20.

Antisthenes, however, occupies a place apart. It is impossible, at least as far as religion is concerned, to group him with the other Cynics, for he almost certainly wrote several works dealing with religion, including *On Injustice and Impiety* (and a *Phusikos,* which can perhaps be identified with the *Peri Phuseōs* and the *Erōtēma peri Phuseōs* found in the catalogue preserved by Diogenes Laertius).[65] Among the Presocratic philosophers, this kind of work dealt with the question of the gods.[66] As far as Diogenes is concerned, the two lists of his works that have been preserved indicate nothing with a specifically religious title. What we know of his views in this area comes solely from anecdotes (or *chreiai*). Among the *Light Poems* of Crates, the *Paignia,* we find an elegy that opens with an invocation to the Muses of Pieria, which could, at least at first sight, be taken as an expression of piety.[67] We also know that Menippus wrote some *Epistolai Kekompseumenai apo tōn Theōn Prosōpou,* a title difficult to translate, for which one might propose *Witty Letters Written as by the Gods;* a *Necyia,* which Lucian used as the inspiration for his *Menippus or Necromancy;* and also possibly a book entitled *On Sacrifices.* Indeed, J. Geffcken showed in a study of a work by Lucian bearing the same title[68] (and some fragments by Varro and Book 7 of Arnobius's *Adversus Nationes*) that Menippus had probably written a book entitled *On Sacrifices.*[69] Finally, from the fragments that remain, there is reason to believe that Bion of Borysthenes tackled religious issues in his diatribes, but we know no more than this.

The inventory is, therefore, rather disappointing, particularly since even looking at the work of later Cynics, we find only one work—albeit an important one—that took up a position on religion: the *Kata tōn Khrēstēriōn* (*Against the Oracles*) of Oenomaus of Gadara.[70] Comparison with the Stoics highlights even more clearly the lack of interest in religion and theology shown by the Cynics, always with the exception of Antisthenes. Persaeus,[71] Cleanthes,[72] Chrysippus,[73] and Posidonius[74] each wrote a work entitled *On the Gods.*

65. These two works are cited in D.L. 6.17. A. Brancacci, *Oikeios Logos: La filosofia del linguaggio di Antistene,* Elenchos 20 (Naples 1990), 23, claims to see in Ἐρώτημα περὶ Φύσεως a subtitle of Περὶ Φύσεως.

66. See, e.g., the Περὶ Φύσεως of Xenophanes (frr. 23, 24, 38 D.-K.), a fragment of which was quoted above (see n. 18).

67. See the verses quoted below at the beginning of the section "Crates of Thebes."

68. J. Geffcken, "Menippos Περὶ Θυσίων," *Hermes* 66 (1931) 347–54.

69. Arnobius goes back to Varro, whose links with Lucian and Meleager bring us round to Menippus.

70. This title is handed down by Julian. It can probably be identified with the Γοήτων Φωρά, extracts of which have been preserved in Eusebius's *Praeparatio Evangelica.* On Oenomaus and his writing, see J. Hammerstaedt, *Die Orakelkritik des Kynikers Oenomaus,* Athenäums Monografien Altertumswissenschaft, Beiträge zur Klassischen Philologie 188 (Frankfurt a.M. 1988); id., "Der Kyniker Oenomaus von Gadara," *ANRW* 2.36.4 (Berlin 1990) 2834–65; and id., "Le cynisme littéraire à l'époque impériale," in Goulet-Cazé and Goulet, eds. (above, n. 6), 403–18.

71. *SVF* 1.448.

72. *SVF* 1.481.

73. *SVF* 3.197.9–21.

74. Frr. 20, 21 Edelstein-Kidd.

We discover also that texts revealing the conceptions and lifestyle of the Cynics make little or no reference to religious questions. Let us look at the example of the fragments of Diogenes' *Republic* as recorded by Philodemus. Of course, these are only fragments, and the possibility cannot be excluded that Diogenes spoke of religion in this work elsewhere than in the fragments selected by Philodemus. These fragments are nonetheless substantial and touch on many areas of social life. Yet all that can be found on religion is one sentence from column 20, which comes straight out of the *Republic:* we should consider that friends are false, faithless, and enemies of the gods. The reader is left dissatisfied. Shocking though it may be in itself, this idea tells us nothing about Diogenes except that he referred to the gods. We might also have hoped to allusions to Diogenes' religious ideas in Diogenes Laertius 6.30–31, where the style of upbringing practiced by Diogenes in regard to the children of Xeniades is outlined by Eubulides. Yet nothing in this passage undermines religious behavior.

It seems, therefore, fairly safe to deduce that religious and theological reflection held no great fascination for the Cynics, or at any rate not for Diogenes and his successors. The bulk of the evidence available consists of tales and anecdotes transmitted by tradition, whose documentary value derives from the fact that their attribution to Diogenes or to one of the other Cynics seems probable.

The Motives of the Cynics

Though they may not have been fired by enthusiasm for theology, the Cynics did devote a good deal of time and energy to criticizing religious practices. What could have been the motives behind this ancient Cynic criticism, which was so virulent concerning traditional religion?

We can deal quickly with one motive that, while it is certainly important, is not peculiar to the Cynics, since it is already to be found in Socrates. The Cynics sought to oblige their contemporaries to reflect on the lack of morality in the way they honored the gods and in the demands they made to them. This desire for purity is found right across the board for Cynic moral behavior. Thus it is that Antisthenes told those who would become immortal to live piously and justly.[75] As far as the contents of prayers were concerned, Diogenes reproached men for asking Fortune for things that seemed good to them but were not so in reality.[76] The second motive already has a more distinctively Cynic air, since it is founded on the distinction—so beloved by Diogenes and his disciples—between the wise and the mad. In religious behavior, as elsewhere, the Cynic makes it a point of honor to denounce the madness of his fellow men

75. D.L. 6.5 (= fr. V A 176 G.).
76. D.L. 6.42 (= fr. V B 350 G.).

(their *anoia*) and to call for reason, common sense, and discernment. We read in Diogenes Laertius:[77] "Diogenes also said that when he saw the lives of steersmen, doctors, and philosophers, he thought that man was the most intelligent living being. On the other hand, when he saw interpreters of dreams, soothsayers and those who listened to them, or those puffed up with pride and riches, he thought there was nothing more foolish than a man." Diogenes was also beside himself when he saw men sacrificing to the gods in order to have good health and, even while the ceremony was going on, eat in a way that was detrimental to their health.[78] He likewise mocked those naive enough to believe that the initiates of the Mysteries had a right to the best places in Hades:[79] "Let me laugh! Agesilas and Epaminondas will be crouching in the mire while any nincompoop—provided that he was an initiate—will be staying in the Isles of the Blessed!"[80]

The third motive is also truly Cynic. Diogenes seeks to show how popular religion and its practices stem from *nomos* and not from *phusis*. These practices, inscribed in the framework of custom and convention under all its forms, domestic, social, or political, were always a favorite target of the Cynics, and to such practices they opposed *phusis,* that is to say, nature. I refer to the famous passage of Antisthenes' *Phusikos* in which he says that according to tradition there are many gods, but according to nature only one.[81] For all the Cynics, popular religion plays a part in social conventions, which is why they criticize it. This is what led to the disrespectful comments of Diogenes, comments which must have shocked his contemporaries. He said, for instance, that there was nothing out of place in robbing a temple.[82] For Diogenes, from the moment temples are a human institution, respect for the goods within them becomes a purely social convention.

A final motive can be explained by the general context of Cynic thought. It concerns their conception whereby the happiness of the wise man consists in his realization of self-sufficiency, freedom, and detachment within himself. Indeed, traditional religion, with its demand for specific forms of worship, with the fear that it inspired in the individual—especially that of death and eternal

---

77. D.L. 6.24 (= fr. V B 375 G.).

78. D.L. 6.28 (= fr. V B 345 G.).

79. D.L. 6.39 (= fr. V B 339 G.).

80. The Spartan king Agesilaus and the Theban general Epanimondas fought at Coronea in 394 and at Leuctra in 371. If we accept traditional beliefs as expressed by Plato (*Phaedo* 69c), these brave generals, through the simple fact that they were not initiates, would not have had the right to a place in the Isles of the Blessed after death and would have been condemned to stay in the quagmire. On the quagmire, see M. Aubineau, "Le thème du bourbier dans la littérature grecque profane et chrétienne," *Recherches de Science Religieuse* 47 (1959) 185–214. A variant on the passage in question is quoted by Julian, *Or.* 7.238a, where it is explained that initiation into the Mysteries of Eleusis was restricted to those inscribed on the rolls of Athenian citizens, be they Athenians by birth or in law.

81. Frr. V A 179, 180 G.

82. Fr. V B 353 G.

punishment—and with its naive and illusory beliefs, must have been seen by Diogenes or Crates as the obstacle to be avoided at all costs, even that of never experiencing true *apatheia* (imperturbability). Let us bear in mind the famous lines of Crates: "You do not know the force of a beggar's pouch, / A handful of lupin seeds and freedom from care [*to mēdenos melein*]." [83]

The Cynic Hierarchy Man–Animal–God

The conception that the Cynics formed of animals is not unconnected with their religious views and the motivations I have just outlined. Whereas, throughout antiquity, animals are placed on a lower register of being, with man higher up and the gods at the top, the Cynics completely overturned this hierarchy. Their reasoning was more moral than religious: it is the condition of the gods to need nothing, that of those who are most like them to need very little.[84] So who then, for the Cynics, are those most like the gods? Quite simply, animals. In a significant number of their writings the Cynics set up animals as an example to man, on the ground that animals have very few needs and provide the best living examples of self-sufficiency. Thus it is, according to Theophrastus's *The Megarian,* that Diogenes was converted to frugal living while watching a mouse living without wants or desires.[85] Again, let us consider the words of Crates in one of his poems: "Far from heaping up fabulous wealth, I crave / For my only affluence the happiness of the dung beetle, the riches / Of the ant." [86] Such is the paradoxical hierarchy whereby the Cynics take gods and animals for their two paradigms.[87]

We may examine the foundations of this hierarchy (man–animal–god) in more depth by looking at a piece of evidence on the happiness of animals. The text in question is rarely included in studies on Cynicism, for the simple reason that its author, the first-century-B.C. Epicurean Philodemus, never mentions by name those he is attacking. The work concerned is his *On the Gods,*[88] and the

83. Fr. V H 83 G.
84. D.L. 6.105 (= V A 135 G.). We find this idea reappearing in Dio Chrysostom, *Or.* 6.31: "Diogenes sought to imitate the lives of the gods. For, as Homer says, only the gods lead an easy life, whilst men live laboriously and painfully."
85. D.L. 6.22 (= fr. V B 172 G.).
86. Julian, *Or.* 7.9.213c (= fr. V H 84 G.). This idea lasted as long as Cynicism did. In Ps.-Lucian, *Cynicus* 12, the Cynic declares: "If you believe that I live the life of a wild creature because I have need of little and demand little, according to your reasoning, the gods are inferior even to the wild animals, because they have no needs at all. . . . As a general rule, in all areas, the weak have more needs than the strong. That is why the gods have no needs and those closest to them have very few."
87. Even if the Cynic philosopher is not mentioned as such, we find an echo of these paradoxical views in Aristotle, *Politics* 1.2.1253a26–29, on the subject of self-sufficiency: "He who is not capable of living in a community, or who, because of his self-sufficiency, feels no need at all to do so, is in no way part of the city and is thus either a wild animal or a god."
88. Philodemus, Περὶ Θεῶν I, col. 15, 17 [*PHerc.* 26], ed. H. Diels, "Philodemos 'Über die Götter,'" *APAW, Philosophisch-historische Klasse,* I. Buch, Jg. 1915 (7 Abh.) (Berlin 1916), 26.

polemic turns on the problem of *tarakhē,* or all that is trouble, agitation, anguish, as opposed to *apatheia,* the ideal of the Cynic sage.[89] Philodemus says: "Many deem the animals blessed because of the hard conditions of their lives [*epi talaipōrismōi tou pantos autōn biou*], and especially because they have no knowledge even of the gods—the gods who, by their very nature, inspire such terror in ourselves." I believe that Diels was wholly correct in identifying the Cynics, in this passage, as opponents of Philodemus and particularly in advancing the argument that *talaipōria* (hard labor, hardship) is a key Cynic concept,[90] related to the Cynic theory of *ponoi,* those efforts to which the Cynics exhorted men with such insistence. For Philodemus's adversaries, if animals, unlike man, are happy, it is because they have a hard life and have no intuition of the divine. This spares them from experiencing anguish, particularly when faced with death.[91] But was it the Cynics of his age who opposed Philodemus? Or was he simply replying to arguments found in Cynic writings of an earlier epoch? At the end of the day, it hardly matters which. The reference to the happiness of animals is one of the most ancient and fundamental tenets of Cynicism. If Diogenes and the Cynics took a dog as their model, it is because they saw advantages in living a life that was *talaipōros* (hard).[92]

---

89. Cf. Teles, *Diatribe* 7, Περὶ ᾿Απαθείας, p. 56.4 Hense: "Thus he who is beyond passion and trouble will be happy" ([ὁ] ἐκτὸς τοῦ πάθους καὶ ταραχῆς ὤν). Likewise in his *Diatribe* 2, Περὶ Αὐταρκείας, p. 12.6–7, Teles opposes τὸν μὲν ἐν τῇ πάσῃ εὐκολίᾳ καὶ ἀπαθείᾳ ὄντα and τὸν δὲ ἐν τῇ πάσῃ ταραχῇ.

90. Diels (above, n. 88) 72–75. He quotes Xenophon, *Mem.* 2.1.18, where Socrates (not Antisthenes as Diels claims) addresses Aristippus: "He who lives miserably by his own choice [ὁ μὲν ἑκουσίως ταλαιπωρῶν] rejoices in his sufferings because he has the hope of happiness." To this text, the testimony of which is not particularly reliable since it is Socrates and not a Cynic who is speaking, we can add Epictetus 3.24.64 concerning Diogenes: "Did Diogenes love no one, he who was always so full of love for other men that for the public good he joyfully put up with so many miseries and bodily hardships [τοσούτους πόνους καὶ ταλαιπωρίας τοῦ σώματος]?" Philodemus's expression may well seem paradoxical to us: How can the animals, with their miserable life, full of πόνοι, be thought to be happy? But the context is polemical; it is Philodemus's way of deriding the Cynic theory of πόνοι.

91. Here is Philodemus's reply (Περὶ Θεῶν 1, col. 15, ll. 21–34, pp. 26–27 Diels): "The reasoning that follows does away with the great additional difficulty that has come to light [namely the idea put forward by Philodemus's adversaries, that animals are happier than we are because of the hard conditions of their lives and the fact that they have no knowledge of the gods], insofar as it makes obviously clear that the animals live with the same terrors as we do and teaches, in addition, that in some ways they know even greater terrors than we do. At the same time, this line of argument does away with the idea of happiness for animals, since it leaves them no way of mitigating their unease for so long as they keep their animal nature. With man it is not thus. Reason enables man to put off infinitely anguish and fear of the future. Similarly, by making us reflect on the passions and the few ways of dealing with them, reason leads us to hold these passions in contempt and to feel that they are easily controlled. Also, we should reflect on one hand on what is good and on the other hand on what is bad, and on what is the commonest cause of misery." In this passage, Philodemus replies, in effect, that all living creatures feel ταραχαί when faced with death and that these ταραχαί are stronger in man than in animals because animals, unlike man, cannot counteract them with reason.

92. We find an allusion to the Cynics' voluntary choice of a life that was ταλαίπωρος in Athenaeus, *Deipnosophistae* 13.611c. Myrtilus reproaches Cynulcus for doing all he can to imitate the negative features of a dog's way of life: "The dog is offensive and voracious; worse, he leads

Another passage we need to look at is of a much earlier date. It is from the treatise entitled *On Irrational Contempt,* edited by Giovanni Indelli (see esp. cols. 21–22).[93] The author is the third-century-B.C. Epicurean Polystratus, who was the second successor of Epicurus. Polystratus's adversaries are not mentioned by name, though today it is generally agreed that they are Skeptics and also in certain passages Cynics.[94] The polemic that opposes Polystratus and his adversaries concerns the psychology of animals. His adversaries, whom Polystratus considers to be full of insolence,[95] observe that moral concepts are not the same for man and for animals, and that those moral values that are generally accepted vary from one culture to another and from one man to another.[96] They conclude that such moral ideas, denuded of *phusis,* have no universal value save that lent them by convention—unlike gold and stone, where the difference is said to be one of nature rather than of convention. In the eyes of Polystratus's adversaries, who are probably Cynics, ethical concepts such as the noble (*to kalon*) or the base (*to aiskhron*) correspond to false beliefs in man and do not deserve to be taken seriously,[97] since they do not exist objectively (*kat' alētheian*).[98] This position obviously shocked Polystratus, implying as it does a fundamental spiritual identification between the human soul and the souls of animals, an idea that Polystratus hotly contested and attempts to ridicule. This passage is similar in tone to the paradoxical hierarchy mentioned above. It supposes that animals have the same souls as men have, while the Cynics go even further when they say, as we have already seen in the case of Philodemus, that animals are happier than man because they have no knowledge of the divine.

Such a hierarchy is so fundamental that for a long time it served to symbolize Cynic attitudes. A trace of this can be found as late as the second century of our era in Tatian's *Discourse to the Greeks* 25.1. While obviously completely unaware of the paradoxical hierarchy of the Cynics, Tatian addresses

---

a miserable, bare existence. These are exactly the two aspects you set about imitating: you say unpleasant things; you are gluttonous, and, what is more, you live without home or hearth."

93. Ed. G. Indelli, *Polistrato sul disprezzo irrazionale delle opinioni popolari: Edizione, traduzione e commento,* La Scuola di Epicuro 2 (Naples 1978).

94. See Gigante (above, n. 6) 203–9. It is true that Polystratus's adversaries are not clearly named, and scholars have not always agreed on their identification. Thus K. Wilke, *Polystrati Epicurei* Περὶ ἀλόγου καταφρονήσεως *libellus* (Leipzig 1905), takes them to be Skeptics, while R. Philippson ("Polystratos' Schrift Über die grundlose Verachtung der Volksmeinung," *Neue Jahrbücher für das Klassische Altertum* 12 [1909] 487–509) and Diels (above, n. 88) take them to be Cynics. The fact that in col. 21.7–10 Polystratus speaks of τῶν ἀπαθεῖς καὶ κυνικοὺς αὐτοὺς προσαγορευσάντων supports Diels and Philippson. Nonetheless, in chap. 5 of his edition (above, n. 93), Indelli showed clearly that in fact Polystratus attacked several adversaries: his main aim is certainly to counter skepticism, but he also takes on Cynics, Stoics, and Megarians. Gigante, who also supports the antiskeptical nature of the text, brings out clearly the passages directed against the Cynics.

95. Col. 23.2.

96. Col. 23.3–5.

97. Cols. 21.17–18; 22.10, 22; 24.3–4; 25.9; 26.25; 28.10.

98. Col. 21.29.

one of them with the following reproach: "You who imitate the Dog, you know not God and have descended to the imitation of creatures deprived of reason [*kai epi tēn alogōn mimēsin metabebēkas*]." This imitation, which Tatian calls a descent, a degeneration, is for the Cynic, on the contrary, an important step in the direction of the stated goal of self-sufficiency.

Cynic criticism thus goes much further than a simple criticism of popular religion and its practices. Certainly the divine may serve as a moral paradigm of self-sufficiency, on a more elevated level than the beasts of the field. The Cynics nonetheless envy animals, who have no notion of gods or of ethical and religious concepts and can therefore know true detachment. We are here far from Socrates, for whom one of the superiorities of man over animals was the very fact of knowing that the gods exist.[99] To Diogenes and his disciples religion seemed to be an obstacle to human happiness, which is why the Cynics considered the state of an irrational creature far preferable to that of men, who suffer the misfortune of having a concept of the gods.

The Criticism of Religion

It seemed to me more useful to start by analyzing the motives of the Cynics, before turning to a catalogue of their criticisms of religion. We need only to open Book 6 of Diogenes Laertius to find numerous examples of these criticisms. At the level of opposition to traditional practices, Antisthenes completely shares the attitudes of Diogenes and his successors. Like them he concentrates his attacks on the traditional and popular notion of divinity—that is to say, on anthropomorphism—while he also strikes at the heart of polytheism. When he maintains that "God resembles no one [or "nothing"]; this is precisely why nobody can grasp him through an image," [100] he means to cast doubt on the worship of statues. In the same spirit, Diogenes refuses to admit that the gods live in temples.[101] This aspect of Cynicism must have influenced the Stoics, notably the two Stoics who were closest to the Cynics: the young Zeno, who says in his *Republic* that it is pointless to build temples, since no work of builder or of craftsman is sacred;[102] and Aristo of Chios, who says that man cannot grasp the form of God: [*Aristo*] . . . *qui neque formam dei intellegi posse censeat.*[103] Finally, we must remember that one of the dogmas of the

---

99. In Xenophon, *Mem.* 1.4.13, Socrates expresses himself thus: "First of all, what other living creature [i.e., what creature other than man] has a soul capable of recognizing that the gods who ordered the universe, the greatest and most beautiful of things, exist? And what other race than man worships the gods?"

100. Fr. V A 181 G.

101. This is the reason that eating his dinner in a temple was no more difficult for him than eating his dinner on the town square.

102. *SVF* 1.264.

103. *SVF* 1.378.

Stoic catechism is [*theon*] *mē einai anthrōpomorphon* (God does not exist in a human form).[104]

Elsewhere Cynic criticism concerns traditional forms of religion, and particularly the Mysteries.[105] What the Cynics object to in the practice of the Mysteries is that once the process of initiation has been completed, the initiated believe they have earned an automatic right to salvation, and that at the end of their lives they will be assured a place in the Isles of the Blessed. This means, or so they suppose, that, if the theory is taken to its extreme, then they can lead a life of debauchery, without fear of retribution, from the moment they become initiated. Such a claim to control the power of the gods shocked the Cynics. Diogenes' reflection on the subject of the noninitiation of Agesilas and Epaminondas at Eleusis has already been quoted. No less relevant is Antisthenes' bitter comment to a priest celebrating the Orphic Mysteries:[106] "While he was being initiated into the Orphic Mysteries, and when the priest had confirmed that initiates enjoyed certain advantages in Hades, Antisthenes replied: 'Why don't you die then?' "[107]

Prayer was another of the preferred targets of our philosophers. As we have already seen, they reproached the faithful for the content of their prayers, since they often demanded things that they thought were blessings but really were not. Beyond that, they reproached them for addressing themselves to the gods before having done all that was in their power to help themselves. Offerings and sacrifices were not spared either. We have seen how Antisthenes said to some priests of Cybele who came to beg from him: "I will not feed the Mother of the Gods; the gods feed her."[108] Diogenes, seeing some people sacrificing to the gods to have a son, said to them: "Do you not sacrifice for the sort of person your son will turn out to be?"[109] And it is this same Diogenes who pokes fun at the commemorative plaques of Samothrace offered in thanks to the Cabiri, protectors of sailors during storms at sea. With his typical sharp wit, he replied to someone impressed by the plaques: "There would be many more if it were those not saved who left them."[110]

104. *SVF* 2.1021.

105. The popular belief was that the Mysteries freed us from Destiny, from the determinist causality known to the Greeks as *Heimarmenē*.

106. Antisthenes did not challenge practicing the Mysteries, but he refused to accept that mere initiation gave an automatic guarantee of future reward.

107. Fr. V A 178 G. See also Bion of Borysthenes (fr. 28 Kindstrand), who ridiculed the punishment inflicted in Hades on those not initiated into the Mysteries. They were expected to fill a barrel with a hole in it with water carried in a sieve. As far as the secret character of the Mysteries is concerned, it is criticized in Lucian, *Demonax* 11. Demonax remarks that if the Mysteries are dishonest, people should be kept away from them, but if they are good they should be revealed to all the world.

108. Fr. V A 182 G.

109. D.L. 6.63 = fr. V B 343 G.

110. D.L. 6.59 = fr. V B 342 G. The Cabiri, divinities who were supposed to protect sailors during storms, had their sanctuary on the island of Samothrace. Custom dictated that when sailors

The same virulence is shown against the interpretation of dreams. Diogenes reproached men terrified by their dreams for not caring at all about what they did when they were awake, yet being curious about what they imagined when asleep.[111] And similar attitudes are adopted toward rites of purification. It would be absurd, according to Diogenes, to imagine that water can cleanse us of our moral errors any more than it can of our errors of grammar.[112]

There remains the question of religious institutions. One day Diogenes saw the guardians of a temple dragging away a man who had stolen a goblet from the temple treasure and said: "Look: big thieves taking away a little one." [113]

In all, then, the Cynics could not abide the tendency to make human happiness depend on practices that had nothing to do with man's moral disposition.

The Originality of Cynic Views

Is there any difference between the criticisms voiced by the Cynics and those of other philosophers? One can certainly say that the Cynics took their criticism of religion to extremes. But the greatest difference is that they made absolutely no concession to traditional religion. This is an original attitude if compared with that of the Stoics or Epicureans. We know that Epicurus wrote a book *On the Gods,* one *On Holiness,* and another *On Piety,*[114] sacrificed piously to the gods, performed all the rituals of religion according to accepted usage, and encouraged participation in public ceremonies.[115] Even if the gods of the Epicureans care nothing for men and do not listen to their prayers, even if they do not engage in any activity, Epicurus supported the idea that they exist and called madmen those who deny them like Prodicus, Critias, or Diagoras.[116] As far as the Stoic sage is concerned, although like his Cynic counterpart he does not restrain himself from criticizing popular religion, he nonetheless avoids cutting himself off from the beliefs of the majority of people. Thus it is that he explains and excuses anthropomorphism and manages to safeguard

---

returned safe and sound from a voyage on stormy seas they should set up commemorative tablets to the Cabiri inscribed with their thanks. The same anecdote is attributed to Diagoras by Cicero, *De Natura Deorum* 3.89.

111. D.L. 6.43 = fr. V B 327 G.

112. D.L. 6.42 = fr. V B 326 G.

113. D.L. 6.45 = fr. V B 462 G.

114. Are the Περὶ Ὁσιότητος and the Περὶ Εὐσεβείας a single work? Or two separate works? On this point, see A. S. Pease's note in his edition (Cambridge, Mass., 1955) of *De Natura Deorum,* 1.41.115, pp. 506–8.

115. See, for example, Usener 12, 13, 169, 387 (= 10.3, 134, 93, 114 Arrighetti²). On the religion of Epicurus see, among others, Festugière (above, n. 9), esp. chap. 4, "La religion d'Épicure"; and J. Salem, *Tel un dieu parmi les hommes: L'éthique d'Épicure,* Bibliothèque d'Histoire de la Philosophie (Paris 1989), 175–79.

116. Cf. fr. 27.2 Arrighetti².

polytheism,[117] while at the same time showing a clear drift toward monotheism. He displays a pious attitude, offers sacrifices to the gods, and performs purificatory rites.[118] In other words, the theoretical revolution of the Stoic sage is accompanied by extraordinarily conservative attitudes, which were completely alien to the Cynics. Yet there is more to it than that. Other philosophers, as we have remarked already, had managed to set up new systems that effectively safeguarded popular religion. This was the case with the Platonic Ideas, the Aristotelian Prime Mover, and the Stoic Logos. Even the Epicureans, with their materialist philosophy, managed to keep a place for the gods, whom they situated in the *intermundia,* as though man had, come what may, a need to preserve his concept of the divine.

In the case of the Cynics, however, we see nothing of the sort. They had neither a rational image of the world nor a providentialist conception of nature. They did not think that the universe was created for the benefit of man or that there was a mystery of the world waiting to be uncovered. Because of this one might consider their vision of things to be somewhat mundane, whereas it is in fact essentially realistic. They understood the artificiality of the world and were resigned to it. They accepted the human condition, while at the same time remaining fully aware that it was not a particularly enviable one. In other words, they submitted to the laws of nature, firmly resolved to reject all illusion and accordingly all the temptations called civilization. So we find in them an acute desire for lucidity and a desire to preach that lucidity. This is why they went out into the streets and marketplaces, insisting that man must return to nature and that it is not difficult to do so. But they refused absolutely to allow that man—whose limits they knew only too well—should abandon his true place and his true nature, and put himself in the hands of the transcendent.

The Religious Positions of Individual Cynics

Even if their criticisms and refusal to elaborate a new religious system are the principal characteristics of the Cynics in religious matters, it is nonetheless possible to examine the particular positions of individual Cynics. When dealing with this matter, it is crucial to differentiate between Antisthenes and other Cynics, since, so far as we can tell from the texts that have survived, Antisthenes' distinction between two levels—one of the unique god, one of the many gods—is not shared by the later Cynics. Furthermore, Antisthenes is the only Cynic to have worked out a theory of the gods, and a language appropriate to

117. The stars, years, months, and changes of year were all gods to him (Zeno, *SVF* 1.165 = Cicero, *De Natura Deorum* 1.36), even if at the same time he upheld the dogma of divine unity in conceiving a god who is at once Fire, Ether, Breeze, Intelligence, Reason, Destiny, and Providence.
118. Cf. Chrysippus, *SVF* 3.604, 608.

speaking of them. In the strict sense of the word, he was the only theologian among them and also the only one, it seems, of whom we can say that he believed in the existence of a divinity.

Antisthenes (ca. 445–ca. 360 B.C.)

Antisthenes can be dealt with more rapidly than Diogenes, since Aldo Brancacci has already produced a sound study of his theology.[119] In his *Phusikos,* which Brancacci qualifies as "a work of speculative theology," Antisthenes affirms that "according to tradition there are many gods, but according to nature there is only one." [120] Placing this sentence in the context of the debates sparked off by Protagoras's *On the Gods,* Brancacci analyzes the different readings recorded for the quotation in order to bring out the oppositions of one versus many and nature versus custom, which he rightly links with another opposition made much of by Antisthenes, that of truth versus opinion.[121] Antisthenes places the single god at the level of unity, nature, and truth, and the many gods of popular religion at the level of multiplicity, tradition, and received opinion.

The position Antisthenes took up is clearly brought out in the second text from the *Phusikos* that we have at our disposal, a text handed down by Clement of Alexandria and by Theodoret,[122] which displays a serious effort on the part of Antisthenes to purify the idea of divinity: "God is not known through an image, is not seen with the eyes, resembles no one [or "nothing"]." The god in question is the one god according to nature, the divine according to custom being the anthropomorphic gods of popular religion.

Can we, then, speak of monotheism in reference to Antisthenes? If Lactantius reports his views correctly when attributing to him the idea that the gods of popular belief are many,[123] but the creator of the universe is singular,[124] then it is difficult, so far as Antisthenes is concerned, not to do so, though I agree with Brancacci's slightly qualified view: "This notion has some legitimacy, provided that the 'monotheistic idea' is given a narrow reading, which is to say that of a philosophical criticism put forward within a context of polytheistic theory and having meaning only within this context. At the same time, if it is true to say that monotheism, according to the strict definition of the term,

---

119. A. Brancacci, "La théologie d'Antisthène," *Philosophia* 15–16 (1985–86) 218–30.

120. Philodemus, *De Pietate* 7ᵃ 3–8 (= fr. V A 179 G.).

121. The quotation was variously recorded by Philodemus, Cicero, Minucius Felix, and Lactantius.

122. Fr. V A 181 G.

123. Lactantius, *Divin. Instit.* 1.5.18 = fr. V A 180 G.

124. *Antisthenes multos quidem esse populares deos, unum tamen naturalem id est summae totius artificem.*

supposes an absolute division between God and the world, then clearly one would not dream of ascribing to Antisthenes a transcendental vision of God, given the close relationship he established between the concepts of 'god' and 'nature.' " [125]

On this point, I would wish to say that Antisthenes' principal contribution to Cynicism lies in the distinction he established between nature and culture, giving greater importance to nature, and downgrading culture or custom. Without this point of departure, on which all Cynic morality is based, Diogenes' philosophy could never have existed, nor could there have been any defacing of the currency.

We have another piece of evidence to support the idea that Antisthenes not only believed in the gods—or, more accurately, a god—but also that he even showed a certain degree of piety. It concerns a passage of Diogenes Laertius that I have mentioned already: "He said that those who wished to be immortal should live in accordance with piety and justice." [126] A second piece of evidence deserves our attention. Even if it is not strictly speaking a proof of piety, it nevertheless shows that Antisthenes made much of the divine: "When someone asked him what he ought to teach his son, Antisthenes replied: 'If he is to live with the gods, philosophy; if he is to live with men, rhetoric.' " [127] One must not be too surprised at the plural "gods," since Antisthenes places himself in the cultural framework of the person he is speaking to. It is interesting, however, that we see here another opposition to add to the ones already discussed, with the divine and philosophy on one side, in the domain of unity and nature, and with men and rhetoric on the other, in the domain of multiplicity and convention. Only philosophy enables man to surpass the human level and reach that of the divine.

We can, then, properly conclude that Antisthenes believed in a god. I would even hold that we cannot exclude the possibility that he had a pious attitude, albeit a piety unlike that of his age.

Diogenes (412/403–324/321 B.C.)

The case of Diogenes turns out to be much more complex than that of Antisthenes, because the evidence, taken as a whole, is inconsistent. Diogenes refers to and speaks of the gods often, which could allow the hypothesis that he believed in them. Yet at the same time he displays an agnostic attitude concerning their existence. Some have even delved into antiquity to try to make him out to be an atheist.

125. Brancacci (above, n. 119).
126. D.L. 6.5 = V A 176 G.
127. Stobaeus 2.31.76 = fr. V A 173 G.

Ancient catalogues of atheists.   If we look at the lists of atheists that survive from antiquity, we see that Diogenes does not figure in them.[128] The first catalogue, which according to Winiarczyk goes as far back as the Neo-Academician Clitomachus, does not seem—insofar as we can reconstruct it—to contain Diogenes' name. Characters such as Diagoras, Prodicus, Theodorus, Euhemerus, Critias, and Protagoras appear, but not Diogenes. The only list of atheists in which a Diogenes is included is the list recorded in Aelian's *Variae Historiae*.[129] But it is extremely unlikely that this Diogenes is he of Sinope, given that the name has the epithet "the Phrygian." [130] In other words, these lists tell us nothing about the atheism of Diogenes.

Double attributions.   There are various cases where the same anecdote is attributed either to Diogenes or to one of the two famous atheists Diagoras and Theodorus. It is a sign of the way that people try to make Diogenes into an atheist. A case in point is the anecdote about the commemorative plaques of Samothrace;[131] Diogenes Laertius attributes the anecdote to Diogenes, but adds: "Others repeat this story of Diagoras of Melos." It is of course possible that the false attribution has been made the other way round, so to speak, and that a story originally about Diogenes has been falsely applied to someone else. Thus it is with the story told in the *Theosophy of Tübingen,* where Diogenes is described throwing a statuette of Heracles into the flames.[132] In this particular case it is plausible, in light of a reference to lentil puree, that the anecdote was of Cynic origin and was only later transferred to Diagoras.[133] But as the same

128. Cf. M. Winiarczyk, "Der erste Atheistenkatalog des Kleitomachos," *Philologus* (1976) 32–46, where it is shown that the catalogues of atheists left by Ps.-Plutarch, *Placita Philosophorum* 880d–e (= Aetius 1.7.1–2; Diels, *Dox. Gr.* 297–98), by Cicero in his *De Natura Deorum* 1.117–18, and by Sextus in his *Adversus Mathematicos* 9.50–58 all have as a common origin the catalogue of the Neo-Academician Clitomachus of Carthage, who lived around 100 B.C.

129. Aelian, *Variae Historiae* 2.31, p. 32.1–2 Dilts.

130. Did the author mean Diogenes of Sinope, and has he perhaps confused the two? This hypothesis is unlikely, given that in other passages of the *Variae Historiae* (e.g., 3.14, 3.29) Aelian definitely means Diogenes of Sinope. Sinope is not in Phrygia, even if Pontus and Phrygia are not far from one another.

131. D.L. 6.59 = fr. V B 342 G.

132. *Theosophy of Tübingen* 70, p. 184.13–17 Erbse (= Diagoras T 29 Winiarczyk).

133. This was the position of C. Buresch, *Untersuchungen zum Orakelwesen des späteren Altertums* (Leipzig 1899) 119; but it was contested by M. Winiarczyk, "Diagoras von Melos und Diogenes von Sinope," *Eos* 64 (1976) 179 and n. 12. The latter believed that lentil puree was not a dish particular to the Cynics, but quite simply the common food of poor people. He adds that no source in antiquity represents the dish as typically Cynic. However, several accounts do in fact let it be seen that lentil puree was much in favor with our philosophers. Thus we read in Plutarch and Athenaeus (V H 41 G.) this remark by Crates: "Do not get us into an argument by vaunting stew at the expense of lentil puree." Likewise, one day Crates gave Zeno a pot of lentils to carry, much to the latter's displeasure (V H 41 G.). But the best piece of evidence is to be found in Athenaeus, *Deipnosophistae* 4.156c–e. Cynulcus here describes the *Banquet of the Cynics* of one Parmeniscus. Parmeniscus tells how he wanted to attend a dinner given by Cebes of Cyzicus. When he

sort of confusion arises over Theodorus, it is doubtless an indication that someone has tried to make Diogenes out to be an atheist. We read in Diogenes
Laertius: [134] "When Lysias the apothecary asked him if he believed in the gods,
Diogenes said: 'How could I fail to believe in them, when I see that you are an
enemy of the gods?' Others say that it was Theodorus who said this." [135] Consequently we must ask in whose interest it was that Diogenes should be perceived as an atheist, and what motive there could be for these altered attributions. Some have seen here the intervention of hedonizing Cynics like Bion,
who was a pupil of Theodorus. [136] This is a possible explanation. Personally, I
think it more likely that enemies of the Cynics, hoping to discredit them, put
into their mouths the words of notorious atheists. [137]

Contradictory positions.   We also have several texts that could be seen to
give weight to the idea of Diogenes as an atheist. For example, in Cicero's *De
Natura Deorum,* [138] we read: "The prosperity and contentment of the merchants
refute, as Diogenes said, all the power of the gods." Or, in a similar vein: [139]
"Diogenes the Cynic used to say that Harpalus, who was taken at the time for
a happy thief, was evidence against the gods by the fact of his living so long
and in such good fortune." The truth is that such statements, where the author
draws commonsensical conclusions from simple facts, cannot be taken as professions of atheism. In this particular instance, he is out to give his contemporaries a lesson in common sense rather than to lead them into atheism. At any
rate, there is not a trace of militant atheism in Diogenes. At the most, and
largely as a result of these anecdotes, one could perhaps speak of a latent or
implicit atheism.

There is, therefore, no unimpeachable argument that Diogenes was an atheist. But are we for that reason entitled to conclude that he was a believer? At a
first glance, some of the texts do seem to point in that direction. First, there is

---

arrived, he found half a dozen Cynics, with Carneius of Megara at their head. And what was eaten
at this dinner? Lentil puree and more lentil puree—"We had hardly emptied one dish of lentils
before it was filled again" (156e; cf. 157b). Later the dish of lentils seems to have been associated
with Zeno: see Athenaeus 4.158b, where the Ζηνώνειος φακῆ is spoken of, as well as part of the
recipe given by the Stoic philosopher for making it. It would seem therefore that a case can be
made for Buresch's hypothesis.

134. Diogenes Laertius 6.42.
135. On Diogenes and Theodorus confused with one another, see M. Winiarczyk, "Theodorus
ὁ Ἄθεος und Diogenes von Sinope," *Eos* 69 (1981) 37–42. As in the case of Diagoras, Winiarczyk believes that the anecdote was first about Theodorus and was only later attributed to
Diogenes.
136. This, for example, is the opinion of Gerhard (above, n. 22) 81.
137. This is also the opinion of Winiarczyk (above, n. 133) 182, 184.
138. Cicero, *De Natura Deorum* 3.35.88.
139. Ibid. 3.34.83. In his annotated edition of the *De Natura Deorum* (above, n. 114: 2.1210),
Pease quotes several passages from Theognis, Plato, Euripides, Epictetus, and Athenagoras where
the same idea is expressed.

the famous oracle of Apollo, of whom Diogenes, when young, asked if he ought to deface the currency, and who enigmatically conceded public money.[140] I shall ignore this for two reasons: at the time when he went to consult Apollo, Diogenes was still living in Sinope and was therefore not yet a Cynic; and it is also possible that the oracle is a later fabrication. It is indeed rather curious that Socrates,[141] Diogenes, and Zeno[142] all consulted oracles before making key decisions in their lives.

Second, in several of his apophthegms Diogenes makes use of the gods as a moral paradigm to illustrate the idea of self-sufficiency, since the notion of divinity implies the realization of self-sufficiency and faces man with the reflection of what he also could accomplish. Thus, "he said that the quality of the gods is to need nothing; that of those most like them, to have need of very little."[143] Expressing himself in this way, Diogenes uses a widely accepted idea that enables him to get his message across more easily. Such an idea had in fact already been formulated by Socrates:[144] "He who is very close to the gods has need of very little." In this kind of declaration the gods serve as a straightforward reference to the culture of the times. This is also the case in the following syllogism proposed by Diogenes:[145]

Everything belongs to the gods.

Wise men are the friends of the gods.

The goods of friends are held in common.

Therefore everything belongs to the wise.

The positive reference to the gods in this reasoning does not, in my opinion, suggest any kind of belief on the part of Diogenes. A syllogism starts from a generally accepted premise—in other words, one that the audience can accept without difficulty. Then, through the chain of reasoning, the audience is led to accept a particular conclusion. What does Diogenes want to demonstrate? He wishes to show that the wise Cynic possesses everything in order to justify his practice of begging. When the sage begs, he is only claiming his due, since everything is his by right. To reach the conclusion he desires, Diogenes starts from received wisdom. The ideas to which he appeals, that everything belongs to the gods, that the wise are the friends of the gods, and that the goods of friends are held in common, were all more or less proverbs, with a vaguely Pythagorean or Platonic flavoring. We cannot, therefore, use these sentences as any kind of proof that Diogenes believed in the gods.

---

140. Diogenes Laertius 6.20–21 = V B 2 G.
141. Ibid. 2.38.
142. Ibid. 7.2.
143. D.L. 6.105 (= fr. V A 135 G.).
144. D.L. 2.27; Xenophon, *Mem.* 1.6.10.
145. D.L. 6.37, 72.

There remains a story from which some have drawn the conclusion—mistaken, in my opinion—that Diogenes held pantheistic views and a positive conception of divinity: "One day he saw a woman prostrating herself before the gods in a particularly indecent position. Wanting to rid her of her superstition, according to Zoilus of Perge, he approached her and said: 'Aren't you afraid, woman, to be in such an indecent position, in case there's a god behind you, since everything is full of his presence?' " [146] In fact, this is more a sally at the expense of the pious woman whom Diogenes had taken for his target that day than the affirmation of a rigorously worked-out pantheism.

There is, therefore, nothing to prove that Diogenes was a confirmed atheist, and equally little to prove that he was pious. How, then, can his attitude be defined? He was an outright agnostic, who had rid himself, once and for all, of the basic problem of religion and succeeded in extricating himself from embarrassing questions with a display of intellectual agility. Harpalus the thief is happy? It is a testimony against the gods. Lysias the apothecary acts like an enemy of the gods? Then the gods exist. But the most interesting passage is to be found in Tertullian: [147] "When Diogenes was asked what went on in heaven, he said: 'I've never been up there.' " Diogenes displays—and I believe that this is his fundamental attitude—not so much atheism as agnosticism about a realm whose secrets no effort of human understanding, nor any human experience, can penetrate. Tertullian continues: "When he was asked if the gods exist, he replied: 'Do the gods exist? I don't know, but I know that it is expedient that they should.' " [148] Thus the philosopher steadfastly refuses to pronounce on the existence of the gods. But he does show that he is well aware of the social role religion can play: the simple fact of believing in the gods instills in man a fear that society is well able to take advantage of.

At the end of the day, we discover that the gods are insignificant in Cynicism and that in Diogenes' philosophy there is no place for religious preoccupations. In the eyes of Diogenes, religion serves no purpose, and is even an obstacle to the Cynic aim of detachment. Man alone has the ability to create his own happiness. He should count only on his will to follow nature, the only power that he admits is stronger than himself. But do we therefore have to suppose that the Cynics saw a god in this same nature? A passage in Diogenes Laertius could allow of such an interpretation: [149] "Diogenes constantly proclaimed that the life the gods had given man was an easy life, but that he spoiled the ease of it by looking for honey cakes, perfumes, and other luxuries of that kind." It is obvious that the gods in question here have become one with nature. But we must not lose a sense of perspective. The Cynic sage does not revere nature as

---

146. D.L. 6.37.
147. *Ad Nationes* 2.2. See Lucian, *Demonax* 43: "When someone asked him, 'In your opinion what is it like down in Hades?' he answered, 'Wait, I'll send you a note from down below.' "
148. *An dei essent, nescio, nisi ut sint expedire.*
149. D.L. 6.44.

one would a divinity. He simply acknowledges it and puts up with it, because he cannot do otherwise, because in the end it is easy to live according to nature. He who refuses all that could compromise his ideal of detachment, who would be master of his own life, recognizes nature and its constraints as the only limits on his freedom. But once these constraints are admitted, he constructs, with the sole aid of his own *iskhus* or will power, a happiness that nothing can threaten.[150]

A confirmation of this interpretation is to be found in the ideas Diogenes expressed on the subject of his burial. There are various versions in circulation of the alleged final wishes of the philosopher.[151] Their limited historical value is of little importance here; what counts is the sentiment behind them. Diogenes variously asked to be left in the open without a tomb so that wild animals could share his body among them, to be shoved into a hole and covered with a handful of dust, or alternatively to be thrown into a river, that he might prove useful to his brothers (which might mean the fish or more indirectly, through them, his fellow men). Diogenes shows thereby that he cares very little about death, that he does not believe in any kind of afterlife, and that he accepts death quite simply as a natural phenomenon and as a normal end to life. In such a system of beliefs the gods can indeed have little part to play.

Crates of Thebes (368/365–288/285 B.C.)

Reading what the emperor Julian had to say about him in his *Against Heraclius the Cynic,*[152] it is very tempting to turn the disciple of Diogenes, Crates of Thebes, into a model of piety. Julian includes eleven lines of an elegy by Crates, claiming that they bear witness to the piety and reverence of the philosopher toward the gods. Here is a translation of the first two lines:

> Noble daughters of Mnemosyne and Olympian Zeus,
> Muses of Pieria, hear my prayer!

And here is one of the last two:

> I will conciliate Hermes and the pure Muses
> Not with luxurious offerings but with my pious virtue.

---

150. We must not look upon the Cynics as sour-minded. They were, on the contrary, passionate about happiness. Diogenes maintained that "there is only one happiness, which consists in truly rejoicing and never getting upset, whatever the place or circumstances you find yourself in" (Stobaeus 4.39.20 = V B 301 G.). He asserted that "true happiness is to be found when mind and soul find themselves in continual tranquillity and gaiety" (ἐν ἡσυχίᾳ καὶ ἱλαρότητι): Stobaeus 4.2.39.21 = V B 300 G.). This is just like Crates, in fact, who saw in life a festival for laughing and joking (Plutarch, *De Tranquillitate Animi* 466e = V H 46 G.). Diogenes reckoned that for man every day is a holiday (ibid. 477c = V B 464 G.).

151. D.L. 6.76–77.

152. Julian, *Against Heraclius the Cynic* 7.9.213b = V H 84 G.

When examining these lines, it does indeed seem perfectly proper to look upon Crates as a pious Cynic. The prayers of request that come between the two couplets have a Cynic quality to them, expressing as they do the wish to live frugally, far from riches and close to animal life. What must be made clear, however, is that this elegy is in fact an imitation of a prayer by Solon;[153] so it is from Solon that Crates borrowed the pious framework of his prayer. The first two lines quoted, which are taken to prove the great piety of the philosopher, are word for word the first two lines of Solon's prayer. The only thing that changes is the content of the prayers themselves: Solon aspires to happiness, fame, and fortune, asking that they should be given to him in accordance with the demands of justice. Should we therefore speak of piety in relation to Crates? The pious framework of the poem is so closely based on that of Solon that one should be wary of seeing in these verses a piety for which we have no other proof, and we should take care not to confuse poetic adaptation and true piety.[154] The fact that Julian uses these lines as evidence for the piety of Crates should not impress us too much, given that Diogenes, who was Crates' teacher, is presented in his writings as a kind of saint invested with a divine mission.

Menippus of Gadara (First Half of the Third Century B.C.)

Menippus, who was a disciple of Crates, wrote most notably *Witty Letters Written as by the Gods,* a *Necyia,*[155] and probably also *On Sacrifices.* Nothing has survived of these works, but we do have Lucian's *Menippus or Necromancy* and a treatise by the same author called *On Sacrifices* that reflects, as Geffcken has shown, an earlier work by Menippus on the same theme. It would of course be impossible to determine how much is original to Menippus and how much is the work of Lucian himself, imitating the Cynic philosopher. We can none-theless discern in Lucian a parodic recreation of Menippus that resonates with what we have encountered in Diogenes. This is why it seems to me to be useful to sketch the broad traits of several of Lucian's works inspired by Menippus.[156]

In *Menippus or Necromancy,* Menippus goes down to Hades to consult Ti-resias on the best way of living. Tiresias advises him to stop speculating on what is going on in heaven and wanting to understand primary and final causes,

---

153. Solon, fr. 13 in T. Bergk, *Poetae Lyrici Graeci,* 4th ed. (Leipzig 1882), 2.41–46.

154. Crates' poem is generally considered to be a parody. However, U. Criscuolo, "Cratete di Tebe e la tradizione cinica," *Maia* 22 (1970) 360–67, thinks that Crates is less concerned with parodying Solon than with showing that happiness founded on αὐτάρκεια is superior to the ideal of social happiness extolled by Solon, founded on a good reputation and on riches of which the enjoyment is equitable. However, even on this hypothesis, plausible as it is, we are not obliged to attribute any true piety to Crates.

155. These two titles are quoted in D.L. 6.101.

156. For a detailed exegesis of Lucian's *Menippus* and *Icaromenippus,* see R. Bracht Bran-ham, *Unruly Eloquence: Lucian and the Comedy of Traditions* (Cambridge, Mass., 1989) chap. 1.

and instead to make his only preoccupation *to paron,* the present situation or what immediately concerns his life.

In his dialogue *On Sacrifices,* Lucian asks whether those who offer sacrifices are pious or, on the contrary, enemies of the gods. Sacrifice implies, Lucian claims, that the gods have need of men, rejoice in flattery, and are angered if slighted. Such a conception can only be impious. In this treatise we thus have a harsh criticism of sacrifices, a criticism that probably comes from Menippus himself. Similarly, there is criticism of anthropomorphism. The pious have temples built and commission Praxiteles, Polyclitus, or Phidias to make statues that look exactly like the gods. But the faithful coming into the temples believe them to be gods in the flesh, not in ivory or gold.

Zeus Refutatus shows the same boldness of thought. Cyniscus, representing the Cynic point of view, asks Zeus questions that are in themselves impious, since he asks whether the gods are subject to *Heimarmenē,* Destiny. Zeus agrees that they are. At this point, Cyniscus remarks that, if the gods are subject to Destiny, if their power is so limited, then it is not worth men's while offering sacrifices to them. Zeus tries to get out of this conundrum by saying that the gods can at least be honored for being soothsayers and for revealing the future. But Cyniscus, who has an answer to everything, retorts that it is useless to know the future without having the power to change it. At the end of the dialogue Zeus finds himself constrained to ask: "Are we then gods in vain, who bring no providence into things, who do not deserve the sacrifices that are offered to us?" [157]

We may also glance at *Zeus Tragicus* and the *Icaromenippus.* The same kinds of ideas are expressed. The gods are powerless. They are afraid that they will no longer receive sacrifices, presents, and honors. The philosophers who claim to know the truth about the gods contradict one another. Wisdom consists in being occupied with one's own life and not attempting to penetrate the secrets of what lies beyond man.

Menippus, the exemplary *spoudogeloios* or seriocomic writer, may well have produced this kind of satire, virulent in its criticism of the gods and of traditional religion.

Bion of Borysthenes (ca. 335–245 B.C.)

To place Bion in context, we must remember that, at the time of his arrival in Athens around 314 B.C., Diogenes and Aristotle were but recently dead and the schools of Zeno and Epicurus did not yet exist, since Zeno arrived in Athens at the same time as Bion, and Epicurus not until 307/306. The position of Bion among the Cynics is somewhat peculiar, for Bion frequented in turn the

---

157. Lucian, *Zeus Refutatus* 15.

Academy, where Crates the Academician was his master; the Cynic school, where he probably listened to Crates of Thebes; the Cyrenaic school with Theodorus the Atheist; and finally the Peripatos with Theophrastus.[158]

As far as Bion's religious views are concerned, should we follow Decharme[159] and Drachmann,[160] who make him out to be an atheist, or Kindstrand,[161] who categorically refuses to speak of atheism in connection with him?

The first thing to notice is that all the criticisms voiced by earlier Cynics are present in Bion. He too pronounces against anthropomorphism, prayers to the gods, amulets, divination, the Mysteries, the idea of punishment after death. Everything suggests he had a sharp tongue when it came to attacking traditional views. For example: "How can men reasonably ask Zeus for good children, when Zeus could not even manage this for himself?"[162] Bion also points out the absurdity of the idea of sacrilege. At one point he constructs the following syllogism: "Whoever steals or destroys or even uses for his own purposes what belongs to the gods commits sacrilege; everything belongs to the gods; therefore to steal anything is always to steal it from the gods, who are masters of all; therefore stealing anything is always sacrilege."[163] The next moment he maintains that "there is no such thing as sacrilege, since anything stolen is only removed from one place belonging to the gods . . . to another place belonging to the gods."[164] His criticism of anthropomorphism was taken up by his disciple the Stoic Aristo of Chios, who in his turn ridiculed the idea of the gods' having human form.[165]

Bion certainly uttered some harsh criticism; but is that a good reason to make him into an atheist? Some anecdotes have been wrongly interpreted: for example, the one where Bion says that religion should not be discussed in the street.[166] While Decharme understood Bion's attitude to imply that he denied the existence of the gods, Kindstrand took it,[167] correctly in my opinion, to mean that he considered a discussion on religion far too important to be con-

158. See J.F. Kindstrand, *Bion of Borysthenes: A Collection of the Fragments with Introduction and Commentary* (Uppsala 1976) 56–78.

159. P. Decharme, *La critique des traditions religieuses chez les Grecs des origines au temps de Plutarque* (Paris 1904) 175.

160. A.B. Drachmann, *Atheism in Pagan Antiquity* (London 1922) 109.

161. Kindstrand (above, n. 158) 240.

162. F 29 Kindstrand.

163. F 33 Kindstrand.

164. Ibid.

165. See Cicero, *De Natura Deorum* 1.37 = Zeno, *SVF* 1.378: *cuius discipuli Aristonis non minus magno in errore sententia est, qui neque formam dei intellegi posse censeat, neque in dis sensum esse dicat dubitetque omnino deus animans necne sit.*

166. "When Crates asked Stilpo if the gods rejoiced in kneeling and prayers, they say the latter replied: 'Idiot, don't ask me about this in the middle of the street, but when I'm alone.' " The same account is given of Bion, on being asked if the gods exist: "Aren't you going to get the crowd away from me, accursed old man?" (D.L. 2.117 = F 25 Kindstrand).

167. Kindstrand (above, n. 158) 225–26.

ducted in public, which is not to exclude the possibility that people might not understand what he had to say. But if we take Bion to have been an atheist, it is above all because of a poem composed by Diogenes Laertius at the end of the chapter on Bion in Book 4 of his *Lives*. The poem begins thus: "We hear it said that according to Bion the gods definitely do not exist." [168] In the following verses, Diogenes Laertius adds his own authority to the rumor current at Chalcis (4.54): when Bion was about to die, so Diogenes tells us, he offered sacrifices to the gods and wore amulets round his neck, although all his life long he had criticized such practices.[169] Are we to believe the professions of atheism that Diogenes Laertius attributes to him, and are we to believe the story that Diogenes tells us of his conversion? Bion had aroused much hostility while he was alive. Diogenes mentions in particular the ill will borne him by Persaeus and by Philonides. What is more, the very fact that he had been a pupil of Theodorus would have encouraged people to make out that he was an atheist. At the end of the day, like Hense, Dudley, and Kindstrand,[170] we should do well to think twice before accepting the truthfulness of the details that Diogenes Laertius has preserved for us in his poem.

Another question is whether we should consider his religious ideas to reflect Cynic rather than Cyrenaic influence, given that he was a pupil of Theodorus. Kindstrand maintains that in Cynic religion we find traces of a positive attitude, even allowing for the scarcity and lateness of the material (Dio, Epictetus, Maximus of Tyre, Julian).[171] Failing to find in his case these positive elements, Kindstrand concludes that Bion, whose views by contrast are negative, must have been under the influence of Theodorus the Atheist. In fact the positive traits in question concern monotheistic belief, but we have already seen that this concerns only Antisthenes and the divine mission of the philosopher, which is present only in Epictetus and in Julian. Without wishing to deny that the influence of his relationship with Theodorus the Atheist may have led Bion to stiffen his attitudes, I nonetheless believe that they are perfectly Cynic, in the clear line of Diogenes' thinking.

Only one of his ideas cannot be attributed to the first generation of Cynic thought. It crops up when Bion expresses himself on the idea of *Tukhē*, Fortune. In fragment 16 Kindstrand, preserved in the diatribe of Teles *On Self-Sufficiency,* Bion compares Fortune to a poet. The poet distributes roles to actors, and the good actors play their roles well. Likewise Fortune attributes roles to men, and good men know how to accept the roles they have been allotted:

168. D.L. 4.55.
169. D.L. 4.55–57.
170. O. Hense, *Teletis Reliquiae,* 2d ed. (Tübingen 1909), LVIII–LIX; D.R. Dudley, *A History of Cynicism from Diogenes to the Sixth Century* A.D. (London 1937) 64–65; Kindstrand (above, n. 158) 16.
171. Id., (above, n. 158) 240.

one is a king, and another a beggar; one rules, and the other is ruled. Consequently Bion advises each man to accept the part he has been given. This attitude is noticeably different from that of previous Cynics, who criticized Fortune and laughed at her attacks. But this is the only aspect, I believe, that is not in keeping with Diogenes.

Thus Bion could perfectly well have found in Cynicism the content of his criticisms, even if he expressed them in his own particular style. Beyond that, it is probable that Theodorus supported him in his opinions, although the testimony of Diogenes Laertius's poem alone is not sufficient to class him as a confirmed atheist, as a hostile tradition, found in veiled form in Diogenes Laertius, would have us believe.

Conclusion

Of the interpretations mentioned at the beginning of my study, I would retain the idea of *Aufklärung* (enlightenment) as formulated by Zeller, qualifying it with the idea of agnosticism. I would challenge Rahn, who fleshed out the piety of the Cynics by using a Diogenes who was not the Diogenes of history, but rather a creation of Epictetus or of Julian. I would reject Gomperz's epithet "colorless," which he used, thinking principally of Antisthenes, to describe divinity as conceived of by the Cynics. If this monotheism seems colorless to us, it is because all we have today are the two fragments of the *Phusikos*. As for the Antisthenean pantheism of Guthrie, on the one hand there is a lack of evidence to support the idea, and on the other hand Brancacci has rightly drawn attention to the fact that neither Antisthenes nor his age made this notion a regular theme of inquiry. And one could say the same of the deism proposed by Bernays.

Working from the preceding remarks we can draw the following conclusions. Antisthenes was not a Cynic in his religious views, but by opposing nature to custom he undoubtedly influenced Diogenes and his successors, particularly in the criticism of tradition. In the end, Antisthenes is the only one of the philosophers we have considered to whom we can ascribe piety, at least of a philosophic kind.

As far as Diogenes is concerned, it would certainly be a mistake to lay at his door an atheism that was very probably the invention of his enemies. Whether or not the gods exist is not his problem, and, indeed, the question does not interest him. He shows a frank agnosticism on the subject. On the other hand he is passionately interested in being happy, whereas the very idea of religion and gods, as perceived by his contemporaries, contradicts his ideal of human happiness as founded on freedom, detachment, and self-sufficiency— which is why he banished such an idea from his thoughts. Diogenes wants to be master of his own destiny. The only limits to his freedom that he recognizes—because he cannot do otherwise—are the constraints imposed by nature. But in no way does he revere nature as one would a god. He simply has the wisdom not to struggle against it in vain.

As far as the later Cynics such as Crates, Menippus, or Bion are concerned, they seem to have remained faithful to the spirit of Diogenes. In the Cynicism of the imperial age, Oenomaus of Gadara, with his virulent criticism of oracles, does no more, with all his talent and conviction, than follow in the footsteps of Diogenes.[172]

I have deliberately not touched upon the various forms of idealization of Diogenes here, as they interfere with the true thought of the philosopher. In Epictetus, our philosopher has actually become a servant of Zeus, sent to earth as an example to man,[173] while Julian represents him as *theosebēs,* a man pious in both words and deeds, always acting in the service of the gods.[174] These authors turn Diogenes into a pious man, with a mission from the gods, and attribute to him a discourse on the divine that certainly did not originate with Diogenes.

172. On *The Charlatans Exposed* of Oenomaus, see Hammerstaedt (above, n. 70).

173. *Diss.* 3.24.64–73; 4.8.30; see Goulet-Cazé (above, n. 7) 2773–76.

174. In *Or.* 7 Julian explains how Diogenes was convinced that the gods looked after him and that they had not sent him to Corinth by chance. The city had, in fact, greater need than Athens of a censor. This is why, even after his enfranchisement by Xeniades—when, in other words, he was in no way obliged to do so—he nonetheless chose to stay in Corinth (*Or.* 7.212d). Julian also goes out of his way to justify the fact that Diogenes never had himself initiated. He explains that a candidate for initiation had to be inscribed on the list of Athenian citizens. Diogenes, however, considered himself to be a citizen of the world; consequently, out of respect for the gods, Diogenes had no wish to transgress the law (*Or.* 7.238). Similarly, Julian allows that Diogenes might be reproached for not going anywhere near sanctuaries, statues, or altars. To this he replies that Diogenes served the gods with his soul, giving the most precious thing he had (*Or.* 9.199b). In the same way he idealizes Crates, who worshipped the gods solely through the holiness of his morals (*Or.* 7.213).

Defacing the Currency:
Diogenes' Rhetoric
and the *Invention* of Cynicism

R. Bracht Branham

Cynicism is the only form in which common souls
come close to honesty; and the higher man must
prick up his ears at every cynicism, whether coarse
or refined, and congratulate himself whenever a buffoon without shame or a scientific satyr speaks out in
his presence.
>   —Nietzsche, *Beyond Good and Evil* 2.26

How, I ask you, can you consistently admire both
Diogenes and Daedalus? Which of these two seems a
wise man—the one who invented the saw, or the one
who, on seeing a boy drink water from the hollow of
his hand promptly took his cup from his knapsack
and broke it, upbraiding himself with the words,
"How foolish I was to carry around superfluous
baggage all this time," and then curled himself up
in his barrel and fell asleep?
>   —Seneca, *Letters to Lucilius* 90.14

The Cynics attacked and ridiculed religion, philosophy, science, art, literature, love, friendship, good
manners, loyalty to parents and even athletics—
everything which tended to embellish and enrich human life, to give it significance and to make it worth
living. The callous amoralism expressed by the word
"cynicism" reflects the impression made by them
upon their contemporaries.
>   —F. Sayre, *The Greek Cynics*

I would like to thank Marie-Odile Goulet-Cazé for causing this article to be written for her
Colloque International: Le Cynisme ancien et ses prolongements (Paris 1991); I would also like to
thank her, Tony Long, Jim Porter, and Dan Selden for reading and commenting on it. It was published in an earlier form in *Arethusa* 27.3 (fall 1994) 329–59.

cyn-ic (sin'ik) *n.* **1.** A person who believes all people
are motivated by selfishness. **2. Cynic.** A member of
a sect of ancient Greek philosophers who believed
virtue to be the only good and self-control to be
the only means of achieving virtue.—**cynic** *adj.*
1. Cynical. **2. Cynic.** Of or relating to the Cynics or
their beliefs. [Latin *cynicus*, Cynic philosopher, from
Greek *kunikos*, from *kuon, kun-*, dog. See **kwon-** in
Appendix.]

—*American Heritage Dictionary
of the English Language*

In his influential study of the ancient Cynics, *A History of Cynicism*, D.R.
Dudley prefaces his account with a list of what he concludes are the three primary features of the Cynic movement in antiquity: [1]

1. the vagrant Cynic life;
2. the assault on all established values;
3. a body of literary genres.

While Dudley concedes that these three features are "separable," they seem to
be reducible to two more basic categories, the expression of an ideology and
its practice; but given the intensely pragmatic nature of Cynicism as an ideology, [2] theory and practice, or discourse and experience, seem in fact to resist
segregation even more stubbornly than usual. Where does the theory of Diogenes end and the life begin? It is true of course that the figure of Diogenes and
the body of genres invented by the Cynics outlive the movement that generated
them. But this only suggests that the rhetorical or literary dimension may have
been more fundamental to Cynicism than to the other philosophical schools
that left no such legacy. In fact, no other philosophical movement in antiquity
had such far-reaching consequences for the institution of literature or extended
its influence so far beyond the domain of written discourse. But what features
of Cynicism as an ideology or a *modus vivendi* made it at once the most liter-
arily inventive philosophical movement as well as the only one to attract a

---

1. D.R. Dudley, *A History of Cynicism from Diogenes to the Sixth Century* A.D. (London 1937)
xi–xii.

2. I am using "ideology" in the neutral sense as defined by R. Williams, *Keywords: A Vocabulary of Culture and Society* (New York 1976): "In fact, historically, this sense of ideology as
the set of ideas which arise from a given set of material interests has been at least as widely used
as the sense of ideology as illusion" (129). Cf. T. Eagleton, *Ideology: An Introduction* (London
1991); L. Althusser, "Ideology and Ideological State Apparatuses," in *Lenin and Philosophy*,
trans. B. Brewster (New York 1971).

significant following among the illiterate majority?[3] As an approach to my main topic—the *invention* of Cynicism—I would like to sketch the rhetorical and literary dimensions of early Cynicism. Then, to support my claims for the rhetorical origins of Cynicism, I will specify those features of Diogenes' own performance that constitute it as a distinctive rhetoric,[4] unlike any other developed in antiquity.

When we think of Cynicism we probably don't immediately associate it with either the theory or the practice of rhetoric. After all, weren't the Cynics the bluntest and least cultured of the philosophical schools—assuming they can even be called a school? One thinks of Antisthenes: "*Aretē* ["excellence"] is a matter of acts [*erga*], not of discourses [*logoi*] or learning [*mathēmata*]" (Diogenes Laertius 6.11). Or Crates: "Do not shun practicing Cynicism, but avoid discoursing, for the long road to happiness is through discourses, but that through the daily practice of deeds is the short way" (*Epistle* 21).[5] And didn't the Cynics teach orally rather than with treatises or formal lectures that might give more scope to the practice of rhetoric and the arts of literacy? In general, their emphasis on practice over theory and deeds over words seems alien to rhetoric. But we need to remember that in an oral culture "great words" no less than "great deeds" were seen as a form of action,[6] and Cynicism remained the most orally oriented of all the ancient philosophical traditions.[7] Yet if we go back to the fourth century B.C. we find that the legendary founders of the movement were invariably associated with a wide range of literary activities and often had close links with the formal study of rhetoric as well.[8] If we take as

---

3. Dudley (above, n. 1): "By the early years of the second century [A.D.] the Cynics were numerous at Rome, and even more so in Alexandria. . . . We hear of Cynics in all parts of the Eastern provinces—they were numerous in Asia and Syria; Athens and Corinth; they were familiar in Epirus and Thrace; even in the remoter parts of Pontus and Moesia the inhabitants knew that a man in a beggar's dress might be a 'philosopher' " (143). It is of course impossible to document how large the Cynic movement was at any given time or what part of it was literate. But Lucilius (*Greek Anthology* 11.154) and Lucian (e.g., *Fug.* 13, *Vit. Auct.* 11), for example, speak of poor illiterate men taking up the Cynic way of life: "C'est là, croyons-nous, un trait sociologique typique du cynisme impérial: celui-ci recrute de façon importante dans les milieux sociaux les plus mal lotis" (M.-O. Goulet-Cazé, "Le cynisme à l'époque impériale" *ANRW* 2.36.4 [Berlin1990] 2736).

4. Of course any verbal artifact will exhibit its own rhetoric, and any text can be analyzed rhetorically. Throughout this study I use the term "rhetoric" of Diogenes' performance in a specifically Aristotelian sense both of its themes (e.g., *parrhēsia*) and of its methods. For an analysis of both, see "Diogenes' Rhetoric," below. For Diogenes' attitude toward rhetoric, see n. 22.

5. Cited by F. Sayre, *The Greek Cynics* (Baltimore 1948) 7.

6. W.J. Ong, *Orality and Literacy: The Technologizing of the Word* (London 1987) chap. 3; R.P. Martin, *The Language of Heroes: Speech and Performance in the Iliad* (Ithaca 1989).

7. This is not of course to deny the orality of Socrates or of post-Platonic Academics who disavowed writing. For Diogenes and writing, see nn. 8, 9.

8. Diogenes' paradoxical stance as an author is the subject of one *chreia*: "When Hegesias asked to borrow one of his writings [*suggrammata*] Diogenes said, 'You're a fool, Hegesias; you wouldn't choose painted figs over real [*alēthinas*] ones, but you're overlooking the real discipline [*askēsis hē alēthinē*] in your eagerness for a written version' " (*gegrammenē*: D.L. 6.48). This

examples the figures Lucian (in the second century A.D.) regarded as canonical—Antisthenes, Diogenes, Crates, and Menippus—we notice that every one is a major literary figure, with the possible exception of Diogenes himself.[9] Antisthenes, of course, is not technically a Cynic,[10] but he was appropriated by the tradition and hence is significant here as part of its self-description. (Neither Diogenes Laertius nor Lucian hesitates to group him with Diogenes and company.) It is an interesting fact, therefore, that he is said to have been a student of Gorgias[11]—as well as of Socrates—and that among his many writings he is credited with works on such "rhetorical" topics as "style and expression," "dialectic," "eristic," "forensic oratory," and "sophists," as well as numerous works on literary topics drawn from myth such as the contest between Ajax and Odysseus for the arms of Achilles.[12] Such a range of interests is not at all atypical of the early Cynics. Nor is it confined to a few major figures. A minor author such as Zoilus of Amphipolis, also active in the fourth century, was known in antiquity as "a Cynic rhetorician and satirist" (*kuōn rhētorikos kai psogeros*: Aelian, *VH* 11.10). He was famous for the bite of his attacks on Isocrates, Plato, and Homer, and was dubbed "Homeromastix." Aristotle took him seriously enough to write a reply to his work on Homer. Dionysius of Halicarnassus (*Pomp.* 1) refers favorably to his critique of Plato. In addition to works of praise and blame, Zoilus wrote a technical treatise on the rhetorical figures, in which he offered one of the earliest formal definitions of the term *skhēma* as "to feign one thing and mean another" (cf. Quintilian 9.1.14). Zoilus was a student of the Athenian rhetorician Polycrates, another pupil of

---

chreia could be taken two ways: (1) as the *chreia* tradition (originally oral) affirming itself against other written accounts by or of Diogenes; or (2) as Diogenes taking a quasi-Socratic stance in favor of actual practice (*askēsis*) over the "written word." For Diogenes' "works," see n. 9. For the essentially oral character of ancient rhetoric, see Ong (above, n. 6) 109.

9. In antiquity Diogenes was alleged to be the author of numerous books. Diogenes Laertius attributes dialogues, tragedies, *chreiai,* and epistles to him but also reports that Satyrus, the Peripatetic biographer (third century B.C.), and Sosicrates, a historian and biographer (second century B.C.), deny that he left anything in writing (D.L. 6.80). On the other hand, several later authors refer to his works by title, including a *Republic.* For a careful assessment of the evidence for Diogenes' literary activity, see M.-O. Goulet-Cazé, *L'ascèse cynique: Un commentaire de Diogène Laërce VI 70–71* (Paris 1986), 85–90; G. Giannantoni, *Socratis et Socraticorum Reliquiae* (Naples 1990) 4.461–84, K. Döring," 'Spielereien, mit verdecktem Ernst vermischt': Unterhaltsame Formen Literarischer Wissensvermittlung bei Diogenes von Sinope und den frühen Kynikern," in *Vermittlung und Tradierung von Wissen in der griechischen Kultur,* ed. W. Kullmann and J. Althof (Tübingen 1993), 337–52. If Diogenes did write books, they would in all likelihood have been parodies and satires directed against the most influential poets and philosophers, not philosophical works like those of Plato, Aristotle, or the Stoics. Compare, for example, Diogenes' interpretation of Prometheus and Oedipus in Dio Chrysostom, *Or.* 6.5–29; 10.29–30.

10. See Giannantoni (above, no. 9) 223–33.

11. I cite this claim as part of the tradition's self-description. It may not be possible chronologically.

12. Of which the speeches of the two heroes survive. For this important fragment, see M.-O. Goulet-Cazé, "L'Ajax et l'Ulysse d'Antisthène," in ΣΟΦΙΗΣ ΜΑΙΗΤΟΡΕΣ, *Chercheurs de sagesse, Hommage à Jean Pépin,* Série Antiquité 131 (Paris 1992) 5–36.

Gorgias, who wrote encomia of Busiris and Clytemnestra and an indictment of Socrates. Zoilus was the teacher of Anaximenes of Lampascus, who wrote histories, and who may have been the author of the *Rhetorica ad Alexandrum* (cf. Quint. 3.4.9). Other than Crates the only Cynic roughly contemporary with Diogenes some of whose work survives is Onesicritus of Astypalaea.[13] He evidently wrote an account of Alexander modeled on Xenophon's *Cyropaedia,* in which the gymnosophists ("naked sages") of India were found to resemble model Cynics!

Even if we exclude prototypical or minor figures such as Antisthenes or Zoilus,[14] we find a remarkable variety of literary activity ascribed to the early Cynics. Certainly no other philosophical "school" engaged in such diverse and original forms of literary production. While most philosophical writing was limited to a relatively small number of familiar forms such as dialogues, symposia, epistles, memoirs, lectures, and treatises, the Cynics struck out in new directions both by transforming the traditional material of myth in burlesques and parodies and by renovating traditional forms such as the proverb (or *gnōmē*), to which they gave a Cynic stamp that would remain a permanent feature of aphoristic writing. But they didn't stop there; they also developed new or marginal forms in both prose and verse, as well as the peculiarly Cynic mixture of the two associated with Menippus (and Lucian). Thus we find Cynics like Crates and Menippus turning low or extraliterary genres such as the will or the diary into full-scale literary productions with satiric motives, or using an established form like the epistle in novel ways, for example by addressing it to a god. The diatribe, often associated with Bion of Borysthenes,[15] is another good example of a form, which was certainly extraliterary or oral in the classical period, that the Cynics established as a distinctive part of their own literary repertoire. It is precisely this expansion of the domain of literature through the transformation of oral, quotidian, and utilitarian forms of discourse that makes the Cynic impact on literary culture truly significant. It is not simply a matter of introducing new styles or Cynic themes or of adapting Socratic forms to new purposes, but rather one of opening up whole new areas of literary activity and using these new forms as a way of critiquing the conventional genres of writing and thinking enshrined in the more established classical kinds rooted in the old oral culture. The map of Greek literature simply wasn't the same after the Cynics. Nor were their innovations confined to prose: Cynics wrote in iambics, elegiacs, and hexameters; and Cercidas invented a new meter, the meliambus, to write a political poem from a Cynic perspective. Other me-

13. Cf. T. S. Brown, *Onesicritus* (Berkeley and Los Angeles 1949).
14. I do not mean to exaggerate the importance of Zoilus, who after all is not even included by Giannantoni in his collection of Cynics. My point is that on inspection even a Cynic as marginal as Zoilus turns out to have been of genuine significance in the literary culture of his time and is still remembered many centuries later.
15. See J. F. Kindstrand, *Bion of Borysthenes* (Uppsala 1976).

ters were put to novel use, such as the iambics of Crates' *Diary,* a form that one might have expected to be cast in prose.

Of course except for Cercidas's poem almost all these multifarious works (and many others I haven't mentioned) are lost or survive only in meager fragments. Otherwise their importance would be self-evident.[16] As a result, the most complete picture we have of the rhetoric of an early Cynic is that preserved in the anecdotal (or *chreia*) traditions about Diogenes.[17] While their historical value is notoriously difficult to assess,[18] they give us an invaluable picture of Diogenes as the Cynic and related doxographic traditions conceived him. It is of course primarily through these anecdotal traditions that Diogenes survived to enter into European literature through the works of Lucian and later writers. As he is represented here, he is already "a deeply novelized figure," as Bakhtin observes, by which he means not just that Diogenes is a storied figure, like a character in a novel, with his tub, his cloak folded double, his broken bowl, knapsack, and lentils—all those trappings that became the defining attributes of the Cynic as a type and that cluster around him giving his image some of the circumstantial detail of daily life. Rather Bakhtin means something much more fundamental, namely that Diogenes is, in his terms, a "dialogical" figure—"a hero of improvisation not of tradition"—one who refuses "to be incarnated in the flesh of existing sociohistorical categories" and who takes the "ideological and linguistic initiative to change the nature of his own image." In choosing to reject the socially produced categories by which his contemporaries organized their lives, Diogenes made of himself "an object of experimentation and representation." [19] The incongruity this refusal of social typing

16. For the literary consequences of Cynicism see H. Niehues-Pröbsting, *Der Kynismus des Diogenes und der Begriff des Zynismus* (Munich 1979); Goulet-Cazé (above, n. 3) 2724–27; R. Bracht Branham, *Unruly Eloquence: Lucian and the Comedy of Traditions* (Cambridge, Mass., 1989) esp. chap. 1; M.M. Bakhtin, *The Dialogic Imagination,* trans. C. Emerson and M. Holquist (Austin 1983), chap. 2; id., *Problems of Dostoevsky's Poetics,* trans. C. Emerson (Minneapolis 1987), chap. 4.

17. The practice of collecting anecdotes about philosophers can be traced back to Metrocles, a "teacher" of Menippus, if not to Theophrastus; while this practice was not confined to Cynics, it was one at which they excelled and that served admirably to propagate their philosophy in a culture that remained predominantly oral. The anecdotes lend themselves to the process of retelling and elaboration characteristic of an oral tradition. They are portable and memorable as jokes. By the time of Diogenes Laertius the retelling of anecdotes (*chreiai*) in written form had long been a basic part of the curriculum in rhetoric. For the *chreia* tradition, see *The Chreia in Ancient Rhetoric,* vol. 1, *The Progymnasmata,* ed. F. Hock and E.N. O'Neil (Atlanta 1986); J.F. Kindstrand, "Diogenes Laertius and the 'Chreia' Tradition," *Elenchos* 71–72 (1986) 214–43; Branham (above, n. 16) 234–35 n. 72.

18. Cf. J. Mansfeld, "Diogenes Laertius on Stoic Philosophy," *Elenchos* 7 (1986) 296–382. Cf. K. von Fritz, *Quellenuntersuchungen zu Leben und Philosophie des Diogenes von Sinope,* Philologus Suppl. 18.2 (Leipzig 1926).

19. Bakhtin, *Dialogical Imagination* 37–38. If Bakhtin is right, as I hope my analysis will show, the thesis of S. Greenblatt, *Renaissance Self-Fashioning from More to Shakespeare* (Chicago 1980) collapses. While acknowledging self-consciousness about the fashioning of identity "had been widespread among the elite in the classical world," Greenblatt persists in defending the

produces is the source of the characteristically Cynic style of humor that makes Diogenes an inherently comic figure continually at odds—often physically—with the social world around him.

The Diogenes of tradition is of course perfectly aware of his status as a contrarian. Once when trying to enter a theater just as everyone else was leaving Diogenes was asked why he was doing this. He replied matter-of-factly: "This is what I practice doing [*epitēdeuō*] all my life" (D.L. 6.64). This moment of comic self-dramatization is typical of the way Diogenes is shown in the *chreia* tradition as going against the grain in a self-conscious and deliberately rhetorical fashion.[20] What I would like to examine now are some of the characteristic strategies by which he pursued this unlikely path, thereby to suggest how inextricably Diogenes' rhetoric and the Cynic *bios* ("way of life") are intertwined.

The Rhetoric of Diogenes

It is impossible to read through the collection of over 150 sayings that purport to represent the actual words of Diogenes in Diogenes Laertius's *Lives and Opinions of Famous Philosophers* (of the third century A.D.) without being struck by the Cynic's rhetorical cunning. Indeed, Diogenes Laertius remarks that Diogenes' persuasive powers (*peithō*) were so great that no one could withstand him in argument (D.L. 6.74–75).[21] Of this main group of anecdotes that cite Diogenes' words verbatim, almost one in six depends for its effect on some kind of pun or wordplay, including some of the most famous (e.g., D.L. 6.24, 32, 33, 35, 45–47, 49–52, 54–56, 61, 62, 66, 68). Many others depend on quotations and parodies of the poets. The remaining *chreiai* that simply paraphrase Diogenes or describe a significant act (rather than quote him) are no less rhetorical in character. Ancient rhetorical theory recognized of course that *chreiai* could pivot on significant deeds as effectively as on words. The picture that emerges from Diogenes Laertius's jumbled, repetitious collection is of one whose philosophy grew out of a continual process of ad hoc improvisation, including even what came to be regarded as its most fundamental tenets. In short, the *chreia* tradition suggests that Diogenes' most brilliant invention was not a set of doctrines, let alone a method, but himself—a concrete yet malleable demonstration of a *modus dicendi,* a way of adapting verbally to (usually hostile) circumstances. It is this process of inven-

---

old idea, which goes back at least to J. Burckhardt, that such self-consciousness "began to be fully articulated only in the early modern period(s)." Such a stance serves to justify ignoring the ancient evidence, an extraordinary approach to a society with obsessive ties to its own cultural past.

20. Cf. Sayre (above, n. 5), citing D.L. 6.64: "These acts may have been the exhibitionism of an egotist or attempts to attract attention and give him an opportunity to solicit contributions (58).

21. Of course Diogenes Laertius makes similar remarks about many of his biographical subjects.

tion, this applied rhetoric, that constitutes the Cynic's discourse, a process in which strategies of survival and rhetorical strategies repeatedly converge and coalesce.[22]

Of course Cynicism differs from all the other ancient philosophical movements—except for Pyrrhonism, which it antedates—precisely in its rejection of high theory. It is based on a few simple principles or axioms rather than a systematic body of abstract argument, which the Cynics disdained as irrelevant to practice if not simply absurd. The Cynic view is brought out clearly in a series of imagined confrontations between Plato and Diogenes. It is significant that Plato occurs far more frequently than any other philosopher in the anecdotes about Diogenes. The tradition designates him, the paradigmatic metaphysician and plutocrat, as a kind of antitype to the Cynic. As such he is a useful tool for defining the Cynic stance by contrast and juxtaposition. Once, after the father of metaphysics had expounded his theory of forms using neologisms such as "tablehood" and "cuphood," Diogenes responded: "Plato, table and cup I see, but your 'tablehood' and 'cuphood'—no way" (*oudamōs*, D.L. 6.53). This story resembles the occasion when Plato deployed his vaunted method of collection and division to define man as "a featherless biped," and Diogenes produced a plucked chicken as a counterexample, saying, "Here is Plato's man!" (D.L. 6.40). Elsewhere, he dismisses Plato's lectures (*diatribē*) as a waste of time (*katatribē*, D.L. 6.24), or ridicules the philosopher for paying court to the tyrant Dionysius (D.L. 6.58), for his aristocratic generosity (in sending him a whole jar of figs when he had asked for a few), and for the vanity of his expensive possessions (D.L. 6.26). A pivotal theme emerges from this group of anecdotes: the Cynic's distrust of abstract argument is merely the other side of his belief that the test of truth is less a matter of logical finesse than of the philosopher's ability to practice persuasively what he teaches. Plato stands condemned on both counts.[23]

If Plato's paradigm is that of philosophy as *theōria* and the philosopher as a spectator of time and eternity, uniquely able to rise above time and chance, Diogenes' is just the opposite—the philosopher of contingency, of life in the

22. This doesn't stop Diogenes from being highly critical of others' rhetoric and of rhetoricians generally, any more than it did Plato. Cf. D.L. 6.47: "Rhetoricians and all who spoke for reputation [Diogenes] used to call 'thrice-human' [*trisanthrōpous*] meaning thrice-wretched [*trisathlious*]."

23. The famous exchange with Alexander is the political counterpart to the confrontation with Plato. The moral: Diogenes needs nothing of either (*autarkeia*) and is willing to tell the truth (*parrhēsia*) even to the "great king." Hence when Alexander says, "Ask me for anything you want," Diogenes replies, "Step out of my light" (D.L. 6.38). On another occasion, Alexander is supposed to have said, "Had I not been Alexander, I would have liked to be Diogenes" (D.L. 6.32; cf. 6.60). Legend has it that Diogenes died in Corinth the same day Alexander died in Babylon (D.L. 6.79). Other potentates were less magnanimous: Perdiccas, Alexander's successor, threatened to put Diogenes to death if he did not come to him. Diogenes replied: "That's no great accomplishment; a beetle or tarantula could do the same" (D.L. 6.44). Perdiccas's response is not reported. For Diogenes and autocrats, see Niehues-Pröbsting (above, n. 16) 87–109; Giannantoni (above, n. 9) 2.237–50. For Diogenes and Plato, ibid. 251–56.

barrel, of adapting to the données of existence, of "minimal living," as Dudley puts it. On this view philosophy is not an escape from but a dialogue with the contingencies that shape the material conditions of existence. Hence the centrality of the body to Diogenes' way of practicing philosophy (which we will come to in a moment). Unlike the metaphysicians of the day, Plato being the prime example, Diogenes was content to derive his thinking directly from his social—or, in his case, antisocial—practice without grounding it in a metaphysical domain remote from experience. This lack of interest in foundations is another significant similarity between Diogenes' practice and that of rhetoricians.

Diogenes would have agreed with William James: "The true is what is good in the way of belief" [24]—if we take this to mean "the truth is what works." This pragmatic stance, which implies that argument is effective only in a highly specific context and is valuable, like an action, primarily for its effects, is distinctly rhetorical in its assumptions. Rhetoricians like Isocrates also shunned theory as remote from the exigencies of moral experience. They had as little use as Diogenes for astronomy and geometry.[25] It is because Diogenes refused to take seriously the theoretical debates that raged in the academies of his day—as his repeated mockery of Plato shows—that the place of Cynicism in the history of philosophy has always been so marginal. For Hegel there was "nothing particular to say of the Cynics, for they possess but little Philosophy, and they did not bring what they had into a scientific system." [26] Their appeal has often seemed to be as much rhetorical (or literary) as philosophical or "scientific." But this may be a way of describing the source of Cynicism's peculiar authority and resilience rather than its methodological deficiencies.

Now if a rhetorician operates by exploring "the available means of persuasion in a particular situation, [trying] them on and as they begin to suit him [becoming] them," [27] as a contemporary rhetorician puts it paraphrasing Aristotle, then Diogenes' performance can usefully be analyzed under the rubric of rhetorical "improvisation" or "invention." [28] For example, when his exile

24. Cited by R. Rorty, *Consequences of Pragmatism* (Minneapolis 1989) 97. Rorty insists that James "was simply trying to debunk epistemology"—a very Cynical thing to do—"not offering a 'theory of truth.'"
25. Isocrates' interest in morals and morality pervades his work (e.g., *To Nicocles, Nicocles or the Cyprians, Evagoras*). Effective encomia (or satires) require the author to don a moral stance the audience will find compelling.
26. *Lectures on the History of Philosophy,* trans. E. S. Haldane and F. H. Simson, vol. 1 (London 1983), 479. Hegel continues: "their tenets were raised into a system by the Stoics," For a concise account of modern scholarship on the Cynics, see M. Billerbeck, ed., *Die Kyniker in der modernen Forschung: Aufsätze mit Einführung und Bibliographie* (Amsterdam 1991) 1–28.
27. S. Fish, "Rhetoric," in *Critical Terms for Literary Study,* ed. F. Lentricchia and T. Mc-Laughlin (Chicago 1990) 208. Cf. Aristotle, *Rhetoric* 1355b26.
28. Invention (*heurēsis*) is of course the first of the five principal tasks (*erga*) of the rhetorician (followed by *taxis, lexis, mnēmē,* and *hupokrisis*). It embraces the general modes of persuasion (*koinai pisteis:* examples and enthymemes) and questions of status or definition (*staseis*). It is important to remember that Aristotle includes invented parallels (e.g., *logoi* and *parabolai*) under

brought him to Athens, Diogenes had originally tried to arrange for a cottage to live in, as anyone else might have. It is only when the cottage fails to materialize that he improvises the idea of living in a pithos ("large wine jar"), like a dog (D.L. 6.23). By devising this practical response to a particular contingency Diogenes takes a large step toward becoming the kind of person who can adapt to almost anything, even to ways of life considered beneath the dignity of his species. In retrospect this was one of the founding acts of Cynicism, an expression through action of an attitude toward conventional culture (*nomos*) that would become fundamental as Diogenes' thought and life evolved. Thus the ideology of Cynicism originates as the set of rhetorical strategies Diogenes invented to make persuasive sense of such "minimal living," so at odds not only with the traditional aristocratic notions of a desirable life, but with the existing models of the philosophic life as well. The practice of "Cynicism"—from "doglike" [29]—came to mean living as circumstances had taught Diogenes to live: in exile both literally and metaphorically. That is why Diogenes is outraged when he is reproached for having been exiled from Sinope (for defacing the city's currency with a chisel stamp): "But that was how I became a philosopher, you miserable fool!" (*kakodaimon,* D.L. 6.49).[30] It is tempting to see Diogenes transforming into an act of conscious defiance the exclusion that he suffered involuntarily when he was forced into exile. Chance circum-

---

"example." The maxim (*gnōmē*), another locus of invention, is considered by Aristotle to be the equivalent of the premise or conclusion of an enthymeme: *Rhetoric* 1397a7–1400b34.

29. For the meaning of "Cynic," see Niehues-Pröbsting (above, n. 16) 15–28.

30. Ancient tradition holds that Diogenes was forced into exile because his father, Hicesias, "was entrusted with the money of the state and defaced the coinage" (D.L. 6.20). Another version (reported in the same paragraph of Diogenes Laertius) claims that Diogenes' father "entrusted him with the money and that he defaced it, in consequence of which his father was imprisoned and died, while the son fled" (D.L. 6.21). It turns out that these stories are probably based on fact. According to C.T. Seltman (*International Numismatic Congress* [1938], summarized by Dudley [above, n. 1] 54 n. 3; cf. also H. Bannert, "Numismatisches zu Biographie und Lehre des Hundes Diogenes," *Litterae Numismaticae Vindobonenses* I [1979] 49–63), there are defaced coins from Sinope dating from 350 to 340 B.C. Other coins minted after 362 B.C. bear the name of the official in charge: *Hikesio.* It remains unclear whether it was Diogenes or his father who decided to deface the coins by smashing them with a large chisel stamp, and exactly what the motive was. Following Seltman, Dudley argues that Diogenes and his father were attempting to defend the credit of Sinope by driving counterfeit currency out of circulation. The problem is that not all the coins so defaced were counterfeit; a small percentage were good Sinopean coins. Be that as it may, this incident provided the Cynics with one of their most powerful metaphors: "to deface the current coin" (*parakharattein to nomisma*) came to refer to the Cynics' attempt to drive the debased currency of conventional thought out of circulation. The story also resonates with Diogenes' defense of Cynic theft and his critique of the rules regulating exchange in other contexts: " 'Very valuable things,' he said, 'are sold for things of no value and vice versa' " (D.L. 6.35).

The related story that Diogenes received an oracle at Delphi instructing him to "deface the currency" (D.L. 6.20–21) is a legendary encrustation on the historical kernel of Diogenes' exile. It is clearly modeled on the oracle Plato's Socrates claims in the *Apology* to have received at Delphi and, as Niehues-Pröbsting suggests, may well be a parody of it. The idea of Diogenes' consulting the oracle to discover his philosophical mission is of course absurd and clearly incompatible with his utterances on traditional religion. This story probably originates in a literary context. For a thorough discussion of both stories, see Niehues-Pröbsting (above, n. 16) 43–63, 77–81.

stances, particularly unfortunate ones, are the wellspring of Cynic pragmatism. So, when asked what good he had gotten from philosophy, Diogenes could reply: "If nothing else, then to be prepared [*pareskeuasthai*] for every kind of luck [*tukhē*]" (D.L. 6.63). *Tukhē*—the random, improvident quality of experience—is the mother of Cynic invention (*pareskeuasthai*), a word that can be appropriated to specifically rhetorical contexts (cf. Isocrates 4.13; Xenophon, *Mem.* 4.2.6). Hence when Diogenes compares himself to a character in a tragedy, citing an unidentified fragment (D.L. 6.38),

> Without a city, without a house, without a fatherland
> A beggar, a wanderer with a single day's bread,

he's not being melodramatic but comically dramatizing the premise of his usual performance by identifying himself ironically as a hero of tradition.

Radical uncertainty is surely conducive to the kind of pragmatic, improvisational thinking that I am ascribing to Diogenes. I am arguing, however, that these qualities are not just implicit in practice. Rather, Diogenes is represented as fully aware of the improvised and thoroughly provisional character of his "philosophy." At least one very important *chreia* seems to suggest as much. To someone who reproached him saying, "Although you don't know anything you engage in philosophy [or "philosophize": *ouden eidōs philosopheis*]," Diogenes responded disarmingly, "Even if I do pretend to wisdom [*prospoioumai sophian*], this too is to practice philosophy [*philosophein*]" (D.L. 6.64).[31] Here Diogenes seems to affirm that the philosophic life is a kind of performance, an act (*prospoioumai*),[32] and thus to anticipate the idea of the philosopher as an adaptable actor,[33] such as Aristo of Chios and others would later espouse.

Insofar as Diogenes is attempting to enact a *sophia,* he is engaged in the activity traditionally termed "philosophy." But the underlying idea that the authority of a philosopher (or sage) is the result of his success at embodying (or enacting) what he teaches antedates philosophy proper and is one of the reasons that Socrates and Diogenes have their peculiar status in the pantheon of philosophers. It is this idea that underlies Diogenes' only observable method, which consists of a continual process of "adaptation" or "improvisation" as circumstances confront him with a series of differing problems. As the

31. Sayre (above, n. 5) misses the point: "This seems to be an admission that the Cynic claim to possess wisdom was not based on learning. The Cynics asserted their superior wisdom by criticizing and denouncing other men" (19).

32. Cf. the translation of L. Paquet, *Les cyniques grecs: Fragments et témoignages* (Ottawa 1948) 77: "Jouer au sage, c'est aussi de la philosophie!" Cf. also D.L. 6.49: "When Diogenes was asked why he was begging alms of a statue he replied: 'To get practice at being turned down.'"

33. Theatricality is not unique to Diogenes but, on the contrary, is another link between the Cynic and those called "sophists" and "rhetoricians," e.g., Hippias at the Olympic Games, Protagoras in Plato's *Protagoras,* etc.

question, the interlocutor, and the specific context vary, so do Diogenes' responses. Such a method does not produce a consistent set of doctrines, as Diogenes' contemporaries enjoyed pointing out. So, when asked if wise men eat cakes, he replies cheerily: "Yes, all kinds [*panta*], just like everyone else" (D.L. 6.56). When reproached for drinking in a tavern he responds punningly: "Of course—and I get barbered in a barber shop!" (*en koureiōi keiromai*, D.L. 6.66). When reproached for eating in the agora he retorts pointedly: "I got hungry in the agora!" (D.L. 6.58). So much for Diogenes' "asceticism." Scholars have of course tried to determine whether the ascetic or the hedonistic tendencies in the Diogenes of tradition are more central.[34] But this project starts from the gratuitous assumption of the unity and coherence of Diogenes' thought. But if any one resisted systems—whether of thought or of social control—it was Diogenes. Moreover, the doxographic tradition generally, and that based on *chreiai* in particular, is as interested in *ēthos* ("character") as in *dianoia* ("thought"). To privilege one aspect of the tradition over another is futile. It is the contradictions Diogenes embodies that have made him an object of fascination. He exerts an authority far beyond that of an advocate of asceticism or hedonism, and, in any event, there is no available criterion by which the true Diogenes can be separated from the false; for whatever criterion we use will entail an interpretation of the very traditions at issue. Instead of speculating about what the traditions would have told us about Diogenes had they been more complete, truthful, or systematic, to approach Diogenes as the rhetorical construct of a tradition of over five hundred years enables us to explore what it does in fact show us—contradictions and all.[35]

In addition to being pragmatic and improvisational, a third feature of Diogenes' performance stands out and in my view is the most fundamental: that is its humor. Why should this be so? Most philosophy is not particularly witty, to put it mildly. Democritus's laughter is legendary, but he left few traces of it behind. It would be a historicizing error to answer this question with reference to Diogenes' personality, for biting and sometimes outrageous humor was characteristic of the whole *eidos* of Cynic discourse, according to Demetrius (*De Eloc.* 259),[36] and it persists in outline right down to Lucian and even Dio Chrysostom. The answer has less to do with personality than (1) with the cultural and social position of Cynics in ancient society, particularly with their attitude toward social convention as it bears on the private life and the body; and (2) with the rhetorical or heuristic style of philosophy that Diogenes practices, which consists of subjecting the rules and customs promulgated by soci-

34. For bibliography and discussion, see Goulet-Cazé (above, n. 9) 77–84: "Nous voulons simplement souligner que déjà chez Diogène hédonisme et rigorisme pouvaient se côtoyer" (84).

35. Cf. Niehues-Pröbsting (above, n. 16): "Die Diogenes-Gestalt ist . . . immer schon in Rezeption übergegangen" (13).

36. For Demetrius on the *kunikos tropos* ("Cynic style"), see Branham (above, n. 16) 234 n. 73.

ety to the test of embodiment and to the vagaries of material existence. Making himself the medium of such arguments often puts Diogenes in direct violation of rules so familiar that they are rarely articulated, let alone enforced. The violation of the countless rules both tacit and explicit that govern our behavior, beginning with our use of language, is basic to any form of humor. As Mary Douglas has argued, the form of a joke "rarely lies in the utterance alone" and can only be understood with reference "to the total social situation." [37] The Cynics' innovation consists of exploiting this fact polemically as a way of defining themselves in opposition—not to this or that rule or this or that group, but to the authority of society to dictate thought and behavior. Mary Douglas and Bakhtin have taught us that the significance of joking as an activity in a traditional society lies in its resistance to the social control of cognition. The Cynic motto—"Deface the Current Coin" (*parakharattein to nomisma*)[38]— makes joking, parody, and satire not merely a useful rhetorical tool, but an indispensable one, constitutive of Cynic ideology as such.[39] Humor is the chisel stamp of Cynic discourse. The work of Douglas and Bakhtin provides us, therefore, with the interpretive framework within which the rhetoric of the Cynics can be most usefully analyzed.

To take just two examples, let us consider reason and ritual in the *chreiai* about Diogenes. It is significant that in spite of the fact that Diogenes is said to have composed written works, there are no extended arguments of any kind attributed to him even of the length attributed to Presocratics. This might lead one to suspect that he didn't use extended arguments. There are of course two formal syllogisms attributed to him by Diogenes Laertius, but both are parodic.[40] One is ostensibly offered as a justification for Cynic theft; the other, to justify transgressive eating (D.L. 6.37, 68)—both violations of common social norms. The former runs:

> All things belong to the gods.
> The wise are friends of the gods.
> Friends hold things in common.
> All things belong to the wise.

Using the form of the syllogism allows Diogenes to invoke the authority of reason even as he parodies its procedures in a single gesture. Of course a

37. M. Douglas, "The Social Control of Cognition: Some Factors in Joke Perception" *Man* 3.3 (1968) 363. Reprinted as "Jokes" in *Implicit Meanings* (London 1975) 90–114. For an interesting critique of her theory, see M. Mulkay, *On Humour* (London 1988).

38. See n. 30 (on Diogenes' exile).

39. Cf. Niehues-Pröbsting (above, n. 16): "Im Kynismus des Diogenes ist das Lachen ein unentbehrlicher Bestandteil" (86).

40. W.D. Ross, *Aristotle* (London 1949) 32: "Aristotle's definition of syllogism is quite general; it is 'an argument in which, certain things having been assumed, something other than these follows of necessity from their truth, without needing any term from outside'" (*An. Pr.* 1.23).

parody does not belong to the same type (or genre) as its model. A parody of a syllogism is no more a syllogism than the parody of a tragedy is a tragedy. I don't think Diogenes offers such syllogisms as serious arguments, but as parodic examples of the kind of reasoning that other philosophers take seriously, and that he routinely mocks. In any event, such arguments are not likely to change the mind of anyone who is not already inclined to accept their conclusions. That cannot be their purpose. The point of the parody lies rather in the jarring contrast between the formal protocols of reason and the paradoxically Cynic conclusions they serve to produce. In the process, the instruments of reason are neatly turned against themselves in a mockery of syllogistic method. The butt of the joke is its form.

The second syllogism is no less a joke; specifically, it works by means of a pun on *atopon*. The first time it is used figuratively, to mean "absurd"; the second, it is used literally, to mean "out of place":

> If to breakfast is not "absurd" [*atopon*],
>
> It is not "out of place" [*atopon*] in the agora.
>
> To breakfast is not "absurd" [*atopon*].
>
> It is not "out of place" [*atopon*] in the agora.

This is one of the types of fallacy catalogued by Aristotle in his *Sophistical Refutations*. In both these instances, jokes—a parody and a pun—are decked out in the trappings of formal argumentation. Cynic conclusions are asserted while the rationality of the philosophers is caricatured as logic chopping and verbal sleight of hand.[41]

In her classic study of jokes and joking, "The Social Control of Cognition: Some Factors in Joke Perception," Mary Douglas develops the argument that "the peculiar expressive character of the joke stands in contrast to ritual as such."[42] For if we consider the joke "as a symbol of social, physical, or mental experience," we are already treating it as a kind of rite. But what kind? As a spontaneous symbol, she says, a joke "expresses something that is happening, but that is all." It stands in contrast, therefore, to the standardized rite or ritual, "which expresses what ought to happen" and thus, unlike spontaneous joking, is "not morally neutral." Douglas spells out the opposition between joking and ritual as follows:[43]

41. It is true that one saying attributed to Diogenes seems to endorse reason: "He used to say repeatedly that to be prepared for life one must have reason [*logos*] or a rope" (*brokhos:* D.L. 6.24). I would point out that this too is a pun and argue that *logos* need mean no more than Diogenes' "opinions" or "beliefs" (see LSJ s.v. III.2, 4, 5; VI.3.b). There are no examples in the *chreiai* that purport to quote him verbatim of Diogenes using *logos* in a philosophically loaded sense as "reason" or "right reason." Cf., however, D.L. 6.38.

42. Douglas (above, n. 37 [1968]) 368–69.

43. Ibid. 369–70, 373.

A joke has in common with a rite that both connect widely differing concepts. But the kind of connection of pattern A with pattern B in a rite is such that A and B support each other in a unified system. The rite imposes order and harmony, while the joke disorganizes. From the physical to the personal, to the social, to the cosmic, great rituals create unity in experience. They assert hierarchy and order. In doing so, they affirm the value of the symbolic patterning of the universe. Each level of patterning is validated and enriched by association with the rest. But jokes have the opposite effect. They connect widely differing fields, but the connection destroys hierarchy and order. They do not affirm the dominant values, but denigrate and devalue. Essentially a joke is an anti-rite. . . . The message of a standard rite is that the ordained patterns of social life are inescapable. The message of a joke is that they are escapable . . . for a joke implies that anything is possible.

If this argument is correct, joking in a traditional society organized by myth and ritual tends to set itself in opposition to the prime embodiments of social reason or ideology. The methods of professional philosophers would be one example of such reason; ritual would be a far more important one. If formal philosophical reasoning is the most convention-governed form of thought, ritual is the most convention-governed form of activity. Insofar as Diogenes is an uninhibited opponent of *nomos*—unlike Antisthenes, for example, he never refers even to a *nomos* of *aretē*—we would expect him to be averse to ritual per se (since it embodies and reinforces *nomos*), and he does not disappoint us. Every single reference to ritual activity—sacrifice, prayer, or purification rites—in the *chreiai* is derisive (cf. 6.37, 42, 47, 59–62, 73). There are several anecdotes which suggest that Diogenes did not believe in the gods of tradition; indeed, it is hard to see how he could have. His ironic response to someone impressed by the quantity of votive offerings in Samothrace comes to mind: "There would have been far more if those who were not saved had made offerings!" (D.L. 6.59). The opposition between Cynic jesting and traditional religion continues down to Demonax (in the second century A.D.), who is put on trial in Athens for not joining the Mysteries, but refuses to take the charge seriously.[44] Where ritual is socially consolidating and conservative, the Cynic parrhesiast is antiritualistic and disruptive. That Diogenes defends stealing from temples and denies the validity of such fundamental dietary and sexual taboos as those against cannibalism and incest coheres with this antiritualistic stance.[45] The contrast with a philosopher like Socrates is striking and significant. The Cynic's rejection of inherited patterns of conduct makes room for his own improvisations; but where do they derive their authority if, as Douglas

44. See Branham (above, n. 16) 57–63.
45. See D.L. 6.73; Dio Chrysostom, *Or.* 10.30. There is of course a difference between questioning the validity of a taboo and advocating the tabooed activity. Diogenes has sometimes been misinterpreted as engaging in the latter.

also argues, joking "merely affords opportunity for realizing that an accepted pattern has no necessity . . . [but] is frivolous in that it produces no real alternative, only an exhilarating sense of freedom from form in general"?[46]

The answer usually given to this question would be "nature." It is typically said, for example, that the Cynic pursues freedom or happiness by "following nature," which means a life devoted to "discipline" (*askēsis*) and "self-sufficiency" (*autarkeia*).[47] While there is much to this characterization, if we examine the *chreiai* in Diogenes Laertius that purport to quote Diogenes verbatim, nowhere does he show any interest in nature as a philosophical concept or a *Lebenswelt*.[48] As for "self-sufficiency" (*autarkeia*), begging for a living—which is very well represented in the *chreiai*[49]—may have many advantages, but autonomy would not seem to be among them. Yet if Diogenes is our model, "life according to nature" means living in the middle of a large city and begging for a living. Given that this is the case, the central Cynic value could be neither "self-sufficiency" (*autarkeia*)—no one is more dependent than a beggar—nor nature as a rationally formulable principle, equivalent to reason, as it is in Stoicism, but freedom, and freedom of speech (*parrhēsia*) in particular. Begging—the rejection of work,[50] of a life considered productive by society—is required by freedom to avoid becoming subject to society's rules and

46. Douglas (above, n. 37 [1968]) 365.

47. See, e.g., s.v. "Cynics," *Encyclopedia of Philosophy,* ed. P. Edwards (New York 1972), 1.284–85; "Diogenes," *OCD*² (348). Contrast Sayre (above, n. 5): "The Cynics accepted the principle of following nature and their amoralism was incidental to it, but 'following nature' was not the dominant idea of Cynicism and does not adequately describe it" (5).

48. Diogenes' statements (D.L. 6.63, 72) that he is a *kosmopolitēs* (citizen of the cosmos) and that the "only good government [*orthē politeia*] is the one in the *kosmos*" are inconsistent with my argument only if they are not primarily a rejection of existing governments. Since the *kosmos* has no citizens, I take Diogenes' neologism *kosmopolitēs* to be a witty rejection of actual citizenship—which had resulted in his exile—and an affirmation of the larger, apolitical allegiances of a Cynic, which are not subject to the same risks or constraints. See Moles's contribution, p. 105.

49. Diogenes was an aggressive beggar and took advantage of every opportunity begging offered to engage in *parrhēsia:* "To a miser who was slow to respond, Diogenes said, 'I'm asking you for food, not for funeral expenses'" (D.L. 6.56). "When he needed money he told his friends not to give something, but to give something *back*" (D.L. 6.46). "When he begged of a grouch who said, 'If you can persuade me,' Diogenes replied: 'If I could have persuaded you, I would have persuaded you—to hang yourself'" (D.L. 6.59). His standard approach was: "If you have already given to someone else, then give to me also; if not, then start with me" (D.L. 6.49). "He once [was seen] begging alms of a statue. When asked why he did this, he replied: 'I'm practicing [*meletō*] getting turned down'" (D. L. 6.49; n. 32 above). "When asked what he did to be called a dog, Diogenes replied: 'I wag my tail at those who give, bark at those who don't, and bite scoundrels [*ponērous*]'" (D.L. 6.60). For Diogenes as beggar, see Giannantoni (above, n. 9) 2.328–33.

50. Cf. Diogenes: "Instead of useless toils men should choose such as nature recommends, whereby they might have lived happily" (D.L. 6.71). Cf. D.L. 6.29: "[Diogenes] would praise those who were about to marry and refrained; those who were going to travel and did not; those who were about to enter politics and did not; those who were about to raise a family and did not; and those who were about to live at court but did not." Like Bartleby the Scrivener, Diogenes "preferred not to."

authority.[51] *Autarkeia* ("self-sufficiency") is a desideratum, but freedom is imperative.[52] Accordingly, when Heracles comes up in Diogenes Laertius's account, Diogenes is said to have claimed that their lives had "the same character"—not because of Heracles' capacity for endurance (*askēsis* or *autarkeia*), but because they both "deemed nothing more important than freedom" (*mēden eleutherias prokinōn*, D.L. 6.71). If happiness is an activity, then the exercise of freedom would be happiness for a Cynic and thus in need of no further justification.[53] The exercise of this freedom in words, *parrhēsia*,[54] is, as Dioge-

51. Sayre (above, n. 5): "Work under the control of an employer was inconsistent with the Cynic conception of freedom" (11). Sayre also derives Cynic "idleness" from Cynic "apathy." He cites the Stoic Chrysippus: "What reason is there that the wise man should provide a living? For if it be to support life, life itself is after all a matter of indifference. If it be for pleasure, pleasure too is a matter of indifference. While if it be for virtue, virtue in itself is sufficient to constitute happiness. The modes of getting a livelihood are also ludicrous" (D.L. 7.189). Cynic freedom rules out marriage as well as work: "Whoever trusts us will remain single; those who do not trust us will rear children. And if the race of men should cease to exist there would be as much cause for regret as there would be if the flies and wasps should pass away" (Ps.-Diogenes, *Epistle* 47; cited by Sayre 9).

52. Of course there is a paradox or contradiction I do not wish to deny in affirming both freedom and begging; but evidently, since begging, unlike work, is nowhere rejected (see above, nn. 49, 51), it was felt to be less inimical to Cynic freedom than was work. As practiced by Diogenes, begging becomes a form of self-assertion and social satire in spite of the obviously dependent position of the beggar (see n. 49).

53. Sayre (above, n. 5): "The object of Cynicism was happiness: it was a form of eudaimonism and it is of interest as a human experiment with that end in view. . . . The Cynics sought happiness through freedom [7]. . . . The Cynic virtues were the qualities through which freedom was attained [9]."

54. *Parrhēsia* ("freedom of speech"), like *isēgoria* ("equality of speech") is of course central to democratic ideology in the classical period. *Parrhēsia* is later (late fifth century) and perhaps stronger, describing forms of speech that may well be offensive to some ears. In time *parrhēsia* also acquired distinctly aristocratic connotations: Aristotle associates it with his aristocratic ideal, the magnanimous man, in the *EN*. Like many such terms, it was used in different ways by different classes. Diogenes' claim to *parrhēsia* and *eleutheria* from the bottom of the social hierarchy—as an impoverished noncitizen—is therefore starkly paradoxical, since such freedoms are among the rights of a citizen (in a democratic state) or the privileges of an aristocrat. The legal status of *parrhēsia* under Athenian democracy is uncertain, but as a citizen's right it must have been protected by custom in some contexts (e.g., in the assembly or in court) but probably not by specific laws. See K. A. Raaflaub, "Democracy, Oligarchy, and the Concept of the 'Free Citizen' in Late Fifth Century Athens," *Political Theory* 11.4 (1983) 517–44; id., "Des freien Bürgers Recht der Freien Rede: Ein Beitrag zur Begriffs- und Sozialgeschichte der athenischen Demokratie," in *Studien zur Antiken Sozialgeschichte: Festschrift F. Vittinghof*, Kölner Historische Abhandlungen 28, ed. W. Ech et al. (Cologne 1980), 7–57; S. Halliwell, "Comic Satire and Freedom of Speech in Classical Athens," *JHS* 91 (1991) 48–70. Cf. also LSJ s.v.: "outspokenness, frankness, freedom of speech, claimed by the Athenians as their privilege" (Eur. *Hipp.* 422); 2, "license of tongue"; 3, "freedom of action"; 4, "liberality, lavishness."

In the Hellenistic and Roman periods speaking freely to or about those in power was risky, and the Cynics courted this danger deliberately. (See Dudley [above, n. 1] chap. 7: "Demetrius: The Philosophic Opposition in the First Century A.D.") The point to emphasize here is that after the disappearance of democracy *parrhēsia* was of course an aspiration, not a right, in ancient society and that to engage in it meant to risk exile, death, or other severe punishments. Diogenes' confrontations with Philip, Alexander, Perdiccas, et al. should be seen in this light. This example shows how precarious the Cynic claim to *parrhēsia* could be in practice. For an exemplary confrontation

nes plainly affirms, "the finest thing in the world" (*to kalliston,* D.L. 6.69).[55] Therefore, certain kinds of rhetorical acts—those that effectively assert freedom in some particular context—will be quintessentially Cynic, constitutive of what it means to be a Cynic, not merely instrumental to an ideology that exists independently of them.

If, as Mary Douglas argues, a joke is an assertion of freedom, it is precisely the commitment to freedom that gives rise to a rhetorical practice characterized by (1) pragmatism, (2) improvisation, and (3) humor. This conception of Cynic rhetoric as a kind of performance premised on freedom helps to explain some of Cynicism's most curious features when considered as some kind of systematic moral philosophy, such as its lack of doctrinal rigor or a systematic method like logic or dialectic. For example, considered rhetorically Diogenes' way of life may be taken as an assertion of nature, of human nature, in the face of culture; indeed, human nature is the only kind Diogenes shows more than incidental interest in. It is safe to say that "nature" according to Diogenes is simply human nature as he embodies it. In this sense, we do find it figuring prominently in the *chreiai;* Diogenes frequently uses his own body as an example of nature and thus as a means of developing his "discourse on nature" by taking advantage of the two principal forms of rhetorical argument, the example and the enthymeme.[56] In this sense, "nature" is rhetorically central: Diogenes' arguments frequently turn on the body as an example of unaccommodated and unaccommodating man; as such it is a fertile source of comic enthymemes that give memorable expression to the most basic tenets—or tendencies—of Cynicism.

Accordingly, Cynic theory is merely the continuation of practice—the exercise of freedom—by other means. "Theory" arises to justify and to rationalize practice, which is based on the commitment to freedom—the refusal to be dictated to by society or external circumstance—and informed by the logic, the *anagkē,* of the body. It is this that gives Diogenes' thought its ad hoc quality as well as its many antinomies.[57] Let us consider in this context Diogenes' defense of the preeminently Cynic practice of doing the works of Demeter and Aphrodite in public. Of his habit of continually (*sunekhēs*) masturbating in public, for example, Diogenes said famously: "I only wish I could be rid of hunger by rubbing my belly" (D.L. 6.69). The humor here derives from the fact that Diogenes tacitly rejects the premise of his audience according to which he is violating well-known rules segregating private and public activities; in its place he has inserted a Cynic premise, the principle of *euteleia:*

---

between Cynic *parrhēsia* and Roman authority, see Lucian, *Demonax* 50. For *parrhēsia* as a generic signal in Lucian's "literary Cynicism," see Branham (above, n. 16) 229 n. 47.

55. When asked the opposite question—"What is wretched [*athlios*] in life?"—Diogenes answered, *Gerōn aporos!* ("A helpless old man": D.L. 6.51).

56. Aristotle, *Rhetoric* 1356a36–1358a35.

57. See, e.g., Plutarch: V B 147.23–25 G.

natural desires are best satisfied in the easiest, most practical, and cheapest way possible. As far as the body or nature is concerned, one appetite is in principle no different from any other. It is culture that creates a hierarchy of desires and the proprieties governing their tendance. Diogenes' response blandly asserts the claims of nature without even acknowledging the restraints of culture. If he had acknowledged them explicitly, his response wouldn't have been a joke—it wouldn't have been funny. As Umberto Eco has argued,[58] the tacit suppression of the violated norm—the social frame—is essential to the comic. Knowledge of it must be supplied by the audience. It is the fact that the audience must simultaneously impose the relevant social frame—the prohibition—and supply the tacit Cynic premise, the principle of *euteleia*, that makes many of Diogenes' jokes work like enthymemes or rhetorical syllogisms. To get their point requires that we collaborate in a process of inference from Cynic premises.[59] The Cynic premise does not merely violate but contradicts the social frame; hence, the laughter it elicits is tendentious. Indeed, virtually every witticism of Diogenes is tendentious in Freud's sense—hostile, argumentative, and subversive of authority.[60]

In *A History of Cynicism*, D.R. Dudley observes that "the stories about Diogenes are decidedly funnier than those Diogenes Laertius tells about other philosophers. Perhaps some of the apothegms . . . did originate with Diogenes." This is an attractive suggestion, but the opposite inference is equally possible: however rooted in the historical person, the humor of the traditions about Diogenes reflects the polish of a self-consciously rhetorical practice that made optimal use of the argumentative resources of the pointed anecdote or *chreia*. What I am stressing here, however, is the fit between ideology and rhetorical practice, between *parrhēsia* and Cynic traditions of philosophical jesting. I have already argued elsewhere that all true humor has an enthymematic character:[61] it requires the audience to perform an act of mental collaboration that can be variously described as bridging a logical gap; moving between alien

58. U. Eco, "The Comic and the Rule," in *Travels in Hyper Reality: Essays* (San Diego 1986) 269–78.

59. See T. Cohen, "Jokes," in *Pleasure, Preference, and Value: Studies in Philosophical Aesthetics*, ed. E. Schaper (Cambridge 1983) 120–36.

60. S. Freud, "Jokes and Their Relation to the Unconscious," in *The Standard Edition of the Complete Psychological Works of Sigmund Freud*, ed. J. Strachey, 24 vols. (London 1953–74), vol. 8: "Tendentious jokes are especially favored in order to make aggression or criticism possible against persons in exalted positions who claim to exercise authority. The joke then represents a rebellion against authority, a liberation from its pressure. The charm of caricature lies in the same factor: we laugh at them even if they are unsuccessful simply because we count rebellion against authority as a merit" (105). Cf. ibid. 133: "In the service of cynical or skeptical tendencies [the joke] shatters respect for institutions and truths in which the hearer has believed, on the one hand by reinforcing the argument, but on the other by practicing a new species of attack. Where argument tries to draw the hearer's criticism over to its side, the joke endeavors to push the criticism out of sight. There is no doubt that the joker has chosen the method which is psychologically more effective."

61. Branham (above, n. 16) 54.

codes, frames of reference, or universes of discourse; or in Arthur Koestler's influential formulation, bisecting divergent matrices of meaning.[62] His analysis of this process convinced Koestler that humor exemplifies "the logical pattern" of inventive thinking generally. In whatever language we choose to describe it, it is precisely this feature that distinguishes the anecdotes (*chreiai*) about Diogenes. Although Dudley acknowledges that Diogenes' "shamelessness" (*anaideia*) was philosophically motivated, he fails to see that the traditions about him insistently make wit or humor essential to his chief didactic method, *parrhēsia*.

If we turn to the *chreiai* collection in Diogenes Laertius with an eye to its rhetorical characteristics, we can isolate a variety of distinct topoi, or rhetorical premises, that are used repeatedly: for example, "When Diogenes was reproached"; "Diogenes thought it funny that"; "Diogenes used to wonder"; "Diogenes begging"; "Diogenes meets a philosopher"; "Diogenes meets a ruler"; "Diogenes and dogs." But the most important trope, both ideologically and rhetorically, is arguably that of Diogenes' body, which continually puts him at odds either with society, as in his defense of masturbation, or with his own professed asceticism, as in the anecdotes about eating cakes and drinking in a tavern. Moreover, many of Diogenes' jokes are aimed at the body or call attention to bodily aspects of his interlocutors and targets: for example, a woman bending over as she prays, a boy exposing his rear, a rhetorician mocked for his physical bulk, effeminate men, brawny athletes, fatiguing lecturers, and so on. The ungovernable body recurs in many forms, upsetting the pretense to serious or civilized behavior. It is the ideal instrument for the Cynic attack on the artificiality and falsity of the official codes of civilized life. Citing Bergson, Douglas argues: " 'Every incident is comic which calls our attention to the physical person when the issue is moral.' . . . All jokes have this subversive effect on the dominant structure of ideas. Those which bring forward the physiological exigencies to which mortal beings are subject, are using one universal, never-failing technique of subversion." [63]

Thus the body is not just a tool for attacking enemies or shocking the public—though it serves both of these eminently rhetorical purposes—it is also a source of the Cynic's authority, his warrant for engaging in *parrhēsia*. He uses it as the visible expression of his exemption from social control, of his immunity to *doxa* or public opinion: it confers on his conduct the sanction of nature. Diogenes' willingness to live with his body in public view, his refusal to hide or disguise the bodily functions conventionally deemed strictly private or obscene, is the clearest example of his commitment to Cynic freedom—"to use any place for any purpose" (D.L. 6.22). The Cynic's *anaideia* and *parrhēsia* meet in this exhibitionistic or performative use of the body. That Diogenes is

62. A. Koestler, *The Act of Creation* (New York 1964) chaps. 1–4.
63. Douglas (above, n. 37 [1968]) 364.

the only philosopher, ancient or modern, we see eating, masturbating, urinating, expectorating, and, as we shall see, defecating in public is of more than incidental interest for understanding Cynic ideology and its reception by ancient audiences.

As a final example of my thesis that there is such a thing as Cynic rhetoric (as Demetrius's phrase *kunikos tropos* suggests) and that it developed a distinctive set of rhetorical topoi, verbal techniques (e.g., pun, parody, obscenity), and physical gestures for advocating Cynic ideology, I would like to consider briefly the figure of Diogenes as reconstructed by Dio Chrysostom (in the second century A.D.) in his performances as a sophist. I have already argued elsewhere that Lucian's portrait of Demonax is continuous with the Cynic conception of the parrhesiast or seriocomic figure, the philosophical jester.[64] While Dio Chrysostom is a far less original sophist, for that very reason he is an excellent example of rhetorical practice in the Second Sophistic. We would expect Dio to flatten out some of Diogenes' eccentricities, as do other writers of the empire, lessening the difference between Cynic and Socratic traditions of moral philosophy in the process. It is interesting that while Dio has made Diogenes into a full-blown and occasionally long-winded moralist, he is very concerned to retain certain salient features that mark Diogenes' performance in the *chreia* tradition, such as his use of humor, obscenity, and *parrhēsia* generally. While the chosen themes, such as "kingship" or "tyranny," tend to reflect Dio's interests as a sophistic and courtier, even in these orations (4, 6) Dio repeatedly refers to Diogenes' *parrhēsia* (4.10, 15) and, to demonstrate it, has Diogenes open his conversation with Alexander (in *Or.* 4) with an ostensibly insulting reference to the king's parentage. Similarly, in *Oration* 6, on tyranny, Dio includes a lengthy digression on Diogenes' philosophy of sex, including a public demonstration of the ready availability of Aphrodite and a comic genealogy of masturbation that traces it back to Pan, who learned it from Hermes when in love with the elusive Echo. (Pan then taught it to the shepherds.) Throughout his intelligent and sympathetic presentation of Diogenes, Dio serves to illustrate how acutely aware skillful practitioners were of utilizing "Cynicism" as a traditional style of rhetorical performance adaptable to their own very different purposes.

Dio's most interesting treatment of Diogenes the rhetorician are *Orations* 8 and 9, where Diogenes is depicted as a public performer at the great games: "For it was his custom at the great assemblies to make a study of the pursuits and ambitions of men, of their reasons for being abroad; and of the things on which they prided themselves" (*Or.* 8.6). The two pieces show frequent parallels in theme and structure. They both begin by emphasizing Diogenes' waspish sense of humor—he is compared to a wasp by Antisthenes (*Or.* 8.3); his use of jokes and jesting is deliberately noted, as well as his *parrhēsia,* which is

64. Branham (above, n. 16) 57–63.

now identified as the serious element in his performance that the jokes serve to lighten (*Or.* 9.7). In sharp contrast to scholars such as Farrand Sayre (whose assessment serves as an epigraph to this article), Dio emphasizes the widely varying responses Diogenes elicits from the public: "Some admired him as the wisest man in the world; to others he seemed crazy; many scorned him as a beggar and a good-for-nothing; some jeered at him; others tried to insult him by throwing bones at his feet just as they would to a dog" (*Or.* 9.8–9). While both pieces skillfully develop a variety of traditional Cynic topoi—for example, "Diogenes as a dog," "Diogenes as a king"—they take one, Diogenes as life's true agonist in contrast to the athletes, as their primary focus; and both conclude with a specifically Cynic joke. Thus, while there is little that is actually funny and still less that is obscene in these polished sophistic presentations of Diogenes, the rhetorical impact of Dio's pieces is seriously distorted if divorced from the basic conventions of Cynic rhetoric, and of Cynic jesting in particular.

Let us consider *Oration* 8 as an example. It recounts Diogenes' visit to the Isthmian Games, a traditional locus for generalizing about human life in the light of the athletes' trials and the motley diversity of the crowd thronging to see them. In Dio's account, Diogenes uses this occasion to develop the theme of the Cynic as agonist, using the traditional but inherently improbable and comic idea of Heracles as a paradigmatic Cynic (*Or.* 8.27–35). Part of what makes Diogenes' diatribe interesting is the rhetorical challenge of finding similarities between the widely disparate terms of his comparison; it is also this feature that makes his mode of argument comic. The process of developing the metaphor gives scope to the moral tenets of Cynic discourse as Diogenes defines the old hero's labors as distinctly Cynic achievements. But it is the final act of his performance that will pull most readers up short, just as, Dio reports, it did the original audience: after completing his praise of Heracles, Diogenes abruptly squats (*kathezomenos*) and does "something disgraceful" (*epoiei ti tōn adoxōn,* 8.36) before the crowd. This might seem a distinctly odd way to conclude a moral homily, but it makes perfect sense in the context of Cynic rhetoric. What may seem an incomprehensible bit of buffoonery, or tasteless clowning, is actually crucial to the reception of Dio's entire oration. It works on several levels. First, it alludes to Heracles' final exploit as just recounted by Diogenes, the cleaning of the Augean stables, which the Cynic interprets as anticipating his own healthy disrespect for common opinion (*doxa,* 8.35). What unites the comic comparison of the lowly Cynic to the ancient hero, on the one hand, with the public act of defecation, on the other, is that both these Cynic transgressions strike directly at the arbitrary, provisional nature of conventional categories, "lifting their pressure for a moment and suggesting other ways of structuring reality." [65] These are deliberately structured Cynic incon-

---

65. Douglas (above, n. 37 [1968]) 374.

gruities and as much a part of the movement as the Cynic knapsack. As Mary Douglas argues of the joker generally, the Cynic jester "appears to be a privileged person who can say certain things in a certain way which confers immunity [i.e., *parrhēsia*]. . . . Safe within the permitted range of attack, he lightens for everyone the oppressiveness of social reality, demonstrates its arbitrariness by making light of formality in general, and expresses the creative possibilities of the situation."[66] Specifically, the surprise ending validates Diogenes' role as a Cynic preacher by dramatizing his commitment to say what is true and to act according to nature undeterred by shame, "the most intimate of social fetters" and the cornerstone of traditional Greek morality.[67] But it is precisely his willingness to make himself an object of ridicule, to engage in unseemly, shameful, or ridiculous acts, that empowers Diogenes as a Cynic moral authority, as one obedient to another set of rules—those of "nature." Otherwise he would just be another philosopher haranguing crowds. His shocking peroration is an act of philosophical jesting directed at the audience. It is an action *chreia* of an unmistakably Cynic kind and serves as a kind of signature authenticating the Cynic nature of Dio's own speech.[68]

Because he is willing to flout the rules that everyone else must observe, the Cynic is a freak, a monster, like every violator of taboos. (Diogenes is also a defender of freaks: according to Dio he argued that Oedipus should simply have legalized incest in Thebes!)[69] Dio says the crowd at the games responded to Diogenes' performance by calling him "mad" (*mainesthai, Or.* 8.36), as had Plato.[70] The price he pays for being a licensed fool is to live as a beggar; the compensation he receives from society is *parrhēsia,* a peculiar kind of privilege conferred, paradoxically, by custom alone. Because he has nothing to lose, he can tell the truth and, therefore, may be worth listening to. (This of course is the point of the imagined encounters between Diogenes and the powerful.) The act of defecation is meant to remind the audience of this fact—the anomalous social status of the Cynic, his privileged perspective on a society he is in and not of, whose *doxa* he need not take seriously.

I would like to conclude by briefly considering the implications of a rhetorical approach for our general assessment of Cynicism, its central values and cultural significance. From the standpoint of rhetorical practice, Dudley's char-

66. Ibid. 372.

67. Peter Sloterdijk, *Critique of Cynical Reason,* trans. M. Eldred (Minneapolis 1988), 168. See B. Williams, *Shame and Necessity* (Berkeley and Los Angeles 1993).

68. Cf. Douglas (above, n. 37 [1968]): "It still remains to distinguish jokes in general from obscenity as such. . . . A joke confronts one accepted pattern with another. So does an obscene image. The first amuses. The second shocks. . . . The joke works only when it mirrors social forms; it exists by virtue of its congruence with the social structure. But the obscenity is identified by its opposition to the social structure, hence its offence" (371–72).

69. Dio, *Or.* 10.30: "Domestic fowls do not object to such relationships [i.e., incest], nor dogs, nor any ass, nor do the Persians, although they pass for the aristocracy of Asia."

70. "When Plato was asked, 'What sort of man do you think Diogenes is?' he replied, 'A Socrates—gone mad'" (*mainomenos:* D.L. 6.54).

acterizations of Diogenes as a "benevolent anarchist," whom he compares to Peter Kropotkin,[71] is certainly far less misleading than (1) the recent attempt of Peter Sloterdijk to associate the Cynic with some form of "Japanese Zen master";[72] or (2) the condemnation of Diogenes by the humorless Sayre as a "megalomaniac rather than a misanthropist";[73] or (3) the tendency to assimilate Diogenes too completely to a Socratic tradition of moral philosophy, which classicists have sometimes succumbed to, following idealizing writers of the empire such as Epictetus and Julian.[74] But any account of Cynicism that ignores or discounts its literary or rhetorical dimension—its link to the arts of philosophical jesting as suggested by the term *spoudogeloios*[75]—is leaving out what made Cynicism different from any other ancient philosophical tradition. Cynicism is the only philosophical movement in antiquity to make freedom a central value, and freedom of speech in particular. This fact is directly linked to the Cynic invention of satiric and parodic forms of literature without classical precedent. It is equally a mistake, however, to think of a body of Cynic doctrines first formulated and then embodied in literary works. Cynicism originates in no small part in rhetorical and literary activity, as the exercise of *parrhēsia*. Aside from its sheer historical accuracy in this respect, a rhetorical approach has the advantage of focusing our attention on: (1) how powerless Cynics like Diogenes gained the attention and won the grudging admiration of ancient audiences, and (2) why Diogenes left so curiously divergent a legacy in antiquity—a mass of irrepressibly opinionated beggars, on the one hand, and a literary tradition cultivated by the most talented sophists in the Roman empire, on the other. If we ask what these two distinct and sometimes hostile parties have in common in virtue of which they can claim to be the heirs of Diogenes—whether as buffoons without shame or as scientific satyrs—the only possible answer is *parrhēsia:*[76] "the finest thing in the world!"

71. Dudley (above, n. 1) 211–12. Cf. P. Marshall, *Demanding the Impossible: A History of Anarchism* (London 1991) chaps. 1, 19; S.J. Gould, "Kropotkin Was No Crackpot," in *Bully for Brontosaurus: Reflections on Natural History* (New York 1992) 325–39.

72. Sloterdijk (above, n. 67) 157.

73. Sayre (above, n. 5) 66.

74. Contrast Sayre (ibid.)—"The Cynics were not Socratics; their teaching was opposed to that of Socrates in almost every respect" (24)—with H.D. Rankin, *Sophists, Socratics and Cynics* (London 1983): "There are in fact distinct Socratic characteristics in Diogenes" (232). Rankin follows Dudley (above, n. 1): "Diogenes represents the Socratic *sophos* with its chief features pushed to extremes" (27–28). Or are they inverted, as Plato's witticism ("Socrates gone mad") could be taken to suggest? Socrates' irony becomes Diogenes' *parrhēsia;* Socrates' indifference to poverty becomes Diogenes' embrace of it; Socrates' respect for the authority of law (e.g., in Plato's *Crito*) becomes Diogenes' indifference to it.

75. For the concept of the *spoudogeloios* or "seriocomic" voice, see Branham (above, n. 16) chap. 1.

76. While writing this article I was unaware of the centrality of the Cynics and the concept of *parrhēsia* to Foucault's late work: see T. Flynn, "Foucault as Parrhesiast: His Last Course at the Collège de France (1984)," in *The Final Foucault*, ed. J. Bernauer and D. Rasmussen (Cambridge, Mass., 1987), 102–18.

Cynic Cosmopolitanism

John L. Moles

How should we interpret Cynicism? A 1991 Paris conference laid the following stern injunction upon its participants:[1] "The material demands both a very precise philological inquiry to take account of the fragments and testimonia and a rigorous philosophical approach to determine the exact originality of Cynic thought." Of course, such traditional methods have their place, but in my opinion the most important thing is to penetrate the spirit of Cynic formulations, which are provocative, paradoxical, and ludic.

Cynic thought is simultaneously easy and difficult to interpret. The first Cynics, Diogenes and Crates, were obviously clever men, but they rejected intellectual subtlety in favor of simplicity, and they expressed this simplicity in paradoxical and ludic forms, which often seemed obtuse but in fact were not. Their aim was to challenge the preconceptions of their audience, and so-called wise men, philosophers, and sophists found themselves particularly targeted.

In the words of Saint Paul:[2] "If any man among you seemeth to be wise in

1. This paper is an English translation of a French version published in Marie-Odile Goulet-Cazé and Richard Goulet, eds., *Le cynisme ancien et ses prolongements* (Paris 1993) 259–80, a collection of the papers delivered at Le Cynisme Ancien et ses Prolongements: Colloque International du C.N.R.S., Paris, 22–25 July 1991. I am grateful to the Comité Scientifique for inviting me to participate and particularly grateful to Marie-Odile Goulet-Cazé and Margarethe Billerbeck for numerous kindnesses. The published versions are close to the paper delivered on 23 July 1991 but incorporate some modifications, developments, and second thoughts. My subsequent paper "The Cynics and Politics," delivered on 20 August 1992 at the Symposium Hellenisticum, Cambridge, 17–23 August 1992, and later published in A. Laks and M. Schofield, eds., *Justice and Generosity: Studies in Hellenistic Social and Political Philosophy* (Cambridge 1995) 129–58, contains further second thoughts on Diogenes, which, however, do not substantially alter my original conclusions.
2. 1 Corinthians 3.18.

this world, let him become a fool, that he may be wise." Many modern scholars are too clever to interpret Cynicism correctly. And since the challenge posed by the Cynics is moral as well as intellectual, modern scholars who misinterpret Cynic cosmopolitanism are, from a Cynic point of view, not simply ignorant but wicked.

Consequently, anyone who tries to interpret Cynic cosmopolitanism should not be discouraged if he is not a philosopher. Indeed, it is an advantage not to be one, provided that one respects the extremely radical nature of Cynic thought and that one appreciates its ludic quality, never forgetting that in the case of Cynicism, because of the concept of the *spoudogeloion* or "serio-comic," one can always uncover a deeper meaning.[3]

This study rests on the following assumptions. First, because Cynic philosophy is fundamentally simple, there comes a point beyond which it does not go. Second, because the evidence is so defective, there comes a point where we must employ the principle *ben trovato*. Third, there nevertheless comes a point beyond which our reconstruction of Cynic philosophy cannot go. Inevitably, therefore, my reconstruction of Cynic cosmopolitanism will be a "story" (*muthos*) rather than a "true account" (*logos*). Fourth, both the cosmopolitan "saying" attributed to Diogenes in Diogenes Laertius (6.63) and the cosmopolitan "thought" attributed to Diogenes in Diogenes Laertius (6.72) are authentic.[4] Fifth, the attribution of virtually identical formulations to Socrates and other philosophers before Diogenes lacks plausibility.[5]

In contrast to the ancient view, the current scholarly opinion of many years has been that Cynic cosmopolitanism, at least as regards Diogenes and the first

---

3. It is with regard to the fundamental seriousness (σπουδή) implicit in Cynicism that I find myself in disagreement with the otherwise excellent study of R. Bracht Branham in this volume. On Cynic σπουδογέλοιον, see for example J. F. Kindstrand, *Bion of Borysthenes: A Collection of the Fragments with Introduction and Commentary,* Acta Universitatis Upsaliensis, Studia Graeca Upsaliensia 11 (Uppsala 1976), 47–48.

4. I do not agree with the arguments of M. Schofield, *The Stoic Idea of the City* (Cambridge 1991) 141–45, 133, 64, against the authenticity of Diogenes Laertius 6.72. My general reasons are implicit in this study as a whole, but one reason that seems to me virtually decisive in itself is the word play on προκοσμήματα and κόσμῳ. In fact, the testimonia that link cosmopolitanism to Diogenes are numerous. See, e.g., Dio Chrysostom 4.13 (V B 582 G.); Epictetus 3.22.45–48 (V B 263 G.), 3.24.64–66 (V B 290 G.); Plutarch, *De Fortuna Alexandri* 10.332b–c (V B 31 G.); Lucian, *Vitarum Auctio* 8 (V B 80 G.); Julian, 6.201c (V B 264 G.), 7.238b–c (V B 332 G.); Maximus of Tyre 36.5 (V B 229 G.). I deal directly with the so-called authenticity problem in "Cynics and Politics" (n. 1 above) 132–37. Also numerous are the passages that attest general Cynic cosmopolitanism. See, e.g., D.L. 6.93 (V H 31 G.; Crates), 6.98 (V H 80 G.; Crates); Plutarch, *De Fortuna Alexandri* 6.329a–d (discussed below); Teles F 3, p. 21.1–22.7 Hense = Stobaeus 3.40.8, p. 738 Hense; Ps.-Heraclitus, *Ep.* 5.2, 36.9.2, 4, 7; *Anthologia Palatina* 7.417 (Meleager); Maximus of Tyre 36.4; Julian, *Or.* 6.201c; Ps.-Lucian, *Cynicus 15.*

5. Socrates: Cicero, *TD* 5.108; Musonius, p. 42.1–2 Hense = Stobaeus 3.40.9, p. 749 Hense; Epictetus 1.9.1; Plutarch, *De Exilio* 6.600f–601a; others: see, e.g., D.L. 2.7 (Anaxagoras); Democritus F 247 D.-K. I stress the terminology "virtually identical *formulations,*" for, as we shall see, *generally* cosmopolitan sentiments are widely attested before Diogenes, and this affects our interpretation of Diogenes' sentiments.

Cynics, is purely negative.[6] That is, when Diogenes answered the question "Where are you from?" with the words "I am 'a citizen of the cosmos' [*kosmopolitēs,* D.L. 6.63]," and when he wrote, "The only good government is that in the cosmos" (*monēn . . . orthēn politeian tēn en kosmōi,* D.L. 6.72), he meant only what he expressed elsewhere in tragic verses (D.L. 6.38): "Without a city, without a house, without a fatherland, / A beggar, a wanderer with a single day's bread"[7]—namely that he had no polis and rejected the polis as "against nature" (*para phusin*).

In combatting this current opinion, I take my stand, like Diogenes himself, on the wisdom of old and not on the sophistry of the *savants de nos jours;* like Diogenes, I intend to deface the currency, and I appeal to an anecdote about Diogenes related by Dio Chrysostom.[8] In typically Cynic fashion, this anecdote shocks and instructs us at the same time. Both "the many" and "the sophists" despise Diogenes' teaching as *kopros* ("shit"), but in reality the sophists do not understand the "opinions" of Diogenes, even though they are on the point of engulfing them, and it is their own false "opinion" that is the *kopros pollōn etōn* ("the shit of many years"). I hope that my study will be the true *kopros,* the "real shit" on Diogenes the Dog. No doubt some of my readers will consider it to be *kopros* pure and simple.

To begin with, can we accept that Cynic cosmopolitanism is negative to the extent that it rejects the polis? The tragic verses already cited, the slogan "Deface the Currency," and numerous fragments and testimonia support the thesis that Diogenes and Crates and the Cynics in general considered the polis to be "against nature."[9] It is true that in the case of Diogenes the controversial passage concerning *nomos* ("law," "custom") in Diogenes Laertius (6.72) poses a problem, but in my opinion those scholars who hold that this passage should not be taken at face value are certainly right.[10]

---

6. See, e.g., the altogether typical discussions of G. Giannantoni, ed., *Socraticorum Reliquiae* vol. 3 (Rome 1985 [hereafter Giannantoni 1985]), 483–92, virtually identical to *Socratis et Socraticorum Reliquiae* vol. 4 (Naples 1990 [hereafter Giannantoni 1990]), 537–47; M.-O. Goulet-Cazé, *RhM* 125 (1982) 229–31 (note her conclusion: "par conséquent, un cosmopolitisme négatif"); Schofield (n. 4 above). Among the very few scholars to believe in a positive Cynic cosmopolitanism are M.H. Fisch, *AJPh* 58 (1937) 144; R. Höistad, *Cynic Hero and Cynic King* (Uppsala 1948) 138–52, esp. 141–43; M. Buora, *AIV* 132 (1973–74) 247; R. Giannattasio Andria, *CronErc* 10 (1980) 148.

7. D.L. 6.38, V B 263 G.

8. Dio Chrysostom 8.35–36, V B 584 G.: ἵνα μὴ δοκῇ . . . τὸν ὕδρον οὐχ ὁρῶντες.

9. See, e.g., D.L. 6.20 (V B 2 G.), 6.29 (V B 297 G.); Epictetus 3.22.45–47, 24.65–66; D.L. 6.85 (V H 70 G.; Crates' *Pēra*), 6.93 (V H 31 G.); Dio Chrysostom 6.25, 28, 31 (V B 583 G.); Philodemus, *De Stoicis, PHerc.* 339.10.4–6 Crönert = 20.3–4 Dorandi; Lucian, *Vitarum Auctio* 9; Maximus of Tyre 36.5; Ps.-Heraclitus, *Ep.* 5.2.

10. περί τε τοῦ νόμου ὅτι χωρὶς αὐτοῦ οὐχ οἷόν τε πολιτεύεσθαι· οὐ γάρ φησιν ἄνευ πόλεως ὄφελός τι εἶναι ἀστείου· ἀστεῖον δὲ ἡ πόλις· νόμου δὲ ἄνευ πόλεως οὐδὲν ὄφελος· ἀστεῖον ἄρα ὁ νόμος. For present purposes, it matters little whether one follows M.-O. Goulet-Cazé, *RhM* 125 (1982) 214–40, who sees Stoic influence on this passage, or Schofield (n. 4 above: 134), who sees a sarcastic note in the word ἀστεῖος. What is important is not to read the passage

It is true also that the Cynics ordinarily lived in cities and exploited their amenities, including the opportunity of begging, but the principle "use what is present" allows a certain moral relativism (compare the hypocritical behavior of Western Marxists),[11] and to some extent also the Cynics' missionary role (to which I shall return) required their presence in the city.[12] The Cynics' hostility to the city is not fundamentally compromised by their behavior in this context.

Another difficulty is posed by the existence of an apparently Cynic tradition that is less hostile to the polis and to political power in general. Antisthenes compared the polis to fire—go too near and you burn; go too far away and you freeze[13]—and theorized about kingship. Onesicritus accompanied and eulogized Alexander.[14] Bion was court philosopher to Antigonus Gonatas, to whom he said, "You rule well" (*arkheis kalōs*), thereby employing a relativist doctrine that allows considerable moral relativism.[15] The philosophical doctrine of Teles was even laxer. Cercidas was a "politician" and "lawmaker." Dio Chrysostom addressed Cynic doctrines to a Roman emperor; and there are other examples.[16]

One must certainly distinguish the attitude of Antisthenes and his like from the more radical attitude of Diogenes and Crates. Should one then suppose that Antisthenes and his like are not true Cynics, or that they represent a less strict form of Cynicism, while still remaining Cynics? In the final assessment, this question is perhaps semantic and without much importance for the present study.[17] It is certain that the Cynicism of Diogenes and Crates, Cynicism at its most typical, rejected the polis.

---

at face value. (My own preference now is to follow Schofield's interpretation: see "Cynics and Politics" [n. 1 above] 130–31.)

11. See, e.g., Teles F 2, p. 6.5–8.5 Hense; Bion FF 16A, 17 Kindstrand, with Kindstrand's commentary (n. 3 above) 218–19.

12. See, e.g., E. Weber, *Leipziger Studien zur Classichen Philologie* 10 (1887) 126; U. von Wilamowitz-Moellendorff, *Aristoteles und Athen* vol. 2 (Berlin 1893) 24; M.-O. Goulet-Cazé, *L'ascèse cynique: Un commentaire de Diogène Laërce VI 70–71* (Paris 1986) 230.

13. Stobaeus 4.4.28, V A 70 G. The attribution of this testimonium to Diogenes should be rejected.

14. See in general T. S. Brown *Onesicritus: A Study in Hellenistic Historiography* (Berkeley and Los Angeles 1949; repr. New York 1974); and my own remarks in *JHS* 103 (1983) 109 and "Cynics and Politics" (n. 1 above) 144–49.

15. See Teles F 2, p. 5.1–6.1 Hense = Bion F 16A Kindstrand; and my own remarks in F. Cairns, ed., *Papers of the Liverpool International Latin Seminar: Fifth Volume 1985* (Liverpool 1986) 43, 58 n. 60.

16. See my remarks in *Classical Antiquity* 2.2 (1983) 268–69 n. 65 and my study "The Kingship Orations of Dio Chrysostom," in F. Cairns and M. Heath, eds., *Papers of the Leeds International Latin Seminar: Sixth Volume 1990* (Leeds 1990) 297–375, esp. 303, 309–11, 319–24.

17. In fact I agree with the arguments of Giananntoni (1985, 203–11 = Giannantoni 1990, 223–33; cf. his "Antistene fondatore della scuola clinica?" in Goulet-Cazé and Goulet [n. 1 above] 15–34) that Antisthenes was not the founder of Cynicism, though this conclusion requires slight modification, as follows: "the ancient tradition that Diogenes was Antisthenes' pupil was effectively refuted by Dudley . . . but Antisthenic influence upon Diogenes has been widely accepted, and is patent" (cf. esp. Xen. *Smp.* 4.34–44, as I wrote in *JHS* 103 [1983] 104 n. 8).

But this does not make their cosmopolitanism purely negative. It also has positive implications, and I give five "proofs" of this:

First, Diogenes did not say, in the context of D.L. 6.63, "I am without a polis" (*apolis eimi*), nor did he write, in the context of D.L. 6.72, "There is no good government" (*oudemia politeia orthē estin*). His formulations were formally positive, a factor to which we must accord its full importance, since he could have answered, "I am without a polis," as he did on other occasions. If in 1996 you are asked, "Are you French or German?" and you reply, "I am European," the reply entails both the rejection of a restrictive nationalism and the assertion of a larger loyalty.

Second, Diogenes' sentiments must be interpreted not in a vacuum but rather against a general tradition in which the polis or the "fatherland" (*patris*) or some similar concept is rejected, or revalued, in favor of an internationalist or cosmopolitan ideal. Given that the various corresponding sentiments of Heraclitus, Euripides, Antiphon, Hippias, Alcidamas, and others have a positive value,[18] it cannot be justifiable to restrict the parallel formulations of Diogenes to a negative sense.

Third, not only do Diogenes' sentiments form part of a tradition: we must also take account of the philosophical rivalry between Diogenes and Aristippus, which I take to be historical, at least to the extent that there is a certain relationship between their philosophical systems and that Diogenes certainly criticized Aristippus.[19]

Scholars have noted a relationship between Diogenes' sentiments and those of Aristippus as reported by Xenophon. Their philosophical rivalry surely indicates some direct relationship, as Plutarch sensed.[20] Aristippus maintains his freedom by not shutting himself up in a *politeia* ("state," "government,"

---

18. See, e.g., Heraclitus F 114 D.-K.; Euripides FF 777, 902, 1047 N.²; Antiphon F 44 D.-K.; Hippias *ap.* Plato, *Protagoras* 337c–d; Alcidamas *ap.* Aristotle, *Rhet.* 1373b18–18a; Plato, *Theaet.* 173e1–174a1; Aristotle, *EN* 1155a21; see also Democritus F 247 D.-K.; Thucydides 2.24.3; *Tr. Fr. Adesp.* 318 N.²; Aristophanes, *Plut.* 1151, and *ap.* Stobaeus 3.40.2a; Lysias 31.6; see also the discussions of I. Lana, "Tracce di dottrine cosmopolitiche in Grecia prima del cinismo," *RFIC* 29 (1951) 193–216, 317–38; H. C. Baldry, *The Unity of Mankind in Greek Thought* (Cambridge 1965) 26–29, 35–45, 58–59; W. K. C. Guthrie, *History of Greek Philosophy* vol. 3, pt. 1 (Cambridge 1969 [= *The Sophists* (Cambridge 1971)]), 152–63; H. Schulz-Falkenthal, *WZHalle* 28 (1979) 29–32; G. B. Kerferd, *The Sophistic Movement* (Cambridge 1981) 154–59.

19. On the problem of the relations between Aristippus and Diogenes, see O. Gigon, *Kommentar zum zweiten Buch von Xenophons Memorabilia* (Basel 1956) 36; G. Giannantoni, *I Cirenaici* (Florence 1958) 47–49, 83–84; E. Mannebach, *Aristippi et Cyrenaicorum Fragmenta* (Leiden 1961) 72; W. K. C. Guthrie, *History of Greek Philosophy* vol. 3 (Cambridge 1969) 492; G. Steiner, *CJ* 72 (1976) 36–46; R. F. Hock, *GRBS* 17 (1976) 41–53, reprinted in M. Billerbeck, ed., *Die Kyniker in der modernen Forschung* (Amsterdam 1991) 259–71; Giannantoni 1985, 138–40 = Giannantoni 1990, 151–53; and my own remarks in Cairns (n. 15 above) 43–48.

20. Xenophon, *Memorabilia* 2.1.12–13: Ἀλλ᾽ εἰ μὲν , . . . καθίσταντες δούλοις χρῆσθαι. . . . [13] Ἀλλ᾽ ἐγώ τοι, ἔφη, ἵνα μὴ πάσχω ταῦτα, οὐδ᾽ εἰς πολιτείαν ἐμαυτὸν κατακλείω, ἀλλὰ ξένος πανταχοῦ εἰμι. It is significant that Plutarch, *De Exilio* 5.601a, uses the word ἐνέκλεισεν in relation to the cosmopolitanism of Socrates.

"polity"), which seems to him "against nature," and by maintaining his status of "stranger" (*xenos*) everywhere—that is, everywhere on earth, among all mankind. Like Aristippus, Diogenes maintains his freedom by rejecting the polis, which seems to him "against nature," but whereas Aristippus is a "stranger" (*xenos*), Diogenes is a "citizen" (*politēs*), and whereas Aristippus operates "among human beings," Diogenes operates "in the cosmos." The attitude of Diogenes is much more positive than that of Aristippus: Diogenes substitutes the positive and the engaged (*politēs, politeia*) for the negative and disengaged, and he extends his sphere of operations beyond the world of human beings. Clearly, Diogenes defeats Aristippus in the debate. In short, the relationship between the sentiments of Diogenes and those of Aristippus is itself sufficient to prove that Diogenes' sentiments have a positive content.

Fourth, let us consider the precise form of these sentiments. They are paradoxes, which provoke and challenge us to find a meaning in apparent absurdities. How can a *politēs,* a member of so small a group as a polis, be a *politēs* ("citizen") of the *kosmos* ("cosmos"), the largest organism imaginable? How can the only true *politeia* ("government"), a single small entity, be coextensive with the cosmos? This is the ultimate "defacing" of "the political currency." [21] As in other celebrated Cynic formulations, the challenge to find a meaning is formulated in terms of polar oppositions. The answers suggested by the majority of modern scholars—"I am a citizen of no polis" and "There is no good government"—are on the one hand intolerably banal and on the other hand take no account of these polar oppositions.

Fifth, the sentiments are paradoxical in another sense. For they seem to contradict Cynic doctrines themselves. How can the Cynic, severe critic of the polis, be a *politēs* ("citizen")? How can this savage outsider advocate a political *kosmos* ("cosmos")? [22] How can the apolitical man *par excellence* be *engagé?* How can the despiser of cosmology embrace the cosmos? [23] These paradoxes also demand substantive answers. [24]

These are my five "proofs." I submit that individually and cumulatively they prove that Diogenes' sentiments *must* have positive content. But they do not yet shed much light on this content.

Let us first recall what the cosmos consists of: the earth and the heavens; on

21. For this formulation of the great Cynic slogan, see D.L. 6.20, V B 2 G.

22. For this concept, see J. Bordes, *Politeia dans la pensée grecque jusqu'à Aristote* (Paris 1982) 493; and also LSJ s.v. κόσμος, I.4, iii.

23. See, e.g., D.L. 6.28 (V B 374 G.), 6.39 (V B 371 G.), 6.73 (V B 370 G.), 6.103 (V A 135 G.); Stobaeus 2.1.11 = Bion F 6 K. (with Kindstrand [n. 3 above] 192–93, 198–99), Stobaeus 2.1.11 (Demonax); in this respect, the position of Onesicritus in Strabo 16.1.65 is altogether heterodox.

24. There is still more to be said about the verbal cleverness of Diogenes' sentiments: see my "Cynics and Politics" (n. 1 above) 136–37, which includes a detailed analysis of the whole of D.L. 6.72; but enough has been said here for the purposes of the essential argument.

the earth, there is both animate and inanimate nature; animate nature consists of human beings and animals; human beings consist of Cynics and non-Cynics, Greeks and barbarians, men and women; the heavens contain the heavenly bodies and the gods who live in them.

Cynic cosmopolitanism has numerous positive aspects, which relate to each of these constituents of the cosmos:

The Cynic, his virtues, and his way of life.   Cynic cosmopolitanism relates to Cynic "freedom" (*eleutheria*) because of the link with Aristippus's concept of "hospitality" or "rights of a foreigner" (*xenia*), which was designed to secure his personal freedom, and because the polis, with all its attendant obligations, is equally an impediment to true Cynic freedom. It relates to Cynic "virtue," a state defined as "to live according to nature," because, as we have seen, the polis is "against nature." This link is implicit in Diogenes Laertius (6.72), where "birth, reputation, and all such things" are linked with "vice," and the "one good government in the cosmos" is linked, by implicit contrast, with virtue; and also, as I have already noted,[25] the false cosmos of this world contrasts with the true cosmos of the Cynic "state" (*politeia*). Of course, Cynic freedom and virtue have negative aspects—freedom partly implies freedom *from* things, including the polis—but they are not *merely* negative: freedom from inessentials is a precondition of positive freedom.

Since rejection of the polis facilitates freedom and virtue, by a typical Cynic revaluation of terms, *patris, patra, polis, politeia,* and so on ("fatherland", "city," "government," etc.), become metaphors for the Cynic way of life itself.[26] In other words—and this is an absolutely fundamental point—the Cynic *politeia,* the Cynic "state," is nothing other than a *moral* "state": that is, the "state" of being a Cynic. And since neither the polis nor racial distinction means anything to the Cynics, it is often claimed that one can live the Cynic life anywhere on earth, and that "the whole earth" is the Cynic's home.[27] Positive or negative? Certain modern scholars hold that to say "I am at home everywhere" is equivalent to saying "I am a stranger everywhere." This is only true if the word "home" is given a narrow meaning, but the truth is that the Cynic expresses a positive allegiance to the whole earth. We may note in passing that this allegiance to the whole earth is sometimes linked to a sense of allegiance to all mankind.[28]

25. See n. 4 above.
26. See, e.g., D.L. 6.85 (V H 70 G.; Crates' *Pēra*), 6.93 (V H 31 G.); Epictetus 3.22.84–85.
27. See, e.g., D.L. 6.98 (V H 80 G.); Bion F 17.8–9 Kindstrand = Teles *ap.* Stobaeus 3.1.98 = F 2, p. 7.5–6 Hense; Ps.-Anacharsis, *Ep.* 5.3; Dio Chrysostom 4.13; Epictetus 3.24.66; Maximus of Tyre 36; Ps.-Lucian, *Cynicus* 15.
28. See, e.g., Dio Chrysostom 4.13; Epictetus 3.24.64–66; of course, these are late testimonia, but, as we shall see, they are faithful to the true Cynic spirit.

The natural world.   Cynic cosmopolitanism implies a positive attitude toward the natural world and all its riches (water, garlic, lupins, etc.!) as opposed
to the world of the polis.[29] This positive attitude may extend to the heavenly
bodies insofar as they affect the Cynic way of life on earth. (We recall Diogenes' pleasure in sunbathing.) It is true that the Cynic attitude toward the natural
world is less lyrical, less developed, less integral to a total system than the
corresponding Epicurean or Stoic attitude. It remains, nevertheless, a positive
attitude.

*Cynic cosmopolitanism implies a positive attitude to the animal world, in
contrast with that of the majority of Greek philosophers.*   As their willing
acceptance of the abusive term "dogs" shows, Cynics upheld animals as models of the true life "according to nature." Of course, Cynics generally ate animals,[30] but animals equally could eat human beings, and it is a notorious fact
that Diogenes was even prepared to envisage cannibalism.[31] This mutual eating
was supported by the theory of the kinship of human beings and animals,[32] and
even by Anaxagoras's physical theory that "there is a portion of everything in
everything" and by Empedocles' theory of "pores." [33] We seem here to be
verging on the idea (which would have very important consequences) that the
universe is a unified physical organism. It is true also that man, or at least the
ideal man, is distinguished by his possession of *logos* ("speech," "reason"),[34]
and in this regard he differs from the animals. We must therefore recognize the
existence of a double attitude: human beings and animals are at once kin and
not kin, but we must assess the kinship at its true value.

*Cynic cosmopolitanism has implications for the relations of the Cynic with
his peers.*   The Cynics recognized the kinship or community of the wise.[35]
We

29. See, e.g., D.L. 6.44 (V B 332 G.), 6.85 (V H 70 G.; Crates' *Pēra*), 6.98 (V H 80 G.); Bion
F 17.7–9 Kindstrand = Stobaeus 3.1.98 = Teles F 2, p. 7.4–6 Hense; Dio Chrysostom 6.12–13,
25, 30 (V B 583 G.); Strabo 15.1.64 = Onesicritus *FGrH* 134 F 17 (cf. Plutarch, *De Fortuna
Alexandri* 10.332b); Maximus of Tyre 36; Ps.-Lucian, *Cynicus* 15.

30. D.L. 6.34, 73, 76, 77 (V B 93 G.); Julian 6.190c–193c; Kindstrand (n. 3 above) 215; for
Cynic food in general, see for example A.O. Lovejoy and G. Boas, *Primitivism and Related Ideas
in Antiquity* (Baltimore 1935; repr. New York 1965) 133–34; R. Vischer, *Das einfache Leben*
(Göttingen 1965) 75–83.

31. See, e.g., D.L. 6.73 (V B 132 G.); Philodemus, *De Stoicis, PHerc.* 339.10.4–6 Crönert =
20.1–3 Dorandi.

32. D.L. 6.79 (V B 101 G.).

33. See D.L. 6.73 (V B 132 G.); discussion in D.R. Dudley, *A History of Cynicism* (London
1937; repr. Hildesheim 1967) 30; Höistad (n. 6 above) 143–44; Brown (n. 14 above) 37; Giannantoni 1985, 429–31 = Giannantoni 1990, 479–81.

34. See, e.g., D.L. 6.24 (V B 303 G.), 6.73.

35. This is admitted by some scholars, for example Dudley (n. 33 above) 35–36; Baldry (n. 18
above) 110; J.M. Rist, *Stoic Philosophy* (Cambridge 1969) 62–63; Giannantoni 1985, 490 =
Giannantoni 1990, 545; see also my discussion *JHS* 103 (1983) 109–11.

may recall, for example, the doctrine that "the wise man is a friend to his kind";[36] and Diogenes' famous syllogism—"All things belong to the gods; the wise are friends of the gods, and friends hold things in common, therefore all things belong to the wise"[37]; the "likemindedness" (*homonoia*) that, according to Plutarch, was the basis of Diogenes' polity (*politeia*)[38]; and Crates' claim to be "a citizen of Diogenes" (*Diogenous politēs*).[39] This kinship transcends the conventional barriers between men and women (cf. the relationship between Crates and Hipparchia)[40] and between the races (cf., for example, the relations between Diogenes and the gymnosophists described by Onesicritus).[41]

Cynic cosmopolitanism has implications for the relations of the Cynics with the gods.   Since the polarized form of Diogenes' sentiments, their link with the thought of Aristippus, and Greek linguistic usage of the fourth century guarantee the word *kosmos* its full force of "universe," Diogenes must be making a statement about the position of the Cynics vis-à-vis the heavens. As we have already seen, the heavenly bodies affect life "according to nature" on earth. But we must also consider the position of the Cynics vis-à-vis the gods. (Here we venture upon dangerous territory that is fiercely contested by modern scholars.)[42]

The gods, who are man's benefactors,[43] provide a paradigm for Cynic self-sufficiency;[44] the Cynic himself is godlike,[45] friend of the gods,[46] their messenger, their agent,[47] and, in being *agathos daimōn* ("tutelary god," "guardian angel"),[48] he is himself virtually divine. We may recall too that "Diogenes"

36. D.L. 6.105 (V A 99 G.).

37. D.L. 6.37, 72 (V B 353 G.).

38. Plutarch, *Lycurgus* 31.2; I do not accept the arguments of D. Babut, *Plutarque et le stoïcisme* (Paris 1969) 201–2, for a reference to Diogenes the Stoic.

39. D.L. 6.93 (V H 31 G.).

40. For sex in Cynicism see, e.g., D.L. 6.72 (V H 353 G.); Dio Chrysostom 6.19–20; the discussion in Rist (n. 35 above) 59–62, seems to me very convincing, despite the judgment of Giannantoni (1985, 482) that "non sembra necessario . . . contestare il carattere genuino e originario della misoginia di Diogene." See also my article "The Woman and the River: Diogenes' Apophthegm from Herculaneum and Some Popular Misconceptions about Cynicism," *Apeiron* 17 (1983) 125–30.

41. Strabo 15.1.64–65 = *FGrH* 134 F 17.

42. See especially the contribution of Marie-Odile Goulet-Cazé to this volume, a rich and stimulating study, whose principal conclusions, however, I am unfortunately unable to accept.

43. See, e.g., D.L. 6.44 (V B 322 G.); Dio Chrysostom 6.25; Ps.-Lucian, *Cynicus* 7, 11, 18.

44. See, e.g., D.L. 6.51 (V B 354 G.), 6.104; Dio Chrysostom 6.31 (V B 583 G.); Ps.-Crates, *Ep.* 16; Ps.-Lucian, *Cynicus* 12.

45. See, e.g., D.L. 6.51 (V B 354 G.), 6.104, 105; Aristotle, *Politics* 1.2, 1253a26–29.

46. See, e.g., D.L. 6.37, 72 (V B 353 G.).

47. See, e.g., Strabo 15.1.63–64 = *FGrH* 134 F 17 (cf. Plutarch, *Alexander* 65.2); D.L. 6.102 (V N 1 G.); Dio Chrysostom 1.58; 32.12, 21; Epictetus 3.22.2, 23, 53, 69; Ps.-Heraclitus, *Ep.* 9.3; see also the discussions of M. Billerbeck, *Epiktet: Vom Kynismus* (Leiden 1978) 78; A. Delatte, "Le sage-témoin dans la philosophie stoïco-cynique," *BAB*, ser. 5, 39 (1953) 166–86.

48. D.L. 6.74 (V B 70 G.); Apuleius, *Florida* 22 (V H 18 G.); Julian 6.200b; Lucian, *Demonax* 63.

means "Born of Zeus" and that Diogenes was hailed as an *ouranios kuōn* (a "godlike [or "heavenly"] dog").[49] This "friendship" (*philia*) and "affinity" (*homoiotēs*) between Cynic and gods should imply that the cosmos is the common home of gods and wise men, and this implication is substantially confirmed by the syllogism of Diogenes already cited. We may note in passing that there are Cynic fragments to the effect that everything is full of the divine—a contention consistent with the physical theories already mentioned[50]—and that human beings in general are endowed by the gods with "intellect" (*nous*),[51] or "reason" (*logos*),[52] or "judgment" (*gnōmē*).[53] The possible implications of these two positions are obviously very important: they seem to weaken the ordinary distinctions between the animate and the inanimate and between gods and men.

Cynic cosmopolitanism has implications for the relationship between the Cynics and mankind at large. Cynicism presents itself as a missionary philosophy.[54] By his characteristically exhibitionist behavior, the Cynic offers other human beings a model to imitate or a demonstration of the falsity of their own values.[55] In innumerable anecdotes and literary descriptions, we see the Cynic energetically trying to convert other human beings (whether one or two individuals, or vast crowds in cities)[56] to the Cynic life of virtue, and he is often followed by pupils.[57] He enjoys a vast range of titles that imply a didactic and proselytizing

---

49. See, e.g., Cercidas *ap.* D.L. 6.76 (V B 97 G.); Ps.-Diogenes, *Ep.* 7.1; for other testimonia and a large bibliography, see J. F. Kindstrand, *Eranos* 82 (1984) 161.

50. See D.L. 6.37 (V B 344 G.), 6.73 (V B 132 G.).

51. See, e.g., Dio Chrysostom 10.27–28 (V B 586 G.); Ps.-Diogenes, *Ep.* 9.3.

52. See, e.g., D.L. 6.24 (V B 303 G), 6.73 (V B 132 G.).

53. See, e.g., Maximus of Tyre 36.1 (cf. Strabo 15.1.65 = *FGrH* 134 F 17); see also the concept of the god within: e.g., Dio Chrysostom 4.139 (with Moles [n. 16 above (1983)] 259–60); *PGenev.* inv. 271.2.45–46.

54. Here I repeat some of the arguments of my article *"Honestius Quam Ambitiosius?* An Exploration of the Cynic's Attitude to Moral Corruption in His Fellow Men," *JHS* 103 (1983) 103–23, esp. 111–18, with some modifications and (I hope) some improvements also.

55. See, e.g., D.L. 6.78 = *Anthologia Palatina* 16.334 (V B 108 G.); Seneca, *Ep.* 20.9.; *De Beneficiis* 7.8.3; Epictetus 3.22.46, 86, 88; 3.24.112; Julian 6.187c, 201c; *THW* 4 (1942) s.v. μάρτυς, pp. 477–520 (H. Strathmann); Delatte (n. 47 above); Billerbeck (n. 47 above) 78, 107; Kindstrand, *Philologus* 124 (1980) 90; also relevant is the important παράδειγμα of Socrates: Plato *Apology* 23a12. Of course, the behavior of the Cynics in this regard can be criticized as τῦφος or *ambitio*, etc.: see, e.g., D.L. 6.26 (V B 55 G.); Epictetus 3.22.50–51, 4.8.34; Tacitus, *Histories* 4.40.3; Seneca, *Epp.* 5.2–4, 7.9; Lucian, *Vitarum Auctio* 10–11.

56. See on this Kindstrand (n. 3 above) 138, (n. 55 above) 90.

57. Of course this claim often depends on the meaning given to the word "pupil": on this topic see H. von Arnim, *Leben und Werke des Dio von Prusa* (Berlin 1989) 37–43; Dudley (n. 33 above); 37–38; Kindstrand (n. 3 above) 10–11, (n. 55 above) 90; Giannantoni 1985, 205–8, 435–39, 504–8 = Giannantoni 1990, 225–26, 485–89, 562–66; M.-O Goulet-Cazé, "Une liste de disciples de Cratès le Cynique en Diogène Laërce 6, 95," *Hermes* 114 (1986) 247–52.

role toward others,[58] a role that seems to bear witness to a profound philanthropy (*philanthrōpia*),[59] "love for mankind," "benevolence." These apparently altruistic aspects of the Cynic's behavior cannot be dismissed as later embroideries inspired by the more humane character of Crates. They are all, or almost all, documented for Diogenes himself, and some indeed for his predecessor Antisthenes. It seems, therefore, that they form an integral part of Cynicism.

Does this mean that the Cynic recognizes kinship with mankind in general? Admittedly, this conclusion presents difficulties, which a good number of scholars judge to be so great either that they vitiate the conclusion, at any rate in regard to the Cynicism of Diogenes, or at least that they render the Cynic position incoherent. What of the criticisms and insults that the Cynic directs at humanity in general, insults that are characteristic of the Cynicism of Diogenes but are far from absent from the type of Cynicism represented by Crates, which is universally admitted to be more moderate? What of the apparently disdainful fashion in which the Cynic divides humanity into a handful of sages and the mass of the foolish or insane? What of the apparent elitism as expressed in the doctrine that "the wise man is a friend to his kind"?[60] And if the Cynic is totally self-sufficient and enters into the affairs of others only through his own free choice (as for example in the sexual sphere, where masturbation and "free love" are equally legitimate), why should he concern himself with the moral state of others? It is true that the Cynics seem to recognize some virtues (for example, "justice"),[61] which entail virtuous dealings with other people; but such virtues are marginal in Cynicism. It is true also that wrongdoing toward others obviously may form part of vice, but Cynic virtue—"life according to nature" in the most primitivist sense, a constant "discipline" (*askēsis*) of "natural labors" (*hoi kata phusin ponoi*)[62]—can surely be a very largely self-contained activity.

In my opinion, these difficulties have been exaggerated. Harsh criticism—even abuse—of the ignorant is not incompatible with a didactic purpose. Diogenes and Crates asserted this explicitly.[63] The apparent conflict between a philanthropic mission (*philanthrōpia*) and elitism is exactly paralleled in Sto-

---

58. κατάσκοπος, ἐπίσκοπος, εὐεργέτης, παιδαγωγός, διδάσκαλος, ἄρχων, ἰατρός, σωφρονιστής, νουθετητής, διαλλακτής, ἀγαθὸς δαίμων, σῴζειν, ὠφέλειν: for a representative documentation of these titles, see Moles (n. 54 above) 112. For the central and fundamental concepts of κατάσκοπος and ἐπίσκοπος, see especially E. Norden, "Beiträge zur Geschichte der griechischen Philosophie," *Jahrbücher für classiche Philologie*, Suppl. 19 (Leipzig 1893), 365–462; and Giannantoni 1985, 457–58 = Giannantoni 1990, 507–8.

59. See especially Kindstrand (n. 3 above) 61, 247; Moles (n. 54 above) 112–14.

60. D.L. 6.105.

61. See, e.g., D.L. 6.16 (V A 41 G.), 6.12 (V A 134 G.), 6.5 (V A 176 G.); Crates F 10 D = 1 Diehl = 84 G.; Bion F 17.7 K. = Teles F 2, p. 7.3 Hense; Kindstrand (n. 3 above) 214–15.

62. See above all the remarkable study of M.-O Goulet-Cazé in n. 12 above.

63. Stobaeus 3.13.44 (V B 149 G.); Crates F 10 D = 1 Diehl = V H 84 G.

icism, and can be resolved by the hypothesis either of differing levels of reality, or of a distinction between the actual and the potential or ideal.

It is true that as a matter of fact there is a great gulf between the sage and the majority, who are victims of illusion, and that only the former is a human being in the fullest sense of the term.[64] Yet vice is a matter of ignorance, and virtue a matter of knowledge;[65] Cynic virtue is "easy" and represents in effect the natural state of human beings;[66] and all men without exception are endowed with "intellect," "reason," or "judgment." Furthermore, many of the conventional barriers that separate human beings are demolished by the fact that the Cynic rejects the family and all distinctions based on sex, birth, rank, race, or education. Consequently, even the imbecilic masses can be regarded as potential human beings. In other words, for the Cynic other human beings are and are not *philoi* ("friends," "kinsmen"). We may recall the Cynic's double attitude toward animals. Of course, this kind of complexity of attitude, based on differing perceptions of similarity and difference, is an integral part of Greek thought, as Claude Lévi-Strauss and other great French structuralists have shown us (or at least some of us). Consequently, the gulf between the Cynic and ordinary human beings, while still immense, is not insuperable. It is of course less great for Cynics like Crates, who (as it appears) held complete "wisdom" (*sophia*) to be an impossibility.[67]

It is the potential bond of humanity between the Cynic and the masses that explains several of his most characteristic roles. He is a "teacher" (*didaskalos*) because it is the fruitful application of Cynic doctrine that will bridge the existing gulf between the two groups. If this is not so, what is the good of Cynic teaching? He is a *kataskopos* ("spy," "inspector") because it is he who searches out the truth and reports it back to men. He is a "mediator" (*diallaktēs*) because he reconciles men, and, if this whole analysis is correct, he must also be a *diallaktēs* because he reconciles men and gods. He is an *agathos daimōn* (a "guardian angel") because he is the mediator between men and gods.

Hence, when Epictetus describes Diogenes as "dear to gods as to men," as "loving all mankind," [68] this is not a late, propagandizing, Stoicizing view, but a conception integral to Cynicism from its beginnings. We must of course concede that in order to put Diogenes' profound "philanthropy" (*philanthrōpia*) into relief, Epictetus implausibly attributes to him the "soft" qualities of Crates, but the distinction between Diogenes' method of teaching and Crates' is one of means, not ends.[69] We must also concede the existence of a genuinely

64. See, e.g., D.L. 6.41 (V B 272 G.), 6.60 (V B 273 G.).
65. See, e.g., D.L. 6.105.
66. See, e.g., D.L. 6.70 (V B 291 G.).
67. See D.L. 6.89 (V H 36 G.), with Moles (n. 54 above) 110 n. 56.
68. Epictetus 3.24.64 (V B 290 G.).
69. See Moles (n. 54 above) 112–13.

misanthropic tendency, but this is not an integral part of Cynicism, nor was it ever more than a secondary tendency.[70]

There are other factors to support the thesis that the Cynics recognized at least the possibility of a common humanity: certain dicta of Diogenes and Demonax;[71] Diogenes' defense of cannibalism, which invokes not, as one might have expected, the differences between Cynics and their fellows, but their essential identity;[72] the Cynics' habit of appealing to the customs of foreign countries;[73] the idea that all human beings are endowed with "reason"; the Cynic anti-Promethean myth, which goes back to Diogenes himself and regards human beings as a unity before the insurgence of vice.[74]

Despite the arguments of certain scholars, I continue to believe that the celebrated passage in Plutarch's *De Fortuna Alexandri* reveals numerous details of the Cynic's attitude toward other men and of Cynic cosmopolitanism in general.[75] It is here that Plutarch develops Onesicritus's thesis of Alexander as a philosopher in action and that he contrasts the purely theoretical propositions of Zeno with the actual achievements of Alexander. Zeno wrote his *Republic* "on the dog's tail" when he was still one of Crates' pupils,[76] and many of the Cynic elements of this work are generally recognized.

Like Diogenes, Zeno rejects the existing *dēmoi* ("peoples," "citizenries") and *poleis* ("states"), even though later Stoics did not agree. Zeno's ideal is that "all human beings should be members of the same people and fellow citizens, and there should be one way of life and one cosmos" (*pantas anthrōpous hēgōmetha dēmotas kai politas, heis de bios kai kosmos:* Plutarch, *De Fortuna Alexandri* 329a–b); Diogenes was himself a "citizen of the cosmos" and in my view regarded all men as his potential *philoi* ("friends," "kinsmen") and con-

---

70. See, e.g., Ps.-Heraclitus, *Epp.* 4.2, 5.3, 7 *passim;* Ps.-Diogenes, *Epp.* 27, 41; Pliny, *NH* 7.19.79–80; G.A. Gerhard, "Zur Legende vom Kyniker Diogenes," *Archiv für Religionswissenschaft* 15 (1912) 80–109 = Billerbeck (n. 19 above) 89–106, esp. 94–95.

71. D.L. 6.56 (V B 189 G.); Lucian, *Demonax* 21, with Moles (n. 54 above) 113.

72. See D.L. 6.73 (V B 132 G.).

73. See, e.g., D.L. 6.73 (V B 132 G.); see further the discussions of Weber (n. 12 above) 117–33; Giannantoni 1985, 467 = Giannantoni 1990, 518.

74. See, e.g., D.L. 6.44; Strabo 15.1.64 = *FGrH* 134 F 17; Dio Chrysostom 6.22–25; Ps.-Diogenes, *Ep.* 32.3; Maximus of Tyre 36; Brown (n. 14 above) 149 n. 152; Moles (n. 54 above) 116; Goulet-Cazé (n. 12 above) 59–60.

75. Plutarch, *De Fortuna Alexandri* 6.329a–d: Καὶ μὴν ἡ πολὺ θαυμαζομένη Πολιτεία τοῦ τὴν Στωικῶν αἵρεσιν . . . δι' αἵματος καὶ τέκνων ἀνακεραννυμένους. Of course this passage has been much discussed, with very varied conclusions. See, e.g., M.H. Fisch, *AJP* 58 (1937) 66–69, 137–38; W.W. Tarn, *AJP* 60 (1939) 65–69; id., *Alexander the Great* vol. 2 (Cambridge 1948) 417–24; H.C. Baldry, *JHS* 79 (1959) 12–13; id., *The Unity of Mankind* (n. 18 above) 159–60; O. Murray, *CR* 16 (1966) 369; Rist (n. 35 above) 64–65; A.M. Ioppolo, *Aristone di Chio e lo stoicismo antico* (Naples 1980) 254; Moles (n. 54 above) 115–16 and nn. 95–98 (which already indicates the main lines of my interpretation); A.A. Long and D.N. Sedley, *The Hellenistic Philosophers* vol. 1 (Cambridge 1987) 429–30 (67A), 435; A. Erskine, *The Hellenistic Stoa* (London 1990) 20; Schofield (n. 4 above) 104–11.

76. The later dating proposed by Erskine (n. 75 above: 9–15) conflicts with the ancient testimonia, which in my opinion should not be lightly discarded.

sequently potential "citizens of the cosmos," like himself. The sole divergence of opinion between the two philosophers is the importance that Zeno attaches to *nomos* ("custom," "law"), but this has nothing to do with the existing *nomos*, which the Cynics scorned: it is the "law" or "reason" of nature, which interpenetrates the cosmos and which in consequence may be compatible with the Cynic principle of "living according to nature." (I shall return to this point.)

By contrast with Zeno, Alexander translated philosophical ideas into reality. On his view, his role was that of a "universal divine governor and reconciler of all things" (*koinos theothen harmostēs kai diallaktēs tōn holōn*, ibid. 329c). Like the Cynic, he is sent by the gods; like the Cynic, he is a governor of men; like the Cynic, he is governor of all men; like the Cynic, he is a reconciler (and we note the presence of this idea in Onesicritus);[77] and he is reconciler not only of men, but also *tōn holōn:* that is to say, of everything that exists—the whole earth, the cosmos, men, and gods.

This passage also demonstrates the double classification of human beings that I have argued for: on one level, for Zeno "all human beings" are "members of the same people and fellow citizens," and for Alexander all men should consider "the inhabited world" as "home" or "fatherland"; yet on another level, Zeno excludes the bad from his state,[78] and for Alexander humanity divides into the good, who are kin, and the bad, who have no kinship with the good. This double classification is also evident in another Cynic text, Pseudo-Heraclitus, *Epistle* 9.2, where the "polity of the cosmos" is defined by virtue or vice, and yet the cosmos is the "place common to all." [79]

Let us come to our conclusion. The Cynic proclaims his allegiance to the cosmos. He can live a virtuous life anywhere: the whole earth serves as his home. He maintains a positive attitude toward the natural world and toward the animal world. He is himself godlike. He recognizes his actual kinship with other sages and his potential kinship with human beings in general, whom he seeks to convert. He is a mediator between men and gods, and this mediation is an important part of his pedagogic activity.

Let me anticipate possible objections. Is this model Stoic rather than Cynic? No—it is the other way round. Stoicism is Cynicism, enriched of course with numerous refinements. Is it anachronistic to hypothesize such a model of cosmopolitanism before Alexander the Great, who, according to some scholars, was the first to give substance to the idea of the unity of mankind? No—the sense of the unity of mankind had already been expressed by Antiphon and Alcidamas (to say nothing of Homer and Herodotus), and Plutarch's thesis in *De Fortuna Alexandri* would founder if it was Alexander who had been the

77. See Strabo 15.1.65.
78. See D.L. 7.32–33.
79. ἀνὴρ δὲ Ἐφέσιος, εἰ ἀγαθός, κόσμου πολίτης. τοῦτο γὰρ κοινὸν πάντων ἐστὶ χωρίον, ἐν ᾧ νόμος ἐστὶν οὐ γράμμα ἀλλὰ θεός, καὶ ὁ παραβαίνων ἃ ⟨μὴ⟩ χρὴ ἀσεβήσει· μᾶλλον δὲ οὐδὲ παραβήσεται, εἰ παραβὰς οὐ λήσεται.

initiator of such ideas. Does this model depend on physical theories, which the Cynics could not accept, given their rejection of physics? There are two possible answers to this question. First, whether logically or illogically, Diogenes did sometimes invoke physical theories. Second, although the physical theories of Anaxagoras and Empedocles serve to give the model coherence, they are not indispensable to it. The essentials of such a model go back to Homer, and similar models were developed by certain of the Presocratics, whose physical explanations could readily have been discarded by nonintellectual philosophers like the Cynics.

Finally, what can one say of the importance, originality, and influence of Cynic cosmopolitanism? The concept clarifies the position of the Cynic in the universe and his relations with inanimate nature, the animals, other men, and the gods. It also offers us a partial answer to the question of why the Cynic should, despite his self-sufficiency, concern himself with the moral standing of other men. As *kosmopolitēs* ("citizen of the cosmos"), he recognizes his potential kinship with others, and he has therefore a certain obligation to help them.

Claims for the originality of Cynic cosmopolitanism require careful formulation. Its most distinctive element—the primitivist, or animalistic, interpretation of the principle "living according to nature"—has parallels in the fifth century, although in general these parallels dissociate animalism and "philanthropy" (*philanthrōpia*).[80] Here again, Antisthenes was no doubt an important intermediary. One is, however, justified in crediting Diogenes with the invention of the word *kosmopolitēs,* a word that in itself marks an important stage in the history of ideas, and with expressing his cosmopolitan sentiments with that combination of verbal virtuosity and arresting exposition so characteristic of this great philosopher.

On my interpretation, Cynic cosmopolitanism influenced Stoic cosmopolitanism far more than current opinion recognizes. The Cynics did not bequeath to the Stoics a purely negative concept to which the latter added a positive value: rather, Cynic cosmopolitanism already contained all the essential positive qualities that the Stoics endowed with a fuller exposition, and that they integrated into a fully developed physical system.

There remains a final problem—the precise degree of convergence between Cynic and Stoic cosmopolitanism. Cynic rejection of the polis contrasts with the Stoic orthodoxy that the polis had a certain value as an imperfect analogue of the true "cosmic polity." Precisely how far can one reconcile the Cynic and Stoic interpretations of the principle of "living according to nature"? Primitivism and animalism remain available strategies within Stoicism at all periods,

80. See, e.g., Lovejoy and Boas (n. 30 above) 112–16; T.A. Sinclair, *A History of Greek Political Thought* (London 1951; repr. 1967) 48 n. 4; Guthrie (n. 18 above) 3.1.104 and n. 4, 114 n. 4; R. Seaford, *Euripides: Cyclops* (Oxford 1984) 52–55.

although they are rejected, at least in their most extreme forms, by certain Stoics. Some modern scholars, notably Höistad, have seen in Cynic cosmopolitanism essentially the same fusion of "nature" (*phusis*) and "custom" or "law" (*nomos*) and transcendental "reason" (*logos*) that is found in Stoicism.[81] One can then link the passage cited from Plutarch's *De Fortuna Alexandri* with certain passages in Philo and elsewhere. On this view, the Cynic and Stoic interpretations of "living according to nature" are almost identical. Höistad's analysis, while flawed in detail,[82] is not thereby totally vitiated.

My own view is rather different. The Cynics and Stoics shared beliefs that could have led them both to the same conclusion—namely that "to live according to nature" means to live in accordance with the whole natural order as divinely ordained. In practice, however, the Cynics gave greater weight to animalistic primitivism and individual self-sufficiency, because these ideas contributed to the simplicity and attractiveness of their message: What could be more natural than to live the life of animals? What more comforting than the conviction that self-sufficiency leads to happiness?

So much for the theory; what of the practice? Was the Cynic *politeia* a reality, a utopia, an ideal, or a community of philosophers? The Cynics diverged from their primitivist fifth-century predecessors in that they practiced their animalistic interpretation of "life according to nature." They also diverged from their cosmopolitan predecessors in that they practiced their cosmopolitanism. The "polity of the cosmos" is already a reality for the Cynics themselves, and they try to turn it into reality for others, who are potential fellow citizens. After all, in the time of Cronus, the "polity of the cosmos" had already been a reality for all men. In its own bizarre fashion, Diogenes' polity was the most practical, the most universalist, and (let us not be afraid to say it) the noblest of all the philosophical states (*politeiai*)—indeed, of all the political states—of all antiquity.

There remains a tension between the simplicity of the primitivist life and Cynic self-sufficiency, on the one hand, and the implications of Cynic cosmopolitanism, on the other hand. In my opinion, Julian appreciates this tension correctly when he writes that the "end" (*telos*) of Diogenes and Crates was their own "happiness" (*eudaimonia*), but that they also helped others as being their "fellow citizens" (*sumpoliteuomenous*).[83] In any case, this tension does not allow us to deny the positive value of Cynic cosmopolitanism, a value that I hope to have established, contrary to current opinion.

---

81. See, e.g., Höistad (n. 6 above) 138–42; R. Anastasi, *Studi in onore di Quintino Cataudella* vol. 2 (Catania 1972) 367–70; Buora (n. 6 above).

82. For example, when he accepts the authenticity of the syllogism on νόμος in D.L. 6.72 (see n. 10 above).

83. Julian 6.201c: Καὶ οὐ τοῦτο . . . ἀλλὰ καὶ τοῖς λόγοις.

Dog Heads and Noble Savages:
Cynicism Before the Cynics?

James Romm

> The nobler of the cynics, for their part, say that great
> Heracles . . . left to mankind the greatest exemplar of
> their way of life. But I, although I wish to speak rev-
> erently of the gods and of those who have reached
> divine status, believe that before Heracles there were
> others, not only among the Greeks, but among bar-
> barians also, who practiced this philosophy.
> —Julian, *Oration* 6.187c–d

In discussions of Cynic philosophy much attention has been paid to the
question of origins—of what Diogenes owed to Antisthenes, and Antisthenes
to Socrates. But even in antiquity the suspicion was raised, as my epigraph
suggests, that Cynicism antedated all three figures, and indeed could be traced
back to the time before Heracles. More recently Farrand Sayre has one-upped
Julian by suggesting that the roots of Cynicism extend into the earliest phases
of human evolution: "It is probable that the first man who shaped a stone ham-
mer was jeered at by cynics who claimed that unshaped stones were better." [1]

While it seems unlikely that any of these stone-age Cynic models are recov-
erable today, it is at least possible that some of the literary antecedents of the
movement can be investigated without venturing too far into the realm of

---

The material in this essay has been adapted from chapter 2 of my recent book, *The Edges of
the Earth in Ancient Thought: Geography, Exploration, and Fiction* (Princeton 1992). I am grateful to Bracht Branham for editorial suggestions.

1. *The Greek Cynics* (Baltimore 1948) 48. Contrast the view of Donald Dudley, who observes
in the opening paragraph of his *History of Cynicism* (London 1937): "Cynicism cannot be shown
to antedate Diogenes of Sinope."

speculation. I hope to show here that at least one early branch of Cynic ancestry is indeed readily available for our consideration, though it has seldom been noticed by students of the Cynic movement per se:[2] the archaic Greek traditions surrounding noble savages and other primitive men, many of which clearly anticipate the Cynic paradigms of later eras. The rise of ethnographic literature in the sixth and fifth centuries B.C., I will argue, allowed the Greeks to see their own culture contrasted, not always favorably, with the cultures of barbarians— in particular the Ethiopians, Scythians, Arimaspians, and *Kunokephaloi* (Dog Heads). Ethnography thus served as an early proving ground for the *parrhēsia,* the freedom to contravene and ridicule established practice, that would later come to characterize Cynic discourse and the Cynic lifestyle.

It should not surprise us to find a close connection between Cynic discourse and early Greek ethnography. Cynicism is, among other things, a form of voluntary cultural estrangement, in which the individual comes to see the customs and values of his society as arbitrary in nature and disdains to observe them. Its most radical practitioner, Diogenes of Sinope, is reported to have written plays challenging even the most basic cultural assumptions, the taboos surrounding cannibalism and incest. But the social alienation that a Cynic had to work hard to attain—by making himself absurd or offensive, and by loudly proclaiming to all around him his outside status—also occurs in nature, as it were, when peoples with different customs (*nomoi*) encounter one another for the first time. In that epiphanic moment of contact, the customs belonging to both groups are necessarily revealed as artificial, perhaps even bizarre or senseless, constructs. Thus, if Diogenes did endorse cannibalism in his lost play *Thyestes,* his position finds its ethnographic correlate in Herodotus's tale of how Darius once brought Greeks and Indians together to investigate their respective burial customs;[3] the Indians, who professed to eat the bodies of their dead, were as much horrified by Greek cremation rites as the Greeks were revolted by Indian anthropophagy. The confrontation between differing value systems robs both of any claim to universal validity, and thus brings about the same sense of cultural alienation that the Cynic writer or speaker sought to instill in his audience.

2. Commentary on the links between Cynics and barbarians mostly focuses on instances of actual contact: thus Sayre (above, n. 1: 39–48) has suggested that Diogenes may have based some of his practices on customs learned from the barbarians in his native Sinope. See also Ragnar Höistad, *Cynic Hero and Cynic King* (Lund 1948) 135–38, for a discussion of Onesicritus's claim to have found a Cynic way of life among the gymnosophists of India (Strabo 15.1.63–65, Plutarch *Alexander* 65); while T. Gomperz (*Greek Thinkers: A History of Ancient Philosophy* vol. 2 [New York 1905]) observes that "not a few of [Antisthenes'] successors belonged to the outer fringes of Greek culture" (148). Marie-Odile Goulet-Cazé also notes the tendency for Cynicism to take root among slaves and other disenfranchised members of society, at least in Roman times ("Le cynisme à l'époque imperiale," *ANRW* 2.36.4, 2720–2833, esp. 2735).

3. On this episode and Herodotus's treatment of it, see J. A. S. Evans, "Despotēs Nomos," *Athenaenum,* n.s., 43 (1965) 142–53; Hans Erich Stier, "Nomos Basileus," *Philologus* 83 (1928) 225–58, esp. 239–44; and now Rosario Vignolo Munson, "The Madness of Cambyses (Herodotus 3.16–38)," *Arethusa* 24 (1991) 43–65, esp. 57–63.

This is not to imply, however, that Herodotus, in narrating the story of the Greek-Indian encounter, can himself be considered a Cynic. His comment on this confrontation of burial customs—"Custom is king"—though susceptible to various interpretations, certainly does not mean that the Greeks are fools for not eating their dead; Herodotus has not attacked anything, nor exercised free speech (*parrhēsia*). Yet the mere recognition that cultural usage has no absolute value, that all judgments about custom are relative, constitutes a first step along the path that leads, ultimately, to the Cynic injunction *parakharaxon to nomisma*, "Deface the currency" ("Violate customs"). We can imagine how a true Cynic, like Diogenes, would recast the Herodotean tale: instead of an evenhanded comparison of customs, mediated both by Darius and by Herodotus's own narrative voice, we would hear a scathing diatribe on the evils of cremation, spoken by one of the anthropophagic Indians. That is, where Herodotus has moved his discourse away from a Hellenocentric position and into neutral middle ground, a Cynic would push it further still toward the anti-Hellenic end of the spectrum.

It is not enough, therefore, that an ethnographic text contain moments of cross-cultural contact or comparison for us to consider it a predecessor of Cynic discourse. It is rather when that comparison is handled in a certain way, adopting a barbarian perspective in order to examine Greek customs, that a recognizably Cynic pattern begins to emerge. Herodotus's *Histories* (to stay with our most prominent example) often compares Greek and foreign customs without evaluating either. The portrait of the Scythians in Book 4, for example, shows a way of life that is in many ways opposite to that of the Greeks (as illustrated by François Hartog in *The Mirror of Herodotus*),[4] but Herodotus does not therefore criticize the Greeks for living as they do. However, when (as we shall see below) the historian allows a single Scythian to visit Greece, and to comment derisively on what he finds there, he employs a form of discourse much closer in spirit to that of the Cynic school. Hence, I shall, in what follows, focus only on cultural encounters in which an alien perspective is privileged over that of natives, giving rise to an implicit note of satire or polemic. There are a surprising number of such encounters still extant in early Greek ethnography, though some are preserved only in fragmentary or secondhand form.

Our first example of an alien attack on native customs is found, like the Greek-Indian confrontation mentioned above, in Herodotus:[5] the remarks made

---

4. First published as *Le miroir d'Hérodote: Essai sur la représentation de l'autre* (Paris 1980); now in English translation by Janet Lloyd under the title given here (Berkeley and Los Angeles 1988).

5. The distinction is hinted at by Gomperz (above n. 2: 144), in a discussion of Cynic primitivism: "The idealization of uncivilized peoples was no novelty in Greek literature. . . . But the Cynics took the savage for their teacher in all seriousness." More recently, the varying degrees of distancing that led the philosophic movements either to remain in the city and attack its vices, or to remove

by the king of the Ethiopians about the Persians, on the occasion of a visit by their ambassadors, the Ichthyophagi (3.17–24). It is paradigmatic of the perspectival shift described above, although we should also note two anomalies: first, the encounter is not direct but takes place through intermediaries, the Ichthyophagi; and second, the role of native people is assigned in this case not to the Greeks but to the Persians. It may seem odd for a Greek author to have cast Persians as representatives of the cultural norm, but what is at stake here is the contrast between natural peoples and cultured peoples;[6] thus the Persians, who are at this stage the most technologically and politically developed of any ancient race, are perhaps best suited to be the standard-bearers of culture. Moreover, the industrial and material values that the Persians here embody, as we shall see below, were shared in common by all members of the Mediterranean community; it seems likely that Herodotus, in constructing the confrontation of Persians and Ethiopians along such universal lines, must have expected that his Greek readers could easily insert themselves into the place of the Persians.[7]

The confrontation begins when the Persian king Cambyses, based in occupied Egypt, decides to invade the Ethiopian land. In preparation for this venture he sends a delegation of emissaries, from a tribe called Ichthyophagi ("Fish Eaters")[8] to present the king with four precious gifts—a dyed robe, gold jewelry, a container of myrrh, and a jar of palm wine—ostensibly as a gesture of friendship but really as a pretext for spying on his adversaries. These Ichthyophagi seem completely uninvolved in the conflict, showing loyalties to neither the Persian nor the Ethiopian side; they function purely as go-betweens, facilitating the confrontation between the two disparate cultures. They also serve, in narrative terms, as the porters of Herodotus's point of view, allowing the narrative to cross the border and see the world from both Persian and Ethiopian perspectives.

Thus, once the Fish Eaters have arrived at the Ethiopian court, the narrative quickly adopts the perspective of the unnamed Ethiopian king. This monarch, with unexplained omniscience, sees through the trick behind the purported em-

---

themselves from it altogether, have been discussed by Heinrich Niehues-Pröbsting, *Der Kynismus des Diogenes und der Begriff des Zynismus,* Humanistische Bibliothek, Abhandlungen, Band 40 (Munich 1982), esp. 81–87.

6. For a discussion of these terms and the overall pattern of nature/culture opposition throughout the *Histories,* see Stewart Flory, *The Archaic Smile of Herodotus* (Detroit 1987) chap. 3.

7. I do not mean to imply by my use of the word "constructing" that Herodotus made this episode up out of whole cloth. There is indeed slender evidence that a Persian invasion of southern Africa actually took place, if we accept that an inscription found in Africa and now housed in Berlin (see R. Hennig, *Terrae Incognitae,* 2d ed., vol. 1 [Leiden 1944] 84–85) refers to Cambyses. However, we can hardly doubt that Herodotus himself is largely responsible for the elaboration of the episode, which must have reached his ears in only the sketchiest outlines (see Torgny Säve-Söderbergh, "Zu den äthiopischen Episoden bei Herodot," *Eranos* 44 [1946] 77–80).

8. The Fish Eaters too were idealized in ancient ethnography, in much the same terms as the Ethiopians; see Diodorus Siculus 3.15–20, Agatharchides 49.

bassy and rebukes Cambyses for his treachery.[9] He sends the Ichthyophagi back to Egypt bearing symbols of Ethiopian defiance, but first pauses, in a bemused frame of mind, to examine the gifts they have brought (Hdt. 3.22):

> Picking up the purple robe, he asked what it was and how it was made. The Ichthyophagi gave him a true account of purple, and the process of dyeing, to which the king said, "These men are fakers, since the colors of their clothing are faked." Then he asked about the gold jewelry (a necklace and some bracelets). When the Ichthyophagi explained the use of gold as ornament, the king laughed, and supposing them to be fetters, said, "We have stronger fetters than these among our people." Third, he asked about the myrrh; when they told him about its production and use in ointments, he made the same reply as he had regarding the robe. Then he came to the wine, and learned about its manufacture, while delighting in its flavor; next he asked what the king of Persia ate, and how long a Persian lived. They said that bread was the chief source of food, explaining the nature of cereal grain, and that the fullest age a man might attain was eighty years. At that the Ethiopian said he was not surprised that they lived such a short time, since they subsisted on dung; they would not live even so long, he said, if they were not sustained by that drink (indicating the wine), a product in which his own people were bested by the Persians.

From the detached perspective of the Ethiopians, Persian customs appear contrived and ridiculous; the conquerors of the known world are here reduced to liars, cheats, fools, and eaters of dung (i.e., cereals raised from the manured earth).

Neither these gifts, nor the Ethiopian king's rebukes of them, are idly chosen: under attack here are the most basic underpinnings of industrial technology and material culture.[10] It is the artifice behind such products as dyed cloth and refined myrrh, echoing as it does the artifice of Cambyses in sending out spies, that the Ethiopian king finds so distasteful; likewise, it is the use of gold for cosmetic rather than practical purposes that he sees as ridiculous. The most esteemed products of a sophisticated, manufacturing-based society suddenly lose their value when viewed through the eyes of *Naturvölker,* for whom the raw materials supplied by nature are sufficient to meet every need. Herodotus carries this contrast further in the next scene, by having the king conduct the Ichthyophagi on a tour of Ethiopian life: he exhibits their food and drink (boiled meat and milk); the spring of rarefied water that gives a glossy sheen, "like that of olive oil," to those who bathe in it; the prison, where wrongdoers are bound in golden fetters; and last the famous Table of the Sun, which holds forth endless quantities of cooked meats. In each case the Ethiopians are seen

---

9. Compare, for example, his resentful reaction to the Egyptians' claim of an epiphany of the god Apis, 3.29.

10. See Flory, *Archaic Smile* (above, n. 6) 98–99.

to obtain from the environment around them the substances that the Persians can only get, ignobly, by manufacture or cultivation.

This *nomos/phusis* (custom/nature) opposition becomes somewhat more complex in the case of the jar of palm wine, the one token of Persian custom that wins admiration from the Ethiopian king. Herodotus here follows a long-standing tradition (dating back at least to the Cyclops episode of the *Odyssey*) according to which primitive peoples are unable to resist the effects of wine, that most sublime of advancements wrought by higher civilizations. Even here, however, we can see an implicit critique of Persian sophistication at work: the Ethiopian king praises wine as a salutary beverage, capable of extending the life span of those who drink it, whereas in fact it has the opposite effect on Cambyses, who (as we learn at 3.34) lapses into madness and violence partly as a result of his overindulgence in wine. Alcohol can be a medicinal beverage to the Ethiopians because, in their golden-age innocence, they do not crave it immoderately; only for advanced races like the Persians does it pose a hazardous temptation.[11]

The narrative now returns with the Ichthyophagi to the Persian side of the cultural barrier, where events begin to move forward at a rapid pace. Cambyses, stung by his emissaries' report of the Ethiopian barbs, recklessly leads his army forward before they have been adequately provisioned; as a result, the Persians begin to starve during the march southward, and Cambyses is forced to turn back before even meeting his foe. This whole section, it must be noted, is narrated rather briefly and summarily by Herodotus, and does not give to Cambyses (or any other Persian) the opportunity for direct or indirect speech. To explore the Persians' perception of the Ethiopians would be redundant; we already know what they must think, based on their general attitude that distant races are more contemptible in proportion to their distance (1.134). Clearly, it is of greater interest to Herodotus to find out what the Ethiopians think of the Persians, and so it is around the speech of the Ethiopian king that the whole episode is structured.

In this speech Herodotus seems to have very nearly taken the step from the cultural relativism of the "custom is king" passage (which follows only a few chapters after this episode) to a direct attack on native usage (*parakharaxon to nomisma*).[12] Indeed, the pointed replies the king makes to each of the descriptions of the Persian gifts can, with only a small effort, be read as *chreiai,* the

11. Much the same contrast emerges from Herodotus's later account of another self-destructing military leader, the Spartan king Cleomenes (6.84), who goes mad after drinking unmixed wine among the Scythians.

12. Although it does not seem that Herodotus is as much concerned with attacking the Persians as with exalting the Ethiopians, whom he portrays as a fairy-tale race with no wants or imperfections. The authorial technique of putting polemical comments in the mouths of naive barbarians is discussed by A. Riese, *Die Idealisierung der Naturvölker des Nordens in der griechischen und römischen Literatur* (Frankfurt 1875) 14–17.

barbed rejoinders for which the Cynics later became notorious: behind them lies a desire to overturn the Persians' cultural presuppositions, to pull the rug of their own customs (*nomoi*) out from under them. It is in this speech, one senses, and not in the desert wastes of central Africa, that the Persian army has been defeated. The power that accrues to an outsider looking in renders him invincible, at least on his own turf; the conquering general is easily bested by the mocking Cynic, as Alexander later discovered in his famous encounters with Diogenes and with the gymnosophists of India.

For other examples of Cynic-like polemics in pre-Cynic ethnographic litera-ture, I turn to the far north rather than the far south, which is to say, to the landscape of hard rather than soft primitivism. In this region were found the one-eyed Arimaspians, a race that, according to archaic Greek legends, dwelt in the northern steppes of central Asia, where they passed their days locked in grim combat with the griffins that also inhabited these lands. Herodotus men-tions the Arimaspians only in passing (since he refuses to believe that one-eyed men really exist: 3.115), but we know from other sources about their dire struggle with the griffins: these reptilian birds were said to unearth mounds of gold in the course of digging their burrows, whereupon the gold would be pilfered by Arimaspian raiders who would then have to run for their lives from the enraged griffins.[13] The story is paradigmatic of hard-primitive life in that it portrays a world governed by raw, Darwinian patterns of interspecies compe-tition, rather than by the sophistication of agriculture and industrial produc-tion.[14] Stories of this type, recounting how men battle wild beasts or harsh climates for survival in distant parts of the earth, can be found throughout Greek (and later Roman) collections of ethnographic lore.

But the Arimaspians seem to be an especially early and especially polemical case in point, to judge by the fragments of the *Arimaspia* of Aristeas of Pro-connesus, an epic poem written perhaps in the sixth century B.C.[15] Most of the poem has been lost, but we are fortunate enough to have Herodotus's account of its composition: Aristeas, possessed by some sort of religious ecstasy, jour-

13. The most detailed account is by Ctesias (*apud* Aelian *Nat. Anim.* 4.27). There is also a sixth-century Caeretan vase depicting a griffin chasing an Arimaspian, discussed by T.B.L. Web-ster in *JHS* 48 (1928) 196–205.

14. See Riese, *Idealisierung* (above, n. 12) for the early history of this topos; for its later development, see E. Norden, *Die germanische Urgeschichte in Tacitus' Germania* (Leipzig 1920), esp. chap. 1.

15. The date has been variously fixed. Herodotus places Aristeas about two hundred years before his own time, a date that seems impossibly early but has nevertheless been defended by J. Bolton, *Aristeas of Proconnesus* (Oxford 1962) chap. 1. The *Suda* puts Aristeas at the beginning of the sixth century, and this has seemed a more reasonable chronology; see the discussion by Walter Burkert in a review of Bolton, *Gnomon* 35 (1963) 235–40. There is no decisive evidence within the poem to support either the earlier or the later date.

neyed to the land of the Issedones in the far north, a place just south of the Arimaspian territory (4.16.1). There he halted, and during his stay learned from the Issedones about what lay beyond; on his return he recorded the whole experience in the epic devoted (as its title suggests) to Arimaspian matters. Whether Aristeas actually undertook such a journey is open to grave doubt;[16] more likely the scenario was contrived in such a way as to permit an extended confrontation of differing cultural outlooks. Like the Fish Eaters of Herodotus's Ethiopian idyll, bearing with them the tokens of Persian *nomoi,* Aristeas here serves both as cultural ambassador and as scout, sallying into the interzone where the values of dominant cultures encounter those of more marginal races.

Aristeas's hosts, the Issedones, seem to have served as a conduit for this cultural confrontation; it was they, as we know from Herodotus's remarks, who described the battles between Arimaspians and griffins, while Aristeas himself only listened, and later transcribed their stories. This fact accounts for the strongly idealizing cast that can be detected in the few surviving fragments of the poem (frr. 4, 5):

> They say there are men dwelling farther up, sharing their northern borders and that they are many, and very noble warriors, rich in horses, with many flocks of sheep, many of cattle.

> Each has a single eye set in his elegant forehead; shaggy they are with hairs, the toughest of all of mankind.

Here the Issedones—who are undoubtedly to be understood as the subject of *phasi,* "they say"[17]—depict their northern neighbors as a civilized people whose life, like that of any true-blooded Homeric aristocracy, is rich with the joys of horsemanship and battle. In fact, the Arimaspians are described as *polurrhēnas poluboutas,* "owning many herds of sheep and cattle," like the wealthy Pylian lords who are given the same formulaic line-ending by Homer (*Il.* 9.154, 296). More remarkable still, the Arimaspians' faces, despite having only one eye—ordinarily a mark of grotesque ugliness—are here seen by the Issedones as *prosōpa kharienta,* "pleasing visages." The Issedones seem to be functioning here as spokesmen for a non-Greek point of view, in which the far-northerly Arimaspians, who might seem to Greek eyes as savage as the Cyclops Polyphemus, are instead elevated to a stature befitting an Iliadic warrior hero.

The flip side of this idealizing attitude might, one supposes, show the Issedones turning their gaze toward the central Mediterranean races and describing *them,* not the Arimaspians, as barbarians. And in fact a moment very much like

16. Ken Dowden ("Deux notes sur les Scythes et les Arimaspes," *REG* 93 [1980] 487–92) notes rather dryly that Aristeas couldn't have gone far in the trancelike state denoted by Herodotus's *phoibolamptos.* On the other hand, see Bolton (above, n. 15) chap. 4 for the view that Aristeas's journey did take place.

17. The same conclusion was reached by C. M. Bowra in "A Fragment of the *Arimaspeia,*" *CQ* 49 (1956) 1–10.

this seems to have been preserved, in a passage of the *Arimaspia* quoted in the treatise *On the Sublime* (10.4), some eight or nine centuries after the poem's initial circulation (fr. 7):[18]

> and this too seems, to our minds, a thing of very great wonder: men reside in water, in the sea, far from land. Pitiful fellows these are, for they endure grievous afflictions: they have their eyes on the stars, their life and soul in the sea. Indeed, one would think, they lift up their hands to the gods and utter many a prayer, while their innards are foully tossed upward.

It is not entirely clear what is being described here, since the author of *On the Sublime* quotes the passage without describing its original context; as a result modern interpretations of it have varied widely.[19] But the most defensible reading sees in this passage the attempt of a landlocked race—presumably the Issedones again—to comprehend the alien idea of seafaring. Having never before encountered this activity the Issedones naively assume that men who sail ships actually dwell in the water, and that the instability of such a life causes them almost constant discomfort (including seasickness, described here as uptossed innards).[20] If this reading is correct, we might further suppose that seafaring had first been described to the Issedones by Aristeas, presumably the only Hellene to visit their remote part of the world, and that therefore the caricature of it that they conjure up constitutes a lampoon not just of seafaring in general but of the Greeks in particular.

It would make sense, moreover, for seafaring to serve as the pivot of a cultural inversion of this kind, since seafaring had long been associated in Greek literature with trade and commerce, social evolution, and resulting moral decline. Thus golden-age races were traditionally thought to be ignorant of navigation, as seen in the so-called last journey of Odysseus foretold by Tiresias in the *Odyssey* (11.121–37).[21] According to Tiresias's prophecy, Odysseus will

18. Cited by the author, conventionally known as Longinus, as a failed description of a storm at sea, to contrast with Homer's more successful version. Longinus does not mention Aristeas by name but refers only to "the author of the *Arimaspia*," and Bolton (above, n. 15: 26–27) believes that he did not have access to the entire poem. See the discussion *ad loc.* by D. A. Russell, *Longinus: On the Sublime* (Oxford 1964). In any event, Longinus cannot have correctly remembered the context of the passage, since it can hardly describe a storm at sea.

19. Bethe (*RE* 1.2, s.v. "Aristeas," col. 877) believes them to be "fabelhaften Meerbewohnern," but there is no evidence elsewhere of such a legend. Karl Meuli, who discusses the passage in "Scythica" (*Hermes* 70 [1935] 154–55), suggests a race of platform dwellers, like those described in *Airs Waters Places* (15), but this interpretation leaves no possible sense for *ommat' en astroisi . . . ekhousin*, "they keep their eyes fixed on the stars." On the other hand, this line takes on a nicely pointed sense if we read it in the context of navigation.

20. The reading was first proposed by Rhys Roberts (*Longinus: On the Sublime* [Cambridge 1899] 219) and has been supported by Bowra, "Fragment" (above, n. 17); and by H. Fränkel, *Early Greek Poetry and Philosophy* (Oxford 1975) 242.

21. Discussed by Jane Harrison, "Mystica Vannus Iacchi," *JHS* 24 (1904) 241–54; A. Hartmann, *Untersuchungen über die Sagen vom Tode des Odysseus* (Munich 1917), esp. 91–92; and F. Dornsieff, "Odysseus's Letzte Fahrt," *Hermes* 72 (1937) 351–55.

end his life by traveling inland carrying an oar on his shoulder until he meets a people who mistake that object for a winnowing fan: that is, he will discover a place so far from the sea that its inhabitants will be innocent of even the most basic navigational tools. Similarly, in the schemes of social evolution described by Hellenistic and Roman philosophic writers, it is often the invention of seafaring that marks the end of the golden age and the start of man's long fall from grace.[22] Thus this Issedonean caricature of seamanship—if that is indeed what the above passage represents—would seem to have a strong ethical, as well as ethnological, point: the virtuous life of primitives who are as yet innocent of navigation is contrasted with that of advanced peoples who greedily chase profit on the seas.

If this seems an overelaborate interpretation to construct on a few fragmentary lines of the *Arimaspia*, I should add that a very similar lampoon of seafaring can be found in the folklore of another hard primitive, the Scythian sage Anacharsis. This northern barbarian was thought to have toured the Greek world as a kind of itinerant moral philosopher in the early sixth century B.C.[23] Unfortunately, the texts that relate to his visit mostly derive from a later period than the one we are here concerned with, but the legend itself seems to date well back into archaic times, perhaps to the same era in which the *Arimaspia* was composed.[24] Thus it is interesting to find the following barbs attributed to Anacharsis by his late-antique biographer, Diogenes Laertius (1.103–4):

> After learning that a ship's thickness was only four fingers' width, he said that those who sail are only that far away from death. . . . On being asked what kind of ship was the safest, he replied, "Those that are hauled up on shore." . . . On being asked which were more numerous, the living or the dead, he replied, "In which group do you place those who are sailing the seas?"

In another text from the same tradition, moreover—the ninth of the *Letters of Anacharsis*[25]—the Scythian sage uses sea travel as a metaphor for greedy profiteering, by describing an incident in which a band of pirates sank their own ship by taking on too much plunder; and we may further see, in the popular notion that Anacharsis had invented the ship's anchor,[26] a token of the Scythian's mistrust of seagoing vessels. In these legends, like that of the *Arimaspia*,

---

22. The most prominent examples are Lucretius, *De Rerum Natura* 5.1004–8; Manilius, *Astronomicon* 1.76–78; Ovid, *Metamorphoses* 1.96–98; Vergil, *Georgics* 3.141–42; Seneca, *Medea* 301–39, 364–79.

23. See R. Heinze, "Anacharsis," *Philologus* 50 (1891) 458–68; W. Schmid, "Anacharsis," *RE* I, cols. 2017–18; and J.F. Kindstrand, *Anacharsis: The Legend and the Apophthegmata*, Studia Graeca Upsaliensia 16 (Uppsala 1981).

24. As demonstrated by P. von der Mühll, "Das Alter der Anacharsislegende," *Ausgewählte Kleine Schriften* (Basel 1975) 473–81.

25. Edited and translated by Abraham J. Malherbe, *The Cynic Epistles: A Study Edition* (Missoula 1977) 36–51.

26. Diogenes Laertius 1.104; Pliny, *Hist. Nat.* 7.56.209.

seafaring serves to demarcate advanced races from primitive ones, in a way that underscores the moral degeneracy of the former.

The above attacks on seafaring may further remind us of the anti-Persian *chreiai* Herodotus puts in the mouth of the Ethiopian king, in that in both cases a barbarian observer focuses his gaze on the most advanced or sophisticated aspects of life in the Hellenic world.[27] In fact, in all the literature surrounding these *Naturvölker,* it is the pursuits that stand out as the highest achievements of Hellenic culture—seafaring, athletic contests, symposia, and the use of the marketplace as a center of trade—that come under the strongest attack. Herodotus himself records an early Anacharsis story in which an attack on Greek sophistication can clearly be discerned (4.77):

> I have also heard another story [regarding Anacharsis] told by the Peloponnesians, to the effect that Anarcharsis was sent by the Scythian king to learn about Greek ways, and that on his return he reported to the man who had sent him that all the Greeks, except the Spartans, were too busy to engage in any kind of intellectual pursuits; but that the Spartans alone were capable of carrying on an intelligent dialogue. But this story is only a frivolity invented by the Greeks themselves.

The satire behind this ethnic joke is easy to spot and certainly was not lost on the Peloponnesians who (as Herodotus informs us) were its most appreciative audience. Here the Spartans, ordinarily the least inclined of any Greek society toward intellectual matters, are seen by an outsider as representing the very school of Hellas. The resulting inversion suggests that all standards of human intelligence are merely subjective to begin with, and that one race's dumb can easily become another's smart.

Such use of hard-primitive figures like Anacharsis and the Arimaspians as distorting mirrors, in which Greek *nomoi* get turned upside down, would later become a standard technique of Cynic epistles and diatribes—many of which actually adopt Anacharsis or other northern barbarians as satiric masks. But the texts discussed above show that this tradition can in fact be traced back to sixth- and fifth-century lore that antedates anything recognizable as a Cynic school. In the last analysis, it may be more accurate to describe Cynicism as the extension and elaboration of a preclassical literary tradition than as a philosophic movement arising, like Stoicism and Epicureanism, during the fourth century B.C. As has long been noted, Cynicism produced much less in the way of written doctrine than did the other schools; what it had instead were role models, the rugged individuals who possessed a sure talent for knocking the *nomoi* of Greek society into a cocked hat. The point I would like to stress here is that Antisthenes and Diogenes were not the first such models, but were preceded

27. See Hartog, *Mirror of Herodotus* (above, n. 4) 12–14, for an assessment of how the Scythians' nomadic way of life made them a cultural antithesis of the polis-based Greeks.

by the satirical barbarian figures of archaic Greek ethnography and travel literature. And the moments in which those barbarians first encountered Greek culture (or advanced culture in general) served to illustrate the kind of estrangement that the Cynic might hope to achieve.

If the Cynics were not as original in their efforts to champion *phusis* over *nomos* and to deface the currency of accepted Greek values as is sometimes suggested, it may also be true that they were not original even as doggish philosophers. Long before they came on the scene the Greeks were already familiar with a face of *Hēmikunes* (Half-dogs) or *Kunokephaloi* (Dog Heads) dwelling (according to most accounts) in the remote regions of India.[28] Recently it has been suggested by David White, author of *Myths of the Dog-Man,* that these curious creatures may have helped give rise to the canine element in the appellation "Cynic."[29] Although this idea must remain only a suggestion, it attests to the remarkable degree of similarity between this bestial race of primitive dog-men, as depicted by Ctesias of Cnidus in the early fourth century B.C., and the Cynic figures who came to prominence later in that century. Let us look briefly, then, at Ctesias's account of these proto-Cynic *Kunokephaloi.*

Ctesias lived at Susa as court physician to the Persian royal family, and thus, like Aristeas among the Issedones, shared the perspective of those who looked in at the Greek world from outside. From this remote location he wrote the *Persica,* a revisionist history of the Persian empire, and the *Indica,* a remarkable whirlwind tour of Eastern nature lore. Unfortunately, the text of both works has been lost, but a detailed summary set down by the Byzantine patriarch Photius preserves enough of their content to allow for useful discussion. It is the *Indica* that interests us here, and in particular, the lengthy[30] description

28. The Hesiodic *Periodos Gēs* mentions *Hēmikunes* or Half-Dogs in the course of its aerial circuit of the earth (fr. 150 Merkelbach-West 1. 8; cf. fr. 153 = Strabo 7.3.6); their location is not clear from this text, but later authors place them in the East. The *Kunokephaloi* appear as semi-human creatures only in Ctesias and writers who follow his account; the word *kunokephalos* later was used to denote the baboon (see Aristophanes, *Knights* 416, where it is not clear in which sense the word ought to be understood; and Plato, *Theaetetus* 161d; also Otto Keller, *Die Antike Tierwelt* vol. 1 [repr. Hildesheim 1963] 7–9).

29. David Gordon White, *Myths of the Dog-Man* (Chicago 1991) 50, in a discussion of the *Kunokephaloi:* "One is tempted here to see the origin of the name of Diogenes of Sinope's fourth-century B.C. 'philosophical sect,' the Cynics (from *kunikos,* 'little dog')." Unfortunately White's mistranslation of the term *kunikos* reveals the limitations of his linguistic skills.

30. Photius's reliability as an excerpter has been attacked by Wilhelm Reese, *Die griechische Nachrichten über Indien* (Leipzig 1914), who reaches the conclusion that "gerade wie in seinem Auszuge aus Philostratos *Vit. Apoll.,* auch hier das Fabuloseste am ausführlichsten [Photius] wiedergab, alles andere aber kurzte" (78). More recently, J.M. Bigwood points out that Photius's summary of the *Indica* is more detailed than his other epitomes, and in cases where we can check it against quotations of the original, often follows Ctesias word for word ("Ctesias' Indika and Photius," *Phoenix* 43 [1989] 302–16).

of the *Kunokephaloi* (or Dog Heads) dwelling in the remote Indian mountains (chaps. 20, 22–23).[31]

As their name implies the *Kunokephaloi* represent an exotic missing link, partaking of both human and canine nature at the same time (20):

> In the mountains dwell men who have the head of a dog; they wear skins of wild beasts as clothing, and they speak no language, but bark like dogs, and in this way understand one another's speech. They have teeth bigger than a dog's, and nails like those of a dog, but larger and more rounded. . . . They understand the speech of the Indians, but cannot respond to them; instead they bark and signal with their hands and fingers, as do mutes.

Here the first feature of the *Kunokephaloi* that Ctesias chooses to focus on is their use of speech; and since speech was often viewed by the Greeks as a definitively human attribute,[32] it is significant that the *Kunokephaloi* possess it only in part, being able to understand language but not replicate it.[33] This taxonomic ambiguity continues to reveal itself throughout Ctesias's description of the *Kunokephaloi,* where the Dog Heads are seen to be stuck midway between the human and animal conditions. They disdain to eat food raw, but, lacking the means to make fires, can only broil it in the hot sun (22); they have no beds but heap up litters of dried leaves to avoid sleeping on the ground (23).

In all this material Ctesias seems not to have looked down on the *Kunokephaloi* as mentally or culturally deficient creatures; he describes them on two occasions as just (*dikaioi*), a quality that in Greek ethnography connotes a state of supreme moral perfection. Beyond simply idealizing the *Kunokephaloi,* moreover, Ctesias seems to have used them as a mouthpiece through which to challenge Greek customs—the move that, as we have seen above, most clearly anticipates later Cynic polemics. Thus, in Ctesias's final note on the *Kunokephaloi* (or at least the one that Photius makes final), we are told:

> All of them, men and women, have a tail above their hips, like a dog's, except bigger and smoother. They have intercourse with their wives on all fours, like dogs, and consider any other form of intercourse to be shameful. They are just, and longest-lived of any human race; for they get to be 160, sometimes 200 years of age.

31. Chapter numbers are those of R. Henry's edition, *Ctésias sur la Perse et l'Inde: Les sommaires de Photios* (Brussels 1947); the same numbers are also used in the English translation by J. W. McCrindle, *Ancient India as Described by Ktesias the Knidian* (Calcutta 1882; repr. Patna 1987).

32. U. Dierauer, *Tier und Mensch im Denken der Antike,* Studien zur Antiken Philosophie 6 (Amsterdam 1977), 12, 33–34; H. C. Baldry, *The Unity of Mankind in Greek Thought* (Cambridge 1965) 15.

33. Later writers used Ctesias's account to classify the *Kunokephaloi* both as animals and as humans. See the note *ad loc.* in Henry's Budé edition of Photius (vol. 1 p. 143), which contrasts Aelian's treatment (*Nat. Anim.* 4.46 = fr. 45p Jacoby) with that of Pliny (*Hist. Nat.* 7.2.23).

To appreciate the satiric tone of this passage we must bear in mind that sexual practices, like speech, form a marker by which the Greeks distinguished civilized from uncivilized races; thus Herodotus, for example, compares sexually aberrant peoples—those who copulate on the ground, for instance, or in public (1.203, 3.101)—to beasts. The *Kunokephaloi,* however, see things from just the opposite perspective; for them the civilized approach to sex becomes a badge of shame, while bestial intercourse is the only variety they deem acceptable. The subsequent observation that the *Kunokephaloi* are just creatures, and enjoy the longest lives of all mankind, forms an ironic pendant to this reversal of sexual mores, showing that despite their contravention of Greek *nomoi,* they have a healthier society than do the Greeks themselves. Although there is no explicit attack on Hellenic culture, the implicit comparison, in which the Greeks come off very much the worse, is inescapable.

Unfortunately, the fragmentary condition of the *Indica* does not allow us to go further in exploring whether Ctesias can truly be called a proto-Cynic satirist. I hope to have shown at least that the *Kunokephaloi,* like other barbarians that inhabit early Greek lore and legend, anticipate in many ways the behavior of later Cynic role models like Diogenes. If we look ahead to the practices of the Cynics in the Hellenistic and imperial eras—dressing in skins, dwelling in the open or in cast-off pots, flaunting sexual mores by copulating in public— we can see the lines along which such figures as the *Kunokephaloi* could develop once they took root in the Hellenic imagination. The Dog Heads, like the dog itself, offered a model of estrangement not only from the mores of a particular society, but—the grandest achievement to which a Cynic could aspire— from those of the human species as a whole.

———•◆•———

With Ctesias's *Indica* we have reached the beginning of the fourth century B.C., the century whose latter years saw the emergence of a movement that can be clearly identified as Cynicism. It is difficult to find ethnographic texts that would bridge the intervening decades, or that would establish direct links between the archaic traditions we have been concerned with here and those that later became associated with Diogenes. My suggestion that the outspoken barbarians of early Greek ethnography can, in some senses, be considered proto-Cynics must remain a suggestion, due to the lack of explicit testimony from ancient sources. Moreover, it is a significant qualification that, of the various barbarian races and figures I have discussed, only Anacharsis went on to play a large part in later Cynic literature (as discussed by Richard Martin elsewhere in this volume).

It may be reassuring to mention, in closing, one additional text that attests to the fourth century's interest in barbarian attacks on native *nomoi.* Theopompus of Chios, a prominent historian of that period whose works are now mostly lost, seems to have glimpsed much the same potential in the traditions of archaic ethnography as I have here claimed was seen by the Cynics. According to a later report,[34] Theopompus, in Book 8 of his *Philippica* (a history of his own times centered around Philip of Macedon), described a land called Meropis situated beyond the waters of Ocean. The inhabitants of this land one day decided to investigate the rest of the earth, and so crossed a vast stretch of Ocean until they came to the Hyperboreans. And upon meeting this foreign race, and learning that it was by far the happiest and most favored of the peoples on that side of the sea, the Meropians became disenchanted. They promptly hoisted sail and returned home, deeming it a waste of time to proceed any farther.

Since we are here once again, as with Ctesias, faced with a secondhand report rather than a complete text, we cannot make any assumptions about the tone or intent of Theopompus's Meropian idyll. It is difficult to imagine that there was not some note of satire or polemic in the scene of the Meropians' scornful departure from the land of the Hyperboreans. One does not bring visitors to an alien world, then have them retreat again in disgust, without intending some sort of attack on the culture of that world. The fact that the Hyperboreans are here made the butt of scorn is especially damning, since they, according to the traditional Greek view, lived a life as pure and blissful as any in the mortal realm. If they appear this wretched to the Meropians, as Theopompus seems to have implied, then the Greeks must surely seem far worse.

I cite this small and mysterious fragment of Theopompus only to show that the tradition of the mocking barbarian was very much alive, and was being put to creative and self-conscious use, during the latter half of the fourth century. The idea of pressing ethnographic models into the service of moral philosophy and social criticism was very much in the air;[35] one can easily believe that it suggested itself as well to those who would later become recognized as Cynics. If so, they would have found, especially in the narratives of cross-cultural contact discussed above, a model of discourse that closely approached their own traditions of self-alienation, free speech (*parrhēsia*), and renunciation of prevailing customs. Perhaps that is as far as we may safely go in reconstructing the history of Cynicism from Heracles to Diogenes.

34. Aelian, *Varia Historia* 3.18 (= Theopompus fr. 75c Jacoby). The legend has occasionally been interpreted as a parody of Plato's myth of Atlantis.

35. Mention might also be made here of the voyage narratives of Iambulus and Euhemerus, though these have a somewhat different character than the works we have been discussing, since they use Greeks to observe and comment on the barbarian world rather than the other way around.

The Scythian Accent:
Anacharsis and the Cynics

R. P. Martin

Why Anacharsis? Of the many potential paradigms for the sage that might have served, what made the semimythical sixth-century Scythian good to think with for Cynic practitioners and fellow travelers up to Julian and beyond?[1]

The short answer was already put succinctly—in what context it is hard to say—in a one-sentence letter supposed to have been written by Apollonius of Tyana, the first-century-C.E. Pythagorean sage, to one Lesbonax: "Anacharsis the Scythian was a sage; and if he was a Scythian, then it was because he was a Scythian that he was a sage."[2] Apollonius means this as a swipe; in the same

---

1. From the outset, I am placing Anacharsis within the bounds of mythic categories, which I take to be cognitive filters, in the mode first developed by Lévi-Strauss and elaborated by Clifford Geertz, Rodney Needham, and, among classicists, G.E.R. Lloyd. I cannot here delve into the fascinating later employments to which the innocent/wise/savage Anacharsis was put, especially in the writing of Barthélemy and the living theater of the eighteenth-century revolutionary "Anacharsis" Cloots. For a brief sketch, see J.F. Kindstrand, *Anacharsis: The Legend and the Apophthegmata* (Uppsala 1981) 85–95 (hereafter "Kindstrand"). For a reading of Cloots, see J. Kristeva, *Strangers to Ourselves,* trans. L. Roudiez (New York 1991) 161–62.

2. *Ep. Ap.* 61, edited and translated by R. Penella, *The Letters of Apollonius of Tyana* (Leiden 1979) 70–71. As Penella notes (103), the chronology of Philostratus's *vita* of Apollonius makes it difficult to believe that this letter was addressed to Lesbonax of Mytilene, whom Lucian (*Salt.* 69) identifies as a pupil of Timocrates of Heraclea and who would therefore have been a second-century contemporary of the sophist Polemo. Penella suggests another Lesbonax, a grammarian of the first century. But if we assume that *Ep.* 61 is a fictionalized representation (or fragment thereof), as at least some of the other letters seem to have been (Penella 28–29), then it may be significant that the Mytilenean Lesbonax had the same teacher as did the Cynic Demonax (Lucian, *Demon.* 3): Apollonius is thus *depicted* as discussing Anacharsis with one probably familiar with Cynicism. The other letter to Lesbonax in the collection (*Ep.* 22) sounds a Cynic theme (one should bear poverty in a manly fashion). Other letters attributed to Apollonius are to Cynic sympathizers whom the historical Apollonius might even have known (*Epp.* 9, 10, 90 to Dio of Prusa; *Ep.* 77e to Demetrius the Cynic, on which see Penella 132–33). It is probable that Anacharsis in the context of Apollonius's letter plays a stock Cynic role.

vein he writes to the wise men in the Museum in *Epistle* 34, explaining with a
wicked paraphrase of Euripides' *Orestes* (line 485) why he has abandoned the
lecture circuit in mainland Greece: " 'I have become barbarous' not 'by being
away from Greece for a long time' but by being in Greece for a long time." [3]
But beyond the joke at the expense of the philistine Greeks is a deeper recognition that barbarian mores could offer a legitimate alternative to traditional
Greek practices and habits of thought. On one level, "Scythian" means "anything but Greek," while on another level it is the specifically *Scythian* associ-
ations of Anacharsis that make him a valuable emblem, probably for Apollonius, certainly for writers of Cynic tendencies in all periods. In this essay, I
shall review the various uses to which the legendary Anacharsis was put, ask
how these might relate to Cynic mind-sets, and suggest two conclusions: that
Anacharsis is both less and more of a Cynic hero than has been thought.

It might have been rewarding to be able to pinpoint where and when Anacharsis became a sage in Greek tradition, and to be able to compare a historical
Anacharsis with his later Cynic employment. As will become clear, neither of
these interpretive tasks is possible. In one way, this is a boon, because, barred
from indulgence in positivist historicism, one has to find ways to investigate
the richer problems involved with *representations* of Anacharsis, borrowing
from folkloristics, ethnography, and literary study. Furthermore, as Apollonius
hints, it is not so much the man whom we should examine as his affiliation with
a specific ethnos, one that represented an extreme otherness, that of semino-
madic races living on the edge of the Greek world. This affiliation allowed a
series of Greek writers, some of them Cynic in various degrees, to use the
figure of Anacharsis as a medium for their critique of Greek institutions, by
constructing an internal outsider with the freedom of speech to say what could
never be put so explicitly *in propria persona*. The underlying technique is as
old as Hesiodic poetry, in which the narrator's self-characterization as a first-
generation Boeotian goes hand in hand with his poetics of free speech (*parrhēsia*).[4] It reappears in the parabatic freedom of Old Comedy, is standardized
in the rhetorical practice of personification (*prosōpopoiia*), and provides the
basic pragmatic structure for the genres of diatribe and iambus throughout ancient literature. Dangerously critical voices are always someone else's.

Nor is what we may call the Scythian strategy uniquely Greek. We might
call to mind the freewheeling commentary on Chicago political life that ema-
nated, with a thick brogue, from Mr. Dooley in Finley Peter Dunne's enormously successful series of stories written in the early part of this century.
Other American examples can help show what this distancing technique ac-
complishes within the rhetoric of social relations.

Will Rogers, the humorist who was, as an Oklahoman (and part Cherokee)
in Washington and Hollywood, himself an embodiment of the informed out-

3. Penella (above, n. 2) 48–49, 108.
4. I have argued this at length in "Hesiod's Metanastic Poetics," *Ramus* 21 (1993) 11–33.

sider, once remarked: "If a distinguished foreigner was to be taken into the Senate and not told what the institution was, and he heard a man rambling on, talking for hours, he would probably say, 'You have lovely quarters here for your insane, but you have no warden to look after their health—to see that they don't talk themselves to death.' " [5] We should notice that the imaginary foreigner in this anecdote uses yet another special social category, the insane, to characterize the behavior of those he sees. Precisely the same comparison is made by Anacharsis when he is quoted making a Cynic point about athletics. The Scythian observes that each of the Greek cities has a designated place in which they go mad every day—the gymnasium.[6]

Alongside the foreigner as political observer in American life is the continuing use of the barbarian—in the form of the Native American—as critic of wider cultural trends. The noble savagery of James Fenimore Cooper's Indians served one set of purposes when *The Last of the Mohicans* was published in 1826 and another in its recent film rendition in the five-hundredth anniversary of Columbus's landing. But both versions share the strength and flexibility one finds in myth. The Indian provides implicit cultural criticism, from the standpoint of a higher ideal, whether it be religiosity or environmental consciousness. It is not impossible that the native himself should make a memorable critique of the (to him) foreign culture. We have, for instance, the apparently authentic testimony of Red Jacket, an Iroquois leader, who in 1828 delivered a speech in answer to one Mr. Cram, a proselytizer from the Boston Missionary Society: "Brother! You say there is but one way to worship and serve the Great Spirit. If there is but one religion, why do you white people differ so much about it? Why do not all agree, as you can all read the book?" [7] No Unitarian tract writer could argue more eloquently than Red Jacket for religious universalism (a fact that makes even this speech suspect). Most often, however, the native only gains a voice when being used as another's mouthpiece. What goes for the Indian applies equally to Scythians—the "Indians" of the Greeks. It would be naive to imagine that any Greek source on Anacharsis, Cynic or not, provides us with the real man rather than an imaginative construct, within a specific context, of a wise Scythian.

We can see this elaborate framing of Anacharsis even within our earliest and, it might seem, most direct account, the *Histories* of Herodotus. In his account of Scythia in Book 4, Herodotus mentions Anacharsis first in an off-

5. *The Best of Will Rogers,* ed. B. Sterling (New York 1979) 38.

6. An extended version is found in Dio (*Or.* 32.44), who cites Anacharsis's view that the oil with which athletes rubbed down induced a mania of running and fighting that disappeared when the oil was scraped off. Lucian's *Anacharsis* (see below) uses this anecdote to build a more sophisticated critique. Shorter versions with similar wording are found in D.L. 1.104, *Gnomologium Parisinum* 343, and Ps.–Dion. Hal. *Ars Rhetorica* 11.4. For these texts with commentary, see Kindstrand (above, n. 1) 117–18, 146–47.

7. B.B. Thatcher, *Indian Biography* (New York 1845), cited in *Native American Testimony,* ed. P. Nabokov (New York 1991), 57–58.

hand comment about the barbarism of people living around the Black Sea (4.46.1): only the Scythians have any *sophia,* and only one Scythian is worthy of mention (*logios*)—Anacharsis; he does not say why. It is significant that the *sophia* of the Scythians as a people, to Herodotus, consists in their ability to defeat any enemy since their nomadic existence does not tie them down to cities or crops. They carry their houses with them (*phereoikoi*) and thus cannot be cornered or even contacted (4.46.3). We assume Anacharsis shares in the distinctive Scythian trait, but his claim to fame is made specific a bit later. Immediately after a digression on the Scythians' religion, Herodotus remarks that they are known to shun foreign customs, especially the Greek. The story of Anacharsis is offered as an example of this. The brief biography that follows might be read better as a variation of the returning-hero plot, akin to the epic tale of the return home from Troy of Odysseus and, even closer, of Agamemnon. Its religious contexts remind one that such stories of barbarians are constructed in socially grounded dialogue, as it were, with Greek stories about Greeks. In this case, perhaps the most relevant sacred tale is that of Orestes' voyage to the Taurians as depicted, for example, in the *Iphigenia in Tauris* of Euripides. Anacharsis's return home is a mirror image of Orestes': the Greek hero, son of a king, in collaboration with his sister, whom he has helped flee from the barbarous devotees of Artemis, plays a central role in the establishment of a cult that is accepted and passed down by the Athenians, the very polis that continues to commemorate him in drama centuries later. His crime in the view of the Taurians—stealing their cult statue—becomes the *aition* (cause) for heroic glorification on the other side of the cultural border. Contrast this with the Scythian Anacharsis, whose return to his homeland is highlighted by his attempt to establish a cult that he, too, has found abroad: ironically, the cult, that of the Mother of the Gods (4.76.3), is explicitly foreign from the Greek point of view, while, from the Scythian perspective, it represents a dangerous *Hellenic* religious innovation (perhaps another hit at Scythian obtuseness). Anacharsis was shot by Saulius after the king saw him, complete with drum and cult clothing, celebrating a *pannukhis* (an all-night ritual) in honor of the Great Mother. He had observed the rites in Cyzicus and vowed to duplicate them if given a safe return home.

At this point in the story, the narrative verges on a violent-rejection tale of the Dionysiac type. In this connection, it is worth noticing that Anacharsis (according to further information that Herodotus now adds) is said to be the uncle of the king Idanthyrsus and grandson of one Spargapithes, bearers of compound names that sound suspiciously Dionysiac.[8] Moreover, the story of

8. For the *sparg-* root, see Euripides, *Ba.* 701, where the verb functions as a synonym of *orgaō* (LSJ s.v.) and describes the swelling of new mothers' breasts as they join in maenadic activity in honor of Dionysus. At *Ba.* 705 one of these Theban women is described as striking the ground with her *thursos,* causing the ground to give forth wine. In Herodotus's report an unnamed Scythian informs the king, who then arrives to view and kill Anacharsis; one is reminded of the dramatic structure of the latter part of the *Bacchae.*

Anacharsis is conjoined at this point in the narrative with a more recent historical episode, that of another unfortunate Scythian traveler, Scyles, who is initiated into Dionysiac *orgia,* hunted down for this by his brother, and eventually beheaded for his Philhellenism. Unlike Scyles, however, Anacharsis after his death is the victim of a sort of cultural amnesia—as Herodotus reports (4.76.5), in his day no one in Scythia professed to know about Anacharsis. Herodotus himself says he found out the genealogy of Anacharsis from an agent of Ariapithes, who was king of the Scythians and father of Scyles. One wonders to what extent the stories of the two Scythian violators are thus codependent fictions.[9]

At any rate, even unaccompanied by diagrams, this double narrative of Anacharsis and his concealed counterpart Orestes could warm the heart of the hardest structuralist: it counterpoints in a seemingly systematic way undervalued/ overvalued kin (since, as Herodotus points out, Saulius must have been Anacharsis's brother), male/female, outside/inside, land voyage/sea voyage, Great Mother/Artemis, and obliteration of memory/immortality. Put another way, in a complete mythopoeic system, one must have such a failure story about foreigners in order to authorize the native-son success tale. To us, the Orestes story is concealed beneath that of Anacharsis, but of course a traditional audience knows a vast range of stories, and Herodotus's public knew about Orestes. It might even be argued that the implicit linkage between the digression on Scythian religion (4.59–75) and Herodotus's use of the Anacharsis story (4.76) is the underlying Orestes tale, a story of a near-victim of near-Scythian rites, which are mentioned by Herodotus at 4.103. Could it be Anacharsis was *unknown* to Scythians because he, like Orestes, was a necessary figment of the Greek mythic imagination?[10]

Part of the fascination of Herodotus, as with Hesiod, lies in his apparently seamless joining of mythic thought and rational analysis.[11] Anacharsis occupies the border between these two equally powerful modes of conceptualizing the world. By the time we first see him he is not only a fictional creation from a vivid, tale-telling culture, but a figure within an intensively schematizing scientific ethnography. Already the Scythian is enmeshed in geopolitics and sub-

9. For a different interpretation of the similarity between the stories, see P. von der Mühll, "Das Alter der Anacharsislegende," *Ausgewählte Kleine Schriften* (Basel 1975) 476. He sees Dionysus as the original cause of a mania that led to Anacharsis's death, and the Great Mother story as the distortion of an original Dionysiac tale. In my view, this reduces to one dimension the complexity of a doubly meaningful story that is enmeshed in two folkloric motifs. The key point is that a Greek audience hearing the Anacharsis tale but already familiar with Dionysus stories, and knowing how Greeks *had* in fact integrated his cult into the polis, would interpret Scythian culture as fixed in a pre-Dionysiac stage. For the importance of the Mother of the Gods here see below.

10. In the slightly different view of M. V. Skrzhinskaya, these Scythian stories are the product of oral traditions current among Greek colonists in Olbia in the fifth century, with whom Herodotus had contact; thus, they are composed close enough to Scythia to contain actual information (e.g., genealogies) while still keeping a Greek outlook. See her article "Skifskije syuzhety v istoricheskikh predanijakh ol'biopolitov," *VDI* 4 (1982) 87–102.

11. The work of J.P. Vernant, especially *The Origins of Greek Thought* (Ithaca 1982) and *Mythe et pensée chez les grecs* (Paris 1965), traces many ways in which the former category actually creates structures for the latter.

ject to an explicit structural analysis—the Greeks of the late archaic age, after all, were the first to carry out a hostile critique alongside their retransmission of myth.[12] There is no overt hostility toward Anacharsis within Herodotus; in fact, Herodotus refuses to credit a joke at the Scythian's expense (4.77), according to which Anacharsis, sent to learn their wisdom, found all the Greeks lacking in *sophia* except the Spartans—a mistake only a foreigner could make. But Anacharsis in the *Histories* does participate in a larger East-West scheme. François Hartog has explicated the important role played in the composition of the *Histories* by Herodotus's consistent juxtaposing of center and extreme, polis and barbarian land.[13] For Hartog's essentially structuralist analysis, Anacharsis happens to be a counter in the game of *nomoi* (customs), one of those transgressive figures (like Scyles) who by their disastrous border-crossing define the limits all the more clearly.[14] Grids and oppositions, not personalities, are at the heart of the Herodotean analysis, in this perspective. It is not surprising, then, that Hartog can see no paradigmatic traits in this early Anacharsis: "Herodotus's Anacharsis is neither at school in Greece nor a martyr to Hellenism, but then neither does he represent the Cynics, despising city life with all its soft ways; he is not held up as a model on which the Greeks should school themselves." [15] Yet, when we consider the alternative paths in the development of the legend, it is hard to believe that the Herodotean Anacharsis bears no relation to the later figure of Cynic propaganda whom we see most clearly in the *Letters of Anacharsis.* Either there was an Anacharsis legend before Herodotus or not; if it existed before, he either ignored it and made up his own, modified the inherited version, or passed it down unchanged; if he did change it, of course, we cannot now on our evidence tell, but unless Herodotus was himself a Cynic—a possibility never imagined—we can be sure the Herodotean Anacharsis picture is not Cynic. And yet the odd thing is, there do not appear to be many shifts in the subsequent depiction of the Scythian, other than obvious changes due to genre (narrative history vs. epistles or dialogues). How should we imagine the relationship between stages?

Some of these points have been much debated. That the Anacharsis legend functioned as an early, pre-Cynic, and even pre-Herodotean form of cultural critique was argued by Peter von der Mühll in 1914.[16] Already essentially that of later times, this Anacharsis, claimed von der Mühll, underwent some Cynic influence but was actually older. He uses later material (mainly Diogenes Laer-

12. On this, see M. Detienne, *The Creation of Mythology,* trans. M. Cook (Chicago 1986) 42–62.

13. F. Hartog, *The Mirror of Herodotus: The Representation of the Other in the Writing of History,* trans. J. Lloyd (Berkeley and Los Angeles 1988), esp. 5–28, 56–82. J. Romm, *The Edges of the Earth in Ancient Thought* (Princeton 1992) 77, affiliates Anacharsis with a number of other figures who mark out for the Greeks otherness at the extremes of the known, and points to their usefulness for satiric inversions.

14. Hartog (above, n. 13) 61.

15. Ibid. 369.

16. Von der Mühll (above, n. 9) 473–81 (originally in *Festgabe für H. Blümner* [Zurich 1914] 425–33).

tius and Lucian) to fill out the picture that he alleges is already current in Athens and Sparta by the fifth century and developed as a legend in sixth-century Ionia.[17] The criticism of Greek athletics attributed to Anacharsis (see Kindstrand A36–37 = D.L. 1.103 and Dio, *Or.* 32.44; Lucian, *Anach.*) can be compared with the elegiac complaints of Xenophanes (2 W.) and even Tyrtaeus (12.1–4 W.) about the excessive privileging of sport, claims von der Mühll— and thus Anacharsis can be their contemporary.[18] But must he be? Similar reasoning marks his observation that the apophthegm credited to Anacharsis about the tongue as the best and worst part of the body (D.C. 1.105, *Gnom. Vat.* 131) is attributed to others among the Seven Sages; Bias, not Anacharsis, who was also present, in the *Banquet of the Seven Sages* by Plutarch, is said to have dramatized this message in the context of a reply to a despot about the parts of sacrificial animals, for instance (*Conv. Sept. Sap.* 146f). Von der Mühll sees this and other similarities of attribution as borrowings from an old Anacharsis tradition. But his method is flawed: in folk materials of this sort, one cannot simply take anything attested early on about several figures—for example, the Seven Sages—and claim that it originates within a particular legend. We cannot distinguish priority in look-alike anecdotes. According to Diogenes Laertius, Solon said laws were like spiderwebs that trap the small and let the great fall through (D.L. 1.58), while Plutarch (*Solon* 5.4) puts the words in the mouth of Anacharsis, on his visit to Solon. Even if we could prove which attribution is original, such isolated and generalized evidence cannot support an argument either for or against the Cynicism of Anacharsis.

Von der Mühll wrote partly to correct the view of Heinze, according to whom the legend of Anacharsis was largely developed by the Cynics for their own purposes.[19] It is significant for Heinze that Diodorus Siculus (9.26) preserves a story in which Anacharsis appears before Croesus and answers that the bravest, most just, and wisest things in the world are the wildest animals, because only they live according to nature, not law (*mona gar kata phusin zēn, ou kata nomous*), and nature is the creation of the gods. Croesus laughs at him and his answers, saying that Anacharsis, as a Scythian, has had a beastly way of life. "Everything here is Cynic," observes Heinze, noting the antinomian flavor of the anecdote. Since Diogenes Laertius (1.40–41) says that Ephorus wrote about a meeting of the Seven Sages with Croesus, and that Ephorus was also the first to have inserted the name of Anacharsis among the Seven Sages, Heinze may well be right when he speculates that Diodorus got this story (as he did much else) from Ephorus and that the fourth-century historian had in turn used a (now lost) Cynic book on Anacharsis.[20] The theme of the superiority of *phusis* to *nomos* in an anecdote about Anacharsis in Athenaeus (613d)

17. Ibid. 481.
18. Ibid. 477–78.
19. R. Heinze, "Anacharsis," *Philologus* 50 (1891) 458–68.
20. Ibid. 462, 466–67.

may stem from the same source: when a monkey was brought into a symposium, the Scythian laughed, although he was solemn when the clowns arrived, because the monkey was funny (*geloios*) by nature, unlike the practiced comedians.[21] But it is harder to believe that no Anacharsis picture existed prior to the Cynics. Probably the most reasonable interpretation of the growth of the Anacharsis tale would be to see in it some archaic roots (as pointed out by von der Mühll) but, more important, to recognize that its survival depended on its being coopted rather early for contemporary ethical critiques, in two stages: a sophistic and a Cynic. What we need to see above all is that these stages are themselves intimately connected.[22] When it comes to cultural analysis, one and the same intellectual stream, expressed in the sixth century in elegiac poetry of an ethical bent, simply forks. It trickles into Herodotus (where until recently it has been overshadowed by his history) and, running parallel to this, through the sophistic movement (where we treat it usually as rhetoric or philosophy). A third branching-off of the stream manages to bypass intellectual articulation within fifth-century history or philosophy and ends up instead on the street, as it were, in the pronouncements and enactments of Diogenes.[23] Von der Mühll's point is well taken, but should be redirected in one way: while it may be true that those elements in the Anacharsis legend that provide a critical assessment of Greek culture do precede Cynicism per se, it is not clear that they precede sophistic trends in the fifth century, trends that are *already* at work in our first attestation, Herodotus's neatly illustrative story of Anacharsis. While we should acknowledge a very old tradition within Greek culture concerning the wisdom of sages, encapsulated usually in stories about the Seven Sages, the study of any number of folk traditions will demonstrate that old conventional motifs—such as the sage—do not prevent innovation: in fact, part of the reason such conventional categories survive is because they are open to new uses. In this context, the one significant piece of corroborating evidence is that previously mentioned, about the status of Anacharsis as sage: if, as it appears, Ephorus was the first to introduce Anacharsis among the Seven Sages, this means that even if he had been as traditional a figure as Solon, Thales, and the rest, he still occupied a more marginal position than they until a period later than Herodotus.[24] The *Histories* tell us as much, in that Herodotus represents

21. Ibid. 463.

22. H.D. Rankin, *Sophists, Socratics and Cynics* (London 1983), is useful in showing continuities.

23. The problems of the origin of Cynicism center on this parallel development as well. Both Antisthenes and Diogenes draw from the archaic ethical tradition, but in different ways, the former as an intellectual, the latter as more extreme actor of wisdom, rather than thinker. Paradoxically, the later figure represents himself as a much earlier type than his predecessor, i.e., as a performing sage.

24. Kindstrand (above, n. 1) 34. In general, Kindstrand leans heavily toward von der Mühll's skepticism regarding a Cynic Anacharsis; see pp. 3, 34–38. Possibly authentic pre-Cynic traits in Anacharsis, according to Kindstrand, are his inventions (Plato, *Rep.* 600a) and his association with the sages.

Thales, Solon, Bias, and other sages as wise advisers—but not Anacharsis.[25]

If the postsophistic Anacharsis was an explicit Cynic model even in the works of Antisthenes and Diogenes, no sign of this survives. For Antisthenes, Cyrus is the barbarian with a message (D.L. 6.2, frr. 19–21B Decleva Caizzi). Diogenes, too, had a fascination with Persian kingship, as emerges from Dio Chrysostom (Or. 6.1). But there are no hints of a similar habit of self-representation by allusion to Scythians. Only three authors provide narratives of any length concerning Anacharsis afterwards in Greek tradition, and these must be used with caution in reconstructing the Cynic traits within the Scythian's legend: Plutarch (Convivium Septem Sapientium, Solon), Lucian (Anacharsis, Scytha), and Diogenes Laertius.[26] After a brief review of this evidence, I shall turn to a richer source, the anonymous third-century Letters of Anacharsis. Finally, I shall suggest that the distinctive feature seen in these letters can lead us to reimagine how Anacharsis might have been used by the first Cynics of the century prior to that in which these were composed.

In Plutarch's Solon, the story of an encounter between Anacharsis and the Athenian lawmaker must stem from an account written by Hermippus in the third century B.C.E., which served as the source for a similar story in Diogenes Laertius, as the latter explicitly tells (D.L. 1.101).[27] Anacharsis comes to Athens seeking friendship with Solon, knocks on his door, and is told by the Athenian that it is better to seek friendship at home (5.2). To this the Scythian wittily replies: "Since you are at home, then, provide friendship and hospitality [xenia] for us."[28] Solon, says Plutarch, marveled at the intelligence of the man (agkhinoia, 5.3) and entertained him as houseguest even though he was busy with public business and drafting laws at the time. His host's occupation gives Anacharsis the opportunity to make another cutting remark, this time about how fruitless is the attempt to control lawlessness and greed through written ordinances, "which are no different from spiderwebs, since they will trap the weak and light but will be ripped right through by the rich and powerful" (5.4). Solon's answer is less cynical: people keep agreements when it is not profitable to either one of the parties to violate the conditions; he is tuning (harmozetai), he says, the laws to suit the citizens, so as to show all doing the right thing is better than acting illegally. Here the narrator intervenes with foreshadowing: "But these matters turned out as Anacharsis had reckoned rather than according to Solon's expectations." The brief story is finished with another Anachar-

---

25. Compare Solon at 1.29; Thales at 1.74–75, 1.170; Bias at 1.27, 1.170; Chilon at 1.59, 7.235.

26. The brief anecdotes and apophthegms found in several other authors most often repeat information in these narratives: see Kindstrand (above, n 1) passim.

27. Plutarch cites Hermippus (6.7) as his source for the next anecdote, concerning another sage, Thales, and Solon. See M. Manfredini and L. Piccirilli, eds., Plutarco: La vita di Solone (Verona 1977) 127. On this writer as a source for Diogenes Laertius, see J. Mejer, Diogenes Laertius and His Hellenistic Background, Hermes Einzelschriften 40 (Wiesbaden 1978), 32–34.

28. Tzetzes (Ep. 1, p. 2.5 Leone) alludes to this incident when asserting his own friendliness.

sis one-liner: while attending the *ekklēsia* he observed that among the Greeks the wise talk but the ignorant do the judging (5.6). Tertullian in the third century thought the remark striking enough to use early on in his *Apologeticus* (1.8).[29] It is hard, however, to place this in any one intellectual context. We might judge Anacharsis's apophthegms preserved by Plutarch to be antiaristocratic in tone, in which case they would dovetail with the views he is supposed to have expressed on merchant trade's being akin to cheating (D.L. 1.105). As Leslie Kurke has shown, Anacharsis represents a predemocratic ideology on this issue, and most likely his figure served as the mouthpiece for a conservative sector of the newly democratized polis.[30] At any rate, there is no need to take the remarks on law, the assembly, or hospitality as exclusively Cynic in tone, since these institutions were subject to analysis and critique already within the Greek poetic tradition from Homer through the fifth century.[31]

Plutarch's other evocation of Anacharsis, in the *Banquet of the Seven Sages,* depicts him as a sage relaxing among companions of similar abilities during a symposium at the Lechaeum in the Corinth of Periander (himself one of the Seven Sages, in some lists). Thales, Bias, and the narrator, a seer named Diocles, who is recollecting the event, arrive at the party to find Anacharsis already there, being groomed by Cleobulina, the daughter of the Rhodian sage Cleobulus. Thales urges her to continue combing Anacharsis's hair "so that, while he is the most gentle sort, he not look a frightful or savage sight to us" (*Conv. Sept. Sap.* 148c). To his companions, Thales explains that Anacharsis has a special friendship with the girl because he is prudent and learned (*sōphrōn . . . kai polumathēs*), and has taught her Scythian medicine—diet and purging (148e).

As the story progresses, we hear more relating to Anacharsis's views on food and drink.[32] To Ardalus, who asks if the Scythians have flute girls, he replies: "No, nor grapevines either" (150e). This apophthegm was known to Aristotle, who criticizes it as an example of a faulty syllogism (*An. Post.* 78b29–31). In context here, and perhaps quite early in the tradition, the remark concerns the Greek institution of the symposium. It assumes that Anacharsis views this social practice from the wrong end, as it were, as the logical end-

---

29. See also *IG* 14.1297 col. 2 recording his visit. On the implications of a coincidence of the visit with Solon's archonship. see Manfredini and Piccirilli (above, n. 27) 127–28; and on the comparison of laws and spiderwebs (also attributed to Zaleucus, Thales, and Solon himself), ibid. 128.

30. L. Kurke, "Καπηλεία and Deceit: Theognis 59–60." *AJP* 110 (1989) 535–44.

31. The problems of *xenia* are thematic within Homer's *Odyssey,* as has often been noticed; the work of Aristophanes (e.g., *Acharnians*) and Thucydides (*passim*) offers many a criticism of the *ekklēsia* in terms not unlike those of Anacharsis. On the connection of these authors with the older poetic heritage, see L. Edmunds, *Cleon, Knights, and Aristophanes' Politics* (Washington 1987) 5–37.

32. Beside the remarks on wine, see his endorsement, for health reasons, of Hesiod's advice to eat asphodel and mallow: 158a. This resembles the Cynic approval of simple food: see Dio Chrys. *Or.* 6.12, 22.

point of a natural condition. The same logic underlies another remark of his about wine, later in the evening, after he attributes Solon's abstemiousness to fear of Pittacus's law that doubled penalties for crimes committed while drunk. "*You* were so scornful of the law," says Pittacus, "that last year at Labys's house in Delphi you got drunk and asked for the prize and a crown." Anacharsis defends himself, saying: "What is the purpose [*telos*] of drinking much unmixed wine, other than to get drunk?" (155f–156a). These and the several other apophthegms on wine in the tradition about Anacharsis could, of course, be read as outgrowths from Cynic preaching on self-mastery (*egkrateia*).[33] But, once again, there is an alternative source, in traditions about proper sympotic behavior that are attested even as early as the *Odyssey*. Ironically, in Homer it is the misbehaving suitor Antinöus who instructs the disguised beggar Odysseus about the dangers of drunkenness, hinting that the wine has gone to the old man's head (21.293). Unrestrained drinking, says Antinöus, began the enmity between Centaurs and Lapiths, since Eurytion the Centaur, mad with drink (*mainomenos*), did evils at the house of Pirithöus (21.298).[34] There is irony but also appropriateness in attributing precepts about moderate drinking to a Scythian. Traditionally these barbarians were expert drinkers of *unmixed* wine—witness the proverb "to drink like a Scythian." But this non-Greek practice, when imported, is depicted as dangerous: Cleomenes of Sparta, as Herodotus reports (6.84), was said to have died after going mad from drinking in the company of Scythians.[35] In other words, like the Centaurs, in Greek mythopoeic thought the Scythians teach Greeks moderation by exemplifying excess. They can always be cited for the other's way of behaving: Anacreon (356 P.) urges his fellow symposiasts to avoid brawls like those at Scythian drinking parties and instead sip wine while listening to hymns.[36] In sum, the tradition about Anacharsis on wine continues an archaic discourse on how to establish sympotic boundaries. The Cynic outgrowth, if there is any here, is part of the general evolution of older Greek practical ethical principles—for example, how to act at parties—into philosophical doctrines, a development not at all confined to Cynicism.[37]

33. In other sayings cited in Kindstrand (above, n. 1: 113–16) he advises interlocutors to learn sobriety by observing the drunkenness of others (D.L. 1.103, Stob. *Flor.* 3.18.34), and characterizes wine as a drink of madness (Ps.–Dion. Hal. *Ars Rhet.* 11.4).

34. He is said to have attempted to carry off the bride of the Lapith hero. Xenophanes fr. 1 (W.) is in the same old tradition: see especially lines 15–24. Significantly, the elegist associates good drinking behavior with a prohibition on telling Centaur stories (1.22).

35. On Scythian drinking, see F. Lissarague, *The Aesthetics of the Greek Banquet: Images of Wine and Ritual,* trans. A. Szegedy-Maszak (Princeton 1990) 7, 11–13.

36. Ibid. 90–91.

37. I cannot therefore agree with the remark of Jean Defradas, ed., *Plutarque: Le banquet des sept sages* (Paris 1954) 19 n. 1, that Anacharsis at this point presents "la figure d'un philosophe cynique." More reasonable is his observation that Plutarch in the last sections of the work portrays a non-Cynic Anacharsis, a possibility I would extend to this earlier section.

Ardalus continues his line of questioning by asking Anacharsis whether the Scythians, then, have gods; the connecting thought, apparently, is that flutes are a natural accompaniment to worship (150e). Indeed they do, replies Anacharsis, and they understand human language, for his countrymen are "not like the Greeks, who think that they themselves speak better than the Scythians but believe the gods find it sweeter to listen to bones and pieces of wood." [38] (I will return to the topic of Scythian speech shortly; meanwhile, it is enough to note that the implicit criticism of Greek liturgical practices fits with a Cynic view of degraded religious behavior: compare D.L. 6.42 on Diogenes' criticisms of prayer and purifications.) But Anacharsis does not get to develop his view, as Aesop breaks in at this point with his own musings on flute making (150e–f). From here until near the end of the dialogue, the views attributed to Anacharsis are hardly to be distinguished from those of the other sage guests: a king or tyrant can be illustrious provided he is not the only one to be wise (152a); the best government is one where what is better is distinguished by virtue (153f). Only on the topic of the household (*oikos*), which naturally flows from such political talk, does Anacharsis have something substantially different to contribute. Aesop points out that the Scythian prides himself on being homeless (155a) and acts like the sun with his chariot, wandering from land to land—a poke at the traditional Scythian house-wagon. Anacharsis picks up the comparison and expands it into what sounds like a Cynic point: "For this reason he [Helios] is free and autonomous and rules all but is ruled by none" (155a). At this stage, we are not far from the expressions of Diogenes, who professed to be a *kosmopolitēs* (D.L. 6.63), compared himself to the sun that shines on good and bad (D.L. 6.63), and described his state as a homeless exile (6.38):[39]

> Without a city, without a house, without a country,
> A beggar, a wanderer with a single day's bread.

This is the closest affiliation between Anacharsis and Cynic notions in the *Banquet,* but two final resemblances are worth noting. First, aside from Aesop, Anacharsis is the sage who most favors animal fables; he even reminds Aesop of his own story regarding the fox and the leopard (155b) to draw the moral that externals do not matter, and adds to this an observation about the possibility of domestic happiness even in a bird's nest or an anthill provided the inhabitants share all (155c). We are reminded of the Cynic fondness for using animals as behavioral paradigms, a trend that begins with Diogenes' admira-

38. The exchange is more pointed if Plutarch assumes knowledge of the story that Ardalus invented the flute and established a Muse cult at Troezen (Paus. 2.31.4–5).

39. Cosmopolitanism, interpreted radically, entails homelessness: on the theme in general see I. Lana, "Tracce di dottrine cosmopolitiche in grecia prima del cinismo," *RFIC* 29 (1951) 193–216, 317–38.

tion for mice and, of course, dogs (D.L. 6.22, 40, 60).[40] Second, the mention of the Scythian bow in Anacharsis's disquisition on the responsiveness of the soul to God's motion (*kinēsis,* 163e–f) might recall to a learned audience an apophthegm attributed to him elsewhere, that a bow continually stretched will break. The comparison, applied to intellectual operations (*logismos*), argues that they are not productive when the mind dwells on the same things.[41] Aristotle (*EN* 10.6, 1176b32–35) seems to have known an apophthegm of Anacharsis that had a similar point: play so that you can work (*paizein d'hopōs spoudazēi*). As Praechter saw, the bow comparison is attested in Herodotus (2.173), in a form that more explicitly links it to the idea that serious work requires intervals of play. Amasis the Egyptian, chided by friends for his unkingly jesting and drinking in midday, replies that bowmen unstring their weapons so that they do not break from constant stretching; he, too, without relaxation (*heōuton anienai*) would grow mad or apoplectic.[42] Putting these pieces together, we might conclude that the bow comparison was associated with Anacharsis (as a Scythian, the ideal archer) in the context of Cynic thinking about play: the Cynic aesthetic of the seriocomic (*spoudogeloios*) comes to mind, as does the self-presentation of Diogenes, whose life, as we read it in Diogenes Laertius, sounds like a series of instructive pranks.[43] But an equally plausible interpretation might be that Anacharsis, as a pre-Cynic paradigm of sympotic behavior (see above, on wine), could be associated easily with the topos regarding the need to play; the depiction of Amasis in Herodotus, then, would be a similar offshoot of Greek sympotic imagination: notice that he is still an important presence in the minds of Plutarch's symposiast sages (*Conv. Sept. Sap.* 151b–c).

We have seen that Plutarch's Anacharsis, however much recycled out of Cynic materials, embodies principles that can already be seen in early elegiac, even epic, ethical contexts. Lucian's depiction of Anacharsis in his dialogue of that name does not bring us much closer to being able to establish a Cynic sage who is at all distinctive from the more general guru type to be found from the sixth century on in Greek lands.[44] There were pragmatic reasons for Lucian's interest in what one critic calls the inherently comic fantasy world of the barbarian: Christopher Robinson notes that the *Scytha, Anacharsis,* and *Toxaris* might all be works prepared for a Macedonian circuit, occasional pieces tossed

40. On animals and Cynics, see M. Onfray, *Cynismes: Portrait du philosophe en chien* (Paris 1990) 36–42.

41. Attested as *Gnom. Vat.* 17 and in other *gnōmologia:* Kindstrand (above, n. 1) 109 (A 10A–D).

42. K. Praechter, "Der Topos περὶ σπουδῆς καὶ παιδιᾶς," *Hermes* 47 (1912) 471–76.

43. On typical Cynic joking style, see J. Kindstrand, *Bion of Borysthenes* (Uppsala 1976) 47–48, with bibliography there; also Heinze (above, n. 19) 466 n. 8; E. Weber, *De Dione Chrysostomo Cynicorum Sectatore* (Leipzig 1887) 86–94, on Diogenes' *paignia,* is still useful.

44. On this type, see A.A. Long, "Timon of Phlius: Pyrrhonist and Satirist," *PCPhS,* n.s., 24 (1978) 70–72.

off by the roving Lucian for audiences who might feel the closer to these topics.[45] In the *Scytha* (9), the satirist makes this occasionally clear, alluding to his own resemblance to Anacharsis: both are barbarians who arrive in a great metropolis and have the good fortune to discover patrons—in Lucian's case, not a Solon but a wealthy father and son, whom he flatters while elaborating on the story of Anacharsis's meeting with the Athenian sage. Given this performance context, it is not unreasonable to read the *Anacharsis* as purely Lucian's invention, a possibility Heinze long ago envisioned, but ultimately resisted.[46] In the Lucianic dialogue Anacharsis shows an inability to see anything of worth in Greek athleticism. The attitude is that of the anecdote found in Dio of Prusa's *Oration* 32.44 (= Kindstrand A37a), where Anacharsis is reported to have said each Greek city had a place where people go mad daily—the gymnasium—and called oil a drug producing madness: as soon as they anoint themselves, "right away some run around, others knock each other down, others stretch out their hands and hit against nobody, others receive blows. After doing these things, and scraping off the drug, they regain their senses immediately, and acting in a friendly way with one another walk away looking down, ashamed at their deeds." [47] Heinze acknowledged that this strain in Greek thought—the antiathletic voice—can be found as far back as Xenophanes and is echoed most famously in Euripides' *Autolycus* (284 N.):

> Out of myriad evils all through Greece
> There is nothing worse than the race of athletes.

In both poets the athlete is devalued in order to privilege political wisdom, prudence, and justice within the polis, claimed Heinze, whereas in his reading, the Cynics from Diogenes to Oenomaus scorned athletics from a different motivation, because they preferred, instead of this waste of time, the practice of virtue. This, asserts Heinze, is more like the Anacharsis we see in Lucian.[48] As a second piece of evidence for a Cynic Anacharsis figure in Lucian, Heinze adduces the high value set by Cynics on nature and animals as models.[49] In this light, the two main figures of Lucian's dialogue appear as expressions of a clash between nature and culture, the staging of the superiority of *phusis* to *nomos*.

But even if Lucian obtained his knowledge of the Anacharsis tradition through the filter of several lost Cynic renditions, as Heinze would have it, a

45. C. Robinson, *Lucian and His Influence in Europe* (London 1979) 61; see pp. 15–16 on fantasies of barbarians. An excellent analysis of the relation between figures such as Anacharsis, the first-person Lucianic narrator, and the author himself can be found in R. Bracht Branham, *Unruly Eloquence: Lucian and the Comedy of Traditions* (Cambridge, Mass., 1989) 13–14.

46. Heinze (above n. 19) 461.

47. Ibid. 459. Compare D.L. 1.104 for a similar anecdote—in the form of an apophthegm = Kindstrand A 37e–f.

48. Heinze (above, n. 19) 460.

49. Ibid. 462. See the discussion above concerning Diod. Sic. 9.26.

straightfoward reading of this dialogue reveals more interest on the part of Lucian in the satiric possibilities of such an imaginary conversation between archaic notables. Anacharsis begins with a characteristically pungent comparison of wrestlers to eels, pigs, rams, and cocks (*Anach.* 1–2). What does this madness serve? To Solon's reply that it brings bodies to perfection, Anacharsis responds that he would rather use his Scythian dagger on himself than be so degraded (7). Solon's next tactic is to argue for the role of athletics in the good maintenance of the polis—after all, Anacharsis has come to learn statecraft, has he not? After a Periclean exposition of the educational function of the state, its dramas, and its music (20–23), Solon shifts to a different tack: athletics prepare men for war (24–30). The reaction of Anacharsis is a masterpiece of comic writing: he ironically imagines the Athenians swarming out, dust-covered and oiled, to meet their enemies' spears and arrows (or, perhaps, with scary tragic costumes); wouldn't it be better to learn how to use a bow or Scythian knife (31–33)? As he presses Solon to explain why Athenians simply do not adopt Spartan practices, inflicting real pain in simulated war games, the dialogue begins to take on a disturbing darker irony. The Scythian has indeed uncovered an inconsistency between rhetoric and practice in this idealized Solonian state. Solon's weak reply, "We do not think it right to emulate foreign things" (39), may remind one of the xenophobia Herodotus ascribed to the Scythians (4.76.1), the very point he had used to introduce the story of Anacharsis into the *Histories.* We never hear Lucian's Anacharsis describe the logic of the Scythian system, as it is put off for another day. Thus, Branham's observation that Lucian eschews a clear authorial judgment is ultimately a more useful and less reductive reading of the total effect.[50] This is no Cynic tract. If anything, one could argue that the Scythian figure plays the same role here as in sympotic usages of the other, for, even if Solon cannot provide a convincing *logos,* the Athenian institution, in which a metaphorical equivalence of war with athletics prevails, does end up sounding at least more enlightened than the alternative, the Spartan model. The sophisticated postclassical satirist offers us something like a postmodern vision, wherein the proponent's reliance on chauvinist natural argument from the current local custom is clearly exposed, but we are left without valid counterclaims.

The account of Anacharsis given by Diogenes Laertius (1.101–5), if composed in the third century C.E., as is usually suggested, would then give us the latest extended ancient rendition of the sage. It is also potentially most useful, as we might expect it to bring into focus, in juxtaposing Anacharsis with other philosophical biographies, what is specifically Cynic, and what could be so but is also attested earlier than Cynic treatments regarding different topoi. As it turns out, the account does not make any overt claims for an affiliation between the Scythian and the Cynics (one would expect to see such claims in Book 6),

50. Branham (above, n. 45) 102.

nor does it give any hints that the Cynics wrote about him. The Anacharsis biography comes toward the end of Diogenes' account of the Seven Sages. Anacharsis was of Scythian royal blood, son of Gnurus and brother to the king Caduidas, and was bilingual (his mother was Greek: 1.101). He composed an eight-hundred-line poem (poetry occupied all the sages, it seems) on military matters and simplicity of life (*eis euteleian biou*). The rest of the account we have seen mostly already in relation to other sources, probably antecedent to it: the visit to Solon, the apopthegms about wine drinking, the antiathletic stance. Some of what looks like new information is also in the *gnōmologia* tradition, where it could either be borrowed from Diogenes Laertius or be older than his account. At any rate, it is not markedly Cynic: Anacharsis does not like boats (1.103–4), in which passengers are four fingers' breadth (i.e., the hull's thickness) from death, and which are safest hauled ashore. Here is an echo of the paradoxical folktale character who has been much traveled yet wants nothing to do with the sea, and wanders about, enduring insults over wine in others' houses (cf. 1.105, of Anacharsis insulted by a boy). Of course, much of the *Odyssey* is built along similar lines. Cynics, from Antisthenes on, admired and imitated Odysseus. This Anacharsis *could* be the last in that long line of copies. More likely, he is part of an independent reuse of free-floating traditional motifs, what folklorists call a multiform.[51] His critique of Greek behavior at many points resembles a Hesiodic stance: his caution against the tongue, for example, as the best and worst part of a person can be compared to Hesiod's depiction of language (at *WD* 719–21), where the tongue is called the best storehouse for humans when used sparingly.[52] Hesiod, too, wrote about simplicity of life (and we should notice Anacharsis's defense of the poet in Plutarch's depiction at *Conv. Sept. Sap.* 158a).[53] More intriguing are the quite specific parallels between the frame stories about these two moralists. Both have problems with their brothers: Anacharsis, more explicitly here than in Herodotus (D.L. 1.102), is the brother of the king of Scythia and (a new twist, which sounds like the Atys story in Hdt. 1.43) is killed by him while they are out hunting together, because his brother did not like his newly acquired Hellenism. Some reported that he was slain while performing Greek rites (D.L. 1.102).[54] Again, Anacharsis's low opinion of sailing resembles that of the Hesiodic persona (at *WD* 618–49), and, if it is tied to a negative view of mercantile trading in the agora, which Anacharsis is represented (D.L. 1.105) as equating with mutual deception, it can be compared with the Hesiodic preference

---

51. On Odysseus as a character in seamen's tales, and multiforms generally, see W. Hansen, "Odysseus and the Oar: A Folkloric Approach," in *Approaches to Greek Myth,* ed. L. Edmunds (Baltimore 1990) 241–72.

52. See Kindstrand (above, n. 1) 53–54. Cf. *WD* 321–26.

53. Kindstrand (above, n. 1) 61–65.

54. Kindstrand (ibid.: 10–11) explores the evidence. This was the main point in the account at Hdt. 4.76. The Herodotean account may place the death near a grove of Hecate, reminding one of the close relation between Hesiod and the goddess in the *Theogony.*

for subsistence farming over the dangers of sea trading (and also against hang-ing about the agora: *WD* 28–32).

To sum up at this point: a survey of the major works dealing at least in part with Anacharsis does not commit us to the view of Heinze, that we are seeing a Cynicized sage; more likely, as von der Mühll observed, the portrait simply preserves a generally archaic quality. The comparanda from epic, didactic, and elegiac poetry point in this direction. Given this rather negative result, it is time to pose our original questions in a new way: If it is impossible to distill a Cynic Anacharsis from the varied versions of his legend, can we pin down, instead, what Anacharsis, as opposed to any other sage, provided for the Cynics? We will want to examine purely Cynic documents, not derived representations that may or may not have been simply colored by lost Cynic treatments. As it hap-pens, we have an excellent control group in the form of the *Cynic Epistles,* dating from the fourth century B.C.E. to the first or second century C.E.[55] These fictionalized letters are all the more valuable because we see depicted in them the views—as at least writers of some periods conceived—of Diogenes and Crates, and, alongside them, of men apparently considered Cynic forerunners: Socrates, Heraclitus, and Anacharsis. Without question, the letters attributed to Anacharsis in this collection are composed for Cynic use, as the most recent editor argues.[56] By comparing the topics and viewpoint of Anacharsis's letters with those found in the others, and putting to one side the generic Cynic quali-ties of the collection, we can obtain the best idea of what it was Anacharsis *brought to* Cynic self-representation, instead of how Cynicism affected the tra-dition *about* him. My method once again is derived from the folklorist's: the comparison of motifs works as a first step, a straining-out of the universal (since it is banal to assert merely that motif X *is* a universal, be it tricksters in folktales or talk of the value of *ponos* in Cynic philosophy). The second step is to examine what is left after the universals, to get at the specific shape of an individual text or performance.

When we do this with the ten extant *Letters of Anacharsis,* which date prob-ably from 300–250 B.C.E., one feature juts out from the terrain—the Scythian's way of talking.[57] In *Epistle* 1 (to the Athenians) Anacharsis starts immediately

---

55. On dating and on the collection generally, see A. Malherbe, *The Cynic Epistles: A Study Edition* (Missoula 1977) 1–34; H. Attridge, *First-Century Cynicism in the Epistles of Heraclitus,* Harvard Theological Studies 29 (Missoula 1976) 3–12; W. Capelle, "De Cynicorum Epistulis" (diss. Göttingen 1896). M.-O. Goulet-Cazé, *L'ascèse cynique* (Paris 1986) 19 n. 8, presents the case for using the *Cynic Epistles* as evidence for practice, with caution.

56. F. Reuters, *Die Briefe des Anacharsis* (Berlin 1963) 5.

57. On the dating, see F. Reuters, *De Anacharsidis Epistulis* (Bonn 1957) 11–14. M. Mühl, "Der 2. und 9. Anacharsisbrief und Isokrates," *AC* 40 (1971) 111–20, sees traces of an early fourth-century debate on barbarian vs. Greek mores in two letters. The letters appear in at least thirty-six manuscripts, from the eleventh century on, mostly in the context of letter collections (including the epistles of Phalaris), sometimes with Lucianic works (e.g., Laurentianus gr. plut. 57.51, saec. xi): see Reuters (1957) 17–25.

with the problem of the language barrier: "You laugh at my voice, because it doesn't pronounce Greek letters clearly" (*ou tranōs Hellēnika grammata legei*). Anacharsis solecizes in the company of the Athenians, but the Athenians solecize when among Scythians.[58] Men differ "not by *phōnai* when it comes to worthiness, but by *gnōmai*." He then goes on to praise the Spartans: "The Spartans are not clear in their Attic speech but are famous and renowned for deeds" (1.6).[59] Next, he shifts to Scythian verbal behavior: "The Scythians do not criticize a speech that makes clear the necessary things, nor do they praise one whenever it does not reach what is needed" (1.7–9). What is more galling, he sees Athenians as paying no regard to a person's speech when importing Egyptian doctors or Phoenician helmsmen, and they do not pay more to people who speak Greek in their marketing (1.11–14). Then there is the example of the kings of Persia, who are forced to solecize when they must speak to monolingual Greek officials—"but you do not despise their counsels or works" (1.16–17). A speech is not bad when fine deeds follow it and it comes out of good intentions (*boulai*). You will be deprived of much, says the Scythian, if you get annoyed at barbarian voices—you will make people fear to bring you useful things; why value barbarian textiles but not language? (1.21–26). He concludes: it is better to be saved by paying attention to solecists than follow at one's harm people who speak perfect Attic.

A similar argument, this time from other sign systems (body adornment, architecture) is at the core of *Epistle* 2 (to Solon). Despite local differences, the signs of ignorance are the same for barbarians and for Greeks (2.16–17). *Epistles* 3 (on sobriety) and 4 (envy) present more standard Cynic topoi; *Epistle* 5 (to Hanno) has been seen to contain older views, cognate with the Herodotean use of Anacharsis as representative of Scythian *nomoi*.[60] *Epistles* 6 and 7, on the freedom of the Scythian and good rule, respectively, are brief advisories to unnamed (6, king's son) and mythical (7, Tereus of Thrace) royal personages; the tone is not as strikingly Cynic. Finally, *Epistles* 9 and 10, to Croesus, give us a letter of introduction (10) and a longer consolation for the Lydian despot, which uses the Scythian's freedom from possessions again as a paradigm for how one escapes care. It might be said that there is little else go on in these letters to distinguish Anacharsis from other Cynic propagandists. But a survey of the letters of Diogenes and Crates, the real Cynics, makes it more obvious that *Epistle* 1 is a uniquely revealing document; nowhere else is foreign speech

---

58. The same sentiment is contained in *Gnom. vat.* 16, with the word *soloikizei* (See Kindstrand [above, n. 1] A 4B–C). Reuters (above, n. 57: 13) notes that the use of the verb in an early meaning helps to date this letter; it still means here "to mispronounce" (as at Hdt. 4.117, Demos. 45.30), not "to misuse rhetoic or grammar."

59. Line numbers as in Malherbe's edition (above, n. 55). As Reuters (above, n. 57: 73) notes, the Spartans are a Cynic topos. He compares also Hdt. 4.77.1 on Anacharsis's experience of the Spartans. We may be reminded of Lucian's *Anacharsis;* see above.

60. K. Praechter, "Der fünfte Anacharsisbrief," *Hermes* 56 (1921) 422–31.

problematized. Yet this letter uses Anacharsis's foreign speech as a way of highlighting the importance of deeds. Though the distinction is as old as Greek literature, its application here should be connected with a broader Cynic focus on the value of actions rather than words. Several letters attributed to Crates elaborate on this idea: *Epistle* 20, to Metrocles, describes how Crates joined in with young men exercising, to make a point about training (*askēsis*). It ends with the advice that his addressee, too, run and frequent the gymnasium, since action (*ergon*) teaches endurance more quickly than speech (*logos*). Again, in *Epistle* 21, to the same man, the point is made: "Long is the way to happiness through words; but that through the practice of deeds each day is a shortcut [*suntomos*]." This is familiar Cynic ground. In this context, Anacharsis's odd language (from the point of view of Athenians) forces one to look at what he does, not what he says. And this reinforces the Cynic message—to follow the shortcut to virtue, without philosophizing in endless talk of dialectic and *elegkhos* (refutation). Anacharsis is the remedy for the threat—apparently quite real in early Cynicism and understandable if Antisthenes is the actual originator of this philosophy—that Platonic-style discourse will drown out the Cynic message.[61]

If Anacharsis in the *Letters* gives us a clue to actual Cynic use, I conclude, it is because of his Scythian accent that Anacharsis is good to think with. Here the representations of narrative lore and the conventions of poetics meet. Anacharsis is characterized by an unmistakable style, which can puncture overblown rhetoric. Diogenes Laertius (1.101) records that the manner of Anacharsis gave rise to a proverb—"Speech from the Scythians"—because he was outspoken (*dia to parrhēsiastēs einai*). At the same time, inscribed on his statues, says Diogenes Laertius (1.104), were the words *Glossēs, Gastros, Aidoiōn Kratein* (Rule Your Tongue, Belly, and Genitals, a saying taken literally in the story he slept with one hand on his mouth, the other on his genitals: *Gnom. Vat.* 136, Plut. *De Garr.* 7.505a). Thus freedom of speech is the complement to the control of speech that he also represents; the one with self-mastery (*egkrateia*) is also the one allowed to cross the boundaries of controlled speech (or proper drinking, as we have seen).

This Anacharsis may well have been traditional before the fifth century. We have no way of knowing, but the possibility does offer one final, intriguing thought. Whether or not he began Cynicism, we can still wonder where Diogenes of Sinope got his notions about street theater—the *paignia* we see him play in the service of effective philosophy, which Dudley maintained belong

61. D. Dudley, *A History of Cynicism from Diogenes to the Sixth Century* A.D. (London 1937) 1–3, sets up a contrast between the Socratic intellectual pursuits of Antisthenes and Diogenes' anti-intellectual traits. We do not need to agree with him that Diogenes began Cynicism, but we can still maintain there were two contrasting tendencies early in the movement. Long (above n. 44: 76) points to the well-known criticisms of Plato by Diogenes as characteristic of Cynic treatment of philosophers in all periods.

rather to an anthology of Greek humor than a discussion of philosophy.[62] It is interesting in this light that Anacharsis, as we have seen, was associated with sayings about the necessity for play, *paidia.* But perhaps more to the point is the fact of Diogenes' coming from Sinope. Sayre once suggested that, as a terminus for eastern trade routes, Sinope enabled Diogenes to hear stories of gymnosophists and other guru types.[63] I would rather point northwards: Sinope was a staging point for traffic across the Euxine toward Scythian lands; it was actually destroyed by the Scythians in the seventh century B.C.E.[64] Could not a young man growing up in this town have heard travelers—or even locals of Scythian descent—tell of the barbarian and his Hellenization? We know that Cynics valued heroic models; who was Diogenes' hero? Could it be a Scythian who acted like a sage, and brought back, to his detriment, the rites of the Great Mother from Cyzicus (two hundred miles to the west of Sinope)? Was it an accident, or by design, that Diogenes of Sinope ended up, living an outdoor life, in the Metröon, cult place of the same Great Mother, in the Athenian agora (D.L. 6.23, *Ep. Diog.* 16.21)?

62. Dudley (above, n. 61) 29.
63. F. Sayre, *The Greek Cynics* (Baltimore 1948) 39–49.
64. A.R. Burn, *The Lyric Age of Greece* (New York 1967) 117; R. Höistad, *Cynic Hero and Cynic King* (Lund 1948) 19.

The Philosophy of Aristo of Chios

J. I. Porter

Heterodoxy

Aristo of Chios stated that the goal of existence is a life led indifferently with respect to what is intermediate between virtue and vice, without our making any kind of discrimination whatsoever among those intermediates, but instead setting all of them on an equal basis. For, he argued, the sage resembles a good actor who, whether he takes up the role of Thersites or of Agamemnon, plays either part as the part demands.

This striking dictum,[1] drawn from one of Aristo's many famous analogies,[2] gives as clear a statement of his moral doctrine as one could hope to find among his scant remains. It also gives us a taste of the philosophical impression he strove to leave behind. Here Aristo earns his modern tag, "heterodox," "heretic," or "radical," for he seems to be swimming hard against the current of a Stoic view that, destined to become mainstream, found no incompatibility in maintaining virtue and vice to be absolute points of reference for moral action while justifying the existence of a separate class of motives in the same realm of moral action, these latter constituting an intermediate, naturally sanctioned set of values (things according to nature, *ta kata phusin*), which in themselves

This paper began in 1989 as an inquiry into Philodemus and Aristo (undertaken with the generosity of the National Endowment for the Humanities) and later developed into a study of Aristo's Cynic tendencies, thanks to the impetus of Bracht Branham. I am especially indebted to Alan Code, Brad Inwood, Tony Long, Sara Rappe, and David Sedley for saving me from many errors, even if I have persisted in others.

1. D.L. 7.160 (*SVF* 1.351).
2. Some of these were collected together by Stobaeus (*SVF* 1.383–87, 391–94, etc.).

make absolutely no difference to the attainment of virtue. Possession of life, health, beauty, and the like is naturally preferable to their loss, but seen from the perspective of virtue's perfection these naturally preferable things have no value for the content of happiness. That content was understood by Zeno, the school's founder, as life led in accordance with nature or virtue.

Aristo sensed a contradiction here: if natural value is essential to goodness (the good is naturally good and naturally valuable), how can any item that has natural value be said to lack goodness? Of course, the risk in conceding goodness to anything with natural value is that things according to nature start looking like mini-goods, and (worse still) like a species of the good—a result that would be unacceptable to both Aristo and Zeno. The Academic Antiochus of Ascalon would later mount a similar objection (to a different end), and the only available defense is to acknowledge that nature is an equivocal notion.[3] Unswayed, and missing a justification, Aristo responded in kind, in effect giving the Stoic teaching a rigorously literal and unambiguous construction. Henceforth, indifferents must be construed unqualifiedly as such, with no grades of natural preferability among them: a virtuous life should be, so to speak, perfectly indifferent to indifferent things, even if under the pressure of circumstances (but not of nature) one might need or wish to choose provisionally among indifferents and thus to act on them without belief in them—with all the savvy of a seasoned theatrical performer. The ultimate status of the good and of happiness as goals is never in doubt. But what is to be said about the nature of virtue and its embodiment by the sage? For virtue seems complicated, if not quite overshadowed, by the sage's exuberant and ethically dubious assumption of the roles allotted to him in Aristo's analogy.[4] Sagehood is the last thing one would look for in a Thersites or an Agamemnon, as the literary tradition before and after Aristo amply illustrates.[5]

More than a streak of cynicism, if not Cynicism, runs through this response to a Stoic nicety. The coldly indifferent analogy to ethical role-playing, with its bluff nonsequitur and its flirtation with deft hypocrisy, is anything but harmless, and anything but ethically straightforward. The source of the image may be the Cynic Bion of Borysthenes (*fl.* early third century B.C.),[6] but the sentiment is vintage Cynic school property. The attitude of equanimity in the face

---

3. Cic. *De Fin.* 4.39; cf. 4.43; Plut. *De Comm. Not.* 1070a; cf. the reformulations by Diogenes and Antipater (*SVF* 3.44–46, 57–58); I. G. Kidd, "Stoic Intermediates and the End for Man," in *Problems in Stoicism,* ed. A. A. Long (London 1971), 150–72 (here, p. 167); A. A. Long, "Carneades and the Stoic Telos," *Phronesis* 12 (1967) 59–90 (here, p. 89).

4. With this active assumption of a role, and even of a debased trait, contrast Plut. *De Comm. Not.* 1058a (the Stoic sage as hunchbacked, "if he should chance to be this").

5. For ridicule of Agamemnon, cf. Bion of Borysthenes *ap.* Cic. *Tusc. Disp.* 3.26.62 (fr. 69 Kindstrand, with commentary *ad loc.*) and Cic. *De Offic.* 3.95 (reflecting a Stoic criticism). For the mock view of Thersites as a proto-Cynic, cf. Lucian, *Dem.* 61; with R. Bracht Branham, *Unruly Eloquence: Lucian and the Comedy of Traditions* (Cambridge, Mass., 1989) 57–63.

6. Cf. fr. 16A Kindstrand (fr. 2, pp. 5.2–6.8 Hense = Stob. 3.1.98).

of adversity and the rule that one should adapt oneself to circumstances can be traced back to the Cynic Crates and earlier still, while casting the sage in the role of active and even truculent indifference to the world about him is a signature piece of Diogenes of Sinope.[7] The depth of Aristo's commitment to Cynicism is difficult to gauge. It is not entirely clear, for instance, whether he is using the image of the actor to project an un-Stoic attitude about ethical behavior, or whether he is exploiting the image to scandalize his audience in another sense, namely to point up—virtually, to dramatize—the unexamined implications of allowing indifference to occupy so central a role in a philosophy otherwise so entirely given over to the careful calibration of moral differences. Let the Stoics have their cake, but they cannot eat it too, Aristo seems to be saying, and not unjustifiably, as he accuses them of a logical hypocrisy: for you cannot posit natural value as essential to goodness while at the same time denying goodness to a class of items that have natural value.[8] The truth about his position may lie somewhere between these two alternatives.

The uncompromising division of the ethical world into virtue, vice, and their excluded middle is in fact a Cynic gesture, and of course it is a Socratic one too. But a word of caution is needed, given the different levels of explicitness that are involved. The Cynics marked their distinction not so much formally, perhaps, but with actions and with words equivalent to actions, and so I take it that the class of indifferent things for them, as for Aristo later, was defined by the dispositional attitude of indifference they showed toward the external world and its conventions, just as virtue and its deficiency were the only objects they regarded with no indifference at all.[9] Aristo could have consistently thought that he was referring to both ways of thinking, Cynic and Socratic, when he embraced his theory of indifference, especially given the Hellenistic reception of the Cynic Socrates.[10] Significantly, though, the later tradition remembered (or chose to remember) Aristo as looking back to the Cynics. Ancient doxog-

---

7. Bion *ap. Teletis Reliquiae,* pp. 16, 4; 52, 2; Teles, ibid. p. 5, 2. Crates: ibid p. 38, 10; Diogenes: D.L. 6.22, 38, 63. (Contrast the Stoic reply to Aristo, Cic. *De Fin.* 3.24 [*SVF* 3.11].) On Aristo's simile, see Epict. *Diss.* 4.2.10 and A.M. Ioppolo, *Aristone di Chio* (Naples 1980) 191, 196–97, 202.

8. For ancient and more recent criticism of the Stoic distinction, see Plut. *De Comm. Not.* 1070a; G. Vlastos, *Socrates, Ironist and Moral Philosopher* (Cambridge 1991) 225 n. 84; cf. p. 304.

9. A.A. Long is right to point out (*per litt.*) that we have no evidence of a formal recognition by the Cynics of the Socratic tripartite division, even though this is widely presumed. Cf. D.L. 6.11–12, 27, 29, 104, etc. (where the division is implicit, rather than formal). The mention of indifferents at 6.105 may be retrojected (J. Mansfeld, "Diogenes Laertius on Stoic Philosophy," *Elenchos* 1–2 [1986] 297–382 [here, pp. 342, 351]), but it may also stem from the Cynic attitude of indifference that Aristo adopted after his own manner (cf. nn. 11, 81, 123 *infra*), as did Zeno and Chrysippus after theirs (using the same term, "indifferent"; cf. Sext. *P* 3.200; *SVF* 1.190, 191, 195, 256; 3.745; Simplic. *In Cat., CAG* 8.410.29–30). For the indifference of external goods in Socrates, cf. Plat. *Gorg.* 467e–468b; and A.A. Long, "Socrates in Hellenistic Philosophy," *CQ,* n.s., 38 (1988) 150–71 [here, pp. 167–71].

10. Long (n. 9 *supra*) 164 *et passim.*

raphy holds that Aristo's theory of indifference is the same theory that the Cynics espoused (D.L. 6.105), but the point must be that Aristo was inscribing back into Stoicism a Cynic tendency that Stoicism in any case displayed, albeit in a weaker form. Presumably, in the eyes of later tradition, and surely in his own, Aristo's dissidence lies not in his falling away from the Stoa, but in his bringing out this recessed trait of Stoicism—which is to say, in resuscitating some of the original and uncompromised force of the Cynic concept, or just attitude, of indifference toward anything save virtue and its opposite.[11] It is this trait that makes Aristo one of the most colorful Hellenistic philosophers, and it deeply pervades his philosophical style.

As is well known, the allegiances of both Aristo and the Cynics, in contrast to those of Zeno, Cleanthes, and Chrysippus, are exclusively and emphatically to ethics, as against logic and physics (D.L. 6.103). This by itself helps to account for his sharp attack on the Stoic concept of natural value, in part just for its being derivative of a theory of nature. The Cynic view of nature and the natural, which Aristo arguably takes over, is far less exalted, and far less determinate, than its Stoic counterpart.[12] (This will be discussed below.) An even more profound comparison between the Cynics and Aristo may be drawn, given the radical philosophical tendencies that both displayed: for instance, the appearance of extreme moral rationalism, which they could put on and off at will. Both flirt with extremism as a matter of course, pushing knowledge claims to uncomfortable limits. But in order to appreciate this fact, further details will first need to be integrated, and a more complete understanding of the consequences, in Aristo's philosophy, of his realignment of the Stoa with its roots in Cynicism will be required as well. That Aristo set out to correct Zeno is well known, though just what this correction amounted to is still a matter of some dispute. By reopening the issue, hopefully we can begin to pave the way for a better understanding of Aristo's Cynic impulses.

Is the theory of indifference as it is laid out above in the quotation from

---

11. Cf. ὁ τὴν ἀδιαφορίαν εἰσηγησάμενος at D.L. 7.37. Somewhat differently, J. Moreau, "Ariston et le Stoïcisme," *Revue des Études Anciennes* 50 (1948) 27–48 (here, p. 46 n. 1); Ioppolo (n. 7 *supra*) 158; see further M. Isnardi Parente, "Una poetica di incerto autore in Filodemo," *Filologia e forme letterarie: Studi offerti a Francesco Della Corte* (Urbino 1987) 90. For background and discussion of Aristo's heterodoxy and his Cynic contacts, see D.R. Dudley, *A History of Cynicism from Diogenes to the Sixth Century A.D.* (London 1937) 99–102; J.M. Rist, *Stoic Philosophy* (Cambridge 1969) 74–80; A.A. Long, *Hellenistic Philosophy: Stoics, Epicureans, Skeptics,* 2d ed. (Berkeley and Los Angeles 1986), 189–99; Ioppolo (n. 7 *supra*) 158–59 *et passim;* M. Schofield, "Ariston of Chios and the Unity of Virtue," *Ancient Philosophy* 4 (1984) 83–95; A.A. Long and David Sedley, *The Hellenistic Philosophers* vol. 1 (Cambridge 1987 [henceforth "L.-S."]) 358–59.

12. H. Schulz-Falkenthal ("Κατὰ φύσιν: Bemerkungen zum Ideal des naturgemäßen Lebens bei den 'älteren' Kynikern," *Wissenschaftliche Zeitschrift der Martin-Luther-Universität, Halle-Wittenberg,* Gesell.- und Sprachwiss. Reihe, 26 [1977] 51–60 [here, p. 53]) notes the lack of positive definition in the Cynic use of "natural." I take this absence, which is conspicuous, to be deliberate and significant.

Diogenes Laertius Aristo's final word on the matter? Cicero, following his source Chrysippus, assumed that it was (*De Fin.* 4.68–70), and until recently modern scholars for the most part went in his wake.[13] Cicero's reaction to Aristo's moral indifference (e.g., at *De Fin.* 3.50) is one of moral outrage, and his verdict is damning. To cite a recent paraphrase of his position, "unless there are intrinsic differences of value" between indifferent things, "the wise man will have no objective criteria for grounding his preferences."[14] Aristo can be saved, or so it has been imagined, by showing that he was capable after all of making rational choices: if indifferents can assume a momentary value (one defined by circumstances and the sage's moral judgment), the problem, it seems, is solved. But the question of momentary value is fraught with difficulties, as is the related notion of assuming value.[15] Worse still, as Cicero saw, it is the *whole* of life (*omnis vita*) that the issue of differentiation among things (*differentia rerum*) touches (ibid.). The question, then, is not how a choice can be grounded among indifferents, but what in the whole of life is *not* morally indifferent, when all things have been set on an equal basis (*rebus omnibus sic exaequatis ut inter eas nihil interesset*). Virtue and vice are the obvious answer. But locating these somewhere in life, and not just on its theoretical borders, is the problem that Aristo's theory makes excruciatingly elusive.

Cicero grasped one of the implications of Aristo's theory, even as he misgauged its thrust. Here, Cicero's instincts can reliably give us an insight into the paradoxical nature of Aristo's flamboyant ethics, and possibly the Cynicism that persists in it. Unless Cicero is exaggerating, which I think is unlikely here, in what way does Aristo threaten to render life *as a whole* completely undiscriminated (*confunderetur*)?[16] Cicero may be reflecting the Stoic view that virtue is a craft concerned with the whole of life (Stob. 2.66.17–67.4 [*SVF* 3.560]). If so, then Aristo's sage merely fails to practice virtue as a rational craft. But this cannot be Aristo's view, surely (Plut. *De Virt. Mor.* 441c); nor does it adequately capture Aristo's challenge to Zeno. To see why Cicero is in fact right, some further unpacking will be needed.

Aristo's notion of indifference (*adiaphoria*) is misleadingly complex, because it comes in two forms that shade off into one another: it characterizes anything that is external to virtue and vice (the so-called material of virtue, which is its sine qua non),[17] and it is the virtuous attitude toward this third, intermediary, and as it were extramoral sphere. Is virtue in the act or is it in

---

13. Rodier ("La cohérence de la morale stoïcienne," *Année philosophique*, 1904, 296 n. 3) and esp. Moreau (n. 11 *supra*) mark the turning point in another direction (see Moreau, ibid. 47, n.2).
14. L.-S. 1, p. 359.
15. For the concept, see Moreau (n. 11 *supra*) 29, 34, 36.
16. L.-S. 1, p. 359, where, however, the question is not squarely confronted.
17. *SVF* 3.114, 3.491 (Plut. *De Comm. Not.* 1069e; cf. Plut. ibid. 1071b and Cic. *De Fin.* 3.61).

the attitude toward the act? The question is not without its dilemmas. The usual solution, in the Stoa, is to distinguish morally indifferent acts that are performed with a virtuous disposition (appropriate acts thereby being perfected into right acts) from those performed with a vicious one. Indifference as a morally relevant disposition—one that is cardinal and decisive—is plainly no option. Aristo's sage, by contrast, will perform all his indifferent acts with a perfect indifference, the very hallmark of virtuousness. Henceforth, virtue threatens to collapse into a sheer and galling indifference: for there is no virtuous act that doesn't have as its descriptive content indifferent choices and acts (a thesis acceptable to a Stoic), and therefore no virtuous act that doesn't involve, centrally, a disposition of moral indifference (a consequence unacceptable on the Stoic perfectionist view). Surely the sage cannot be indifferent to all of his acts? At this point, Aristonic indifference reveals a further, pragmatic function, inseparable from its relation to virtue. Not only is indifference a moral criterion. Its prominence, both theatrical and rhetorical, has a strategic value, for it seems calculated to provoke moral reflection. Aristo's virtuoso sage, like the Cynics before him, can hardly have remained indifferent, in this sense, to his acts; nor can Aristo have been insensible to the unsettling effects his theoretical construction would have on those who received it. Indifference, in short, is difficult to read. And that is part of its virtue.

Aristo's role, as he conceived it, was to foreground the difficult semantics of indifference, in part by insisting on the strict identity of virtue and indifference.[18] Rather than make things in accordance with nature internal to virtue, as Antiochus would propose, Aristo pushed the view that indifference is internal to, and exhaustive of, virtue. It may be that actions, like circumstances, are morally indifferent (neither good nor bad) "when considered in abstraction from their agents."[19] If so, the problem is not just to point out what is morally indifferent, but to show how virtue consists in more than being able to make this abstraction. Aristo frustratingly offers little in the way of help, for to do so (he reasons) would make virtue itself into an abstraction. Meanwhile, the question of the nature of virtue is left dangerously open. In part as a consequence of the so-called Cynic shortcut to virtue, instead of showing a way to the good, indifference creates an abyss in front of it and even within it.[20] To state the issue in its most concentrated and most insoluble form, the form that Aristo gave to it, in what sense is the sage qua actor to be considered good? The same question could be put to Diogenes as he went about his daily exhibitionist routine. Nei-

18. For this identity without this particular paradox, see G. Striker, "Following Nature," *OSAP* 9 (1991) 1–73 (here, pp. 16–18); Ioppolo (n. 7 *supra*) 187; differently, Mansfeld (n. 9 *supra*) 341–42; and see *infra* n. 77.

19. L.-S. 1, p. 367.

20. D.L. 7.121; Plut. *Amat.* 759d; Cic. *De Fin.* 4.70. Cf. M.-O Goulet-Cazé, *L'ascèse cynique: Un commentaire de Diogène Laërce VI 70–71* (Paris 1986) 22–28.

ther Diogenes nor Aristo is exactly forthcoming with an answer. It is arguable that they were less interested in supplying an answer than in provoking the question. It is this question that will be our focus in all that follows.

An Anonymous Stoic Theory of Indifference (Philodemus, On Poems 5)

I wish to suggest that in order to understand why Aristo couches his theory in the way that he does we must look into a somewhat neglected side of his interests, namely his theory about the linguistic expression of value, which is palpable in some of the ancient doxography that preserves (and often distorts) the relatively few traces of him that we have. But as if matters weren't complicated enough, there is yet another source of evidence that is of great potential relevance but of uncertain value: some eight columns of papyrus from Herculaneum (*On Poems* 5, cols. 16.28–24.22 Mangoni) containing a polemic by Philodemus of Gadara, the Epicurean watchdog from the last century B.C. The target of that polemic was identified as Aristo of Chios by the first editor of the papyrus, Christian Jensen, based on a partial reconstruction of Aristo's name and on inferences drawn from Philodemus's secondhand report. As Jensen was the first to point out, the view exposed in Philodemus intersects neatly with a theory of moral value, indeed with a theory that resembles what we know of Aristo's theory of indifference from other sources.[21] Even so, the connections between the columns of Philodemus and the fragments of Aristo remain strangely untested.[22] True, there is something counterintuitive about the possibility that Aristo would have ventured into the theory of poetry, given his rejection of logic and physics. On the other hand, Aristo was not innocent of logic, despite his protestations to the contrary, any more than the Cynics were defenseless before the snares of dialectic, which they both mimicked and detested.[23] His interest in poetry, if not in poetics, is well attested (and this will be discussed below), while his keen interest in language, never quite for its own sake but for the kinds of limits on human rationality that it both imposes and reveals, will be argued for in virtually all that follows. Moreover, the two sets of evidence, the fragments of Aristo and the columns from *On Poems,* can be mutually illuminating regardless of the identities involved (consensus has never been achieved): some theory of indifference and some dissident Stoic are

21. C. Jensen, *Philodemos über die Gedichte, fünftes Buch* (Berlin 1923) 128–45.

22. Cf. Schofield (n. 11 *supra*) 86, without any arguments as to *On Poems* 5. Ioppolo (n. 7 *supra:* 258–78), Isnardi Parente (n. 11 *supra*), and E. Asmis ("The Poetic Theory of the Stoic 'Aristo,'" *Apeiron* 23 [1990] 147–201) all discuss the Philodemus columns but offer no parallels to Aristo (apart from *SVF* 1.377).

23. See below on Antisthenes and Diogenes; and *infra* n. 42 on Aristo's rebuttal of Alexinus the Megarian, nicknamed *Elegxinos* for his sophisms (frr. 74, 76 Döring).

exposed in the Philodemus columns. Given the complexity of the material, only the salient points of comparison can be summarized here.[24]

The opponent under attack is said to be an adherent of the Stoics, but the fact that A. (the anonymous opponent in question) doesn't quite fall in with the mainstream Stoics (hoi panu Stōikoi) is an inference that can be made based on another fragment (*PHerc.* 403 fr. 4), possibly from the same book. The Herculaneum papyri give a glimpse of the orthodox Stoic view (esp. *PHerc.* 403, 407). One fragment puts the Stoic criterion of good poetry in the content alone (*sophēn dianoian,* "wise meaning," viz. "philosophically acceptable," and probably "morally good" meaning); another posits that the author of such poetry, who, needless to say, is the *sage,* is a good poet *in the proper sense* (*kuriōs*) of the term "good."[25] There are several indications that A., whose language may well be coloring this report, would have contested the presumption that goodness in the proper sense can be satisfied by poetry, which for him is morally indifferent regardless of its content, and therefore can (in his own, stipulative terminology) by considered good only *in an improper, figurative* sense (*katakhrēstikōs*), but not properly speaking. Poems may be instructive, and possibly morally instructive, at least in tendency; but this does not make them good in a moral sense (nor does it clearly make us, as readers, morally virtuous—not even in tendency). A. would have further pointed out that it is not qua sage that a poet is good qua poet, nor are poems philosophical to the extent that they are poetry; even Cleanthes had the sense to concede this.[26] Poems can only improperly be called good, because strictly speaking they are morally indifferent (viz. not good in the relevant, nonderivative sense of the word); hence, they are neither good nor bad. And the same holds for their makers, who cannot be called good poets except in an extended sense of "good."[27] A. goes on to justify his proper/improper distinction with a distinction of another kind: for "speaking *in absolute terms* (*kathap[ax leg]ōn*), ⟨poems⟩ are not good but are neither good nor bad, he claims, ⟨but if we judge them to be good⟩ they are good *in some respect* (*kat[a] ti*)," which is to say relative to their poetic and aesthetic merits (*On Poems* 5, col. 19 Mangoni).

What is striking about A.'s poetics is first of all the subtlety of his distinctions, which are aimed at extracting the moral and nonmoral senses of good-

---

24. For a fuller treatment of the papyrus columns, see J.I. Porter, "Stoic Morals and Poetics in Philodemus 403," *CErc* 24 (1994) 63–88.

25. *PHerc.* 403 fr. 4.12–18 (cf. C. Mangoni, *Filodemo: Il quinto libro della Poetica* [Naples 1993] 251–52) and fr. 3.7–15 (F. Sbordone, "Ancora un papiro ercolanese," in *Sui papiri della Poetica di Filodemo* [Naples 1983] 254–55); *PHerc.* 407 fr. 1 Mangoni ("Il *PHerc.* 407 della *Poetica* di Filodemo," *CErc* 22 [1992] 131–37). On the provenance of this report, see Porter (n. 24 *supra*) 76 n. 70.

26. Philod. *On Music* 4 col. 28 Neubecker.

27. See *PHerc.* 407 frr. 1–3.

ness from the ambiguities of ordinary language; second, his seemingly deliberate habit of passing back and forth between the two senses of goodness without explicit warning (without the aid of his disambiguating qualifications); and third, his studied denial of the unconditional sense of "good" to poems generally. The first two points touch his unstated strategy of argumentation, which seems designed to provoke a series of questions about the meaning of value terms in different contexts (such as the question, What does it mean to call an object like a poem good or bad?). The third issue in particular is a sticking point that touches Stoic doctrine. For, while the Stoics from whom he dissents would have accepted his overall framework, they would have resisted his conclusion that meanings, just by being in a poetic context, are in the first instance *poetic* meanings (the term is his), and that their moral relevance is therefore anything but clear. A.'s formal logic and even his distinctions are impeccably Stoic, but they are also more unyielding, and they lead to un-Stoic results. His fussiness over the labels used in value judgments and his admission, positively rare in ancient contexts, that suspension (*ephexein*) of moral judgment is a viable response to poetry suggest that more than most critics he was sensible to the frailties of moral abstraction as applied to poems.

With moral values thus suspended, A.'s gaze next falls upon all that remains, the genuine counterpart in his poetic system to the indifferents of his ethical system (if we can even talk about the existence of two distinct systems): verbal composition (*sunthesis*) or, in a word, the aesthetic qualities of language. *Sunthesis,* unlike meaning, is intrinsically and incontrovertibly adiaphoric—it makes absolutely no difference to one's moral happiness. And here A. surprisingly suggests that good *sunthesis* is practically sufficient to make a poem good in the restricted sense (col. 21). Hence the astonishing (but, in view of the above, intelligible) stress laid by A. not on meaning but on irrational pleasure, euphony, and composition, all of which serve as his privileged criteria of poetic excellence. But the complexity of his position does not end here. For A.'s embracing of the moral indifferents of poetry reveals a series of requirements that bear on the larger definition of moral indifference, of the sort that will reappear in the philosophy of Aristo of Chios.

What attracts A. to compositional features, as opposed to features of meaning, is ultimately the allure of the detail. Meaning, in the Hellenistic lexicon (for literary critics and philosophers alike) has something common or universal about it: it is a *koinon,* unless it is viewed, aspectually, for its linguistic properties, in which case it is *poetic* (qua element of *lexis*). But the aesthetic properties of poems, which are gauged by the ear, are constituted in the opposite way: they are an *idion,* uniquely specific to their immediate environments, and especially to their moment of sensation; they cannot be transported from their location without dislocation, whereas meanings are intelligible in virtue of their ability to mean across contexts. Hence A.'s view that the function of the critic's judgment is to register the idiosyncratic features (*idiotētes*) of poetic language (col. 24). *Idiotētes* here are a perceptual property. But even more important, they are an entirely *contingent* property, specific to the material event of a given sensation (involving this object, viz. this poem or verse, and this sense). Each poem in effect requires its own criteria of judgment, just as (and perhaps because) each has a distinctive set of sounds and other material and phenomenal attributes—not ideas, for these are in the public domain—that make it unique.

The admirable thrust of this position, which is adopted wholesale from a minor and unconventional school of thought in ancient literary criticism (exemplified by the euphonist critics known to us from Philodemus simply as the *kritikoi*),[28] lies in its recognition that there is something irreducibly particular about individual poems. In keeping with his bias in favor of poetic particulars, A. rejects the concept of absolute standards for judging poems, and instead rules in favor of aesthetic idiosyncrasy, though not exactly pluralism. A kind of ad hoc and circumstantial mode of judgment appears to carry the day, for only so can the (as it were) proprietary features of individually crafted lines and even words be fully appreciated. We might call this position A.'s absolutism of the particular—of this particular poetic effect in this poem, which exists per se, is incomparable to any other, and is not bound by evaluative rules, apart from the empirical criterion of euphony (viz. pleasure). In consequence, A.'s theory of poetic excellence gives us an excellence in a figurative sense: *poems are not so much good as they are absolutely unique.* Finally and remarkably, aesthetic values, which exist as much in the perception of a work as in the work itself, are never wholly intrinsic to the work, or intrinsically preferable; nor are they simply natural. Poems are not naturally beautiful, even if their beauties are apprehensible only through natural acts, such as empirical sensation. Why one poem is preferred to another, or warrants the label "good," ultimately has to do with literary tastes and sensibilities that are tied to an awareness of artistic techniques, practices, and conventions. The same ought, one should think, to apply to the very perception of poems as bearers of unique properties. But that paradox is another story. In any event, natural inclinations are not irrelevant, but neither are they all-decisive, on this theory about poetic *sunthesis.*

A.'s theory can be said to pave the way for a Stoic appreciation of the art of poetry for its own sake (*kath' hautēn*), and not for what poetry contains. Only, the price to be paid for this appreciation is the provisional surrender of the tag "Stoic" itself. At this point, A. is himself a *kritikos,* enjoying the particulars of poems viewed apart from their moral relevance. And here, within the frames

28. D. Blank, "Diogenes of Babylon and the κριτικοί in Philodemus: A Preliminary Suggestion," *CErc* 24 (1994) 55–62; J.I. Porter, "Content and Form in Philodemus: The History of an Evasion," in *Philodemus and Poetry: Poetic Theory and Practice in Lucretius, Philodemus and Horace,* ed. Dirk Obbink (Oxford 1994), 97–147, esp. 133–42; id., "Οἱ κριτικοί: A Reassessment," in *Greek Literary Theory after Aristotle: A Collection of Papers in Honour of D.M. Schenkeveld* (Amsterdam 1994) 83–109.

of a qualified perception, he can throw himself—not as a Stoic, but as a connoisseur of poetic phenomena—into his aesthetic appreciation, with an enthusiasm as unconditional as any literary critic could show. It is an enthusiasm that was mistaken by Philodemus for an uncritical zeal, whereas in fact it may have been no more than a pose, masking (or just marking) a deeper, moral, indifference.[29]

The Philodemus columns at the very least offer a pretext for an investigation into the meaning and implications of indifference in Stoic contexts. Aristo, its most energetic proponent, was famous for expressing his divided allegiance to the Stoa with the concept.[30] But what evidence is there that he was even interested in literary questions? For Aristo, poetry would have doubtless fallen under the vast category of the ethically indifferent. Even so, poetry everywhere marks his style of philosophizing. His arresting literary similes, the poetic diction of his writing (Sext. *M* 7.12), and his nickname of "Siren," earned on account of his bewitching rhetorical powers (D.L. 7.160), all suggest a considerable literary flair. Some of the evidence may reflect his Cynic tastes: his parodies of Homer, his epigrams (if they are his) and other verses, possibly a diatribe.[31] Much of this would have been aired in the famous Cynosarges, traditionally linked to the origins of Cynic teaching, and even to the origins of the name "Cynic" itself.[32] Strabo indicates the influence Aristo exercised on Eratosthenes.[33] Was it also for the elevation of aesthetic pleasure over didacticism that Philodemus's opponent commends?[34] It is not only conceivable but probable that Aristo would have sided with Eratosthenes against the long-hallowed view that poetry is a kind of first philosophy, the earliest source of moral instruction and discipline (Strabo 1.2.3; Plut. *Mor.* 15f, 36d–37f). Aristo's antipathy to moral instruction of any kind is well known, and essential to understanding his philosophy. Finally, no titles of works by Aristo devoted exclusively to poetry survive, but several are broad enough to have included such a discussion (D.L. 7.163). That they may have is supported by the tantalizing mentions, in connection with Aristo, of tragedy, catharsis, Homer, and

29. This gives the answer to the puzzle stated most bluntly by Robert Philippson in his review of Jensen's edition (*Philologische Wochenschrift* 44 [1924] 417–21; here, p. 420): Why is it that *euphony,* an indifferent, could be made a requirement of good poems?

30. Cf. [Philod.] *Ind. Stoic. Herc (PHerc.* 1018) col. 10.8–13 Traversa (*SVF* 1.39).

31. Ioppolo (n. 7 *supra*) 82; cf. Bion of Borysthenes, fr. 7 Kindstrand (D.L. 4.52); J. F. Kindstrand, *Bion of Borysthenes: A Collection of the Fragments with Introduction and Commentary,* Acta Universitatis Upsaliensis, Studia Graeca Upsaliensia 11 (Uppsala 1976), 79–82; further evidence is cited in Porter (n. 24 *supra*) 66–67.

32. D.L. 7.161, 6.13.

33. Strabo 1.2.2 (*SVF* 1.338); cf. *SVF* 1.341.

34. Eratosthenes wrote a work with the title *Aristo.* It dealt with pleasure and its positive relation to virtue (φιληδονία: Athen. 7.281d [*SVF* 1.341]; cf. *SVF* 1.375, 408). Eratosthenes' affinity for Bion (D.L. 4.52) is remarked upon by Strabo (1.2.2), possibly in connection with Aristo. See further Ioppolo (n. 7 *supra*) 183–87; Jensen (n. 21 *supra*) 145.

possibly of mimetic arts in another papyrus from Herculaneum, a work in all likelihood composed by Philodemus, and one that deserves to be reread (*Ind. Stoic. Herc.* [*PHerc.* 1018], cols. 33–36 Traversa).

None of this is decisive, however suggestive and tantalizing it may be.[35] There are gaps in our evidence as well.[36] In addition, there is the precedent of Zeno's own excursions into poetics. From Dio Chysostom we know that Zeno apparently went to great lengths to save Homer from self-contradiction, by distinguishing the truths from the false opinions contained in his poems. Zeno established that he could find nothing to fault Homer by, and his method was subsequently taken up by his disciple Persaeus and unnamed others.[37] Now, Aristo had every reason to confront Zeno on this issue, given that he made a point of doing so in everything else. (Nor were his relations with Persaeus always harmonious.)[38] Again, the correction would have amounted to a clarification of Stoic logic, around the question of what it means to discover truths in a poet like Homer. Zeno's starting point would have appeared badly misconceived to Aristo: the only relevant truths are moral truths, and these will be found written down in no book (not even in Aristo's own writings).[39] Aristo has a much more elegant way of saving Homer's appearances: by viewing them indifferently—even if this should mean conceding to poetry a pleasure of its own and apart, or confessing to a fondness for the vehicle of literature in his own philosophizing.[40] As the quotation above from Diogenes Laertius shows, Aristo's own moral theory already gestures toward the domain of the literary (epic and drama), not to say the theatrical.

It is, at any rate, questions like these that A.'s theory of poetic judgments addresses. Indeed, that theory is best seen as an exercise in value determinations, and perhaps as an experiment in the application of a general theory or critique of value, of the sort implied (or possibly inspired) by Aristo's ethical framework, to which we now return.

---

35. Note, however, that while much of the evidence for the mainstream Stoic interest in poetry is at worst damning and at best equivocal, none of the evidence for Aristo points to a condemnation of poetry. See Porter (n. 24 *supra*).

36. Diogenes' catalogues of titles, for instance, can be incomplete (cf. R. Blum, *Kallimachos: The Alexandrian Library and the Origins of Bibliography,* trans. Hans. H. Wellisch [Madison 1991], 62). Zeno's pupil Persaeus of Citium is said to have written on Homer (*SVF* 1.456), though there are no titles on record to show for this (D.L. 7.36). On Aristo's possible grammatical interests, see Ioppolo (n. 7 *supra*) 279–90.

37. Dio Chys. *Or.* 53.4 (*SVF* 1.274, 456); cf. A. A. Long, "Stoic Readings of Homer," in R. Lamberton and J. Keaney, eds., *Homer's Ancient Readers: The Greek Epic's Earliest Exegetes* (Princeton 1992) 41–66 (here, pp. 59–60).

38. D.L. 7.162, Athen. 251B. Persaeus's disciple Hermagoras wrote a dialogue bearing the title *Anti-Cynic* (*Suda* s.v. "Hermagoras")—one further index of alignments within the older Stoa.

39. Cf. Sen. *Ep.* 94.2–4, and below.

40. The anecdote related in Ael. *Var. Hist.* 3.33 (*SVF* 1.337) is consistent with this position: nothing but philosophy withstands comparison with philosophy.

Contingencies and Value
Aristo's Critique of Stoic Semantics

A passage from Sextus (*M* 11.64–66 = L.-S. §58F) is often taken to show that despite Cicero's claims to the contrary (as witnessed at the outset of this essay) Aristo was able to ground his choices and actions in a rational way. The passage represents a continuation of Aristo's defense of the indifferents. Against the Stoics, Aristo denies that health and everything similar to it are preferred indifferents: there are circumstances in which a sage would opt for sickness over health, for instance (on the scenario he paints) when sickness is the price to be paid for freedom from tyranny and release from destruction, as against servitude and destruction, the consequence of being healthy. Aristo's claim is that indifferents, which are said to be preferred, are not unconditionally (*pantōs*) preferred. But neither are they naturally (*phusei*) or necessarily (*kat' anagkēn*) preferred. Quite the contrary, indifferents, being absolutely (*katholou*) without difference as between virtue and vice, have no difference at all; only circumstances vary, and the sage must adapt himself to these.

The claim that indifferent things absolutely have no difference amounts to the claim that indifferents, viewed absolutely, cannot be distinguished on intrinsic criteria or on natural grounds: their differences reside, rather, in their contingent relation to circumstances and, what is equally important but insufficiently heeded in discussions of Aristo, in their linguistic expression as well. Aristo is not denying that indifferents can become preferred or dispreferred. His point is that if and when the sage selects an indifferent, he won't commit the mental error of judging a preferred indifferent to be unconditionally, naturally, or necessarily preferred, let alone good (in the unrestricted sense of "good").[41] Indeed, to mislabel health as naturally preferred would be to commit an error of moral judgment. Compare his criticism of Zeno from the same passage (11.64–65): "To call (*legein*) [health] a preferred indifferent is *equivalent to judging it to be good and different* [from what is good] *practically in name alone.*" Clearly, labeling our judgments correctly is as important as making correct judgments, and in fact these amount to the same thing. Hence the particular stress in the passage on the problem of naming in moral language and in philosophical discourse. (It is an emphasis that will recur in other, unrelated testimony as well.) Aristo is in effect correcting Stoic logic and semantics, in part by recasting Zeno's language in terms of a *distinguo* not employed by him, namely the contrast between relative and absolute meaning.[42] But in

---

41. Cf. Sext. *P* 3.192–93.

42. See discussion *infra* in text at n. 62. On the Stoic exegetical revision of Zeno, see M. Schofield, "The Syllogisms of Zeno of Citium," *Phronesis* 28 (1983) 31–58. That Aristo defended Zeno's logic seems likely: see Sext. *M* 9.109–10; the title preserved in D.L. 7.160, *Reply to Alexinus's Objections* (*SVF* 1.333); von Arnim, *SVF* 1, p. 76 n.; Ioppolo (n. 7 *supra*) 41, 69–72; Schofield, "Syllogisms" 38 ("*via* Aristo's attack").

confirming indifference in its strictest possible sense, Aristo is doing more than clarifying Zeno's words; he is reconceptualizing the category itself, and broadening its application. The revisions go right to the heart of Zeno's teaching. For in their absolute indifference relative to everything save virtue and vice, the scope of indifferent things now maps onto the whole circumstantial fabric of life, which forms the background and the occasion for virtuous behavior. By viewing moral differences as constituted exhaustively in relation to what is, absolutely speaking, morally indifferent, Aristo raises the question of what it is that makes a difference a moral one, and how it is that virtue expresses itself in action. As we shall see, pressing these issues to a disturbing extreme is characteristic of Aristo's way of philosophizing.

How does Aristo's supremely indifferent sage make rational choices (and not just rational judgments)? The answer is far from evident, although Aristo's position is often viewed as if it were. Zeno apparently held that preferred values approximate somehow (*suneggizein pōs*) to the nature of good things.[43] No such approximation is tolerated on Aristo's ethics (just as he has no patience for Zeno's notion of prokopē, or moral progress), in the light of which Zeno's preferred health would have to be acknowledged to be a catachrestic good, in the sense we encountered above in Philodemus. Perhaps this is all that "somehow" above is meant to say; if so, then "approximate" requires explanation.[44] For Aristo, indifferents never do, properly speaking, have a value. If nature is no criterion of their value, then what is? At most, indifferents can be thought to be possessed of a value that is not properly or objectively theirs. Consequently, on Aristo's reasoning (which goes against Zeno's express intentions), Zeno's sage will have chosen health *as if* it were a good. In that case, momentary value (what Moreau calls *valeur de circonstance*) just comes improperly with the expression of the judgment that an indifferent is choiceworthy in a given circumstance.[45] It may be that it is psychologically unavoidable not to assign or express some kind of value whenever a choice among indifferent things is to be made in a given set of circumstances. But this only begs the

43. *SVF* 1.192. Further, Long (n. 3 *supra* [1967]) 66 with n. 20.

44. Chrysippus's defense of the equivocal use of "good" in moral discourse, especially as applied to indifferents, may be a retrospective defense of Zeno: some of Zeno's value terms are properly meant (κυρίως); others have a more relaxed sense (Plut. *De Stoic. Rep.* 1048a, D.L. 7.122), especially those statements that give the appearance of Cynic absolutism. Chrysippus may well be responding to Aristo. The claim that all words are naturally ambiguous (*SVF* 2.152) is part concession and part counterargument, since Aristo denied any natural status to language (see below).

45. For a defense of Zeno's logic, see *SVF* 3.698, 3.137; and M. Frede, "The Affections of the Soul," in M. Schofield and G. Striker, eds., *The Norms of Nature* (Cambridge 1986) 108. I regret that C. Atherton's relevant study *The Stoics on Ambiguity* (Cambridge 1993) appeared too late for me to take it into account in the present essay; but see her discussion of the coherence in Stoicism of linguistic, moral, and psychological considerations, particularly as regards the indifferents (pp. 55–61). Further, Plut. *De Stoic. Rep.* 1048a; and cf. B. Inwood, *Ethics and Human Action in Early Stoicism* (Oxford 1985) 95, 199.

question of what it means for something to assume value. And it still leaves unclear what a *proper* ascription of value ("good" in the proper sense) will amount to. Aristo's sage may be capable of rational selection, but the basis of his choices (the source of their value) is nowhere spelled out, beyond the formal appeal to a knowledge (of good and evil things) that, in the absence of any reference to particulars, is conspicuously lacking in content. This is no accident of doxography: Aristo simply never fills in the blanks. The logic of circumstantial value, and thus of virtuousness in the face of circumstances, is hardly self-evident, and so too the Sextus passage takes us a little further than the simile of the actor from Diogenes Laertius (7.160), but not much.

Language and Nature

Having established the proximity of judgment and language, Aristo goes on to demonstrate the elusiveness of both, especially as concerns the problem of naming virtue in its particular manifestations or expressions. As we shall see, language for Aristo is nothing if not a realm of provisional differences (if you like, of choices made according to circumstances but not nature); and the field of ethics has something equally and ineluctably provisional about it as well. Such considerations disturb the concept of value.

Value (*axia*) enjoyed a privileged criterial position in the Stoa, standing as it did in an intricate relation to goodness, virtue, and choice, and being reducible moreover to two kinds, relative or absolute.[46] In taking a hard look at the semantics of value ascriptions and especially at the incommensurability of these two kinds of value, Aristo is attacking some of the foundations of ethical theory from two different directions at once. On the one hand, he is asking us to reflect on a conception of virtue that lies beyond the contingencies of value and expression (virtue's absolute condition). But on the other, he is asking us to question what the value of such a virtue is, if it indeed does lie beyond our power to describe and account for it.[47] How adequate is language to the task of moral evaluation? This is Aristo's guiding worry. The question is aimed primarily at the class of professional moral philosophers he would gladly have labeled ethicists, but it occasionally takes the form of a reflection on the nature of language itself.

Now, language for Aristo is a paradigmatic but also pivotal realm of contingency. Located within us, as a central component of rationality, its vagaries strongly resemble external contingencies. At best, it is a conventional instrument, not participating in any natural order. By taking such a view, Aristo

---

46. Stob. *Ecl.* 2.83.10 [*SVF* 3.124], D.L. 7.89, Cic. *De Fin.* 3.33–34. The distinction could be reapplied to the indifferents themselves; ἅπαξ: D.L. 7.104; πρός τι: Stob. 2.79.18–82.21 (*SVF* 3.140), a distinction possibly forced into the open by Aristo, as the Sextus passage and *SVF* 3.137 suggest.

47. *Pace* Bréhier, "Sur une théorie des valeurs" in É. Bréhier, *Études de philosophie antique* (Paris 1955) 229–32.

could not diverge any further from orthodoxy even had he wished to do so.[48] Stoicism, by contrast, holds to a naturalist theory of the relation between language and reality. The natural world is rationally coherent, and language is naturally, not conventionally, coherent too.[49] A nice illustration of Aristo's clash with Stoic orthodoxy comes in the sequel to the Sextus passage quoted earlier, where the focus turns primarily to linguistic difference, which is to say to the conventions of linguistic usage and names. For in the case of names "we put different letters first at different times, adapting them to the different circumstances (*pros tous diaphorous peristaseis artizomenoi*)," as with "Dion," "Ion," and "Orion," "*not* because some letters are chosen over others by nature but because the circumstances (*tōn kairōn*) compel us to do this" (*M* 11.67).

Once again, Aristo is attacking Zeno's theory of natural preferences and its nomenclature, this time through the analogy of language itself. The denial of the role that nature plays in both cases (moral and linguistic) does not seem to leave room for a fundamental and positive role for nature, which is on the contrary left hanging desperately in the balance. I take it that there is something especially paradigmatic about this conception of the way in which language operates: it runs implicitly against the grain of Stoic beliefs; and, at least in its intention, it has an obvious analogy to moral choices and acts. Is the sage, in Aristo's hypothetical case, performing virtuously? It would seem that he is, just as a matter of definition: the sage is being shown to be self-consistent in his actions (self-consistently indifferent to indifferent things). If so, this raises a new set of considerations. Aristo is not affirming that whatever makes a moral difference is natural, necessary, or unconditional. Virtue is unconditionally good; but goodness and virtue are not realized in unconditional ways: they obtain only with reference to particular circumstances (*kata touton ton kairon*), and, in a crucial sense that still needs to be explored, they are necessarily conditioned by this reference.[50]

The mention of necessity ("compel") in the analogy draws attention to this ineluctable point of reference in the performance of virtue (which for Aristo is not distinct from a virtuous disposition, but is just its active possession). Available choices are a constraining factor, and no choice is without some constraints. But neither is Aristo suggesting that, even if virtue is one thing, there

48. Cf. Long (n. 11 *supra*) 125.

49. Cf. A.C. Lloyd, "Grammar and Metaphysics in the Stoa," in Long (n. 3 *supra* [1971]) 58–74 (here, p. 62): "So too, a lesson in 'orthography' was [in the Stoa] as objective as a lesson in nature study." Further, D. Blank, *Ancient Philosophy and Grammar: The Syntax of Apollonius Dyscolus* (Chico 1982) 8, 12–13, 16–17, 30–31, on the natural necessities governing the formation of words from letters in Stoic grammar (cf. *SVF* 2.148 [Chrysippus]; and, e.g., Ap. Dysc. *Synt.* 2.3–3.2; cf. ibid 16.6–11: language in its rational essence is not a thing constituted by chance). The premium put on etymologies and on original, natural meanings by the Stoics is symptomatic of their general view of the fit between world and word; nothing of the kind is to be witnessed in Aristo's philosophy.

50. Cf. Gal. *De Plac. Hipp. et Plat.* 7.2.434.31–436.7, 438.6–8 De Lacy (henceforth, *PHP*).

is necessarily only one way to respond virtuously in a given situation.[51] There is nothing fatalistic or deterministic about Aristo's ethics (on his scheme of things there is no natural order, and no objective totality, to which to appeal), whereas Chrysippus could write, in marked contrast to Aristo: "If I knew I was fated to be sick now, I would pursue sickness" (Epict. *Diss.* 2.6.9 [*SVF* 3.191]). Plainly, Aristo is contesting the Stoics' metaphysical nature as a way of grounding moral inquiry: the cosmos and its nature stand revealed to our senses as they are, or to the degree that matters to us (cf. Eus. *Praep. Ev.* 15.62.7 [*SVF* 1.353], Min. Fel. *Oct.* 19.13).[52] Aristo can appear a pure pragmatist and an agnostic on the question of nature, and this is partly a Socratic position. We will want to return to this question in a moment. But let us briefly take stock.

Two considerations seem to be relevant to anyone whose business it is to be a sage, and these seem to be radically opposed: virtue requires a correct knowledge of the moral qualities (absolutes) at play in any situation (most conspicuously, the status of indifferents); virtue materializes only in relation to the particularities of the situation at hand. This already points ahead to Aristo's theory of the virtues as relations, and of virtue itself as an absolute. But first let us consider the opposed tendencies just outlined. Only virtue makes a difference to one's happiness. Circumstances, by contrast, give grounds for choosing among morally indifferent things, in part just by differentiating them (*para tas diaphorous tōn kairōn peristaseis,* Sext. *M* 11.65); but those grounds are not morally decisive grounds. On Aristo's scenario, you may believe that it is better to be sick and free than to be healthy and in a state of servitude, all things being equal, but it is not strictly better, in a moral sense, to be these things: the sage's virtue will not be diminished or increased on either course of action.[53] On what rational grounds does the sage decide? In the present case, freedom preferred over sickness may reflect a purely *conventional* valuation; the sage, then, is an agent who performs his acts with a self-conscious adherence to a convention that others follow without reflection, confusing it (say) with their nature: this constitutes the moral superiority of the sage's role-playing, the tranquillity of his disposition and his supreme indifference. This is one way to construe the compulsion of circumstances: it is what results whenever you pair up occasions and conventional values, dictating no more than the way you sign your name. This may leave us to wonder to what degree conventional valuations come already scaled, let alone commensurable with circumstances that are unforeseeably unique, but more crucially, whether virtue for Aristo is reducible to acting on conventions. In an important sense it is (as we shall see below); but this doesn't account for the whole of Aristo's thinking, specifically the strain of

51. Cf. Striker (n. 18 *supra*) 20.

52. Also D.L. 7.162–63. For Zeno's foundationalist appeal to nature, see, e.g., D.L. 7.86–87, with Mansfeld (n. 9 *supra*) 332.

53. That is, unless *moral* destruction is meant. But this seems unlikely, since the sage, so long as he acts rationally, is in principle morally incorruptible. See further at n. 115 *infra*.

moral absolutism that is detectable even here, in the Sextus passage. Either way, Aristo's counterargument against Zeno not only is incomplete (he fails to give us enough of the relevant information to retrace the sage's decision); it seems to advertise its incompleteness. This too is, I believe, a calculated part of his philosophical strategy, which throws us, uncomfortably, into deeper, more searching reflection. Ultimately, the question Aristo would have us ask comes down to one issue: How do we name the moral qualities, the goodness, displayed by a sage at any given moment? This problem will be developed in the following pages.

Naming Virtue

First, a few quandaries. For Aristo health may be a natural item. But is it naturally indifferent? He nowhere denies that the good is naturally such. Yet what is its nature? If Aristo steers clear of questions like these (nature is conspicuously absent in his definition of the *telos*), it is not due to his fixation on the moral absolutes of his system (as he is so often portrayed), but due to his obstinate focus on values as they are deployed, in philosophy and in life. As a safe first approximation, we might say that for Aristo value determinations are in an important sense conventionally expressed even if they are not conventionally determined. The problem, however, is getting back to a value that is nonconventionally determined when the only language of evaluation available to us is itself so thoroughly convention-ridden. This needs to be expanded. Let us go back to the problem of names, which as we saw for Aristo are conventional in their appearance, and necessarily contingent.

Moral values are conventionally expressed if the language in which they are couched is a matter of convention. It is easy to infer from what we know about Aristo that he held this innocuous view, which he complicates in interesting ways. Compare his claim that virtue is like money (*SVF* 1.376): a drachma used to pay a shipmaster is called a fare, while the same drachma paid to a tax farmer is called a tax; to a landlord, rent; to a teacher, fee; to a seller, earnest money; and so on. Its exchange values, like its names, vary with the use, but the drachma apart from its transactions has no obvious function. The logic of the simile, one among several of its genre (fire, naturally one thing, burns various woods; a single knife cuts different objects at different times), may be playing off a Cynic conceit: the conventionality of monetary value and its plural (and debased) expressions was a staple of Cynic teaching.[54] Aristo may not

---

54. Aristo's claim is paradoxical: virtue and money ought to be antithetical. Contrast Sext. *M* 11.60 (*SVF* 3.122), where the drachma is used in a Stoic analogy to represent the indifferents. On the Cynics' contempt for received value and currency, see, e.g., D.L. 6.71; G. Calogero, "Cinismo e stoicismo in Epitteto," in *Scritti minori di filosofia antica*, ed. G. Giannantoni (Naples 1984), 395–408 (here, pp. 402–3); H. Niehues-Pröbsting, *Der Kynismus des Diogenes und der Begriff des Zynismus* (Munich 1979) 55–79; Branham (this volume).

have gone so far as to proclaim a defacing of the currency; but his comparison of virtue's appearances with various financial transactions, and of virtue itself as their betokened identity, points directly to the ultimate pragmatic relevance of any *summum bonum.*

If these somewhat heterogeneous examples are meant to suggest that virtue has a single nature but different conventional names, we are nonetheless left in the dark as to what its single nature might be. It ought to be like the nature of money. But what is that? Other texts go further than this in casting doubt on the viability of nature as a criterion of identity. From Plutarch as we know Aristo's view that *"by nature* there is no native land, just as there is no house or cultivated field, smithy or doctor's surgery: each one of these comes to be so, or rather *is so named and called, always in relation (pros)* to the occupant and user." [55] Cynic cosmopolitanism comes directly to mind, not orthodox Stoic views of exile and the reassurances of transcendental law. As Ioppolo observes,[56] Aristo is not interested in erecting a positive, natural ideal over the deficiencies of local examples of cultivated existence, as Zeno was. Aristo is affirming that where natural distinctions can no longer be said to obtain—and this appears to be everywhere one looks—linguistic considerations take over, not all by themselves, but as crucially *paired* with the range of circumstances that supply the ultimate distinguishing marks (*differentiae*) of any action or object of choice. In this respect, virtue behaves no differently, as the testimony on the relativity of the virtues elsewhere shows: it is crucially conditioned by its use. From this it follows that Aristo is a kind of nominalist; but then his own description of virtue begins to look suspiciously general too.[57]

If virtue's names are conventional (the word "virtue" being one of them, we might note), what about their meaning? I think Aristo deliberately leaves this question open: it touches, after all, the very substance of ethics. I doubt that Aristo wanted to claim that moral value is conventional or relativistic, even if he held that what passes as moral behavior, among the foolish mob or in more exalted circles, often is. His appeal to the unconditional nature of virtue is too insistent to be simply explained away like that. Similarly, I doubt whether he wanted moral value to be natural, if appealing to nature is supposed to exhaust what value (or virtue) is. Rather, it seems likely that Aristo's idea of nature is akin to the Cynic concept of the same: it is whatever comes naturally to the sage, as he adapts himself virtuously but indifferently to circumstances. (He may have termed this capacity "excellence of natural endowment," *euphueia.*)[58] If so, then Aristo and the Cynics had no concept of nature in some

55. Plut. *De Exil.* 600e (*SVF* 1.371); tr. L.-S. (§67H).

56. Ioppolo (n. 7 *supra*) 255.

57. On Aristo's nominalism, cf. Ioppolo (n. 7 *supra*) 228; Inwood (n. 45 *supra*) 204. Cf. also Cic. *De Fin.* 3.12–14.

58. *CPF* 1.1.22.1 T. The background to this polemical fragment is obscure, as is the precise position taken by Aristo (which may be dialectical only). See Schofield (n. 11 *supra*) 91; Ioppolo (n. 7 *supra*) 120–23, 234–36.

grand sense, as the Stoics did, but only of nature in this minor, and to all appearances ad hoc, sense.[59] It may be that nature is at bottom indifferent; more
likely, though, Aristo and the Cynics are simply indifferent as to its real nature.[60] As a consequence, both nature *and* convention come under attack. But
where the Cynics arraign popular and philosophical conceits for being unnatural (all the while promoting their own shockingly hormonal practices as natural), Aristo is content to attack the conceits of philosophers, and their views of
nature, for being conventions. (These, in turn, prove to be at least partly based
on popular and conventional intuitions: what counts as naturally appropriate is
a case in point.) In both cases, once the decks are cleared, so to speak, all that
remains is the difficult relation of virtue to individual acts and specific circumstances. Aristo, I believe, argued a version of the Socratic thesis about the unity
of virtue so as to expose this difficult relation, upon which the necessary coherence of any ethical project has to be premised.[61] Affirming the unity of virtue, in other words, accounts for only half of his argument.

The evidence for Aristo's version of the thesis is troubled: the reports seem
to come by way of Chrysippus, and Chrysippus seems to be contaminating the
language used to describe Aristo's own views. It may be that Aristo was re-
sorting to the Stoic category of the relatively disposed (*pros ti pōs ekhon*) to
express the way in which virtue comes to be known as particular virtues. Or it
may be that behind Chrysippus's polemical distortions, in Aristo's original account, lay the older and simpler (and broader) Academic distinction between
what something is or is called with reference to itself and what it is or is called
with reference to something else (*pros ti*).[62] I'm not sure the difference makes
much of a difference in the end. (Galen admits both kinds of distinction and
uses them interchangeably.)[63] Aristo's most general point would have been that
virtue is essentially one, but that it is in reference to individual circumstances
that we derive virtue's many names, the names of virtue in specific applications
(courage, practical wisdom, moderation, etc.). The problem brings us back to
the question of labels and language in moral philosophy.

One of the two versions of Aristo's thesis that are retailed by Plutarch speaks
to this question directly: "It was *by relativity* (*tōi pros ti*) that he named the
virtues in a way (*pōs*) different and plural." [64] "In a way" is a way of acknowledging the breach of linguistic propriety (catachresis) that using relative predi-

---

59. See Branham (this volume).

60. Perhaps tellingly, no consensus about the Cynic conception of nature exists today. Calogero (n. 54 *supra:* 402–3) and Moreau (n. 11 *supra:* 46) argue that the Cynic reduction of nature
is a way of securing moral autonomy; for a somewhat different restriction on the concept, see Long
(this volume).

61. Previous treatments include Dudley (n. 11 *supra*) 108–9, Ioppolo (n. 7 *supra*) 208–43,
and Schofield (n. 11 *supra*).

62. Cf. D. Sedley, "The Stoic Criterion of Identity," *Phronesis* 27 (1982) 255–75 (here,
p. 273 n. 21); Schofield (n. 11 *supra*) 89.

63. E.g., *PHP* 7.1.430.33 (κατὰ τὴν πρός τι σχέσιν), 438.8 (ἐν τῷ πρός τι).

64. Plut *De Virt. Mor.* 440e (*SVF* 1.375).

cates can entail. But the insight goes more deeply than this, for in this case *it is the virtues themselves,* and no longer qualities like goodness, that are being shown to be the relative predicates. Relative to what? If the virtues were relative only to virtue—that is, if they were its mere *skheseis* (Chrysippus *ap.* Plut. *De Stoic. Rep.* 1034d)—Aristo would be guilty of establishing a purely logical nuance. Chrysippus surely thinks that he is, but his translation (if that is what we have) of Aristo's meaning into category relations has a more damaging effect, because it reverses Aristo's point. The virtues are not relations *of virtue;* they just are what virtue is when it stands *in relation to things.* Now, it would be absurd, and a trivialization, if virtue stood in a merely logical relation to its objects and, what is even more important, if it could stand outside any relation to them. (Perhaps Chrysippus has too eagerly made an equation between indifference and such lack of relation.) Even if Aristo has in mind the Academic distinction between what something is (called) with reference to itself and with reference to something else, behind that distinction, in Aristo's mind, is the question, What does it mean to name virtue *without* the reference to this something else—that is, to the circumstances that enter into individual moral judgments? It would seem obvious, moreover, that taking such circumstances into consideration is what individuates particular judgments both from the generic disposition of virtuous knowledge and from each other: for virtue when it concerns what is to be done or not to be done is *phronēsis;* when it concerns desires it is *sōphrosunē;* when it concerns communal and contractual matters it is *dikaiosunē;* and so on.[65]

If that is Aristo's point, it is strangely put even in his own terms. For if what is being exercised in the virtue called justice is virtue in the proper sense, is justice a proper or improper name for virtue? The answer seems to be that justice improperly names what virtue properly is. In the same way (Aristo argues) any act of vision is always contingent on the objects seen, and is therefore properly speaking an exercise of vision (an unqualified seeing), while improperly speaking it is a this-seeing: for example, a white-seeing or a black-seeing.[66] The different names for virtue are clearly improper, but not so the reference to virtue they contain. It is tempting to read this thesis as a reduction of the virtues to their singular essence (and this, presumably, in the name of a return to Socratic, unitarian rigor). But however much the analogy points up the absurdities of naming vision by its objects, it does bring out in equal measure a paradoxical antithesis. Vision is not anything unless it is of something; we do not see unless we also see things. But then, we cannot be virtuous unless we put ourselves in relation to the practical circumstances by which our judgments, and possibly

65. Plut. *De Virt. Mor.* 440e–f.

66. Plut. *De Virt. Mor.* 440E–41D. Cf. Schofield, (n. 11 *supra*) 89, 91; L.-S., I 179. I agree with Schofield (*ibid.* 89) that the position presented here is Aristo's even if Plutarch is expounding it in his own language. The visual analogy, whether authentic or in Aristo's spirit, points to a dispositional change (see Galen, *PHP* 436.4–7; 438.6–7; L.-S, I 384).

our acts, come to be known, and mislabeled, as distinct virtues. It is crucial to realize that in affirming the unity of the virtues Aristo is not negating them; otherwise, the theory would make no sense. If virtue is one, it is identical with its relations: they do not vanish before virtue; in some sense, it is virtue that vanishes in them.

We should perhaps see their unity as a dialectical one. In Aristo's argument we find an emphasis that points us in two directions at once: toward virtue apart from its relations, and toward the relativities of virtue. The distinction is between virtue in and of itself (in relation to itself and, as it were, in the absolute) and virtue in relation to circumstances, which impinge on it and in crucial ways delimit it. There is a Socratic tension here, one that needs to be underscored. If virtue is a matter of knowledge, it is not an inert activity: whatever its content might be, it is ultimately aimed at action. Thus, if Socrates is the inspiration, we cannot appeal to virtue's oneness unless we also acknowledge the practical dimension of Socratic virtue, not to mention its complete absence of dogmatic content.[67] Significantly, Aristo, like Socrates, nowhere tries to *collapse* the basic distinction between virtue and the virtues: virtue is not privileged over its applications (they are, after all, its instances); rather, their tension is preserved, which by itself reveals quite a lot about the way Aristo felt moral problems ought to be analyzed. And as a result, it is *virtue* that is now beginning to look like an abstractly logical nuance, not its relativities, which serve to underscore the inescapably contingent nature of virtue. To resort to plainer language: a virtuous subject is like a navigator who knows how to face the changing conditions about him by adapting himself relative to them (*pros tauta pōs ekhonta*). The simile, evidently, is once again from Bion of Borysthenes, and Aristo is known to have used the same analogy for his own purposes elsewhere.[68]

Aristo's position is complex, because it combines a more or less open attack on the conventions of moral language—the virtue words—with an implicit attack on the place of virtue in them. In one sense, the virtues are "*only* different relations in which virtue itself stands to the different intentional objects one has from time to time to consider in the exercise of virtue." [69] In another sense, virtue is *nothing other than* its multiple relations—to objects, we must add, whose criterion cannot be that they exist only in our minds. To know that virtue is virtue, and is properly called virtue, qua knowledge of good and evil things, is not to know very much, and this is surely part of Aristo's point: such knowledge does not appear to give content to virtue, because it appears to be its

---

67. See Calogero's salutary reminder of this (n. 54 *supra*: 397).

68. *Teletis Reliquiae,* pp. 9.8–10.2 Hense (Bion; not in Kindstrand, but cf. Hense's note *ad* 53.15); *SVF* 1.396 (Aristo).

69. Schofield (n. 11 *supra*) 92 (emphasis added); similarly, Ioppolo (n. 7 *supra*) (e.g.) 228–29.

synonym; cast your eyes anywhere else, and you cannot avoid the conclusion (which Cicero grasped) that the whole of life is a domain made up by morally indifferent things.

Is performing virtue an indifferent act? At times it would appear to be, given Aristo's professions that virtue is invulnerable to fortune and his indifference to externals. His position is arch, but intriguing. Indifference appears to go all the way down. There are no appropriate acts in the Stoic sense; no circumstantial values in an objective (and therefore binding) sense; no one way to respond virtuously in a situation; no choices—of the kind Aristo seems willing to entertain, at any rate—whose consequences are so intolerable that a different result might be preferred to them.[70] "Ask Aristo if freedom from pain, riches, and health are good; he will deny it. Then are their opposites evils? No, by the same token" (Cic. *De Fin.* 4.69). Instead of helping us find our way as we seek to act on a moral impulse, Aristo leaves us with the problem, precisely, of identifying (naming) virtue in the particular actions of the sage, and indeed of identifying just what a moral impulse might be. The trouble is that whenever we think we can put our finger on some virtue, we find that we have only named it improperly; and, conversely, whenever we think we have named virtue (outside of its relations), we cannot quite put our finger on what it is that we have named.

Aristo's labeling virtue "health" (*SVF* 1.375) is another instance of improper naming, this time flagrantly flouting Stoic convention and, curiously, or just ironically, even his own (as reported by Sextus, above), the better to be able to make a point about the boundaries of all such conventions. As with the uses of money, or with fatherlands and smithies, Aristo seems to hold that language tends toward a nominalism when left to itself; that philosophers like Zeno tend to steer things back toward universal concepts; and that the proper task of the moral philosopher is to contemplate this dissonance, even if this means directing attention back again, and again somewhat nominalistically, to the world of particular actions, away from the more rarified world of ethical postulates and essences—and ultimately, too, away from language itself: for happiness is not something said in respect of the names that we attach to the happy life or man; it lies in the combined use (*kata tēn sugkhrēsin*) of all the virtues, each of which is the cause of its own particular effect (Clem. *Strom.* 1.19.98.1–2 [*SVF* 1.376]). Perhaps virtue is not only its abstract relations after all.

Aristo's theory of virtue needs to be further fleshed out. It may be that the theory is designed to be constitutively incomplete, forever in need of fleshing out, because questions about virtue can never be put to rest. Bernard Williams

70. See *infra* n. 114.

has written that "the road from the ethical considerations that weigh with a virtuous person to the description of the virtue itself [viz. whatever particular virtue is in question] is a tortuous one." [71] I do not believe that Aristo meant to suggest anything less important or even very different with his categorical refusal to remove any of the obstacles on the road from the virtues as denominated in the plural to virtue understood as a total characteristic. And yet, that road will of necessity be cluttered with descriptions, because moral reflection is immediately bound up with language (and the prolific quantity of evaluative terms in everyday language—words like "good" or "bad"—only serves to remind us of this fact). Aristo seems to be playing both ends of his dilemma at once, and at the extreme limits of Socratic moral discourse: there seem to be either too many names for virtue, or not enough to capture it adequately.

So, for example, the sage who chooses sickness over health in Aristo's hypothetical case above is exercising an unnamed virtue (one that would at least allow him to continue to exercise virtue). Aristo studiously, and characteristically, avoids filling us in on the content of virtue in the example given, and we are left with the implication, which is plainly circular, that a virtuous man will choose to be virtuous. (Chrysippus would attack him for such evasions.) [72] Here as elsewhere, Aristo's reticence is his way of making us hunger after the meaning or content of virtue, which is never exhaustively filled in, either in theory or in practice: not in theory, because theoretical virtue (knowledge in the abstract) is all but empty; not in practice, because (arguably) no single act consummates the whole of virtue, nor does any other additional act either. Virtue is inescapably relational—not just with respect to the way it is named, but to the circumstances from which it takes its hues. Here, Aristo successfully distinguishes himself from the reductive ethical monism of the Megarians or from the apparent Platonism of Menedemus of Eretria. [73] Aristo's thesis gives us a way to identify the relations of virtue as its momentary expressions, without revealing the single identity of virtue that stands behind (but not apart from) them. [74] They are, to use his own phrase, or its paraphrase, different (from virtue) in name alone. [75] Far from embracing a reductive thesis about the logical unity of the virtues, he is pointing to the requirements of action in life, and thereby to the difficulties of naming virtue from a philosophical point of reference. Virtue is anything but self-evident.

71. *Ethics and the Limits of Philosophy* (Cambridge, Mass., 1985) 10, a title that would have appealed to Aristo.

72. Plut. *De Comm. Not.* 1071f–1072a. Plutarch correctly calls Aristo's position an aporia.

73. D.L. 2.106, 7.161; Plut. *Virt. Mor.* 440e.

74. In this, it recalls sophistic puzzles about virtue, such as at Eur. *Pho.* 499–502 (with the scholia on vv. 501, 502).

75. Cf. *SVF* 1.376: "Each virtue is synonymously called [*sc.* "virtue"]" in addition to being called by its own (improper) name.

Aristo Cynicus

Put this way, Aristo's moral theory is no longer innocuous. It raises funda-mental questions, not just about how we call virtue by its many names, but about what it is that we call virtue, and how it is to be achieved. His aim may indeed have been "to weaken the hold the virtue words have on us";[76] it was surely not to sever the connection entirely. Rather, Aristo is pointing out the necessary but ineluctable dangers that pertain to moral discourse and to moral analysis generally. Far from revealing a continuity between the disposition of virtue in the abstract and its engagement in particular cases, his theory lays stress on the problematic gap between these two spheres; and bringing indif-ference centrally into the realm of virtue only intensifies the problem. I suggest that in placing the emphases in the way that he does, Aristo is reverting to a Cynic aporia, and powerfully challenging his Stoic peers to reexamine the question of virtue and value from the ground up. His approach to moral theory is anything but simple, and leaves one anything but complacent about the major concerns in moral theorizing. In short, Aristo's moral theory is not only turned against the Stoa; it is partly turned against itself. Ultimately, it is perhaps best seen not as a positive theory but as a strategy, one that reveals some of the pragmatic features of philosophy as it was waged in Hellenistic times.[77]

Aristo not only carved out a terrain of indifferents; he made living indiffer-ently the very *goal* of a life well lived (its *summum bonum*): such indifference is a decidedly moral goal, perhaps even the only legible mark of a virtuous man.[78] This alone would have sent palpitations through Zeno's heart. (For him, living harmoniously with nature was the ethical goal.)[79] Some overtones with Pyrrho's own version of skeptical indifference are perhaps audible here (the two are not infrequently mentioned in one breath by Cicero and others), nor can the ethical implications of Pyrrhonism be denied.[80] But Aristo is also ap-propriating the style and rhetoric of the Cynic philosophical attitude, which relies upon shocking its audience out of complacency and into genuine moral

76. Schofield (n. 11 *supra*) 89.

77. I use "Cynic aporia" in default of any better term. The aporetic side of Cynicism ought to fit well with readings of the Cynics as radically questioning all dogmatic assertions, e.g., those by M.-O Goulet-Cazé (n. 20 *supra*), M. Onfray (*Cynismes: Portrait du philosophe en chien* [Paris 1990]), and R.B. Branham (this volume). The notion of philosophy as praxis in antiquity is sorely in need of exploration (and definition).

78. D.L. 7.160, Cic. *Acad.* 2.130.

79. On this clash of perspectives, see Kidd (n. 3 *supra*) 165; and (e.g.) Sen. *Ep.* 89.13.

80. Cic. *De Fin.* 2.43. Cf. A. Brancacci, "La filosofia di Pirrone e le sue relazioni con il cinismo," in G. Giannantoni, ed., *Lo scetticismo antico* vol. 1 (Naples 1981) 213–42; L.-S. 1, pp. 21–22; and H.W. Ausland, "On the Moral Origin of the Pyrrhonian Philosophy," *Elenchos* 10.2 (1989) 359–434. On the Cynic roots of Pyrrhonian skepticism, see Brancacci, *op. cit.;* and A.A. Long, "Timon of Phlius: Pyrrhonist and Satirist," *PCPS,* n.s., 24 (1978) 68–91.

reflection.[81] How can indifference make a difference in life? How does one realize virtue in one's daily existence? The only matter for reflection that counts, for Aristo or a Cynic, is the always difficult relation between virtue and its place in the world.[82] The Cynics challenge us to find a solution, each exhibitionary act crying out for an answer to the question, If virtue is all that matters, where can it actually be seen and identified as such? It is upon this same problematic link that Aristo, practicing a kind of philosophical shamelessness, has us fasten our gaze.[83]

The problem of virtue's many names flows directly into Aristo's famous critique of precepts for conduct, known to us from Sextus Empiricus and, in a more expansive form, from Seneca.[84] Precepts (*praecepta*) are too general to apply *ad singula*, to particular circumstances (or even kinds of circumstances), which quickly exhaust them with their sheer contingency.[85] Dissatisfied with rules, Aristo resorts to paradoxes. If precepts must exist, then in a sense each individual kind of situation calls for its own precept (*atqui singulae* [sc. *species*] *propria* [sc. *praecepta*] *exigunt*, Sen. *Ep.* 94.15). Knowledge of what to do in any given case (*quid in quaque re faciendum*) is the province of the sage, who furnishes himself, so to speak, with precepts (*sibi ipse praecipit*, 94.2). Precepts are superfluous for the wise and ineffectual for the rest: for the wise are in no need of them, and the unwashed masses (the fools), if they could make use of them, would no longer need them either. General rules for conduct must, accordingly, go out the window. And the lever by which they are ousted turns out to be the particular, the contextual, the immediate, and the kairotic (cf. *kata touton ton kairon* in Sextus, above), which require not precepts but judgments. It is, after all, toward the uneven but concrete realm of human situations that ethical theorizing must in the end be aimed.[86] The sage does not simply know what is good and bad in principle: he knows *what he should do* in any given case, and can supply reasons for his actions. In fact, supplying reasons and knowing what to do may amount to the same thing. It doesn't follow that the

81. On indifference as the Cynic way of life (τὸ ἀδιάφορον τῆς ζωῆς), cf. Elias, *In Aristot. Categ. Prooem.* in *Aristotelis Opera* vol. 4, *Scholia in Aristotelem*, ed. C. A. Brandis (Berlin 1836), 23 = fr. I H 9 G.; Sext. *P* 1.152–55, 160; and see Calogero (n. 54 *supra*). Nietzsche knew how to realize the potential ironies of Cynical indifference (*Beyond Good and Evil* §9).

82. If the position is skeptical, it is in the constructive sense defined by Sextus, *P* 1.7, viz. "zetetic" (searching, reflective) skepticism. I owe this reference to Sara Rappe.

83. Shamelessness and philosophical *parrhēsia* are closely connected in the Cynics and in Aristo (cf. *SVF* 1.383). Cf. Zeno's ridicule of Aristo's glibness (D.L. 7.18), a charge elsewhere leveled against Diogenes the Cynic (F. Buffière, *Les mythes d'Homère et la pensée grecque* [Paris 1956] 375 n. 34).

84. Sen. *Ep.* 94 (the text shades off into commentary and critique); Sext. *M* 7.12 (*SVF* 1.356).

85. *Praeterea si praecepta singulis damus, incomprehensibile opus est* (94.14).

86. This is the inverse of the going view: "Mais c'est la moral pratique qu'il sacrifie" (Moreau [n. 11 *supra*] 43).

sage knows the one thing that ought to be done in a certain case; he simply knows how to act and how to justify his acts in a rational way. This ought to be true even if his acts are, in their immediate description, impulsive, or if they merely represent a personal or conventional preference—with the proviso, of course, that he will never mistake an indifferent for a good. In the end, the sage is accountable not to the public at large, but only to himself (*sibi*).

Specific precepts (rules) are thus shown to be incoherent or vacuous, but not because they are insufficiently general. Broader philosophical principles (*decreta*) fare no better if they are like rules, as Seneca himself thinks they are (*Epp.* 94.31, 95.10–12). But it is more likely that *decreta philosophiae* (94.31) refer to principles concerning the nature and identity of virtue (*constitutionemque summi boni*, 94.2) as Aristo conceived it,[87] and these, as we have already seen, yield no rules of conduct and still less any informative accounts of virtue itself; they verge instead on tautology (virtue is virtue).[88] Aristo's argument is deceptive. Arguing against particulars (as tied to rules), he is in fact arguing for them (minus the rules): for it is only in relation to particulars that philosophy receives the only content that matters in the end. A glance back at the theory of indifference we encountered in Philodemus can be illuminating. There, we found a rejection of generic standards for judging poems in favor of the irreducible phenomenal richness and particularly (*hai idiotētes*) of poetic language—what might be called an absolutism of the particular. Here, we find an equally frank recognition and promotion of the singular. There, the requirement of specificity led to the paradox that only the empirical sense of hearing and not some abstract criterial standard could provide an account of (or judge) a poem's phenomenal specificity; and implicitly to the further question of how individual instances could be measured by *any* standard. Here, Aristo reaches a parallel conundrum: judgments can be cast, but the language of the virtues will never be fully adequate to the job; indeed, if each instance calls for its own precept, commensurability across the lot of them becomes an overwhelming problem too.[89] But as we are seeing, such paradoxes go to the heart of the issue of criteria for judgment. Indeed, one of the primary aims of the moral philosopher appears to be to restrict the scope and even the presence of moral philosophy: *sine ulla doctrina, naturam ipsam secutus;* unburdened by any doctrine, even of nature, the philosopher aspires only to sage-

---

87. Cf. Sext. *M* 7.12—ὁ πρὸς ἀρετὴν λόγος, according to which life must be led.

88. "Aristo seems to have thought there could be no such general account, and hence refused to attempt one,"(Striker [n. 18 *supra*] 21); cf. Rist (n. 11 *supra*) 77–78; N. White, "Nature and Regularity in Stoic Ethics," *OSAP* 3 (1985) 289–305 (here, p. 305).

89. A similar problem of commensurability exists on the Stoic theory of preferred indifferents; see I.G. Kidd, "Moral Actions and Rules in Stoic Ethics," in *The Stoics*, ed. J.M. Rist (Berkeley and Los Angeles 1978), 250.

hood.[90] The Cynics' shortcut to virtue looms large here, for they were the true minimalists of morals in antiquity.[91]

In his return to the radical spirit, if not quite the letter, of the Cynics, Aristo strikes an uncompromising stance. He holds out on the one hand the image of the virtuous man, purged of philosophical and other obstructions,[92] who in response to changing circumstances effortlessly casts his morally unimpeachable judgment;[93] and, on the other, the image of the bungling, diseased, even mad fool who exhibits the widespread *insania publica*—with no ground intervening.[94] Indeed, one of the sage's fleeting thoughts might be to behave as a Cynic would.[95] But it is the absence of a middle ground, perhaps more than the Cynicizing image of the philosopher become a loose cannon, that Seneca finds inhuman and intolerable in Aristo's position. Aristo would reply that he has given us a middle ground, the area of the indifferents. But here, what emerges is that this zone covers the whole area of human conduct (Cicero's *omnis vita*), which can be acted upon by the virtuous or the vicious: it is the entire realm of particular circumstances, which escape generalizations and prescriptions but which nevertheless demand them. This realm of human exigency is the intolerably wide realm of human conduct:[96] one that is morally unsurveyable, but only visible in the way a pointillist painting dissolves into discrete (and, typically, difficult) moments. Seen in this light, virtue is no longer a sublimely simple affair, because it is intelligible and meaningful only when diffracted into virtues, and these are contingent on particular acts, like vision: this is their irreducible particularity.[97]

Likewise, Antisthenes had argued, nominalistically, that definitions of singular essences only touched intangible qualities (e.g., horseness), but not the thing itself (e.g., this horse, which I see with my eyes). Diogenes displayed a similar penchant for the concrete particular—spectacularly, everywhere he went, but closer to home, in his reported rejection of Plato's tablehood and cuphood in favor of visible and palpable tables and cups.[98] So perhaps it is in his bracing acknowledgement of the contingent and the particular, of life's circumstantial nature, that Aristo most approximates to his Cynic forebears.[99]

90. 94.12; Cic. *De Fin.* 3.11.

91. Cf. Antisthenes *ap.* Stob. 2.31 [fr. 21b Caizzi], D.L. 6.11.

92. Plut. *De Aud. Poet.* 42b (*SVF* 1.385), Sen. *Ep.* 94.5.

93. Cic. *De Fin.* 4.43; cf. 4.69: *quod erit cumque visum ages.*

94. Sen. *Ep.* 94.17, Cic. *De Fin.* 4.43 (cf. 4.69).

95. Cic. *De Fin.* 3.68 (it is clear to which camp Aristo belongs).

96. Cf. *De Fin.* 4.70.

97. Cf. White (n. 88 *supra*) 298.

98. For Antisthenes, Arist. *Met.* 1043b26; Simplic. *In Cat.* 8b25; frr. 44a–46, 50a Caizzi. For Diogenes, D.L. 6.53.

99. The pervasiveness of circumstantial logic in Cynicism is well brought out by Onfray (n. 77 *supra*), even if Nietzsche is too often summoned as doxographical evidence for the Cynics' views.

Aristo's evasions on virtue and its expressions are to be connected with this approximation; and so are other similarities between his views and those of the Cynics, some of which have already been signaled above.[100] It follows that a certain agnosticism, if not indifference, toward virtue in the theoretical abstract (as existing in isolation) is likewise incumbent upon the philosopher. Of course, the Stoics and especially Zeno in his youth were not untouched by Cynicism, as is well known. The extent of their commitment to Cynicism—a perpetual embarrassment to themselves and to others—is not always easy to ascertain, fraught as this history is with doxographical complication.[101] It is safe to say, however, that starting with Zeno himself the Stoa increasingly distanced itself from the more disreputable elements of the Cynic program. In other respects, though, a world of difference separates their outlooks.

Take circumstances. For Zeno and his followers, circumstances, unless they make no difference at all, define exceptional *departures* from morally appropriate conduct. The phrase used to mark the reference to circumstances, *kata peristasin* (likewise found in Cynic contexts),[102] is always mitigating—as is the attitude of indifference that accompanies acts made under their cover. Implied in this special pleading is a contrast with actions according to nature (*kata phusin*).[103] The only other contender, opportuneness of action (*eukairia; opportunitas*), is normative and deterministic, not circumstantial: it exists to prove the underlying conformity of nature and natural actions (*De Fin.* 3.45, 61; Plut. *De Stoic. Rep.* 1037e). For Aristo, by contrast, consideration of circumstances and a corresponding indifference toward them unexceptionally define the *condition* upon which all morally acceptable actions are predicated: nature is no criterion (unless acting with a view to circumstances just is natural, as the Cynics held), and it provides no framework into which to insert, and justify, actions. To borrow a later phrase (cf. D.L. 7.109), we might say that for Aristo actions are right if they are appropriate, never without reference to circumstances (*aneu peristaseōs*), but always in relation to them (*peristatika*). But if so, then we must add the following caveat, which stands Zeno's view of moral action on its head: where Zeno held that right actions are always appropriate, Aristo took the opposite view, that *there is no right action that is unconditionally appropriate.* This view he chose to express with the paradox that virtue is not an action, but virtuous beings must, nonetheless, act. Hence, for Aristo, virtue inescapably stands in some relation to action—one that is forever

---

100. *SVF* 1.353, D.L. 7.16, and Cic. *De Nat. Deor.* 1.37 (cf. Min. Fel. *Oct.* 19.13) all have parallels in Cynic thought. See Ioppolo (n. 7 *supra*) 251.

101. See Mansfeld (n. 9 *supra*).

102. The term itself is, I suspect, one of the traces they left behind them; see the epitome of Teles' work Περὶ Περιστάσεων (pp. 52–54 Hense); and *infra* n. 123.

103. κατὰ περίστασιν: D.L. 7.121. Indifference therein: Sext. *P* 3.200, etc. Cf. Mansfeld (n. 9 *supra*) 343; Philod. *De Stoic.* in T. Dorandi, "Philodemo, Gli Stoici (*PHerc.* 155 e 339)," *CErc* 12 (1982) 91–133.

submitted to ethical reflection, if not quite definition.[104] His impulse is a Cynic one, and he leaves us to contemplate the circumstantial facets of individual and social life, in all their disparity and contingency (and as mirrored in language). His distaste for moral precepts is of a piece with this critique.

One point of contact in particular needs to be mentioned, namely the mannerisms of predication practiced by Aristo, which are likely to have roots in the theory of Antisthenes and in Cynic practice. Antisthenes' puzzles about restrictive predication are both fascinating and bizarre. "Man is good," he would hold, is an improper predication, while (e.g.) "Man is man" and "Good is good," which answer to *ti esti?* ("What is X?"), are the only proper kind. (Cf. fr. 44B Caizzi.) This follows from the fact that the definition of a thing (its *logos*) is in principle impossible, because definitions, which are complex, may be analyzed into predicates, and these latter, listing only qualifications of a thing, do not bring us to the object itself, which is singular, like its name (frr. 47A–B). Hence, nothing can be described except by its proper name (*plēn tōi oikeiōi logōi*, fr. 47A). Only identical predications are admitted as proper by Antisthenes: differences, which can be expressed all day long, ultimately fade away into the horizon of false statements,[105] while the only genuine predications are mere stuttering tautologies ("X is X," "Virtue is virtue"; cf. fr. 60 Caizzi). The effect is to render the subject of the predication absolute and beyond compare. This, too, ought to have a familiar ring (compare Aristo's insistence that virtue's only proper name is itself).

Antisthenes' dialectical puzzles seem to be aimed at ethical applications; indeed, they raise fundamental questions about the status of moral discourse and instruction.[106] Antisthenes is laying stress not on the stability of eternal

104. The underlying logic of καθήκοντα (cf. D.L. 7.109), as described by G.B. Kerferd in "What Does the Wise Man Know?" in Rist (n. 89 *supra*) 125–36 (here, pp. 134–35), might appeal to Aristo, but not the Stoics' arguments for them, which are tied to intermediate values (cf. L.-S. §59 with discussion *ad loc.*). It is sometimes claimed that the orthodox Stoic view is that right actions receive their content according to circumstances, which vary, and hence κατορθώματα can't be specified in advance (so, e.g., B. Inwood, "Goal and Target in Stoicism," *The Journal of Philosophy* 83 [1986] 547–56 [here, pp. 553–54]). But no ancient text says this; and the position is essentially Aristo's, once we subtract the notion of objective rightness or εὐκαιρία. An interesting possibility, one that would have to be inferred, is that for both Aristo and the Stoics rightness of action is constituted only in the *retrospective account* of the action (a position recently hinted at by B. Williams in *Ethics and the Limits of Philosophy* [n. 71 *supra*]; cf. "Nietzsche's Minimalist Psychology," *European Journal of Philosophy* 1.1 [1993] 4–14). This, however, would again crucially compromise the objectivity of the account, and would make for a more dynamic account of moral explanation (one more suited, I think, to Aristo's tastes).

105. Frr. 47A–B Caizzi (ἁπλῶς and κυρίως appear in the same context). Antisthenes argues that contradiction is impossible if words are properly used, because "to contradict one needs to state a difference, but it is impossible to bring different *logoi* to bear on the one *logos* proper to each thing" (fr. 47B). The same holds for the impossibility of false claims.

106. Cf. F. Decleva Caizzi, "Antistene," *Studi Urbinati* 1–2 (1962) 48–99 (here pp. 58–59), on the moral implications of Antisthenes' puzzles, followed by A. Brancacci, *Oikeios Logos: La filosofia del linguaggio di Antistene* (Naples 1990). Antisthenes has not committed a fallacy of

truths, but on their remoteness from us. His constraints on signification, which are anything but naive, only press meaning—especially the meaning of ethical speculation—into nonsense; our focus is instead driven away from definitions and toward the realm of human activity and praxis (not least because propriety cannot be verified in language).[107] At any rate, such devices may have earned him the nickname *Haplokuōn,* or the Dog *Simpliciter,* if that is its meaning;[108] and they inspired Diogenes of Sinope to take up the equivalent thesis that it is impossible for a king to rule badly any more than a man can be good badly, because it is impossible for a king to rule in an unkingly way (*basileuein mē basilikōs*), or for a good man to be anything but virtuous.[109] In the wake of the Cynics, and more distantly Socrates, Aristo would press the limits of language into identical straits, achieving the same results. Aristo and his forerunners are in effect posing a rather shrill and disquieting version of the Socratic "What is X?" problem.[110] But neither are they carbon copies of Socrates.

Everything so far seems to point, interrogatively, toward the status of virtue itself. Aristo's reticence with regard to its content is equal only to the implication that its content is all that matters in life. In his double-edged rhetoric, Aristo appears to be reminding the Stoa once more of its Cynic roots. Goulet-Cazé describes the Cynic position on the goal of life as a deliberately untheorized one; the various definitions given for it—virtue, happiness, freedom from moral illusion, apathy—are so many aspects of the one end.[111] One might add that this reticence, which is both aporetic and negative (note their heaping of privative terms: *adiaphoria, atuphia, apatheia, adoxaston einai;* and compare the negative freedoms celebrated by the Cynics),[112] drives us to the other extreme, away from universals and toward the problem of specifying virtuous

---

confusion, but only an intentional (and sophistic) aporia, *pace* Decleva Caizzi, *op. cit.* 57; and W.K.C. Guthrie, *A History of Greek Philosophy* vol. 3 (Cambridge 1969) 215; cf. G.M.A. Grube, "Antisthenes Was No Logician," *TAPA* 81 (1950) 16–27. He receives more credit from M. Burnyeat, "The Material and Sources of Plato's Dream," *Phronesis* 15 (1970) 101–22 (here, pp. 112, 117).

107. D.L. 6.11 (fr. 70 Caizzi). See Long's remarks (in this volume) on what he describes as the Cynic challenge to unreflective views on the relation between language and ethical judgment.

108. D.L. 6.13 ("véritable chien": C. Chappuis, *Antisthène* [Paris 1854] 12); cf. Dio Chrys. *Or.* 1.61 (πεπαιδευμένος ἁπλῶς, οὐ πολυτρόπως), which may be Antistheneian (R. Höistad, *Cynic Hero and Cynic King: Studies in the Cynic Conception of Man* [Uppsala 1948] 180). Other speculations are possible. Cf. G. Giannantoni, ed., *Socratis et Socraticorum Reliquiae,* 4 vols. (Naples 1990), vol. 4, p. 229. That of LSJ (s.v.) is weak.

109. Dio Chrys. *Or.* 4.24–26 (fr. V B 582 G.); Decleva Caizzi, (n. 106 *supra*) 60. Cf. D.L. 6.40 (indicting accounts of essences); also, Plat. *Soph.* 251b; Stilpo frr. 197–98 Döring (where the same argument reappears); with Long (n. 80 *supra*) 72, 86 nn. 34, 35 on the uncertain relation between Antisthenes, the Cynics, and Stilpo.

110. Cf. the Socratic analysis of virtue at *Euthyd.* 278e–281e (unconditional ["strictly speaking"] and conditional goods); Long (n. 9 *supra*) 167; Vlastos (n. 8 *supra*) 228–31.

111. Goulet-Cazé (n. 20 *supra*) 35.

112. Cf. *SVF* 3.639 and, on Diogenes, Max. Tyr. *Phil.* 32.9 (fr. V. B 298 G.): ἀλλὰ ἄφετος παντὸς τοῦ δεινοῦ, ἐλεύθερος, ἄφροντις, ἀδεής, ἄλυπος, κτλ.

actions. Aristo, it seems, follows suit exactly. The radical insistence by both that *only* virtue is good in the proper, unrestricted sense (in other words, that virtue is the only good)[113] has the effect of reminding us how rare if not impossible to locate are the instances of virtue in the world, and how essential such location ultimately is. Conversely, putting indifference under the same constraints (of being absolutely and unqualifiedly [*haplōs*] indifferent: *SVF* 1.360) has the same effect. Virtue looks to be as indeterminate as the meaning behind the motley appearances of the word "dog," that ubiquitous leitmotif, counterideal, and virtual koan of the Cynic attack on the conventions of virtue, whether these are to be found in the lecture room or on the street.

In Aristo's wake, the foundations of Stoic dogmas could from now on be seen to rest on paradoxical grounds, or to call for an energetic defense. Some of that defense was offered first by Aristo himself. Perhaps Aristo's real point in the passage from Sextus above is not that the sage opts for freedom from tyranny and destruction (it is disputable whether, on Aristo's own terms, these so-called goods are intrinsically choiceworthy),[114] but that he opts, again in Cynic fashion, for freedom from the tyranny and strictures of moral dogma, the greatest anxiety to afflict any soul.[115] In one respect Aristo reapproximates Stoic ethical teaching, by vigorously facing the dilemmas it poses and from which it then compromisingly backs down. But in another respect he decisively parts company with Zeno and others, in his reconception of the way virtue and vice bound and define the indifferents absolutely and yet contingently in relation to them. And as such, absolutes can only with supreme difficulty, perhaps even only with supremest hypocrisy, pass into the conventional language of evaluation, which is the only language we know.

These two aspects of the problem as it was posed by Aristo perhaps go some distance toward explaining the oddity from which we set out: the sage as actor. Here at last we see why Aristo could illustrate his ethical teaching at his ethical best only through the example of his own theoretical practice (as opposed to dogmatic precepts) and through the aesthetic language of analogy: that is his version of the Cynic shortcut to virtue.[116] Here too we can better comprehend why Aristo's version of the Stoic sage might choose the part of Thersites or

---

113. D.L. 6.11–12; Schol. Lips. *ad Il.* 15.123 (fr. 56 Caizzi; fr. V A 192 G.): "If the sage does anything, it is in accordance with every [viz. the whole of] virtue [κατὰ πᾶσαν ἀρετήν]" (Antisthenes); Cic. *De Fin.* 3.11–12, 4.48–49 (Aristo).

114. Circumstances might conceivably turn these particular freedoms into constraints (if, say, my liberty is contingent on your servitude or destruction). Cf. D.L. 7.122 on moral and nonmoral servitude.

115. Cic. *De Fin.* 4.69. This motif is widespread in the Cynic literature, but cf. Diog. *Ep.* 37.6; Dio Chrys. 4.60; Clem. Alex. *Strom.* 2.20.121.1. "Servitude" has a strong and a weak sense for a Cynic too; cf. D.L. 6.74.

116. Cf. Sen. *Ad Luc.* 6.5: *quia longum iter est per praecepta, breve et efficax per exempla.* Cf. Jul. *Or.* 7; and H. Niehues-Pröbsting, " 'Der kurze Weg': Nietzsche's 'Cynismus,' " *Archiv für Begriffsgeschichte* 24.1 (1980) 103–22.

Agamemnon with equanimity: they describe the only course of action available to any moral agent (sage or fool), which is precisely that of acting.[117] The image, which is meant to shock, is cynical only in its dispassionate and disturbing exploration of the foundations of categorical frameworks. Moral absolutism, conjoined with pragmatic realism, naturally seems to bring in its train a certain cynicism and a polemically minded indifference. We saw evidence of this blend earlier in the Philodemus columns, where identical commitments drove a dissident Stoic to the brink of the implausible in his theory of poetry and morals. As both thinkers conceive it, indifference may be so powerful and so unstable a concept that it lies at the limit of our means of comprehension and expression. Is language adequate to the task of moral evaluation at all?

The answer would be yes in Aristo's case if we could be sure that language is a rational instrument. Is Aristo a hyperrationalist? Or is he an irrationalist? The exact place of reason in Aristo's philosophy is as controversial today as it must have been in his own time. Aristo's position reveals and then radicalizes a strain inherent in the origins of the Stoa: with reason absolutized to such a degree, it can no longer even be completely instantiated.[118] Thus, "perhaps there are no sages. This is the dilemma of Stoic ethics. Nature promises a destination which is approachable by no known road." [119] The thought is Kafkaesque, but it is also characteristically Cynic.[120] Aristo clearly does flirt with the limits of rational conduct and explanation, to the point where rational choices look to be indistinguishable from irrational ones. But it is with the limits of reason, not with what lies beyond them, that Aristo is exclusively preoccupied.

The Stoic Zeno, faced with the choice of declaring himself (impossibly) a sage[121] or taking the scandalous route of playing the Cynic,[122] would retreat to a middle ground of intermediate values, where action could find a safe haven from the rigorous absolutism of Stoic moral reason and from the freedoms of Cynic circumstantial logic (itself a paradoxical embrace of contingency in the name of freedom from contingencies).[123] Aristo, by contrast, found a stunning

117. Here I must take issue with Ioppolo (n. 7 supra: 202), who attempts to soften Aristo's point: "Aristone svaluta la parte [viz. the dramatic role assumed by the sage] completamente, poiché accentua l'importanza del giudizio della ragione in ogni circonstanza."

118. Cf. Moreau (n. 11 supra) 35.

119. A.A. Long, "The Logical Basis of Stoic Ethic," *Proceedings of the Aristotelian Society* 70 (1970–71) 85–104 (here, p. 102); cf. also L.-S. 1, p. 383; Moreau (n. 11 supra) 35–36. On Antisthenes' role in the idealization of the sage figure in post-Socratic philosophy, see Dudley (n. 11 supra) 12. Ironically, Antisthenes (with Diogenes) comes to embody this ideal for the Stoa (D.L. 7.91).

120. Cf. Crates' location of the sage on the Isle of Pera (frr. 4–6 Diels [*Poet. Phil. Frag.*]); and see Goulet-Cazé (n. 20 supra) 38, on the reluctance of the Cynics to specify the positive content of virtue.

121. *SVF* 1.44, 3.245.

122. ἔτι τε μὴ δοξάσειν τὸν σοφόν, . . . κυνιεῖν τ᾽ αὐτόν (D.L. 7.121).

123. Cic. *De Fin.* 68. Circumstantial indifference is associated with the very *origins* of Cynic thinking; cf. the anecdote about Diogenes and the mouse (D.L. 6.22: πόρον ἐξεῦρε τῆς περιστάσεως). Indifference to circumstances just is the means of adapting oneself circumstantially to them.

solution to the dilemma, which he gripped firmly by both horns. In ways more of a Cynic *and* more of a Stoic than Zeno, he would take the step that his teacher could not have dared even to imagine. Henceforth, the sage will not be a Stoic (at least not by nature), though he might choose the part of the Stoic philosopher or the Cynic crank with equanimity, and then play out this choice to the hilt, as the part happens to demand—if not appropriately (*kathēkontōs*) then at least fittingly (*prosēkontōs*).[124]

124. According to L.-S. 1, p. 427, Panaetius's theory of ethical role-playing (Cic. *De Off.* 1.107–17) was unprecedented in antiquity. If the clues to Aristo's theory are reliable, there may have been a number of precedents to Panaetius, not least among them Aristo and the Cynics.

Cynicism and the Romans: Attraction and Repulsion

Miriam Griffin

In attempting to recover the facts about the Cynics of the Roman period we encounter problems, different from but comparable to what we face in studying the earlier history of the sect. Whereas no works by Cynics of the early period are preserved, for the first century A.D. we have Dio Chrysostom, but his philosophical credentials are often difficult to establish. We now have descriptions of Cynics from writers of comedy, mime, and satire, but they are suspect on various grounds: not only are they clearly exaggerated, but it is unclear if they imitate life or just Greek literary models. Finally, we have descriptions of Cynic teachers from Stoic writers, but, as Margarethe Billerbeck has demonstrated, such writers tend to make them cleaner and more seemly than they were in reality.[1]

Fortunately for me, however, my purpose here is not to uncover the actual facts about Cynic teachers and teaching, but to discuss the attitudes of others toward Cynicism. This is an easier task, for all would agree that, even in the first and second centuries B.C., when it can be doubted whether there was a Cynic presence in Rome,[2] there was an image of what a Cynic teacher was like, an image based on the model of Diogenes and expressive of attitudes toward

---

1. M. Billerbeck, *Epiktet: Vom Kynismus* (Leiden 1978); ead., *Der Kyniker Demetrius* (Leiden 1979). M.-O. Goulet-Cazé, "Le cynisme à l'époque impériale," *ANRW* 2.36.4 (Berlin 1990) 2720–2833, collects the evidence on the imperial period, including the meager testimony of the historians.

2. For a summary of the problem and different views concerning it, see J. Moles, "'*Honestius quam ambitiosius?*' An Exploration of the Cynic's Attitude to Moral Corruption in His Fellow Men," *JHS* 103 (1983) 120–23.

Cynicism. For example, not only did Varro call his satires Menippean and give some of them titles like *Hippokuōn* (Half Mare, Half Bitch) or *Hudrokuōn* (Water Dog), but Cicero makes him say in the *Academica* (1.8) that these satires had some recognizable philosophical content, some of it presumably Cynic, a label later writers applied to them (Gellius, *NA* 2.18.7, 13.31.1). Moreover, in his *De Philosophia,* where Varro classified 288 philosophical schools by *telos* (ultimate goal), he included Cynicism, though not as a *hairesis* or school of thought, but as a way of life (Augustine, *CD* 19.1.2–3). At the other extreme, the mime writer Laberius could dignify the school as *Cynica haeresis* while associating it with toilets (*Compitalia* fr. 3 Ribbeck[2]).

One of the incidental benefits of approaching Cynicism through the attitudes of others may turn out to be the resolution or clarification of some conflicts in our evidence about the identity of certain philosophers or philosophic views, conflicts that may be more *in verbo* than *in re*. That phrase leads me to the first of three puzzling cases that I shall use as a starting point for my inquiry.

Sometime during the period 46–44 B.C. Cicero wrote to his Epicurean friend Papirius Paetus a letter rightly described by Shackleton Bailey as a *jeu d'esprit* (*Fam.* 9.22, SB 189). Provoked by an obscene word in Paetus's letter, Cicero discourses on the freedom of speech (*libertas loquendi*) that consists in calling a spade a spade. He gives the Stoic argument against the use of euphemisms, namely, that their use implies that we do not find shamefulness in the things denoted by them and that it is absurd to think that it is the denotation of a nonshameful thing that is shameful. Though Cicero first ascribes the view to Zeno of Citium in the past tense (1), he goes on to assign it to Stoics in the present tense: "There is the Stoic school for you: the Wise Man will speak plainly" (*habes scholam Stoicam: ho sophos euthurrhēmonēsei,* 4; cf. 1). Naturally, he illustrates the view with Latin examples, but we cannot be sure if they are his own or taken from contemporary Stoics. However, in *De Officiis* (On Duties), written at the same time or a year or two earlier, Cicero says, *nec audiendi* sunt *Cynici, aut si qui* fuerunt *Stoici paene Cynici,* when issuing his warning: "We must certainly not listen to the Cynics, or to those Stoics who were almost Cynics, when they criticize and mock us for thinking that, though some things are not themselves dishonorable, the words for them are shameful, while we call by their own names those things that are dishonorable" (1.128). This occurs in his discussion of seemliness (*decorum,* Panaetius's *to prepon*).

We have here an interesting contrast. Cicero, whether or not he really knew of contemporary Stoics who maintained this view, labels it as characteristic of the *schola Stoica* in a letter to an Epicurean and written not from the Stoic point of view, but from that of Cicero's *Academica nostra* (*Fam.* 9.22.1; cf. 4: "I preserve and will go on preserving—for this is my habit—the modesty of Plato," *ego servo et servabo – sic enim adsuevi – Platonis verecundiam*). In *De Officiis,* however, where he is writing from the Stoic point of view and probably agreeing with Panaetius, Cicero attributes the view to Cynics or early Stoics, alluding in particular, we may imagine, to Zeno, whose *Republic* was written "on the dog's tail." Philodemus tells us that Stoics of his period tried to excuse or even deny the authenticity of this work, though Chrysippus had no doubts of its authorship and indeed admired it.[3] We might surmise that Stoics or those favorable to them ascribed the embarrassing parts of the Stoic heritage to the Cynics or to the Cynic influence on their founders, while critics of the Stoa might identify these same notions as Stoic without qualification.

Another interesting point emerges, common to both Cicero passages. Cicero's remarks in the letter fit into a well-known pattern of Roman prudishness about obscene language, which even extended to accidental combinations of syllables.[4] In *De Officiis,* though Cicero is probably following Panaetius to a considerable extent, he enters into his views with enthusiasm and may well go beyond them. Nature itself, he argues, by hiding certain parts of the body, shows that their use and description should not be public (1.127).[5] This *verecundia* he then exemplifies by the Roman custom according to which, contrary to Greek custom, adult sons do not bathe with their fathers or fathers-in-law (1.129).[6] The disowning of the characteristic Cynic *anaideia* (shamelessness) is here reinforced by Roman prudery and respect for social convention.

Finally, a third point emerges from this example, which will become important later on. In *De Officiis,* after Cicero has continued his discussion on *decorum* at great length and in considerable detail, adumbrating rules for polite conversation and appropriate houses and finally talking about *mos et consuetudo civilis* (custom and civic practice) as the proper guide in social relations (1.148), he adds that Socrates and Aristippus can be pardoned for acting against custom because they enjoyed the license accorded to great and divine good men; the *Cynicorum ratio* (the Cynic way), however, must be rejected as hostile to *verecundia.* This concession to Socrates, the great model of the Cynics and Stoics, and to his pupil Aristippus, the man Diogenes called the royal dog,[7] for enjoying what pleasures came to hand without looking further, anticipates the later portrayal of idealized Cynics in Stoic teaching. Thus Epictetus (*Ench.* 15) will say that we should wait patiently for wife, wealth, and office (clearly the orthodox Stoic view of the *adiaphora* or indifferents) but that to refuse these things even when they are set before you is not just to share the banquet of the gods, but to rule with them—an ascription of divinity to Diogenes and Heraclitus similar to that Cicero made to Socrates and Aristippus.

---

3. Philodemus, *De Stoicis* cols. IX, X, D.L. 7.34 (cf. 7.187).

4. Cicero, *Orat.* 154; cf. Quintilian 8.3.44–47; and Fr. Ritter, "Uebertriebene Scheu der Römer vor gewissen Ausdrücken und Wortverbindung," *RhM* 3 (1835) 569–80.

5. Compare the view of Zeno that no part of the body should be entirely concealed (D.L. 7.33; Philodemus, *De Stoicis* col. XVIII).

6. Cf. Plutarch, *Cat. Mai.* 20.

7. D.L. 2.66; cf. Hor. *Epist.* 1.17.13.

The second case also comes from the late Republic. Favonius, a Roman senator who rose at least to the rank of praetor, was a close associate of the younger Cato (Plut. *Cato Minor* 46). In Tacitus's *Annals* (16.22), during an attack on the Stoic Thrasea Paetus, *ista secta* (that sect: i.e., the Stoa) is said to have produced Tuberones and Favonii who gave trouble in the Republic, just as their current adherents make a display of *libertas* as a way of undermining the Principate. The Stoic credentials of Q. Aelius Tubero are confirmed by Cicero (*Brut.* 117), but no other source explicitly assigns Favonius a sect—not even Plutarch, who, however, mentions him as philosophically inclined (*Brut.* 12.3, 34.2, 34.4), shows him collaborating in the austere regimen Cato designed for his aedilician games (*Cato Minor* 46), and indicates (*Pomp.* 60, *Brut.* 34.5) that Favonius's temperament led him to exaggerate the *parrhēsia* (frank speaking) of Cato into *akairia* (unseasonableness), *authadeia* (insolence), *hubris* (outrageousness). Plutarch calls this behavior Cynic in his *Life of Brutus* (34.3–4), where Brutus himself is shown castigating Favonius as a *haplokuna* (a mere dog) and *pseudokuna* (a false Cynic)—or perhaps *pseudokatōna* (a false Cato). As Geiger has argued, we cannot harmonize the conflicting evidence of Tacitus and Plutarch, as both items are tendentious and neither may be reliable.[8] But if Favonius really was a Stoic, then it may be Plutarch's respect for the Stoics, his *adversaires privilégiés,*[9] and his particular regard for Cato,[10] one of the very few Romans he calls a philosopher (*Brut.* 2.1),[11] that inclined Plutarch to call this reprehensible conduct of Cato's admirer Cynic, using it as a term of abuse. In this he was following the attitude of the subject of his biography, for Brutus revered Cato (*Brut.* 2) and was a follower of Antiochus, who was sympathetic to the Stoa, as Plutarch knew (*Cic.* 4.2, *Luc.* 42.3–4).[12] Brutus and his biographer had behind them a long Greek tradition of using offensive behavior as the criterion to distinguish a Cynic from a Stoic: hence Lucian's joke about the Stoic philosopher Thesmopolis, who was soiled by a lapdog and thereby earned the insult from a rival client of his patroness, "Our Stoic has suddenly become a Cynic" (*Merc. Cond.* 33–34), and Juvenal's verse about Stoic doctrines differing from Cynic ones by dress alone (*Stoica dogmata . . . a cynicis tunica distantia,* 13.121–22).

In addition to confirming what the Cicero example shows about the necessity for the Stoics in a Roman context of disowning certain kinds of action and

---

8. J. Geiger, "M. Favonius: Three Notes," *RSA* 4 (1974) 161–70. I am not convinced by Moles (above, n. 2) 121 n. 129.

9. D. Babut, *Plutarque et le stoïcisme* (Paris 1969) 531.

10. Ibid. 173–75.

11. S. Swain, "Hellenic Culture and Roman Heroes of Plutarch," *JHS* 110 (1990) 134.

12. Swain notes (ibid. 134 n. 71), however, that the Stoic sympathies of Antiochus are not mentioned by Plutarch in the *Brutus* itself. The emphasis there is on Brutus's Platonism, which is the basis of the comparison Plutarch makes between Brutus and Dion (*Dion* 1).

speech as Cynic, Plutarch shows how particularly important this was for the acceptance of Stoicism by the Roman governing class. For Plutarch, in speaking of Favonius, characterizes his undignified, even comic, behavior as evidence that he attached no value to being a Roman senator (*Brut.* 34.3). Though the Cynic conduct of Favonius disarmed Cassius and others by making them laugh, Plutarch makes it clear that men sympathetic to Cato and the Stoa were among those who thought of Cynic behavior generally, or at least the popular conception of it, as unsuitable for a Roman of his social class. There is a similarity here to the attitude of the Stoic senator Seneca, who explains to his correspondent Lucilius (*Ep.* 29.3) that it detracts from the *auctoritas* of a great man to preach to passersby unheeded like Diogenes and other Cynics exercising their *libertas promiscua* (indiscriminate freedom of speech).

With our third case we move to the Principate and the early 70s A.D. In 75 the historian Cassius Dio (here preserved in excerpts) reported verbal attacks on Vespasian's son Titus for his amorous liaison with the Jewish princess Berenice, who had come to Rome in the company of her brother Herod Agrippa (66.15.5). Two Cynics, Diogenes and Heras, who gave public harangues on the subject were punished. They are said to have returned to Rome, eluding the ban on philosophers passed several years before. Dio, discussing that ban in a part of his narrative datable between 71 and 75 (66.13–14), tells us that Mucianus had attacked those who, induced by Stoic principles, were publicly teaching doctrines unsuitable to the time, using philosophy as a pretext. Among them was Demetrius the Cynic. Dio then recounts the charges that Mucianus made against the Stoics, whom he described as barefoot, wearing a long beard, dressed in the *tribōnion* (cloak) thrown back (presumably leaving the shoulder bare), and making exaggerated claims to virtue and hurling insults at everybody. Vespasian is then said to have expelled all the philosophers from Rome except Musonius Rufus and to have called the defiant Demetrius a barking dog (66.13.3; cf. Suet. *Vesp.* 13). One of the philosophers here associated with him, Hostilianus, may be the Stoic C. Tutilius Hostilianus (*CIL* 6.9785; *PIR*[2] H 222),[13] while Helvidius Priscus, whom Dio rightly described as a Stoic earlier in his narrative (66.12.1), is here brought into association with these philosophers, criticized by Mucianus as Stoics, for similarly insulting Vespasian and his friends and for denouncing monarchy (66.12.2).

The historical facts behind this account are difficult to unravel. Helvidius's opposition to Vespasian, even before the new Princeps returned to Rome in the autumn of 70, is recorded in Tacitus's *Histories* (4.4–9), and Epictetus reports a confrontation between the two that may belong to Vespasian's censorship of

---

13. F. Bücheler, who proposed the identification in "Prosopographica," *RhM* 63 (1908) 194 (*Kleine Schriften* 3.387), adduced in support the younger Pliny, *Ep.* 6.32.1, where Pliny refers to a Tutilius as the grandfather of a girl of marriageable age and implies that he advocated *continentia*.

73–74 (1.2.19–22). The way his behavior is described by these authors makes it highly unlikely that Helvidius was a republican attacking monarchy under Cynic influence. The evidence of Dio is hostile and tendentious. In his account Mucianus is made to describe classic Cynic conduct and appearance but call it Stoic, even going so far as to say that Demetrius the *Cynic* is acting on *Stoic* principles. Indeed, as we have seen, the later part of Dio's narrative implies that the Cynic philosophers Diogenes and Heras came under the ban that resulted from Mucianus's complaints against the Stoics. Clearly Dio's Mucianus has no desire to tell us the truth about the philosophical allegiances of those he attacks. Moreover, Dio may here not be entirely false to history, for Mucianus's concern would clearly have been to silence criticism of the regime, particularly from senators like Helvidius Priscus. Like Cossutianus Capito and Eprius Marcellus under Nero, he might well have been prepared to misrepresent the Stoic teachings and attitudes of these senators.[14] To that end not only is conventional Cynic behavior ascribed to undoubted Stoics like Helvidius Priscus, but the offending philosophers (whether they were actually Stoic or Cynic or some of each) have conventional Cynic behavior attributed to them even while being labeled as Stoics.

The problem for Vespasian and his regime was that the eventual punishment of Helvidius Priscus was embarrassing for the new Princeps, who laid claims to friendship and family connections with the so-called philosophical opposition under Nero.[15] Indeed Vespasian had exempted from the banishment of philosophers Musonius Rufus, after allowing him, in the first year of his reign, to take vengeance on the Stoic friend of Barea Soranus who had given evidence against him.[16] The note of self-justification comes through in Suetonius's account of Vespasian's last-minute attempt to reverse his sentence (*Vesp.* 15), and the form of that self-justification is apparent in Dio's account (66.12.3), where it is said that Helvidius aimed to imitate his father-in-law Thrasea Paetus but fell far short of his high standards of conduct. The contrast falls along the lines of the conventional Cynic/Stoic contrast: Helvidius's *parrhēsia* (frank speaking) was *akairos* (unseasonable), thus an offense against the Stoic virtue of *eukairia* (appropriateness);[17] he went in for abuse, he harangued the crowd in public, he refused to respect authority (66.12.1, 2–3). So once again, the enemies of the Stoics, or rather, here, of a particular Stoic, deliberately confuse them with Cynics and imply that such conduct was unbecoming to a Roman senator.

It is not surprising to find that these puzzles over Cynic identity concern the Stoa, given the historical origins of Stoicism and the evidence that the Stoa continued to think of a *koinōnia* (communion) existing between the two

14. Tacitus, *Ann.* 16.22, 28.
15. Tacitus, *Hist.* 4.7.
16. Cassius Dio 66.13.2; Tacitus, *Ann.* 16.32, *Hist.* 4.10, 40.
17. Cicero, *Off.* 1.142.

schools (D.L. 6.104), both of which continued to see Socrates as an important model.[18] According to Diogenes Laertius (7.3), it was precisely because of his natural aversion to Cynic *anaiskhuntia* (shamelessness), the quality prominent in our examples, that Zeno disagreed with his teacher, the Cynic Crates.[19]

Whatever difficulties the Stoa had with the Cynic adherence to an opposition between nature and social convention was, I believe, greatly intensified by contacts with Rome. It is not an accident that the disowning by the Stoa of Zeno's *Republic* is first attested for Philodemus's time. The Roman obsession with *gravitas* (dignity) and *decorum* (seemliness) and the energy that Cicero puts into giving them a Stoic content have already been stressed. Both Seneca (*Ep.* 5.2) and Musonius Rufus (fr. 6 Hense) insist that the philosopher should not seek to live a life at variance with normal custom. Even Horace, though he often depicts forthright Stoic teaching from bearded staff-carrying philosophers lower down the social scale (e.g., *Sat.* 2.3, 2.7)—clearly unrefined *Stoici rustici*—still distinguishes the *sordidus victus* (squalid way of life) of the Cynic from the *tenuis victus* (simple way of life) of the Stoic *sapiens* (*Sat.* 2.2.53–69). Horace also criticizes the Cynic inability to adapt to circumstance (*Epist.* 1.17.13–32) and propensity for causing offense (*Sat.* 2.2.65).[20]

The Romans also had other objections to Cynicism of which Stoics in this period had to take note. Related to their disregard of social conventions was their disregard of reputation.[21] The Stoics themselves differed over whether *eudoxia* (good repute) had any value even as a positive indifferent,[22] and Cicero himself was prepared to accept that only true *gloria* based on solid virtue and accorded by good men was worth pursuing (*Off.* 2.43). But Cicero's own choice of *honestum,* etymologically connected with *honor,* as the Latin equivalent for the Greek *to kalon* (the morally beautiful) reveals an assumption that he makes explicit in the first of the *Paradoxa Stoicorum:* there, after saying that our ancestors agreed with the Stoics that only *quod rectum et honestum et cum virtute est* (what is right and honorable and accompanied by virtue) is good, he enumerates deeds of these Roman paragons that demonstrate their beliefs that the only thing in life worth seeking is what is worthy of praise and renown (*quod laudabile esset et praeclarum*). The Romans could not accept that the conduct of the individual should not be governed in any way by the estimation of others.

The problem was aggravated by Cynic arrogance and exhibitionism, which

18. D.L. 6.104; A.A. Long, "Socrates in Hellenistic Philosophy," *CQ* 38 (1988) 150–71.

19. Zeno also realized that to give content to the life according to virtue and the life according to nature advocated by the Cynics he had to root his ethics in metaphysical views about the nature of the universe and the nature of man. See J. Rist, *Stoic Philosophy* (Cambridge 1962) chap. 4.

20. On Cynics in Horace, see J. Moles, "Cynicism in Horace's Epistles I," *Papers of the Liverpool Latin Seminar* 5 (1985) 33–60.

21. D.L. 6.72, 85, 104.

22. Cicero, *Fin.* 3.56–57.

their critics thought showed that they suffered from the same *tuphos* (vanity) that they claimed to despise.[23] Sources in the Roman period speak of their *kenodoxia* (conceit), *epideixis* (showing off), and *tuphos*.[24] This exhibitionism, it has been argued, may have had the pedagogic purpose of challenging conventional values by outrageous public conduct, including paradoxical defense of the indefensible.[25] In that case Tacitus (*Hist.* 4.40) may have been unfair when he criticized Demetrius for showing more selfish interest than honorable purpose, though claiming to be a Cynic. In taking on a hopeless case, the defense of the Stoic Egnatius Celer, who had been bribed to give evidence against his friend Barea Soranus (*Ann.* 6.32, *Hist.* 4.10), Demetrius may have thought he was behaving virtuously. Even the Stoic Thrasea Paetus thought one should take on *causae destitutae* (cases no one else would take) to demonstrate one's *constantia* and *humanitas*.[26] But even if Demetrius did act for virtuous motives, Tacitus's claim to be giving the reaction of Demetrius's contemporaries is plausible, for he was certainly not the only Roman to think that such behavior on the part of a Cynic was hypocritical in that it exhibited just that desire for fame (here based on oratorical virtuosity) that the Cynics claimed to despise.[27] Seneca as a Stoic criticizes (*Ben.* 2.17.2) the Cynic pursuit of renown through poverty (*gloria egestatis*), and expressly repudiates (*Ep.* 5.1–5) the kind of perverse ambition that leads philosophers to parade their sordid simplicity (*incompta frugalitas*).

Another objection the Romans had to Cynicism was that its emphasis on self-sufficiency combined with its contempt for social convention led to an avoidance of ordinary forms of social life and, *a fortiori,* of participation in politics.[28] Even if the role of the Cynic as teacher and admonisher of mankind can be construed as a social role, it was clearly not one compatible with a career in public life, for which even a rigid adherence to Stoic principles was thought to render one unsuitable.[29]

Yet there is another side to the story of how the Roman context affected the attitude of the Stoa to its Cynic heritage, a more positive side. It is well known

---

23. D.L. 6.7–8, 86.

24. Lucian, *Peregr.* 4, 34 (cf. 38, 42); *Demon.* 48, 13; *Reviv.* 30 (cf. *Vit. Auct.* 11).

25. Moles (above, n. 2) 103–20.

26. Pliny, *Ep.* 6.29.1–2. For *constantia* here, cf. *Ep.* 5.13.2. Pliny clearly did not think that Thrasea Paetus advocated taking these cases in order to acquire fame (in the manner of Cicero, *Off.* 2.51; cf. Plutarch, *Cic.* 3, 5), since he himself goes on to add a category of cases that would confer *gloria* and *fama,* the pursuit of which he did not condemn (*Ep.* 6.29.3). Would Tacitus, however, have interpreted what Thrasea thought as Pliny did? For the oratorical challenge involved, see A.S. Pease, "Things Without Honour," *CP* 21 (1926) 27–39.

27. Thus Lucian, *Vit. Auct.* 11, attributes to Diogenes the view that the Cynic way is the shortest route to fame instead of the shortest way to virtue (the traditional Cynic slogan). See Goulet-Cazé (above, no. 1) 2767. Cf. Galen, *On the Errors of the Soul* 3, 71 Kühn: σύντομον ἐπ᾽ ἀλαζονείας ὁδόν.

28. D.L. 6.29, 72; Lucian, *Vit. Auct.* 9; Cicero, *Fin.* 3.68.

29. Cicero, *Mur.* 60–67; Seneca, *Clem.* 2.5.2; cf. Plutarch, *Cat. Min.* 30.6.

that the Romans felt an affinity with Stoic ethical teaching, which they saw as inculcating values close to Roman traditional values, though naturally they thought the example of the *maiores* a more potent form of instruction, especially as they had a better record than Stoic philosophers of putting theory into practice.[30] It is significant that the founder of the one native school of philosophy that developed in Rome, Quintus Sextius, is described by Seneca (*Ep.* 64.2) as "a Stoic, deny it though he may" (*licet neget, Stoicus*). This blend of Roman and Stoic values Posidonius found in P. Cornelius Scipio Nasica Serapio, the consul of 111 B.C. (*FGH* 87, fr. 112.8); Tacitus (*Ann.* 14.57) has Tigellinus identify the same blend in Rubellius Plautus, though with less sympathy: "mimicry of the Romans of yore with the arrogance of the Stoics thrown in" (*veterum Romanorum imitamenta, adsumpta etiam Stoicorum adrogantia*).

Nonetheless there were obstacles to the establishment of a complete rapport between the Roman and Stoic traditions, other than the taint of Cynic shamelessness. At least three other interrelated reservations about Stoicism are prominent in Roman sources.

The intellectualism of Stoicism.   The Stoics insisted on the coherence of all their doctrines, so that ethics could not be properly mastered without metaphysics and logic. In addition, their attitude toward the passions led them to prefer the appeal to reason through logical proof over oratorical persuasion, which roused the passions. The members of the Roman governing class, who thought of themselves as practical men with more important things to do than theorize, regarded training in rhetoric as the vital preparation for political life. The logic chopping of the Stoics and their oratorical inadequacies were frequently attacked in the Roman period.[31] Epictetus, like his teacher Musonius Rufus, believed in the importance of logic (1.7, 1.17) when properly used in the service of ethics (2.21.21–22, 2.23.46), not as a means of showing off (1.26, 2.19.9–10). Marcus Aurelius too is grateful that his love of philosophy did not lead to involvement with syllogisms and problems in the clouds (*Med.* 1.17).

The use of the sapiens *as a model for conduct and the focus of ethical discourse.*   This struck the Romans as both unrealistic and excessively abstract, for the Stoics tended to say that the *sapiens* had never actually existed. The Romans preferred moral instruction through *exempla*, the examples that

---

30. Cicero, *Tusc.* 2.11–12, *Fin.* 3.67.
31. E.g., Cicero, *Paradoxa Stoicorum* 2–3, *Tusc.* 3.13; *Fin.* 4.5–7; Seneca, *Ben.* 1.4, *Ep.* 82.8–9, 113.1, 123.15–16; Lucian, *Vit. Auct.* 20, 23, *Reviv.* 45.

their own history furnished in abundance. When Quintilian wrote, "Greek superiority in moral precept is matched by Roman preeminence in examples of conduct—which is the greater thing" (*Inst.* 12.2.30), he was, of course, making a point about Roman superiority in moral conduct, but he reflects a pedagogical attitude as well: real *exempla* not only showed what it was right to do but proved that it could be done. Not only did Cicero, in writing his handbook of practical ethics (*Off.* 1.4, 3.15) *De Officiis,* choose as a guide Panaetius, whose concern with the *imperfectus* is attested by Seneca (*Ep.* 116.5), but in Book 3, where he no longer had help from Panaetius, he went further in that direction in a distinctively Roman way: he adopted as his ideal M. Atilius Regulus, a real *exemplum,* not an abstraction.

It is interesting to see how an educated Roman of the governing class in the first century A.D., a man without any explicit philosophical allegiance, sees the ideal philosopher. The younger Pliny (*Ep.* 1.10) gives an encomium of the philosopher Euphrates, a pupil of Musonius Rufus. He is seemly in appearance, bearded but elegantly so; he does not scold but improves and instructs; he castigates vices, not men (*insectatur vitia, non homines*).[32] He is married with children and accepted as son-in-law by a man of high social position, clearly a man at home in high society. He does not despise public service. But not only is he without the conventional Cynic defects (from the Roman point of view), but he is also without the conventional Stoic blemishes: he is eloquent, even achieving Platonic sublimity, and his instruction is realistic, taking account of the obligations men actually have. Finally, Pliny presents him as an *exemplum,* a living *sapiens.*

A strong dose of Cynicism of the right kind could help the Stoa overcome these obstacles to Roman acceptance. Cynicism was famous for neglecting, indeed despising, the other two branches of philosophy, logic and physics, and for concentrating on practical ethics.[33] Whereas the Stoics could claim that their concern for logic fit with Socrates' concern with definition[34] and his general emphasis on knowledge as the key to morality, the Cynics claimed to be the true heirs to his insistence on human conduct as the proper concern of philosophers.[35] Epictetus's insistence on keeping interest in logic within the bounds of usefulness is an adaptation of the Stoic attitude in the direction of Cynicism. Indeed Seneca, who likes to argue that problems like the fear of death cannot be cured by syllogisms (*Ep.* 82.19–24), expressly indicates the Cynic credentials of his anti-intellectualism in *De Beneficiis* (7.1.2–5, 7.8.2),

---

32. Epictetus 4.8.21 stresses the fact that Euphrates rejected the ostentation and outward trappings of philosophers.

33. D.L. 6.103; Galen, *On the Errors of the Soul* 3, 71 Kühn; Apuleius, *Apol.* 39; Lucian, *Vit. Auct.* 11.

34. Epictetus 1.17.4–12.

35. D.L. 6.103; Long (above, n. 18) 164.

when he embodies it in a discourse attributed to Demetrius the Cynic. Seneca says that once one has said what affects *mores* (conduct) there is no point in examining questions that do not contribute to healing the *animus* (mind) but only exercise one's *ingenium* (intellect). Then he quotes Demetrius giving examples of useless knowledge from natural history and human biology and proclaiming that nature only hides those truths that have their own discovery as their only advantage. Seneca praises Demetrius as a man endowed with *sapientia,* though making no claim to it, and as a speaker possessed of direct and effective eloquence.

The oratorical inadequacies of the Stoics.   We have mentioned complaints by Roman writers like Cicero and Seneca about the arid style of the Stoic writers. Now, the Cynics laid claim to a distinctive form of eloquence. Their forthright speech, with its use of ridicule and metaphor, appealed to the native Roman taste for satire, as the Menippean satires of Varro and Seneca and the contribution of Bionic wit to Horatian satire demonstrate. Later still, Apuleius explicitly associates satire with Crates (*Flor.* 20).

Seneca, who admired the eloquence of Demetrius the Cynic (*Ben.* 7.8.3), created a philosophical style with a strong admixture of these ingredients, and Musonius Rufus, Epictetus, and even Marcus Aurelius show a similar approach in Greek. Marcus, by his own account, was inspired to asceticism and the toleration of *parrhēsia* in youth by the preaching of a teacher, Diognetus, with strong Cynic tendencies (*Med.* 1.6). He continued to admire the *paidagōgikē parrhēsia* (educational free speech) of Old Comedy and of Diogenes the Cynic (11.6). Moreover, he practiced it in his moral exhortations to himself. Rutherford has indicated the affinity of the *Meditations* to diatribe and pointed to passages where Marcus not only eschews euphemism but revels in gruesome language for the processes of the body (5.28, 6.13, 10.19, 11.15). By means of grim satire he strips off conventional attitudes and faces up to reality, and the rare touches of humor in his work tend to be of the *spoudogeloios* (jesting-in-earnest) variety (3.3).[36]

By following the Cynic approach, the Stoics could also accommodate the Roman preference for real *exempla.* Cynicism had so little in the way of theoretical foundations that, as we have seen, it could be regarded as a way of life rather than a school of thought. What took the place of doctrine was precisely *exempla,* starting with Antisthenes' emulation of the ἰσχύς (rigor) of Socrates.[37] Diogenes, whom Plato called Socrates gone mad,[38] and his pupil Crates,

36. See R.B. Rutherford, *The Meditations of Marcus Aurelius: A Study* (Oxford 1989) 21–39, 143–55.
37. D.L. 6.2, 11.
38. D.L. 6.54.

whom Zeno was told to follow when he looked for a man like Socrates,[39] became *exempla* in their own right. Much of Cynic teaching took the form of anecdotes about its heroes. Lucian in the *Demonax* imitates that method in portraying his hero largely through a series of anecdotes in which he is seen scoring one-liners in the manner of Diogenes.[40] His *Peregrinus,* on the other hand, is a wonderful satire on the Cynic method of teaching by example. Here the Cynic Theagenes, who imitates everything Peregrinus does (24), goes beyond comparing Peregrinus to Socrates, Antisthenes, and Diogenes, and adduces Zeus. Peregrinus himself, before immolating himself on a pyre, compares himself to Heracles and says that his purpose is to teach men to despise death (23, 33). Lucian encourages the Cynic followers of Peregrinus to imitate him and put an end to themselves (24).

In this Cynic spirit, Roman Stoics adopted as models for conduct, alongside the *sapiens,* Socrates and Diogenes and, for Seneca, Demetrius the Cynic. There also feature prominently in their writings Roman philosophical heroes, notably Cato for Seneca, Helvidius for Epictetus and Marcus Aurelius. To what extent a Roman Stoic like Marcus Aurelius believed that the most effective form of moral instruction was through real examples is shown by his *Meditations.* There, writing for his own benefit, he starts with a catalogue of friends alive and dead from whose example he could learn, the chief being his adoptive parent and imperial predecessor Antoninus Pius.

There were other ways too in which their Cynic heritage could help the Stoics acquire native Roman dress. Dudley suggested that the native tradition of *antiqua virtus* (ancestral virtue) contributed to the relative eclipse of Cynicism in the second and first centuries B.C. by making it otiose.[41] But, as adopted and adapted by the Stoics, the Cynic form of austerity could be an asset. An important element of similarity between the Cynic and Roman traditions was the belief in the role of physical training in developing tolerance of pain and hardship generally. From the elder Cato to Augustus, Romans voiced their belief in the importance of physical education for the young.[42] Cicero, with due allusion to Spartan training, much esteemed by the Cynics,[43] and Roman *exempla,* advocates its contribution to moral education (*Tusc.* 2.35). As M.-O. Goulet-Cazé has shown, the Stoics of the Roman period tried to retain, along with the notion of spiritual exercise traditionally advocated by their school and still stressed by Epictetus (3.12, 3.13.2), some element of the Cynic physical *askēsis:* Seneca advocated temporary periods of asceticism (*Ep.* 18.5–13) and, following his teacher Attalus, abstained from certain luxuries and comforts at

39. D.L. 7.2.
40. See R. Bracht Branham, *Unruly Eloquence: Lucian and the Comedy of Traditions* (Cambridge, Mass., 1989) 57–61.
41. D.R. Dudley, *A History of Cynicism* (London 1937) 119.
42. Plutarch, *Cat. Mai.* 4.1–3, 20.4, 12; Suetonius, *Aug.* 64.2–3.
43. D.L. 6.27, 59; cf. 7.172 (Cleanthes, an ascetic type of Stoic).

all times (*Ep.* 108.15–16, 23); Musonius Rufus gave *ponos* (effort and hard work) a positive value and insisted on the necessity of continual training for the body as well as the mind.[44] What approval this received at Rome can be judged from the praise that another follower of Musonius Rufus, in fact his son-in-law Artemidorus, earns from the younger Pliny for his physical endurance and abstemiousness (*Ep.* 3.11.7).[45]

Another important element of similarity in the Cynic and Roman outlooks was, of course, the value accorded to frugality, even poverty, which the Romans felt had been the key to the achievements of their ancestors. It might seem, however, that the Stoics could draw on their own continuous tradition with no need of a fresh injection of Cynicism. Certainly, Cicero found ample scope for deploying traditional Roman *exempla* when rendering the Stoic paradoxes in the high oratorical style: they are particularly in evidence in his treatment of the first, second, and third paradoxes, where the denial of the value of wealth and pleasure was an important theme. In treating the third, that only the wise man is rich, he could make copious use of the contrast between the present and the paragons of the hallowed Roman past. Posidonius clearly learned from his Roman friends to admire and celebrate the physical toughness, austerity of diet, and general frugality of the ancient Romans (Athen. 6.273–75a frr. 265–67 E.-K.), while the parallel between ancestral morality and that advocated by the Stoa is clearly drawn by Apuleius in praising the governor of Africa Claudius Maximus for his aversion to luxury: he is described as a man espousing a severe creed and with such long service as a soldier behind him (*vir austerae sectae tamque diutinae militiae, Apol.* 19; cf. *PIR*[2] C 933–34).

Yet the Roman attitude toward Stoic teaching of austerity was complex. For one thing, no aspect of Stoic teaching so exposed the school to charges of hypocrisy. For another, if carried to the point of asceticism, austerity was thought unsuitable for men in public life. Marcus Aurelius, who had been dissuaded by his mother from sleeping without a cover (see n. 45 above), praises Antoninus Pius for being, like Socrates, equally able to abstain from or to enjoy what many are too weak to abstain from and too self-indulgent in enjoying (*Med.* 1.17). In general, a rigid adherence to unworldly Stoic principles about virtue being the only good and all sins being equal was thought to render one unsuitable for a public career, a fact Cicero had exploited to Cato's discredit in the *Pro Murena*. Even later, in the *Paradoxa Stoicorum,* where he was making amends to Cato and called the Stoic paradoxes "Socratic in the highest degree and absolutely true" (*maxime Socratica longeque verissima*), he also said they were difficult to make acceptable to the general public because they were so contrary to common opinion (4): it was a rhetorical tour de force on Cicero's part to try to turn them into *loci communes* (commonplaces) for the

---

44. M.-O. Goulet-Cazé, *L'ascèse cynique: Un commentaire de Diogène Laërce VI 70–71* (Paris 1986) 172–91.

45. Compare also the habits of Marcus Aurelius, *HA Marc.* 2.6; cf. *Med.* 1.6.

orator trying to persuade an assembly or a jury. Again, Seneca had to counter the reputation of the Stoa for being too harsh to give good advice to rulers (*Clem.* 2.5.2).

Here the contribution of Cynicism was to be rather different, allowing the Stoics to operate what was essentially a two-tier system of morality. The Stoics had adopted the Cynic notion that virtue was the only good while accommodating more ordinary conceptions of value in the notion of the *adiaphora* (indifferents). Carneades had attacked this doctrine as a mere verbal maneuver to avoid calling good what ordinary men thought of as the good things of this world. The problem was not only theoretical, however, but presented difficulties in giving practical moral instruction. Cicero says he followed the Stoics in *De Officiis* because their view was *splendidius* (*Off.* 3.20), more noble than that of the Peripatetics, who admitted there were other goods than virtue, but his discussion there of the obligations and choices made by ordinary men seems a long way away from the high morality of the *sapiens*. He was in this work, as we saw, hostile to Cynic shamelessness, but aware of the license owed to exceptional men to depart from social custom. Ultimately it was by accommodating the Cynic way of life as one option within Stoicism that the Stoics of the Roman period were able to keep the rigor and nobility of their doctrines without sacrificing realism and practicality.

The view we find in *De Officiis* may have been inspired by Panaetius. His contemporary the Stoic philosopher Apollodorus of Seleucia is credited with the definition of Cynicism as a "shortcut to virtue."[46] The famous passage in Cicero's *De Finibus* (3.68) shows that the Stoa in his day was discussing the question of whether there were circumstances in which the Cynic way of life was appropriate to the Stoic *sapiens,* a question to which Arius Didymus in the same period attempted to give an answer: if the *sapiens* had achieved his virtue by the shortcut, he could stick to that way of life—neglect of the social duties of marriage and political life are in question—but he should not start behaving like that when already a *sapiens* (Stob. 2.7.118, p. 114.24 W.).

Diogenes is reported to have compared himself to the trainers of choruses who set the note a little too high in order to insure that others hit the right note.[47] Seneca does justice to this conception when he describes (*Brev. Vit.* 14.2) the choice offered by the two philosophies as overcoming human nature with the Stoics or exceeding it with the Cynics (*hominis naturam cum Stoicis vincere, cum Cynicis excedere*). For Seneca, Diogenes (like Socrates) was a man of outstanding virtue (*Ben.* 5.4.3–4, 5.6) who showed that nature imposes nothing on men that is hard to bear (*Ep.* 90.14) and who, by stripping himself of all the gifts of fortune, made himself as independent and thus as happy as the gods (*Tranq.* 8.3–5). But he goes on (8.9–9.2): "Since we do not have such strength of character, we ought at least to reduce our possessions so as to be less exposed

46. D.L. 7.121.
47. D.L. 6.35.

to the blows of fortune," and he finally recommends practicing the *parsimonia* (frugality) of the *maiores* (ancestors), but not true *paupertas* (poverty). Seneca also had a contemporary Cynic to offer as an *exemplum* (*Ben.* 7.8.3). Demetrius the Cynic, not a teacher of truth but a witness to it (*non praeceptor veris sed testis, Ep.* 20.9), is offered as a demonstration of how easy it is to despise wealth (*Ep.* 62.3). He may be *seminudus* or *nudus,* but Seneca does not feel obliged to undress or surrender his wealth in order to acquire the same attitude of detachment. Seneca also feels free to describe the lesson he learns from Demetrius as not condemning but leaving wealth to others.

The next step was taken by Epictetus, who set out to describe the ideal Cynic, making explicit which elements of Cynicism the Stoa could endorse. M. Billerbeck's studies of Demetrius the Cynic and Epictetus's ideal Cynic (see n. 1 above) show how impudence and immodesty have been removed, while just those qualities are retained that we have argued above would seem advantageous in the Roman context—concentration on practical instruction by example, eloquence, physical toughness, general austerity. The result is an ideal clearly admirable by Roman standards, especially as the function of this teacher of mankind is still for Epictetus (3.22, 4.8.30–43) what it was for Seneca, a source of inspiration rather than a model for imitation.

I am aware that I have not contributed toward finding an answer to the burning question: Did Cynicism in the Roman period have an independent existence as well as being an option within Stoicism? But I hope I have made more intelligible why the Stoics of the period embraced it as an option with such enthusiasm. The new, sanitized Cynic ideal helped Stoicism to shed unacceptable features of its historical heritage (Cynic and Stoic) and to exploit Cynic notions that appealed to the Romans. The value of this ideal in a world dominated by Rome is shown by the fact that it was adopted by others who were in general critical of Cynic ignorance and rudeness but who were not Stoics. And thus we find it celebrated and promoted by Lucian in the *Demonax,* by Apuleius in the *Apologia* (22), and later in the discourses of the emperor Julian.[48]

It can be argued, however, that this is not the whole story and that such an elevated and uncompromising ideal also enabled the Stoa in the early Principate, its period of greatest popularity, to deal with the problem that confronts any creed when it becomes identified with the establishment. How can it avoid becoming merely the mouthpiece of current values and practices? Just as there was a role for prophets that the Jewish priesthood could not fulfill, just as there was a role for ascetics and mystics that the church hierarchy of the Christian empire could not fulfill, so it was the Cynic strain in Stoicism that enabled that creed to retain its critical function as the conscience of society.

---

48. Platonists, like the Stoics, objected to the squalor, rudeness, and lack of culture of the Cynics. See Goulet-Cazé (above, n. 1) 2813–16.

The Ideal Cynic
from Epictetus to Julian

M. Billerbeck

In the history of ancient Cynicism the portrayal of Diogenes and his successors is far from being uniform. Whereas the *chreiai,* the oldest stratum of the Cynic tradition, represent him as the Dog in all his aspects of shamelessness (*anaideia*) and in his unrestrained freedom of speech (*parrhēsia*),[1] the emperor Julian, toward the end of the movement, ascribes to Cynicism a sublime character and surrounds it with an almost religious aura. In his eyes Diogenes is a model for a universal and divine philosophy, which, founded on the Delphic maxim *gnōthi sauton* (Know Thyself), results in action (*erga*) rather than in a system of doctrines (*logoi*).[2]

This conception of Cynicism, as we shall see, represents a construction of the later times and reflects the influence of syncretism. The tendency to idealize the founder of the movement and to purge his portrait of any features that might shock or keep off potential followers can in fact be traced back to a much earlier period of Cynicism. Because their ultimate origins were to be found in

---

1. This aspect of the Cynic tradition has often been dealt with. Among the most important studies dealing with it are those of K. von Fritz, *Quellenuntersuchungen zu Leben und Philosophie des Diogenes von Sinope,* Philologus Suppl. 18.2 (Leipzig 1926), esp. 1–63; G. Rudberg, "Zur Diogenes-Tradition," *SO* 14 (1935) 22–43, and "Zum Diogenes-Typus," *SO* 15 (1936) 1–18, both reprinted in M. Billerbeck, ed., *Die Kyniker in der modernen Forschung,* Bochumer Studien zur Philosophie 15 (Amsterdam 1991), 107–26, 127–43; cf. also ibid. 11–12. For more recent discussions, see G. Giannantoni, *Socratis et Socraticorum Reliquiae,* Elenchos Suppl. 18 (Naples 1990), 4.413–41; and especially M.-O. Goulet-Cazé, "Le livre VI de Diogène Laërce: Analyse de sa structure et réflexions méthodologiques," *ANRW* 2.36.6 (Berlin 1992) 3880–4048, esp. 3978–97.

2. Julian, *Or.* 9.5.184c; 8.187d; 9.188c, 189 Rochefort.

Diogenes, it remained a problem for the Stoics in particular to justify their Cynic heritage.

Although in this essay we shall limit ourselves to outlining the history of the ideal Cynic from Epictetus to Julian, it will be useful to survey briefly earlier attempts to make the Cynic movement respectable. The beginnings of an idealization, as M.-O. Goulet-Cazé has suggested,[3] may perhaps be seen in the meliambic verses composed by Cercidas of Megalopolis in praise of Diogenes and quoted by Diogenes Laertius in his account of the different versions of how the Cynic died.[4] He died, the poet says, as a result of holding his breath and went to heaven, "for in truth he was rightly named Diogenes, a true-born son of Zeus, a hound of heaven" (*Zanos gonos hēs gar alatheōs, / ouranios te kuōn*).[5] That Cercidas in the Hellenistic manner is playing on the etymology of the name should of course be borne in mind when we take these verses as an early example of intended idealization. That there was a tendency to idealization receives support from a letter falsely ascribed to Diogenes in which in proclaiming his divine mission among men he calls himself a "hound of heaven" (*kuōn ho ouranou, Ep.* 7.1).

So far as we can judge from Book 1 of Cicero's *De Officiis* the elimination of the Cynic heritage of Stoic ethics was the aim of Panaetius. It is certainly with Cynicizing Stoics in view that Cicero (*De Off.* 1.128: *Stoici paene Cynici*) not only criticizes their lack of decorum but completely rejects the Cynic way of life, since in his view it proves to be incompatible with man's natural feeling of shame (§148: *Cynicorum vero ratio tota est eicienda: est enim inimica verecundiae*).[6] In Book 3 of *De Finibus* Cicero's disapproval of Cynic ethics is less pronounced and reflects the lack of unanimity in the attitude of the Stoics toward Diogenes and the inheritance of his rigorism.[7] When faced with the crucial question whether the wise man should play the Cynic, some would answer that the decision rests with him alone (so Apollodorus of Seleucia, D.L. 7.121 [= *SVF* 3, p. 261.20]; cf. also Arius Didymus, Stob. 2.7.11 [S], p. 114.24 W.),[8] whereas others would emphatically deny that Cynicism as a shortcut to virtue

---

3. Goulet-Cazé (*supra*, n. 1) 3913–14.

4. D.L. 6.76–77 (= fr. 1, p. 202 Powell = fr. 54 Livrea). See E. Livrea, "La morte di Diogene cinico," *Filologia e forme litterarie: Studi offerti a F. Della Corte* vol. 1 (Urbino 1987) 427–33.

5. Cercidas, fr. 1.7–8 Powell (rightly following von Arnim, *pace* L. Lomiento, *Cercidas* [Rome 1993] 308). See von Fritz (*supra*, n. 1) 40; F. Williams, "Two Notes on Cercidas of Megalopolis," in *Apophoreta Philologica*, Mélanges M. Fernández-Galiano, Estudios Clásicos 26, no. 87 (Madrid 1984), 354–57; Giannantoni (*supra*, n. 1) 4.493 n. 9. For the notion of the hound of heaven cf. *AP* 7.64.4, 11.158.6 (Antip. Thess.), with the commentary of A. S. F. Gow and D. L. Page, *The Garland of Philip* (Cambridge 1968) 2.98.

6. See M. Billerbeck, *Der Kyniker Demetrius: Ein Beitrag zur Geschichte der frühkaiserzeitlichen Popularphilosophie*, Philosophia Antiqua 36 (Leiden 1979), 3–4; M.-O. Goulet-Cazé, "Le cynisme à l'époque impériale," *ANRW* 2.36.4 (Berlin 1990) 2750; and M. Griffin in this volume.

7. *De Fin.* 3.68: *Cynicorum autem rationem atque vitam alii cadere in sapientem dicunt, si qui eiusmodi forte casus inciderit, ut id faciendum sit, alii nullo modo.*

8. See M.-O. Goulet-Cazé, *L'ascèse cynique: Un commentaire de Diogène Laërce VI 70–71*, Histoire des Doctrines de l'Antiquité Classique 10 (Paris 1986), 22–24.

was an alternative to Stoicism. In fact, the tendency to a rigoristic way of life, such as was preached and practiced by Diogenes, had its followers within the later Stoa. They are the target of Seneca's *Epistle* 5 to Lucilius and also serve as the negative counterpart to his friend Demetrius, who is praised not only for the austerity of his life and his independence of both men and circumstances but, above all, for loyalty to his own principles. This refined ideal of an uncompromisingly resolute but noble character in Seneca's portrait of Demetrius contrasts sharply with the real imitator of the Dog that emerges from the testimony of others.[9]

Epictetus

From a survey of the extant literary sources, Epictetus's *Diatribe* 3.22 (*Peri Kunismou*) and its summary in 4.8.30–43 emerge as the first texts that present a coherent outline of the Cynic way of life and its prerequisites.[10] Modeled on the examples of Heracles, Socrates, Diogenes, and Crates, the portrait of the ideal Cynic consists of two parts. In the first place Epictetus deals with the training of the Cynic adept (3.22.13–22). In following a divine calling, the adherent of true Cynicism will undergo a total conversion and free himself from any false idea of values that he still might have. Instead of concealing his vices behind excessive shamelessness and an ostentatious display of independence as the sham Cynics do, the sincere follower of Diogenes will find his best protection in a genuine feeling of respect and shame (*aidōs:* 3.22.15, 4.8.33), the absence of which was regarded as the most characteristic feature of Cynicism.[11]

The second and longer part of *Diatribe* 3.22, which describes the Cynic's mission to mankind, can be divided in three sections: the message of his moral values, his way of life among men, and his personality. It is important to note that the doctrine of the messenger of Zeus as it is delineated in 3.22.23–44 (and summarized in 4.8.30–32) contains nothing that qualifies as exclusively Cynic. It is in fact the example of Socrates that the Cynic will have to follow when he is called upon to show men "that in questions of good and evil they have gone astray, and are seeking the true nature of the good and the evil where it is not, but where it is they never think" (§23; transl. W. A. Oldfather). The motif of the Cynic who raises his voice and addresses the people from the tragic stage (§26) is derived from the Platonic dialogue *Clitophon* and accordingly reflects the Socratic coloring of the passage.[12] The same tradition is fol-

9. See Billerbeck (*supra,* n. 6) esp. 15–16, 54–56; ead., "La réception du cynisme à Rome," *AC* 51 (1982) 151–73 (English version in Billerbeck [*supra,* n. 1] 147–66); Goulet-Cazé (*supra,* n. 6) 2730–31, 2768–73.

10. See M. Billerbeck, *Epiktet: Vom Kynismus, hrsg. und übersetzt mit einem Kommentar.* Philosophia Antiqua 34 (Leiden 1978); Goulet-Cazé (*supra,* n. 6) 2773–76.

11. Cf. Lucian, *Vit. Auct.* 10; on the idea of αἰδώς in Epictetus, see Billerbeck (*supra,* n. 10) 67–68.

12. Ps.-Plato, *Clit.* 407a; see M. Kokolakis, *The Dramatic Simile of Life* (Athens 1960) 12.

lowed by Dio Chrysostom, who in the speech *On His Exile* (*Or.* 13) has Socrates present a Cynicizing prosopopoeia.[13] When dealing with the personality of the ideal Cynic in the final part of 3.22 (§§90–106), Epictetus draws on anecdotal material about Diogenes. Apart from purging the anecdotes of any provocative points, he even gives the Cynic features of Crates' philanthropic character.[14]

Based on anecdotes and *chreiai,* the long passage on how the ideal Cynic will live among men (§§45–89) serves to illustrate the extraordinary character of this vocation. For whereas the credo of frugality and of virtue put to the test harmonizes perfectly with the principles of Stoicism, self-sufficiency such as was demonstrated by Diogenes seems to clash sharply with the doctrine that even the wise man will fulfill his civic duties. Accordingly, the rejection of friendship, marriage, begetting of children, and engagement in politics called for positive reinterpretation,[15] if Cynicism, especially among Romans, was not to become suspect as a subversive movement. The ideal Cynic, therefore, will not withdraw from his duties as citizen because he rejects them; on the contrary, he renounces them in order to put himself in the service of the whole of mankind (§§69, 81, 85). His mission among men is a divine one; his task, universal—a true vocation, which follows its own rules. By raising Cynicism to a religious level and to the status of an exceptional existence within the human community, Epictetus not only idealizes the spiritual filiation Diogenes–Crates–Zeno but at the same time relieves the Stoic sage of having to choose whether or not he will play the Dog. It is for Zeus alone to call him to an imitation of Diogenes (§§1, 53, 56) and to appoint him to the post of messenger (*aggelos,* §§23, 38, 69), scout (*kataskopos,* §§38, 69),[16] witness (*martus,* §88),[17] and herald of the gods (*kērux tōn theōn,* §69).[18]

13. *Or.* 13.14–28. Whereas H. von Arnim, *Leben und Werke des Dio von Prusa* (Berlin 1898) 255–60, while acknowledging the affinity between the Σωκρατικὸς λόγος and the *Clitophon,* denies that there exists a direct link between the two speeches, P. Desideri, *Dione di Prusa: Un intellettuale greco nell'impero romano* (Messina 1978) 253 n. 3, supposes "che Dione abbia liberamente rielaborato il *Clitofonte* . . . , ne più ne meno di quello che ha fatto Epitteto nell'analogo passo." The passage *Clit.* 407a–e also served as a model for Ps.-Plutarch, *De Lib. Educ.* 4e, and Themistius, *Or.* 26.320d.

14. Cf. also *Diatr.* 3.22.64–65; see Billerbeck (*supra,* n. 10) 7.

15. Cf. Lucian, *Vit. Auct.* 9: γάμου δὲ ἀμελήσεις καὶ παίδων καὶ πατρίδος, καὶ πάντα σοι ταῦτα λῆρος ἔσται . . . [10] μόνος καὶ ἀκοινώνητος εἶναι θέλε μὴ φίλον, μὴ ξένον προσιέμενος. Maximus of Tyre, *Or.* 36.5.140–42 Trapp: οὐχ ὑπὸ πολιτείας ἀσχολούμενος, οὐχ ὑπὸ παιδοτροφίας ἀγχόμενος, οὐχ ὑπὸ γάμου καθειργμένος. See Billerbeck (*supra,* n. 10) 128, 131, 145.

16. On the notion of κατάσκοπος see E. Norden, "Beiträge zur Geschichte der griechischen Philosophie," *Jbb. für Classische Philologie,* Suppl. 19 (Leipzig 1893), 377–82; Giannantoni (*supra,* n. 1) 4.507–8, however, expresses some reservations; see also F. Decleva Caizzi, "La tradizione antistenico-cinica in Epitteto," in G. Giannantoni, ed., *Scuole socratiche minori e filosofia ellenistica* (Bologna 1977) 111–12.

17. On the notion of μάρτυς see A. Delatte, "Le sage-témoin dans la philosophie stoïco-cynique," *BAB,* ser. 5, 39 (1953) 166–86.

18. See Billerbeck (*supra,* n. 10) 6–9; ead. (*supra,* n. 9) 161–66; Goulet-Cazé (*supra,* n. 6) 2775–76. This line of interpretation was also followed by G. Calogero, "Cinismo e stoicismo

The *Cynic Epistles*

In contrast to Epictetus and his tendency to give his portrayal of the ideal Cynic a Stoic coloring, the pseudepigraphic letters of Diogenes and Crates continue the popular tradition of the anecdotes and deal with the more familiar concepts of ancient Cynicism: training (*askēsis*), self-sufficiency (*autarkeia*), frugality, the positive evaluation of effort and labor (*ponos*), and the disdain of pleasure. Both the dating of the letters and their authorship are disputed.[19] Equally problematical is the negative picture of Odysseus in Crates' *Epistle* 19, which stands in marked contrast to the high esteem that that hero enjoyed among the Cynics.[20] But in general it may be said that Cynicism as conceived in the corpus of the letters reflects neither a change of Cynic principles nor a break within the Cynic tradition. Antisthenes appears as the teacher of Diogenes (Ps.-Diogenes, *Ep.* 28.8, 30, 34.1, 37.6; Ps.-Crates, *Ep.* 6), but Diogenes himself is given the credit of having put into practice the shortcut to virtue (Ps.-Diogenes, *Ep.* 30).[21] In fact, Antisthenes is depicted as having begun Cynic philosophy, whereas it is Diogenes who perfected it (Ps.-Crates, *Ep.* 6). The Cynic way of life appears to be something exceptional (Ps.-Diogenes, *Ep.* 41), founded on the conformity (*akolouthia*) of words with deeds (Ps.-Diogenes, *Ep.* 15).[22] More interesting for us are the letters falsely ascribed to Crates, which often convey a tendency to idealization.[23] Diogenes is frequently mentioned, but his way of life is recommended in a slightly apologetic tone. There is no reason, writes the author of *Epistles* 16, 21, and 23, to fear the name "Dog" or to shun the cloak and the wallet that are "the weapons of the

in Epitteto" (1933), *Scritti minori di filosofia antica*, Elenchos suppl. 10 (Naples 1984), 395–408, and by R. Laurenti, "Il 'filosofo ideale' secondo Epitteto," *Giornale di Metafisica* 17 (1962) 501–13.

19. For an introduction to the letters and their special problems see A.J. Malherbe, *The Cynic Epistles: A Study Edition*, Society of Biblical Literature, Sources for Biblical Study 12 (Missoula 1977), 10–21; the basic study on the letters of Ps.-Diogenes remains V.E. Emeljanow, "The Letters of Diogenes" (diss. Stanford: Ann Arbor [University Microfilms] 1968). Still important for the problems of date and authorship is W. Capelle, "De Cynicorum Epistulis" (diss. Göttingen 1896); see also Goulet-Cazé (*supra*, n. 6) 2743–45, and Giannantoni (*supra*, n. 1) 4.551–53. The text of the *Cynic Epistles* is now to be used in the new critical edition by E. Müseler, *Die Kynikerbriefe*, Bd. 1, *Die Überlieferung, mit Beiträgen und dem Anhang 'Das Briefcorpus Ω' von Martin Sicherl;* Bd. 2, *Kritische Ausgabe mit deutscher Übersetzung*, Studien zur Geschichte und Kultur des Altertums, n.F., 1. Reihe, Monographien 6, 7 (Paderborn 1994).

20. On this problem see especially Norden (*supra*, n. 16) 394–95. On the figure of Odysseus in the Antisthenic tradition see R. Höistad, *Cynic Hero and Cynic King: Studies in the Cynic Conception of Man* (Uppsala 1948) 94–102; F. Decleva Caizzi (*supra*, n. 16) 102–3; A. Brancacci, *Oikeios Logos: La filosofia del linguaggio di Antistene*, Elenchos Suppl. 20 (Naples 1990), 45–55, 83, 115–16, 157 n. 19.

21. See V. Emeljanow, "A Note on the Cynic Shortcut to Happiness," *Mnemosyne*, ser. 4, 18 (1965) 182–84.

22. The Cynic elements in the letters of Ps.-Diogenes have been discussed in detail by V.E. Emeljanow; see above, n. 19.

23. For a study of these letters the article by A. Olivieri, "Le epistole del Pseudo-Cratete," *RFIC* 27 (1899) 406–21, is still important.

gods." [24] The cloak of Diogenes, indeed, is not held in esteem (so the opening of *Ep.* 13), but compared with elegant robes, it is at least secure (*asphalēs*).

Much attention is given to the topos of begging. The figure of Diogenes asking for food or money is a stock theme of the anecdotes (cf. D.L. 6.26, 49, 56, 57, 59, 67) [25] and could well be interpreted as an early component of the Cynic tradition. [26] Since mendicity had become very popular among the sham Cynics, [27] Epictetus suppresses this feature of Diogenes in his *Diatribe* 3.22, as does Seneca, who stresses the fact that his model Cynic Demetrius refused to go begging. [28]

Although they draw heavily upon the anecdotes and *chreiai,* the *Cynic Epistles* avoid presenting extreme positions and adopt a somewhat compromising attitude. In *Epistle* 10 ascribed to him Diogenes is reported to have encouraged Metrocles to ask people for things because in doing this he would imitate the sages who, as Socrates used to say, do not beg but demand back what belongs to them. [29] This positive revaluation of Cynic mendicity occurs three times in the letters of Crates, where we encounter the motif no less than seven times. [30]

Diogenes' negative attitude toward marriage and procreation is well documented in the anecdotes and is reflected in *Epistle* 47. [31] It should not surprise us that this rigoristic point of view appears somewhat softened in the letters of Crates that are addressed to Hipparchia. Apart from encouraging his wife to continue in the Cynic way of life (*Ep.* 28–32), Crates in his *Epistle* 33 congratulates her on the speedy and easy birth of a son. Emeljanow in dealing with the Diogenian tradition is certainly right when he insists on the fact that the relation between Crates and Hipparchia, both of whom were following their philosophical vocation, was always regarded as an exception and would not invalidate the general Cynic rejection of marriage. [32] Nevertheless, the advice that Hipparchia is given (Ps.-Crates, *Ep.* 33.2) seems to point to the idea of family life among Cynics. [33] The baby, he instructs his wife, should be bathed

24. Ps.-Crates, *Ep.* 16: τὰ θεῶν ὅπλα. Cf. also *Ep.* 23: τὰ Διογένεια ὅπλα.

25. Cf. also Diogenes V B 247–63 Giannantoni (*supra* n. 4).

26. On the Epicurean polemics against the Cynics (οὐδὲ κυνιεῖν . . . οὐδὲ πτωχεύσειν) see the detailed study by M. Gigante, *Cinismo e epicureismo,* Memorie dell'Istituto Italiano per gli Studi Filosofici (Naples 1992), esp. 39–42 (reprinted in M.-O. Goulet-Cazé, ed., *Le cynisme ancien et ses prolongements: Actes du Colloque international du C.N.R.S.* [Paris 1993] 177–79).

27. This is a favorite subject of Lucian; cf. esp. *Fug.* 14, 17; *Pisc.* 35.

28. *Vit. Beat.* 18.3; see Billerbeck (*supra,* n. 6) 29–31.

29. Ps.-Diogenes, *Ep.* 10.2: Σωκράτης δὲ ἔλεγε μὴ αἰτεῖν τοὺς σπουδαίους, ἀλλὰ ἀπαιτεῖν· εἶναι γὰρ αὐτῶν τὰ πάντα ὡς καὶ τῶν θεῶν. Cf. Emeljanow (*supra,* n. 19) 29–30, 64, 112.

30. Ps.-Crates, *Epp.* 2, 26, 27; cf. also 17, 19, 22, 36; Olivieri (*supra,* n. 23) 417.

31. Cf. D.L. 6.29, 54, 72; and *supra,* n. 15. See Emeljanow (*supra,* n. 19) 67–70; Billerbeck (*supra,* n. 10) 130–31.

32. Emeljanow (*supra,* n. 19) 70; cf. Epictetus, *Diatr.* 3.22.76.

33. Ps.-Crates, *Ep.* 33.2: ἔστω οὖν λουτρὸν μὲν ψυχρόν, σπάργανα δὲ τρίβων, τροφὴ δὲ γάλακτος ὅσον γε μὴ ἐς κόρον, βαυκαλήσεις δὲ ἐν ὀστρακίῳ χελώνης· τοῦτο γάρ φασι καὶ

in cold water, clothed in a *tribōn,* and fed on small quantities of milk. It should sleep in a cradle made from a tortoise shell, which is said to protect against childhood diseases.[34] And when he is able to speak and to walk Hipparchia should dress him with a staff, cloak, and wallet. Insignificant as it might seem at first sight, this program of Cynic education echoes a passage of Epictetus's *Diatribe* 3.22. In the present state of things, Epictetus says, the ideal Cynic will renounce marriage, for he would be driven from his profession to act as nurse in his own family, to heat the bathwater for the baby, and to provide blankets, oil, and a cradle when his wife has borne a child (§71). In a city of wise men, however, even the Cynic will marry and raise children, since his wife would be like himself and his children would be brought up in the same fashion (§68).[35]

This thematic link between Epictetus and the *Cynic Epistles* allows no conclusions to be drawn about either the dating of the pseudepigraphic corpus or its authorship. Yet the few examples given seem to confirm our observation that the letters show a tendency to make Cynicism acceptable as a moral philosophy, as a rigorous way of life, a shortcut to virtue. Hence the slightly apologetic tone in the formula of consolation *mē aniō,* "Do not be upset" (e.g., "to see me in the Cynic dress"), or when censuring in the proviso *heōs an phobēi,* "So long as you fear" (e.g., "to be called Dog").[36] Conveyed in the form of a short note or a letter, the message of Diogenes and of Crates pretends to be composed for a specific occasion and—compared, for example, with Seneca's in the *Letters to Lucilius*—lacks any systematic outline of doctrine. Drawing as they do from the anecdotes about Diogenes and Crates as well as from the impact of these personalities on the behavior of the later Cynics, the *Cynic Epistles* serve as a sort of all-purpose vade mecum for followers of this philosophy.

The Diogenes Speeches of Dio Chrysostom

As a source for Cynicism in the imperial period the Diogenes speeches of Dio Chrysostom (as well as *Or.* 4, the *Fourth Oration on Kingship*) have been the subject of much dispute.[37] In the wake of *Quellenforschung* they have been regarded as a source of Antisthenic doctrine and a valuable testimony of the

---

πρὸς νοσήματα παιδικὰ διαφέρειν. ἐπειδὰν δὲ ἐς τὸ λαλεῖν ἢ περιπατεῖν ἔλθῃ, κοσμήσασα αὐτὸ ... βακτηρίᾳ καὶ τρίβωνι καὶ πήρᾳ. See Olivieri (*supra,* n. 23) 418.

34. The νοσήματα παιδικά against which their "puppy" (σκυλάκιον) is to be protected are presumably those caused by the evil eye; on the apotropaic use of the tortoise against this ever-present danger to small children see Otto Keller, *Die antike Tierwelt* vol. 2 (Leipzig 1913) 251–52. Normally they were given an amulet to be hung around their neck, on which see E.M. Stern, "Kinderkännchen zum Choenfest," in *Thiasos: Sieben Archäologische Arbeiten,* ed. Thuri Lorenz (Amsterdam 1978) 29–30.

35. Epictetus, *Diatr.* 3.22.67–76; see Billerbeck (*supra,* n. 10) 130–40, and, on the Cynic view of the οἶκος in general, D. Dawson, *Cities of the Gods* (New York 1992) 134–39.

36. Ps.-Diogenes, *Epp.* 7.1, 34.1; and Ps.-Crates, *Epp.* 21, 23; cf. also 16.

37. On the problem and its history see Desideri (*supra,* n. 13) 537–47; Giannantoni (*supra,* n. 1) 4.553–59; Billerbeck (*supra,* n. 1) 19.

ancient Cynic tradition; however, more recently scholars have tended to see in the Diogenes speeches a device of the sophist that allows him to make the Cynic a mouthpiece for his own convictions.[38] In fact, we find Dio adopting on occasion the persona of Odysseus,[39] Socrates,[40] or Diogenes whenever this fits the message he has to convey.[41] Whether he actually became a Cynic during his years of exile has been much disputed.[42] In the speech *To the Alexandrians,* for example, he violently attacks contemporary Cynics who discredit philosophy through their ignorance and ostentation (*Or.* 32.9). In the *Second Tarsian Oration* he complains that because of his cloak he is taken for a sham Cynic (*Or.* 34.2).[43] Why then, we may ask, did the sophist have recourse to the figure of Diogenes if he wished to refute the bad reputation of Cynicism and make the pose of the Dog respectable? The Diogenes speech *On Tyranny* (*Or.* 6) deals with the Cynic's self-sufficiency, his faculty of adapting to any circumstance, and his unrestrained sense of independence. It is particularly in this last point that the oration shows an affinity with the *Fourth Oration on Kingship.* There Dio, exploiting the anecdote of the Cynic's unbridled freedom of speech (*parrhēsia*) in the presence of Alexander the Great, veils his own criticism of Trajan's rule.[44] The *Isthmian Oration* (*Or.* 9) and the oration *On Servants and Oracles* (*Or.* 10) deal with main points of Cynic doctrine while retaining the appearance of addresses composed for a specific occasion. Finally, in the speech *On Virtue* (*Or.* 8) the various topoi, such as the comparison of the Cynic

38. For the *Quellenforschung* cf. especially E. Weber, *De Dione Chrysostomo Cynicorum Sectatore,* Leipziger Studien zur Classischen Philologie 10 (Leipzig 1887), 77–268; Höistad (*supra,* n. 20) esp. 150–220. An early reaction against this approach can be seen in the work of K. Hahn, *De Dionis Chrysostomi Orationibus, Quae Inscribuntur Diogenes (VI, VIII, IX, X)* (Bad Homburg 1896); see also von Fritz (*supra,* n. 1) 82–83. This line of interpretation was followed and developed by J. Moles, "The Career and Conversion of Dio Chrysostom," *JHS* 98 (1978) 96–100; id., "The Date and Purpose of the Fourth Kingship Oration of Dio Chrysostom," *ClAnt* 2 (1983) 251–78; less convincing is Moles's Cynic interpretation of the *First Oration On Kingship,* "The Kingship Orations of Dio Chrysostom," *Papers of the Leeds International Latin Seminar* 6 (Leeds 1990) 297–375, esp. 305–37. Further see C. P. Jones, *The Roman World of Dio Chrysostom* (Cambridge, Mass., 1978) 46–50; A. Brancacci, "Tradizione cinica e problemi di datazione nelle orazioni diogeniane di Dione di Prusa," *Elenchos* 1 (1980) 92–122; id. *Rhētorikē philosophousa: Dione Crisostomo nella cultura antica e bizantina,* Elenchos Suppl. 11 (Naples 1985), 50–62. In an earlier article, however ("Le orazioni diogeniane di Dione Crisostomo," in Giannantoni [*supra,* n. 16 (1977)] 141–71), Brancacci had shown some sympathy for the *Quellenforschung.*

39. See Desideri (*supra,* n. 13) 174–75 n. 2, 261–62; Moles (*supra,* n. 38 [1978]) 97. In impersonating Odysseus, Dio was imitated by the sophist Favorinus; see M. W. Gleason, *Making Men* (Princeton 1995) 153–58.

40. See Desideri (*supra,* n. 13) 298, 449 n. 51.

41. On the Diogenes orations in general see von Arnim (*supra,* n. 13) 260–67. For a detailed discussion of Dio's adoption of the pose of Diogenes see F. Jouan, "Le Diogène de Dion Chrysostome," in Goulet-Cazé (*supra,* n. 26) 381–97.

42. See Moles (*supra,* n. 38 [1978]) 93–96; id. "Dio Chrysostom: Exile, Tarsus, Nero and Domitian," *LCM* 8 (1983) 130–34. Desideri (*supra,* n. 13: 200–201) and Jones (*supra,* n. 38: 49–50) remain very skeptical.

43. On Dio's polemics against the Cynics see Desideri (*supra,* n. 13) 150–51.

44. See Moles (*supra,* n. 38 [1983]).

with a physician, the need of training, the rejection of pleasure, and Heracles as a model, are developed at the expense of Diogenes' persona without, however, giving the diatribe a definite moral program.[45] Those speeches, as M. Szarmach has well demonstrated,[46] draw upon the legendary tradition about Diogenes, but in contrast to the *Cynic Epistles,* Dio's aim is neither propaganda nor conversion to the Dog's way of life.[47] The tendency to idealization is unobtrusive and consists solely in the fact that Diogenes, like Odysseus and Socrates, serves as a persona possessed of authority. The sophist is concerned not with contrasting the false Cynics with the idealized portrait of their alleged model but rather with assuming the role of the philosopher who was admired for his independence and freedom of speech.[48]

Oration 36 of Maximus of Tyre and the *Kunikos* of Pseudo-Lucian

A survey of the Cynic literature of the first and second centuries A.D. reveals little difference between the sophist who adopts the pose of Diogenes and the rhetor who composes a panegyric of the Cynic way of life. In fact, the Diogenes speech *On Tyranny* (*Or.* 6) of Dio Chrysostom has been claimed as a model not only for the Pseudo-Lucianic dialogue *Kunikos,*[49] but also for *Oration* 36 of Maximus of Tyre.[50] The two works reveal some points of resemblance and thus invite comparison. Like Dio, who contrasts the fainthearted tyrant with a fearless Diogenes,[51] both authors use the device of *sugkrisis* (comparison).

Maximus opens his oration with an elaborate comparison between the Golden Age and the Iron Age (§§1–2). In a second *sugkrisis* he opposes debauchery to a life of discipline (§§3–4). After these moral and literary commonplaces Maximus introduces Diogenes and presents him as the model of a perfectly happy life (§5). The praise of the Cynic way of life, which emphasizes

---

45. On the structure of *Or.* 8 and the origin of its various elements see Hahn (*supra*, n. 38) 38–49; M. Capone Ciollaro, *Dione Crisostomo: Sulla virtù (Or. 8)* (Naples 1983) 9–16.

46. "Les Discours diogéniens de Dion de Pruse," *Eos* 65 (1977) 77–90.

47. This does not exclude the possibility that in content and style the *Cynic Epistles* were influenced by the Diogenes orations; see Brancacci (*supra*, n. 38 [1985]) 61–62. Hahn (*supra*, n. 38: 27–31, 33) assumes a common source.

48. See Jouan (*supra*, n. 41) 386–89, 394.

49. See R. Helm, "Lukianos," *RE* 13.2 (1927) 1734; according to Hahn (*supra*, n. 38: 31–33) the resemblance derives from the use of a common source; see also *supra*, n. 47. On the problem of dating the dialogue see Goulet-Cazé (*supra*, n. 6) 2743 n. 168.

50. See R. Hobein, "De Maximo Tyrio Quaestiones Philologae Selectae" (diss. Göttingen 1895) 92–93, and more generally, Brancacci (*supra*, n. 38 [1985]) 58–60. For a short discussion of *Or.* 36 see M. Szarmach, *Maximos von Tyros: Eine literarische Monographie* (Toruń 1985) 39–41; id. "Wie Maximus von Tyrus den Kynismus und den Epikureismus interpretiert," *WZRostock* 34 (1985) 59–60.

51. On the device of *sugkrisis* see M. T. Luzzatto, *Tragedia greca e cultura ellenistica: L'or. LII di Dione di Prusa,* Opuscula Philologa 4 (Bologna 1983), 33–37; still useful is F. Focke, "Synkrisis," *Hermes* 58 (1923) 327–68, esp. 328–39.

self-sufficiency and complete independence from all civic and social obliga-tions,[52] is expressed in a series of negative concepts: "without fear of tyrants," "not bound by the rules of law," "without engagement in politics," "not re-sponsible for maintenance," "not attached by bonds of marriage," and so on.[53] Moreover, Diogenes even ridicules people who burden themselves with duties and become the slaves of all sorts of obligations.[54] (The anaphoric *doulos* in §6 emphasizes this idea.) The praise of the Cynic way of life is highly rhetorical, with an abundant use of negative expressions echoing original Cynic diction. In the anecdotes Diogenes displays self-sufficiency and complete freedom from emotions (*apatheia*), posing as banished (*apolis*), as houseless (*aoikos*) and homeless (*anestios*), as having no slaves (*adoulos*) and without possessions (*aktēmōn*).[55] In contrast to Epictetus's idealized Cynic, who because of his uni-versal mission has given up all claim to social status,[56] Maximus presents an encomium of a Diogenes who contents himself with parading his independence and a moral superiority even to Socrates (§6).

In the Pseudo-Lucianic *Kunikos* the *sugkrisis* between the independent life of the Cynics and those who live a life of fear and false conceptions is less explicit than in Maximus's oration.[57] The praise of Cynicism follows the so-phistic tradition rather than the philosophical and concentrates on the Cynic's garb, especially the cloak (*tribōn*).[58] The author refers to the heroic precursors of Cynicism (notably Heracles) and inserts various comparisons with animals in the tradition of Diogenes and his ancient followers. But instead of outlining a coherent portrait of the Cynic profession, Pseudo-Lucian is more concerned with embellishing his style. That the dialogue shows some affinity with the *Cynic Epistles* may be correct;[59] it lacks, however, the freshness and the fervor of Cynic propaganda that characterize the pseudepigraphic corpus.[60] The pose of a sophist advocating Cynicism cannot replace the missionary zeal of a Cynic adherent.

---

52. *Or.* 36.5.137–38 Trapp: τὰς περιστάσεις πάσας ἀπεδύσατο καὶ τῶν δεσμῶν ἐξέ-λυσεν αὐτόν.

53. *Or.* 36.5.140–42 Trapp: οὐ τύραννον δεδιώς, οὐχ ὑπὸ νόμου κατηναγκασμένος, οὐχ ὑπὸ πολιτείας ἀσχολούμενος, οὐχ ὑπὸ παιδοτροφίας ἀγχόμενος, οὐχ ὑπὸ γάμου καθ-ειργμένος.

54. *Or.* 36.5.144–45 Trapp: τούτων ἀπάντων τῶν ἀνδρῶν καὶ τῶν ἐπιτηδευμάτων κατ-εγέλα.

55. Cf. Diogenes V B 263 Giannantoni (*supra*, n. 1); Epictetus, *Diatr.* 3.22.45, 47; 4.8.31. Giannantoni (*supra*, n. 1: 4.544–45) rightly refers to the negative character of these attributes; see also Billerbeck (*supra*, n. 10) 9; Goulet-Cazé (*supra*, n. 8) 20 n. 10, 56–57.

56. See *supra*, n. 55, on Epictetus (Diatr. 3.22.69, 81, 85).

57. Ps.-Lucian, *Cyn.* 8–20.

58. See R. Helm, "Lucian und die Philosophenschulen," *NJbb für das klassische Altertum* 9 (1902) 360–61.

59. See Hahn (*supra*, n. 38) 33–34.

60. Goulet-Cazé (*supra*, n. 6) 2744.

Lucian's *Life of Demonax*

Compared with the pseudepigraphic *Kunikos,* Lucian's *Life of Demonax* glows with the moral engagement of its author.[61] Full of admiration for his teacher and the kind of life he led (§1), Lucian recommends this model philosopher for the imitation of the young (§2). What were his convictions and his moral qualities? Although eclectic in his doctrine,[62] and favorable to the notion of a general education (§4), Demonax practiced the Cynic credo of independence, freedom of speech,[63] training, and self-sufficiency. He is said to have imitated Diogenes in his dress and in his frugality, but in contrast to his professed model he rejected ostentation and conformed to the life of the community, even engaging in politics.[64] Known for his peaceable and affable character, he became the friend of many people. The predominant quality of his philosophy is described as kind, gentle, and cheerful;[65] the personality that emerges from the apophthegms and the anecdotes about Demonax invites comparison with the philanthropic nature of Crates.[66] But Lucian avoids comparing the two men, insisting instead on the fact that his master tended to eclecticism. Possessed of a reverence for Socrates, an admiration for Diogenes, and a love for Aristippus, Demonax combined personal culture with moral determination, matching affability with firmness, with a resultant softening of Cynic rigorism in favor of a more balanced philosophical attitude.[67] Similarly, he did not indulge in Socratic irony but conversed with his friends with Attic urbanity (§6), and far from displaying Cynic aggressiveness he remained sociable even when he was assailing vice and felt compelled to rebuke it (§7).

61. See K. Funk, *Untersuchungen über die lucianische Vita Demonactis,* Philologus Suppl. 10 (Leipzig 1907), 559–674; H. Cancik, "Bios und Logos: Formengeschichtliche Untersuchungen zu Lukians 'Demonax,' " in H. Cancik, ed., *Markus-Philologie: Historische, literargeschichtliche und stilistische Untersuchungen zum zweiten Evangelium,* Wissenschaftliche Untersuchungen zum Neuen Testament 33 (Tübingen 1984), 115–30; C.P. Jones, *Culture and Society in Lucian* (Cambridge, Mass., 1986) 90–100; R.B. Branham, *Unruly Eloquence* (Cambridge, Mass. 1989) 57–63; Goulet-Cazé (*supra,* n. 6) 2763–64; D. Clay, "Lucian of Samosata: Four Philosophical Lives," *ANRW* 2.35.5 (Berlin 1992) 3425–29.

62. *Dem.* 5: φιλοσοφίας δὲ εἶδος οὐχ ἓν ἀποτεμόμενος, ἀλλὰ πολλὰς ἐς ταὐτὸ καταμίξας οὐ πάνυ τι ἐξέφαινε τίνι αὐτῶν ἔχαιρεν· ἐῴκει δὲ τῷ Σωκράτει μᾶλλον ᾠκειῶσθαι.

63. *Dem.* 3: ὅλον δὲ παραδοὺς ἑαυτὸν ἐλευθερίᾳ καὶ παρρησίᾳ. On verbal duels between Demonax and the sophist Favorinus see Gleason (*supra,* n. 39) 135–37.

64. *Dem.* 5: τῷ σχήματι καὶ τῇ τοῦ βίου ῥᾳστώνῃ τὸν Σινωπέα ζηλοῦν ἔδοξεν, οὐ παραχαράττων τὰ εἰς τὴν δίαιταν, ὡς θαυμάζοιτο καὶ ἀποβλέποιτο ὑπὸ τῶν ἐντυγχανόντων, ἀλλ' ὁμοδίαιτος ἅπασι καὶ πεζὸς ὢν καὶ οὐδ' ἐπ' ὀλίγον τύφῳ κάτοχος συνῆν καὶ ξυνεπολιτεύετο.

65. *Dem.* 9: τοιοῦτός τις ἦν ὁ τρόπος τῆς φιλοσοφίας αὐτοῦ, πρᾶος καὶ ἥμερος καὶ φαιδρός.

66. See Funk (*supra,* n. 61) 619–20.

67. Despite his eclecticism, D. Sedley ("Philosophical Allegiance in the Greco-Roman World," in M. Griffin and J. Barnes, eds., *Philosophia Togata* [Oxford 1989] 119 n. 48) considers him "a committed Socratic of some kind"; but see the reservations of Funk (*supra,* n. 61) 595–96.

In the *Life of Demonax,* as in the speeches of Diogenes by Dio Chrysostom, Cynicism recommends itself by its concept of self-sufficiency and freedom of speech—both qualities rooted in the Socratic doctrine. On the other hand, the Cynic features in the portrait of Demonax are applied very discreetly and provoke neither derision nor satire. Such imitation of Diogenes as Lucian describes in the portrayal of his master is restrained and may well be an idealization of Demonax's actual behavior. It is through his eclecticism that the predilection of Demonax for Cynicism gains respectability and can serve as a model for young followers.[68]

Julian and Cynicism

The last author whom we shall deal with in this essay on the ideal cynic is the emperor Julian. A declared enemy of luxury (*truphē*), he liked to pose as a boorish and intractable character (so in the *Misopogon* in his conflict with the Antiochenes)[69] and to impute his austere attitude to his "Scythian" tutor Mardonius, who had educated him with rigorous methods.[70] The emperor's propensity to asceticism emerges also from the description of Ammianus Marcellinus, who praises *temperantia* as Julian's most prominent virtue. His self-sufficiency, the historian points out, not only marked the life he led when on military expeditions, but was a concomitant of his everyday existence, with its inclination to philosophy.[71]

In fact, Julian's idea of austerity seems to coincide perfectly with his conception of the true Cynic, whom he describes in *Oration 7 (Against the Cynic Heraclius)*: "He avoids any excess in food and renounces the pleasures of sexual intercourse. . . . That is the true shortcut to philosophy. A man must completely come out of himself and recognize that he is divine and keep his mind untiringly and steadfastly fixed on divine thoughts, which are stainless and pure. He must also utterly despise his body and regard it, in the words of Heraclitus, as 'more deserving to be thrown out than dung.' "[72] Julian's comparison of the human body with dung reflects the Neoplatonic coloring of the

---

68. On the portrayal of Demonax as an ideal philosopher and its relation to Epictetus, *Diatr.* 3.22, see Funk (*supra,* n. 61) 668–72.

69. See M. Billerbeck, "L'empereur bourru: Julien et le 'Dyscolos' de Ménandre," in G. Hering, ed., *Dimensionen griechischer Literatur und Geschichte: Festschrift für Pavlos Tzermias zum 65. Geburtstag* (Frankfurt a.M. 1993) 37–51.

70. *Mis.* 20.351a–24.353d; on Mardonius and his Gothic origin see P. Athanassiadi-Fowden, *Julian and Hellenism: An Intellectual Biography* (Oxford 1981) 14–21.

71. Amm. Marc. 25.4.4: *namque in pace victus eius mensarumque tenuitas erat recte noscentibus admiranda velut ad pallium mox reversuri.*

72. *Or.* 7.20.226a, 226b–c Rochefort, an intensification of *Vorsokr.* 22 B 96, νέκυες γὰρ κοπρίων ἐκβλητότεροι, with which cf. also Ps.-Epich. *Vorsokr.* 23 B 64, εἰμὶ νεκρός· νεκρὸς δὲ κόπρος. See J. Bouffartigue, *L'empereur Julien et la culture de son temps,* Collection des Études Augustiniennes, Série Antiquité 133 (Paris 1992), 264, 278.

speech, just as does a passage in *Oration* 9 (*Against the Uneducated Cynics*), in which the true followers of Diogenes seem to subscribe to the Platonic doctrine of the soul's superiority to the body.[73] A certain disdain for the physical component of man, it has been argued, can also be traced in the *Meditations* of Marcus Aurelius,[74] whom Julian revered as a model of self-sufficiency.[75] Moreover, that the human body was not held in high esteem by the Stoics as well might be implied from the diatribes of Epictetus, who speaks of it as a *sōmation* (diminutive of "body"), *pēlos* (mud), and a *nekros* (corpse).[76] In contrast, however, to Eduard Zeller, who interpreted these expressions in the light of Platonic influence,[77] Adolf Bonhöffer rightly pointed out that such terms of contempt result from the Stoic definition of the body as a thing neither good nor bad (*adiaphoron*).[78] In addition, we should keep in mind that the Cynic doctrine of training refers to the body as well as to the soul.[79]

The lively interest that Julian took in true Cynicism and the attacks that he launched against the sham Cynics are displayed in two speeches composed in Constantinople during the year 362. Both works seem to have been prompted by the populistic activities of street philosophers whose possibly subversive influence on soldiers in camp and on the lower-class population the emperor could hardly have ignored. "The Cynics," he complains, "go up and down in our midst subverting the institutions of society, and that not by introducing a better and purer state of things but a worse and more corrupt state."[80] Julian compares them to the wandering monks and calls them *apotaktitai*, obviously a term of abuse if we take into account his invective against the members of this Encratite sect.[81] Julian, no less than Libanius[82] or Eunapius,[83] reveals his deep irritation when he directs his attacks against the itinerant monks, rebuking them for the discrepancy between what they preach and what they do. The comparison between the sham Cynics and the monastic ascetics is no novelty

73. *Or.* 9.11.190b; see also 9.16.198b Rochefort.

74. Cf. e.g., *Med.* 3.3.6; 4.41; 7.68.1; 8.37.2; 10.38; see E. Zeller, *Die Philosophie der Griechen in ihrer geschichtlichen Entwicklung,* 6th ed. (Darmstadt 1963), 3.2.259–61; R.B. Rutherford, *The Meditations of Marcus Aurelius: A Study* (Oxford 1989) 239–44. On Marcus Aurelius as precursor of Neoplatonic concepts see also H.R. Neuenschwander, *Mark Aurels Beziehungen zu Seneca und Poseidonios,* Noctes Romanae 3 (Bern 1951), 28–33.

75. *Caes.* 17.317c, 34.334a; see also Eutropius, *Brev.* 10.16.3; see Bouffartigue (*supra,* n. 72) 73–76.

76. Cf. e.g., 1.1.11, 13.5; 2.19.27; 3.10.15, 22.41; 4.11.27.

77. Zeller (*supra,* n. 74) 258–59.

78. A. Bonhöffer, *Epictet und die Stoa* (Stuttgart 1890; repr. Stuttgart 1968) 33–36. See further A. Jagu, "La morale d'Épictète et le christianisme," *ANRW* 2.36.3 (Berlin 1989) 2169–71.

79. See Goulet-Cazé (*supra,* n. 8), esp. 210–22.

80. *Or.* 7.5.210b–c, 18.224a–d Rochefort.

81. *Or.* 7.18.224a Rochefort.

82. *Or.* 2.32; 30.8, 31, 48; see A.J. Festugière, *Antioche païenne et chrétienne: Libanius, Chrysostome et les moines de Syrie* (Paris 1959) 235, 237–39.

83. *VS* 6.11.6 Giangrande.

but follows an established tradition.[84] In the *Acts of Philip*, for example, Philip is taken for a philosopher because of his dress (*skhēma apotaktikou*),[85] while for the *Life of Serapion* in Palladius's *Historia Lausiaca* and, more generally, for the literary genre of Christian aretalogy R. Reitzenstein has demonstrated an indebtedness to the Diogenes legend.[86]

Although in the speech *Against Heraclius* (*Or.* 7) Julian mentions several names, the Cynics whom he assails cannot be identified. Were they Christians?[87] Gregory of Nazianzus, for example, whose penchant for the Cynic idea of training can be clearly traced in his work,[88] nevertheless criticized Diogenes and Crates because they put on a display of their self-sufficiency and sought glory (*philodoxia*).[89] Julian's speech *Against the Uneducated Cynics* (*Or.* 9) was provoked by a Cynic who had accused Diogenes of vanity because he died from eating raw octopus, as though by a draft of hemlock.[90] The reproach of vanity (*kenodoxia, tuphos*), it is true, is a topos in the polemics between the different philosophical schools and was also exploited by Lucian when he ridiculed the suicides of Empedocles and Peregrinus.[91] But the evidence of Gregory as well as of Julian seems to suggest that disapproval of Diogenes' ostentation was particularly at home with Christian Cynics.

The polemical tone of *Oration* 9 owes much to Lucian's satires, but in contrast to the sophist, Julian does not limit himself to invective. Using the sham Cynics and their behavior as a foil he goes on to outline the program of true

84. G. Dorival, "Cyniques et chrétiens au temps des Pères grecs," in Goulet-Cazé (*supra*, n. 26) 425–27. On the relations between pagan and monastic asceticism in the fourth century see also J. H. W. G. Liebeschuetz, *Antioch: City and Imperial Administration in the Later Roman Empire* (Oxford 1972) 234–39; Goulet-Cazé (*supra*, n. 6) 2788–95; and see *infra*, n. 87.
85. *A. Phil.* 6, p. 4.4 Lipsius-Bonnet.
86. R. Reitzenstein, *Hellenistische Wundererzählungen*, 3d ed. (Darmstadt 1974), esp. 64–74.
87. That Christianism and Cynicism were not incompatible is implied by the figure of Maximus-Hero; see Goulet-Cazé (*supra*, n. 6) 2792. On Christian Cynics see P. Courcelle, "La figure du philosophe d'après les écrivains latins de l'antiquité," *Journal des Savants*, 1980, 94–98; and, more generally, Norden (*supra*, n. 16) 395–410. See also Dorival (*supra*, n. 84) 432–43.
88. R. Asmus, "Gregorius von Nazianz und sein Verhältnis zum Kynismus," *Theologische Studien und Kritiken* 67 (1894) 314–39 (reprinted in Billerbeck [*supra*, n. 1] 185–205); for a useful survey see B. Wyss, "Gregor II (Gregor von Nazianz)," *RAC* 12 (1983) 822–24. See further Goulet-Cazé (*supra*, n. 6) 2791–93.
89. *Or.* 4.72: (Crates) πομπεύει τὴν ἐλευθερίαν τῷ κηρύγματι ὡς ἄν τις οὐ φιλόσοφος μᾶλλον ἢ φιλόδοξος. *Or.* 25.7: ταῦτα τῆς Ἀντισθένους ἀλαζονείας καὶ τῆς Διογένους ὠμοφαγίας [Goulet-Cazé: ὀψοφαγίας mss.] καὶ τῆς Κράτητος κοινογαμίας. *De Virt.* 270 (*PG* 37.699): πλεῖον γὰρ ἦν ἔνδειξις ἢ καλοῦ πόθος. On the reproach of vainglory (κενοδοξία) made against the Cynics by patristic writers see Dorival (*supra*, n. 84) 423, 428–30.
90. *Or.* 9.1.180d–181a Rochefort.
91. Lucian, *Peregr.* 1, 2, 4; *DMort.* 6.4. In Palladius, *Hist. Laus.* 37.16, an ascetic Christian woman is criticized for her τῦφος. On the notion of pride see F. Decleva Caizzi, "Τῦφος: Contributo alla storia di un concetto," *Sandalion* 3 (1980) 53–55 (reprinted in Billerbeck [*supra*, n. 1] 273–85).

Cynicism,[92] the principal points of which are the following: anyone who wishes to take up the calling of a Cynic must give proof of his self-sufficiency and freedom from emotion before he exposes himself to social intercourse and to the amenities of life (*truphē*); license of speech and rebuke of people's vices are not for one who fails to keep a tight rein on himself; imitating Diogenes in his provocative deeds and unmasking the vanity of fellow citizens alone suits the man who displays an ability to learn (*eumatheia*), quick wit (*agkhinoia*), independence (*eleutheria*), self-sufficiency (*autarkeia*), justice (*dikaiosunē*), moderation (*sōphrosunē*), reverence (*eulabeia*), gratitude (*kharis*), and a genuine concern not to act at random or without a purpose or irrationally, since all these qualities characterized Diogenes and his philosophy.[93]

In Julian's eyes Cynicism is a universal philosophy based on the principle of "Know Thyself." [94] Accordingly, it is neither Antisthenes nor Diogenes who was its founder but Apollo, the god of truth. Therefore it demands no special study whatsoever but simply requires the practice of virtue and the avoidance of evil.[95] In this syncretistic view of philosophy the old antagonism between Plato and Diogenes is reduced to a matter of mere difference of intent: whereas Plato chose to achieve his aim through words (*logoi*), for Diogenes actions (*erga*) were enough.[96] The ideal Cynic will not let himself be influenced by other people's opinions, but everything he does will first be put to the test of experience. When Diogenes ate the octopus, he did it not out of vanity (*kenodoxia*) but because he wanted to verify whether eating raw meat was in fact unfit for man, while cooked meat is considered a natural diet.[97] This explanation is a tour de force and serves primarily to put Diogenes out of the reach of criticism. The Cynic program of Julian reflects the emperor's own penchant for austerity and conforms with his reformistic vision, which also pervades the self-tormenting satire of the *Misopogon*.[98] Confronted with monastic asceticism and rigoristic movements within the Christian church, the reformer who

92. The thematic relations with Epictetus, *Diatr.* 3.22, are striking, but do not allow us to conclude that the Stoic served as direct model for Julian: *Or.* 9.18.200b Rochefort, the Cynic adept (sim. Epict. *Diatr.* 3.22.1); 200c, reorientation and conversion (sim. §13); 220d, comparison with the bull, training (sim. §§6.99, 51–52); 200d, the Cynic outfit is not sufficient (sim. §§10–12, 50); 201a, the concomitants of the Cynic philosophy are the rules of life (sim. §19); 201a, the freedom of speech (sim. §§90–96); 201b, being without fear (sim. §49); 201b–c, philanthropy (sim. §§72, 81–82); 201c, the happy life of the Cynic (sim. §§45–48, 61, 87); 201d, Cynicism is based on good sense and intelligence (sim. §§19–20, 103–4).

93. *Or.* 9.19.202a.

94. See *supra*, n. 2.

95. *Or.* 9.8.187c, d.

96. *Or.* 9.9.189a.

97. *Or.* 9.11.191b–193c.

98. On the didactic character of this speech (cf. 2.181d–182a, 20.203c) see C. Prato and D. Micalella, *Giuliano imperatore, Contro i cinici ignoranti,* Studi e Testi Latini e Greci 4 (Lecce 1988), xxix–xxxii.

nourished the idea of *Hellēnismos* was seeking a pagan counterbalance. Just as he refers to the model of the clergy when he admonishes his priests to worship the gods and practice philanthropy,[99] so too does he borrow from the portrayal of the Theban anchorite when he depicts the pagan holy man.

Conclusion

After having traced the main lines of the idealized concept of Cynicism from Epictetus to Julian, we see that it was the qualities of independence (*autarkeia*) and freedom of speech (*parrhēsia*) that commended the imitation of Diogenes. On the other hand, shamelessness (*anaideia*), which is a prominent feature of the anecdotes about Diogenes and which characterized the actual behavior of the ancient Cynics, tends to be suppressed.

In the idealization of the Cynic way of life two traditions may be distinguished: the literary or rhetorical and the philosophical. The former is exemplified by *Oration* 36 of Maximus of Tyre and by the *Kunikos* of Pseudo-Lucian, where in both cases the encomium of the Cynic life follows from a *sugkrisis* with other types of lives. This sophistic tradition is less marked in Dio Chrysostom, whose more personal engagement with Cynicism is reflected in his use of Diogenes as an authoritative persona and as a spokesman for his own message. The models of Diogenes and Crates are also evident in the letters ascribed (by a convenient literary fiction) to the Cynics, which serve to propagate the Dog's way of life. While they make use of the parainetic topoi and *bons mots* of the ancient Cynics, the letters nevertheless lack any systematic presentation of Cynic doctrine. In his *Life of Demonax*, which stands between the literary and the philosophical traditions, Lucian strives to depict his master as a philosopher who genuinely practiced Cynic asceticism. Through his eclectic use of the imitation of Diogenes coupled with a reverence for Socrates and Aristippus, Demonax made Cynic rigorism philosophically respectable. Above all in the rhetorical tradition the idealization of Cynicism remains sporadic and reveals no distinct line of development. It is the individual features of Diogenes and Crates that are idealized, combined with praise of their life as happy and independent, as the needs of the authors and the occasion dictate.

In the philosophical tradition, on the other hand, idealized Cynicism is presented as a concept of practical philosophy and as a guideline for ethics. Epictetus and, in his wake, the emperor Julian developed a sympathetic, idealized portrayal of a Diogenes who denounces the offensive behavior of the false Cyn-

99. Cf. Julian, fr. 89b Bidez; Gregory of Nazianzus, *Or.* 4.111–12; and see A. Kurmann, *Gregor von Nazianz, Oratio 4 gegen Julian,* Schweizerische Beiträge zur Altertumswissenschaft 19 (Basel 1988), 367–78. More generally on this subject, J. Kabiersch, *Untersuchungen zum Begriff der Philanthropia bei dem Kaiser Julian,* Klassisch-Philologische Studien 21 (Wiesbaden 1960), remains the basic study.

ics while resolutely refusing to compromise his own principles. Both authors were known for their tendency to austerity and their religious commitment. Whereas Epictetus interprets the profession of the Cynics as a true vocation, which relieves them as philosophers from civic duties so that they may be placed at the disposal of all men, Julian is concerned to defend the rigorism of Diogenes and to oppose it to Christian asceticism. In their insistence on the Cynic principles of self-sufficiency and of the harmony between words and deeds, the Stoic teacher no less than the Neoplatonic philosopher-king employs the figures of Diogenes and Crates to proclaim his own message.[100]

100. For a short survey of the notion of the respectable Cynic (Seneca's Demetrius, Epict. *Diatr.* 3.22, the *Cynic Epistles,* Dio Chrysostom, Lucian's *Demonax*) see now also Dawson (*supra,* n. 35) 246–48.

The Bawdy and Society

The Shamelessness of Diogenes in Roman Imperial Culture

Derek Krueger

"Who has not heard of the Sinopean dog?" asked Gregory of Nazianzus, former patriarch of Constantinople, in a poem composed in the 380s after his retirement to Cappadocia. The question, of course, was rhetorical. Every educated late-Roman gentleman knew about Diogenes the Cynic.[1] Learned culture employed stories about Diogenes to reinforce social values, presenting him at times as an example to emulate, at others an example to avoid. But because he was neither simply praiseworthy nor unambiguously reviled, the figure of Diogenes prompted multiple traditions of interpretation of his peculiar behavior, allowing him to become an instrument of social criticism.

According to legend, the Cynic movement had started in Athens in the fourth century B.C.E. during the time between the Peloponnesian war and the rise of Alexander. Later, ancient historians and philosophers would argue whether the movement started with Antisthenes, a contemporary of Plato, or with Diogenes, an exile from Sinope in Pontus, who followed him. There can be no doubting, however, that Diogenes embodied the tradition in the imagination of the ancients. By the time of the Roman empire, Diogenes had become

---

1. Greg. Naz. *Carm.* 1.2.10, line 218. Major pagan sources for the reactions to Cynicism are available in the Loeb Classical Library (hereafter "LCL"). A notable exception is the corpus of pseudepigraphic letters available with translation in Abraham J. Malherbe, *The Cynic Epistles: A Study Edition* (Missoula 1977). Christian sources are cited from standard editions. Except when noted, translations are mine. On reactions to Cynics and Cynicism in late antiquity, see Derek Krueger, "Diogenes the Cynic among the Fourth-Century Fathers," *Vigiliae Christianae* 47 (1993) 29–49; F. Gerald Downing, *Cynics and Christian Origins* (Edinburgh 1992) 278–97; and Gilles Dorival, "L'image des cyniques chez les Pères grecs," in Marie-Odile Goulet-Cazé and Richard Goulet, eds., *Le cynisme ancien et ses prolongements* (Paris 1993) 419–43.

a stock literary type.[2] He featured prominently in a large body of Cynic sayings and tales that circulated not only in philosophical circles, but in educated circles generally.

The portrait of Diogenes remained remarkably consistent from the first century C.E. on, a composite of asceticism and shamelessness. Renowned for his unique personality and behavior, Diogenes was identified by his simple clothing, his wallet and staff, and his outspoken manner. He attracted crowds in public places while haranguing passersby. From time to time, he would perform shocking deeds: eating in the market or at lectures; farting loudly in crowded places; urinating, masturbating, or defecating in sight of all.[3]

The preservation of traditions about Diogenes in the Roman empire owes much to the place of the *chreia* in the curriculum of the schools of rhetoric.[4] In his textbook on rhetoric written in the second half of the first century C.E., Theon of Alexandria defined the *chreia* as "a concise statement or action that is attributed with aptness [*eustokhia*] to some specified character [*prosōpon*] or to something analogous to a character."[5] At an early point in a young gentleman's rhetorical education,[6] his teacher introduced him to *chreiai* and taught him to perform a number of exercises on these sayings. He recited them, inflected them in the various cases, and was taught to comment on the content of the *chreia,* raising objections where appropriate.[7] The eventual goal was to be able to use the *chreiai* to compose an entire speech, or to use a *chreia* effectively in the course of a speech in order to illustrate a point. *Chreiai* formed the

2. On the history of Cynicism, see Donald Dudley, *A History of Cynicism from Diogenes to the Sixth Century A.D.* (London 1937). Dudley still found it possible to discuss Diogenes as a historical figure, although he realized that anecdotes and teachings attributed to Diogenes by Epictetus, Dio Chrysostom, and Julian were of little value in the attempt to reconstruct the origins of Cynicism (20). For Diogenes traditions and cultural history, see Gunnar Rudberg, "Zur Diogenes-Tradition" and "Zum Diogenes-Typus," *Symbolae Osloenses* 14 (1935) 22–43, 15 (1936) 1–18. For more specialized discussion of Cynicism in gnomic anthologies, see J. Barns, "A New Gnomologium," *Classical Quarterly* 44 (1950) 127–37, 45 (1951) 1–19; and Henry A. Fischel, "Studies in Cynicism and the Ancient Near East: The Transformation of a *Chria*" (*sic*), in *Religions in Antiquity: Essays in Memory of Erwin Ramsdell Goodenough*, ed. J. Neusner (Leiden 1968), 372–411.

3. The full range of such details can be found in Diogenes Laertius's life of Diogenes, *Lives and Opinions of Famous Philosophers* 6.20–81.

4. On Diogenes *chreiai* in the school curriculum, see Krueger (above, n. 1) 30–33. Ronald F. Hock and Edward N. O'Neil, *The Chreia in Ancient Rhetoric*, vol. 1, *The Progymnasmata* (Atlanta 1986), contains all the chapters on the *chreia* found in ancient textbooks, with English translations. The comments of Donald Lemen Clark (*Rhetoric in Greco-Roman Education* [New York 1957] 186–88) are still valuable for placing the *chreia* within the larger rhetoric curriculum.

5. Hock and O'Neil (above, n. 4) 82–83 (text and translation). Cf. Aphthonius's (late-fourth/early fifth-century) definition: "A chreia is a concise reminiscence aptly attributed to some character" (Hock and O'Neil 224–25).

6. In some cases, the *chreia* was introduced late in the student's grammatical education. See Krueger (above, n. 1) 46 n. 14.

7. Treatises on rhetorical education vary concerning the exercises to be performed with the *chreia*. See Hock and O'Neil (above, n. 4) esp. 35–41.

building blocks of rhetorical education. At the teacher's disposal, preserved in a range of textbooks and anthologies, were literally thousands of sayings and anecdotes attributed or attributable to various ancient personages such as Socrates, Isocrates, and Menander. Perhaps the greatest number were attributed to Diogenes. Henry Fischel estimated that, in all their variations and permutations, the *chreiai* attributed to Diogenes number more than a thousand.[8] In Theon's discussion of the *chreia,* seven of the twenty-nine *chreiai* that he uses as examples are attributed to Diogenes. Diogenes is also well represented in later textbooks: Hermogenes in the second century, Aphthonius in the late fourth or early fifth century, and Nicholas of Myra in the sixth century.[9] Over sixty Diogenes anecdotes appear in John of Stobi's fifth-century anthology of passages from Greek authors compiled for the edification of his son.[10] Thus Diogenes emerges as perhaps the most familiar figure of grammatical and rhetorical education.

In the *Lives and Opinions of Famous Philosophers,* Diogenes Laertius makes use of a number of earlier collections of *chreiai* specifically concerned with Diogenes of Sinope in compiling his anecdotal life of Diogenes, but because there was little concern that the *chreiai* should be accurate, only that they should be apt, attempts to establish the authenticity of various sayings and deeds attributed to Diogenes are particularly problematic.[11] The requirement of apt attribution, however, suggests that the conception of a given character (*prosōpon*) was well developed and widely known. In order to attribute a saying to Diogenes, for instance, one first had to consider whether it was appropriate to his character. This character was based in large part on what had been attributed to Diogenes in other *chreiai,* the materials that formed a Diogenes tradition. *Chreiai* attributed to Diogenes shared a family resemblance, in that they portrayed Diogenes as a certain sort of character. This character was determined by a set of loosely related biographical events that featured prominently in Diogenes' portrait, such as his exile from Sinope, his arrival in Athens, the fact that he carried a wallet and a staff and wore a white robe. Chief among these characterizations were witty sayings, an ascetic way of life, and shameless acts.[12]

8. Fischel (above, n. 2) 374.

9. See Krueger (above, n. 1) 46 n. 17.

10. *Joannes Stobaei Anthologium,* ed. C. Wachsmuth and O. Hense, 5 vols. (Berlin 1884–1923 [2d ed. 1958]). Cf. Photius, *Bibl.* cod. 167; Krueger (above, n. 1) 32–33.

11. Diogenes Laertius cites a certain *Sale of Diogenes* by Menippus (6.29) and a book of the same title by Eubulus (6.31), as well as books of *chreiai* by Hecato (6.32) and Metrocles (6.33) as his sources. On Diogenes Laertius's sources for Diogenes of Sinope see K. von Fritz, *Quellenuntersuchungen zu Leben und Philosophie des Diogenes von Sinope,* Philologus Suppl. 18.2 (Leipzig 1926); R. Höistad, *Cynic Hero and Cynic King* (Lund 1948), 116; Richard Hope, *The Book of Diogenes Laertius* (New York 1930). See also Rudberg (above, n. 2 [1935, 1936]).

12. Conceptions of shamelessness and obscenity in Greek-speaking Roman imperial culture and among both Greek- and Latin-speaking Romans in late antiquity lack systematic study. I have

In the course of the Roman empire, reactions to the character of Diogenes were mixed. Pagans and Christians alike praised Diogenes for his life of voluntary poverty and condemned him for obscenity.[13] Origen pointed to Diogenes to defend the poverty of Jesus, and John Chrysostom drew on widespread appreciation of Diogenes' simple life to justify Christian monasticism.[14] In the second quarter of the fifth century, Theodoret of Cyrrhus praised Diogenes for his renunciation of riches,[15] but condemned him as "a slave to pleasure," who lived "lewdly, without restraint," setting a bad example for others.[16] Theodoret's judgment was not novel, nor was it particularly Christian in motivation. Centuries before, Cicero had attacked the Cynics for being a threat to conventions of propriety and accused them of confusing modesty and shamefulness;[17] he wrote: "The whole philosophy [*ratio*] of the Cynics must be rejected; for it is an enemy of modesty." [18] This criticism was also echoed by Augustine. In discussions of the moral life, Diogenes was a bivalent figure, serving alternatively as a positive or as a negative example. While the favorable valuation of Diogenes' positive attributes in Greco-Roman traditions of moral exhortation can be understood as part of the general use of exemplars in the inculcation of virtue, the place of Diogenes' shameless behavior in Roman literary culture remains somewhat puzzling.[19]

The portrayal of Diogenes that emerges from ancient texts reveals that shamelessness (*anaideia*) was an integral component of Cynic lore. Diogenes Laertius's life of Diogenes of Sinope, compiled during the third century C.E., dependent on a number of first-century-C.E. sources, includes the following account: "When masturbating in the marketplace, Diogenes said, 'If only one could achieve the same effect by rubbing an empty stomach!' " [20] Stories about

---

found remarks in the revised editions of the following works helpful: Jeffrey Henderson, *The Maculate Muse: Obscene Language in Attic Comedy,* 2d ed. (New York 1991), 2–3, 240–42; and Amy Richlin, *The Garden of Priapus: Sexuality and Aggression in Roman Humor,* rev. ed. (New York 1992), 1–31, 274.

13. For examples of praise of Diogenes' voluntary poverty, see Dio Chrys. *Or.* 6.6-16; Plutarch, *Mor.* 499b, 604c; Origen, *Cels.* 2.41, 6.28; Basil of Caesarea, *Leg. Lib. Gent.* 9.3, 4, 20; John Chrysostom, *Ad. Op. Vit. Monast.* 2.4. For condemnation of Diogenes, see Tatian, *Orat.* 25; John Chrys. *De S. Babyla* 9, *Hom. in 1 Cor.* 35.4.

14. Origen, *Cels.* 2.41; John Chrys. *Ad. Op. Vit. Monast.* 2.4, 5.

15. Thdt. *Provid.* 6, *PG* 83.649.

16. Thdt. *Affect.* 12.48. Text: Theodoret of Cyrrhus, *Graecarum Affectionum Curatio,* ed. with French trans. Pierre Canivet, 2 vols., Sources Chrétiennes 57 (Paris 1958). On the date of the work, see P. Canivet, *Histoire d'une enterprise apologétique au Vᵉ siècle* (Paris 1957) p. v.

17. Cicero, *De Officiis* 1.128.

18. Ibid. 1.148.

19. Our concern with Cynics and moral education is underscored by the fact that in the 190s Athenaeus (cf. *Deipn.* 3.113d–e) portrayed a contemporary Cynic, Cynulcus, as a critic of the school tradition's preoccupation with words rather than with the teaching of virtue. See R. F. Hock, "A Dog in a Manger: The Cynic Cynulcus among Athenaeus's Deipnosophists," in David Balch, Everett Ferguson, and Wayne Meeks, eds., *Greeks, Romans, and Christians: Essays in Honor of Abraham J. Malherbe* (Minneapolis 1990) 34–35.

20. D.L. 6.46; cf. 6.69.

Diogenes' masturbating in public are also found in a discourse by Dio Chrysostom, composed near the turn of the second century, and in pseudepigraphic epistles of Diogenes generated sometime before the end of the second century C.E.[21] Laertius's collection includes a story in which Diogenes urinates on someone, in the manner of a dog.[22] Both Dio Chrysostom and the emperor Julian relate that Diogenes defecated publicly.[23] He is said to have spat on people as well: "Someone took him into a magnificent house and warned him not to spit, whereupon having cleared his throat he spat into the man's face, being unable, he said, to find a baser place."[24] Displaying horrendous manners, Diogenes was said to sneeze from the left.[25] He was often accused of advocating incest and cannibalism.[26]

The theme of eating in public is found more than once in Diogenes Laertius's collection. Diogenes distracted the audience at a public lecture by displaying some salt fish.[27] Diogenes could be found eating in the marketplace, and when once he was reprimanded for doing so, he explained that it was in the marketplace that he had felt hungry.[28] In another anecdote he was having breakfast in the market when bystanders gathered around him and called him a dog. He replied, "You are the dogs, you who stand around and watch me while I have breakfast."[29] Julian knew stories about Diogenes' farting in public, and Laertius claims that Diogenes wrote a work entitled *Pordalos,* the title of which is surely derived from the Greek word *pordē* (fart).[30] Epictetus bemoaned that the second-rate Cynics of his time mimicked their masters in nothing other than cutting farts.[31] Farting also features in a story recounted about Diogenes' successor Crates, who converted Metrocles, the brother of Hippar-

---

21. Dio Chrys. *Or.* 6.16–20; *Epp. Diog.* 35, 42, 44. See also Athenaeus, *Deipn.* 4.145f. *Ep. Diog.* 44 says: "It is not only bread, water, a bed of straw, and a coarse cloak that teach moderation and patience, but also, if one may speak this way, the hand of the shepherd" (trans. Fiore in Malherbe [above, n. 1] 175). On problem of dating the Diogenes epistles, see Malherbe 14–18.

22. D.L. 6.46.

23. Dio Chrys. *Or.* 8.36; Julian, *Or.* 6.202c.

24. D.L. 6.32.

25. D.L. 6.48.

26. Incest: Dio Chrys. *Or.* 10.29–30; cf. 7.188. Cannibalism: D.L. 6.73; Dio Chrys. *Or.* 8.14; Theophilus of Antioch, *Ad Autolycum* 3.5; and possibly *Ep. Diog.* 28. In a tirade against Cynic indecency, Philodemus's treatise *On the Stoics* accuses Cynics of masturbating in public, transvestism, pederasty, being penetrated in homosexual acts, group marriage, rape, incest, prostitution, and adultery. Text: *PHerc.* 339 and 155, published in W. Crönert, *Kolotes und Menedemos: Texte und Untersuchung zur Philosophen und Literaturgeschichte* in *Studien zur Paläographie und Papyruskunde,* ed. C. Wessely (Leipzig 1906), 55–67, esp. 64–65. Bibliography: Marcello Gigante, *Papiri ercolanesi* (Naples 1979) 89–90, 130–32.

27. D.L. 6.57.

28. D.L. 6.58.

29. D.L. 6.61.

30. Julian, *Or.* 6.202b; D.L. 6.20 (cf. 6.80). On ancient farting generally, see Ludwig Radermacher, "*Pordē*," in *RE,* ed. A. von Pauly and G. Wissowa, 22.235–40. Cf. Henderson (above, n. 12) 195–99; and J. N. Adams, *The Latin Sexual Vocabulary* (Baltimore 1982), 249–50.

31. Epictetus, *Disc.* 3.22.80.

chia, to Cynicism after eating lupines and breaking wind.[32] Lupines are a leg-ume that were notorious for causing gas, with the cultural valence of our baked beans.[33] Diogenes and his followers appear to have eaten lupines religiously, especially at public lectures, where they created a visual distraction and, in time, could be expected to provide an audible and olfactory one as well.[34]

The figure of Diogenes was urban, and his deeds public. Diogenes' behavior was only remarkable because it took place where it could be observed. Dio Chrysostom remarks that the cities were Diogenes' home and the public build-ings were his dwelling places.[35] Diogenes used any place for any purpose, for breakfasting, sleeping, or conversing.[36] Diogenes did not adhere to conven-tional distinctions between public and private space and the activities assigned to each. Thus Diogenes performed inevitable activities, such as farting, urinat-ing, ejaculating, and defecating, normally carried out in the privacy of the home, in full view. In Lucian's *Philosophers for Sale!,* the Cynic on the auction block says: "Do in view of all what you would not do in private. Do it brashly, and choose the most ludicrous of sex acts." [37] Diogenes Laertius explains: "It was [Diogenes'] habit to do everything in public, the works of Demeter and Aphrodite alike." [38] According to Dio, Diogenes gave a public demonstration in order to show the folly of those who spent money to be rubbed "when they needed to eject sperm." [39] Dio sets Diogenes' harangues in public places, in front of the temple of Poseidon at Corinth in one instance, before the Corin-thian gymnasium in another, in both cases turning out just to meet the crowds attending the Isthmian Games.[40] Both Origen and Gregory of Nazianzus asso-ciated Cynicism with the marketplace.[41] As one modern scholar has aptly put it, "Diogenes belongs to the city." [42]

Twentieth-century scholarship on the Cynic movement has at times dem-onstrated squeamishness with regard to the elements of obscenity preserved among the traditions about Diogenes. Mounting a quest for the historical Di-ogenes among the various imperial sources, some such as Farrand Sayre have

32. D.L. 6.94.

33. Cf. Derek Krueger, "The *Life of Symeon the Fool* and the Cynic Tradition," *Journal of Early Christian Studies* 1 (1993) 432–33. On lupines and flatulence, see Ps.-Hippocrates, *Regimen in Acute Diseases (Appendix)* 47 (*Hippocrates,* vol. 6 [LCL] 308). Cf. Hippocrates, *Regimen* 2.45 (*Hippocrates,* vol. 4 [LCL] 314–16). In what appears to be a parody of the Pythagorean practice of avoiding broad beans (κύαμος) because they cause flatulence and interfere with breathing (cf. D.L. 8.24), Lucian mentions a precept against eating lupines (*The True Story,* 2.28).

34. D.L. 6.48. Cf. Krueger (above, n. 33) 432.

35. Dio Chrys. *Or.* 4.13.

36. D.L. 6.22.

37. Lucian, *Philosophers for Sale!* 10.

38. I.e., defecation and sex, D.L. 6.69.

39. Dio Chrys. *Or.* 6.17: "[Diogenes] found Aphrodite everywhere, and for free."

40. See Dio Chrys. *Or.* 8, 9.

41. Origen, *Cels.* 3.50; Greg. Naz. *Or.* 27.10.

42. Wayne A. Meeks, *The Moral World of the First Christians* (Philadelphia 1986) 55.

judged Diogenes a sort of madman,[43] while others have attempted to excise the tales of shamelessness from the portrait of the real man from Sinope. Ragnar Höistad discounted the validity of the accounts in question, claiming that a "burlesque, vulgar and anti-Cynic portrait of Diogenes" was generated during the Roman empire,[44] and that "the most absurd accounts of the proletarian traits of Diogenes' personal way of life must be regarded with great suspicion."[45] On the other hand, Höistad argued for the historicity of the traditions about Diogenes' philosophical positions that are preserved in the Stoic writings of the Roman empire. The doxographical literature, however, was heavily influenced by the concerns of those Stoics who preserved it.[46]

An issue separate from the portrait of Diogenes but certainly related is the fact that literature generated during the debate within first- and second-century-C.E. Stoicism concerning the validity of Cynic teachings presented at least two divergent images of Cynicism.[47] Höistad attempted to resolve the lack of consensus in the sources by tracing two or more branches of Cynic tradition in order to account for inconsistent reports concerning the behavior and teachings of Cynics, and regarded what he called the obscene and burlesque versions of Cynicism to have had a pedigree separate from what he deemed the serious and pedagogical versions of the tradition.[48] And as Margarethe Billerbeck has shown, the imperial Stoics, especially Epictetus, tried to rid the Cynicism of their own day of what they considered a false Cynicism characterized by shamelessness by attempting to set specific standards for acceptable Cynic behavior.[49] The problem was well recognized in antiquity. Cicero refers disparagingly to Stoics who might as well be Cynics, and Julian understood the rise of Stoicism as a mitigation of Cynicism.[50]

43. Farrand Sayre, *Greek Cynicism and Sources of Cynicism* (Baltimore 1948).

44. Höistad (above, n. 11) 15.

45. Ibid. 117, esp. n. 7. The Soviet scholar I. Nachov ("Der Mensch in der Philosophie der Kyniker," in *Der Mensch als Mass der Dinge*, ed. R. Müller [Berlin 1976], 361–98) overstates his case for the relevance of a Marxist class analysis for understanding the Cynics against the political crises of late fifth-century-B.C.E. Athens.

46. See M.-O. Goulet-Cazé, *L'ascèse cynique: Un commentaire de Diogène Laërce VI 70–71* (Paris 1986) 159–91. On the reception of Cynicism into Latin Stoicism, see Margarethe Billerbeck, *Der Kyniker Demetrius* (Leiden 1979).

47. See Abraham Malherbe, "Self-Definition among Epicureans and Cynics," in *Jewish and Christian Self-Definition*, vol. 3, *Self-Definition in the Greco-Roman World*, ed. B.F. Meyers and E.P. Sanders (Philadelphia 1983), 46.

48. See especially the diagram included by Höistad (above, n. 11) 178. For further discussion of the variety of Cynicisms in the Roman empire, see A. Malherbe, " 'Gentle as a Nurse': The Cynic Background to 1 Thess. 2," *NovTest* 12 (1970) 203–17; id. (above, n. 47) 46–59. Both essays now appear in his *Paul and the Popular Philosophers* (Minneapolis 1989) 11–24, 35–48.

49. Billerbeck (above, n. 46) 18.

50. Cicero, *De Officiis* 1.128; Julian, *Or.* 6.185c. M. Billerbeck (*Epiktet: Vom Kynismus, herausgegeben und übersetzt mit einem Kommentar* [Leiden 1978] 4) has highlighted Epictetus's importance in this debate by showing him to be responding to the problem of the lack of a Cynic canon.

The conception of an obscenity-free Cynicism, largely independent of the traditions of the shameless Diogenes, has proven particularly popular among scholars exploring affinities between Cynicism and the origins of Christianity. Concentrating on the doxographical and philosophical materials, such as Dio Chrysostom and Epictetus, Abraham Malherbe has shown how Paul took over the hortatory style of, as well as the ideal types described in, the Cynic literary tradition.[51] In general, Malherbe's Cynics reflect the assimilation into the imperial Stoa and are consequently quite tame. Meanwhile F. Gerald Downing and others have explored the relationship between the collections of Cynic sayings and the collections of traditions about Jesus, suggesting a common genre for the sources that lie behind Diogenes Laertius's lives of various Cynics and the synoptic sayings source Q. These scholars have also argued that the historical Jesus himself should be understood to have been a Jewish Cynic preacher.[52] It is not surprising that studies attempting to draw parallels between texts about Diogenes and texts about Jesus are unlikely to focus on stories of Cynics' spitting, farting, or defecating.[53] In short, interest in the Cynicism reflected in the imperial Stoa has conspired to deflect attention from the shamelessness integral to the portrait of Diogenes. At the same time, twentieth-century models of various branches of Cynicism beg the question of the role of widespread traditions about Diogenes' shameless behavior in each of these types.

The shamelessness of Diogenes was already well established in the first century. As Epictetus's reference to the farting of the early Cynics demonstrates, Stoics' attempt to define a Cynicism free of shamelessness for their own day did not affect their portrait of Diogenes. Dio Chrysostom created dialogues using Diogenes as his main character in order to give a serious exposition of Cynic teachings. Yet at the end of Dio's *Oration* 8, after Diogenes has given an

51. Malherbe (above, n. 47); "Antisthenes and Odysseus, and Paul at War," *HTR* 76 (1983) 143–73; "Exhortation in First Thessalonians," *NovTest* 25 (1983) 238–56; and "'In Season and out of Season' 2 Timothy 4:2," *JBL* 103 (1984) 235–43.

52. F. Gerald Downing, "Cynics and Christians," *NTSt* 30 (1984) 584–93; "The Social Contexts of Jesus the Teacher," *NTSt* 33 (1987) 439–51; "Quite like Q: A Genre for 'Q': The 'Lives' of the Cynic Philosophers," *Biblica* 69 (1988) 196–225. See now Downing (above, n. 1). Cf. J. S. Kloppenborg, *The Formation of Q* (Philadelphia 1987) 306–25; and Burton Mack, *The Myth of Innocence* (Philadelphia 1988) 67–69.

53. Cf. Downing (above, n. 1) 51. While Downing stresses the importance of *parrhēsia* (outspokenness) in the Cynic model with which he works, he has downplayed shamelessness, arguing that "in the material coming clearly from the first and second centuries C.E. there is very little indication that this range of deliberately shocking behavior was *in practice* part of the Cynic repertoire, even if it remained *open to discussion*" (my emphasis). In the next paragraph he points out that Epictetus and Dio Chrysostom refer to the shamelessness of Diogenes and his followers in their writings. Since we are concerned here not with the practice of Cynicism, but rather with the perceptions of Diogenes, the fact that shamelessness was discussed is sufficient. In general, I find the proposition of a Jewish Cynic Jesus intriguing. However, I believe the implications of the shamelessness within the Cynic tradition for such a reconstruction deserve rethinking.

impromptu public lecture on virtue, he squats in front of his listeners and defecates. Moreover it is generally agreed that Diogenes Laertius's life of Diogenes (of the mid-third century) draws on collections of *chreiai* compiled over the three earlier centuries, meaning that the anecdotes in this text that deal with Diogenes' shamelessness were most likely circulating in the first century C.E.[54]

The acknowledgment of the shamelessness of Diogenes in the so-called serious literature occurs in the context of criticism of those who would imitate Diogenes' behavior. Dio Chrysostom portrayed vulgar Cynics standing on street corners, in alleyways, and at temple gates, passing the hat while making coarse jokes and using foul language.[55] During the second century, Lucian claimed (probably exaggerating): "Every city is filled with such upstarts, particularly with those who enter the names of Diogenes, Antisthenes, and Crates as their patrons and enlist in the army of the Dog." [56] Within the Roman Stoa, the debate concerning Cynicism centered on distinguishing the true from the false practitioners of their own day.[57] The philosopher Epictetus hoped that contemporary Cynics would maintain a respect for God and not regress into atheism.[58] The ideal Cynic of his handbook looks significantly more dignified than the Cynics of the *chreia* traditions, practicing none of the shameless acts recorded elsewhere. In the fourth century, Julian was concerned about those who merely adopted the long cloak, the wallet, and the staff and grew their hair out without adopting the ethical concerns that he ascribed to Diogenes.[59] Underlying these authors' concerns is an attempt to dissuade or even prevent people from acting out in reality those most troubling things embedded in anecdotes about Diogenes and transmitted, among other places, in the school curriculum.

What would be offensive in reality can be instructive in narrative. The controversy was not over whether Diogenes had been shameless. This was taken for granted. Rather, the debate in antiquity was over the meaning of the peculiar behavior of the archetypal Cynic. Thus, even while some sought to vilify Diogenes' shamelessness, they also sought to understand it. Julian relates that his rather sophisticated understanding of the Cynics came from his teachers.[60] Just as there were traditions about Diogenes' deeds, there were also traditions about how to interpret them. The Diogenes *chreiai* and the pseudepigraphic letters posit a range of interpretations. Some regarded Cynicism as a shortcut to virtue

54. Von Fritz (above, n. 11); Höistad (above, n. 11) 116; M.-O. Goulet-Cazé, "Le cynisme á l'époque impériale," *ANRW* 2.36.4 (1990) 2726–27; Downing (above, n. 1) 60–61.

55. Dio Chrys. *Or.* 32.9.

56. Lucian, *Runaways* 16.

57. Cf. Billerbeck (above, n. 50) 2–3.

58. Epictetus, *Diatr.* 3.22.2. This view is also found in Julian, who argued that it was Oenomaus's disregard for the sacred that made him shameless and impudent (*Or.* 6.199a).

59. Julian, *Or.* 6.201a–d; cf. *Or.* 7.223d.

60. Ibid. 6.181d.

(although it is not always clear what is meant by "virtue" [*aretē*] in these contexts),[61] while others said that Cynicism was a shortcut to happiness.[62] Some were less inclined than others to see the characteristic actions in a favorable light. Some thought that Cynicism was a form of madness. Tradition held that Plato had termed Diogenes "a Socrates gone mad." [63] Dio Chrysostom relates that while some admired Diogenes, others thought that he was crazy.[64] This understanding of Cynicism was assimilated into Rabbinic circles such that the Hebrew word *kinukos* (*sic*) appears in two passages in the Palestinian Talmud that discuss the "signs of a madman." [65] Similarly in his seventh-century Christian *Life of Symeon the Fool,* Leontius of Neapolis depicts the Fool for Christ's Sake with obvious gestures toward the portrait of Diogenes; Symeon defecates in public, consumes enormous quantities of lupines, and eats raw meat in public, among other things.[66] Another interpretation of Cynic behavior is seen in the commonplace that Cynics had acquired the name "Dog" because their animal-like behavior was not worthy of humans.[67] These various readings of Diogenes need not, of course, exclude one another. The point is that the Diogenes material carried interpretive traditions with it.

Equally prevalent was the understanding that Cynicism was a form of social criticism. Tradition held that Diogenes had consulted an oracle (either at Delphi or the Delian oracle at Sinope) and was told by Apollo to deface the currency (*parakharattein to nomisma*). Like all oracles, this was open to misinterpretation, and according to one tradition Diogenes was exiled from Sinope for counterfeiting.[68] As time passed, Diogenes understood that he was to deface the political and social currency, the exchange of notions that constituted general opinion.[69] The Cynic critique claimed that the conventions by which the

61. D.L. 6.104; cf. 7.121. Also Julian, *Or.* 7.225; Lucian, *Peregrinus* 2. Cf. Sayre (above, n. 43) 1–2.

62. *Ep. Diog.* 12; *Epp. Crates* 13, 21.

63. D.L. 6.54; also Aelian, *Varia Historia* 14.33. Lucian is full of praise for his teacher Demonax. Yet while Demonax followed the manner of dress and the easygoing ways of Diogenes, Lucian claims he had more in common with Socrates (*Demonax* 5). Lucian is careful to stress that Demonax behaved in a sane manner, leading an irreproachable life and "setting an example to all who saw and heard him by his good judgment and the honesty of his philosophy" (*Dem.* 3).

64. Dio Chrys. *Or.* 9.8–9; cf. 8.36. The slave Monimus, who was a student of Diogenes and a follower of Crates, is said to have been regarded by his master as mad (D.L. 6.82).

65. yGittin 38a, yTerumoth 2a. See M. Luz, "A Description of the Greek Cynic in the Jerusalem Talmud," *Journal for the Study of Judaism* 20 (1989) 49–60.

66. On the allusion to Diogenes in Leontius's text, see Krueger (above, n. 33) 423–42; on Cynicism as madness, see esp. 438–40.

67. Κυνικός, in fact, looks like an adjectival form of κύων, and can also mean "doglike." Cf. LSJ s.v. On Cynics as dogs, see Sayre (above, n. 43) 4–5. Serious doubts concerning the etymology of the term "Cynic" and a discussion of the ancient (non-Christian) interpretations of the title can be found in Heinz Schulz-Falkenthal, "Kyniker—Zur inhaltlichen Deutung des Namens," *WZHalle* 26.2 (1977) 41–49. Krueger (above, n. 33: 435–38) provides an extended discussion of "Cynic" as a definition of the word "dog" in late antiquity and Byzantium.

68. D.L. 6.20.

69. Cf. Julian, *Or.* 6.188b. Dudley (above, n. 2: 20–24) discusses the oracle at length.

majority led their lives were unnatural and therefore foolish. One letter attributed to Diogenes explains that "Cynicism, as you know, is an investigation of
nature," [70] and Julian later held that Plato and Diogenes were pursuing the same
goal "not to follow vain opinions [*doxai*] but to track down truth among all
things that are." [71] What Plato achieved through words, Diogenes achieved
through deeds; thus for Julian, Diogenes' behavior—including his shamelessness—had philosophical content.[72] Cynic behavior carries explicitly religious
content for the authors of two Cynic epistles. One letter explains that one
should not shun the cloak and the wallet, because they are weapons of the
gods; [73] while another says quite boldly: "Nature [*phusis*] is mighty and, since
it has been banished from life by appearance [*doxa*], it is what we restore for
the salvation of mankind." [74] Thus Julian drew on traditional modes of interpretation when he argued that the key to understanding the Cynics was understanding the difference between those things that humans do because of convention (*nomos*) and those things that humans do because they are essential to
human nature (*phusis*).[75] Julian's opponent in his speech *Against the Uneducated Cynics,* an unnamed fourth-century Cynic, had ridiculed Diogenes for
eating raw octopus, which according to some traditions had killed him.[76] Julian
explains that, while many debated whether eating meat was natural to humans,
Diogenes believed that in eating uncooked meat, one behaved according to the
same pattern that nature had assigned to all the other animals.[77] The best life,
the one that would result in happiness, was not the life that was led according
to conventions that were upheld according to common opinion, but the life that
was led according to the principles of nature (*kata phusin*).[78] In this argument,

70. *Ep. Diog.* 42.
71. Julian, *Or.* 6.188c.
72. Ibid. 6.189a.
73. *Ep. Crates* 16.
74. *Ep. Diog.* 6.
75. Discussion of the *nomos/phusis* distinction was a standard in Socratic and sophistic debate. See especially Plato, *Gorgias* 482e–484c. On the history of the concept in ancient philosophy, see F.P. Hargar, "Natur," *Historisches Wörterbuch der Philosophie* 6 (Basel 1971) cols.
421–41.
76. Other writers from antiquity who record stories of Diogenes' eating raw meat include
Plutarch (*Whether Water or Fire Is More Useful* 956b and *On the Eating of Flesh* 995d), while
Diogenes' death by ingesting raw octopus is found in Lucian (*Philosophers for Sale!* 10) and
Diogenes Laertius (6.34: "He even attempted to eat raw meat but he could not digest it"). But
Laertius also writes: "Regarding his death, there are several different accounts. One is that he was
seized with colic after eating an octopus raw and so met his end. Another is that he died voluntarily
by holding his breath. . . . Another is that, while trying to divide an octopus among the dogs, he
was so severely bitten on the sinew of the foot that it caused his death"(6.76–77).
77. Julian, *Or.* 6.191c, d.
78. Ibid. 6.193d; cf. 6.207. It is curious to note in passing, however, that in this specific case
the burden of proof remains with Julian, who never refutes the claim that the eating of raw octopus,
supposedly in accord with nature, in fact led to Diogenes' death. Instead Julian only argues that
we cannot know for sure that death is an evil (*Or.* 6.181a).

Diogenes stands as an example in a long tradition of Greek reflection concerning virtue and happiness.

Julian's Diogenes felt it was his duty to refute common misconceptions about the behavior natural to humans.[79] The instruments of this refutation were the functions natural to the human body itself. Julian relates the following anecdote: "Once when Diogenes was in a crowd of people, a certain youth farted. Diogenes poked him with his staff and said, 'And so, vile wretch, though you have done nothing that would give you the right to take such liberties in public, are you beginning here and now to show your scorn of opinion [*doxa*]?'"[80] Here Diogenes himself explains indirectly the Cynic method for criticizing conventional opinion: he regards the fart as a social comment, equal to outspokenness or any other form of human expression of dissatisfaction. Diogenes attacks the young man not for the act of farting in public, but for farting in public without expressing contempt for society. The Cynics claim the bodily functions as a language of protest. Yet as this example shows, vulgarity alone does not make one a Cynic. The youth had not earned the privilege to perform such an act, since he had not done anything else to reject common life. The irony of the anecdote, of course, is that the youth had no intention of registering an objection to the social order. His act was, if you will, innocent. For Diogenes, however, such a deed was an explicit element in his vocabulary. So we are left with Diogenes performing yet another vulgar deed: poking a youth in public and thus calling attention to a natural act that the youth would no doubt have preferred had gone unnoticed.

It is not banal to say that in behaving as he does the figure of Diogenes makes a statement. Diogenes' acts of shamelessness function like his outspokenness, as a form of criticism. In challenging the social norms that regulate the boundaries of the body, Diogenes challenges the order of society. In another oration Julian states explicitly that "Cynics go around in public subverting the institutions of society [*koina nomima*]."[81] Citing Diogenes' bodily functions as a critique of urban morals, Julian relates how the Cynic attacked the unscrupulous practices of Athenians in the market:[82]

> Let Diogenes trample on conceit; let him ridicule [*katapaizetō*] those who although they conceal in darkness the necessary functions of our nature—I am speaking of the expulsion of excrement—yet in the center of the marketplace and of our cities carry out most violent deeds that are not proper to our nature: robbery of money, false accusations, unjust indictments, and the pursuit of other such vulgar [*surphetōdōn*] business. When Diogenes farted [*apeparden*] or went

79. Cf. ibid. 6.191d.
80. Ibid. 6.197c.
81. Ibid. 7.210c.
82. Julian, *Or.* 6.202b, c.

to the bathroom [*apepatēsen*][83] or did other things like this in the marketplace, which they say he did, he did these things to trample on the delusion of those men and to teach them that they carried out deeds far more sordid and dangerous than his. For what he did was according to our common nature, while what they did was not, so to speak, in accord with everyone's nature [*pasi kata phusin*], but was all carried out because of perversion [*ek diastrophēs*].

Julian values Diogenes as an exemplar of the moral life; stories about Diogenes' shamelessness could be used to teach virtue.

Fourth-century interest in Diogenes as a moral exemplar is not limited to pagan writers. Basil of Caesarea, close friend of Gregory of Nazianzus, defended the use of *chreiai* about Diogenes alongside the texts of Homer and Plato in the curriculum for Christian gentlemen. In his influential letter "To Young Men on How They Might Benefit from Pagan Literature," Basil cites Diogenes favorably as a critic of ostentation and particularly of those men who spend too much time on the care of the hair or on dress.[84] Basil, however, avoids mentioning Diogenes' most unseemly behavior.

Late-Roman authors also used Diogenes as a negative example in the teaching of virtue. In the *City of God,* in the course of explaining that humans should be ashamed of their sexuality, Augustine condemned the Cynics for advancing "an opinion directly opposed to human modesty, an opinion truly canine, that is to say, filthy and indecent." Nevertheless, Augustine explained that Diogenes had sex in public "because he imagined that his school of philosophy would gain more publicity if its indecency were more startlingly impressed on the memory of mankind."[85] Diogenes' shamelessness was an advertisement that demonstrated the content of his theories. Augustine also claimed that, in time, modesty prevailed over "the mistaken idea that men should make it their ambition to resemble dogs," and later Cynics abandoned immodesty. Augustine's further musings on the Cynics reveal a concern to rescue even Diogenes from scorn: "I am inclined to think that even Diogenes himself went through the motions of lying together before the eyes of men who had no means of knowing what was really going on under the philosopher's cloak. I doubt whether the pleasure of that act could have been successfully achieved with spectators crowding round."[86] Despite Augustine's attempt to deny Diogenes' success, both he and Julian share a view of the ancient Cynics, and of Diogenes in particular, that integrates their shameless appearance with their critique of urban values. Practice and theory go hand in hand (or under the same cloak).

---

83. ἀποπατέω, a common euphemism, literally meaning "go off the path." Its use here is ironic; Diogenes does not go off, but rather stays in public view. Julian no doubt intends his audience to appreciate the onomatopoeic qualities of the scatological words in this passage.

84. Basil, *Leg. Lib. Gent.* 9.3, 4, 20. See Krueger (above, n. 1) 35–36.

85. Augustine, *Civ. Dei* 14.20; trans. John O'Meara, *Augustine: Concerning the City of God against the Pagans* (London 1984) 582.

86. Aug. *Civ. Dei* 14.20; trans. O'Meara (above, n. 85) 582.

Behavior according to nature was for Diogenes a form of symbolic action that relied on the human body as the instrument of expression. The stories about Diogenes were revelations of the natural state. Further consideration of the things that the Cynic heroes did with their bodies in the traditional accounts allows us to situate Cynic shamelessness within the larger context of Cynic *askēsis*. Cynics were held to advocate nudity, since humans do not need the amenities that separate them from the animals.[87] Putting the body through trials was an integral part of Diogenes' behavior. Diogenes embraces statues covered with snow,[88] walks barefoot in the snow,[89] and consumes the plainest food and water.[90]

It was a matter for debate whether Cynics disregarded the body. Epictetus, seeking to make Cynicism respectable, tried to argue that the Cynic was no longer identified with his body, and although his body might be reviled, beaten, and insulted, the Cynic remained unaffected.[91] But Dio Chrysostom defended Diogenes by suggesting that the Cynic way of life made one more sensitive to simple pleasures:[92]

Diogenes was not careless with respect to his body as certain foolish people thought. When they saw him shivering and living outside and being thirsty, many believed that he did not care about his health or his life. However, the rigor made him better in health than those who were always stuffing themselves, better than those who remained indoors suffering neither cold nor heat. And he had more pleasure feeling the warmth of the sun, and more pleasure eating his food than they did.

In general, however, commentators agreed that the goal of Cynic behavior was to achieve indifference, both to the elements and to the opinions of others.[93] An anecdote preserved in Diogenes Laertius's life of Zeno levels criticism at Stoic concerns with appearances. Crates felt that his pupil Zeno of Citium was too

---

87. *Ep. Diog.* 35; Epictetus, *Disc.* 1.24. See also Lycinus in Ps.-Lucian, *The Cynic* 1, 14; and the marriage of Crates and Hipparchia (D.L. 6.96): "[Crates] took off his clothes in front of her and said, 'This is the bridegroom; here are his possessions. Make your choice accordingly, for you will not be my companion unless you take on my practices.'" In a version known to Apuleius (*Florida* 14), Crates was hunchbacked, and Hipparchia agreed, stating she was not likely to find a handsomer or wealthier husband. Then they consummated their marriage publicly in broad daylight. (In Apuleius's account Crates' prudish student Zeno, the founder of Stoicism, covered them with a cloak out of respect for modesty—a cipher perhaps for the efforts of the imperial Stoa to "clean up" Cynicism.) For other references to the wedding of Crates and Hipparchia, see Clement of Alexandria, *Strom.* 4.19; and Tatian, *Ad Graecos* 3. Cf. Dio Chrysostom in Philostratus, *Lives of the Sophists* 488.

88. D.L. 6.23; cf. Plutarch, *Sayings of the Spartans* 233.16.

89. D.L. 6.34.

90. D.L. 6.31.

91. Epict. *Diatr.* 3.22.100.

92. Dio Chrys. *Or.* 6.8–9.

93. On indifference in Cynicism, see Julian, *Or.* 6.192a; *Ep. Diog.* 21; D.L. 4.52 (explaining how Bion became a Cynic). On the role of *askēsis* in achieving indifference, see D.L. 6.71. This interpretation, of course, betrays the Stoic assimilation of the figure of Diogenes.

modest and wanted him to adopt the Cynic way of shamelessness. He therefore gave him a pot of lentils to carry through a prominent district of Athens, the Ceramicus. Zeno was ashamed and tried to conceal the pot, eventually breaking it with his staff. Zeno ran away with the lentil mush running down his leg while Crates tried to explain to him that nothing terrible had happened.[94]

Through the derisive lens of his satire, Lucian reads a Cynic's shamelessness as part of his conditioning toward indifference. According to Lucian, while Peregrinus Proteus studied the Cynic way of life in Egypt with Agathobulus,[95]

> he practiced that wonderful asceticism [*askēsis*], shaving half of his head, rubbing his face with mud, erecting his penis [*aidoion;* literally: shameful thing][96] in front of all the people standing around, thereby demonstrating what they call indifference; and then striking and being struck with a rod on his rump, and performing many other things, even more wanton acts of wonder-working.

In this description of apparently antiascetic asceticism, which shares many elements with the stories about Diogenes,[97] Peregrinus becomes inured to the opinions of others through violating commonsense notions of the behavior proper to those wishing to detach themselves from the conventions of society; that is, Peregrinus achieves indifference through violating Stoic precepts for philosophically minded aristocrats.[98]

Diogenes' shamelessness can be read as social criticism mediated through an ascetic inversion of *askēsis*.[99] Diogenes' body was out of step with the world as a whole. He wished it to be buried face down,[100] demonstrating disregard not only for the body but also for common ritual practice. The reason Diogenes gave for this request was that "after a little time down will be converted into up."[101] In short, Diogenes' body is used as a symbol of the social order, an order that from the Cynic point of view is inverted.

Many of Diogenes' acts of shamelessness focus attention on substances that pass regularly into or out of the human body: food, saliva, gas, urine, semen, and feces. The very centrality of bodily functions and fluids in the Cynic literature attests to and derives from general Greco-Roman concerns about the boundaries of the body, a concern reflected in the careful regulation of acts of eating, spitting, farting, urinating, masturbating (and other sex acts), and defe-

---

94. D.L. 7.3.

95. Lucian, *Peregrinus* 17. Agathobulus had also been Demonax's teacher (Lucian, *Dem.* 3).

96. For this euphemism, see Henderson (above, n. 12) 3–4, 113.

97. D.L. 6.33 records that Diogenes once attended a party with a half-shaven head.

98. Cf. Michel Foucault, *The Care of the Self,* trans. Robert Hurley (New York 1986), 37–68, 97–144.

99. In this observation I am indebted to Evelyne Patlagean for her remarks concerning Symeon the Fool ("Ancient Byzantine Hagiography and Social History," in Stephen Wilson, ed., *Saints and Their Cults: Studies in Religious Sociology, Folklore and History* [Cambridge 1983] 110).

100. D.L. 6.31.

101. D.L. 6.32.

cating. Roman society's concern with bodily orifices and the fluids (liquids and gases) that may pass into and out of them demonstrates the relationship that Mary Douglas has observed, namely that "the human body is never seen as a body without at the same time being treated as an image of society." [102] Attitudes about bodily control correspond to attitudes about social control. These substances draw attention because they challenge the distinction between the inside and the outside of the body and may therefore be regarded as polluting or dangerous. [103] Diogenes actively rejected the conventions prescribed for these natural functions. By rejecting bodily control, the Diogenes of the anecdotes rejected social control. The authors of some texts considered here make this critique explicit; others leave the power of Diogenes' behavior encoded.

The audience *within* the stories reacts to Diogenes' behavior as to an abomination. In a discourse on virtue mentioned earlier, Dio Chrysostom has Diogenes the Cynic praise Heracles before a crowd. At the end of his speech, Diogenes refers to the labor of Heracles in which he cleaned away the dung in the Augean stable, a task that had not been performed for thirty years. He claims Heracles did this "because he believed that he should fight hard no less in the battle against common opinion [*doxa*] than against wild beasts and the evil deeds of humanity." [104] The crowd was pleased with Diogenes' oration. Whereupon, Dio continues, "thinking of the deeds of Heracles, and having finished his speech, he squatted on the ground and did something indecent [*ti tōn adoxōn*]. At this point the crowd scorned him and called him crazy." [105] Similarly, Julian relates that "the cities [of Greece] fled [*apodidraskousas*] from the excessive plainness and purity of the Cynics' freedom of manners." [106] He makes it clear that, unlike the Cynic impostors of his day, the true Cynics, and especially Diogenes, were not popular: "One or two, indeed, used to applaud Diogenes in his own day, but more than ten times ten thousand had their stomachs turned by nausea and loathing, and went fasting until their attendants revived them with perfumes and myrrh and cakes." [107] According to Julian, not only was the raw food that Diogenes ingested regarded as polluting by conventional opinion, but, in eating it, Diogenes himself became, in the eyes of many, contemptible and disgusting (*bdeluros*). [108] Within the context of these narratives, people found Diogenes shocking and revolting. Diogenes attacked the

---

102. Mary Douglas, "Social Preconditions of Enthusiasm and Heterodoxy," in *Forms of Symbolic Action: Proceedings of the 1969 Annual Spring Meeting of the American Ethnological Society,* ed. Robert F. Spencer (Seattle 1969), 71.

103. See Mary Douglas, *Purity and Danger: An Analysis of the Concepts of Pollution and Taboo* (London 1966) 114–28. This discussion is further developed in ead., *Natural Symbols: Explorations in Cosmology* (New York 1982), esp. pp. xxiii, 70.

104. Dio Chrys. *Or.* 8.35.

105. Ibid. 8.36.

106. Julian, *Or.* 6.185c.

107. Ibid. 6.190a; cf. 7.214a.

108. Ibid. 6.193a. These boundaries are similar to the categories of pollution described by the anthropologist Mary Douglas.

social order, and the members of society were offended and angered. Elsewhere the public expresses its loathing and disgust toward Cynic shamelessness by beating and torturing Cynics.[109] Augustine explains that if the Cynics of his own day started to behave like Diogenes they would be "overwhelmed, if not with a hail of stones, at any rate with a shower of spittle from the disgusted public."[110]

Diogenes is abominable because he transgresses the categories considered proper to humans; that people would find his behavior disgusting is plain enough. Given that reaction, what is not so readily comprehensible is the popularity of the Cynic tales among educated Romans. Roman intellectuals did not uniformly condemn Diogenes; instead, he was for many a cultural hero. Diogenes Laertius claims that the Athenians loved the man from Sinope,[111] and the stories about him and his imitators were told again and again. The wide range of sources in which they are found attests to the popularity of Cynic anecdotes. In an apparent paradox, if Diogenes' behavior was obscene by virtue of its opposition to the social structure, narrating stories about Diogenes evidently was not.[112]

The meaning of the stories of Cynic shamelessness was not the same as the acts they described. Telling about defecation in public is not the same as defecating in public. For this reason, we may not reduce the stories' narrative meaning to their ostensive reference. Without such insight, one might well wonder at the place of obscenity in the teaching of virtue. Far from functioning as an attack on those who adhered to societal conventions for appropriate behavior, the stories about Diogenes communicated a judgment concerning appropriate behavior both explicitly and implicitly. Perhaps some who practiced Cynicism during the Roman empire by behaving in a shameless way thought of themselves as subversive; in the absence of their writings, we cannot know their motives. What is clear is that no extant ancient writing employs the stories about Diogenes to advocate subversion of the social order through obscenity. Instead, as has been seen, many authors presented Diogenes' behavior as an example to be avoided. Those who condemned Cynic shamelessness, such as Epictetus, John Chrysostom, and Theodoret of Cyrrhus, were thus expressing a conviction that conformity to social codes was of great importance to wellborn gentlemen, whether Stoic or Christian. That shamelessness was unacceptable was the essence of attacks on contemporary Cynics. Even when the anecdotes about Diogenes stood alone, as they did in collections of *chreiai*, they used humor to articulate the boundaries between the acceptable and the unac-

---

109. Cf. D.L. 6.33, 41; *Ep. Diog.* 20; Lucian, *Philosophers for Sale!* 10; Athenaeus, *Deipn.*, 4.164a; Epictetus, *Diatr.* 3.22.52, 54–55.

110. Aug. *Civ. Dei* 14.20; trans. O'Meara (above, n. 85) 582.

111. D.L. 6.43.

112. The observations here owe much to Mary Douglas's analysis of jokes in *Implicit Meanings: Essays in Anthroplogy* (London 1975) 106–7.

ceptable. Diogenes was not to be emulated; and to the extent that Diogenes *chreiai* were used in a educational tradition that was ultimately concerned to transmit aristocratic values to the next generation of privileged Romans, the stories about Diogenes helped to insure social conformity. One of the school exercises performed on the *chreiai* involved passing judgment on an anecdote, refuting it, in the words of Theon's handbook, "because of unsuitability . . . because of shamelessness [*ek tou aiskhrou*]." [113] Schoolchildren were not taught to imitate Diogenes, but rather to distinguish appropriate modes of behavior from inappropriate ones.

If the use of Diogenes as a negative example is explicit, another function of the traditions is implicit, namely the ability of these stories to reduce societal tension. While the use of Diogenes traditions does not challenge the social structure, it does provide perspective on it. The order of society defined and confined the world in which upper-class Romans led their lives. But in contrast to Diogenes within the stories, those who recounted the stories did not seek to overturn the often frustrating order of their world; they merely sought to come to terms with it. The Cynic stories reduced the tensions inevitable in any system of social organization by giving those who shared the stories and the system an opportunity to achieve critical distance and to laugh.

The stories of Diogenes' shamelessness were transformative because they revealed that the ways in which a Roman gentleman lived his life were based on human constructs that had no basis in a reality beyond human social interaction. For the Greco-Roman authors we have considered (and for their audiences) the order of society was real, even if it was not grounded in nature. Diogenes, of course, did not invent bodily functions, but in focusing attention on them, he was able to recreate them as a form of language. The enacted language of physical movement was translated into the verbal language of the storyteller. Diogenes' behavior, then, involved a process of infusing with meaning the most natural and apparently meaningless human activities. The antics of the Cynic hero exposed those petty rituals that governed the bodily functions.

The Cynic anecdotes denied the ontological basis of social conventions, but the use of Diogenes traditions was not revolutionary. Across the wide variety of purposes for which ancient authors cited them and despite their latent kernel of subversion, the use of these stories bolstered a largely conservative agenda. Cynic tales did not propose an alternative structure for society; instead their critical perspective recast the status quo. As an assault on the most basic conventions, Diogenes' shamelessness revealed Roman imperial manners and mores as a social construct freighted with the ability to define membership in Greco-Roman society. Bad manners were culturally significant. The stories of this marginal icon helped to tell Roman gentlemen how to be who they were.

---

113. Thus Theon, *On the Chreia* I. 338 (cf. 370, 375); Hock and O'Neil (above, n. 4) 102–5.

Cynicism and Christianity from the Middle Ages to the Renaissance

S. Matton

The Cynic philosopher was not a wholly new character on the cultural stage of the Renaissance. Represented principally by Diogenes, the Cynic had long been a character familiar to the Middle Ages. What people knew of the Cynics came from two main sources. There were first Latin authors, both pagan (Cicero, Valerius Maximus, Seneca, Macrobius; to a lesser extent Aulus Gellius) and Christian (Jerome, Augustine, Tertullian, Sidonius Apollinaris). The second source was an Arabic one. The *Mukhtār al-hikam wa-mahasin al-kalim* (1048/49) of Abū 'l-Wafā' al-Mubashshir ibn Fātik included several of Diogenes' sayings not otherwise known from Greek or Latin sources.[1] Sometime before 1257 an anonymous translator at the court of Alfonso the Wise produced a Spanish version of this work under the title *Bocados de oro*.[2] A Latin translation was made from the Spanish version in the last decades of the thirteenth century, possibly by Giovanni da Procida (d. 1299). Some manuscripts

This essay has been translated from the French by Helena Caine-Suarez. A more detailed study of Cynicism during the Renaissance will appear in the series edited by Professor J.-C. Margolin, "De Pétrarque à Descartes" (Paris: Vrin), where the texts referred to in the present essay will be reproduced and the majority of them translated.

1. Those sayings not figuring in Greek or Latin sources have been listed and translated by D. Gutas, "Sayings by Diogenes Preserved in Arabic," in M.-O. Goulet-Cazé and R. Goulet, eds., *Le cynisme ancien et ses prolongements: Actes du Colloque international du C.N.R.S.* (Paris 1993) 475–518.

2. The first edition was prepared by H. Knust, *Mittheilungen aus dem Eskurial*, Bibliothek des Litterarischen Vereins in Stuttgart, 141 (Tübingen 1879). A new edition was established by M. Crombach, *"Bocados de oro": Kritische Ausgabe des altspanischen Textes*, Romanisches Seminar der Universität Bonn (Bonn 1971).

give the Latin version of the title as *Liber Philosophorum Moralium Antiquorum;* others call it *Dicta et Opiniones Philosophorum.*[3]

These sources were taken up and reused in encyclopedic works, anthologies of moral instruction, and biographies of the philosophers. To name only a few of the most important of these collections, there were, in the twelfth century, John of Salisbury's *Policraticus sive De Nugis Curialium et Vestigiis Philosophorum* (completed before 1159), and in the thirteenth century the *Speculum Maius* by the Dominican Vincent of Beauvais (1184/94–1294), both the *Speculum Doctrinale* and the *Speculum Historiale.* From the *Speculum Historiale* passages concerning ancient philosophers were summarized and translated into Italian by an unknown author around 1270 or 1275 under the title *Fiore e vita di filosafi e d'altri savi e d'imperadori.*[4] Still in the thirteenth century, there were two treatises by the Franciscan John of Wales (ca. 1220/30– ca. 1285), namely his *Breviloquium de Virtutibus Antiquorum Principum et Philosophorum* and his *Compendiloquium de Vitis Illustrium Philosophorum.* Both these works were probably composed during his stay in Paris (ca. 1270/ 85). Later still, and even more influential, was the *De Vita et Moribus Philosophorum,* attributed to Walter Burley, but in fact written by an unknown author working in northern Italy around 1315 or 1320.[5] This treatise enjoyed considerable popularity, if we are to judge from the 270-odd manuscripts that have preserved one or the other of two different versions of the work. Along with Vincent of Beauvais's *Speculum Historiale,* the *De Vita et Moribus Philosophorum* was widely used by two historians in Petrarch's circle, both by Giovanni Colonna, one of Petrarch's correspondents, author of a *De Viris Illustribus,* and by Petrarch's friend the Veronese jurisconsult Guglielmo da Pastrengo, who produced a *De Viris Illustribus et de Originibus,* published in 1547 in Venice under the title *Libellus de Originibus Rerum.* In Guglielmo's work Antisthenes, Diogenes, and Crates are placed among the philosophers, while Menippus is put among the poets.[6]

3. See E. Franceschini's edition, "Il 'Liber philosophorum moralium antiquorum': Testo critico," *Atti del Reale Istituto Veneto di Scienze, Lettere ed Arti* 91 (1931–32) 393–597; see also, by the same editor, "Il *Liber philosophorum moralium antiquorum,*" *Atti della Reale Accademia Nazionale dei Lincei,* Anno 327, ser. 6, Memorie della Classe di Scienze Morali, Storiche e Filologiche 3 (1930), 355–99, reprinted in *Scritti di filologia latina medievale* 1 (Padua 1976) 109–65.

4. See A. D'Agostino's edition, *Fiore e vita di filosafi e d'altri savi e d'imperadori* (Florence 1979); see also H. Varnhagen, *Über die Fiori e vita dei filosofi ed altri savii ed imperadori: Nebst dem italienischen Texte* (Erlangen 1893), who edited on facing pages the Latin texts of the *Speculum Historiale.*

5. See M. Grignaschi, "Lo pseudo Walter Burley e il 'Liber de vita et moribus philosophorum,'" *Medioevo* 16 (1990) 131–90; " 'Corrigenda et addenda' sulla questione dello ps. Burleo," ibid. 325–54.

6. Cf. *De Viris Illustribus et de Originibus,* ed. G. Bottari, Studi sul Petrarca 21 (Padua 1991), 5, 6, 47, 151–52.

The rediscovery of Greek literature during the Renaissance naturally led to an improved understanding of ancient Cynicism. Among the new sources of information was one that even today is the most important. This is Diogenes Laertius's work, translated into Latin in 1433 by the Camaldulite Ambrogio Traversari under the title *Vitae et Sententiae Eorum Qui in Philosophia Probati Fuerunt.* By 1472, Traversari's translation had been printed in Rome. The Greek text was not to be printed until 1533, in Basel. Diogenes Laertius's work cannot properly be counted among medieval sources for knowledge of the Cynics since the translation perhaps made by Henricus Aristippus (d. 1162), if indeed it existed at all, went no further than Book 5, possibly only as far as Book 2. This explains why, of the authors whom one might expect to have had access to the translation, none in fact made any use of it in their treatment of such Cynic philosophers as Antisthenes, Diogenes, or Crates. The other principal source, almost equal in importance to Diogenes Laertius, was Plutarch's *Moralia,* which began to be translated into Latin at the end of the fourteenth century. The first printed edition was published by Aldus Manutius in Venice in 1509. The works of Lucian, Julian, Dio, Stobaeus, the Greek Fathers and the *Suda* must also be taken note of, as should Theophylact Simocatta's *Epistolae Morales, Rusticae et Amatoriae* and various apocryphal texts that were long considered genuine. As early as the fifteenth century, Diogenes' *Epistles* were translated into Latin, with a dedication to Pius II, by Francesco Griffolini Aretino, while Crates' *Epistles* were among the first texts to be printed at the Sorbonne, in 1471.

The new outlook on Cynicism made possible by the discovery of these new texts found its way once more into encyclopedic works such as Coelius Rhodiginus's *Lectionum Antiquarum libri triginta* (1516), Alessandro d'Alessandro's *Genialium Dierum libri sex* (1522), Lucio Domizio Brusoni's *Sententiarum liber* (1518), and especially Erasmus's *Apophthegmatum sive Scite Dictorum libri sex* (1531). The third book of Erasmus's apophthegms is the one that makes greatest use of Plutarch and treats in turn of Socrates, Aristippus, and Diogenes the Cynic. Diogenes is given the lion's share, with 218 apophthegms, as against 91 for Socrates and 61 for Aristippus. We should not forget the 1555 *Apophthegmatum sive Responsorum Memorabilium Loci Communes* of Conrad Wolffhardt, known as Lycosthenes, a work that was as popular at the time as was that of Erasmus. Like Erasmus, Lycosthenes gives considerable space to Diogenes, who takes up a large part of the book, with 226 index references compared with 160 for Socrates, 64 for Plato, and 56 for Aristotle. Lycosthenes completes the portrait gallery of Cynic philosophers by putting Antisthenes (80 references) and Crates (27 references) alongside Diogenes, as well as bringing in a new name, Lucian's Demonax, with 52 references.

Given the demonstrable renewal of interest in ancient Cynics, it would nonetheless be a mistake to suggest too complete a break between the medieval and Renaissance images of Cynicism. Despite the rediscovery of classical literature in general, and that of the Greeks in particular, the Renaissance continued to feed off medieval writings, which were published and republished throughout the whole of the period.

Cynicism Between Philosophical Ethics and Christian Edification

The Middle Ages inherited the ambivalent attitude of early Christian authors, who vacillated between condemning the Cynics and praising them.[7] On the one hand, there was respect bordering on admiration, as shown by Saint Jerome in his *Adversus Jovinianum* (2.14), for Antisthenes, Crates, and particularly Diogenes (a "victor over human nature").[8] On the other hand, the Cynics were roundly condemned by Sidonius Apollinaris (*Epistolae* 9.9, 15; *Carmina* 2.164–68, 15.124–25)[9] and by Claudianus Mamertus (*De Statu Animae* 2.9).[10] As M.-O. Goulet-Cazé has pointed out, Claudianus merged Cynicism and Epicureanism, only to decry the resulting amalgam. However, the most widely held position in the Middle Ages was probably that of Saint Augustine. Augustine reproached the Cynics for their lack of *verecundia,* decency and modesty (*De Civitate Dei* 14.20.43), but like Varro accepted their lifestyle, excepting only what was frankly indecent (ibid., 19.19.397).[11]

This ambivalent judgment, which Augustine shared with most or all of the Greek Fathers as well as with many pagans, chiefly Cicero,[12] is to be found in various encyclopedic works. When Vincent of Beauvais in his *Speculum Historiale* (3.68) undertakes a treatment of Diogenes and the Cynic school, he begins by quoting Augustine's condemnation of the Cynics' encouragement of copulation in public. He goes on to quote Cicero, who saw Epicurus as a successor of Antisthenes. However, after these expressions of disapproval, he carries on with quotations from Seneca, Valerius Maximus, Macrobius, and Helinant of Froidmont,[13] all of whom wrote in praise of Diogenes.[14] Above all, in

---

7. See D. Dudley, *A History of Cynicism from Diogenes to the 6th Century* A.D. (London 1937; repr. Hildesheim 1967); M.-O. Goulet-Cazé, "Le cynisme à l'époque impériale," ANRW 2.36.4 (Berlin 1990) 2720–2833.

8. Migne, *PL* 23.304b. Cf. Goulet-Cazé (above, n. 7) 2795.

9. Cf. ibid. 2799.

10. Cf. ed. Engelbrecht, p. 1333, 15. See Goulet-Cazé (above, n. 7) 2799 n. 510.

11. Cf. ibid. 2798.

12. Cf. *De Officiis* 1.35.128, 41.148.

13. The only reference the *Speculum Historiale* gives is "Helinadus 17." I have been unable to find the text, possibly now lost, to which he refers. The passage was apparently not included in Helinant's *Flores,* compiled by Vincent de Beauvais himself (cf. Migne, *PL* 212).

14. Cf. the edition of Venice, 1591, f. 38r.

the following chapter (69, "De Eodem et Morte Eius"), he reproduces in full the relevant passage from Jerome's *Adversus Jovinianum*.[15] The author of the *Liber de Vita et Moribus Philosophorum* takes a similar approach in the section (chap. 50) he dedicates to Diogenes.[16] This section is one of the most substantial of the work. It is shorter than the one on Socrates, but longer than those on Plato and Aristotle. Like Vincent of Beauvais, whom he also uses, pseudo-Burley begins his account with the text taken from the *De Civitate Dei*, though he quotes it much more extensively. He continues with a collage of quotations from all the usual sources: Valerius Maximus, Cicero, Macrobius, Seneca, Saint Jerome, Pseudo–Caecilius Balbus, and others. The overall impression he gives of Diogenes is a favorable one.

Apart from such encyclopedic works, and insofar as there was not much need to counter a sect with no active members, the medieval world made little effort to express or develop criticism of what seemed to be the negative aspects of Cynicism. Instead, several authors highlighted the positive aspects of Cynicism in considering Antisthenes, Diogenes, and Crates, along with most of the other philosophers of antiquity, in a series of writings characteristic of medieval humanism. As Ph. Delhaye points out, these tended to develop a philosophical system of ethics founded not expressly on Scripture nor on Christian theological teachings, but on classical moralists, especially Cicero and Seneca, without, however, giving allegiance to any one philosopher in particular, as the Scholastics had done with Aristotle.[17] In these writings Cynic philosophy is presented as a secular model for rejection of the materialism of this life. William of Doncaster takes just such an approach in his *Explicatio Aphorismatum Philosophicorum*, composed in the first decades of the twelfth century, when he explains that such contempt provides a solid basis for happiness. He offers the examples of Crates' throwing his worldly goods into the sea,[18] and of Diogenes' contenting himself with his tub and refusing Alexander's offer of a Tyrian robe.[19] The author of the *Moralium Dogma Philosophorum*, attributed to William of Conches, likewise bases himself on Seneca (*De Beneficiis* 5.4). He makes use of the episode of the Cynic who asked Antigonus for a talent and then for a denarius, and was refused the first as being unworthy of a Cynic, and the second as

15. In a similar way Vincent of Beauvais in his *Speculum Doctrinale* denounces the impudicity of the Cynics (1.12: "De Diversis Generibus Philosophorum," *ed. cit.* [above, n. 14] f. 3), but quotes Diogenes' life as an example of *sufficentia sive paupertas voluntaria* (4.104; *ed. cit.* f. 65v).

16. Knust (above, n. 2) 192–212.

17. See P. Delhaye, "Un dictionnaire d'éthique attribué à Vincent de Beauvais dans le ms. Bâle B.IX.3," *Mélanges de Science Religieuse* 8 (1951) 65–84 (here 84).

18. For *Socrates* of the mss. we should obviously read *Crates*.

19. Cf. *Explicatio Aphorismatum Philosophicorum*, ed. O. Weijers, Studien und Texte zur Geistesgeschichte des Mittelalters 11 (Leiden 1976), 37.

unworthy of a king (ibid. 2.17).[20] He also makes play with Diogenes' superiority over Alexander, as the former could refuse much more than the latter could offer.[21] John of Salisbury likewise dwells on the question of poverty and asceticism in his *Policraticus* (3.17) when he reproduces verbatim, though without naming his source, the entire passage from Saint Jerome's *Adversus Jovinianum* that deals with Antisthenes and Diogenes. In the *Policraticus* (3.14) he also highlights the Cynics' indifference to what others might say, taking up the tale of Diogenes from pseudo–Caecilius Balbus where Diogenes is told that his friends were complaining about him and replies that it is only to be expected that the wise should be denigrated by the ignorant and that scandalmongers serve merely to illuminate the goodness of those whom they attack.[22]

Diogenes, symbol of Cynicism, is thus represented as a man "of very great virtue," [23] in the words of the anonymous author of *Fiore e vita di filosafi e d'altri savi e d'imperadori*, a work from which all traces of the Augustinian criticism present in Vincent of Beauvais have been excised. In *La divina commedia*, Dante places Diogenes among the greatest philosophers in the first circle of Hell, the Limbo that holds the souls of the innocent and virtuous unbaptized.[24] Petrarch's position is more circumspect than Dante's. In his *Triomphus Fame*, Petrarch places Diogenes, in contrast to Heraclitus, among those who won as much glory through letters as others did by feats of arms. Yet Diogenes' status here is ambiguous, since he is described as doing publicly things that others took great care to hide: *in suo' fatti / Assai più che non vuol vergogna aperto*.[25] At the same time in his *Rerum Memorandarum libri* (2.51) Petrarch passes over this absence of *vergogna* in silence, preferring to portray Antisthenes' disciple as holding in contempt the worldly goods everyone else was craving. Boccaccio has no qualms about Diogenes in his *De Casibus Virorum Illustrium* (1355/60), even citing him alongside Saint John the Baptist.[26] Lau-

20. Cf. J. Holmberg, ed., *Das Moralium Dogma Philosophorum des Guillaume de Conches, lateinisch, altfranzösisch und mittelniederfränkisch* (Uppsala 1929) 15. According to Plutarch, *Reg. et Imperat. Apophthegmata* 182e, §15, the Cynic in question is Thrasyllus; cf. also *De Vitioso Pudore* 531e–f, §7, where Plutarch simply writes merely "a Cynic" (Giannantoni V M). L. Paquet's identification of this Cynic as Diogenes is groundless (*Diogène*, 53 n. 70 [p. 65]).

21. Cf. *Moralium Dogma Philosophorum, ed. cit.* (above n. 20) 63–64.

22. Cf. E. Wölfflin, ed., *Caecilii Balbi De Nugis Philosophorum Quae Supersunt* (Basel 1855) 8.7-9: "Sed et Diogenes, cum ei nunciasset amicus, Te [amici] cuncti vituperant, Oportet, inquit, sapientiam ab insipientibus feriri; esse enim meliorem indicat mala lingua quem carpit." This is repeated by John of Wales (*Compendiloquium*) and the pseudo-Burley (*De Vita et Moribus Philosophorum*, ed. Knust, 202).

23. Cf. *Fiore e vita di filosafi e d'altri savi e d'imperadori* IX, ed. A. D'Agostino, 126–27 (= ed. H. Varnhagen, 6).

24. *Divina commedia,* Inferno, 4.130–44, ed. T. Casini (Florence 1917) 31–32.

25. *I trionfi,* "Triomphus Fame," 2.82–84, ed. F. Neri, *Rime e Trionfi* (Turin 1953) 587.

26. Cf. *De Casibus Virorum Illustrium* 1.16, 3.17, 7.7, ed. P.G. Ricci and V. Zaccaria, in V. Branca, ed., *Tutte le opere di Giovanni Boccaccio* 9 (Milan 1983) 84, 273–76, 630.

rent de Premierfait expresses still more fulsome approval in the free paraphrase that he made of Boccaccio into French between 1400 and 1409, where he calls Diogenes "a friend of poverty" who "had in him neither delectation nor covetousness." [27]

A favorable attitude toward Cynicism is not peculiar to medieval works that give pride of place to moral philosophy founded on a study of the classics. The same attitude is to be found in other treatises, anchored firmly in a Christian ethical tradition, but equally concerned with principles of moral philosophy insofar as their authors encourage Christians not to show themselves morally inferior to pagans. Christians should obey Jerome's injunction (*Adversus Jovinianum* 2.14): "All those who know nothing of or lack respect for the poverty of the apostles and the rigor of the Cross should at least imitate the temperance of the pagans." This is especially so in the works of John of Wales. Flattering references to the behavior of ancient Cynics are frequent in his writings, for example in his *Communiloquium sive Summa Collationum ad Omne Genus Hominum,* where he recalls Diogenes' wish not to have a tomb of any kind (7.3.3). In his *Compendiloquium de Vitis Illustrium Philosophorum* John of Wales exploits even more fully the idea of the Cynic Diogenes as an example for Christians to follow. John of Wales held that pagans were able to lead virtuous lives guided solely by the principles of reason, and it is the avowed intention of his *Compendiloquium* to stir the young to a more Christian life, instilling in them a proper sense of shame by placing before them the example of the lives and teachings of pagan philosophers. In this spirit he praises philosophy as a medicine of the soul and briefly describes Solon and the Seven Sages before going on to the life and teachings of Diogenes of Sinope, albeit sometimes confusing him with Diogenes of Seleucia, called the Babylonian. He dwells at length on Diogenes' virtues, in the course of fourteen chapters, eloquently titled: "On Antisthenes, the Master of Diogenes" (1), "On the Life of Diogenes and His Virtues, Namely His Willing Acceptance of Poverty, His Firmness of Soul and His Constancy" (2), "On His Refusal of Alexander's Gifts and How He Proved More Powerful than the Latter" (3), "How According to Seneca He Was like the Immortal Gods" (4), "How He Wished to Become a Slave Again and Then Met a Better Fate than the King of Persia" (5), "On His Patience When Slandered" (6), "On His Patience and Courage in Captivity" (7), "On His Patience When in Pain" (8), "On His Self-control in Suppressing Vices and Inner Cravings" (9), "On His Frankness in Criticizing Others and Flattering No One" (10), "On His Compassion for the Sufferings of Others" (11), "On His Various Sayings" (12), "On His Discussion with

27. Cf. *De Casibus Virorum Illustrium, Des cas des nobles hommes et femmes,* 16.12–13, ed. P. M. Gathercole, University of North Carolina Studies in the Romance Languages and Literatures 74 (Chapel Hill 1968), 200.

Antipater on the Selling of Goods" (13),[28] "On His Office and His Legation to the Roman Senate" (14).[29] Amid so much praise, Diogenes' disdain for *humana verecundia,* needless to say, is passed over in silence.

John of Wales was far from being alone in his call to imitate Diogenes' frankness in criticizing others and his total avoidance of flattery. Some went so far as to wish he had a few successors ready to be similarly outspoken on the subject of corrupt churchmen, especially those of the Curia. In the *Carmina Burana* there is a poem to this effect called *Diogenis cum Aristippo Dialogus.*[30]

While the *Compendiloquium* certainly represents the most fully worked-out attempt of the Middle Ages to reconcile Cynicism with Christian ethics, we should not forget the work of Jacques Legrand (ca. 1365–1415), an Augustinian inspired by John of Wales.[31] Legrand not only composed a number of important treatises in Latin, but also made adaptations of them into French, thus ensuring their dissemination beyond the circles of the clergy and an educated elite. This is important because he often refers to the Cynics, as he does for instance in *Archiloge Sophie,* adapted from his own *Sophilogion.* Here he transcribes what he calls a proverb:

> Philozophes jadis furent par sapience
> Gens sur tous reputez de grande excellence,
> Comme fut Socrates, Platon et Democrite.
> Ainsi le nous tesmoingne leur vie bien descripte.

These verses he follows with the comment "Diogenes too refused everything in order to acquire understanding, as Saint Jerome says, answering Jovinian." [32] Likewise, in his *Livre de bonnes meurs,* he elaborates on the asceticism of wise Diogenes, who "despised copious meals and all excess," [33] who was in this way richer than the greedy rich, since, like Crates,[34] he possessed "spiritual poverty and true sufficiency." [35] Legrand stresses that the poverty of the Cynics was genuine and not just for show, as is underscored by his pointedly comparing them to the poor in spirit whom Scripture tells us are blessed by God (Matthew

---

28. This is obviously a case of confusion with Diogenes of Seleucia.

29. Also a case of confusion with Diogenes of Seleucia.

30. *Carmina Burana,* no. 189, ed. A. Milka and O. Schumann (Munich 1985), 560–64.

31. See E. Bertan, "Christine de Pizan, Jacques Legrand et le *Communiloquium* de Jean de Galles," *Romania* 104 (1983) 208–28.

32. Cf. E. Beltran, ed., *Jacques Legrand, Archiloge Sophie, Livre de bonnes meurs,* Bibliothèque du XVᵉ Siècle 49 (Paris 1986), 38.

33. Cf. ibid., *Livre des bonnes meurs,* part I, 324.

34. Cf. ibid. chap. 18 ("Comment l'estat de povreté est moult agreable et plaisant a Dieu"), 339.

35. Cf. ibid. 337–38.

5.3).[36] The close link between Cynicism and Christianity is equally clear in the lack of interest that should be shown for one's own tomb:[37]

> On this same subject, we read in the second book of the lives of the Fathers how one day a good man saw an evil one buried with all honors in a lavish tomb while another good man was left in the fields, eaten by beasts. And then an angel said to the man, who was astonished and angered by this sight: "My friend, be not angry, for the tomb is the wage of the evil man who did no good while he was alive, whereas the good man who is eaten by dogs is rewarded quite otherwise in paradise." And so it is clear that the coveting of a tomb is in no way good. And thus it is that we read how Diogenes ordered that, after his death, his body be given to the birds and the beasts to feed upon. And when he was asked why, he replied that after his death the beasts would do him no harm by tearing apart and eating his body, that in this way they could be greatly benefited by feeding on him, and that it were better to be taken for nutrition than left for decomposition. This tale is told by Cicero in the first book of his *Tusculan Disputations.*

The unknown illustrator of the fifteenth-century manuscript of the *Livre de bonnes meurs* kept in the Musée Condé at Chantilly (ms. 297) found this image so striking that he depicted Diogenes, next to his tub, being pecked at by birds while still alive.[38]

Cynicism and Christian Humanism

The various risqué or downright scandalous anecdotes that embellished the life of Diogenes of Sinope in the writings of Diogenes Laertius and Athenaeus did not prevent the Renaissance from continuing the tradition of the Middle Ages in taking over and continuing features from Cynicism. The poet and moralist Maffeo Vegio (1407–58), famous for his continuation of the *Aeneid,* is a particularly interesting example. He was an Augustinian, a canon of Saint Peter's in Rome, and enjoyed the favor of the popes Eugene IV and Nicholas V. He was one of the first people to make use of Ambrogio Traversari's Latin translation of Diogenes Laertius. He does so especially in his major work on education, *De Educatione Liberorum et Claris Eorum Studiis ac Moribus.* Despite his new knowledge of the life of Diogenes, Maffeo Vegio continues to quote the Cynics as an exemplary model, and Diogenes is almost made out to be a universal symbol of the philosopher. Maffeo Vegio even refers to Diogenes when he explains how the young should study philosophy not for any speculative understanding it might give them, but in order to have an immediate

---

36. Cf. ibid. part II, chap. 15 ("Comment l'estat de povreté doit estre agreable a Dieu"), 365.

37. Cf. ibid. chap. 34 ("Comment nul ne doit estre curieux de sa sepulture"), 395–96.

38. This painting is reproduced on the cover of the paperback edition of L. Paquet, *Les cyniques grecs* (Paris 1992).

intuition of the just and honest aims one should have in life, and of how these may be achieved, as well as learning how to react to both happiness and misfortune with equanimity. He praises Diogenes for what he said when asked what he had learned from philosophy: "If nothing else, at least I am ready for anything." [39] He likewise approves of the way Antisthenes, Crates, and Diogenes denounced flatterers and were on their guard against them.[40] He also takes the trouble to excuse the Cynics for their lack of *verecundia,* which he explains by the simple moral code of their age, though taking a less serious example than their sexual practices: "Eating in public places, as the Cynics did, goes against decency, though the ancients did so often. While we hardly praise them for it, neither do we condemn them, since such behavior stemmed from a generally simpler and more humane way of life. The times were so much more humble that people then did not prepare meals so sumptuous that you would be ashamed to be seen eating them in public." [41] In his *De Perseverantia Religionis* Maffeo Vegio goes on to make a rather daring comparison between perseverance in religion and Diogenes' determination to follow Antisthenes and be taught by him.[42]

Robert Gaguin also highlights the numerous points that Cynicism and Christianity have in common. Gaguin was a humanist and a diplomat and belonged to the Trinitarian order, of which he was elected vicar general in 1473. He wrote to Florimond Robertet, the secretary of King Charles VIII of France, sending him the 1486 Paris edition of the apocryphal letters of Crates:[43]

> Don't think I don't know that you are far too busy to be able to devote much time to letters. You have many pressing worries at court. That is why I'm not sending you anything too lengthy. These letters of Crates are short enough for you to read through them all twice over in an hour or each individually in no time at all. In fact it must be the slimmest of my books. If by any chance you should find the time to look them over, you'll see that there is a lot that is in keeping with Christian law. You will be astonished that a Cynic who lived centuries before our Lord could have had such contempt for riches and lived in such absolute poverty, all for the love of philosophy.

Thus Christian humanism does not hesitate to highlight the elements it perceives to be morally unimpeachable and passes more discreetly over the rest, though it does occasionally make efforts to interpret these in a more acceptable light. For example, Alessandro d'Alessandro maintains that, if Diogenes, like

39. *De Educatione Liberorum* 3.8 ("Vt Adolescentes ad Studia Philosophiae Invitentur"), ed. *Bibliotheca Veterum Patrum* 15 (Cologne 1622) 865.
40. Ibid. 3.11, 866.
41. Ibid. 6.3, 885.
42. *De Perseverantia Religionis* 1.6, ed. *Bibliotheca Veterum Patrum* (cit. above, n. 39) 897.
43. Cf. L. Thuasne, ed., *Roberti Gaguini Epistole et Orationes. Texte publié sur les éditions originales de 1498, précédé d'une notice biographique et suivi de pièces diverses en partie inédites* (Paris 1903) 316–17.

Plato, was in favor of holding all women in common, it was only to avoid the serious crime of adultery.[44] About sixty years later Hieronymus Wolf will say more or less the same thing, adding, however, that it was intended ironically (*eirōnikōs et per ridiculum*).[45] Scientific excuses were also found for certain kinds of behavior: Mario Equicola explains in his *Libro di natura d'amore* (1525) that if Diogenes, who was "a person of great severity and continence, had several times made use of Venus," it was because he felt "the retention of his seed was obnoxious and damaging to him." This was in keeping with the teachings of the learned doctors who know that "some small quantity of matter enclosed in one place is damaging to the whole body, which the moving semen harms when it is not expelled." [46] There arose in this way a certain conception of the Cynic philosopher, which eventually crystallized into the image of Silenus popularized by Erasmus. With Christ and his apostles, Socrates ("Saint Socrates, pray for us"), and Epictetus, Erasmus places Antisthenes and Diogenes among the Sileni ranged against the masses of *mundani,* the sophists, the turgid Aristotelian doctors, all those for whom only appearances counted. In one of his *Adagia* (from the edition of 1515 onwards) he explains who the Sileni of Alcibiades were and goes on to say:[47]

> Antisthenes, with his stave, pouch, and cloak, was such a Silenus, richer than a king. Diogenes was such a Silenus, whom the plebs called a dog. Alexander, the first and the finest among princes, recognized something divine in him and said that if he were not Alexander he would wish to be Diogenes—although Alexander, just because he was Alexander, should have wished to have Diogenes' qualities of soul.

Furthermore, justifying the order of presentation of the authors in his *Apophthegmata,* Erasmus confides that he values Diogenes and Aristippus as highly as he values Socrates:[48]

> It does not seem to me misplaced, following the playful sanctity [*faceta sanctimonia*] of Socrates and the joyful freedom of Aristippus, to move on to Diogenes of Sinope, who far surpasses all others with the inexhaustible charm of his words. In the end, though, with all their differing qualities, I have to put these three on a par. Different though they are, they are nonetheless each other's equals.

In the dedicatory letter of the *Apophthegmata* Erasmus had explained that the very tone of their words, light and pleasant as it was, made them infinitely more

---

44. Cf. *Genialium Dierum libri sex* 6.1 (ed. Leiden 1673), vol. 1, 863.

45. Cf. *Tabula Compendiosa . . . a G. Morellio Tiliano collecta. Cum Hier. Wolfii annotationibus . . .* (Basel 1580) 84.

46. Ed. Venice 1563, 216.

47. *Adagia,* no. 2201 ("Sileni Alcibiadis"), ed. S. Seidel-Menchi in *Opera Omnia,* vol. II-5 (Amsterdam 1981) 159–60.

48. *Apophthegmata,* in *Opera Omnia,* ed. J. Leclerc, 10 vols. (Leiden 1703–6), vol. 4, 172B.

suited to the education of princes and the young, leading them more easily to rigorous wisdom than their detractors Xenocrates and Zeno would have been able to do. This is in spite of the fact that, in the *Moriae Encomium* (1509) at least, Erasmus accepts the version of Diogenes' death that has him commit suicide. Dame Folly exclaims: "But who are they who killed themselves because they were disgusted by life? Were they not those who were close to wisdom? We find among their number, apart from Diogenes, Xenocrates, Cato, Cassius, and Brutus, the famous Centaur Chiron, who chose death at the very moment when he could have become immortal."[49]

Nonetheless, in other works from the same Christian humanist background the praise of Cynicism is considerably diluted. So it is in the writings of the Carmelite poet Giovan Baptista Spagnoli, called the Mantuan. In his short *De Vita Beata* (1463), one of his earliest pieces, composed while he was still a novice, as well as in his *De patientia* Spagnoli praises the Cynics' disregard for riches as well as their rigor in criticizing evil doings,[50] those shadowy enemies who shunned the Cynics as they shunned satirists, comic writers, and other critics of society.[51] It would have been ungracious of Spagnoli to hold against them their verbal violence, as he was himself an adept of invectives against women and corrupt ecclesiastics, invectives that later ages would judge obscene. Spagnoli did, however, place Cynics at a distance from Christianity. Much like other ancient philosophies such as those of Pythagoras, Socrates, Plato, or Aristotle, Cynicism, lacking as it does the "condiment" of faith, can be no more than a shadowy light by which man can see only that he knows nothing.[52] In addition, Cynic asceticism does not go far enough as it still shows too great an interest in the body. Explaining why God so slights the body, Spagnoli writes: "Now I come to the pagans. The Pythagoreans did not eat meat. Diogenes, begging with his pouch and his stave, taught his disciples to beg. I believe it was an answer to this that Christ said [Luke 10.4], *Do not carry beggar's pouch or stave,* in order to show us that we should have even less care for our bodies than Diogenes had."[53] We should, however, note that Spagnoli changes the *sacculum* (purse) of the Vulgate text to *baculum* (stave), though it is impossible to tell whether this is a deliberate misrendering or a simple misremembering. Either way, it is one of the first times that this text (and by implication the corresponding texts in Matthew and Mark)[54] was taken to have the Cynics for its target.[55]

49. *Moriae Encomium* 31, ed. C.H. Miller, *Opera omnia* vol. IV-3, 108.

50. *De Vita Beata*, in *Opera Omnia* (Antwerp 1576) vol. 4, f. 185v.

51. *De Patientia* 1.29, in *Opera Omnia*, cit., vol. 4, ff. 43v–4r.

52. Ibid. 3.2, f. 124v.

53. Ibid. 2.24 ("Cur Deus Floccipendat Corpus, Rationes Naturales"), f. 106v.

54. Cf. Matthew 10.9-10, Mark 6.8-9; see also Luke 22.35. These verses do not mention the stave either.

55. For these verses, see F.G. Downing, *Christ and the Cynics: Jesus and Other Radical Preachers in First-Century Tradition* (Sheffield 1988) 47–48.

Though not very clearly written, Spagnoli's *De Patientia* also includes disparagement of the Cynics' much-vaunted *apatheia*. He says that such detachment cannot be fundamentally moral if its sole aim is to escape from our passions. Passions like pain, sadness, or joy are not in themselves acts, though they lead to or are accompanied by acts, whether acts of will or acts of feeling. Passions therefore do no more than disturb our actions, which is why *apatheia* is to be desired. But, he continues, it is not the disturbance that is sinful, but the action itself.[56] Thus the *apatheia* of the Cynics has no moral value, as it does not concern itself with actions: it does not take into account the morality of an act and is connected only with the accompanying passion, which itself has no ethical charge.

A similar position is held by Gianfrancesco Pico della Mirandola in his *Examen Vanitatis Doctrinae Gentium et Veritatis Christianae Disciplinae* (1520). There are points in common between Christianity and some moral teachings of the ancient philosophers, such as the Cynics' condemnation of pleasure or their disdain for splendor and vainglory.[57] But these are not enough: perfect human happiness does not consist of living like a dog but of losing oneself in Christ, and all schools of philosophy that hope to survive can do so only by bowing down before Christianity.[58]

Despite such reservations, which covered all moral teachings from the ancient world, the attitude of early Christian humanists to Cynicism, like that of their medieval predecessors, was generally positive.

Cynicism in Apologetical Literature and in Sermons

This positive attitude toward Cynicism spread to a number of ecclesiastical authors throughout the sixteenth century. For example, in his *De Republica Christi dialogi tres* (1556), Alexius Salamanca praises Diogenes for his condemnation of flatterers, his temperance, and his sobriety.[59] This attitude was given new impetus with the publication in 1571 of the *Collectanea Moralis Philosophiae* by the famous Spanish Dominican Luis of Granada. His anthology of maxims for the use of preachers, taken principally from the works of Plutarch and Seneca,[60] also left an important place for the Cynics, Diogenes in particular.[61] In all his work, even his sermons,[62] Luis of Granada stresses the pedagogical content of Cynicism.

---

56. *De Patientia* 1.23, *ed. cit.* (above, n. 51) f. 35r–v.

57. Cf. *Examen Vanitatis Doctrinae Gentium et Veritatis Christianae Disciplinae* 3, in *Opera Omnia* (Basel 1573) 808.

58. Cf. ibid. 1008.

59. Cf. *De Republica Christi* 30, 122, 133.

60. As the full title suggests: *Collectanea Moralis Philosophiae tomis III, Quorum I. Selectissimas Sententias ex Omnibus Senecae Operibus; II. Ex Moralibus Opusculis Plutarch; III. Clarissimorum Principum et Philosophorum Insigniorum Apophtegmata Complectitur.*

61. Cf. lib. 2, clas. 1, cap. 10.

62. Cf. *Canciones de tempore*, Wednesday of the third week of Lent, serm. 3.

This use of the Cynics alongside other classical philosophers continued into the first quarter of the seventeenth century. The Jesuits encouraged widespread use of an Asiatic style, as ingenious as it was colorful, and which much influenced preachers of the time, who gave free rein to their taste for secular knowledge, displayed in and out of season, with the result that contemporary sermons give the impression of leading one through endless galleries, where are grouped, higgledy-piggledy, persons and authorities who have no real connection between them. So it was that preachers like Pierre de Besse, in a sermon on evangelical justice,[63] or the now forgotten Antoine de Lor, in a sermon on anger,[64] would make play with the way in which a Cynic like Diogenes was able to master his passions. Jacques Suares de Sainte Marie, a Portuguese Observantine, went so far as to apply Antisthenes' praise of fraternal harmony to the powers of the soul in a sermon on the expulsion of demons.[65] Needless to say, the voluntary poverty of the Cynics was compared to that of the Christian, as in the example of a sermon on the evil rich man attributed to Gaspar de Seguiran,[66] the Jesuit preacher and confessor to Louis XIII. Despite the reputation for atheism sometimes given him by classical authors,[67] Diogenes was even recruited as a defender of belief in an immortal soul. The Benedictine André Valladier explained in a sermon that Pherecydes was the first philosopher to hold this belief. Pherecydes taught it to Pythagoras. "Without a doubt, Diogenes, Socrates, and all the other Cynics and Stoics" upheld the same truth after them.[68] The Cynics were also referred to in even more unlikely contexts by some preachers. One example is found in a sermon on the Nativity by a Spanish Augustinian, Pedro de Valderrama, when he speaks of the New Jerusalem as "head" of the world. "The hair and beard," he explains, "mean the inhabitants of this city. Brave and valiant men were symbolized by the beard that Diogenes cultivated, as he said, to remind himself that he was a man and obliged therefore as such to do nothing effeminate."[69] The image of Diogenes with his lantern also crops up time and again and is occasionally put to imaginative use. The Carthusian Polycarpe de la Rivière tries to show in his *Ange-*

---

63. *Conceptions theologiques sur tous les dimanches de l'annee* (Paris 1618) vol. 1, 198.

64. *Sermons salutaires sur tous les jours de l'Advent, pour conduire les Ames pecheresses au chemin du Ciel* (Toulouse 1622) 378.

65. *Tresor quadragesimal, enrichi de plusieurs relevées et admirables considerations tant de l'escripture saincte que de la doctrine des SS. Peres pour les sermons de tous les jours du Caresme* (Paris 1608) 740.

66. *Sermons doctes et admirables sur tous les jours de Caresme et feriees de Pasques, preschez à Paris par un celebre personnage de nostre temps* (Paris 1613) 323. This work has also been attributed to Phillippe Bosquier.

67. See M.-O. Goulet-Cazé, "Les premiers cyniques et la religion," in Goulet-Cazé and Goulet (above, n. 1) 117–58 (here 145 sqq.).

68. *La Saincte Philosophie de l'âme, sermons pour l'Advant preschez à Paris à S*t*Medric l'an 1612* (Paris 1614) 176.

69. *Sermons sur toutes les festes de Nostre-Dame . . . traduicts en François par F.A. Simeon* (Paris 1609), Second Sermon of the Nativity, 185–86.

lique (1626) how hard it is for a man really to know himself, knowing, as he does, not the essence but only the accidents of things. He claims that if Diogenes went about in broad daylight with a lantern, saying that he was looking for a man, it was precisely to show that, in order to reach a true understanding of what a man is, it was necessary to go beyond the external shape and form by which we normally judge and define him.[70] Again, in his *Trois discours pour la religion catholique: Des miracles, des saints et des images* (1600), the Jesuit Louis Richeome denounces the blindness of men, adding that a "Christian Diogenes, using his lantern to seek out those who venerated miracles, would have trouble finding one man in a thousand."[71]

Cynicism and Monasticism

We know that even in antiquity similarities were established between Cynicism and monasticism, notably when the emperor Julian denounced the contempt for the world that the Cynics held in common with the anchorites of the Thebaid in their solitary retreats.[72] This similarity was subject to renewed scrutiny during the Renaissance. In Book 5 of his popular *Hieroglyphica, sive De Sacris Aegyptiorum, Aliarumque Gentium Literis Commentarii* (1556), Piero Valeriano compares the Cynics to the Franciscans, though without actually naming the latter.[73]

> It was with the dog that the Egyptians principally indicated those whose role it was to teach religion. This is because he who would teach sacred writings must be prepared continually to bark like a dog and never stop attacking vice. He must be fierce, and never end up in the good graces of an impious character, in much the same way as a dog behaves with those he recognizes with his eyes or his nose as being not of his master's household. Elias, Jeremiah, Ezekiel, Hosea, and many others were such among the Jews. Among the Greeks, Diogenes was one of the greatest. Indeed, he was commonly nicknamed the Cynic, which comes from the word "dog." Since then, the whole group of Cynics has been famous for its great austerity. There is another group, not dissimilar, which has spread almost throughout all the world right up to the present day. Yet it is famous for

70. *Angelique: Des excellences et perfections immortelles de l'ame* (Lyons 1626) 14.
71. *Trois discours pour la religion catholique: des miracles, des saints et des images* (Rouen 1600) 122–23.
72. Cf. Goulet-Cazé (above n. 7) 2776; G. Dorival ("Cyniques et chrétiens au temps des Pères grecs," in *Mélanges Spanneut* [Lille, 1994], 70 n. 46) criticizes the material used by P. Courcelle ("La figure du philosophe d'après les écrivains latins de l'antiquité," *Journal des Savants,* 1980, 85–101) in support of his thesis. According to Courcelle, anti-Christian polemicists presented these monastics as philosophical successors of the Cynics.
73. *Hieroglyphica* 5, "De Iis Quae per Canem Significantur ex Sacris Aegyptiorum Literis" (Basel 1556), f. 39r.

observing rules we find holier and professing a truer doctrine as well as scorning in a worthier fashion everything profane. They dress in coarse cloth and go about always in bare feet. There have indeed always been men who hold pleasure and luxury in contempt, are satisfied with little or nothing, live an impeccable life, and reproach those who live sinfully. Thus the good preacher should not be embarrassed to reprimand the dissolute for fear of being considered impudent.

Justus Lipsius, in his *Manuductionis ad Stoicam Philosophiam libri III* (1604), expressly compared Cynics not with Franciscans in general, but with Capuchins in particular. They were, he said, men of true virtue, patience, and poverty, distinguished from the Cynics by a piety that the ancients lacked.[74]

The Christian Denunciation of Cynicism

Not all religious authors were willing to believe that a Cynic philosopher could be a model, no matter of what kind, for a Christian, or that there might be any other than superficial resemblances between the two beliefs. Some must have considered the very expression "a Christian Diogenes" impious and frankly aberrant. Just as the Christianization of Cynicism belonged to a larger effort of humanism that wished to reconcile the philosophy of antiquity with Christianity, so the condemnation of Cynicism fitted in with the Pauline rejection of human, and especially pagan, wisdom (1 Cor. 3.19–20).

This wariness, bordering on downright hostility, toward the authors of antiquity had been present throughout the Middle Ages. For example, in the anonymous fourteenth-century *De Divisione et Laude Philosophiae Quae ad Mores Pertinet,* the Cynics are called an "execrable sect." [75] At the dawn of the Renaissance, this attitude was taken much further by the Dominican Giovanni Dominici in his *Lucula Noctis* (1405). Dominici's work was written to criticize humanism, which he saw as a return to antiquity, and to counter the arguments of Coluccio Salutati promoting the study of the classics and their culture in the service of Christianity. Dominici begins by setting out Salutati's arguments, two of which are directly related to our subject. The first is that the Christian should not be inferior in knowledge to the ancients. He who would wish to explain Ecclesiastes should also know the teachings of the Academicians, Stoics, Peripatetics, Ionians, Epicureans, the so-called Mathematicians, Cynics, and other philosophers; for if Ecclesiastes does not expound these teach-

---

74. *Manuductio ad Stoicam Philosophiam* 1.13 ("Cynicos Originem Stoicis Dedisse, et Dogmata Fere Convenire. Illi ex Professo Laudati") in *Opera* (Lyons 1613) vol. 1, 759.

75. Cf. chap. 5: "De Inhonesta Vita Philosophorum, et Quomodo Aliter Vixerunt, Aliter Docuerunt, et de Execrabili Secta Cynicorum," ed. G.C. Garfagnini, "Da Seneca a Giovanni di Salisbury: 'Auctoritates' morali e 'vitae philosophorum' in un ms. trecentesco," *Rinascimento,* ser. 2, 20 (1980) 201–47 (here 213).

ings, he does at least presuppose knowledge of them.[76] The second argument is concerned with Cynicism in particular. Salutati aims to encourage the examination of Cynic ethics by pointing out that, long before the first Christians, the Cynics had been passionate partisans of poverty and had chosen a mendicant way of life.[77]

Having rehearsed Salutati's arguments (chaps. 1–12), Dominici proceeds to demolish them. He maintains that, at the end of the day, studying the texts of classical antiquity is a futile exercise compared with many that are more urgent. ("It is more useful for a Christian to toil in the fields than to read books written by pagans.") The study of pagan writers should be kept, if at all, for a better and holier age to come. The philosophy of the ancients is useless, particularly as far as the community is concerned. For "it often happens that he who would know all, knows nothing, and we certainly never hear of philosophers being of use to the people, nor of any of those in government giving themselves over to philosophy. Socrates disdained public office, Diogenes the royal courts, Plato the masses, Anaxagoras riches, while Plotinus took refuge in unfrequented places." It is by following divine law, and not by submitting to the precepts of philosophers, that rulers will succeed in being powerful and effective in the service of their people.[78] As for similarities between the teachings of pagan philosophers and their Christian counterparts, these are purely superficial. The similarity between Cynic and evangelical poverty is merely external: the two types of poverty are separated by the wide gulf of faith. When Christ is not within us, no behavior can be truly Christian. Moreover, it would be unrealistic to think it possible to pick and choose between the teachings of any and every philosopher, "cultivate friendship with Cicero, regulate your morals along with Seneca, eat herbs like Epicurus, or learn from Diogenes to hold the world in contempt, from Aristotle to be an agile reasoner, from Plato to be a theologian, from Zeno to be constant, from Socrates to take adversity lightly, from Cato to await calmly the gentleness of death, and from Christ to become generally perfect." Such eclecticism leads to something false, confused, chaotic, where whatever is good is mixed inextricably with obvious evils.[79] So much chaos is typical of philosophy itself. As Saint Augustine pointed out (*De Civitate Dei* 18.41), philosophers never agree about anything. For example, Aristippus holds the sensual pleasure of the body to be the greatest good, while for Antisthenes the highest good is to be found in a virtuous soul.

76. *Lucula Noctis* 9, ed. E. Hunt, *Iohannis Dominici Lucula Noctis,* Publications in Mediaeval Studies, The University of Notre Dame, 4 (Notre Dame 1940), 80.

77. *Lucula Noctis* 9, *ed. cit.* 97.

78. *Lucula Noctis* 18, *ed. cit.* 150.

79. *Lucula Noctis* 20.

Cynic Heresy: Beghards and Turlupins

Dominici not only reproached the Cynics with their sexual immodesty; he links them on this ground to a heretical faction of the day:[80]

No one can deny that the Cynics, or rather the Dogs (of whom the noble Diogenes was the father), should also be venerated in the name of holy philosophy. For the ancients called them philosophers, and they differed from others chiefly in that, like the patricide Absalom of long ago, or like hypocrites of the present day, they abandoned all modesty and shame. They claimed that it was right to have carnal relationships in public with wives, while others made the same claim for concubines and female followers. These great men preached moderation, temperance, and patience, with many a refined discourse; but, since their speeches contradicted their acts, their words were not those of a philosopher.

By "hypocrites of the present day" Dominici certainly meant Beghards, Turlupins, and other sects of the Free Spirit. We know that the Beghards (also castigated as hypocrites by Nicholas Eymerich, the inquisitor of Catalonia and Aragon)[81] taught that the perfect man, the man united with God in spirit, is completely without sin and can do with his body as he wishes. Thus he does not sin when he commits a carnal act under the influence of nature and temptation. The link between the Cynics and the Society of the Poor, as they called themselves, had already been made by Jean de Gerson. In a sermon delivered in Paris on the Feast of Saint Louis, probably in the year 1393, the Very Christian Doctor lists the qualities of a good educator:[82]

Fourthly, he should speak often of what is honest and good, in contrast to those who not only name, with no trace of shame, the immodest parts of the body and disgusting acts, but who, with even greater impudence, dare maintain that, in the name of reason, it is right to do so. They do not see that when they say these things they fall into the heresy of the Beghards and Turlupins, who claimed that nothing that is natural should be able to embarrass us. They are like the Cynics, who said that we should live as dogs do, naked, and disport the shameful parts of the body. Such an attitude is condemned by Cicero in his *De Officiis* [1.35] when he discusses beauty and propriety. Seneca too says: "You should say nothing indecent, as the very words will gradually make us less ashamed of the thing itself." "Evil talk corrupts good morals," adds the Apostle [1 Cor. 15.33].

Possibly Giovanni Dominici knew the text by Gerson. Be that as it may, Gerson's judgment of the Cynics was widely disseminated through Gabriel Du

---

80. *Lucula Noctis* 42, *ed. cit.* 362–63.

81. See my edition of his *Contra Alchimistas* in *Chrysopoeia* 1 (1987) 93–136 (here 126).

82. *Sermo Factus Parisiis in Die Sancti Ludovici Francorum Regis,* ed. P. Glorieux in *Jean Gerson, Œuvres complètes* 5 (Paris 1963) 163.

Préau, in the last quarter of the sixteenth century. Du Préau was a zealous adversary of the Reform, and published a dictionary of heresies in 1569, the *De Vitis, Sectis et Dogmatibus Omnium Haereticorum*. In his article "Turilupini," he reproduces, with slight modifications, the passage quoted above, along with another text by Gerson, who had called the Turlupins "Epicureans in the clothing of Christ." [83] Du Préau goes further than Gerson in emphasizing the links that joined the Beghard and Turlupin heretics to Cynics and Epicureans, even making out these latter groups to be heretics and giving each of them a separate entry in his dictionary. The entry on the Cynics runs as follow:[84]

> The Cynics were philosophers of the sect of Antisthenes, who was the first to introduce this new type of philosophy. They derived their name either from the gymnasium of Cynosarges, where Antisthenes taught, or from the doglike bite with which they attacked the lifestyle of all and sundry, or because of their habit of copulating in public like dogs, which is what Diogenes Laertius reported Crates and Hipparchia as doing.
>
> Those carnal and bestial philosophers, who believed that it was acceptable to copulate with women as shamelessly as dog with dog, were imitated by the Waldenses and similar heretics several centuries later. In accordance with the prophecies of Peter [2 Pet. 2], their debaucheries were copied by many, who scorned all authority and blasphemed against sovereign power, as we shall see.

In the seventeenth century Gabriel Du Préau's text and his extract from Gerson's sermon were used by various writers. These included the Protestant theologian Josua Arnd in his *Lexicon Antiquitatum Ecclesiasticarum* (1669), who lets us know of the existence of a Cynic sect around 1567,[85] the pastor Paul Stockmann in his *Elucidarius Haeresium, Schismatum Aliarumque Opinionum et Dogmatum cum Fide Orthodoxa Pugnantium* (1692),[86] and Pierre Bayle's article "Turlupins" in his *Dictionnaire historique et critique* (1697). Thanks to Bayle, the two texts were known to André-François Boureau-Deslandes, who considerably exaggerated the number of heretical sects descended from the Cynics in his *Histoire critique de la philosophie* (1737):[87]

83. See *De Vitis, Sectis et Dogmatibus Omnium Haereticorum, Qui ab Orbe Condito, ad Nostra usque Tempora, et Veterum et Recentium Authorum Monimentis Proditi Sunt, Elenchus Alphabeticus* . . . (Cologne 1569) 482.

84. Ibid. 136.

85. *Lexicon Antiquitatum Ecclesiasticarum* (Greifswald 1669) 497: "Cynici. Philosophi fuerunt, et quidem carnales et bestiales, dicentes: Licere cuique commisceri foeminis instar canum omni pudore sublato. Vixere c. A.D. 1567." Arnd writes of the Turlupins (ibid. 495): "1372. Turilupini. Cynici professione, docebant, de nulla re, quae nobis a natura data est, erubescendum esse. Gerson contra illos nonnulla scripsit."

86. *Elucidarius.* . . (ed. Leipzig 1697) 181–82.

87. *Histoire critique de la philosophie* (Amsterdam 1737) vol. 2, 192–93.

I must add at this point that the Cynics were in no way so inseparable from ancient philosophy as not to have spawned offspring in all later ages, right up to the middle of the Christian era. For can we not give this name to many of the sects that have sought to debase and dishonor a religion that is as much to be respected for the mysteries of faith it proposes as it is to be loved for the moral practice it teaches? To refer to the oldest among them, such are the Ebionites, the Manicheans, the Adamites, the Beghards, the Turlupins, the Waldenses or Paupers of Lyons, the Flagellants, the Humiliati, the Cathars or Patarines, the Anabaptists, the Mennonites, the Quakers or Shakers, as well as the Little Prophets who escaped from the Cevennes and whom we have seen spread to an extraordinary degree in England at the present day. The ongoing history of these sects could just as well be called the history of Christian Cynics or the history of fanaticism in Christianity.

Stupid and Depraved Buffoons

We will now leave the sphere of heresy and return to the specific criticisms leveled by Giovanni Dominici at ancient philosophers in general and the Cynics in particular. One that was to turn up time and again during the Renaissance took issue with their inability to control worldly affairs as they should. This argument was even used by Dominici's enemies, the humanists. For many humanists Cynicism did not conform to one of their fundamental criteria, namely that of utility.[88] Such is the criticism of Lorenzo Valla, who hardly distinguishes Cynics from Stoics, in his *De Voluptate* (1431). He reproaches both alike with failing to link virtue to pleasure and usefulness, and likens the interest they can hold for us to that of monkeys or jesters who make us laugh.[89] This approach was developed in the ironic but detailed criticism of Leon Battista Alberti in his *Momus* (written between 1443 and 1450)[90] and in his *Epistolae septem Epimenidis Nomine Diogeni Inscriptae* (ca. 1462).[91] The idea for this latter came from his reading of the letters falsely attributed to Diogenes, which were translated into Latin by Francesco Griffolini. For Alberti, Cynicism is a truly inhuman doctrine, in that behind all the sophisms it employs to push away the pleasures of society and civilization lies a refusal to accept the human condition, a refusal that has its roots in a profound self-hatred. The uselessness of

88. For a more detailed account, see my forthcoming book on Cynicism in the Renaissance.

89. *De Vero Falsoque Bono* 2.29 (= De Voluptate 37, "De Tranquillitate Mentis"), ed. M. de Panizza Lorch (Bari 1970), 83–84 ("Ipsi vero ea ratione habuerunt quod erant illis miraculo ac voluptati novitate vite, sicut, quidam magni viri simias ac quedam monstruosa ob id ipsum quod ridicula sunt in pretio habent, nec bestias modo sed etiam homines fatuos ac deliros").

90. Cf. R. Consolo, ed., *Leon Battista Alberti, Momo o del principe, edizione critica e traduzione* (Genoa 1986) 50, 188–90.

91. Cf. L. B. Alberti, *Opera Inedita et Pauca Separatim Impressa,* ed. G. Mancini (Florence 1890) 267–71.

Cynicism is again the burden of the ninth dialogue of Giovanni Pontano's *Charon* (ca. 1470), in which the ferryman of the underworld converses with Diogenes and Crates.[92] In his *De Magnanimitate* Pontano contrasts the disinterestedness of Fabricius and Crates:[93] he particularly denounces the Cynics' rejection of riches, which he perceives more as unconsidered vainglory than as a sincere feeling likely to benefit others. Pandolfo Collenuccio also singles out for criticism the uselessness of the Cynic philosophy in his *Agenoria* (1497), where he denounces Cynicism as the philosophy *par excellence* of inertia, as well as the mother of fraud, hypocrisy, and vice, and says that the true font of virtue and truth is work and the arts.[94]

The humanists' criticism was put forward within the framework of philosophical ethics and was, as such, secular, though never, or almost never, entirely disentangled from Christianity. It was also to be found in a number of religious authors, such as Jean Des Caurres, canon of Saint Nicholas of Amiens, who wrote *Œuvres morales et diversifiées en histoires* (1575). Des Caurres, an apologist for the Saint Bartholomew's Day massacre, believed that it would be best for society and humanity if philosophers were statesmen, or statesmen philosophers, and it was for this very reason that he so castigated the Cynics for their refusal to deal with the realities of life and social values, and for the way they would rail against things rather than the use that was made of them.[95] Even more vehement, and indeed abusive, was the criticism voiced by the Jesuit François Garasse in *La doctrine curieuse des beaux esprits de ce temps ou prétendus tels* (1623),[96] a criticism that Bayle quoted in the notes to his *Dictionnaire* article "Diogenes the Cynic," although he saw it as "a tirade of impertinences." The gist of Garasse's text is that Diogenes was nothing but a hypochondriac, a madman, a dolt and an idiot, a buffoon, an ill-mannered and self-conceited fool, and an atheist to boot. Garasse refuses to admire antiquity unreservedly and "canonize every word and deed" of the ancients as though "God had granted them infallibility." He criticizes Diogenes Laertius and Plutarch for describing the lives of Diogenes the Cynic and Democritus in great detail, saying that this is like "describing the acts and words of Brusquet or Maître Guillaume, who were at least as wise as they were." For "one of them, Democritus, was a joker, and the other, Diogenes, a beggar," and it "was

92. Cf. *Charon Dialogus,* in *Opera* (Basel 1566) vol. 2, 1162–65. See also the fifth dialogue, ibid. 1142–43.

93. *De Magnanimitate libri II,* in *Opera* (*ed. cit.* above, n. 93), vol. 1, 781.

94. Cf. *Agenoria,* ed. A. Saviotti, *Pandolfo Collenuccio, Operette morali, poesie latine e volgari* (Bari 1929) 5–6.

95. Cf. *Œuvres morales et diversifiees en histoires, pleines de beaux exemples, enrichies d'enseignemens vertueux, et embellies de plusieurs sentences et discours. Tiré des plus signalez et remarquables Autheurs en latin* 5.5, "Plusieurs choses estre mauuaises par le seul abus des hommes: et de la vilanie de Crates Philosophe Cynique" (ed. Paris 1584), ff. 455v–456v.

96. See H. Niehues-Pröbsting, *Der Kynismus des Diogenes und der Begriff des Zynismus,* Humanistische Bibliothek, Reihe I, Abhandlung 40 (Munich 1979), 104, 223–24.

principally those two who introduced atheism into gentile society." If Diogenes lived in a barrel, it was because he was overfond of wine. In this he was like the old woman in Aristophanes who "gave orders that she should be buried in the cellar, with a barrel above her to keep her bones fresh," or like Buchanan, who "had a hogshead of Bordeaux wine brought to his bedside during his last illness, so that he could nourish his soul with the scent of this delicious liquor." To go looking for a man in broad daylight with a lighted lamp shows "a melancholic temperament in a bout of madness," and it is "enormously conceited to see all men but himself as animals." His manner of address to Alexander could not be considered anything but unpardonable rudeness when the latter had been gracious enough to visit him in his tub. He must also have been feebleminded to reach old age and see a cattle drover drinking from his cupped hand before realizing that a cup is not a piece of indispensable equipment! Religiously, he was "an out and out atheist, who laughed at the gods the people generally worshipped, lived like a dog, a brute beast, and preached that we should have no shame about anything natural. We should do whatever our senses tell us, though it be in the middle of the street, like dogs, who relieve themselves and do everything else in public." This is how the Cynics lived, "using impious language and doing disgusting things that even Tapinambours and cannibals would be ashamed of." [97] This diagnosis was valid not only for Diogenes but for other Cynics, for instance Menedemus.[98]

We find this position echoed by another Jesuit, Nicholas Caussin. He had already used Diogenes' atheism as an example for his theory of definition in his *De Eloquentia Sacra et Humana libri XVI* in 1619.[99] In *La cour sainte* (1624) he denounces "buffoons and those who seek to stuff themselves for free with food," users of coarse language, whose every act, "on the pretext of nature," is similar to those of Diogenes the Cynic.[100] More significantly, Garasse's position is repeated in Jean-Louis Guez de Balzac's *Socrate chrestien* (1652),[101] a text taken account of by Bayle.[102] We know that Guez de Balzac quarreled with Garasse, his former teacher at Poitiers, because of Garasse's attacks, in *La doctrine curieuse,* on Guez de Balzac's friend Théophile de Viau. The unpleasantness was, however, short-lived, and Guez de Balzac accepted much of what was in *La doctrine curieuse.* He borrowed its criticism of Diogenes, which he directed at those religious writers who set up scandalous parallels between

97. *La doctrine curieuse des beaux esprits de ce temps ou prétendus tels* 2.5 (Paris 1623) 33–137.

98. Ibid. 2.11, 170–71.

99. *De Eloquentia Sacra et Humana* 12.31, § "Status Finitivus, et de Eius Tractatione" (Lyons 1637) 802.

100. Cf. *La cour sainte,* "Traicté 3, Passion unziesme: De la honte, section 3: Excellence de la pudeur, et l'opprobe de l'impudence" (Paris, 1647) 139.

101. See Niehues-Pröbsting (above n. 96) 103, 104, 124.

102. Cf. P. Bayle, *Dictionnaire historique et critique* s.v. "Diogène," note E.

Cynicism and Christianity. Guez de Balzac accepted that antiquity was better provided for in moral philosophy than in speculative philosophy, where the ancients were hopelessly lost, but he nonetheless maintains that there was a wide gap between Christianity and the moral codes of the ancients, even those that appeared similar to it, such as Stoicism. It seems to him unfitting therefore for a Christian to draw false comparisons, as did a certain preacher he refers to but does not name, telling us merely that his unnamed source had had several sermons printed at Lyons in 1623 and that he had dared to write: "If Alexander had not been Alexander, he would have wished to be Diogenes. So highly in virtuous poverty esteemed even by royalty and greatness." Unlike the unnamed preacher, Balzac finds Alexander's words "extremely poor." For what does it mean to be Diogenes? "It is to violate laws and established customs; it is to be without shame or honesty; it is to recognize neither family nor friends; it is to be always yapping or biting; it is to eat a raw sole or a bleeding lump of meat in the marketplace; it is to shock people with worse acts than that, acts so shocking and disgusting that they cannot be hidden by enough secrecy and privacy." Since that was so, the preacher "could not do worse by those he seeks to praise than in indulging in such an odious comparison." For "the modest poverty of Christian philosophers has nothing in common with the barefaced beggary of the Cynics. These wild philosophers were full of pride, impudence, and impurity. They hated men while pretending to hate vice. They wanted people to admire their beards, their destitution, and their very filth." In all things they were "far from gentleness, chastity, humility, and Christian spirit." [103]

Garasse's attack on Diogenes, which was at the root of this polemic, was almost exactly contemporary with another attack, though one much more cogent and more scholarly. Francesco Collio was a member of the oblate congregation of Saint Charles and was the Cardinal Penitentiary of Milan. In 1622 he published there *De Animabus Paganorum libri quinque. In quibus de iis qui veteri saeculo in utroque sexu celeberrimi fuerunt disputatur, ac de eorum sempiternis praemiis, aut suppliciis, pro ea quam de rebus divinis hauserant cognitione, et pro cuiusque vitae institutis, ac moribus, ex Sanctorum praecipue Patrum, et gravissimorum Scriptorum decretis, atque auctoritate copiosissime disseritur.* This massive work sought to determine which pagans were damned and which destined for salvation. Collio's examination included Diogenes and other great philosophers, such as Hermes Trismegistus, Thales, Pythagoras, Heraclitus, Anaxagoras, Plato, Socrates, the Seven Sages, Aristotle, Seneca, Epictetus, Apollonius of Tyana, and Plotinus.

Collio's imaginary trial of Diogenes is particularly interesting,[104] as he puts the Greek Fathers in the witness box as often for the defense as for the prose-

103. *Socrate chrestien* (Paris 1652) 242–45.
104. *De Animabus Paganorum*, par. II, lib. I, cap. IV–V (Milan 1622), vol. 2, 11–16.

cution. Beginning with the defense (chap. 4), he analyzes those of Diogenes' acts that seem to be based on virtue. He explains that, as Clement of Alexandria believed (*Stromateis* 1), the Cynics were so called because they "bit" men, as dogs did. He goes on to recall the esteem in which Diogenes was held by Saint Jerome and accepts that many of the philosopher's maxims can be cited in his favor. First among these he places those that deal with God: namely that he is omnipresent and that his knowledge is boundless; that men owe him the greatest respect and humility; that they offend him with evil doings and crimes (as shown by the Lysias anecdote);[105] that his favor cannot be won through superstitious practices, sacrifices, and so on. As far as the crucial issue of religion is concerned, then, Diogenes' doctrine is sound. Furthermore, he condemns vice and wishes to see an inner harmony in men. This is where his contempt for the body seems to come from, as manifested by his poverty, frugality, sobriety, neglected hair, rough clothes, and bare feet. As far as his principles were concerned, a number of Fathers had seen fit to praise them. Origen, Saint John Chrysostom, and Saint Jerome all cited his example when they attacked the enemies of faith and of the monastic life. Collio himself ends by saying: "I have no need to tell the reader how far that is in accordance with our religion. I cannot deny that this way was similar to the one taken by the early Fathers of the Church, who came thereby, with the grace of God, to heaven. Diogenes himself would certainly be there, had he but acted in the state of mind necessary to all virtuous behavior and had he but taken steps to keep well clear of other actions, which are an outrage to God and to man."

In the following chapter (5), Collio moves on to the case for the prosecution in an attempt to show that everything that seemed to be virtue was in fact vice. It is only on the surface that Diogenes' actions can be approved. The nearest they get to goodness is in appearance and in name. There are two reasons for this. The first is a general point: as Saint Augustine said, pagan virtue can never be completely genuine. The second reason is that Diogenes' behavior was dictated not by virtue but by necessity. He lived soberly only when he had no choice in the matter: whenever he got the opportunity, he indulged his greed more than the next man. This is proved by his death, caused by gluttonously gulping down a raw octopus. According to Gregory of Nazianzus (*Oration* 25) and his commentator Elias of Crete, the same can be said about his tub, though they are not very clear on this point. His way of dressing and his choosing to live in a tub were no more than displays of pride and vanity, according to Tertullian, while Chrysostom (*Homily* 35, on 1 Cor. 4) says it was pure ostentation: Saint Paul, he observes, lived and dressed like everyone else.[106] For Gregory of Nazianzus and Saint Basil, if Diogenes lived in a tub in the middle of

105. Diogenes Laertius 6.42.

106. Cf. G. Dorival, "L'image des cyniques chez les Pères grecs," in Goulet-Cazé and Goulet (above, n. 1) 423.

the marketplace, it was to make use of things that did not belong to him. So, all in all, his life was a tissue of vices, and the greatest of them was the dishonesty of his morals. As Chrysostom, Augustin, and Lactantius all pointed out, he had no qualms about doing things repellent to nature. Finally, not only did he never really repent of debasing the currency, but he was also a nasty piece of work, bore grudges, was always looking to avenge himself, and took care to give as good as he got, in direct conflict with the injunction of the Gospel to accept injustice with equanimity and to turn the other cheek. To conclude, it seems likely that Diogenes will not be saved and will have to pay the price for his crimes for all eternity. One thing is certain: to follow his precepts is to obey the Prince of Darkness.

The violent attacks of Collio and Garasse could not go unchallenged. They were answered from the milieu of learned libertines. Diogenes and the Cynics found themselves a worthy advocate in the person of the Skeptic François de La Mothe Le Vayer. He defended the Cynics at length, though without approving of them on every point, in his treatise *De la vertu des payens* (1642).[107] In the conclusion to his defense, La Mothe Le Vayer writes, alluding to Garasse: "It is above all the great severity and, dare I say, injustice with which Diogenes has recently been treated that has led to my trying to show what kind of man he was and how right were those, Christians and pagans, who held him in such high regard."[108] As we have seen, this "great severity" was doubtless rather less new and recent than La Mothe Le Vayer believed it to be. Yet it was indubitably in his age that the religious criticism of Cynicism reached the height of its virulence. Such criticism contributed powerfully to the essentially pejorative image of Cynicism to be found in the everyday language and collective consciousness of several Western countries today, where Cynicism is synonymous with impudence and immorality.

---

107. Cf. *De la vertu des payens,* part II, chap. "De Diogene et de la secte cynique," in *Œuvres* (Paris 1662) vol. 1, 613–23. See Niehues-Pröbsting (above n. 96) 223–25.
108. *De la vertu des payens (ed. cit.* above, n. 107) 620.

Menippus in Antiquity
and the Renaissance

Joel C. Relihan

Lucian cannot be relied upon to tell the whole truth about the nature of Cynicism in the imperial era. As his *Fugitivi* shows, he can be surprisingly disparaging of Cynicism in general, despite his strong affinity to and affection for Diogenes and Menippus; the *Cynicus* has great fun at the expense of those clichéd Cynics for whom all is hypocritical display.[1] But his Menippean works, primarily the infernal fantasy of the *Necyomantia,* the celestial comedy of the *Icaromenippus,* and the funereal *Dialogues of the Dead,* show a real appreciation of one vital aspect of the Cynic movement and Cynic literature. This is the subversive nature of Cynic criticism, which invests authority in a character who cannot be taken seriously without qualification, and which toys with the idea of an absolute or transcendent truth and those who would proclaim it.[2] This allows Lucian to have his cake and eat it too: he enjoys the logically rigorous but ultimately ironic paradox of exploring Cynic truths through the

I am pleased to acknowledge my several debts in the preparation of this essay. My former colleague Linde Brocato at the University of Illinois at Urbana-Champaign offered much useful advice concerning Spanish literature; David Kinney (in matters of neo-Latin literature) and the editor R. Bracht Branham (in matters of Lucian) guided it through its revision. I hope that my errors do not vitiate their efforts.

1. M.-O. Goulet-Cazé, "Le cynisme à l'époque impériale," *ANRW* 2.36.4 (1990) 2763–68, discusses Lucian in this regard.

2. This Cynic stance is abundantly in evidence throughout the history of Menippean satire, as I document in *Ancient Menippean Satire* (Baltimore 1993), where also will be found my arguments for limiting the number of Lucian's Menippean satires by the exclusion of the comic dialogues, which I view as constituting a separate genre (pp. 12–21). But the origins of Menippean satire are Platonic, and I argue that the myth of Er in Plato's *Republic* inspires a Cynic genre that agrees radically with Plato: words and myths cannot express transcendent truths (pp. 33–34, 179–84).

medium of Cynics who cannot command our respect, particularly that Cynic fakir Menippus. This is an aspect of Cynic writing that the Renaissance knows well, and that it learned from Lucian and from the Menippus he presents.

My topic here is not Lucian's influence in the Renaissance, or even the nature and history of Menippean satire, though both shall be addressed and, I hope, illumined in the pursuit of a different goal: an understanding of the surprising transformations of the character of the unreliable Menippus himself.[3] For in the literature of Protestant-Catholic debate, in controversialist and imaginative literature, Menippus puts in an appearance that is not what we should have extrapolated from our reading of Lucian: we see a Menippus who is a scribe in the underworld, a Spanish Menipo who goes to Hades to discover the meaning of his grandfather's will, a Rosicrucian who assumes the name of Menippus to exalt the values of religion over those of philology, and a psychopomp Menippus who leads the souls of scholars to debates on Mount Parnassus. These appearances are few, but fascinating; and I hope to offer here an account of the multiplicities of the Renaissance Menippus and to suggest the logic behind his metamorphoses. The majority of the texts discussed below will be neo-Latin fantasies, works not much brought to bear in the studies of Lucian in the vernacular literatures. I am limited by the contents of the rare-book rooms at my disposal; I hope that what follows may inspire others to examine texts that have been unavailable to me.

Though much may now be said about his originality, it is worthwhile to remember that in a number of ways Lucian is a rather calculating author. The *True History,* for example, with its opening caveat that all that follows is lies, shows what is to the modern taste a lack of nerve: Could he not have written a

---

3. In the vastness of Renaissance literature I am constrained to take as guides those works whose concern with the person of the Renaissance Menippus is merely as a proof of the presence of Lucian, or as a shibboleth to identify Renaissance Menippean satire. The following works will be cited by the last name of the author only: O. Gewerstock, *Lucian und Hutten: Zur Geschichte des Dialogs im 16. Jahrhundert,* Germanische Studien 31 (Berlin 1924); E.P. Kirk, *Menippean Satire: An Annotated Catalogue of Texts and Criticism* (New York 1980); E. Mattioli, *Luciano e l' umanesimo* (Naples 1980); C.-A. Mayer, *Lucien de Samosate et la Renaissance française,* La Renaissance Française, Editions et Monographies 3 (Geneva 1984); C. Robinson, *Lucian and His Influence in Europe* (Chapel Hill 1979); A. Vives Coll, *Luciano de Samosata en España* (Valladolid 1959); M.O. Zappala, *Lucian of Samosata in the Two Hesperias: An Essay in Literary and Cultural Translation,* Scripta Humanistica 65 (Potomac 1990).

Kirk is especially helpful in cataloging this material, and although I do not agree with his very broad definition of Menippean satire, which has primarily thematic and few structural components, his prefatory material is a good introduction to the later traditions of Menippean literature. For Menippean satire in the Renaissance, see J. IJsewijn, "Neo-Latin Satire: *Sermo* and *Satyra Menippea,*" in R.R. Bolgar, ed., *Classical Influences on European Culture, A.D. 1500–1700* (Cambridge 1976) 41–55; additions and corrections in *Humanistica Lovaniensia* 25 (1976) 288, and *Humanistica Lovaniensia* 26 (1977) 245. We await the completion of the second edition of IJsewijn's *A Companion to Neo-Latin Studies* for the most up-to-date summary on neo-Latin satire; J.W. Binns, *Intellectual Culture in Elizabethan and Jacobean England: The Latin Writings of the Age,* Arca 24 (Leeds 1990), does not discuss satire, Menippean or otherwise.

parody of the traveler's tale without announcing to us that that is what it is? He fears, perhaps, to be misunderstood, while we prefer a more gullible Gulliver; or perhaps the conditions of oral performance can excuse such a prologue. Yet Lucian's caution is general, and has had some unexpected benefits for the history of Western literature. The fact that there is a Menippus to talk about at all is largely due to the fact that Lucian decided not to make himself the narrator of the *Necyomantia* and the *Icaromenippus,* or become the dead hero of the *Dialogues of the Dead.*[4] It is a point made by one of his scholiasts: Lucian prefers to put upon the person of Menippus the burden of the incredible, and not upon himself.[5] But what the scholiasts do not note, and what shall be of great importance to us here, is how Lucian fashions a new Menippus from the traditions and potentials of the many Menippuses that lay before him: Menippus the author, Menippus the scandal, Menippus the bogeyman, and Menippus the fantastic voyager. For in writing fantasies about Menippus, Lucian does not follow Menippus's own literary example of *self*-parody, but maintains a laughing distance from his comic hero.

Renaissance literature does not much share Lucian's literary interest in galvanizing Menippus and bringing him back to life anew *in propria persona.* A rare exception is the Golden Age *El crótalon* (The Castanets). In it, Lucian's *Gallus* is extended, and the rooster who is the reincarnation of Pythagoras speaks of his previous incarnations in nineteen cantos, only to die and be mourned in the twentieth. In cantos 12 through 16, he is Icaro Menipo, who traveled to heaven and to hell; the substance of the *Icaromenippus* and the *Necyomantia* is reprised, but from the serious point of view of a Christianized Menippus.[6] The Renaissance typically suppresses the name of Menippus: the great early imitators of Lucian, such as Erasmus, Alberti, and Rabelais, feel no need to resuscitate Menippus himself and hardly speak of him. Alberti's total silence is especially remarkable. To be sure, the absurd Menippus who travels to the other world for truth, the proud Menippus who mocks the rich and arrogant, the demonic Menippus who haunts hell, all survive under a thousand pseudonyms and, like the Lucian in whose pages he survives, can be praised or despised throughout the Renaissance. Some of the most famous of these sub-

---

4. The first of these works is properly titled *Menippus; or, Necyomantia;* I refer to it by the subtitle in accordance with the standard classical abbreviation, and to avoid confusion with Menippus himself. Most of the secondary sources listed in n. 3 above use the proper title, *Menippus.*

5. H. Rabe, ed., *Scholia in Lucianum* (Stuttgart 1906; repr. 1971) 98.8–12: "The work under discussion is fashioned *Icaromenippus* because the principal in the story is brought on wearing wings, likened to Icarus, the son of Daedalus; but because of its great adventure, over-curiosity, and fantasy the story is accommodated to Menippus the Cynic philosopher." Here as elsewhere, all translations are my own unless otherwise noted.

6. J.J. Kincaid, *Cristóbal de Villalón* (New York 1973) 23–50, summarizes the work and argues for Villalón's authorship (it was pseudonymously published in 1552 under the name of Christophoro Gnosopho). Vives Coll, pp. 89–110, gives a more detailed account of its Lucianic borrowings; see also Robinson, pp. 121–25.

limations or assimilations of Lucian's Menippus are such characters as Pasquil and Pasquin, the narrator of Doni's *I marmi,* and Rabelais's Frère Jean.[7]

It is not surprising then that, in name if not in deed, Lucian's Menippus has largely disappeared. If he is the type of a charlatan, his personality may underlie the satiric presentation of some pretentious person; if of a fearless seeker of truth, the authors may prefer to substitute their own names. Renaissance topicality, in contrast to Lucianic generality, has little interest in making Menippus himself a butt, or a champion, of a satire. A faceless and nameless person may on rare occasions be another Menippus; his personality thus abstracted can be used as a type of the shameless Cynic, for whom there is little respect.[8] But there is little need to assess the person of Menippus, or to make him part of the scenery of the afterlife; for the latter purposes the more strictly mythological Momus and Mercury stand in for Menippus in the guise of mocker or of the man who knows the path to the world below.[9]

In those few works in which Menippus does survive as an active character rather than as a proverbial example of the voyager or critic, he is quite different from his Lucianic personalities. A good example is found in a work of Daniel Heinsius, *Cras Credo, Hodie Nihil* (1621). Its critical ambivalence toward the value of Menippus and Menippean criticism will allow us to define the parameters of our inquiry into the fortunes of Menippus in the Renaissance. The title ("I'll Believe You Tomorrow, But Not Today") is taken from one of Varro's *Menippean Satires;* it further asserts its generic allegiances and affiliations by following the lead of Justus Lipsius's *Somnium* (1581), the first modern work to style itself a Menippean satire, in concerning itself with the state of contemporary learning and philology.[10] Its topic, that one ought to preserve some sort of moderation in scholarship, particularly in theological scholarship, is general enough that it avoids the controversialism of some of Hein-

---

7. Mayer, pp. 41–44, cites Philibert de Vienne, *Le philosophe de court* (1547), who says that Rabelais's Frère Jean is like Menippus; Mayer adds the qualification, the Menippus of Lucian, a "witness from home" against those of his own kind (p. 44): "Frère Jean est une machine de guerre contre les moines, tout comme Ménippe avait été une machine de guerre contre les sophistes."

8. Mattioli, pp. 108–9, refers to a character in Pontano's dialogue *Charon* (1491) as a "Menippo quattrocentesco." This unnamed shade (from Etruria) tells Charon that he used to mock princes, and cared only not to feel anything himself, but to laugh at others. Text in H. Kiefer et al., eds., *Giovanni Pontano, Dialoge,* Humanistische Bibliothek 2.15 (Munich 1984) 118–24. For a particularly interesting use of a mocked Menippus figure in the *Intercenales* of Alberti, see below, n. 56.

9. The Protestant Pasquil appears in Pseudo-Hutten's *Momus* (published around 1520) in the company of both Momus and Menippus. The latter describes himself as a mocker: *Ego Menippus ille calumniator hominumque divumque,* "I'm the Menippus you've heard about, the reviler of mortals and gods." His friend is Momus Asianus, a *hominomastix;* Momus is the critic, and Menippus is largely silent. Text in E. Böcking, ed., *Vlrichi Hutteni . . . Opera* vol. 4 (Leipzig 1860) 555–60; see Gewerstock, pp. 120–21; Kirk, pp. 79–80.

10. Text in C. Matheeussen and C.L. Heesakkers, eds., *Two Neo-Latin Menippean Satires,* Textus Minores 54 (Leiden 1980); see also C.L. Heesakkers, "De eerst Neolatijnse Menippeische satire," *Lampas* 12 (1979) 315–39.

sius's other Menippean works. We may view it safely from a literary perspective alone.

The author himself takes on the role of Menippus: in a dream vision, he goes to the moon, speaks to Luna herself, and observes from the moon the vanity and madness of human life and endeavor. Unlike Menippus in the *Icaromenippus,* he is to some extent capable of this vision without any aid; but for a closer inspection he avails himself of a telescope that Luna provides him, and this gives him the miraculous sight afforded Menippus by Empedocles in Lucian (*Icar.* 13–16).[11] Now our author can make out quasi-people: *quasi-nobiles* and *quasi-Theologi;* Luna discourses upon *quasi-virgines.*[12] As the narrator turns his attention to the moon itself and its Lunatic inhabitants, Heinsius seems to draw on the *True History,* but is still within the confines of the *Icaromenippus.* There is a fountain that in its refractions gives images of multiple worlds; and the neighboring fountain gives a universal view of the moon by showing reflections of the daily lives of its Antoeci, Perioeci, and Antipodes.[13] This is the miraculous universal vision of Menippean satire, and, as usual, universal vision is ultimately quite limited: the narrator sees that death is everywhere.[14]

Heinsius may ramble, but his invention is unfailing; the narrator next speaks to a comet.[15] Behind him to the end of his tail is a vast tract of space that encompasses seven cities, each inhabited by a particular sect of philosophers, and each with its own star. But some wander outside these regions: Democritus's soul is between the atoms in the sun; Epicurus cooks his doves and figpeckers in the fourth region of the *intermundia.* Then we hear from the comet about the Cynics:[16]

> Diogenes rules over the Cynics to the south, but Menippus holds sway over the rest. The commoners and the run of the mill, I'm ashamed to say, give themselves over to Venus in the open, just as they once did; in the open they piss, shit, and

11. Further on Menippus's involvement with the New Science of the Renaissance (cf. Kirk, pp. xxviii, 137–43) below, nn. 15, 40.

12. The humor here echoes the disparaging discussion of Epicurean divinities in Cicero, *De Natura Deorum* 1.71–74: they have no blood but quasi blood; not a body, but a quasi body (*quasi sanguis, quasi corpus*).

13. Cf. Lucian's account of the mirror over the well on the moon, *VH* 1.26.

14. Universal vision, which seems a modern and Bakhtinian formulation, is an explicit fascination of Renaissance Menippean satirists. Cf. Cunaeus's *Sardi Venales* (text in Matheeussen and Heesakkers [above, n. 10]), in descriptions of the constitution of an otherworldly assembly of authors and critics, section 23 ("all those born in every age, for it made no difference when or where they lived") and section 32 ("in a word, whoever was outstanding for genius and learning in any age or in any place").

15. This may be influenced by Kepler's *Conversation with Galileo's Sidereal Messenger* (1610). Kepler (1571–1630), in this work and his *Somnium* (this published after his death in 1634), displays a happy conflation of Lucianic fantasy and New Science; Menippus appears in neither.

16. *Cras Credo,* p. 298 (I cite the text by the page numbers of the 1629 Leiden edition of the *Laus Asini,* number 136 in the checklist of Heinsius's publications in P. R. Sellin, *Daniel Heinsius and Stuart England* [Leiden 1968]).

excrete. When this falls to the ground we have our idiots [*moriones*] born; the ancients called them crappers [*copreas:* "jesturds"?]. Beware of them this year! They are scribblers, generally. Cynics are never pleased except with lies, and the genius has never smiled upon them.

Various scenes follow, but Menippus makes no further appearance except implicitly in an inscription set up on the moon in the narrator's honor. It is both self-parodic and self-assertive; he may write nonsense, but it is more sensible than the nonsense of others: "I have forgotten all my triflings; all day and every day I mull over my *Menippeans,* and there is nothing missing in them now but the plot." [17] The Menippean *Cras Credo* is thus labeled as short on substance, but it is long on vituperation. The author/narrator will go on to learn what his detractors say about him; he has the satisfaction of having one of his detractors turned into an ass so that the narrator, impolitely ridiculed as a Silenus, may ride on him. He drinks nepenthe, and witnesses the wedding of a grammarian's daughter; he opens a box containing a chameleon on whose back are written words of humility and caution. There is a concluding moral after he wakes from his dream, expanding on the satire's theme of moderation in learning.

Heinsius has been careful to define his own work as being in the tradition of Menippus and consequently not an apt vehicle for much learning. This aggressive humility by itself would be merely Lucianic and not so surprising, perhaps; but we must wonder how, in a work that aligns itself with Varro's *Menippeans* and Lucian's *Icaromenippus,* the person of Menippus can be so thoroughly assimilated that the narrator becomes him, and how at the same time his reputation can be so low that he is the master of the majority of the Cynics, from whose excrement are born some of the fools that afflict the world. In fact, there are many Menippuses, and in what follows I will try to disentangle them. First, I will consider the various Menippuses that were, so to speak, at Lucian's disposal, and some of the Renaissance reflections of each of them. I proceed then to Lucian's own transformation of Menippus from Cynic charlatan into Everyman and universal observer, and the primacy of this Menippus in Renaissance assimilations of Lucian. I conclude with some neo-Latin illustrations of a Menippus who is an active character in literary works, living a life inspired by, but at a remove from, Lucian's example and practice.

Ancient Faces of Menippus

At the end of his life of the Cynic Menippus, Diogenes Laertius notes that five other men were also called by that name. Pauly's *Realencyclopädie* documents many more. As so little is known of Menippus the renegade Cynic, an-

17. Ibid., p. 305.

cient confusion with his homonyms accounts for some of our traditions about him. The scholiasts confuse him with the young and impressionable aristocrat known from a good ghost story in Philostratus's *Life of Apollonius of Tyana;* this Menippus falls in love with an Empusa (a sort of succubus), and Apollonius brings him to his senses by causing her and her wealth to disappear.[18] One also has to wonder whether our Menippus, known as a mad dog, is somehow related to Menippus the doctor whose cure for rabies has been preserved.[19] Antiquity knows little about Menippus, and we must be aware of the sources of its invention. There are in fact five fairly distinct aspects of our Cynic.

There is the historical Menippus, the flesh-and-blood person of the third century B.C.   About him little may be known, as the hostile and anecdotal life by Diogenes Laertius makes quite clear. Antiquity is uncertain of the time of his life and death, and such details as it assigns to his physical self are clearly modeled on Diogenes the Cynic; Lucian has Pollux refer to Menippus as an old, bald man in rags at the beginning of the first of the *Dialogues of the Dead.* It is quite likely that Menippus himself encouraged this confusion, possibly through the medium of his (hagiographic?) *Sale of Diogenes.*[20] This historical Menippus is largely independent of Lucian. The Renaissance has little to do with him but for the significant exception of the Spanish *Menipo litigante* (ca. 1590) of Bartolomé Leonardo de Argensola (1562–1631), whose picture of an ironic Menippus who advises a dying man to bequeath all of his money to lawyers, since they will only get it anyway, may draw some inspiration from the stories of the Menippus who wasted all of his inheritance.[21]

18. *Vit. Ap.* 4.25; the scholion quoted above (n. 5) continues in this vein. See also the scholiast on Lucian, *Pisc.* 26 (p. 135.13–17 Rabe): "This Menippus was a Cynic philosopher in the time of Augustus[!], having a noble and reproving and severe nature, following the Dog well and philosophically; consequently he obtained a glorious reputation in the eyes of all."

19. Hippocrates Περὶ Ἀντιδότων 2; vol. 14, pp. 172.14–173.3 Kühn. Our Menippus is never specifically called a *rabid* dog.

20. See G. Donzelli, "Una versione menippea della Αἰσώπου Πρᾶσις?" *RF* 38 (1960) 225–76, for the thesis that early versions of the *Life of Aesop* influenced Menippus's *Sale of Diogenes,* and that the *Sale* subsequently influenced the later versions of the *Life of Aesop.* That the popularity of Menippus's work may account for some accommodation of the details of the lives of Menippus and Diogenes, cf. p. 270. See also J. Hall, *Lucian's Satire* (New York 1981) 74–79, for a convenient account of the external evidence for Menippus.

21. Vives Coll, pp. 137–39; Zappala, pp. 193–95; the connection to the stories of the wastrel Menippus is not made by either. For another possible Renaissance allusion to this Menippus, see the anonymous *Ulysses upon Ajax* (1595; cf. Kirk, p. 168). The title is a pun on the word "jakes" (roughly, *Ulysses upon a Chamber Pot*); in it a distinction is drawn between Menippus's wit and his misfortunes (evidently the legend of his suicide); cf. D.L. 6.99–100, where Menippus amasses a great fortune through moneylending but loses it all through some sort of plot and hangs himself. *Anth. Pal.* 9.367 tells of a son of Menippus who wastes his inheritance; cf. my "Menippus the Cynic in the Greek Anthology," *Syllecta Classica* 1 (1989) 58–61.

There is Menippus the Cynic.   Although Menippus is frequently assigned to this movement in antiquity, it is difficult to convict him of the charge on hard evidence. Lucian is surprisingly ambiguous: at *Piscator* 26 Diogenes the Cynic accuses him of betraying the Cynics while in Lucian's employ; and at *Fugitivi* 11, when Philosophy speaks of the Cynics as those who made her prolong her stay on earth (and thereby her suffering), Menippus is grumblingly added at the end of the list: "Antisthenes and Diogenes, and after a little while Crates and that notorious Menippus." In the *Dialogues of the Dead,* Menippus and Diogenes are never seen together, as if in this iconoclastic movement Diogenes is orthodox and Menippus heterodox.[22] In *Icaromenippus* and *Necyomantia,* Menippus is not a Cynic philosopher but a naive sojourner; I shall return to this point.

I do not deny that Menippus is a Cynic; neither does Laertius, who begins his life with the words "Even Menippus is a Cynic." We may in fact find ourselves particularly sympathetic to Menippus's wrestling with a serious problem of self-definition: How can one be a loyal follower of a Cynic who is notorious for his profession of defacing the currency? Strict imitation would be disloyalty; the Menippus who, in the words of Lucian's scholiast, "follows the Dog well and philosophically" (above, n. 18) may be compelled by the nature of Cynicism itself to deface what the personality and example of Diogenes had suggested. Menippus may prove his Cynicism, in effect, by laughing at Cynic certainties. But the point I make here is that antiquity, with a conservative notion of what philosophical schools are and a conservative dislike of what Cynics are fundamentally about, considers Menippus beyond Diogenes's pale and bristles at the notion of any real connection between Menippus and the Cynics. The scandalous details in Laertius's life are only one proof of this. Further, antiquity assigns no *chreiai* (anecdotes) to Menippus, and no words of wisdom; he is only vaguely related to the Cynic succession.[23] We have the feeling that Menippus professed allegiance to the example of Diogenes (his *Sale of Diogenes* would attest to this), but that few accepted the claim. Menippus becomes the dog of the underworld, while Diogenes, according to his epitaph in the *Greek Anthology,* is the dog who lives in heaven.[24] The Renaissance is generally loyal to this division: Diogenes is the example of the true Cynic, and

22. For the distance maintained between Diogenes and Menippus in Lucian's underworld, see my "Vainglorious Menippus in the Dialogues of the Dead," *ICS* 12 (1987) 185–206.

23. Diogenes Laertius seems to place him among the followers of Metrocles, but actually assigns him to those of Crates: see M.-O. Goulet-Cazé, "Une liste de disciples de Cratès le cynique en Diogène Laërce 6, 95," *Hermes* 114 (1986) 247–52. The usual vocabulary of discipleship (μαθητής, ἤκουσεν, διήκουσεν) is absent, and Menippus is only said vaguely to have become notable (ἐπιφανής) among them. Relations between Menippus and Diogenes are discussed at greater length in *Ancient Menippean Satire* (above, n. 2) 42–44.

24. *Anth. Pal.* 7.64.4. For an extended study of this epigram and its literary and philosophical connections, see Helmut Häusle, *Sag mir, o Hund — Wo der Hund begraben liegt: Das Grabepigramm für Diogenes von Sinope,* Spudasmata 44 (Zurich 1989).

Menippus is something else, as in the passage from Heinsius above.[25] As we shall see, Cunaeus's *Sardi Venales* (1612) can exalt Menippus's mockery of human truths over Diogenes' search for Truth personified. But the reluctance of Renaissance authors to put truth in Menippus's mouth, a reluctance learned from Lucian, is in Cunaeus seen in the fact that the Cynic moral of this work is pronounced not by Menippus, our narrator's guide, but by Sophrosyne, Moderation personified.

There is Menippus the author.   Here we seem to be on safer ground, although the fact that we have attached a genre of literature to his name does not limit his literary productions to a single genre.[26] We can assign to him a range of literary productions and innovations: the *Necyia,* his signature work, deserves the label "Menippean satire," but his *Letters from the Gods* seem to be the first in the tradition of the heroic epistle; he has some claims to the symposium genre; he also wrote some sort of biography of Diogenes, and certain polemical works. This Menippus was an influence on the young Meleager.[27] He is the author most particularly labeled *spoudogeloios,* appropriate for a Cynic and his subversive mixture of the serious and the comic;[28] but the slur preserved by Laertius, that Menippus acted as a sort of literary front-man and passed off as his own works that others wrote attests a quality in them not in keeping with the expectations aroused by his personality. Perhaps Menippus's parodies aroused in ungenerous or unperceptive readers suspicions of plagiarism; perhaps they seemed too good for the lowlife Menippus.

Antiquity may not be much interested in Menippus qua author, but the Renaissance is. The Renaissance names the genre of Menippean satire after him with Lipsius's *Satyra Menippea. Somnium. Lusus in Nostri Aevi Criticos* (1581: "A Menippean Satire. The Dream. A Satire on Contemporary Philologians"); the French *Satyre ménippée* belongs to this era; and Casaubon, who prefers to speak generically of Varronian satire, knows him as an author who mixes prose and verse.[29] In a few places he is thought of as an author who actually wields a pen. The Italian historian Lorenzo Pignoria (1571–1631;

25. In Villalón's *El scholástico* ("The Schoolmaster," or, in Kincaid's translation, "The Scholasticate"; Kincaid [above, n. 6] pp. 113–41), Menippus is described as a "so-called philosopher who said he had nothing to learn from men" (translation in Kirk, p. 86).

26. *Ancient Menippean Satire* (above, n. 2) 39–42.

27. *Anth. Pal.* 7.417.3–4: "I came forth from Eucrates, I, Meleager, who with the Muses first ran along with the Menippean Graces"; similarly, *Anth. Pal.* 7.418.5–6.

28. R. B. Branham, "The Wisdom of Lucian's Tiresias," *JHS* 109 (1989) 160 and n. 6.

29. I. Casaubon, *De Satyrica Graecorum Poesi et Romanorum Satira* (Paris 1605; repr. New York 1973); relevant passages translated in Kirk, pp. 231–33. Further details concerning the origin and use of the term "Menippean satire" may be found in my "On the Origin of 'Menippean Satire' as the Name of a Literary Genre," *CP* 79 (1984) 226–29; *Ancient Menippean Satire* (above, n. 2) 12.

Kirk [n. 3 above] 132) writes under the pen name of Menippus the eccentric *Attestation of Julius Paulus,* a demonstration through underworld evidence recorded by Menippus the infernal scribe that the third-century jurisconsult of the title was in fact of Italian stock. The Spanish humanist Vives, in a letter to Cranevelt (of 1524) evidently in response to the receipt of some fantastic poem, likens its author to Menippus just back from Hades.[30] And there are quite a few authors who call themselves Menippus. The Rosicrucian Johann Valentin Andreae (1586–1654; Kirk, pp. 140–41), author of the utopian *Christopolis,* published in 1617 a volume called *Menippus; or, One Hundred Satiric Dialogues Which Are a Mirror of Our Vanities;* these dialogues, which lament the loss of Christianity in philology, are followed by ten more in which either Democritus or Heraclitus speaks; there is other material in the volume as well. Menippus is here only as Andreae's pen name, and he does not appear as a character in the dialogues, which are on the whole rather dry and unappealing. The dialogues are answered by the *Antimenippus* of Caspar Bucher (*fl.* ca. 1605; Kirk, pp. 141–42), which condemns the lies told by Menippus about philologians and speaks of the value of pagan literature. Alexander Torquatus à Frangipani (*fl.* ca. 1630–65?) wrote a *Satyricon Asini Vapulantis* (The Satyricon of the Ass That Gets the Drubbing) under the pen name of Menippus Redivivus. Perhaps the latest pseudonymous Menippus is found in what is in effect an early draft of Samuel Butler's *Hudibras,* called *Mercurius Menippeus; or, The Loyal Satirist in Prose* (1649–50).

These latter fanciful uses are reflections not so much of how Menippus is known as an author in his own right but of how he appears at the end of the *Icaromenippus* and *Necyomantia,* as a prophet with a message to impart. From this derives the idea that Menippus is Lucian's *source* for his otherworld fantasies. This view is first found in the Greek scholia.[31] Famianus Strada (1572–1649), in his *Momus, sive Satyra Varroniana,* tells us who his authorities will *not* be: "Nor Menippus, that garrulous and inquisitive creature, who often revealed to Lucian the secrets of the gods." [32] In the second of Octavius Ferrarius's *Prolusiones* of 1655, the *Artium ac Disciplinarum Auctio* (an imitation of Lucian's *Vitarum Auctio*), there is a prologue telling of the recent events on Helicon. If anyone wants to know his source, he can ask Lucian, who heard it from Menippus; the work ends when the academic convention is dismissed by Apollo, and Lucian by Menippus.[33]

---

30. Zappala, p. 171.

31. Scholiast on Lucian, *Icaromenippus* 27 (p. 108.25–27 Rabe): "You buffoon! You parasite! Just as Homer saw the things in heaven, so did Menippus; and just as Menippus did, so do you, Lucian."

32. *Elegantiores Praestantium Virorum Satyrae* vol. 2 (Leiden 1655) 467. This compendium, unavailable to Kirk (p. 109), is an unfortunate gap in his bibliography; I shall return often to this great repository of Renaissance academic Menippean satire.

33. *Elegantiores Satyrae* vol. 2, pp. 758, 776.

There is Menippus the character in his own writings.   This is the source
of what is most popularly known about Menippus: not the person or the philosopher or the author who wrote the *Necyia,* but the character portrayed within
the *Necyia:* a man who died and came back to life as a walking absurdity, the
bearded Fury known from the *Suda,* the agent of the powers below:[34]

> Menippus the Cynic went so far in his hocus-pocus that he took on the appear-
> ance of a Fury and said that he had come from Hades as an observer of sins and
> would go back down again to report them to the divinities there. This was his
> attire: a gray ankle-length cloak with a purple belt around it; an Arcadian cap
> with the twelve signs of the zodiac woven into it on his head; tragic boots; an
> immense beard; and an ashen staff in his hands.

This one terrific imposture forever associates Menippus with the land of the
dead, and earns him the enmity of the philosophers. He is the bogeyman, the
werewolf who scrabbles among the tombs, whom Laertius calls a Cretan cur,
and whom Lucian is said to have dug up (*Bis Acc.* 33), a galvanized corpse.[35]
We may say here that at this point a number of traditions about Menippus
coincide: he is a poseur, pretending to be what he is not; but we may be more
willing than antiquity to see this as Menippus's self-conscious attempt to be
radically Cynic and not as flagrant hypocrisy. Menippus the character invites
disbelief, as his self-portrayal is clearly self-parodic; and those who come after
him, primarily Lucian but also Marcus Aurelius, feel free to continue this
abuse, and to make Menippus the butt of fantastic humor. As was Menippus to
Diogenes, so are his followers to Menippus—loyalty to the example creates
not pious adulation but criticism and ironic distance, a willingness to mock
Menippus's pretensions as a mocker. Neo-Latin authors will continue this tradition, as we have already seen in Heinsius's *Cras Credo.*[36]

Last, there is Menippus the mocker, closely related to the Menippus above.
Menippus is so much the dog that he loses the name of Cynic and becomes a

---

34. *Suda* s.v. φαιός: see Relihan (above, n. 22) 194–95 for discussion of the attribution of
this fragment.

35. Bogeyman: *infernus tenebrio,* Varro, *Men. Sat.* fr. 539 (from *The Burial of Menippus*).
Hypocrite, D.L. 6.100: "Perhaps you know Menippus: Phoenician by birth but a cur from Crete, a
lender of money by the day, as his nickname proves. When he was robbed and lost everything once
at Thebes, and did not know what it meant to be a dog, he hanged himself." "Cretan cur" seems
to label Menippus not as a Cynic but as a cynanthrope or werewolf; by dying Menippus returns to
the tombs where he belongs. Tales are told of such a "dog disease" on the island of Crete; for this
interpretation of a very strange phrase, see my "Menippus, the Cur from Crete," *Prometheus* 16
(1990) 217–24.

36. Menippus the buffoon figures notably in Heinsius's *Hercules Tuam Fidem* (Help Me, Hercules!), which is briefly treated at the end of this essay.

growling dog without a tail, a dog who always bites.[37] Laertius's life makes it clear that Menippus's Cynicism could be thought of as a thing carried not to a logical but to an *illogical* extreme. This mockery is typically associated with the world below, and the vehicle for its transmission is primarily Lucian's *Dialogues of the Dead.* But Lucian is not content with an endorsement of Menippus's mockery. Note that in the *Necyomantia* Menippus is not a mocker but a pilgrim who witnesses the humiliation of the pompous dead; and while Menippus in his own *Necyia* may have presented himself as an emissary of the powers below come back to mock us all, Lucian directs Menippus's mockery in the *Dialogues* toward an absurd, mythological underworld from which he does not return, and that is real enough to put an end to him and all his (ultimately ineffectual) criticisms and enlightened attitudes. Instead of bringing Menippus back to life, Lucian sardonically leaves him down below.[38]

But it is Marcus Aurelius who has the more poignant thought (*Meditations* 6.47). In his list of men who vainly struggled for greatness against the inevitability of death, Menippus comes as the concluding example, the capstone, as it were: even those who make it their business to mock human fears and mortal superstitions are swallowed up by the death that they affect to master and despise.[39] It is, no doubt, for us the living to be improved by such realizations and so come to despise our pretensions of wisdom and our exaggerated sense of self-importance; but ancient authors, whether sympathetic to Menippus or not, see death and not Menippus as having the last laugh.

The mocking Menippus of the Renaissance is less in evidence than one would suspect, possibly because of the realization that Menippus's mockery can miss the point. In Andreae's *Menippus; or, One Hundred Satiric Dialogues,* the critical Menippus is a pseudonym for a carper, not a realization of the character. And because of such works as this, Menippus himself becomes something of a byword for a bad critic, used by those who do not appreciate the criticisms; so Bruno complains of the ill-founded objections of Menippuses to the inquiries of the New Science.[40] The anonymous *Momus* (once attributed to Ulrich von Hutten [1488–1523]), a colloquy of Menippus *calumniator,* Pasquil, and Momus *hominomastix,* has already been referred to (above, n. 9); note

---

37. *Canis sine coda:* Varro, *Men. Sat.* fr. 518 (from *The Burial of Menippus*); the dog that always bites: Lucian, *Bis Acc.* 33.

38. I argue for this reading of the *Dialogues of the Dead* in "Vainglorious Menippus" (above, n. 22).

39. R. B. Rutherford, *The Meditations of Marcus Aurelius: A Study* (Oxford 1989) 128–29, notes that Marcus's belittling treatment of the deaths of great men is at home in the epigram and the *Anthology;* but Rutherford does not note that Menippus is not present in this *Meditation* as a great man. For further discussion, see my "Vainglorious Menippus" (above, n. 22) 192–94.

40. Giordano Bruno, *De la causa, principio et uno,* ed. G. Aquilecchia (Turin 1973) 55. Mercury is the head professor who decides scientific questions, and the Menippuses only screw up their noses in disgust at the deeds of scientists.

that it is Momus who does the criticizing, not Menippus, whose presence largely adds color and comic detail.[41]

Lucian's Menippus

When we consider the fortunes of Menippus through the centuries, we are primarily tracing the trajectory of Menippus's *Necyia* and its reputation, of a fantastic land of the dead and its critic who is just as absurd as these phantasms, and just as much a charlatan as those whom he would warn of the vanity of their wishes. For Menippus as he is found in Lucian is not one who comes to warn the rich of the reversals that await them after their deaths but a self-proclaimed mocker and rationalist who disputes the reality of the things before his eyes.[42] He is a fantastic experimenter, to borrow a term, who goes to the edges of the world to see truth for himself, and who discovers absurdity rather than truth, and who comes back not as a prophet or a redeemer but as an impostor. Lucian's Menippus asserts the values of simplicity against wealth, learning, and vanity, but the discordance between his absurd medium and his humble message is at the heart of Lucian's humor. When Lucian wishes to endorse Cynic truths through a Cynic critic, the character Cyniscus is right for the job, as in the dialogue *Zeus Refutatus,* which is like a watered-down *Icaromenippus,* without the fantasy and the irony. But when Menippus is on the stage, the simple is rendered implausible.

We must see Lucian as playing with Menippus the impostor in the three major works in which he is enthroned.[43] The *Necyomantia* is the starting point, the text most closely related to the example of Menippus's *Necyia*. The truth that Menippus learns from Tiresias in the underworld, that the life of the private person is best, is the truth he knew before he left on his quest. It seems ridiculous for having been proved, and Menippus returns to the upper air through the oracular cave of the false prophet Trophonius. His appearance similarly invites disbelief: the work begins with his explaining to the interlocutor why he wears Odysseus's hat and Heracles's lion skin, and why he carries Orpheus's lyre. Whatever may have been the particulars of Menippus's self-parody in his *Necyia,* Lucian carries on the idea by making the critic laughable. But I would claim that Lucian's greatest contribution to the legend of Menippus is not so

41. This work is imitated by the anonymous *Menippus* (1603) published in the Netherlands; in it, Diogenes is substituted for Pasquil (Kirk, p. 131). I regret I have had no access to it.

42. In this I cautiously disagree with R.B. Branham, *Unruly Eloquence: Lucian and the Comedy of Traditions,* Revealing Antiquity 2 (Cambridge, Mass., 1989) 25. Branham does observe that the Cynic truths are often put in the mouths of characters other than Menippus in Lucian's Menippean fantasies (cf. p. 22); I expand on this here.

43. I summarize here the conclusions drawn in my "Vainglorious Menippus" (above, n. 22) and in the chapter on Lucian in my *Ancient Menippean Satire* (above, n. 2) 103–18.

much the adaptation of the *Necyia* that is the *Necyomantia,* but the creation of the *Icaromenippus* as a companion piece to the *Necyomantia.* This is most probably Lucian's own variation on his own *Necyomantia,* and not an imitation of an otherwise unattested Menippean work; and in it we find a somewhat different Menippus than we find in the exemplar. The structure is more complicated: Menippus learns to fly in order to take his dissatisfaction with contradictory natural philosophers to the court of Zeus himself; resting on the moon, he observes human folly through the tutelage of the philosophical fraud Empedocles, and becomes the messenger of an animate Moon who herself complains of the natural philosophers; Menippus in heaven is only an observer, and the heavenly council, while suitably enraged about the philosophers, is powerless to find an effective remedy. The *Icaromenippus* is consequently easier on Menippus, not so much making fun of as gradually stifling him, stripping away his personal indignation and making him observe the folly of fantastic creatures who feel the same way that he did when he started on his journey. He becomes the naïf who observes but does not influence an impossible heaven.

These two works form as fast a dipytch as Browne's *Urne-Burial* and *Garden of Cyrus,* and fashion out of the mocker a universal observer. Quite different is the sequence of the *Dialogues of the Dead,* thirty dialogues in which Menippus is sent to Hades and not allowed to return, a Menippus who must, at the end of the collection, take his place among the indistinguishable bones of Nireus and Thersites. Menippus's mockery of the rich and powerful does not serve to separate him from them, and the abuse that he heaps on the absurd and mythological characters of the underworld (Tantalus, for example, in *Dialogue* 7; see also Diogenes' treatment of the schizophrenic Heracles, who lives both in Hades and on Olympus, in *Dialogue* 11) does not cause them to evaporate. Menippus discovers that he is just as real as the fantasies with which fevered brains populate the underworld of their nightmares. Lucian's mockery of the mocker is a brilliant job, and those who find the *Dialogues of the Dead* repetitious have not seen the plot unfolding within it.

There are a number of points to stress. The first is that Menippus is not the paradigmatic Cynic in Lucian, but a particularly problematic one, whose fantastic adventures undercut his message. Second, Menippus is not monolithic in Lucian, but can be manipulated. As a character in Lucian's fictions, he can be either naive observer or mordant critic, and can in either event be made fun of; Menippus's own self-parody inspires Lucian to take the humor a step further. Third, the Menippus of the *Dialogues of the Dead* is different from the Menippus of the diptych: in the former we see his death as a mocker; in the latter we see his life as an observer of folly. The fourth and final point is that the pairing of the *Necyomantia* and the *Icaromenippus* creates out of the infernal Menippus a man of many voyages. Thus he becomes less a critic of mortal error and more a symbol of the restless, if ultimately fruitless, quest for a single, all-embracing truth. The Menippus of the *Dialogues of the Dead* is a social critic, as it were, and a traditional sort of satiric persona, albeit subjected to most unusual circumstances; but the Menippus of the diptych is a critic not of personalities and societies but of ideas: his home is not in the world but beyond it; his medium is apocalyptic, not the jeremiad.[44] The Renaissance typically assimilates this Menippus of the universal vision, but does not choose to exalt him by name. The comic treatment accorded to the person of Menippus, which we can see in Lucian as the reflex of Menippus's own self-parody, inspires Renaissance authors to abuse the Menippus that they do not choose to assimilate, and this Menippus is Lucian's mocker or dweller below.

I grant that Lucian's Menippus exists as a point of reference, the fantastic moralist who sat on the moon, or who made the journey to the world below. For example, Erasmus's *Praise of Folly* (1509) has Folly survey the idiocies of mortals upon the earth in a scene reminiscent of Menippus's observations from the moon in the *Icaromenippus*.[45] In Richard Harvey's *Plaine Percevall* (1590; Kirk, p. 165), he is the "Man in the Moone"; and in Ben Jonson's *News from the New World Discovered in the Moon* (1620; Kirk, p. 174), Menippus's ascent to the moon "by wing" is given as one of the three ways to get there.[46] In *El diablo cojuelo* of Luis Vélez de Guevara (1579–1644; roughly, "The Club-foot Devil"), we read that the hero, Don Cleofás, observing the world below with a magic mirror from the height of a Christian tower, is like Menippus in the *Dialogues* of Lucian.[47]

For Menippus the dweller below we have John Dickenson's *Greene in a Conceipt* (1598; Kirk, p. 162), in which he is named in passing. The word *redivivus* in the *Satyricon Asini Vapulantis* by Menippus Redivivus by itself conjures up the Menippus of the land of the dead. Lipsius's *Somnium* preserves only a brief reference to Menippus at its conclusion, where he is delegated to go down to hell to plead the case against those incompetent editors of classical texts who are dead; Menippus is ideal for the job not only because he is a mocker, but because he knows the way.[48]

But the satiric targets that draw the interest of the universal Menippus in

44. So Northrop Frye (*Anatomy of Criticism: Four Essays* [Princeton 1957] 310–13) distinguishes the primary focus of Menippean satire as the *philosophus gloriosus,* who personifies error not as a social malady but as a disease of the mind.

45. *Praise of Folly* 48. Despite his intimate acquaintance with Lucian, Erasmus does not animate the person of Menippus in his other works, though one of the *Colloquies,* the *Peregrinatio Religionis Ergo,* has a Menedemus as one of its characters; Menedemus and Menippus are confused in Diogenes Laertius 6.102, where Menedemus is said to have dressed like the bearded Fury.

46. Robinson, p. 105, notes the similarity between this masque and the *Icaromenippus.*

47. Zappala, p. 209; the work is described at some length by Vives Coll, pp. 167–74.

48. *Somnium* 20.41 (p. 74 Matheeussen-Heesakkers). In the argument of the *Carolus* of Pseudo-Hutten (4.561 Böcking) Lucian's stories of Menippus, alongside Vergil's about Aeneas, are given as parallels for a tale of the descent of Charles V to the underworld to consult Maximilian. At the conclusion of Doni's *I marmi,* Menippus is listed along with Vergil, Dante, Orpheus, and others as the narrator's guides to the Inferno: E. Chiòrboli, ed., *I marmi* vol. 2, Scrittori d'Italia 107 (Bari 1928), 218.

Renaissance fictions and fantasies are not those that outrage the underworld mocker. What emerges is a close association between Mercury and Menippus, the logical inference to be drawn from Lucian's pairing of *Icaromenippus* and *Necyomantia,* for Menippus and Mercury are equally at home above and below; each is concerned with writing and the word; each is a trickster, a charlatan, and a messenger from beyond. While Momus and Mercury are far more frequent in the scholastic fantasies of the Renaissance than Menippus, Menippus does become, like Mercury, a learned man, a man of letters who is the guide to Helicon and to other learned debates in the next world. The desire to make of Menippus not a despiser of academic culture but a master of philosophical, philological, or scientific lore owes something to Lucian's reinterpretation of Menippus's antidogmatic character. Because Menippus the Cynic was never the simple spokesman for Cynic truths, the Renaissance fascination with Cynicism as an irreverent means of criticizing the vainglory of humanist philological passion and error could never rely on a Menippus who merely thumbed his nose at all things bookish.[49] Menippus must become a scholar in such a scheme, and in doing so he is himself liable to the criticisms that he will direct against other scholars.

Ultimately, the Menippus bequeathed by Lucian to the Renaissance resembles in a number of respects the Alexander of romance, who flies to heaven on eagles or is drawn by griffins, who descends to the bottom of Ocean, who travels to the land of the dead, and who has an inordinate interest in his own mortality, always investigating, and often digging up, tombs and corpses. He sees the smallness of the earth and of earthly ambition, and is frequently told not to search out answers to things beyond mortal knowledge: the Menippus who sees from the moon an earth the size of an Epicurean atom (*Icar.* 18) may not be much different from the Alexander who sees from heaven an earth that is a snake coiled around a threshing floor (*Romance* 2.42). In the romance, Alexander's perpetually frustrated desire to transcend his mortal limits is coupled with his often comic attempts to follow the precepts of his all-knowing teacher Aristotle as he tries to catalogue and understand the strange peoples and lands in the new worlds that he discovers. Neither scholar nor prophet, he returns to Egypt to die amid signs and wonders. The imperfectly known prehistory of the Alexander romance will not allow us to say which work influenced the other, though influence there certainly is. Whatever the exact relation between these fictions may be, the Menippus of Lucian's diptych has been embraced, as has Alexander, by Everyman.[50]

49. For this view of the function of Cynicism in Alberti (though without reference to Menippus), see David Marsh, trans., *Leon Battista Alberti: Dinner Pieces,* Medieval and Renaissance Texts and Studies 45 (Binghamton 1987) 5–7.

50. For the Hellenistic origins of the Alexander romance, see the introduction to R. Stoneman, trans., *The Greek Alexander Romance* (Harmondsworth 1991) 8–17. Stoneman, p. 22, also ob-

The Menippuses of the Renaissance

It is not surprising that, to reach the Renaissance, we must bypass the Latin West; it is more remarkable that we must also bypass Byzantium. Lucian has his great influence there, but Menippus does not appear.[51] The best-known examples of Byzantine Lucianic satire, *Timarion* (of the first half of the twelfth century) and *Mazaris* (of the beginning of the fifteenth century),[52] are journeys to the underworld in which Lucian's *Necyomantia* provides a framework, but not the main character, who is in each case an assimilated Menippus. Curious is *Timarion* 43–44, in which Diogenes appears, not as he does in Lucian's *Dialogues of the Dead,* but as Menippus does: a dog who always barks, a brawler, a buffoon, and the sum total of Cynic outrageousness. Here we have the Diogenes who is the mad Socrates, as he is in Lucian's *Vitarum Auctio* 10, and especially in *True History* 2.18, in which he is paired with Aesop the jester, and is presented as a drunkard who has in the Land of the Blessed now married Laïs the courtesan.[53] The Renaissance produces something similar in Erich van Put's cumbrously titled *The Revels; or, A Sensual Symposium in the Land of the Dead. A Dream-Vision* (1608: *Comus, sive Phagesiposia Cimmeria. Somnium*).[54] In this work, Lucian himself is the dog in the company of the Puritan intelligentsia, who are at a sensual feast in the cave of Cumae with Epicurus and others.

Menippus does not become an active character in neo-Latin imaginative fiction until sometime after Lipsius's revival of the literary genre that bears his name in 1581. But it is not to be imagined that Menippean satire is a revival, after a long interval, of Varro's original form, as deduced from ragged fragments. Varro's 150 *Menippean Satires* could hardly have been uniform in theme or even in genre, given that experimentation could lead him to particular attempts at specific literary parodies in any given *Menippean;* we noted above that Menippus himself probably wrote only one Menippean satire, and a number of other thematically related, but less ambitious parodies of individual literary genres. But it does seem central to Varro's *Menippeans* that that author presents himself as a critic who, despite laudable sentiments and intentions,

---

serves that Aesop, whose *Life* and Diogenes' may have intersected according to Donzelli (above, n. 20), is, like Alexander, a clever inventor who makes a trip to heaven in an eagle-chariot, and is also involved in a number of stories with the last Egyptian pharaoh Nectanebo, presented in the romance as Alexander's physical father.

51. The Byzantine Lucian is discussed most fully by Mattioli, pp. 9–38; see also Robinson, pp. 68–81; Kirk, pp. 39–44; Zappala, pp. 20–31.

52. Both available in English translation: Barry Baldwin, trans., *Timarion,* Byzantine Texts in Translation (Detroit 1984); Seminar Classics 609, trans., *Mazaris' Journey to Hades,* Arethusa Monographs 5 (Buffalo 1975).

53. Baldwin, *Timarion* p. 134 n. 240, points out that Diogenes' oath "by the Cynic philosophy" is to remind us of Socrates' oath "by the dog."

54. Kirk, pp. 124–25; the work is included in the *Elegantiores Satyrae* vol. 2, pp. 311–408 (above, n. 32).

fails to understand the incomprehensible world around him and suffers for his presumptions. In Varro, I think, we have tales of a would-be satirist who finds himself satirized: it is a nice cross-fertilization of Menippus and Lucilius, and is the font of the late classical academic Menippean satirists Julian, Martianus Capella, Fulgentius, and Boethius.[55]

Academic self-parody is Varro's most important contribution to the history of the genre that has been named after his collection; Menippus the heavenly philologue of the Renaissance stands firmly in this tradition, transformed from the antidogmatist that Lucian inherits from the works of Menippus himself. But the Renaissance is more comfortable, in its tales of the inadequacy of academic culture, with a narrator who is a serious critic, or at least a silent follower of a comic guide. Authorial self-parody, already seen in Heinsius and which is one of the nicer aspects of Erasmus's otherwise elephantine *Praise of Folly,* is not as frequent, at least in the earlier stages of the Renaissance. The Renaissance loves to look down with disdain on the spectacle of wrangling philosophers, invoking the contemptuous *catascopia* of the Menippean tradition that is prominent in Varro, Lucian, and elsewhere in the ancient genre. But Renaissance authors and narrators are reluctant to make fun of themselves when they do so. Consequently, Menippus becomes not a narrator but a comic guide, a comic feature on the fantastic landscape of another world. It is worth pointing out as a parallel that what is true of Menippus in Renaissance Menippean satire is also true in Renaissance dialogues of the dead. These too tend to avoid Lucian's gloomy underworld panoramas, to prefer the seriously crucial to the ironic, and to avoid the commingling of trivial fictions and eternal truths. On all three counts, we may say, Menippus is excluded from these more modern underworlds: neither Fontenelle, for all his paradoxes, nor Fénelon reanimates Menippus himself.[56]

Menippean satire, viewed as intellectual rather than social satire, comes to be seen in the Renaissance as a proper envelope for the comic presentation of scholarly wrangling and debate, but what reshapes it as a thing different from Varro's *Menippeans* is a different, specifically humanist, literary genre: the long tradition of fantasy and intellectual criticism embodied in the *praelectio.* In it, students are introduced to a classical text by a speech, often fantastic,

---

55. I argue this view of Varro's *Menippeans* in *Ancient Menippean Satire* (above, n. 2) 49–74.

56. See F.M. Keener, *English Dialogues of the Dead: A Critical History, An Anthology, and a Checklist* (New York 1973) 14, 21–24. A similar seriousness prevails in Alberti's Cynic dialogues, the *Intercenales.* A nice example is "The Dream" (*Somnium*); cf. Marsh, *Dinner Pieces* (above, n. 49) 66–69. In it Lepidus (Mr. Witty, Alberti's Cynic persona) plays straight-man to Libripeta (Mr. Mad-for-Books, behind whom lurks Niccolò Niccoli), who tells a tale of his voyage to the land of dreams, from which he could only escape by a sewer, whence his unpleasant appearance. Note how the author takes on the role of Menippus's friend (a virtual nonentity) in *Icaromenippus* or *Necyomantia,* and makes it his vantage point for serious criticism of the impostures and pretensions of the Menippus character Libripeta.

describing its nature and importance, and the errors of interpretation to which it has been subjected at the hands of critics less enlightened than the author.[57] This is well illustrated in the works of Vives, such as his *Preface to Cicero's Laws; or, The Temple of the Law,* and the *Dream and Vigil on Cicero's Dream of Scipio,* which show a hybrid of comic fantasy and intellectual curiosity as directed toward specific texts.[58] Humanist Menippean satire can therefore be seen as a breaking-free from the reins of the *praelectio.* Works entitled *Somnium* become very popular, and dream visions of critical utopias are frequent.

The great repository of such neo-Latin Menippean material is the two-volume *Elegantiores Praestantium Virorum Satyrae* (Leiden 1655). Its preface, spoken by a Satyra who largely discourses about the spelling of her name (so much for the influence of Casaubon!), suggests that the printer will soon produce, perhaps on the model of the *Letters of Obscure Men,* a volume of *Refined Satires of Anonymous, but No Less Excellent, Men (satiras elegantiores tōn anōnumōn, neque tamen minus praestantium, virorum)*: this was not achieved. The collection's first offerings are Lipsius's *Somnium* and Cunaeus's *Sardi Venales,* and it effectively recognizes these two as the cream of the crop of humanist Menippean satires. But ancient and modern jostle each other here in the first volume: there are also Cunaeus's translation of Julian's *Caesars* (as well as a Greek text and earlier translation of the same work by Cantoclarus), Petrus Martinus's translation of Julian's *Misopogon,* Seneca's *Apocolocyntosis,* and a few academic *Somnia:* Petrus Nannus's *Somnium, sive Paralipomena Virgilii: Res Inferae à Poëta Relictae;* his *Somnium Alterum: In Lib. II Lucretii Praefatio;* and an *Oratio* of Franciscus Bencius beginning *Narrabo somnium, auditores.* Volume 2 is a mine of underappreciated texts in which Varro, Seneca, Petronius, Lucian, Martianus Capella, and Boethius form the literary substratum for comic discussions of the problems with contemporary learning and contemporary critics. It contains Nicolaus Rigaltius's *Funus Parasiticum;* Erycius Puteanus's *Comus;* Petrus Castellanus's *Ludus, sive Convivium Saturnale;* Famiana Strada's *Momus, sive Satira Varroniana;* also his *Academia Prima* and *Academia Secunda;* Janus Bodecherus Benningius's *Satyricon, in Corruptae Juventutis Mores Corruptos;* Vincentius Fabricius's *Satyra, Pran-*

---

57. W. S. Blanchard, "O Miseri Philologi: Codro Urceo's Satire on Professionalism and Its Context," *Journal of Medieval and Renaissance Studies* 20 (1990) 91–122, discusses *praelectiones* as vehicles for criticism of philology and critics: "Urceo's *Sermo Primus* (1494–95) transformed the traditional humanist *praelectio* into a vehicle for a creative satire upon the professional activities of all men, an encompassing mirror of human follies which extended its focal range to include the activities of the humanists themselves" (pp. 95–96).

58. The *Praefatio in Leges Ciceronis: Aedes Legum,* ed. C. Matheeussen (Leipzig 1984), describes how the narrator met an old man who spoke in hyperarchaic Latin and kept the tower of law; the comic possibilities of such an introduction are further developed in the *Somnium et Vigilia in Somnium Scipionis* (1520), a mildly self-parodic account of a scholar in the land of sleep. For this work see E. V. George, "Imitatio in the *Somnium Vivis,*" in *Juan Luis Vives,* ed. A. Buck, Wolfenbütteler Abhandlungen zur Renaissanceforschung 3 (Hamburg 1982), 81–92.

sus Paratus, in Poëtas, et Eorum Contemptores; nine *Prolusiones,* under the general title of *Satyrica Quaedam,* of Octavius Ferrarius; and the two books of Ioannes Sangenesius's *De Parnasso, et Finitimis Locis.*

As in the case of the descendants of the *Dialogues of the Dead,* the absence of Menippus helps to define the peculiarities of Renaissance satire. For example, in Rigaltius's *Funus Parasiticum* (1596) our narrator meets both Lucius Apuleius and Lucian on Onirocrene, the Font of Dreams that is the Island of Asses; the parasite L. Biberius Curculio, a friend of the emperor Heliogabalus, makes arrangements for his will and then dies. This resembles a continuation of Petronius's *Satyricon;* the *musteus poeta* who delivers the funeral poem is specifically compared to Eumolpus, and the concluding funeral feast has the *Cena Trimalchionis* as a model.[59] The narrator is in fact a Menippus-type character, but Menippus travels to philological heavens and hells, not to comic dystopias, and so is unwanted here.

The publication of the *Elegantiores Satyrae* in 1655 lends an impression of uniformity to Renaissance Menippean productions. But the contents are written over a number of decades, and vary not only in vehemence, topic, and tone, but also in their particular uses of Menippus when he does appear. Nor is this the sole source of Menippean literature or appearances of Menippus. But while we are not in a position to speak of a historical progression in the Renaissance from one type of incarnation to another, we can use this collection to illlustrate the unity that exists among the three distinct uses to which our Cynic is put. In what follows I offer briefly three specific examples of the various manifestations of the neo-Latin Menippus; each is deserving of a fuller and separate study. Whether an impossible buffoon, a philologue against philology, or a growling guide to Helicon, Menippus is, after Lipsius's *Somnium* shows the way, a seriocomic literary critic in later neo-Latin literature. The societies that he observes are learned societies, and his viewpoint is that of one who knows the true value of literature; the villains are writers of bad books, or those who exalt love of learning beyond its rational boundaries. From the foregoing considerations of Menippus's variegated reputation and Lucian's manipulation of Menippus's literary personality, we are in a position to appreciate just how it comes to be that the neo-Latin Menippus is so far from his underworld persona of universal moral critic.

---

59. In his modest way Rigault (1577–1654) anticipates by a hundred years the hoax of the completed *Satyricon* associated with Nodot (1693; for this affair see now W. Stolz, *Petrons Satyricon und François Nodot: Ein Beitrag zur Geschichte literarischer Fälschungen* [Stuttgart 1987]). For the fortunes of the *Satyricon* in the Renaissance, see A. Grafton, "Petronius and Neo-Latin Satire: The Reception of the *Cena Trimalchionis,*" *JWI* 53 (1990) 237–49, who makes the interesting point that it is neo-Latin satire that inspires increased interest in Petronius (p. 245). Ass-literature is also closely associated with Menippean productions; an example is Heinsius's *Laus Asini,* which follows on the heels of his Menippean *Hercules Tuam Fidem* (Kirk, p. 124).

Menippus the Buffoon in Daniel Heinsius

The *Cras Credo, Hodie Nihil* of Heinsius has already been discussed. But he has a number of other satires of Menippean affiliation, the most important of which is *Hercules Tuam Fidem* (Help Me, Hercules!). This sets out to record the humiliations in the afterlife of Caspar Schoppe, whose *Scaliger Hypobolimaeus* (Scaliger the Bastard), a recasting of Apuleius's *Metamorphoses,* had claimed that the father of Joseph Scaliger was not a descendant of the princely house of La Scala but was the illegitimate son of an Italian schoolmaster named Burdone (The Ass).[60] The *Hercules* is a lengthy work, a sort of underworld *Apocolocyntosis* with all the stops pulled out; within it we see a Menippus who is the reductio ad absurdum of the mocker of the dead whom we see in Lucian's *Dialogues of the Dead.*

Early in the proceedings we find Schoppe being hauled off to face his trial. The company passes through some doors, and Menippus in the entryway makes everyone laugh by acting like a court jester, in a way reminiscent of Diogenes rolling his tub:[61]

> Not far from the vestibule that same Menippus forced a laugh out of everyone when he was trying to drag behind him a certain dwarf, barely a foot and a half tall, who was toiling in Hercules' boot while trying, with the great effort typical of those in a hurry, to slip away from the throng of the dead and burst into the conclave next door. Now face down, now face up, he was knocking himself against the ground now with his head, now with his forearm, now with his whole body. And when we were asking the reason why, he would say that he was imitating a Stoic, a vainglorious man, who, while trying for fame by whatever means he could, had recently put his foot in Lipsius's work, possibly mad, possibly blind; he had now found instead of praise either ridicule or contempt.

This Menippus, who feels that he must amuse the machinery of the underworld, is found again some twenty pages later, after Schoppe has been stripped, humiliated, and forced to reveal his own origins. Menippus offers a wild rebuttal of Schoppe's speech of self-defense. Aeacus ultimately calls for an end to Menippus's nonsense, demands a final answer about origins, and reveals on

---

60. For a brief account of Schoppe's writings and the various Menippean satires (including John Donne's *Ignatius, His Conclave*) written in response to this outrageous work, see Kirk, pp. 119–22; further on Heinsius's satiric productions in Kirk, pp. 123–24. A. Grafton's intellectual biography of Scaliger (*Joseph Scaliger: A Study in the History of Classical Scholarship,* 2 vols. [Oxford 1983–93]) is not particularly concerned with such texts.

61. The text is that of *Satirae dvae Hercvles Tuam Fidem sive Munsterus Hypobolimaeus. Et Virgula Divina, cum brevioribus annotatiunculis. . . . Accessit his accurata* BVRDONVM FABVLÆ CONFVTATIO, *quibus alia nonnulla hac editione accedunt* (Leiden 1617) 41.

Schoppe's back an inscription that gives Schoppe's initials, home town, and what seems to have been a common *explicit* in his writings, We Trojans Exist No Longer.[62] Menippus immediately leaps on this poetic claim of noble lineage, and indulges in a few pages of abuse: Schoppe is a mad dog like Hecuba, and is as unbelievable as Cassandra. Normally Menippus is an unbelievable mad dog; there is some humor here at our critic's expense. Menippus has little more to do with this fantasy.

It is at first strange that a work so obviously interested in the vilification of Schoppe should invest Menippus, rather than Momus, with critical robes. But note that Heinsius's Menippus is a fixture of a comic afterlife, and neither a witness nor a guide to heaven. This Menippus is a combination of criticism and comic relief, an extreme version of the Silenus who is the heavenly jester and critic in Julian's *Caesars* (cf. 308c–309a) and the drunken embarrassment in Martianus Capella's *De Nuptiis* (cf. 8.804). Menippus's vulgarity is an integral part of Schoppe's humiliation; so too is the fact that this vulgar man knows Schoppe's writings. The other world that ponders his merits treats Schoppe with disgust, and no proprieties need to be maintained; a similar humor motivates Claudius's ejection from the disreputable heaven of Seneca's *Apocolocyntosis.*

Menippus the Philologue in Petrus Cunaeus

While Lipsius's *Somnium* has pride of place in the *Elegantiores Satyrae,* being the starting point of a conscious revival of Varronian satire, it has little to offer us here. Menippus is only mentioned as the one who knows his way to the underworld, and the philological debates proceed without his comments or his ridicule. Much more interesting is Cunaeus's *Sardi Venales. Satyra Menippea, in Huius Seculi Homines Plerosque Inepte Eruditos* (1612: "Sardinians on the Slave Block. A Menippean Satire on the People of This Age, Most of Them Badly Educated").[63] Cunaeus, like Lipsius, is intimately acquainted with the works of Lucian;[64] Cunaeus has the added advantage of being an editor of Julian's *Caesars,* a Menippean satire much akin to the *Sardi Venales* in spirit.

The narrator meets Menippus himself in the Epicurean *intermundia,* and Menippus introduces himself in a long speech (21–26). Although he often

---

62. P. 72; *G.S. A Munster. FUIMUS TROES.*

63. The main title refers to a Roman proverb, *Sardi uenales, alius alio nequior:* "Sardinians on the slave block, each one worse than the other." *Sardi Venales* is also the title of one of Varro's *Menippeans,* of which one fragment survives.

64. The dream vision is prefaced by the *True History*'s warning that all that follows is a lie; less obvious parallels to Lucian are not noticed in the apparatus to the edition of Matheeussen and Heesakkers (above, n. 10) which identifies many of the Latin sources.

travels on the earth, he is now going home to the land of the shades of the literati.[65] There is faction there, however, and disagreement concerning who is to be allowed to dwell among them. Menippus will escort the narrator to this nearby island; Menippus seems at this point to go as an observer, and is not a voting member. Though the membership question makes us think of Lucian's *Jupiter Tragoedus* and *Deorum Concilium,* the meeting of narrator and strange guide mirrors that of Menippus and Empedocles on the moon in his *Icaro-menippus.* They pass through a frightening wood and cross with a ferryman over rivers that clearly suggest the Styx; Menippus greets this novel under-world, part Hades and part Olympus, as his home (27: *Salve . . . gratissima tellus et vos, fratres mei, eruditae animae*). The shades admire the narrator after Menippus sings his praises; a discordant note is sounded when they say, "Who-ever you are, you shall be one of us," words spoken by the luckless Trojans to Vergil's Sinon (*Aen.* 2.148–49). There follows a lengthy account of this coun-cil (over which Erasmus presides) concerning incompetent critics and their rights of access to this island; Menippus appears only sporadically, now stop-ping the mouth of a long-winded speaker (51–53), now refusing to be a phi-losopher's patron (67–70). A final decree is to be made, but an invasion by the citizens of Hades puts the scholars into comic confusion, and there is no formal decision proclaimed (121).[66] Menippus now aids the narrator's escape. There is no need to stay, he says, as the deliberations do not require him, and death is still the force that rules over all. We continue to read him in Vergilian terms, for he parts with a pointed quotation from the *Georgics* (122): " 'No need for us to stay,' he said; 'Troy will be defended even without us. And anyway, it's not the first time that I've heard messengers of this sort. "These spirited pas-sions and these great debates shall be settled by the tossing of a handful of dust and shall fall quiet" ' " (cf. *Georg.* 4.86–87). Our Sinons leave this Troy; the narrator's passion for sightseeing leads them to discover a cave full of drunken scholars who decide, at the very end of the work, to attack as well, and threaten the narrator when he insults their high priest (131–32).

Against all precedent, both Menippus and Diogenes appear in the *Sardi Venales.* Diogenes has been successful in his search for wisdom, and enters with Sophia, who proceeds to declaim against theologians and their wranglings (78–88). But the most intriguing thing here is the speech of Sophrosyne, the handmaiden of Sophia, who enlarges on Sophia's attacks (90–92). She praises those who do not look too deeply into things; her speech to the narrator is

---

65. *Ego Menippus sum, famae celebritate super astra notus. E terris autem venio; quo saepe excurrere soleo, uti res hominum visam.* Note the similarity of this to Satan's opening speech in Job; note too that Menippus is not calling himself anything like a *hominomastix.*

66. In Cunaeus's source for this (Lucian, *VH* 2.23) the attack on the Islands of the Blessed is successfully repulsed, and Socrates is rewarded for his bravery.

worth quoting as a fitting summation of the Cynic principles of the Menippean genre:[67]

> [90.] I shall not hide from you the greatest secret. There is a certain race of people, and a very clever race at that, who inquire deeply neither into the first causes nor into the ends of things, and love as fairest wisdom not to know anything to the limit. Most of you call these people slow-witted, dull, and lazy. Quite the other way around! For they are knowledgeable of things, and they alone of mortals are wise, but not beyond what is enough. But you turn these particular virtues on their head and have long ago lost the real names of things. [91.] You, who love a sound mind, shall praise few things, shall undertake nothing yourself, shall be a spectator of all things, so that you may be like them. . . . [92.] I assure you, this shall be your most exquisite pleasure, when you realize that there is nothing that stands firm, nothing that is beautiful or even proper from all this exertion of wrangling people. Great is this void that has been placed in things. Wherever you turn, you will come up against "a picture studio, nothing true, everything false." Whatever they think they know is less than nothing. This one thing is certain: most things are hardly certain. If you will make this observation, if you will have your revenge on everyone's efforts not in anger but in laughter, indeed, you will be on my side, and, if the great gods are willing, you will merit all approbation.

This is primarily directed against theological knowledge; the verse quotation, from Lucilius,[68] specifically refers to the images of the gods. Yet by its generality the advice spills over into the realm of classical studies as well, and the Cynic moral of section 91, reminiscent of the advice given to Menippus by Lucian's Tiresias (*Nec.* 21), seems to recommend an ironic detachment from the world at large. And like Tiresias's advice in *Icaromenippus,* this too vanishes into smoke as the narrator, again in Vergilian terms, tries to embrace Sophrosyne, who immediately disappears like a dream. He wonders whether he has been deceived and adds that if he ever had such joy *again,* he would finally have something to thank heaven for (93). The revealed truth is more than he can accept; he remains, as Lucian's Menippus does at the end of the *Icaromenippus,* a naïf in a comic paradise.

Diogenes and his search for Sophia are tacitly criticized; what is recommended is the Menippean alternative to the Cynicism of Diogenes, but this is

---

67. The beginning of Cunaeus's dedicatory epistle speaks similarly of the need for observation of the world without striving for arcane knowledge, and of the joy of contemplating another's errors (*Praefatio* 1, p. 80 Matheeussen-Heesakkers): "It is a great and blessed thing to see what has been put at one's feet, to walk through the cities and homes of people, and observe their vices and errors one by one. Whoever does this seems alone to use the intelligence correctly, and to deserve well from humanity at large."

68. Fr. 495 Krenkel (489 Marx), Book 15, from Lactantius, *Inst.* 1.22.13; the text is that printed by Matheeussen and Heesakkers, with *falsa* for *ficta.*

an elusive quantity. Our narrator takes on the role of Lucian's Menippus, a witness to otherworldly stupidity who is not quite aware of what it all means; Cunaeus's Menippus is not the observer, but a guide to a land of learned spirits, a land where he belongs, but whose virtues he does not embrace. Menippus is not entrusted with the Cynic wisdom pronounced by Wisdom herself. Menippus's presence is subversive, and the debate to which he leads the narrator is inconclusive. Cunaeus understands through Lucian's example that wherever Menippus is, there dogmatic truth cannot exist also; but he who was a Cynic fighting against Cynics, or a sophist fighting against sophists, is now a philologue implicating himself in a criticism of professional philology. This shows a confidence that Lipsius's *Somnium* lacks. When a learned author can wish a pox on both the houses of a debate on the value of learned debate, he can show himself in the company of Menippus, the ironic scholar.

Menippus the Guide to Helicon in Octavius Ferrarius

Also to be found within the *Elegantiores Satyrae* are the *Prolusiones* of Octavius Ferrarius, a suite of nine mildly critical satires bemoaning philological incompetence, the laziness of students, the lack of respect and patronage afforded men of letters, and the growing importance of doctors.[69] The nine have a logic and ask to be read as a whole: the eighth is a sort of apology for the nasty things said about doctors in the earlier *prolusiones,* and the ninth is a palinode, the goal of which is actively to dissuade his readers from the life of letters. While Menippus does not appear in all, he appears at significant intervals in different capacities so that, as is the case with the *Dialogues of the Dead,* he casts his shadow over the whole.[70]

Prolusio 6, *Quo Pretio Viri Principes Literas ac Literatos Habuerint* (The Regard of Rulers for Literature and Scholars), is most to our purposes. Here

---

69. Ferrarius wrote a total of twenty *prolusiones,* the last, on Alexander the Great, appearing in 1655, the year the *Elegantiores Satyrae* was published.

70. In the second *prolusio,* the *Artium ac Disciplinarum Auctio,* a fantasy concerning the sale of Theologia, Eloquentia, and other abstractions in imitation of Lucian's *Vitarum Auctio,* Menippus makes two crucial appearances: one is as a mocker of the doctors and pseudophilosophers who gather as potential buyers; in the other, in the company of Mercury and the Muses, he pitchforks down Parnassus those who have bought Poesis and think themselves poets, a scene based upon the conclusion of Lucian's *Piscator,* but also recalling the Menippus in the *Dialogues of the Dead* who helps Charon row his boat. The fourth *prolusio, De Causis Pereuntium Literarum* (The Decline and Fall of Literature), casts Menippus into yet another role, that of actual, but not very active, narrator concerning a gathering of literati on Helicon, with Turnebus and Joseph Scaliger as censors. *Prolusio* 9, *Literatorum Infelicitas* (The Lucklessness of Scholars), is the palinode; it is fascinating in that, while Menippus does not appear by name, the *viri docti* who are deprived of the financial rewards that are their due lead lives that are to remind us not only of Juvenal's unsuccessful clients but also of the Cynics in general, and possibly Menippus in particular: "They alone are praised and freeze: they are lifted up to the stars, and they lie dead; . . . it is uncertain whether people point them out because of their wit or their filthiness" (pp. 891–92).

our sick narrator has a dream, and without the aid of either Mercury or Pegasus travels to Helicon, where Apollo in his temple is expected to give answers directly to the crowd of petitioners about him. Apollo stands still as a statue, evidently numbed by the venality of their wishes; but Menippus is not silent. In a role compounded of literary critic, the mocker of the *Dialogues of the Dead,* and Jesus cleansing the temple, Menippus takes it upon himself to tell these people what is wrong with them (pp. 837–38):

> But in the meantime Menippus and others from that same sect were taunting with Cynic freedom of speech those who were making their supplications; they were yelling insults, and were on the point of smashing their raised walking sticks down on their heads. Menippus himself, in a loud and grating voice, said: "You sleepyheads, drowsy in idleness and vice, why, damn you, do you shamelessly call for the rewards of exertion and sleeplessness? Why have you made his temple a shambles? Why do you vainly weary the ears of Phoebus that pay less and less attention? Why do you seek from the god what you can get by yourselves? Are you so stupid as to think that that wisdom can be had by these womanish pleadings? Or is it to fall from heaven into your sleepy minds, so you will also of a sudden emerge as learned men while you keep your fingers laced together? Those times are long gone, if there ever were such times, when old Hesiod was made a poet in his dreams and was instructed by the Muses; or when that other, Latin old man [*sc.* Ennius], obviously insane, was practically made a peacock and the Muses' little chick. You have lost wisdom completely, for you have spent your best years drowned in wine and debauchery; you have wasted them in gaming and sleep as if you were merely passing through them, and you think that by one tiny prayer you can emerge on the brow of Helicon? To cure a madness like that would take, I'm sure, quite a few acres of hellebore. But your ancestors, the glory of the written word, who gained for themselves an undying name, wrestled in this arena with Herculean effort and unimaginable struggle. But you, swollen with the soft potbelly, eyes that droop in slumber, raised on dice throwing and dancing, the shame of a feeble begetting, do you dare to hope for wisdom? Apollo, why don't you get out your bow and kill on the spot these dogs, these beasts . . . ? Is there anything worse that I can call them?"
>
> Everyone thought the Cynic's harangue, while not unfair, was certainly too harsh, and practically rabid. Consequently, with unanimous shouting and threats, he was thrown out of the temple.

Menippus suddenly becomes a spokesman for the necessity of labor in scholarship, a dog declaiming against dogs much as the dilettante Encolpius declaims against dilettante orators at the beginning of Petronius's *Satyricon.* Menippus here knows the prologue of Persius, whence the complaints about the dreaming Hesiod and Ennius's previous life as a peacock; Menippus can speak of literature in comic terms. We are surprised to see Menippus actually ejected from Apollo's temple, and perhaps this reflects a general feeling that Menippus ought to have nothing to do with such topics; but he does not leave without having had his effect. One of the virtuous scholars admits that the speech of this dog was shameless and crude, but he too is ashamed of the laziness of this age, and goes on to praise those in times gone by who combined their passions for intellectual and political excellence (beginning with Alexander the Great). Menippus does not reappear; a convulsion reminiscent of the end of Aeschylus's *Prometheus Bound* terminates the proceedings.

Menippus plays here the full range of his roles: psychopomp, mocker, witness, and source. But the *Prolusiones* as a whole present themselves as a failure, and the Menippus who presides over them is closest to the Menippus of the *Dialogues of the Dead,* who cannot change the vices that he sees. Ferrarius himself as narrator plays the universal observer of Lucian's otherworldly satires, and sees visions that he no longer wants to see. From Lucian comes the insistence that Menippus's truth is not only uncomfortable, but also ineffectual. The heavenly debates on literature to which Menippus has access have settled no questions; the travel to heaven has been pointless; and it is Menippus the author and inspiration of authors, Menippus the literary man, who is ultimately invoked here.

Conclusion

The literature of the Spanish Golden Age assimilates Lucian's Menippus frequently, but Spain seems also to have had a greater interest in Menippus the person, the character outside Lucian, than other countries and literary traditions in the Renaissance. Leonardo de Argensola's *Menipo litigante* is one proof of this; the flights of Icaro Menipo are another; Velázquez's portrait of Menippus is an important third.[71] With its companion piece, the portrait of Aesop (both ca. 1640), it gives us the image, if not of the bearded Fury of the *Suda,* at least of a bearded rogue. Wrapped in an ample robe instead of rags, he seems to conceal something from us, and he does not look us full in the face.[72] The books scattered at his feet show his interest in words as well as his devil-may-care attitude toward literature and learning; the jug of water is a sign of Cynic simplicity and self-sufficiency. A classical figure made to live in the picaro's world, he is a scholar's rogue.[73] Spain has a greater interest in sending this Menippus

71. Inscribed with the curious orthography "Mœnippus"; a reproduction of it graces the dust jacket of Branham's *Unruly Eloquence.*

72. See the description of the painting in Kurt Gerstenberg, *Diego Velázques* (Munich 1957) 221–24.

73. Cervantes' *Colloquy of the Dogs* (publ. 1613) deserves mention here because of a similar, curious Cynic fantasy: two dogs, each a mendicant's assistant, each accustomed to carry a light at night in a search for alms, discover to their surprise that they have powers of speech. The nasty Berganza tells his stories to the proud Scipio; Scipio will tell his the next night, though these are not recorded. Like other picaresque fictions modeled on *The Golden Ass,* it provides a low-life view of contemporary society; but my suspicion is that Cervantes is in effect bringing the Cynics Menippus (Berganza) and Diogenes (Scipio) back to life together in their capacities as moralists. To make these two Cynics actually speak to each other is a brilliant innovation that allows for moderation in other aspects of a Menippean fiction: the fantasy is restricted to miraculous speech, and the miraculous journey is avoided altogether.

on other voyages, and in considering how the world looks through his eyes; the literary critic, the philological psychopomp, and the infernal buffoon of the neo-Latin works considered above are all at some remove from this.

In general, earlier neo-Latin literature strips Menippus of his wings. When he is later allowed to fly, he inhabits a corner of a fantastic world, and is no longer the naive voyager to it, who sees all of human existence from a fantastic point of view. Menippus the author, the renegade Cynic, and the mocker take the place of Menippus Everyman, a role ceded to other narrators. As a critic of the comic microcosm of philology and its humors, he loses sight of the macrocosm. His Lucianic functions are variously apportioned: Mercury is the typical guide to the other world, and Momus is the archcritic in satirical texts based on Lucian. Menippus, in effect, is transformed into Silenus, that heavenly wise fool known through Julian's *Caesars* and Martianus Capella's *De Nuptiis.*

This is an intelligent transformation, presenting much of what is true about Lucian's Menippus in a different guise. Silenus is an ideal instrument for self-parody, for eccentric (possibly unreliable) criticism, for comedy at the expense of the pretentious in the mouth of the grotesque. In the works of Heinsius, Cunaeus, and Ferrarius, we see Menippus as a mad man of letters. In order to criticize the world of letters and see its inanities he needs to be a literary man; and because the criticism of letters in letters involves in our neo-Latin authors a certain amount of self-parody, Menippus becomes an unreliable critic, a character who may say the truth but not absolutely.

We associate Menippus, and the Lucian who preserves him, with the concept of the *spoudogeloios* (seriocomic). We have expectations that Menippus will tell the truth with a laugh, that he will subvert our expectations of knowledge and meaning. Certainly the Renaissance has its seriocomic literature, but its Menippus is not primarily a seriocomic figure in the Renaissance use of that term. "Seriocomic" is used for taking trivial things seriously, and Menippus does rather the opposite. The great compendium of mock encomia and other literary trifles compiled by the self-styled doctor and philosopher Dornavius (Hanover 1617) announces that the seriocomic is a whole new branch of learning: *The Amphitheater of Socratic, Serio-Comic Wisdom: That is, Encomia and Commentaries of Practically All Authors, Ancient as well as Modern: in which Subjects Commonly Considered Unworthy or Pernicious are Justified and Made Elegant by Means of the Pen: A Work for Understanding the Mysteries of Nature, of the Greatest Practical Use, Public and Private, for Complete Enjoyment, Wisdom, and Virtue.*[74] In Cunaeus there is a hint that Menippus is the master of a rival sort of wisdom, but the speech of Sophrosyne does not mention him by name.

74. *Amphitheatrum Sapientiae Socraticae Joco-Seriae, hoc est, Encomia et Commentaria Autorum, qua Veterum, qua Recentiorum prope Omnium: Quibus Res, Aut pro Vilibus Vulgo Aut Damnosis Habitae, Styli Patrocinio Vindicantur, Exornantur: Opus ad Mysteria Naturae Discenda, ad Omnem Amoenitatem, Sapientiam, Virtutem, Publice Privatimque Vtilissimum . . . a Caspare Dornavio Philos. et Medico.*

Heinsius suggests in the *Cras Credo* that all Menippean works fail to make a point. In this, neo-Latin literature understands Lucian and his Menippus perfectly. But who shall shoulder the burden of incomprehensibility? The Everyman Menippus of the *Icaromenippus* and the *Necyomantia* bears paradoxical messages from a ridiculous place. When the Renaissance splits this Menippus up again, the universalist, who is admired, is subsumed in characters and narrators who go by other names as they search for less equivocal truths; the unreliable Menippus, who may be fleshed out with details known from other sources, is similarly out of place when the questions are those of vigorously championed right and wrong. But in the later stages of the Renaissance, when there is some room for self-parody, and for a more detached contemplation of the classical world and the philology that seeks to understand it, Menippus may reclaim from Momus and Mercury his sharp tongue and his sharp pen. Lipsius's *Somnium* is the immediate cause of this revivification; we may allow that Renaissance interest in the Menippean *Satyricon* has its hand in inspiring tales of a crazy scholar. If Menippus is allowed to breathe in the 1600s, it is perhaps because there is some fresher air, and the ironist who doubts the value of philosophy, scholarship, and learning may once more survey, if not the entirety, at least one field of human activity.

Heirs of the Dog: Cynic Selfhood in Medieval and Renaissance Culture

Daniel Kinney

As Diogenes went into a theater meeting face-to-face
those coming out, being asked why he did so, he
said, "This is my standard role throughout life." [1]

There are two almost equally venerable, though not equally dignified, notions of what it takes to make a Cynic. The first notion is almost entirely a matter of principle: if one swears by the values of autarky, frankness, and bold spontaneity, taking animal nature as a standard or at least as a point of departure for cultural skepsis as well as didactic "indifference," by this notion that makes one a "proper," or in English an uppercase Cynic.[2] The second notion is sensationally and symptomatically *un*principled: if one sees nothing basically wrong with behaving indecorously (though not as a rule criminally) on all manner of public occasions, espouses outlandish habits, displays general contempt for ideals of all stripes, or, as Oscar Wilde puts it, demonstrates that one knows the price of everything and the value of nothing, by this notion that makes one (in German) not *kynisch* but *zynisch,* and in English a lowercase "cynic." Though these matching distinctions in German and English are clearly quite modern, an analogous saving and damning distinction between styles of playing the *kuōn* or dog, imitating dogs' virtues and vices respectively, may be

---

1. Diogenes Laertius (hereafter "D.L.") 6.64, ed. R.D. Hicks (London 1950), whose own translation I sometimes revise; for Diogenes "the Dog" see esp. 6.60, 85.
2. On the first view of Cynics see esp. A.A. Long's essay in this volume; on the tensions as well as the links between *kynisch* and *zynisch* or Cynics and "cynics" see the essay in this volume by H. Niehues-Pröbsting. Cynics clearly cultivated indifference to externals in both thought and act, though the term *adiaphora* ("things indifferent") may come in with the Stoics; see D.L. 6.2, 11–12, 14, 22–23, 29, 34, 38, 44, 58, 63, 69, 71–73, 79, 86, 88, 93, 97, 104–5, along with n. 47 below; Lucian, *Hermot.* 18 (on the "exaggerated indifference" that sets Cynics apart from the Stoics); and G. Giannantoni, *Socratis et Socraticorum Reliquiae,* 4 vols. (Naples 1990; hereafter "*SR*"), I H 9.40, n. 47(4, p. 491), n. 50(4, p. 521). Cynics turning to crime become criminals or at the very least hypocrites, occupational hazards perhaps, but at odds with effective outspokenness. Oscar Wilde's bantering (cynical) gloss is from Act 3 of *Lady Windermere's Fan.*

traced to an early opponent of Cynics who may even have once known Diogenes.[3] The more dignified image of the uppercase Cynic is austere, self-denying, and thus readily conflated with the stock virtuous pagan or indeed the stock Christian ascetic; not so with the second and less dignified image, which keeps far more disreputable company among truants and worldlings of every description from antiquity down to the present.

In this essay I first note the interdependence of these opposed images in Diogenes' own self-portrayal; I then follow out the generative history of the latter, unashamedly scandalous image through a standard medieval reference-entry concerning the Cynics to a series of jest-earnest transvaluations of cynic (and Cynic) unruliness among Renaissance and Reformation writers from Valla to More and More's archenemy Luther, to name but a few. In the structuralists' wake we are quicker than ever to seek out and define complementary yet opposite aspects of cultural phenomena, and in one sense this essay extends a long-standing tradition of characterizing the culture of Renaissance Europe in terms of a new, less uneven, but more volatile style of alliance between pagan and Christian directives than the more serene union now routinely called "medieval humanism."[4] What requires stressing here is the solvent and volatilizing effect of the Cynics' own self-conscious canine performance, not just in the sense that for men to play dogs confounds cultural categories, but, much more to the point, in the sense that for men to play dogs, making dogs' marginal nature a center of cultural concern, is to make both explicit and patent the weak grip of culture and culture's directives upon even dogs' nature, that is, upon nonhuman, non*verbal* nature at its most receptive. This account of dogs' nature is positional more than essential, even if dogs' own cultural positions may appear to be virtual constants; dogs are after all apt to seem marginally human and feral by turns, and the Cynics (like Freud) make dogs' casual indiscretions something more like a structurally pointed demonstration of how even culture's most fundamental distinctions can routinely constrain or distort.[5] As binary distinctions in Montaigne, for example, can serve mainly to highlight infixity,

3. Aristotle's disciple Clearchus of Soli, b. *ca.* 340 B.C., for whom Cynics were simply "bad dogs," merely barking and gluttonous (Athenaeus 13.611b [*SR*, V B 151; and n. 47, n. 8]; cf. Lucian, *Fugitivi* 16, and Epictetus, *Disc.* 3.22.50).

4. See R. W. Southern, *Medieval Humanism* (Oxford 1970); cf. also the writings of P. Courcelle, J. Leclercq, and D. W. Robertson. For the less easy interdependence of Christian and pagan directives (not simply "unworldly" and "worldly") in Renaissance contexts, see Bouwsma's fine study, here cited in n. 53, of competing Augustinian and Stoic identities in Renaissance humanism; cf. Stephen Greenblatt's kindred discussion of "self-cancellation" and "self-fashioning" as cited below in n. 80.

5. See Freud's *Civilization and Its Discontents,* trans. J. Strachey, *Standard Edition,* 24 vols. (London 1953–73), 21, p. 199, n. 1: "It would be incomprehensible, too, that man should use the name of his most faithful friend in the animal world—the dog—as a term of abuse if that creature had not incurred his contempt through two characteristics: that it is an animal whose dominant sense is that of smell and one which has no horror of excrement, and that it is not ashamed of its sexual functions"; cf. also K. Thomas, *Man and the Natural World* (New York 1983) esp. 102–13, and n. 31 below.

so in Cynic performance just as in the present essay an opening binary distinction like "Cynic" and "cynic" is as likely to end up transformed or reversed as sustained throughout in the same form; indeed this test of terms by impertinent Socratic inversion and self-schooled "indifference" may well be the most constant and generative feature of Cynic address to be traced anywhere in this survey.

Though the "bad" cynic's image never ceased to provoke, the extent to which reputable writers and thinkers were willing to patronize, countenance, and license this image in their own expressions did change rather dramatically as the Middle Ages drew to a close, a change signaling more basic shifts in the functional self-understanding of culture, at least Western culture, at large. For the Renaissance cult of transformative rhetoric unsurprisingly meant the jest-earnest ascendancy of an unrestrained new cultural skepsis as well, showing up or "defacing" all manner of overblown cultural norms as *mere* rhetoric, what cynics and Cynics since Crates routinely deride as mere *tuphos* ("hot air"); this same cynics'-corrective of mocking indifference as compounded unstably with Cynic and saintly detachment is what makes Cynic selfhood in its various styles an important if always unruly constituent of the rhetoric of modern identity, counterpointing as it does the ready-made Self of autarkic essentialist dogma or faith with an improvised self-on-the-make, with emergent, self-conscious contingency.[6]

Some may feel moved to discount this disreputable countertradition of cynic effrontery as a caricature more than a profile of what Cynics are or have been, and since medieval authors were fond of such partial and ad hoc descriptions it may seem not surprising at all that this image and the noble Christian-Stoicized Cynic exemplars surveyed here in S. Matton's work shared one cultural stage for so long without more efforts made to correct for their crucial discrepancies. What is rather more telling is how closely the same rogue-image shadows or dogs more presentable Cynic designs even outside the Middle Ages, to the point we may fairly suspect that at least some of its shocking lines have been drawn from live models after all, and that what passes now and again for the more dignified reality (the ascetic ideal as contrasted with cynic license in the Middle Ages) is in fact an alternative caricature. For whoever regards this same scandalous image as exposing its subjects conclusively, not much less than whoever neglects it *tout court,* simply misconstrues how scandal bears on a practice that after all rates ill repute (Greek *adoxia*) as another paradoxical good on a level with *ponos* or "toil" (D.L. 6.11); citing such ill repute to damn bona fide Cynics' rehearsed indiscretions is as captious or pointless as charging a Cynic with half-civilized canine behavior when half-civilized canine behavior

6. For a richly suggestive rogues'-history of early modern rhetorical identity which, however, omits to take note of the Cynic tradition, see W. A. Rebhorn, " 'The Emperor of Men's Minds': The Renaissance Trickster as *Homo Rhetoricus*," in *Creative Imitation: New Essays on Renaissance Literature in Honor of Thomas M. Greene* (Binghamton 1992) 31–66; cf. here also nn. 40, 51, 57.

is what frames Cynic skepsis in the first place. It is futile to attempt an ad hominem exposé of Cynic principle based on this or that shocking Cynic practice when the point of the practice in question *is* partly to shock, testing current decorum in the process. This is how Cynics (largely by way of Lucian's writings) helped to shape the reforming and critical agenda of a wide range of Renaissance humanists, and in one sense, at least, this exemplary testing represents a more vital extension of Cynic tradition than the tenuously continuous line of stock, morally uplifting citations that perpetuates some Cynics' names, in a sense, from antiquity down through the Middle Ages.[7] Worth suggesting, at least, is that since Cynics swear by "defacing" canonical values, canonized Cynic sayings and anecdotes may well falsify Cynic realities; a tame Stoicized-Christianized Cynic may be further from Cynic originals than no professed Cynic at all. Indeed, as we shall see, at times Cynic unruliness can deface or outface canonized Cynic values no less than the rest; Cynics routinely volatilize in their practice the same absolute self they assert, and their didactic postures are often, instructively often, just that. The most our vexed ad hominem critic can salvage from this exposé in good conscience is the charge that Cynics are (or were) merely theatrical, with less interest in what they are doing than in how it flouts workaday norms; but this mere Cynic theatricality, or the social-performative aspect of Cynicism and the Cynical aspect of social performance, is precisely the generative embarrassment for self-contained methods and systems of thought that gives rise to the Cynic tradition addressed in this essay.[8]

"Being asked what creature's bite is the worst, he [Diogenes] said, 'Of those

---

7. For the nondescript saintliness of a stock Christian-Stoicized Cynic see *The Dicts and Sayings of the philosophers*, ed. C.F. Bühler, EETS, no. 211 (London 1941) 62–73; also see Gower's *Confessio Amantis* 3.1201ff., 7.2229ff., and texts canvassed by S. Matton in this volume, along with J.L. Lievsay ("Some Renaissance Views of Diogenes the Cynic," in *Joseph Q. Adams Memorial Essays*, ed. J.G. McManaway et al. [Washington 1948], 447–55), G.D. Monsarrat (*Light from the Porch: Stoicism and English Renaissance Literature* [Paris 1984] 122–25), and F.G. Butler ("Who Are King Lear's Philosophers? An Answer," *English Studies* 67 [1986] 511–24).

8. Cf. also n. 80. Systematic solemnities are of course a prime target of Cynic jest-earnest or *spoudogeloion;* see esp. Branham's *Unruly Eloquence: Lucian and the Comedy of Traditions* (Cambridge, Mass., 1989), and on "defacing the currency" of workaday norms cf. Long's essay in this volume. On *parrhēsia* or "license" as a privilege habitually claimed by the Cynics and elsewhere often linked with dramatic or festive impertinence—with folk-jesters' and tricksters' impertinence, and Old Comic impertinence in particular—see H. Niehues-Pröbsting, *Der Kynismus des Diogenes* (Frankfurt 1979) 170–80 (citing Marcus Aurelius 11.6.4), Branham n. 47, and C.O. Brink, *Horace on Poetry: Epistles Book II* (Cambridge 1982), *ad Ep.* 2.1.145, 147. On the mainly bawdy license conceded or merely imputed to mimes in particular see esp. Ovid, *Tristia* 2.494–515, Martial 1.4.5–8; and E.K. Chambers, *The Medieval Stage*, 2 vols. (Oxford 1903), 1, p. 5 n. 3, with n. 61, below; cf. John of Salisbury, *Policraticus* 1.10, on those scurrilous mimes "who expose to all eyes turpitude even a Cynic would blush at." Diogenes himself in several anecdotes counterpoints his own extratheatrical practice to tragic performance (D.L. 6.24, 38, 64), and it clearly makes sense to connect at least some of his acts to the sort of informally "licensed" sympotic diversion provided by beggars in the *Odyssey*. Cf. n. 20, below, D.L. 6.27, 43, 54 (further calling Diogenes a "mad Socrates"), and Maximus of Tyre, *Disc.* 36.5–6 (*SR* V B 299), where flamboyant performance is what seems to win tolerance for Diogenes where the less flamboyant Socrates was persecuted.

that are wild a sycophant's; of those that are tame, a flatterer's" (D.L. 6.51).
"Being asked what he had done to be called a hound, he said, 'I fawn on those
who give me anything, I yelp at those who refuse, and I set my teeth in ras-
cals' " (D.L. 6.60). I do not wish to debate the authenticity of either or both of
these sayings; indeed my sole concern in relating the two is to mark the ambivalent position of dogs and their namesakes, the Cynics, between slanderers
and flatterers or "wild" and "tame" threats to a person's or culture's well-
being. What makes these the worst possible threats, wild and tame, is presumably just the dissembling, the lying and playacting, that typifies each; human
sign-use makes humans distinctively dangerous and treacherous even if it does
not necessarily make them distinctly humane. In the first of these sayings, Diogenes' own Cynic *parrhēsia* (plain speaking or license) seems to form an
indifferent and natural corrective for tendentious role-playing of either sort; in
the second, however, the stress shifts to the learned, rehearsed character of the
dogs' own responses, in which the Cynics' *own* vaunted spontaneous indifference is to say the least shockingly compromised. The importance of such tellingly unsettling shifts in the Cynics' self-representations does not rest on the
textual authority of this or that anecdote; the same pattern emerges again and
again, from the choice of the beggar's existence as a model for Cynic sufficiency to the layabout Cynic's celebration of *ponos* or "toil" to the transvaluation of "dog" from a term of abuse to a watchword. As distinguished by one
rhetorician at least, "Cynic style" can indeed involve still more emphatic ambivalence; "Cynic style," says Demetrius, is a style that fawns while it offends,
"wags its tail" while it "bites." [9] Cynic cultural skepsis begins at home (such
as it is), with ironically "shameless" self-exposure, and though Cynicism may
owe relatively little to Socrates the doctrinaire moralist, Socrates as a practical
ironist is perhaps its most crucial antecedent.[10] Nor is it just a question of con-
flating the sophistic and Socratic traditions as reflected in Cynic cultural skepsis; Socrates like the Cynics—but unlike most sophists— cultivated a lifestyle
or pose of unseriousness to see how much or little of what then passed for
serious could be shown up as merely a pose. Testing what can be said to accredit the ethos of beggars and dogs is a basic approach to what might be called
practical paradoxy, validating the conventionally valueless or endowing the
conventionally unprincipled with a more or less plausible set of principles,[11]
and not seldom the very effrontery of such a performance is what does most of

---

9. Demetrius, *De Eloc.* 261, on which see Branham (above, n. 8) 234. Cf. P.B. Corbett, *The
Scurra,* Scottish Classical Studies 2 (Edinburgh 1986), 4, on "the apparent paradox of the *scurra's*
personality, now pleasing entertainer, now social menace."

10. See Niehues-Pröbsting (above, n. 8), esp. 34–35, 63, 82–84, 171–74.

11. On the general practice of paradoxy see Rosalie Colie, *Paradoxia Epidemica: The Renaissance Tradition of Paradox* (Princeton 1966), esp. 3–71, 461–81 (on *King Lear*); cf. also n. 62,
below. For Antisthenes' rhetorical and practical transvaluing of poverty see Xenophon, *Mem.*
4.34–44; cf. *SR* NN. 23, 38, and 49 (4, pp. 511–12). For the ancient Cynics' skeptic affinities see
Branham (above, n. 8) 55, 225.

all to dispel the illusions of everyday. Placed on trial for his life, Socrates, for example, can treat his own impertinent engagements with workaday norms as corrective instead of corrupting, and can even demand a state stipend in lieu of the death sentence he actually gets. Cynics go even further in asserting didactic unseriousness (now reduced to the marginal ethos of beggars and dogs), yet consistently claim still more public rewards for *their* trying performances than did Socrates.[12] Worth remarking again is the social, staged character of at least this assertive scurrility: impudence is the mask the wise-fool and the Cynic, or the virtuous because self-confessed parasite, put on to speak truth.[13]

The bare mention of Cynics in this sort of company, notably in the company of professional fools and buffoons, *moriones* and *scurrae*, those egregiously trifling bit-partners in lordly or tawdry excess, may well seem to surpass even Cynic confusions of categories. Yet the link between Cynics and professional parasite-jesters is as ancient as Plautus and Horace at least; Plautus likens the professional outfit of the parasite-jester Saturio to that of a Cynic (*Persa* 123–26), while in Horace the timeserving hedonist Aristippus jokingly represents his own calling and that of Diogenes as just two rival styles of buffoonery: "While I play the buffoon for my own good, you play to the crowd" (*scurror ipse mihi, populo tu, Epist.* 1.17.19). Nor is this line of Cynic hangers-on just a Roman invention; "bad-dog" parasite-Cynics abound in Greek writers from Diogenes' day on down, as well. The point of such conflations is not just to stress dubious Cynics' disgraceful dependency in the face of their claims to autonomy; entertaining buffoonery is a trademark as well as not seldom a meal ticket for good Cynics—including Diogenes—and conventional parasites alike.[14]

Some regard Cynic shamelessness as a more extreme version of Socrates' irony; since aggressive shamelessness is at least as distinctive of parasite-*scurrae* as it is of Cynics,[15] the slur one later rival directed at Socrates is especially telling for our purposes: "Using the Latin term, Zeno the Epicurean . . .

---

12. See Plato's *Apology of Socrates,* esp. 36b–38b, and for Socrates' didactic shamelessness especially in the *Gorgias* see Long's essay in this volume. Begging Cynics, too, ask for their "due," not a dole (D.L. 6.46, 62).

13. For a comment comparing the antic truth-telling of the satyrlike, *atopos* Socrates with that of the Cynics see Branham (above, n. 8) 48–57. For Erasmus the image of the Silenus-box applies equally well to the sudden, unsettling disclosures of figures like these and to the discrepant literal and figurative meanings of Christian sacred Scripture; see his long adage-essay of 1515, "Alcibiades' Sileni."

14. For affinities between Cynics and Roman *scurrae* in particular see Corbett (above, n. 9) 24, 40–42, 56, 59, 62–64; for Greek writers on Cynic hangers-on see n. 3, above; Lucian, esp. *Symp.* 12–14, 19, *De Parasito* 53–54; and *Anth. Pal.* 11.154–58. For Diogenes himself as a battle-hardened parasite-jester see D.L. 6.46, 54–56, 58. More elaborately links parasites, Cynics, and *scurrae* in his own 1520 rebuttal of the French court-poet Brixius; see More's *Latin Poems,* in *Complete Works,* ed. R.S. Sylvester et al., 15 vols. (New Haven, 1962–; hereafter "*CW*"), 3/2, pp. 650–52, and *Epig.* 43 in that volume (with nn.) on a gluttonous-sounding Diogenes (D.L. 6.56).

15. See *Rhet. ad Her.* 4.10.14 and Pliny the Younger, *Epist.* 9.17; and cf. E. Welsford, *The Fool: His Social and Literary History* (New York 1936) esp. chaps. 1–3.

called Socrates, the very father of philosophy, the '*scurra* of Athens' " (Cicero, *De Nat. Deor.* 1.93). A crash course in translating this difficult word is afforded by Nicholas Udall in his 1542 translation of Erasmus's *Apophthegmata* (sig. xxx$_{ij}$), rendering *scurra Atticus* "the scoffer or hicke scorner of the cittie of Athens"; in his comments on §84 of the entries for Socrates (a saying taken from Plutarch, *Moralia* 10d, likening Old Comic mockery of Socrates to banqueting-license) Udall adds that professional "scoffers" or fools are a feature of many English banquets, as well. Just *how* Socrates scoffed is spelled out in the Christian apologist Lactantius's creative account (*Div. Inst.* 3.20) of how Socrates earned the title *scurra Atticus,* notably (says Lactantius) by swearing "by Dog" not "by God" (*ma ton kuna* and not *ma ton Zēna*); though the word *scurra* comes to mean mainly professional parasite-jesters or "trenchermen," "ribalds," and rogues, then as now one could play an impertinent "corrupter of words" without earning one's living as a *scurra.*[16] Ancient usage in Latin confirms that the *scurrae* themselves were both social and professional types; then as now, there were amateur scoffers as well as professionals, these last commonly doubling both on and off stage for an amateur "fast set" of dandies and wits. Perhaps casually hinting at this very convergence, Aristotle in his *Ethics* (*EN* 1108a20–26, 1127b24–1128b4) presents ironic self-deprecation and "buffoonery" or *bōmolokhia* in Greek as adjacent conversational vices; though he ties the two "vices" to the different mean-virtues of "straightforwardness" and decorous wit, it is not hard to class them instead as two more or less genial disparaging-styles that would later mark two sorts of *scurrae.*[17] Given also the ancient traditional links between "barking" and satire or verbal aggression in general, it is scarcely surprising to find "bad-dog" parasite-Cynics converging in their most definitive traits with those "wandering scoffers" whom one fourteenth-century churchman proclaims "good for nothing but eating and bad-mouthing." [18]

---

16. The fool Feste in Shakespeare's *Twelfth Night* styles himself at 3.1.36 a "corrupter of words," and thus takes after Udall's Diogenes (§3, loosely rendering D.L. 6.23): "the scholastical exercitacion and conferryng of *Plato* called in greeke *diatribên, Diogenes* by deprauyng and corruptyng the woorde [depravata voce *Er.*] called *katatribên,* that is, myspendyng of muche good labour and tyme. . . ." Concerning Socrates' oath, see Dodd's notes on Plato, *Gorg.* 482b5, 489e2.

17. Argyropoulos's Renaissance translation of the *Ethics* uses *scurra* to render *bōmolokhos;* see *CW* 4, p. 345. Self-disparaging jokes were thought equally typical of such *bōmolokhoi* ("altarhaunters" or "host-stalkers") and Roman *scurrae;* see Quintilian 6.3.82. Though the real derivation of *scurra* is uncertain, the medieval abundance of professional *scurrae* makes vague "parasite"-glosses quite common, e.g., *sequens curias, scutellam radens, discurrens,* and More's own punning *expers curarum.* Udall's "hicke scorner" renders the word with the like-sounding name of a well-known theatrical Vice (from *Hickscorner,* a play thirty years old as of 1542). More's associate John Palgrave equates "scoffers" with parasites, jesters, and wise-fools (*saigefols*) or "disours" in his 1530 *Lesclaircissement* and his 1540 *Acolastus;* see the *OED's* entries s.vv. Other glosses of *scurra,* e.g., "harlot" and "lecher," are less flattering still. See the 1570 *OED* entry, which makes "scoff" = *scommari* or *skōptein,* a "host-stalker's" trademark.

18. Thomas of Chobham, bishop of Worcester, *summa conf.,* d. 2 q. 2a "De histrionibus." As Corbett (above, n. 9: 81) notes, most of Chobham's remarks on this second class of "actors" (after

Clearly Socrates was not "just" a buffoon, nor were principal Cynics; but among other forms of rehearsed indiscretion, the Cynics quite clearly did practice didactic transgressions against conversational decorum of every sort. As Orlando Patterson has recently noted, the Cynics' against-the-grain code of misconduct (a code clamorously privileging "shamelessness," "ill repute," and, in practice, didactic indifference) is the "perfect antithesis" of Aristotle's own linkage-subjection of even courage itself to decorum and public perception (*EN* 1115a10–18); for the Cynics at large, even if they do dwell "not beneath shame but rather above it," shamelessness or effrontery and courage in general are indeed very closely akin.[19] Cynics sacrifice "face" to gain freedom, a fool's bargain by workaday reckonings, or a mystic's, or merely a rogue's; major Cynics' behavior has at times been regarded in each of these ways, and in view of the Cynics' own taste for transvalued contempt the most unprepossessing of these frames of reference may well prove as revealing as any. In their generous recourse to the roguish correctives of wit, major Cynics surpass even Socrates, and the volatile, leveling impertinence of the Cynics' rehearsed indiscretion comes still closer perhaps than the decorous wit authorized in the *Ethics* to the "educated insolence" (*pepaideumenē hybris, Rhet.* 1389b11) Aristotle elsewhere equates with wit proper.[20] Where they thrive, notably in the festive and carnival contexts they both share and shape,[21] such impertinent

mimes) are a paraphrase of Horace, *Ep.* 1.15.28–30, also written against *scurrae vagi* or free-ranging scoffers; Chobham's last phrase (*ad nihil utiles . . . nisi ad devorandum et maledicendum*) instead foregrounds the same "bad-dog" traits most routinely imputed to Cynics (cf. Bartholomaeus Anglicus 18.26; Rabanus Maurus, *De Universo, PL* 111, 224, on dogs; and my n. 3, above). On the canine affinities of invective and the poetry of blame see G. Nagy, *The Best of the Achaeans: Concepts of the Hero in Archaic Greek Poetry* (Baltimore 1979) 226–27, 315; Branham (above, n. 8) 234, 266; and Erasmus's discussion of the adage "*Canina facundia*" (*Adagia* 1234). Even Latin verse satire is *mordax* and *latrans*, like Cynics; see Horace, *Serm.* 1.4.93, 2.1.85, *Epist.* 1.17.18; Martial 4.53.1–8; and the further citations in Persius's *Satiren*, ed. W. Kissel (Heidelberg 1990), *ad* 1.107–15. Varro's prose-verse Menippean confections were called "Cynical satires" by some; one of them bore the title *Cave Canem* ("Beware the Dog" [Aul. Gell. 2.18.7, Nonius 75.22]), and Pompeii's *Cave Canem* mosaic affords an apt cover illustration for M. Coffey's *Roman Satire* (London 1974). For such canine satiric / satyric personas in England see A. Kernan, *The Cankered Muse* (New Haven 1959) 91, 96, 105–6, 122–23, 155; and the *OED* entries for "cynic." "Satyrs" standardly figure with "dog-headed men" or baboons, on which see Pliny, *Nat. Hist.* 8.216; Plato, *Theaet.* 161c; and above, n. 13.

19. O. Patterson, *Freedom* (New York 1991–) 1, p. 185; for the saving distinction "not beneath shame but rather above it" see *SR*, I H 9.49–51; cf. here also n. 46.

20. On this gloss in relation to banqueting-license see N.R.E. Fisher, *Hybris: A Study in the Values of Honour and Shame in Ancient Greece* (Warminster 1992) 12, 91, and index s.v. "symposia"; cf. also my nn. 8 and 17. In the *Ethics* (*EN* 1128a34) Aristotle speaks of the buffoon as being "mastered" by laughter; one could stress just as well (see Quintilian 6.3.8), how buffoons' laughter even masters others. On Cynic wit as accommodation as well as defiance see Niehues-Pröbsting (above, n. 8) 85–87, 182–83, and Branham (above, n. 8) esp. 22, 25, 50, 60–62. At Eph. 5.3 the Vulgate translates *eutrapelia* or "wit" as *scurrilitas*.

21. Cf. C. Clifford Flanigan, "Liminality, Carnival, and Social Structure: The Case of Late Medieval Biblical Drama," in *Victor Turner and the Construction of Cultural Criticism,* ed. K.M. Ashley (Bloomington 1990); 42–63. On the other hand, Cynic performance is often at odds with the more or less ritual containment of carnival release in Bakhtin's, and indeed "anti-structure" in Turner's sense.

cynic (and Cynic) "corrupters of words" affront not so much persons as personal limits, indeed recognized limits in general. This same vast yet offhand recreational feat of suspending as well as revising such limits, bringing "strained expectations to nothing" as Kant once suggests, is what widely gains jokers like these both the outrage of formally vested authorities and the tolerance or license informally shared by fools "natural" and fools "artificial" alike, *moriones* and masters of staged indiscretion not seldom including the Cynics.[22]

I am scarcely the first to suggest a connection between Cynics and various traditional "licensed" fools; perhaps less routine here is the ongoing argument that in recasting so much of personal freedom in terms of fool's license and antic impertinence Cynics not only claimed a more absolute negative freedom but enlarged the rhetorical boundaries of self-recognition to make room for revised understandings of positive freedom as well.[23] Cynic license was freedom-in-the-making as opposed to the ready-made freedom attending on birth, reputation, and rank; by discounting such status-linked freedoms completely, the Cynics made sure that "that which was called freedom in some" would seem outlandish "license" in Cynics per se.[24] The same flouting of outward constraints that makes more than a few major medieval authors construe Cynic license as merely an outrageous sham of sublime unconstraint is an antic unsettling-device of a sort that proves far more congenial to rhetorically playful Renaissance humanism, though still frequently under attack from conservatives both new and old; between glamorous rhetorical game and intently subversive display, Cynic license along with Socratic dissembling in Renaissance writers

22. Kant, *Critique of Judgment* §54. More and Luther both clearly refer to fool's license in virtually those words, while Erasmus's much-copied defense of the *Folly* in a letter to Dorp of May 1515 clarifies that both fools and buffoons, *moriones* and *scurrae,* by long-standing tradition are free to mock even "the most violent tyrants"; he refers to Suetonius's *Vespasian* 20 as a typical ancient example. Cf. Shakespeare's *Troilus and Cressida* 2.3.54 on the "privileged" detractor Thersites (a both "good" *and* "bad" Cynic-exemplar in Lucian [*Demonax* 61, *Fugitivi* 30]; a satiric exemplar in M. Seidel, *Satiric Inheritance: Rabelais to Sterne* [Princeton 1979] 4–5). On Diogenes, Thersites, and the Renaissance "licensed fool" see R.H. Goldsmith, *Wise Fools in Shakespeare* (E. Lansing 1955) 8–10, and R.C. Elliott, *The Power of Satire: Magic, Ritual, Art* (Princeton 1960) 133; Bakhtin similarly links Menippean invention with carnival license and the carnivalesque, in *Rabelais and His World,* trans. H. Iswolsky (Bloomington 1984).

23. On this Cynic reduction, or seeming reduction, see esp. D.L. 6.69, 71; along with Theophrastus, *Characters* 28 (*Kakologia*), on the (probably Cynic) *kakologos* ("ill-speaker") who "calls ill-speaking *parrhēsia* and 'democracy' and 'freedom,' and makes this out as the best thing in life" and on positive and negative freedoms and what each has to do with the Cynics cf. Patterson (above, n. 19) 3, 192, and 220. I share Patterson's sense of the interdependence of positive and negative freedoms ("self-fulfillment" distinguished from sheer unconstraint) but doubt his sense that Cynics professed a "purely negative freedom"; rather they sought a way to shed outward selves' spurious fulfillments in case these obscured others less false. Cf. also R. Sorabji, *Animal Minds and Human Morals* (Ithaca 1993) 158–61.

24. See Quintilian 3.8.48, a discussion of speakers' personas, concluding, "That which is freedom in some is called license in others, and while some get by on sheer authority, certain others are barely brought off safely by reason itself."

of more than one cultural stamp would transform the decorums of authoring, with all that implies.

To frame our overview of the Cynics' medieval retreat we should note well one crucial affinity between culture from Plato to Lucian and the culture of Renaissance Europe: both of these were distinctly rhetorical cultures, each unusually apt to consider itself as rhetorically constructed, and hence as potentially *re*constructed.[25] For all their discontents, which were many, and often remarked on by Cynics and others, these intensely rhetorical cultures were at any rate far less intent than the medieval Christian establishment on sustaining a view of their own institutions as given, not made, providential, not merely provisional.[26] It is here in the free play of Renaissance rhetorical showmanship that the anti-institutionalism of the earliest Cynicism finds a public again despite medieval heresy-law and despite all the sanitized trappings of Christianized Stoicism; Christianized Cynic sages and doomed cynic scoundrels regroup on the frontier and indeed in the clamorous forum of Renaissance culture, quick to make the most out of the general confusion when two such safely disparate profiles of social eccentrics turn out to be two sides of one.[27] Nonetheless the chief basis of this Cynic resurgence is not just some ecstatic revival of pagan exuberance but a cool, sometimes grudging reacquaintance with Socrates' insight (Plato, *Apol.* 38a) that a culture impervious to skepsis is a culture finally out of control. Though the changing sociology of marginal types toward the end of the Middle Ages meant that commonplace representations of beggars and dogs, for example, could sometimes take on opposed cultural valences, more than ever these came to supply twinned alternative visions to reckon with, one of them the perspective of sinless instinctiveness (animal primitivism in Erasmus's *Praise of Folly* or Montaigne's *Apology for Raymond Sebond*) and the other of roguish adaptiveness (picaresque self-exposure and the pageants of would-be rogue-heroes and master-pretenders from More's Richard III to the latter's redoubtable doubles in Shakespeare's self-styled player-kings).[28] In between lies—or *lies*—the unstable theatrical space where

25. Cf. Rebhorn (n. 6 above), J. Altman, *The Tudor Play of Mind* (Berkeley and Los Angeles 1978); and *CW* 15, "Introduction," esp. chaps. 2–3.

26. R. A. Markus (*Saeculum: History and Society in the Theology of St. Augustine* [Cambridge 1970]) notes how later medievals turned Augustine's distinction between the City of God and the City of Man into a more or less absolute charter for Christian hegemony; likewise A. Kemp elaborates a parallel between steady Apostolic succession and unbroken *translatio imperii* as twin charters for medieval church and state (*The Estrangement of the Past* [New York 1991] chap. 2). On provisional attempts to approximate Providence see *CW* 15, pp. lxvi–lxxviii.

27. See P. Stallybrass and A. White, *The Politics and Poetics of Transgression* (Ithaca 1986) 27–28, on the Renaissance market as a scene for transgressive performances; and Rebhorn (n. 6 above) on the rhetorician as trickster.

28. On More's would-be rogue-hero and his twins in Shakespeare see my forthcoming article, "The Tyrant Being Slain: Afterlives of More's *History of King Richard III*," and cf. Rebhorn's account (n. 6 above) of the trickster as *homo rhetoricus*. On the altering status of marginal types in this period see N. Z. Davis, *Society and Culture in Early Modern France* (Stanford 1975)

most moderns transact their identity in good faith or bad, the precarious scene of a self on the make that is still at least make-believe Self, if not Self in the making.

Again taking Diogenes as a point of departure, a kind of antithetical complementarity connects Cynic performance on the margins of seriousness with more solemn performances at the center. The Cynic rhetoric of antirhetoric[29] is remarkably enough more congenial to rhetorical culture than it is to a culture professing some more secure grounding than rhetoric, since rhetorical culture can register Cynic critiques and correctives as a limit on its own ungrounded excesses, and thus as a practical warrant of its own good faith. The Cynic's overt subversiveness mocks and counters the covert subversions performed by abusers of rhetoric, and thereby in a qualified way vindicates rhetoric's business-as-usual. In the meantime, what warrants the good faith of the Cynic "control" is precisely its stubborn unruliness, its refusal to go along peacefully even with the persistent attempts to coopt and idealize its project we noted above. For along with the canine "indifference" that is commonly stressed in the commentaries there is also a stress on dogs' excellent native discernment;[30] it is less that dogs fail to discriminate where it matters most than that dogs have a different idea of where it matters most to discriminate. To set this protocol of unruliness in a context of (virtual) sociology, Cynics stage a strategic confusion of marginal categories; indeed this is what makes the largely gestural, occasional character of unruliness or demonstrative nonconformity more germane to the study of Cynics than such relatively static conceptions as transgressiveness or even marginality. Likewise, one can interpret Diogenes' own unconventional style as a disruptive medley or muddle of marginal types undertaken precisely to call centering ideals into question. Topographically marginal watchdogs and bona fide exiles alike, economically marginal beggars, psychologically marginal madmen and fools, and of course ontologically and ethically

---

chap. 2; A.L. Beier, *Masterless Men: The Vagrancy Problem in England 1560–1640* (London 1985); P. Burke, *The Historical Anthropology of Early Modern Italy* (Cambridge 1987) chaps. 6–7; A.F. Kinney, ed., *Rogues, Vagabonds, and Sturdy Beggars,* 2d ed. (Amherst 1990); and M. Koch, "The Desanctification of the Beggar in Rogue Pamphlets of the English Renaissance," in *The Work of Dissimilitude,* ed. G. Allen and R.A. White (Newark 1992), 91–104; and Scase (n. 38, here). Cf. also A.C. Spearing, "The Poetic Subject from Chaucer to Spenser," in *Subjects on the World's Stage,* ed. D.G. Allen and R.A. White (Cranbury, N. J., 1995), 13–37.

29. Cf. Branham's essay in this volume and G. Braden's account of unreconciled Stoic invention in Renaissance contexts, *Renaissance Tragedy and the Senecan Tradition: Anger's Privilege* (New Haven 1985). In addition see P. Valesio's "The Rhetoric of Antirhetoric," a discussion of Cordelia's expressive rejection of rhetoric in Shakespeare's *King Lear* 1.2 (*Novantiqua: Rhetorics as a Contemporary Theory* [Bloomington 1980] 41–60). It seems telling that one book distinctly averse to chief humanists' view of persuasion as a cultural artifact (see *CW* 3.2, pp. 578–84) also slights what could be called the rhetoric of Cynic impertinence; see K.J.E. Graham, *The Performance of Conviction: Plainness and Rhetoric in the Early English Renaissance* (Ithaca 1994).

30. Noting dogs' gifts for "outspokenness, examination, and discernment" (*to parrhēsiastikon kai elegktikon kai diakritikon*) is a quite standard way to gloss "Cynic"; cf. *SR,* I H 9; and *SR,* V B 27, 149; and see Plato, *Rep.* 2.376a, on dogs' quasi-philosophical discerning faculty.

marginal trickster-performers and buffoons either challenge or reinforce centering ideals to the same extent each keeps its cognitive place;[31] yet the ritual
fixity of these marginal states actually dwindles at every new stage of the series
just sketched, and a posture of Cynic (or upstart) "indifference" flouts not only
these saving and damning distinctions but moreover the putative absolutes they
serve to guard.

The degrading of rhetoric in medieval culture is indeed more a parallel
symptom than a cause of the Cynic retreat. A rhetorical approach to conviction
itself as an artifact is quite clearly at odds with implicit, embedded, essentialist
assumptions of the sort that sustained most medieval institutions; it is also quite
clearly the complement as well as the converse of the rhetoric of exposé favored by cultural skeptics from Diogenes to Montaigne and beyond. Similarly,
an essentialist habit of thought is unlikely to grant more than a strained, or
occasionally depraved, allegorical interest (and in terms of new cultural insights, no interest at all) to a penchant for "playing the dog." To the very extent
that what publicly passes for fixed in the marginal status of dogs, or men treated
"like" dogs, limits what can be learned from such marginal rhetorical postures,
it also rules out the Cynic cultural skepsis that makes these its own points of
departure; thus the breakdown of rigid, theoretically bolstered distinctions between sanctioned and unsanctioned marginal types at the end of the Middle
Ages did as much to advance Renaissance Cynic performance as it did to per-
plex early modern responses to real vagrants and other outsiders.

The traditional disjunctive reception of Cynics outside their first forensic
milieu might be called in one sense an exemplary instance of medieval
Christian "charitable reading," in another, tendentious misprision or descriptive dividing-and-conquering.[32] What has come to be known after Erwin Panofsky as the medieval "rule of disjunction," a phrase usefully glossing the
piecemeal medieval reception of classical themes and motifs, applies in an especially precocious, determining way to the Cynics' medieval *fortuna*,[33] and

31. See D. Krueger's discussion in this volume linking Cynic transgression of cultural boundaries to Mary Douglas's treatment of structuring taboos; cf. my own n. 6, on the Cynic as trickster,
and Stallybrass and White (above, n. 27) 44–48, on the Renaissance carnivalesque and unclean
beasts, esp. pigs and dogs, as symbolic or *model* confounders of cultural categories. For the symbolic linkage, see also here n. 47.

32. For medieval Christian "charitable reading," see esp. D. W. Robertson, *A Preface to
Chaucer: Studies in Medieval Perspectives* (Princeton 1962) 342–43; for broader perspective on
the stakes of such normalization see R. Simon, "The Moral Law and Discernment," in *Discernment of the Spirit and of Spirits,* ed. C. Floristán and C. Duquoc (New York 1979), 74–83.

33. On this generally unconscious and chronically medieval style of defacing a cultural currency see C. F. Stinger, *Humanism and the Church Fathers: Ambrogio Traversari (1386–1439)
and Christian Antiquity in the Italian Renaissance* (Albany 1977) 72: "In these medieval accounts
Socrates and the other Greek philosophers appear strangely transmogrified into the guise of contemporary sages, . . . a phenomenon Erwin Panofsky has termed the 'principle of disjunction.' "
For specific examples of such transformed Cynics see n. 7, above. Panofsky's well-known
principle (*Renaissance and Renascences in Western Art* [New York 1969] 85–90) is regularly

that fact itself may tell us much about just how unsettling the first Cynics' (self-) disclosures could be; for a kind of forced accommodation of Cynics construed in a way that rules out or makes something quite alien of Cynic affronts to conventional proprieties seems to start long before the great age of such piecemeal reception in medieval Europe, and indeed not long after Diogenes' death in the writings of Zeno the Stoic. Renaissance rhetoric's teasing reassertions of Cynic "indifference" helped expose and reverse such tendentious disjunctions not just in this one local tradition of piecemeal reception, but elsewhere as well, until Cynic rehearsed indiscretion could once more set or upset the stage for still bolder displays of unauthorized cultural discovery.[34]

The medieval reception of Cynicism salvaged (so to speak) all that it could of the Cynics' nonconformity, and consistently savaged or demonized the rest; this ambivalent form of reception reveals not just authentic convergence between Cynic and Christian cultural skepsis as far as the latter extends, but moreover a more general tendency on the part of medieval Christianity to delimit the scope of a Christianized cultural skepsis as well as the province of orthodox charity by adopting some marginal types as unworldly, and therefore deserving, while rejecting the rest as unnatural, hence rightly suppressed. Christian cultural skepsis, as the functional exposure of rival ("un-Christian") conventions, is end-stopped, programmatic, and conducive to stable recentering; Cynic cultural skepsis runs instead to more dogged, "indifferent" affronts to the cultural center per se. As for actual convergence with Cynic concerns, Christian teaching begins with its own style of practical paradox; what else are we to make of the sayings that the last shall be first or that God has elected the foolish of this world to confound the wise?[35] Institutional Christianity could scorn all forms of Cynic excess very much the way Lucian scorns that of "poor" Cynics, to play down its own links to the Cynics' unruly propensities; nonetheless, the two clearly continued to share a great deal. At some moments

invoked to distinguish between medieval fragmenting of classical culture and Renaissance efforts to reintegrate it, but to reintegrate it in a way that restores its distinctness; of course this is disjunction as well, but now recognized rather than randomized. Cf. here also nn. 26, 40, 53, 54. Thus the newly acknowledged or "featured" convergence of Cynic license and theatrical fool's license helped revive Cynic "teaching impertinence" elsewhere in the Renaissance; cf. Goldsmith as cited in n. 22 above.

34. Cf. *CW* 3/1, pp. 5–7, and *CW* 15, pp. 90–92, and nn. (Lucianic irreverence along with philological skepsis as a platform for cultural self-scrutiny). On the Stoics' dilutions of Cynic principles see texts cited in nn. 2, 42, and 47.

35. On the early convergence of Cynic and Christian see F. G. Downing, *Cynics and Christian Origins* (Edinburgh 1992), and n. 1 to D. Krueger's essay in this volume. "Antinomian" and "libertine" are first used to refer to extreme antilegalist Christians in Luther's own era; both these terms are now often employed for antilegalist early Christians as well. See, for instance, H. Maccoby, *The Myth-maker: Paul and the Invention of Christianity* (New York 1987) 191–202, likening Saint Paul, the Gnostics, and much later antinomian Christians. My "unworldly"-"unnatural" contrast has a half-punning analogue in the terms *mundo mortui / immundi* routinely employed for monastics and Cynics, respectively.

Augustine can sound very much like Diogenes, for example in mocking the faulty perspectives of readers who fret about Dido's *malheurs* while forgetting to look to their own or in characterizing all manner of noble exertions as merely the trappings of pride.[36] Other Christian Fathers clearly admired Cynic asceticism and took Cynic disaffection with secular custom as a kind of example for their own; Cynics not seldom feature with "gymnosophists," the Brahmins or "naked philosophers" of India, as models of noble contempt for the trappings of worldly authority.[37] Among begging or mendicant orders the Dominicans called themselves *Domini canes,* "the Lord's dogs," the foes of heretical foxes or wolves; but still more reminiscent of Cynic rehearsed indiscretion, as of ancient Cynic sermonizing, was the crowd-pleasing style of Franciscan street-preachers, whom Saint Francis himself once described as the "jesters of God."[38] Even so it is none too surprising that the Renaissance Cynic resurgence proceeded with blast after blast at the ultimate cultural complacency of these very preachers, "vested Cynics" whose unworldliness, much like that of Lucian's Cynic-impostors, could at times seem more like a new costume for secular custom than an apt uniform for dismantling it.

We have already seen how the medieval Christian establishment could take

---

36. See *Confessions* 1.13.20 with P. Brown, *Augustine of Hippo* (Berkeley and Los Angeles 1967) 305–10; and Downing (above, n. 35) 224–27 (cf. *CW* 15, pp. xlviii–xlix), summarizing the cultural exposé of the *City of God* (though the *tuphos/superbia* connection suggests a still closer Cynic link; for especially close analogues see Diogenes in D.L. 6.27 and 6.72. The latter passage on nobility as the trappings of villainy became almost a motto for Cynic cultural skepsis in the face of Christian-Stoic civic humanism; see, for instance, A. Rabil, Jr., ed., *Knowledge, Goodness and Power: The Debate over Nobility among Quattrocento Italian Humanists* (Binghamton 1991) 83, 219, 283, and cf. *CW* 3/1, p. 168, and here n. 60, with L. Valla's (and Machiavelli's) deciphering of *honestum* or "decency" in terms of expediency. For the Lutheran-Augustinian gloss of pagan virtues as *splendida vitia* see C. Thompson's edition of Erasmus's *Inquisitio de Fide* (New Haven 1950) esp. 106–7. Rabil's first quote is from Poggio Bracciolini's *De Nobilitate* (*Opera* [Basel 1538] 79); for another pair of references derogatory to Cynics see *Opera* 385.

37. Cf. *SR* 2, V B 529, H 8–12, and P. Brown, "The Challenge of the Desert," in *A History of Private Life,* vol. 1, *From Pagan Rome to Byzantium,* ed. P. Veyne, trans. A. Goldhammer (Cambridge, Mass., 1987), 289: "The monastic paradigm drew on the more radical aspects of the pagan philosophic counterculture, most notably on the magnificently asocial lifestyle of the Cynics." The traditional pairing of Cynics and gymnosophists apparently began with Diogenes' student Onesicritus, who accompanied Alexander to India; see Strabo 15.1.65. St. Jerome links the gymnosophists and Diogenes as similarly saintly disdainers of great rulers' homage (*SR* 2, V B 175, abridging *Adversus Iovinianum* 2.14).

38. On Dominicans see W. P. Eckert, "Der Hund . . . und andere Attribute des h. Dominicus," *Symbolon,* n.s. 5 (1980), 31–40 (and more generally *The Book of Beasts,* trans. T. H. White [New York 1954], 66); on street-preaching see Downing (above, n. 35) 21–23, and on preaching in general, G. R. Owst, *Literature and Preaching in Medieval England* (Oxford 1961); and on the Franciscans as God's jesters see J. Saward, *Perfect Fools* (Oxford 1980) 84–88, with J.-M. Fritz, *Le discours du fou au Moyen Age* (Paris 1992) pp. 189, 317–18. For prehumanist invective against friars, see W. Scase, *"Piers Plowman" and the New Anti-Clericalism* (Cambridge 1989); cf. More in *CW* 15 (s.v. "friars") and Erasmus, *Praise of Folly* (*Opera Omnia,* ed. J. Waszink et al. [Amsterdam 1969–; hereafter *"ASD"*]), 4/3, esp. pp. 159–68 (friars as shameless play-actors and part-time parrhesiasts), with the colloquy *Ptōkhoplousioi* ("The Rich Beggars," *ASD* 1/3, p. 397) on Franciscans as *mundi moriones.*

up or incorporate not just Cynic assertion but street-preachers' impertinence, as well. Catholic sorting of sanctioned and unsanctioned Cynic behavior was of course a reflection of more general doctrinal imperatives, and the actual standard of sorting could change with the times; thus Franciscans' flirtations with popular unruliness more than once brought them close to being treated not as unworldly zealots but rather as unnatural subversives and heretics. The church nonetheless found similar saving distinctions for several other marginal types, from the virtuous poor to the innocent foolish or mad, and even to the idea of the reverent theatrical player, though the church generally chose to recruit its own amateur players before trusting its pageants to those cynics-at-large, the professionals.[39] What could not be absorbed was, however, ejected, and as Cynic expansive indifference was wholly at odds with the church's selective approach to critiquing and testing specific institutions, Cynicism with its outspoken code of misconduct, at least in the West, was consigned to the fringes of orthodox discourse, or even beyond. One should not after all fetishize one "legitimate" tradition for an antitraditional point of view; what we have is repeated emergence, a long history of disconnected jest-earnest feints, and a war of doctrinal attrition in which even the occasional bid to condemn cynic impertinence completely could do no more than lend a new topical aptness to old "scoffs." In its wayward and masterless way, cynic discourse indeed not uncommonly thrived on the margins to which it was forced, thrived not least because it was *not* heresy despite frequent suspicions to the contrary, and because it shunned autos-da-fé no less keenly than the flames of unquestioning zeal.[40] Even uppercase Cynics had shown scant taste for martyrdom, though some Christians did find something of the same sort to admire even in this or

39. On the poor see n. 28 above; on the foolish see n. 15, W. Willeford, *The Fool and His Scepter* (Evanston 1976), and Fritz (above, n. 38); on the mad see further P. Doob, *Nebuchadnezzar's Children: Conventions of Madness in Middle English Literature* (New Haven 1974); on professional actors see E. K. Chambers (n. 8 above); W. Hartung, *Die Spielleute: Eine Randgruppe in der Gesellschaft des Mittelalters* (Wiesbaden 1982); S. Mullaney, *The Place of the Stage: License, Play, and Power in Renaissance England* (Chicago 1988) chaps. 1–2; and my n. 40.

40. On these wayward and masterless cynic inventions *sans titre,* which of course admit more than one critical approach, see, for instance, M. Bakhtin, *Rabelais and His World,* trans. H. Iswolsky [Cambridge, Mass., 1968]), and R. H. Bloch, *The Scandal of the Fabliaux* Chicago 1988); cf. also B. Taylor, *Vagrant Writing: Social and Semiotic Disorders in the English Renaissance* (Toronto 1991). As peripheral and collateral to proper traditions (cf. *Adagia* 1211: *Qui semel scurra, nunquam paterfamilias!*) the whole history of cynic invention, at least, is a model compromised and contingent, *novelistic* tradition or a history of discontinuities; cf. nn. 18 and 33 above; and on such novelistic or "bastard" descents see esp. M. Robert, *Origins of the Novel,* trans. S. Rabinovitch (Bloomington 1980), 21–37, 187. For the *jongleurs* and actors as a "church of the wicked" (*ecclesia malignantium,* Ps. 25.5; cf. 21.16) or a "school of abuse" (cf. Tertullian, *De Spec.* 17) see Owst (n. 38 above) esp. 93, 327; Hartung (n. 39 above), esp. 42 n. 44, E. K. Chambers, *The Elizabethan Stage* (London 1923; hereafter "*ES*") vol. 4; and J. Barish, *The Antitheatrical Prejudice* (Berkeley and Los Angeles 1968); for the Cynics as a heresy and not merely a pre-Christian sect see nn. 47–49, below, and Matton's essay in this volume. For Tertullian's praise of Cynic suicides see Downing (above, n. 35) 205, and cf. my n. 60.

that Cynic suicide. Matton's learned account (also found in this volume) of a rich Latin Cynic anecdotal tradition shows how much praise routinely attached to particular Cynics and Cynic ideas once detached from their unruly backgrounds, that is, once recast in terms dear to medieval Christian humanism: the same study shows just how much hate and suspicion attached to the Cynics en masse (not just lowercase cynics) once aligned with unruly or heterodox groups closer to the same authors' realities. In what may be the most telling contrary legacies of the piecemeal medieval reception that we have just sketched, renowned Cynics like Diogenes himself could end up virtual saints while their sect, mainly named as a front for generic unsavory abuse, could seem merely a monstrous excuse to go straight to the dogs. Indeed most authors seem to have known very little about Cynicism as an ethical stance or a coherent practice, though implicitly sharing at least some Cynic viewpoints; what they generally do seem to have known, as the glosses attest, is the Cynics' reputed, or at least ill-reputed, affinity for foul speech and foul acts, and in both these foul playacting. Trying on our own practical paradoxy, let us see what there is to be said for this scurrilous pack of bad-mouthers, loose-livers, and shape-shifting rogues.

Christian Fathers had no lack of precedents for linking the Cynics in general with foul speech (*turpiloquium*), and foul speech with some inner depravity; yet foul speech in the sense of unseemly expression may be just what a mind in the grip of false seeming has most need to hear. The long-standing connection of Cynics with satire suggests that what frequently passes for Cynic abusiveness may be just an unflattering rhetorical mirror;[41] certainly the unflattering mirror the Franciscans routinely held up could seem no less abusive than this, and at times even more so. Here the difference between edifying and abusive may be strictly dependent on a higher institutional authority, and the scope of such higher authority is just what the Cynics set out to test. We might offer a similar accounting for the Cynics' celebrated foul *acts,* generally breaches of sexual decorum, from Diogenes' reported masturbation in public to the no less notorious Dog-duo of Crates-Hipparchia and their alleged trysts in the street: bizarre conduct by virtually any standard, but not ill conceived as a way of exploring the difference as well as the affinities between natural and cultural dictates or indeed, for that matter, between sanctity and civil routine. Christian Fathers detested the "utterly vain turpitude" of such acts, treating them as affronts to august institutions in general including the church.[42] In a treatment of

41. See n. 18 above.
42. For Diogenes' public masturbation see D.L. 6.46, 69; cf. *SR*, N. 51 (4, pp. 533–35), and Niehues-Pröbsting (n. 8, above) 157–67. For Crates and Hipparchia, who supposedly consummated their "dog-marriage" (*kunogamia,* var. *koinogamia*) in public, see D.L. 6.97 and *SR*, V B 529, V H 19, 21–24, and *SR*, N. 54 (4, pp. 565–66). For the orthodox disgust at Diogenes' unseemly solo see *SR*, V B 426–27 and Jerome on Ephes. 5.3 (*PL* 26.519). Orthodox Christian authors appear to be at least as sensitive to how "dog-marriage" flouts the conventional proprieties, and indeed almost

sexual shame as a token of original sin Augustine even goes so far as to speculate (*Civ. Dei* 14.20) that the first Cynics merely staged play-acts or just went through the (blanketed) motions of sex in the street; their residual shame would have stopped them from having real sex, or if they had, the mob would have stoned them, that is, would have martyred or made an example of them for displaying a Cynic sexual freedom that went beyond what Augustinian dogma could countenance, that is, beyond show.

It seems clear where the problem lies here: the same regimen of shame that Augustine presents as a transcendent mandate of social control is assailed by Diogenes, for one, as a cultural construct that the Cynic may show up at will. In its tactically shocking assertions of natural freedom, but not only there, Cynic practice presented a real, even fundamental credal affront, an affront Petrarch saw even in the considerably more decorous independence displayed by the autarkic gymnosophists. To the extent that autarkic ascetics could actually dispense with the world, they could also dispense with a transcendent make-good for their inner worth;[43] self-reliance pursued to extremes made church doctrine seem worldly as well. Active Cynic displays of disdain for conventional marriage and conventional sexual reserve, scorning privacy as essentially a mask for embarrassment and enslavement to public perception, further challenged the rule of *honestum* or "decency" as a charter of cultural dependency and as the sanction conferred by mere standard procedure on dynastic institutions in general. The simplest orthodox counter to such Cynic displays, though completely at odds with the ethos of ironic self-deprecation and indeed of all practical paradox, was to play to the casual, orthodox or lay-cynic's assumption that there are no sane self-exposers but only poseurs, and that whoever courts ill repute deserves all that he or she gets if not more, reading Cynic rehearsed indiscretion in public as merely the last and most desperate symptom of a more general self-uncontrol.[44] Not surprisingly, then, shocking Cynic behavior was

---

equally sensitive whether it involves Cynics or dogs; to the Christian texts cited in V B 524, V H 25 add Augustine, *Civ. Dei 14.20* [title] (*De Vanissima Turpitudine Cynicorum*); *Contra Iul.* 3.7.16 (*ut remota honestate nuptiarum omnes indifferenter ac passim canino more concumberent*); *Serm.* 8.4.5 (*caninum est parentes non cognoscere*); Jerome, *Ep.* 69.4 (*ut passim caninas nuptias iungeres*); and nn. 47–49 below. Many of these attacks have sectarian motives, but also sustain a traditional invective against Cynic disrespect and indecency that was already well under way in the writings of Cicero (*De Off.* 1.26.128, 1.41.148; cf. *De Fin.* 3.57 and Braden (above, n. 29) 73–80, on eventual Stoic rejection of the Cynic pursuit of *adoxia*. Here but not only here Stoic claims to a Cynic affinity become more and more partial with time; a Diogenes might have lampooned the Stoa as a doghouse reserved for ex-dogs.

43. Petrarch, *De Vita Solitaria* 2.6.1, in *Opera Omnia* (Basel 1554; repr. Ridgewood 1965) I, p. 313. The inordinate self-reliance of the gymnosophists links them to the Stoics as well as Pelagians; on autarky and the sage's political mastery (*sapientis imperium*) see *SR*, N. 50 (4, p. 522) with n. 28 above, and for Pelagius and the Stoics in relation to orthodox Christianity see P. Brown (above, n. 36) 367. Julian the Pelagian took a Cynic approach to contesting the global predominance of sexual shame; see Augustine, *Op. Imperf.* 4.43–44 (*PL* 45.362–64).

44. Hence the commonplace judgment that makes public licentiousness, as pernicious *unguardedness,* conduct that others have every right to restrict. But the Cynic's self-mastery starts at home, hence if true (*alēthēs*) will have nothing to hide or to guard from the public; cf. D.L. 6.69;

habitually cited to no other end than to make a portentous example of Cynics and their style of selfhood, just as one major medieval source crowns its brief against "blasphemous," "atheistical" Lucian with the claim that dogs ate him alive for his blasphemous words, a portentously tidy example of a biter well bit.[45]

Something like the Cynic challenge to conventional marriage along with other ruling conventions of secular social decorum was allowed, indeed even prescribed, in the confines or spiritual privacy of monastic and clerical institutions. Prohibition of marriage for monks, nuns, and eventually priests helped confirm their ascent beyond common mortality by God's common grace, not their own strength, so that they themselves posed no real threat to dynastically ratified hierarchy; recognizing this highly prestigious, unthreatening priestly way out was one point of the change when Aegidius Romanus, a student of Saint Thomas Aquinas, took the claim that a stateless existence is for either a beast or a god and referred it instead to unmarried existence or celibacy.[46] But in flouting conventional marriage without first disavowing all fleshly desire, even a pre-Christian Cynic was much apter to sound like a heterodox "beast"—the notoriously beastly Carpocratians, for instance—than an orthodox godly ascetic.[47] The same tendencies that serve to explain the Cynics' interest for Renaissance authors engaged in their own reappraisal of standard mind-body and gender economies and the rites by which these are sustained

---

Seneca, *De Benef.* 7.1.7 (from Demetrius the Cynic), and Epictetus, *Disc.* 3.22.13–18 (expressed here with a striking new twist: "modesty" is the trait that guards true Cynics' nakedness from indecency). All this also supports a potentially subversive account of the true Cynic's life as no less an incessant *performance;* thus the Cynic's commitment to counterimposture and counter-hypocrisy can seem mere virtuous *show* in (almost) its own terms, and not only according to the lay-cynic's working assumption that where there is shame, there is doubtless sham, too. On the pretense of frankness see also here, n. 63. The dynamic self-exposure that not seldom links Cynics and cynics can at best protect both from the lure of a fixed, well-defined credal niche or a standardized role of their own.

45. *Suda,* s.v. "Lucian"; cf. Lucian, *On the Death of Peregrinus* 5, and *Alexander or the False Prophet* 55.

46. Aegidius Romanus, *De Regimine Principum* 2.1.7 (*Quod homo est naturaliter animal conjugale: et quod nolentes nubere non vivunt ut homines: sed vel vivunt ut bestiae: vel vivunt ut dii*), paraphrasing Aristotle, *Politics* 1.2, 1253a2–6. Cf. the proviso (*SR*, I H 9.49–51) that Cynics *un*like dogs should be not beneath shame but above it; cf. also Diogenes and Crates on philosophical exile at D.L. 6.40, 49, 63, 85, and 93, and Epictetus 3.24.66–69 on Cynic freedom-in-alienation.

47. Civic-minded Stoic treatments of marriage as a means of containing erotic desire while refining it into dispassionate friendship were as crucial to orthodox Catholic perspectives on marriages as to such Stoics' own routine "civil defense" of *honestum* or "decency"; on this link see esp. J.L. Brundage, *The Law, Sex, and Christian Society in the Middle Ages* (Chicago 1987); and on orthodox urging of sexual guilt as a counter to libertine anticonventionalists cf. E.H. Pagels, *Adam, Eve, and the Serpent* (New York 1988). On the notoriously licentious Carpocratians, Nicolaites, and Valentinians as disciples of Cynic indifference along with Epicurean voluptuousness see Irenaeus's *Contra Haereses* 1.25.5, 1.26.3, and esp. 2.14.5 and 2.32.2; for further alleged or hinted ties between Cynics and Epicureans ("Dogs" and "Pigs" in polemical slang) see D.L. 10.3; Lactantius, *Div. Inst.* 3.8.9; Isidore, *Etym.* 8.6.14–15; and below, nn. 48, 49, 61; cf. also nn. 31 and 72.

also help to explain why medieval descriptions of Cynics—though not Stoics—keep expanding on their subjects' most shocking traits till at last they converge with descriptions of demonized heretics.[48]

An especially outrageous expansion of the commonplace case against Cynics occurs in the *Catholicon* of the Dominican Joannes Balbus, an alphabetically arranged etymological encyclopedia first issued in 1286 and in general use till the Renaissance. Balbus's claims are in general unfounded though not unprovoked, and in pushing those negative claims to the point of thick caricature Balbus readies the way for the Renaissance recuperation of Cynic self-abasement as a radically empowering humility.[49]

> *Cinaedus* [literally, an obscenely loose male]. From *cinos* [i.e., Gk. *kuōn* or "dog"] derives *cynicus, -a, -um,* and *cinaedus, -a, um,* with the same sense, that

---

48. For the general pattern of such damning descriptions (initially applied to Christianity in general), almost always involving indiscriminate sex, sometimes more than a casual suggestion of cannibalism, and quite often a dog-mascot trained to pull over the lights, see esp. Downing (above, n. 35) 171–72. For the specifically Cynic character of one such heretical love-feast (even in the original contemptuously hailed as "a true congregation of swine and dogs") see P. Sloterdijk, *Critique of Cynical Reason,* trans. M. Eldred (Minneapolis 1987), 257–59. A similar nexus of outlandish teaching and scandalous gossip may account for the graphic accounts of specifically Cynic "dog-marriage" which are furnished so often by scandalized orthodox Christians (above, n. 42; *SR,* N. 54 [4, p. 566]), and since similar stories are not told against all philosophical sects it seems clear there is more at stake here than the standard polemical gambit of lumping together new heresies and outworn philosophical fads. Nonetheless Cynic naturalism is quite clearly no simple equivalent of the pantheist and dualist-occultist traditions most often arraigned in such terms, and the case is not finally complete for explicitly branding the Cynics as heretics until Balbus employs his inventive semantics to "show" Cynics engaging in what counted as outright perversion as well as professing mere shamelessness. Cf. M. Goodich, "Sexual Deviation as Heresy in the XIII–XIV centuries," in *Modernité et non-conformisme en France à travers les âges,* ed. M. Yardeni (Leiden 1983), 14–22; J. Richards, *Sex, Dissidence, and Damnation: Minority Groups in the Middle Ages* (London 1990); and J. Dollimore, *Sexual Dissidence, Augustine to Wilde, Freud to Foucault* (Oxford 1991) esp. 119–23, 237–38.

49. I here translate from Balbus's *Catholicon* (Mainz 1460; repr. Westmead 1971) s.v. "*Cinedus.*" Balbus is among the medieval lexicographers most often attacked by Erasmus; see the refs. in *CW* 15, p. 507, and R. Klinck, *Die lateinische Etymologie des Mittelalters* (Munich 1970) 20. The last third of Balbus's article *Cinedus/cinicus* is expanded from Isidore, *Etym.* 8.6.14; the discussion of marriage as "lawful" in turn comes from Augustine, *Civ. Dei* 14.19–20. Similar links between *cinedi* (as if "*kunoeideis*") and *cinici* are attested in Albertus Magnus, *De Animalibus* 1.2.22, and s.vv. in J. W. Fuchs, ed., *Lexicon Latinitatis Nederlandicae Medii Aevi* (Amsterdam 1970–); Thomas of Chobham, *summa de arte praedicandi,* ed. F. Morenzoni (Turnout, 1988) 71 (cf. Juvenal 4.106). Jean Gerson attacked libertine heretics as Cynics a bit more than a century later; see G. Leff, *Heresy in the Later Middle Ages,* 2 vols. (Manchester 1967), 1 p. 356, and more generally on the libertine doctrines imputed at various times to a (largely trumped-up) Heresy of the Free Spirit, Turlupins, the Bohemian Adamites, and of course the Beghards (often rendered *Picardi*), source of Modern English "beggar" and quite possibly cognate with "*pícaro.*" Under "Turlupins" Bayle cites promiscuous sex "in the manner of dogs or of Cynics." Calvin blasts (as "mad dogs") later Spiritual Libertines; see P. Zagorin, *Ways of Lying: Dissimulation, Persecution and Conformity in Early Modern Europe* (Cambridge, Mass., 1990), furthermore citing Calvin against various "Lucianist" scoffers, including Rabelais (in Calvin's *De Scandalis* likened to both "dogs" and "pigs"). Beggar counterproprieties could be likened in early seventeenth-century England to those of the libertine Family of Love (Koch [n. 28 above] 101) and the "Jovial crew" of the Ranters.

is to say, "doglike" [*caninus*]. Soft, effeminate, and impure men [*immundi*] are also called *cynici* and *cinaedi,* like dogs, who both have public sex and return to their vomit [2 Peter 2.22]. Or else satirists and critics are so called, who wound with their criticism as a dog with its bite.—Juvenal [2.10]: "Do you castigate vice, you the best-charted asshole among the Socratic *cinaedi*"? And hence certain heretical philosophers were called Cynics for their impurity *par excellence;* for they had sex with their wives openly and in public, preaching that men ought to have sex with their wives publicly in the road and the street the way dogs do, since marriage is lawful.

There is something almost Rabelaisian in this gallimaufry of garble. Doubtless prompted in part by the bare hope of bettering Isidore (Isidore, who is copied and amplified here, takes on only the Cynic philosophers), Balbus also deploys certain powers of satiric invention, or rather demonizing projection, that indicate more than a trivial sense of the challenge such Dogs as Diogenes pose to medieval institutions in general.

In the Renaissance there is a general if less than unanimous revulsion from this damning perception of the Cynics and a general revaluing of the shocking Diogenes no less than the "atheist" Lucian.[50] Even for classicizing Renaissance authors, however, a slight faltering of nerve can abruptly set back in polemical play Balbus's outrageous romp of bohemians, detractors, and heretics; the same freedom that beckons at one moment threatens the next, and appears to converge, as repeatedly in Plato, with unmastery, misrule, and enslavement by uncontrolled appetites.[51] Yet for many different Christians in differing degrees, antinomian freedom could claim scriptural support of its own. The Platonic reform-school construction of selfhood in terms of constraining, self-divided hegemony has some obvious analogies in mainstream Christianity; on the other hand, the Good News of Christian Evangelical liberty itself seemingly points toward a state of affairs where such models no longer obtain. Though for Cynics the terms of exchange are most clearly this-worldly, not otherworldly, it is hard not to see some analogy between Christian self-denial

---

50. On the Lucianic-Menippean revival see, for instance, *CW* 3/1, "Introduction," and J. Relihan in this volume; on the objections of social conservatives both Catholic and Protestant see esp. Zagorin (above, n. 49). On Diogenes see n. 7, above; Balbus's dispraise of Cynics in general appears to impinge on Erasmian praise in the translator's comment on a bowdlerized version of D.L. 6.69 in Erasmus-Udall (above at n. 16), *Diogenes* §210.

51. For example, see More (*CW* 5, p. 414) on the Lutherans "whom the devil has called to his servile liberty"; and for two related problematics of rebellion and internal chaos see Jonathan Sawday, "'Mysteriously Divided': Civil War, Madness and the Divided Self," in *Literature and the English Civil War,* ed. Thomas Healy and Jonathan Sawday (Cambridge 1990), 127–43, and more recently Martin Jay, "Abjection Overruled," *Salmagundi* 103 (1994) 235–51. For especially telling Platonic instances see *Gorgias, sub fin.,* and *Republic,* esp. Books 4, 10, and the discussion by C. Taylor (*The Sources of the Self: The Making of the Modern Identity* [Cambridge, Mass., 1989] chap. 6, "Plato's Self-Mastery"). Plato's rationalistic self-control never fully accommodates the more willful, thymic aspect of self-mastery according to the Cynics.

for the sake of one's immortal soul and the Cynics' preparedness to shed one sort of external selfhood or "face" for the sake of a deeper autonomy. By reversing the implicit logic of Balbus's indictment (from "Lack of inward control condemns Cynics to outward debasement" to "Cynic self-abasement, like saintly humility, may help free the mind") many Renaissance authors adapt claims clearly founded in Evangelical paradoxy to head off several threats to new freedoms at once, using those claims to buttress and hedge Cynic claims for autonomous selfhood as well as vice versa, and dramatically fusing the two exposés of both freedom and unfreedom in a single utopian mode that has aptly been called "Christian Cynicism." [52]

This amalgam of Christian Evangelical liberty and Cynic autonomous selfhood is clearly more like yet another syncretistic pastiche than a wholly new cultural ideal. What distinguishes this Renaissance Evangelical syncretism from the many other tamer varieties of Christian syncretism is that radical revaluation is no longer merely an occasional necessity as a non-Christian outlook is Christianized; in this new syncretism a general reversal of traditional cultural priorities represents a dramatic first step toward recasting old rules for discerning between unredeemed and redeemed modes of life or between error "then" and enlightenment "now." Something similar already occurs in Paul's disjunctive treatment of the "folly of God" and the wisdom of man, and in Augustine's more general disjunctive account of the aims and ideals of the City of God and the City of Man; indeed this Augustinian model seems basic to most of the bolder revisionist movements of Renaissance Europe.[53] For when Augustine's typological stasis centered on the First Coming is recast to allow

52. On the Christian exchange or conversion paralleling the Cynic's rejection of cultural "standing" and "face" in exchange for autonomy see especially Matt. 16.25, Mark 8.35, Luke 9.24, and John 12.25, and cf. *SR* V H 8–12; losing selfhood in order to save it makes better sense once, like the Cynics, we can choose between *meanings* of selfhood. M.A. Screech calls Rabelais a "Christian Cynic" (*Rabelais* [Ithaca 1979] 441) with a primary reference to the long exploration in Rabelais's Book 4 of the Cynic-satirical dictum, "The belly is the master of arts" (Persius, *Sat.,* proem 10). In imputing "new freedoms" to Renaissance authors, I chiefly refer to the new, larger scope for free inquiry left by the weakening or fall of at least some traditional certainties.

53. On two styles of Renaissance self-definition in terms of two rival, inclusive descriptions of Christian and secular virtue see W. J. Bouwsma, "The Two Faces of Humanism: Stoicism and Augustinianism in Renaissance Thought," chap. 1 of *A Usable Past: Essays in European Cultural History* (Berkeley and Los Angeles 1990). Christian Stoicism propounds an essential equivalence between the two versions of virtue, though their working realms (inner and outer) may be quite at odds; Augustinianism connects an essential unlikeness between the two versions of virtue with an epochal difference between two forms of human community, so that noting a "then"-"now" disjunction (again recognized rather than randomized) between the two virtues can help integrate the self in the human community as now reconceived or "redeemed." Thus even civic-minded Christians-as-Stoics might be less free to act and react to an imperfect world than a born-again Christian revisionary; and, as Bouwsma goes on to suggest, the same sort of disjunctive revision that at first licensed cultural progressives like Valla would soon do just as much, if not more, to accredit fundamentalist militants like Luther. For Paul's own qualified antinomian leanings see n. 73.

for another all-inclusive renewal (*renascentia*) or another dramatic release from conventional error even after the church is established, Augustine's own model can be taken to furnish at least a provisional sanction for quite shocking revisionist experiments.[54]

We have here a surprising development in which, of all things, Augustinian and Cynic directives appear to converge; but is this after all so surprising? For Augustine's account of the faith could be put to more uses than one, and an anticonventionalist, separatist use of Augustine's account is what for a time brings a reformer like Luther so close to the cultural skepsis of a humanist critic like Erasmus.[55] Among other distinctions between humanists and major reformers we might well indeed cite just these variants of one much-broadened cultural skepsis: what the humanists pursue with the mental reserve and the studied unseriousness of a Lucian is much like what reformers pursue with the doctrinaire seriousness of an anticonventionalist Augustine. Thus though Valla the humanist and Luther both treat the Middle Ages as a massive, surreptitiously pagan impediment to the spread of authentic Christianity, and though Luther and Luther's lieutenant Melanchthon both champion determinist views once dismissed as the frivolous theses of "that jester" Valla (*festivus nugator*), Valla tends to construe Evangelical liberty as a concomitant of revitalized rhetorical culture whereas Luther considers this last (if at all) as a minor concomitant of the former.[56] Similarly, though both movements are committed to a more or less rigorous review of what pass for sustaining traditions, each is apt to discern in the other an eventual betrayal of its skepsis; for besides the well-known competition of skepsis and faith throughout cultural debate since the Renaissance there is arguably also a long-running contest of Cynicisms. The example of Sir Thomas More, Catholic humanist martyr, makes it clear that strategic unseriousness may indeed coexist with more basic and heartfelt traditionalism, but that their compound forms a third stance of reserve and discreetly expressive dissent, anything but the frivolously cynical timeserving ruse More's reforming opponents impute to him. For the leveling and demystifying operation of laughter and irony that is favored by this Cynic-Lucianic tradition, we have in the more militant reforming tradition a quite different touchstone of

54. On this contrast of epochal "Renaissance" themes (Christian "rebirth" succeeding "medieval" decay) and a far more traditional theme of continuous reform see *CW* 15, p. lxxvii; cf. also Kemp (above, n. 26) chap. 3, and n. 33 above.

55. The opposing integrationist and separatist uses to which Augustine's views could be put are well characterized by F. Oakley, *The Western Church in the Later Middle Ages* (Ithaca 1979) 206–8.

56. On Valla as *festivus nugator* and his riddling *Dialogus de Libero Arbitrio* see Philipp Melanchthon's *Loci Communes* of 1521 (*Melanchthons Werke in Auswahl*, ed. R. Stupperich et al., 5 vols., 2d ed. [Gütersloh 1978; hereafter "*MW*"], 2/1, p. 26), and Luther's *De Servo Arbitrio* of 1525 (*Werke*, 60 vols. [Weimar 1883–1980; hereafter "*WA*"], 18, p. 639), and more generally the high praise in Luther's *Tischreden*, 6 vols. (Weimar 1912–21), nos. 259, 1470, and my n. 59, below.

new truthfulness, namely, intense but evolving prophetic conviction or an as-
surance of a personal stake in transcendent-historic finality. Once again we end
poised between openly volatile selves-on-the-make and (revised) timeless
Selves in the making.[57]

At this point it makes sense to examine in somewhat more depth two or
three crucial chapters or exemplary crises in the Renaissance history of Cynic
selfhood. There is certainly no shortage of cases in point; numerous ambitious
Renaissance essays in a practical paradoxy work to heighten and sharpen the
challenge to normative values represented for instance by the throwaway
mockery of medieval fools and *fols sages*. Poised somewhere between merely
academic and merely uncouth, or perhaps rather shuttling between them, is
where most of these Renaissance jest-earnest challenges situate their own unruly styles; the degraded knight-clown Sir John Falstaff for instance is almost
as at home misapplying learned axioms as deploying his own vast array of
"low" jokes. There is nothing indeed altogether unprecedented in this style of
demoting the high by promoting the low; and no less than the rhetoric of Christian transvaluing, or indeed than Prince Hal in his many mock-reckonings with
Falstaff, Renaissance-Cynic verbal designs for "reclaiming" the low patronize
it in ways that may not seldom leave it the poorer. Cynicism-by-halves is a
nearly ubiquitous strategy for both channeling and taming Cynic skepsis; nonetheless we may still fairly clearly distinguish between old and new styles of
invoking the Cynics, between calling on this or that sanitized Cynic exemplar
to offset the too-carnal allure of the present and reviving the whole repertoire
of impertinent transvaluing by which Cynics themselves sought to settle accounts with idealized tradition in general and thus the whole past. One especially crucial attempt in this jest-earnest vein is a seminal argument, paradoxical yet not frivolous, that has been called "a decisive 'transvaluation of
values' . . . in the theory of morals," the common Renaissance defense of
(higher) hedonism first espoused as a jest-earnest "cause" by philologist-
reformer L. Valla.[58]

Controversial, pugnacious, and iconoclastic, Lorenzo Valla (1407–57) won
his singular eminence among Renaissance humanists and reformers alike by a

57. For a stark opposition between Lucianic ironic reserve and reforming assertiveness see
Luther's much-studied response to Erasmus, *De Servo Arbitrio*, WA 18, p. 606. Though without
any reference to Cynics of either description, others offer a similar account of this bipolar "worldly–
unworldly" recasting of self in the age of estrangement and skepsis: see T. Reiss, *The Discourse
of Modernism* (Ithaca 1982) esp. chap. 3; C. Whitney, *Francis Bacon and Modernity* (New Haven
1986) esp. 43–49; and C. Taylor, *The Ethics of Authenticity* (Cambridge, Mass., 1991) with n. 51,
above; cf. also the *double entendre* of "Renaissance self-fashioning" or "self-styling" as well as
"self-authoring."

58. Edgar Wind, *Pagan Mysteries in the Renaissance*, rev. ed. (New York 1968), 68. In
Dante's *Inferno*, Canto 10, hedonistic Epicurus is punished as an arch-heretic for setting bod-
ies on a level with souls; Diogenes fares better, ending up with the other virtuous pagans in
Canto 4, 135.

stance often noted for the same sort of scandalous willfulness he himself once condemns, or appears to condemn, in the Cynics.[59] Valla starts out his *De Voluptate* (On Pleasure) with a sweeping declaration of polemical intent: to establish that even according to pagan philosophy "paganism has done nothing according to virtue, nothing rightly" (1 pr. 4, p. 50). Valla also overtly embraces the cultural skepsis of the "least arrogant" of pagan philosophies, the Middle Academy, a more moderate anticonventionalist posture that Cicero along with a number of Christians had praised as supporting a chastened and circumscribed regimen of secular custom; but instead of presenting this moderate "oratorical skepticism" as no more than that, Valla promptly joins it in the dialogue itself with an "Epicurean" vindication of pleasure that is actually more Cynic than Epicurean in its palpable eagerness to shock. A purportedly Stoic arraignment of Nature for assailing mankind with so many temptations and hardships is soon answered by a poet speaking here as an "Epicurean" who proceeds (as he notes) with considerable "license" to unmask all behavior as pleasure-seeking, to dispense with all shame and to praise all pleasure-seeking alike as a matter of principle, to elaborate some shocking extensions of this shameless ethic including a ban on all workaday sexual taboos, and at length to reinstate workaday decency and sexual restraint in the terms of enlightened but still strictly worldly self-interest (1.35–48, pp. 116–30). In Book 2 he continues a hedonist unmasking of all "honest," unselfish motives, including the highest; nonetheless he is praised in Book 3 by a pious rhetorical judge for defeating the falsely self-righteous, self-satisfied Stoics so that not even they can now claim to improve on the ethics of higher self-serving represented by Christian expectancy. This may look like a tame typing-up of the case; actually it is not. Not content to present the poet's hedonist discourse as a glib foil for fideist Christianity, Valla turns the speech into a sweeping exposé of conventional pieties as no better than self-serving blinds, and then follows this up with an equally radical charter for a Christian higher hedonism, a new model for what might well be christened a new Epicureanism of hope. Two

---

59. For Valla's vastly influential reinvention of rhetoric as an instrument of cultural analysis see *CW* 15, "Introduction" and notes; for the *De Voluptate* as a model for Erasmus's *Praise of Folly* see my "Erasmus and the Latin Comedians," *Actes du Colloque international Érasme (Tours),* ed. J. Chomarat et al. (Geneva 1990) 64, 67–68. On Valla's dialogue (also titled *De Vero Falsoque Bono*) see Stinger (above, n. 33) 242 n. 55, and the editors' introduction to *On Pleasure/De Voluptate,* trans. and ed. A. K. Hieatt and M. di Panizza Lorch (New York 1977), the edition to which my citations refer, though I sometimes revise the translation. In Erasmus's *Praise of Folly* (*Moriae Encomium, ASD* 4/3, p. 130; cf. *CW* 15, commentary at 174/2–3), Folly calls Academics the "least arrogant" of pagan philosophers (*quam minime insolentes*). *Epokhē* or suspension of judgment, the avoidance of arrogant assertion, and rhetorical license and free inquiry all contribute to Cicero's much-copied model of a moderate cultural skepsis; see Cicero, *De Off.* 2.3.7 (probably more influential than Cicero's own *Academica*); Augustine, *Contra Academicos* (actually more sympathetic to Academic skeptics than to most other pagan philosophers); Valla, *De Voluptate* 1.10.3 (pp. 74–76); and L. di Panizza, "Lorenzo Valla's *De Vero Falsoque Bono [De Voluptate]*: Lactantius and Oratorical Skepticism," *JWCI* 41 (1978) 76–107.

consecutive moments of *déprise* and *reprise,* dispossession and repossession, orchestrate a dramatic return—in a sense—to the same sort of communal calm and agreement that the work started out to contest; but this seeming return to community faiths can no more undo Valla's residual challenge to established perceptions and pieties than utopian schemes for a Cynic *Politeia* could obscure a Diogenes' ongoing challenge to his own era's cultural establishment.

Valla's explicit references to the Cynics in this text are as telling as they are misleading. What is crucial to note in the judgments of pagan philosophy to be found in the *De Voluptate* is that Valla essentially reverses the very authors he cites for support. While Augustine and Lactantius both had limited patience with pagan Stoicism as well as its closest Christian cognates, neither had the least patience with either radical Cynicism or hedonism, postures these Christian authors, and not only these, very often condemned as a pair, viewing them as overt and covert interchangeable forms of a single subversive disdain for the standard of secular custom—even Christianized secular custom— that both radical Cynicism and hedonism do indeed in their own ways discount.[60] Valla's principal targets are clearly the same Christianized Stoics, the same legalist Christians and uniformed would-be ascetics, that Erasmus and Valla among other Evangelical humanists oppose as a matter of course; indeed what Valla does in this text is find cause to transfer the ill fame of "unnatural" Cynic-subversives to the unworldly Cynic-recluses approved by the medieval Church, not a difficult feat—though a mischievous one—if indeed (as it seems) the first Cynics of those opposed cultural styles were historically one and the same. In a real tour de force, or de farce, of tendentious transvaluing, Valla's hedonist

---

60. Valla's references to Diogenes rely more than once (at 1.12.6 and at 2.29.8) on Jerome, *Adversus Iovinianum* 2.14 (*PL* 23.345, partly cited in *SR,* V B 175); Valla turns Jerome's praise for Diogenes' courage in the face of death into all-out invective against Diogenes and his supposed suicide. Valla must actually have worked from Jerome's text as it is excerpted and expanded in, e.g., John of Salisbury's twelfth-century *Policraticus* (5.17); on the strength of an ambiguous phrase in Jerome (*eliso gutture,* "with his throat constricted"/"constricting his throat" [cf. also D.L. 6.76]) it is John not Jerome who proceeds from Diogenes' brave struggle with fever to a standard Christian invective against pagan suicide (cf. Augustine, *Civ. Dei* 1.17ff.). Also at 2.29.8 Valla mockingly mentions Diogenes' "will" as described by Cicero, *Tusc. Disp.* 1.108. Despite knowledge of Greek Valla never cites Greek Cynic sources. In connecting the Cynics and Stoics so closely to start with, Valla doubtless proceeds from such standard conflations as Juvenal 13.121–22 (*Stoica dogmata . . . A Cynicis tunica tantum distantia*), and in associating "some Stoics" with public sex and *inverecundia* at 1.46.2 doubtless Valla again conflates Stoics with the Cynics whose loose conduct the Christians so often deplore (cf. n. 42 here; note that Valla maintains the pejorative rendering of "Cynic" as "doglike" [*caninus*] at 1.12.6). But Valla's frequent allusions to Cicero's *De Officiis* and *De Finibus* (the *De Finibus* in particular) make it clear that he also knew texts like *De Off.* 1.128, 148, and *De Fin.* 3.57, 68, where the Cynics' rejection of *honestum* as a standard of conduct is named as precisely what sets them at odds with the Stoics of Cicero's own day; the repeal of *honestum* as a standard is also distinctive of Valla's own licentious spokesman, most notably at 1.35.1–45.12 (and conversely at 160 [honor-seeking as whoring]), a deliberately shocking declaration of what Sloterdijk would call sexual Cynicism. On the Cynics' perceived ties with the Stoics and the Epicureans see nn. 34 and 47, and Long's essay in this volume.

persona faults the Stoics for their beastly ties with the Cynics, though the Cynics' presumed beastly ties with the Epicureans were what made Cynics seem so disreputable to conservative readers from the start. Even so, the persona several times cites Diogenes by name as the Stoics' "monstrous" mascot, with whom they are depicted as lurking inertly on the margins of civilized rhetorical discourse just as they lurk or posture ineptly on the margins of human society (1.12.6, 1.46.2, 2.29.5–10, pp. 78, 128, 212–14); in the last of these texts he attempts to unmask Cynic-Stoic austerity in general as no more than an antic and apish sham self-overcoming, exemplified here by Diogenes' theatrical suicide. In their fruitless austerity these Stoics, or Stoicized Christians, fall short not just of bona fide Christian redemption but of good-faith attainment in general. While the Stoics are exuberantly heckled as Cynics, the main Cynic points here are all made by the Stoics' opponents; and though the victory in this philosophical face off officially goes to the anti-Stoic hedonists, what survives and continues to resonate at the end of the transhedonist Christian Book 3 (in its way no less shocking in treating *honestum* or "decency" as at best an accessory device of enlightened self-interest) is a ringing assertion of Evangelical liberty combined here with a model experiment in Cynic free-thinking outspokenness.

Certainly Valla's own spokesman for pleasure, the professed adversary of Diogenes, is as fond of crowd-pleasing impertinence as any ancient Cynic. The historical figure once cast for this role was the poet Panormita, whose main work was the scandalous *Hermaphroditus,* and the poet who ends up with the role, Maffeo Vegio, has a no less licentious conception of "poetic license" if we are to judge by the case Valla here has him make; the same "license" effectively links both these hedonist spokesmen to the Cynics condemned by Augustine.[61] The historical Vegio's high esteem for the Cynics as explored in Matton's contribution to this volume makes his role in the *De Voluptate* as the Cynic's professed archdetractor seem still more like an intricate joke. At one point in the earliest draft of the text (1.9.1 *var.,* p. 356) the poet banters about his own role as a Cynic exposer, stalking his Stoicized quasi-Cynic opponents *tanquam canis venaticus,* "like a hunting-dog"; a bit later (1.28.1 *var.,* p. 365) he brings up yet another charged topic for practical paradox by explicitly praising *scurrae,* parasites, actors, and panders. There is patently something quite scurrilous, at least by traditional standards, in the speaker's own bounty of scandalous theses, and when the Christian moderator at length tries to salvage the poet's personal standing by telling the rest of the group that the poet

---

61. On Augustine's equation of "poetic license" and pagan licentiousness see *Civ. Dei* 2.9, 12; cf. *De Fide et Op.* 18 (whores and actors as *publicae turpitudinis professores*) along with John of Salisbury in n. 8, above. For the damning conflation of Cynic and sensualist license cf. n. 47, Ps.-Aug. in *SR*, V B 525, and *Civ. Dei* 14. 20 (*De Vanissima Turpitudine Cynicorum*) with 19.1 on the *horribilis turpitudo* of making pleasure the highest good.

does not live as he talks (3.7.2–3, p. 258), we see how close his talk comes to that of the *scurra,* whom Valla's own handbook of usage defines as a clown or buffoon with no reverence for personal dignity (*Elegantiae* 4.51). The further claim that the hedonist was speaking not seriously but rather jokingly, like a Socratic *eirōn,* is just one more reminder of the intricate tactical kinship linking scurrilous excess and irony in all manner of Cynic performance;[62] for this sort of wise-foolish performance, as the author's own cautious disclaimers attest, is disarming precisely by virtue of being prima facie unserious, even as it hints at meanings *beyond* workaday seriousness that may make it seem plausible, as well. Valla volatizes conventional seriousness through his hedonist spokesman's assault on *honestum* or "decency" as arrogance, something close to Augustine's *superbia* or "pride" not to mention Cynic *tuphos* or "vanity"; this derisive-defacing re-vision of workaday seriousness is at least as intrinsic to this text's historic *succès de scandale* as its final sublimation of vilified "pleasure" into salvific Christian expectancy. We find accommodation for the sake of neat closure in Valla's Book 3 but paradoxical confrontation for the sake of broad cultural skepsis virtually everywhere in Books 1 and 2, and even given the text's final championing of true Christian piety as a restlessly hopeful expectancy it might well be more accurate to say that the accommodation of Book 3 is appended as a foil for the unsettling argument than that all the unsettling is merely a foil for some ultimate harmony. In this text's dextrous linkage of a more or less radically anticonventional content and a governing style of conventional flippancy we see Valla making room for a new cultural skepsis partly at the expense of persona-Diogenes, but more crucially thanks to a kind of conventionally licensed impertinence more routinely connected with Cynic philosophers than with any other comparable movement in pagan antiquity.[63] Far from countering the governing style of the *De Voluptate,* "Cynic style" may in some sense determine it.

With his primary target the arrogance of all worldly systems including the church, Valla radicalizes oratorical skepticism to maintain an even sharper disjunction than his own Christian models routinely presume between ignorance or error in the past and enlightenment "now"; and for Valla, this past includes even the era in which these very models emerged, so that this new, more radical

62. Cf. nn. 10–17; B. Bowen, *The Age of Bluff: Paradox and Ambiguity in Rabelais and Montaigne* (Urbana 1972); *CW* 3/1, p. 5 (on Menippus's bravado as irony); *CW* 3/2, p. 577; *CW* 15, p. 107, and nn. (declamation, disclaimers, and practical paradoxy in *Utopia* and Erasmus's *Praise of Folly*). Similarly the whole hedonist discourse in Valla is described in 3.7.2 (p. 258) as an argument merely for show, undertaken "for practice or novelty," and in 3.7.5 (p. 260) as a mere speaker's joke undertaken entirely *iocandi causa.* This is also what Valla describes in the beginning of Book 1 (52; cf. 122) as the "more entertaining and almost licentious content" (*hilariora et prope dixerim licentiosa*) of Books 1 and 2.

63. See esp. n. 8 above; for *parrhēsia* reduced to conventional rhetorical gesture ("If I may speak freely") see, for instance, *Rhet. ad Her.* 4.37.49.

break represents a new style of release from such error and not just a new view of the singular, church-mediated release that by then had been proffered so frequently. It is not after all so surprising that Luther and Luther's lieutenants recognized such a kinship with Valla; for both Valla and Luther were deeply committed to expanding the temporal framework of Augustine's disjunctive enlightenment. But for Valla, at least, this expansion brings Christian enlightenment—or at least the mechanics of Christian enlightenment—remarkably close to the process of Cynic disenchantment.

A good sequel to Valla's humanistic-reforming engagement with the rhetoric and general thematics of Cynic dissent is a sketch of what might well be called the lifelong Lucianic collaboration of Erasmus and Sir Thomas More. More's engagement with Lucian begins with a volume first published in 1506 of Erasmus and More's Latin renderings of various short pieces by Lucian (or "Lucian") including *The Cynic;* other ventures in Lucianic masking and didactic impertinence by More include (naturally) *Utopia,* a riddling *History of King Richard III,* and a series of long, often tactically arch letter-essays expounding the cultural stakes of Erasmian humanism.[64] Were it not for our previous look at the *De Voluptate* of "that jester" Valla, in some ways an exemplary jest-earnest text for both More and Erasmus, we would have a hard time doing any sort of justice to Erasmus's many notable essays in practical paradox, from the early *Enchiridion Militis Christiani* of 1503 to its "as-if" rebuttal, the *Moriae Encomium/Praise of Folly* of 1511, to the 1515 adage-essay "Alcibiades' Sileni" (*Adag.* 2201) with its startling alignment of Socrates and of Valla's social-misfit Diogenes with eventually no less a colleague than Christ.[65] As it

---

64. There is much to be said on *Utopia* as a Cynic invention; for the time being, on practical paradox in *Utopia* from redemptive extolling of pleasure to didactic debasing of gold, see E. McCutcheon, "More's *Utopia* and Cicero's *Paradoxa Stoicorum,*" and on Lucianic joking, see R. Bracht Branham, "Utopian Laughter: Lucian and Thomas More," *Moreana* 86 (1985) 3–22, 23–43; for Lucianic games of truth in *Utopia* and other works by More see *CW* 3/2, p. 664, and *CW* 15, esp. pp. l–li, lxviii–lxix, lxxi, 50–54, 272, 482, and nn. The *ingens inane* or "great void" on which More situates his island republic links *Utopia* in interesting ways with the mock-epic squib in which Crates the Cynic celebrates his own state—that of Beggary—as an insular haven from *tuphos,* that is, as an isle in a "wine-dark" expanse of Illusion or Pride (D.L. 6.85); More's Utopian reporter Hythloday of course rails against pride although prideful (or at any rate *insolens*) himself, and this willful exponent of Utopian values would no doubt be expelled from Utopia if it were an actual state, *not* an essay in Cynic transvaluing.

65. On Erasmus and Valla see nn. 59, 61; for Erasmus and the Cynics see further *Adagia* 1234 ("*Canina facundia*"), 2070 ("*Ad Cynosarges*" [Cynic "roots" in a precinct for bastards, especially the archbastard Heracles]), *Enchiridion Militis Christiani* (1503), "Canon Sextus" *sub fin.,* with the late discourse *Lingua* (*ASD* 4/1, p. 62, on untimely reforming outspokenness), the two colloquies *Ptōkhologia* ("Beggar Talk") and *Ptōkhoplousioi* ("Rich Beggars [Franciscans]"), and the book-length Diogenes section in Erasmus's still later *Apophthegmata* (in this case chiefly gleaned from D.L., *cum commento*). In the still fuller English of Nicholas Udall (London 1542) this last text probably furnished the main "Diogenical" source for such authors as Shakespeare. The illegitimate Erasmus identified closely with Heracles; see *Adagia* 2001 ("*Herculei labores*"; see esp. *ASD* 2/5, p. 23 n., and the jest-earnest praise [415] of compilers-emenders combining dung-beetles and Heracles).

is, we can fairly distinguish between Christian-Cynic perspectives developed by Valla no less than Erasmus and the firmer control of *decorum personae* or in-character decorum insulating Erasmus from some, though not all, of the disrepute dogging preposterous causes however well urged, such preposterous causes as that of the *De Voluptate* or as that of Erasmus's equivocal *Praise* of both Folly and More. As a sample of Erasmian Christian-Cynic invention at work, this last text's dedication derives the whole *jeu d'esprit* simply from the ironic discrepancy between what More's name *means*—namely "Fool"—and the wise man dissembling his wisdom that More really *is;* More and this text, like More the "wise fool" or the "foolish wise man" who made jest-earnest play even of his own death on a scaffold in 1535, are thus matching instructive examples of practical paradoxy.[66]

One significant check for the claim of at least More's enduring commitment to Cynic-Lucianic reforming impertinence is afforded by More's bitter *Responsio ad Lutherum* of 1523, a work written pseudonymously on behalf of the outraged King Henry VIII in which Luther is cast as a doubly bad Cynic or the bad Cynic *par excellence*.[67] For a decade, in book after book published in his own name, More continues to blast various Reformers' impertinence in much the same terms. Yet remarkably, even in the last of these works, even as he renounces his own early Lucianist essays in Cynic dissent and impertinence, More reserves no less Cynic and skeptical license than ever for his fellow Lucianist Erasmus, as if More's own demise in defense of the faith could afford just as good a defense for his "second self's" mission of questioning;[68] and indeed this "good" Cynic whom More in a sense vindicates with his death represents an authentic if wavering and beleaguered alternative to both Lutheran debasements of Cynicism. For the play of rhetorical masking in which Luther himself sees Erasmus as hiding or lost is in part an attempt at achieving a both flexible and answerable selfhood, a "part of one's own," reconciling

66. For Erasmus's dedication see *ASD* 4/3, p. 67, and nn., a ludic "honor roll" of sorts in which More is explicitly linked with Democritus (cf. Niehues-Pröbsting [above, n. 8] 182–83) and less explicitly with Aristippus, another "man for all seasons" whom Diogenes once called "the King's Dog" (D.L. 2.66). Not long after More's death Edward Hall criticizes More's scaffold performance as that of a "wise fool" or "foolish wise man" (*Chronicle,* ed. H. Ellis [London 1809], 317).

67. More's *Responsio* is cited according to the text readily available in *CW* 5, ed. J. Headley, trans. Sister Scholastica Mandeville, though at times I revise the translation. For More's own pseudonyms (one of them borrowed from Baraballo, the *scurra* of Pope Leo X) see *CW* 5, pp. 794–801. For More's Cynic perception of Luther see pp. 180 and 464 [*sidenote*] (*Cynicus Lutheri mos*), and for Luther as "dog" or as doglike, pp. 20, 74, 132, 220, 346, 438, 574, 676, 680; More calls Luther *impudens, parasitus* or *scurra* (at times playing on *scriptura,* as well) far too often to list, and eventually restyles Luther "Luder" or "jester" as if trying to improve the punning pen name once adopted by Luther himself, *Eleutherius* or "Freeman" in Greek.

68. See *CW* 15, pp. lxxxiii, xci–xcii, 568 (More's last praise of Erasmus and Erasmus as More's "second self").

without compromising the gaze of the world and the scope of the self, and displaying a "self on the make" in a way that indeed can converge on, if not clearly end in, substantial integrity. Such dramatic projections and heuristic expansions of self are a mainstay of standard rhetorical training, as well as of Cynic *ascēsis;* but in More's view the point of the Lutheran recourse to such truculent Cynic extremes of self-dramatization, to assertive conviction as well as to jeering effrontery, is in fact just *becoming invisible,* or unanswerable because radically false, not an essay in truth-telling impudence at all, but an impudence armed with a new personal dogma against the whole truth.

Is this view of the case fair to Luther? It would be a huge understatement to say that More's view is occasionally unfair to Luther, or indeed for that matter that Luther's own view of his foes (from which More takes his stylistic cue) is no more than occasionally unfair; hyperbolic abusiveness is so much the established decorum of early Reformation debate that refraining from this sort of abuse could seem more indiscreet, even *tactically* so, than engaging in it. It is here we should pause first of all, for indeed, sympathetically canvassed, this same doubly embattled and doubly unbending commitment to skepsis-by-simple-restraint may do much to explain how Erasmus can remain a reforming ideal for More even as he himself launches into ever more violent rejoinders against such reformers as Luther, More apparently views his own violence of style as just canceling out that of his radical opposites so that more balanced styles of appraisal and skepsis, a more balanced Erasmian style, for example, can once more prevail.[69] More's performance as watchdog against what he views as mad-dog depredations by figures like Luther does not alter the need he perceives for a guardian or watchdog-at-large like Erasmus, whose role More himself actually defends in distinctly Cynic terms from the start.[70] The rehearsed indiscretion of both More and Erasmus in their Lucianic engagements is the mark and the mask of a deeper self-irony or a tempered and wary discernment especially trained against all forms of personal complacency, an ironic self-exposure that may savor no less of provoking mock-arrogance than it does of engaging self-mockery; from a scurrilous quirk to a heuristic norm, this Socratic and Cynic self-disprizing or "bluffing" *esprit,* the same wit Aristotle once aptly described as an "educated insolence," forms a regimen for internal balance and accommodation with perhaps more to do with the shape of both Renaissance and Enlightenment selfhood than all else generally viewed

69. See *CW* 5, p. 692, and *CW* 15, pp. 166, 310.

70. For Erasmus as satirist-watchdog of culture see *CW* 15, pp. 106–10, 118, 266, 274, 290–92, and nn. The fierce-friendly ambivalence of dogs' nature (*Rep.* 375c; cf. 416a, *CW* 3/2, no. 115 [kings and tyrants as "watchdogs" and "wolves"]) seems a cultural asset or not mainly based on how highly one rates those whose interests dogs serve to defend; the shared interest More serves seems to him far less partial than the separatist interest to which Luther caters, but (at least in the long term) perhaps still less broad than Erasmus's cosmopolitan Christian humanism.

as a legacy of Renaissance humanism.[71] Put more coyly (as Montaigne at least hints in his teasing preamble's half-promise to bare all), there are versions and versions of nakedness; humanist writers' ironic self-exposure in Renaissance texts is as much a profession or proffer of modesty as an essay in true or false shamelessness, so much so that exposures of this sort at least in some Renaissance contexts replace the stock modesty-topoi of earlier rhetoric. It is this saving, or at least humanizing, ingredient of self-irony not merely pro forma that More finds wholly missing in Luther's own cynical-seeming amalgam of vehemence and scorn.

What is genuinely Cynic in Luther? If we trust his brief passing attacks on the Cynics, not much; but by 1526, when he launched his first blast against Cynics and their unconventional ways, the ex-monk clearly felt he had cause to suspect *both* extreme Cynic styles of resistance to business-as-usual, both ascetic withdrawal and the bold antinomian activism that he saw as one cause of the German peasants' bloody rebellion in 1525.[72] In a second blast dating from 1541–42, while addressing alleged "Jewish" readings of Genesis 26.8, Luther simply confounds Cynic sexual shamelessness with the sort he imputes to the Jews, or more strictly, to "those Jewish swine"; as in numerous traditional texts, "Cynic" here stands more crudely for whatever piquant suggestion or peccant behavior the author sees fit to condemn. Based on this pair of slurs it might seem rash to claim to detect any more than generic Christian-Cynic affinities even in Luther's earlier work; they are nonetheless definitely there, and in forms that at times surpass even Saint Paul's most outspoken assertions of Christian liberty. In a comment of 1532 Luther still celebrates his own knack for offending religious traditionalists, treating it as a case of "provoking them for their own good"; in a comment of 1539 he still gladly avows his own role as a "smasher" of law in the Pauline sense.[73] Luther's masters of the practical

71. On these aspects of wit see nn. 17 and 20, above. On ironic self-exposure and Erasmian modesty see esp. *CW* 15, s.v. "modesty," and *ASD* 4/3, pp. 67–68. Opposites to such modesty can include chauvinistic complacency no less than sectarian arrogance, whence the close links between More's responses to chauvinist French poets and later to Luther; see the references to Luther in *CW* 3/2. Renaissance cognates of this antithetical pairing include Silenus-"bluffs," *sprezzatura,* "hastening slowly," and "prudent simplicity"; cf. here also n. 62, and Wind (above, n. 58), esp. 199, on rhetorical "trimming" or balancing-acts as a standard constituent of Renaissance reading and mythmaking.

72. For Luther's two chief anti-Cynic pronouncements see his 1526 commentary on Ecclesiastes (*WA* 20, p. 103) and his 1541–42 commentary on Genesis (*WA* 43, p. 449). On Luther's ultimate revulsion from pronounced antinomianism, which he clearly linked closely to the 1525 Peasant's War (called in *WA* 18, pp. 357–58, an assault or revolt of "mad dogs"), see esp. his *Tischreden,* nos. 3554 (1537) and 4007 (1538). The views he there condemns sound much like views advanced in his early Galatians commentaries and his own *Babylonian Captivity of the Church* (1520), probably the most seditious text More reckons with in *Responsio.*

73. *Tischreden,* nos. 395, 4577. Cf. Paul in Rom. 14.14–23, 1 Cor. 6.12, 9.19–23, 10.23–33, 2 Cor. 3.17, Gal. 2.2–14, 3.10–14, 28, 5 *passim,* and Tit. 1.13–16; for discussion see Downing (above, n. 35), Patterson (above, n. 19) chap. 19, and here, n. 35. Luther (*Tischreden,* no. 146

paradoxy that was so closely linked with the new Christian Cynicism were Paul, Valla, and the finally much-hated Erasmus; for, regarding his own new autarkic insistence on justification by faith (*sola fide*) as the ultimate tool for "destroying" Christians' bondage to ill-grounded rituals and empty external traditions, a standard complaint for Erasmus as well, Luther took it as proof of Erasmus's own perfidy when he failed to embrace the new fideist "dogma" on which Luther had raised his new paradoxy.[74] Simply put—the way Luther himself often puts it in his early works—if mere faith is sufficient, all else is "indifferent," not just "inessential," as Stoics construed the "indifferent," but Cynically "free and indifferent," intrinsically *neutral* in its bearing on one's spiritual health, though occasionally scandal is salutary.[75] One well-known scandalous passage by Luther, to which More responds, even argues that a wife with an impotent husband should be free to take on a new mate and raise children with him at the husband's expense unless he offers her a divorce; this seems not so much serious advice about changing the law as a saucy though poignant joke at the expense of routine casuistical hairsplitting.[76] One more Lutheran blow for assertive impertinence that More may well have learned of by hearsay, at least, was the *hoffnar* or "court-fool" persona adopted by Luther (complete with a once again saucy appeal to fool's license) in the German *An den christlichen Adel* of the year 1520, a shrewd tract in which Luther urged Germany's nobility to cast off the gilt shackles of Rome;[77] here again, though in Luther's inimitable way, self-assured Cynic license suggests both sublime unconcern for the taste of the times and adroitly timeserving scurrility.

[1531–32]) calls Galatians his "darling epistle," his "Katy von Bora," the name of the ex-nun he married in 1525.

74. For this view of the doctrine of justification by faith as a "thunderbolt" shattering the papacy see *Tischreden*, no. 3502; the *Tischreden* abound in attacks on the dextrous Erasmus as an "Epicurean"and a "skeptic"; cf. also here n. 57.

75. It seems Luther himself draws the formula *libera et indifferentia* (addressed by More *CW* 5, pp. 96, 164, 254–56, and 418) from old glosses describing the Gentiles in Gal. 2.4, 14 as *libere et indifferenter victitan[tes]*; see *PL* 104, p. 861a, *PL* 112, p. 275a, and cf. Luther's 1516–17 and 1519 Galatians commentaries (*WA* 57, pp. 17, 63–64; *WA* 2, p. 451 [*Nam in Christum credentibus omnia munda, indifferentia, licita sunt*]) along with Melanchthon's *Loci Communes* (*MW* 2/1, pp. 144–57, 183–84). Not least galling to More was the definite convergence of such statements as these with Erasmus's and More's own more measured critiques of such "human traditions," notably Erasmus's *Enchiridion* and More's long letter-essays directed to Dorp and a monk. For a valuable contrast between Cynic and Stoic-eclectic, confrontationist and conciliationist "indifference" as each of these bears on the Age of Reform see B.J. Verkamp, *The Indifferent Mean: Adiaphorism in the English Reformation to 1554* (Athens, Ohio, 1977) esp. chap. 2, and cf. my nn. 2, 47, and 73. For didactic impertinence see *Tischreden*, nos. 344, 395, with the scandalous tales in nos. 1326, 1472, and 5418.

76. *Babylonian Captivity* (*WA* 6, p. 558; cf. *CW* 5, p. 688, and n.). In his handling of marriage as well as confession in this 1520 pronouncement, we find some of Luther's most extreme attacks on the "bondage" of customs and "circumstances."

77. *WA* 6, pp. 404–5, 442 ("und sag das fur mein hoffrecht frey").

A brief look at one lengthy dismantling-aside in More's own scurrilous answer to Luther's effrontery makes it clear how far More both trumps up and
trumps down Luther's prospects en route to the truth, how indeed he still works
toward a Cynic and ludic dismantling of his own partial, wrangling performance no less than his separatist adversary's. More repeatedly toys with a figure of speech in which Luther imagines what great fools it would take to match
some of the foolery he gibes at in Henry VIII's well-known tract against Luther.
More has reason to joke about Luther as a *stultifex* ("fashioner of fools");
More himself, the "wise-fool," takes his stylistic lead here from Luther, the
fool-supposed-wise. But most striking of all in this passage (*CW* 5, pp. 434–
38) is a balked, largely wishful correction of Luther's own heedlessly preening
effrontery, evoked in what by now are familiar theatrical terms:

> But since he glories so in his kind of fool-offspring that he either believes or at
> least makes-believe no one sees his own folly, let this singular fashioner of fools
> fashion us one, at least, who first finds a brass ring, then at some prankster's
> prompting persuades himself it is the gold ring of Gyges . . . with which they say
> that he went invisible wherever he pleased. . . . How this moron puffed up with
> his marvelous good fortune . . . will strut, laugh, and dance with delight, while
> the onlookers turn their eyes elsewhere to further his folly! . . . But lest this
> honored father not like the name "fool," let us fashion another, not clear-fool,
> but near-fool, and beyond that . . . a hireling-buffoon . . . who comes on in a feast
> of Bohemian village-rustics and starts his buffoonery . . . [and] to stage a first-
> rate show of folly, walks out in the feast naked and covered with only a net, as if
> someone has got him persuaded that none can see through his enchantment. Hav-
> ing come on this way . . . with obscene moves he angles for laughs till so foul a
> show outrages even those hinterland-rustics who publicly mate in their churches
> [rumored Adamite "dog-marriage" (*kunogamia*); see p. 220 n.], while the one
> out for laughs is the only one laughing—the same way a dog "laughs" when
> provoked—and the rest in disgust finally tear off the net and throw out the buf-
> foon with a beating. . . . [So] this scoundrel of ours, [though] aware that his filthy
> chicanery is quite obvious to everyone everywhere . . . still so mimics a fool, and
> in that fool's persona so shamelessly abuses the license of reckless buffoonery,
> not in some rustics' feast but the theater of the whole world, not on some trifling
> score but the ground of religion and faith, that he proves himself clearly deserv-
> ing not only of public chastisement by all decent folk as a public corrupter of
> decency, but moreover a marketplace drubbing by all the buffoons for buffoonery
> so odious it makes the whole class of buffoons appear hateful, not merely
> ridiculous.

From almost every angle, this scene is a party gone horribly wrong, perhaps
not least because of the violent collision or pell-mell confusion of so many
crossed pre-texts and paradigms. Not to dwell on odd foretastes of Brueghel or
memories of Bosch, we have first an insistence that Luther's rhetorical effrontery is no better, indeed worse, than fools' blithely oblivious nakedness, then a

crude folktale made a thin pretext for bawdy display,[78] then an inset as if from the Balbus compendium of heretical-Cynic depravity, then bizarrely enough a restating in Adamite terms of that already strange Augustinian sketch in which even a pack of licentious Greek pagans would feel morally bound to home in and destroy any Cynics affronting their vision with sex in the street. In each case the enforcer is (oddly) a wolf-become-watchdog or watchdog-turned-wolf, and none here seems distinctly worth salvaging.

As if that were not already more than enough, the whole passage is also a curious recasting of what may well be More's favorite image of all, the well-known Cynic trope in which life is all "show," and the whole world a stage or its "scene."[79] More's first humanist counsels for making the best of this image of life emphasize both the wisdom of silent detachment and the prudence of "playing along"; in this late, extreme instance, though, what makes the best of a life finally verging on outrageous farce is precisely the wanton disruption that mars the whole show, shaming shameless transgressors from their entertainments with still greater shame—something Luther, of course, on More's reading at least, would be clearly the last man to do. The true tactically indiscreet spoiler in this scene must surely be More the wise-fool, but undoing-undone, willingly self-effaced and consumed as he seems in the act (or the *act*) of outscandalizing even a Luther, swallowed up tragic passions and all in his own Socratic Silenus-masque of ironic and comic transvaluing.[80]

To do Luther some part of the justice that More never outwardly does, we should add that More "trumps" or outfaces his enemy's impudence in a way that makes More much *like* Luther, "above" shame as well as beneath it, justified "not in other men's eyes but [he hopes] in his God's,"[81] staking all on a feat of transvaluing reversal that turns worldly disgrace into gain, flouts all outward appraisers indifferently, and when valid, *can* arm a discountenanced selfhood—like Gyges—to hide in plain sight. Unlike Luther's, however, More's form of this saving and saved Christian-Cynic indifference subjects even the insular self thus secured to the same sort of skeptical handling as anything else culture comes to set up as a primary good; in this sense Cynic laughter for More, and not only for More, reconciles even more than it flouts, since above all it flouts the abusive self-seriousness that all fetishized values including the

78. On the blithely self-ignorant fool as an inverted Gyges, see Henri Bergson, "Laughter," in *Comedy,* ed. W. Sypher (Garden City 1956),71; cf. also Stith Thompson, *Motif-Index of Folk-Literature,* 11 vols. (Bloomington 1932–36), no. J2312 ("Naked person made to believe he is clothed"), and the 1578 sermon-excerpt in Chambers, *ES* 4, p. 200, against all sorts of plays and—the final straw—"men naked dauncing in nettes, which is most filthie" (a reference, the context suggests, to a Maygame or Midsummer-skit that took place in or close to a churchyard).

79. See the note in *CW* 15, pp. 630–31, and on Lucian, Branham (above, n. 8) esp. 24.

80. For More's crossings of tragedy and comedy even in his most violent polemics see the refs. in n. 69; cf. also n. 8, *CW* 15, pp. 50–54, and S. Greenblatt on More with the answer in *CW* 15, lxxviii.

81. Luther's 1515 lectures on Romans, *WA* 56, p. 268; cf. More, *CW* 15, pp. 302–4, and nn.

new, absolute, faith-sufficed Selfhood promoted by Luther enthrone.[82] We have seen Cynic selfhood deployed in licentious as well as ascetic departures from workaday norms; what we see in this unseemly two-in-one faceoff of Luther and More "in the theater of the whole world" is more like a now-standard if endlessly open exchange between bold born-again self-assertion and pious denial, overstatement and reflex-retrenchment, in which in effect self-affirmation leaves nothing untried and tradition itself in the long run leaves nothing uncriticized. In this epochally unmoored exchange the ironic hyperboles of Cynic autonomy, self-exalting and self-compromising at once, are both ballast and buoys for the new floating norms of dogmatically supple modernity.[83]

82. Cf. Bergson (above, n. 78) 74, on laughter as a social antidote to "rigidity."

83. On the antithetical complementarity of scientific and skeptical discourse in post-Renaissance contexts, see texts cited here in nn. 6, 29, 57, 59, and the essay by Niehues-Pröbsting in this volume; on a similarly uneasy interdependence between "systematic" and "edifying" philosophical discourse, see Richard Rorty, *Philosophy and the Mirror of Nature* (Princeton 1979) esp. 367–72. In my view, it is not hard to read much of renaissance rhetorical discourse in the same way that Nietzsche, for instance, reads Shakespeare as well as Montaigne, as intently "reactive" as well as self-questioning or as precociously edifying in Rorty's sense.

For what might be described as another, still more problematic descent of Cynic practical paradoxy, see Martin Jay, "Abjection Overruled," *Salmagundi,* 103 (1994), 235–51.

The Modern Reception of Cynicism: Diogenes in the Enlightenment

Heinrich Niehues-Pröbsting

The first problem encountered by anyone dealing with the history of the reception of Cynicism is the problem of the sources. I am not referring to the fragmentary state in which ancient documents have been handed down to us, but rather to the literary form of those texts in which Cynic thought was formulated, transmitted, and actualized. What sort of texts are we dealing with here? Where could one search for the relevant documents? Where would they be found? And how does this situation present itself particularly in modern contexts? Before I turn to the discussion of contents, I would like at least briefly to address this formal aspect of reception.

Philosophy produces itself mostly in theories and theoretical treatises. This is even more the case in modern than in ancient times. The continuation of a philosophy takes place essentially in its transmission and in commentaries, in the discussion and the criticism as well as the elaboration of its theories. Such a foundation of tradition and reception is absent from Cynicism, for it did not produce theories. The material on Cynicism handed down from antiquity—in particular by Diogenes Laertius—is mostly of an anecdotal-biographical and sententious kind. The anecdote and the apophthegm are the most important media of Cynic tradition, and they are the literary forms most suitable to Cynicism and its representation.

An abundance of such material enters the early modern historiography of philosophy. This is due to the fact that this historiography still relies for the most part on the paradigm of the ancient historiography of philosophy, namely

Translated by Peter Gilgen, Stanford University. All translations from other texts also by Gilgen unless noted. I would like to thank my friend Conrad Curtis for many invaluable stylistic suggestions.

the *Lives and Opinions of Famous Philosophers* by Diogenes Laertius. And like Diogenes Laertius, who dedicated a whole book to Cynicism, early modern histories of philosophy give ample space to the description of the Cynic school or sect and in particular to Diogenes. Indeed, the Cynics occupy more space than many philosophers who for theoretical reasons are considered more important in the contemporary historiography of philosophy.

In the modern period, the transmission of Cynicism on the basis of anecdote and apophthegm was twice seriously questioned and shaken,[1] first by historical criticism as practiced in an exemplary and influential fashion by Pierre Bayle. He and his successors subjected the copiously transmitted anecdotal-biographical material to the standard of historical credibility. Thus, they reduced it to a steadily decreasing stock of anecdotes that were believed to be true. Only later, in reaction to historical-philological criticism, was it recognized that the value of an anecdote—its philosophical and moral meaning—does not necessarily depend on its historical truth. At least the requirements of historical criticism for the time guaranteed the continued examination of the untrue stories, the fables or fairy tales, even if the aim was solely to devalue them by demonstrating their ahistoricity and to withdraw them from circulation. Precisely this intention necessitated a thorough study of these stories, such as Bayle's study of certain versions of the Diogenes-Alexander anecdote, or that of Christoph August Heumann (a German successor of Bayle) of the anecdote about Diogenes and the tub.

When the anecdotal-biographical basis of the reception of Cynicism was shaken for the second time, the consequences were even graver and more devastating than those of historical criticism. This second challenge was ushered in through the understanding of the history of philosophy that Hegel formulated, as a consequence of which he criticized the earlier historiography of philosophy as unphilosophical. After this, the history of philosophy is reduced to the history of ideas: only the theoretical products of philosophers, not their biographies, are of importance for the history of philosophy. Before this shift, the transmission of biographies had a large place in the historiography of philosophy, for the life of the philosopher was believed to be of exemplary character and was considered the verification of the doctrine. Now, biographical transmission becomes an inessential and superfluous accessory: "The bodies of these spirits who are the heroes of this history, their temporal lives, have passed, but their works did not follow them; for the content of their works is the rational [*das Vernünftige*]," writes Hegel. Only the works count, and moreover, the more they have left behind the individual signature of their creator, the more they "belong to free thinking, the universal character of man as man,

---

1. Cf. H. Niehues-Pröbsting, "Anekdote als philosophiegeschichtliches Medium," *Nietzsche-Studien* 12 (1983) 255–86.

the more this thinking free of peculiarities is itself the producing subject." [2]
For those philosophers who did not leave behind theoretical works and who
became part of the tradition only by virtue of their exemplary individuality
or their idiosyncratic personalities, this meant exclusion from the history of
philosophy. Reduced to a mere history of theories or ideas, a historiography
of philosophy does not know how to deal with them. This primarily affects
the Cynics and their chief exemplar, Diogenes. Even though they were still
dragged along in the histories of philosophy in the nineteenth century and have
begun to be excluded from them at an increasing rate only very recently, it was
in fact the Hegelian understanding of the history of philosophy that pushed
them aside into the curiosities at the margin of this history.

While the treatments found in histories of philosophy are the most obvious
documents of the reception of Cynicism, they are not always the most interesting, at least not for someone studying the connection between classical Cynicism and modern cynicism and analyzing the genealogy of the modern concept. In this kind of context, the historically distancing and objectivizing
treatments are usually less illuminating than the topical reception. I am not
referring to the practical imitation of the Cynic lifestyle, although one can find
sporadic examples for this in modern times as well. Rather, the evidence may
be found in the conscious imitation of particular Cynic gestures, in the avowal
of Cynic maxims and attitudes, in the literary relation to Cynic motifs and the
figure of the Cynic, in the use of this figure as one of projection and identification, and in many other forms. Such references can be found less in
theoretical-philosophical than in literary-philosophical or even purely literary
texts—for example, in moral, satirical, and aphoristic literature. After some
time, a reader develops a feeling that indicates to him which authors might have
used Cynic motifs and quotations. The contexts that give rise to such references
are those of, for example, sexuality and satire, misanthropy, the social exclusion of outsiders and extreme individualism, the critique of culture and the
advocacy of natural conditions free of civilization. In the modern period,
shameless sexual speech as well as biting satire and insulting sarcasm were
perceived as being decisively Cynic; and, not surprisingly, the roots of the modern concept of cynicism are to be found there. Modern cynicism was originally
sexual and comical. [3]

2. Georg Wilhelm Friedrich Hegel, *Vorlesungen über die Geschichte der Philosophie,* in
Werke, ed. H. Glockner, vol. 17 (Stuttgart 1959) 28; cf. 68.
3. In contrast to other European languages, the form *Cynismus,* which up to this point had
been uniform, was given up in German in the nineteenth century and replaced by the distinction
between *Kynismus*—which exclusively designates the philosophy of Antisthenes and Diogenes
and their classical successors—and *Zynismus* as a name for an attitude that does not recognize
anything as sacred and that insults values, feelings, and decorum provocatively, with biting sarcasm, or even just by deliberate indifference. About the emergence of the modern concept of

I would like to present the modern reception of Cynicism and its connection to the modern concept of cynicism by following the thematic thread that is the most rewarding from a philosophical perspective and has been the center of attention in the most recent reception and actualization of Cynicism: the relationship between the Enlightenment and Cynicism. I start with a quotation that alludes to the most important aspects of this topic and can therefore serve as a motto of what is to follow: "Diogenes the Cynic was one of those extraordinary human beings who indulge in excesses in whatever they do—even in matters of reason—and who confirm the principle that there is no great mind whose character is free of all folly." With this sentence, Pierre Bayle, an important precursor of the Enlightenment, opens the article "Diogenes" in his *Dictionnaire historique et critique*.[4]

I would like to underline four points in this summary evaluation of the figure of the proto-Cynic. First, Diogenes is an "extraordinary human being" and a "great mind"—someone to whom Bayle dedicates a great deal of attention and a long article. Second, Diogenes is a representative of reason, considered to be the highest and most decisive authority by the Enlightenment. This provides the basis for the Enlightenment philosophers' sympathy for the Cynic, and it makes him an effective figure for identifying Enlightenment ideals and motifs. Ideals that the Enlightenment associated with Cynicism are, for example, the freedom from prejudice and the open criticism of secular and religious authorities; the autonomy of the individual and the separation of morality from religious constraints; universal philanthropy [*Menschenliebe*] and cosmopolitanism.

Third, Diogenes nevertheless represents not only reason but also its opposite, the other of reason, folly. That turns him, or rather his acolytes, into the target of Enlightenment sarcasm and the word "Cynic" into a term of abuse that Enlightenment philosophers apply to the outsider in their own ranks, Rousseau.

A history of names of philosophers and philosophical schools must include the rhetorical-polemic function that is often connected with them and usually ignored by a pure history of ideas and a doxography merely interested in factual contents and their meanings. "Epicureanism," "Idealism," "Positivism," to mention just a few, are not the names of pure facts, but rather represent controversial positions and programs. Furthermore, they serve as polemical terms and even insults. Often enough, someone is made into an Epicurean, idealist, or positivist only to be attacked and exposed publicly.

This is particularly true for the classical terms "Cynic" and "Cynicism"

---

cynicism (*Zynismus*) from the reception of Cynicism (*Kynismus*), cf. H. Niehues-Pröbsting, *Der Kynismus des Diogenes und der Begriff des Zynismus*, 2d ed. (Frankfurt 1988).

4. *Peter Baylens Historisches und critisches Wörterbuch*, trans. J.C. Gottsched (Leipzig 1741–44), 2.310.

and even more for the modern "cynic" and "cynicism." The colloquial use of "cynic" and "cynicism" almost always highlights the polemical intention at the expense of a precise meaning. Whatever it means when, for example, one politician accuses another of cynicism, surely something pejorative is meant by it, and it indicates the greatest indignation on the part of the person making the accusation.

Once one has noticed the rhetorical potential and the polemical virulence that can be found in the figure of the Cynic and the early modern concept of Cynicism, one also will notice the important role the figure of Diogenes and Cynicism played in the self-definition of the philosophers of the Enlightenment qua philosophers, in arguments among them, and in resistance to them and the Enlightenment. As long as the Enlightenment cannot be considered historically dead and gone, the quarrels and discussions within and about it are of more than merely historical interest. Not least, the history of the reception of Cynicism provides a vital insight into the polemical style of the Enlightenment as well as of that of the Counter-Enlightenment. Here, a phenomenology of polemics and the expression of contempt can find rich illustrative material.

Fourth, and finally, in cynicism, folly is not a contingent moment, but a consequence of reason itself, the consequence of the excesses of reason. Cynic folly is the dark and seamy side of reason. In Cynicism, the Enlightenment discovers the danger of reason being perverted, reason turning into irrationality and madness, reason being frustrated because of its own far too exalted expectations. The Enlightenment becomes aware of this menace to itself through its affinity with Cynicism. The reflection on Cynicism provides a necessary piece of self-recognition and self-criticism. Consequently the failure of the Enlightenment—or of one part of it—leads to cynicism in the modern sense of the word. "Cynicism is *enlightened false consciousness.*" [5]

In his evaluation of Diogenes, Bayle refers to the ancient anecdote in which Plato called Diogenes a *Sōkratēs mainomenos,* a Socrates gone mad. We will be repeatedly reminded of this story below, when I illustrate the last three aspects just listed of the reception of Cynicism in the Enlightenment, all of which are of far-reaching importance for the understanding of the Enlightenment itself. This anecdote is so striking because it expresses not only the exaggerating, lampooning side of Cynicism, but also the reverse, the topsy-turvy perspective that marks Diogenes' relationship with Socrates, especially the Platonic Socrates. It is well known that Socrates is one of the great guiding figures of the Enlightenment. The identification with him is not problematic. This changes with the mad Socrates: if the Enlightenment mirrors itself in this figure, it cannot perceive itself exclusively as an ideal or a success, but also as failing and failed.

---

5. P. Sloterdijk, *Kritik der zynischen Vernunft* (Frankfurt 1983) 37.

We find the absolute idealization of the Cynic from the Enlightenment's point of view in Christoph Martin Wieland's literary adaptation of the Diogenes figure, which first appeared in 1770 under the title *Socrates Mainomenos; or, The Dialogues of Diogenes of Sinope* (*Sokrates mainomenos oder die Dialogen des Diogenes von Sinope*). The book had a quick and enormous but short-lived success. Already in 1772, it appeared in a French translation, *Socrate en délire, ou Dialogues de Diogène de Synope*. Diderot knew it and liked its author because of it. The most eminent man of letters of the German Enlightenment besides Lessing had intertwined the Diogenes tradition of antiquity with fictional stories and expanded the whole fantastically in the contemporary styles of rococo and sentimentality.

The main point Wieland pursues in his *Diogenes* is the representation of the free and independent personality. "I therefore admit," says Wieland's Diogenes, "that many years ago I studied explicitly 'how I could make myself as independent as possible.' I found out 'that this is possible under certain circumstances' and 'that these circumstances are in my power.' " [6] Frugality and distance from society serve to achieve independence, and only because of this do they seem desirable to the Cynic Wieland. Wieland adjusts the Cynic concept of virtue to his own ideal of enlightened humanity (which in turn is influenced by Winckelmann's idealization of the Greeks) and juxtaposes it with the suppression of joy and the senses in Stoic-Christian morality. This Cynic's virtue does not lack grace. Diogenes is presented neither as an ascetic and grim fanatic of virtue nor as a rigorous moralist. He is—in his own words—no despiser of the beautiful, no enemy of pleasure, no hater of joy. If the Platonist preaches that voluptuousness enervates, he counters that virtue does likewise. Joy as such cannot be claimed by the devil, for the simple reason that doing good is itself the highest joy, a divine joy.

Since virtue is essentially a function of humanity, vice is not a matter of pleasure or desire but a crime against human nature and a lack of humanity, whether from wickedness, selfishness, envy, or indolence in the face of others' needs. The Cynic's distance from society therefore does not make him a misanthrope. He does not belong to any particular society or nation; rather he is a cosmopolitan. Cosmopolitanism, however, is the fullest realization of the Enlightenment: whoever is a member of and identifies with a particular society is subject to its prejudices and restricted opinions. His actions are determined by unilateral interests. Every society has its particular moral views, and whatever is considered a virtue according to those views "often turns out to be merely a splendid vice before the tribunal of nature." By distancing himself from prejudices and biases, which integration into a particular society necessarily entails,

---

6. *Wieland's Werke* (Berlin 1879) 24.22. On this topic, cf. H. Niehues-Pröbsting, "Wielands Diogenes und der Rameau Diderots: Zur Differenz von Kyniker und Zyniker in der Sicht der Aufklärung," in *Peter Sloterdijks "Kritik der zynischen Vernunft"* (Frankfurt 1987) 111ff.

the cosmopolitan has privileged access to truth. This enables him to tell others the truth. He can therefore be of great benefit, if only others make use of his insights. Thus the existence of the Cynic is positively legitimized in the universal human sense.

The Cynics' harshest criticism attacks the rich, the drones of society. Protected by the civil constitution and its institutions, they acquire and increase their property by exploiting the labor of others. And the order of the state even protects property against the demands of those who created it in the first place. But the civil constitution is not identical with natural law; for natural law does not know slaves by birth. By nature the worker is not distinguished from the master, but all are equal. It is therefore no far-fetched idea that the people against whom society discriminates one day will unite against the privileged in order to bring about a revolution. As if he wanted to appease the authorities, Wieland has his Diogenes soften this revolutionary thought: the case presented must be indeed considered possible, "for many reasons not all too alarming." [7]

In the criticism of the inequality of social relations, Wieland's Diogenes shows the most concrete affinity to the Enlightenment and its political ideals. Here he is most radical, and his idea of a possible revolution—twenty years before the French Revolution—turns out to be downright prophetic. Here, where he talks like a modern theoretician of the state, he seems the most modern and thus the most anachronistic. Nevertheless, the background is provided by a motif that is central to Diogenes' Cynicism, namely the antithesis of law and nature, of *nomos* and *physis*. In the practical application of this antithesis, the Cynic of antiquity represents himself as the heir and executor of the sophistic Enlightenment. For Wieland's Diogenes, the antithesis becomes the difference between positive, civil law and natural law. In the iconography of the French Revolution, Diogenes becomes nothing short of a civil hero; and a German count, Gustav von Schlabrendorf—who out of philanthropic and republican enthusiasm for the revolution moved to Paris in 1789, was an intimate acquaintance of Mirabeau's, escaped the terror, and criticized Napoleon's expansion of power—this Gustav von Schlabrendorf became the "Diogenes of Paris." [8]

Wieland wove a series of satires on religion, philosophy, and political theory into his Diogenes novel and privately sneered at the fact that most readers had not recognized the contemporary objects of the satire—church, metaphysics, and social utopias in the tradition of Rousseau—underneath the disguise of antiquity. The use of Diogenes as a persona in satire that cultivates the satirical tendency of classical Cynicism is common and widespread in the eighteenth century.

---

7. Ibid. 70.
8. Rich material about Diogenes in the reception and iconography at the time of the French Revolution can be found in K. Herding, "Diogenes als Bürgerheld," *Boreas* 5 (1982) 232ff.

In Wieland's Diogenes novel, the identification of the author with his pro-tagonist is significant. In a letter to his friend Sophie von la Roche, he explicitly admits: "You see that the philosophy of Diogenes is much more my own than you would like to believe." [9] In the ideal of Cynic *autarkeia* (self-sufficiency), Wieland, who had just become a professor of philosophy, expresses his desire for the freedom that is the condition of intellectual independence. The Cynic's mode of existence becomes the model for the social position of the modern intellectual.

From the third edition onward, Wieland changed the title of the novel into *The Legacy of Diogenes of Sinope*. The original *Sōkratēs mainomenos* (Socrates Gone Mad) seemed too disreputable to him, for his Diogenes should not be a shameless fool, as he is represented by Diogenes Laertius and Athenaeus. If one believed these two, "Diogenes the Cynic would have to be the most despicable and foolish, the filthiest and most unbearable lad who ever defaced the human figure." Only as an improved and idealized Cynic, as described by Epictetus or by Lucian in the *Demonax,* was Diogenes Wieland's ideal. The negative, filthy, and crude Cynicism was despised and excluded by the urbane representative of the Enlightenment. Wieland, wrote his biographer Gruber, describes Diogenes "as an eccentric, but with a good measure less Cynicism and more wisdom than one usually ascribed to him." [10] Wieland himself justi-fied the rest of the Cynicism in the novel as necessary to the historical frame needed to make his protagonist recognizable in spite of all the idealization. When a single offensive word uttered by the protagonist was pointed out to him, he argued that the word "would not be in my book, if *I* were speaking; however, it is Diogenes the Cynic who speaks and whom I idealized to such a degree that I had to add a trait of Cynicism now and then in order not to distort this man beyond recognition for the scholars." [11]

Wieland's whole disposition was not inclined to Cynicism, as Goethe, who was thrilled with the Diogenes novel in his youth, once observed astutely. On the one hand, Wieland was too moderate for the extremes of Cynicism. Humor, irony, and satire are the essential elements of his literary works; for this reason, Laurence Sterne and Lucian were the crucial models for him. But the increased sharpness of a cynical type of humor was far from the courtesy and civility of his character. He certainly had a taste for the erotic as he found it in contem-porary French literature—for example, in Diderot's novels—and he was there-fore reproached for being obscene. But he avoided the pronounced Cynic the-matization of sexuality.

9. "Vous voyez que la philosophie de Diogène est beaucoup plus la mienne, que vous m'avez paru vouloir la croire": 20 March 1770; quoted after F. Martini's afterword in Christoph Martin Wieland, *Werke* 2 (Munich 1966) 843.

10. J.G. Gruber, *C.M. Wielands Leben* (Leipzig 1827) 4.569.

11. Cf. ibid. 571f.

On the other hand, Wieland displayed an entirely skeptical attitude toward the Cynic critique of culture and civilization as it was spectacularly revived, in particular by Rousseau. It is telling that Napoleon, well instructed by his intellectual advisers, addressed him as the German Voltaire. Wieland had no taste for Cynic asceticism and the minimal and crude Cynic satisfaction of needs, but leaned toward a temperate hedonism. He had his roots in the rococo; its refinement of manners was second-nature to him and diametrically opposed to the Cynic coarseness, as Goethe remarked astutely: "It is therefore no wonder that Wieland's tender nature leans toward Aristippic philosophy; on the other hand, his decisive dislike of Diogenes and all of Cynicism for this very reason can be very satisfactorily explained. A mind like Wieland's, in which the gracefulness of all forms is born, cannot possibly be delighted in a continuous and systematic undoing of these forms." [12]

Since Wieland distanced himself from and even opposed himself to all these aspects of Cynicism, the one aspect that enticed him to study Cynicism and to identify with the proto-Cynic carries all the more weight: the independence of the person. That was the essential element of his understanding of Diogenes, and as he grew older he proceeded to reduce it to this one point. Even in retrospect, after almost three decades he judged the *Diogenes* to be one of his best works: "I don't know whether I ever wrote a better one in prose." (This evaluation was not shared in the field of German literary scholarship.) "In it I have idealized Diogenes in my own way, for of the old Diogenes only the tendency to independence remained." [13]

At this time, the decade of the French Revolution, Wieland also had a historical-political reason to think highly of the *Diogenes.* In it he predicted, as I mentioned above, the emergence of a revolutionary situation. In 1787, two years before the French Revolution, he repeated this prediction in the Lucianic dialogue *A Pleasure Trip to Elysium* (*Eine Lustreise ins Elysium*).[14] With the figure of Menippus, the author's fictional partner in the dialogue, Wieland again refers to the literary tradition of Cynicism. One year after the beginning of the revolution, he opens his essay "Unparteiische Betrachtungen über die dermalige Staatsrevolution in Frankreich" (Impartial Reflections on the State Revolution in France) with a recollection of this prediction.[15]

By 1797, the year of the retrospective remark about the *Diogenes,* the great expectations excited by the revolution had been disappointed. Wieland, however, saw the political content of his *Diogenes* confirmed by the course of the revolution. Besides the satire on speculative metaphysics, his favorite part of

---

12. J. Falk, *Goethe aus näherem persönlichen Umgange dargestellt* (Leipzig 1832) 80f.

13. Böttiger's notes from 26 February 1797 on a conversation with Wieland, in T.C. Starnes, *Christoph Martin Wieland: Leben und Werk,* vol. 2, *1784–1799* (Sigmaringen 1987) 568.

14. *Wieland's Werke* (above, n. 6) 33.252f.

15. Ibid. 34.65f.

the novel was the added *Republik des Diogenes.* Wieland knew of course that the *Republic* ascribed to Diogenes could have only been a satirical, parodic antithesis to Plato's *Politeia.* Therefore he makes his Diogenes too into a representative of a decisive anti-Platonism, particularly where the regulation of sexual matters is concerned. But Wieland's satirical intention aims at the classical utopia of an ideal state only on the surface. Beyond that, it is primarily directed at the contemporary critique of civilization and the idealization of a state of society in which humans who are mostly untouched by the achievements of culture supposedly live in accordance with nature and in happy harmony with each other. Such an ahistorical state excludes any development and is incompatible with the needful nature of man. Human needs are the engine of perfectibility, and perfectibility can be avoided only at the price of artificially limiting the needs. An ideal state of society is a paradox, since human nature excludes the immutability and immobility of the ideal. There cannot be an ideal republic. The republic of Diogenes must be made invisible by its creator in order to be preserved in its ahistorical immutability: "They will not find it in eternity," reads the ironic closing sentence, which is supposed to warn everybody who wants to search for and realize this construct of the imagination in reality. Wieland regretted that the French had not taken note of this warning: "If the French had read my *Republic of Diogenes,* they would have been cured from their addiction to republics at once. For there I provided a proof as clear as daylight that the conditions under which the true republic would be possible in this world are not at all sublunar." [16]

Eleven years after this retrospective, history led the old Wieland once more back to the *Diogenes.* In the *Diogenes,* he had had the premonition of a revolution. The novel had been confirmed in his eyes by the course of the French Revolution. Now, in 1808, Napoleon, the executor of the revolution, brought up the topic of the *Diogenes.* The emperor himself barely knew Wieland, as he admitted in conversation with Goethe. That he nevertheless wished to see him as well as Goethe testifies to Wieland's high popularity in France. There, his works were cherished, and he was called Germany's Voltaire. With this compliment, Napoleon, according to Talleyrand's notes, opened the conversation. Among the works he mentioned by name was the *Diogenes:* "Tell me, Monsieur Wieland, why did you write your Diogenes, your Agathon, and your Peregrinus in such an ambiguous form, which makes the novel switch over into history and history into the novel? As important a man as you should treat each genre on its own and for itself. Such a mixture easily causes confusion." Wieland justified the criticized mode of representation with his pedagogical aims and eventually talked about the didactics of history *and* the novel: "Voltaire's *The Century of Louis XIV* and Fénelon's *Telémaque*—in the first case the history, in the latter the novel—both contain in their own ways the best instruction

16. Starnes (above, n. 13) 568.

for kings as well as for peoples. My Diogenes is also purely human, even if he only lives in a tub." [17]

The reference to Diogenes at this point only seems unexpected: *Diogenes* contains the best instruction as well, not only for kings—this view of Wieland's we already know—but also for peoples. His Diogenes is not one of those Cynics, hated especially at the courts, who excel in loud insults and provocative contempt for power and the powerful. "The Cynicism that more and more seems to become a fashion and among whose comical symptoms we also find the fact that we view our kings with such pride—this Cynicism will, like all fashions, pass," wrote Wieland in 1777 in his essay "Über das göttliche Recht der Obrigkeit" (On the Divine Right of the Authorities).[18] Wieland's Diogenes does not display this arrogant Cynicism toward power and the powerful. If Napoleon had read the novel, he who liked to see himself as the new Alexander would have recalled the dialogue between Diogenes and Alexander. In the novel, Diogenes turns down the king's request to be his adviser and inseparable companion, but agrees to a conversation. He expresses his appreciation for the man who is about to conquer the world as well as his fear of a possible misuse of power; he reminds him of the duties of humanity and warns him of the dangers of power.

The dialogue between Diogenes and Alexander immediately precedes the *Republik des Diogenes;* both parts correspond with each other: in one case, the extremes of power are thematized; in the other, the republic, the utopian society free of all domination. Wieland was skeptical about both extremes.

If one compares the real scene of 1808 with the literary scene of 1769, one notices that Wieland's behavior toward Napoleon parallels the behavior of his Diogenes. This behavior is determined neither by arrogant Cynicism nor by subservience, but rather by calm self-confidence. Wieland does not turn down the emperor when he asks him for a meeting; but at the same time he does not impose himself on the emperor, and he is not willing to be ordered around. Furthermore, *he* ends the meeting. Wieland behaves toward Napoleon "by no means like a courtier—even when Napoleon is a victor fresh from battle. Wieland is the one who must be entreated to show up and who determines when he will take leave." [19]

———•◆•———

The Diogenes novel marked the starting point of Wieland's discussion of Rousseau and Rousseauism. In the same year as the *Diogenes,* a series of

17. *Memoiren des Fürsten Talleyrand,* ed. Duke of Broglie, German ed. A. Ebeling, vol. 1 (Cologne 1891) 326.

18. *Wieland's Werke* (above, n. 6) 33.117. In the essay *Gedanken über eine alte Aufschrift,* Wieland juxtaposed the despotic and the Cynic consciousness of independence as two extreme types of arrogance toward the opinions of others (ibid. 32.43–63).

19. H. Blumenberg, "Das Erschrecken des Aufklärers vor dem Vollstrecker der Revolution: Zum 250. Geburtstag von Christoph Martin Wieland," *Neue Zürcher Zeitung,* 2 September 1983.

smaller literary works and theoretical essays were published under the title *Contributions to the Secret History of Human Understanding and the Human Heart, Drawn from the Archives of Nature* (*Beiträge zur geheimen Geschichte des menschlichen Verstandes und Herzens, aus den Archiven der Natur gezogen*). The transition from Diogenes to Rousseau suggested itself, especially since Rousseau seemed to follow the tracks of the Cynic in his cultural critique and the idealization of untouched nature in the first and second *Discours*. "As a matter of fact, in his first *Discourse* Rousseau continues a tradition that is associated with names like the Cynic Diogenes, Socrates, Jesus, Seneca, or even Saint Francis of Assisi." [20] "For an ear trained in the classics Diogenes' accent in the *Discourse on Inequality* could not go unnoticed." [21] The contemporaries noticed this accent immediately and called Rousseau a new Diogenes.

Inversely, the influence of Rousseau, the "subtle Diogenes," led Kant to represent Cynicism as thoroughly Rousseauist. In his lectures on ethics he divides up classical ethics into the Cynic, the Epicurean, and the Stoic ideal. The Cynic ideal is "the ideal of innocence or rather simplicity. Diogenes says the highest good consists of simplicity, of moderation in the enjoyment of happiness." The sympathy with which Kant pondered the Cynic ideal had its roots not least in the Rousseauist influence: Kant's positive understanding of Rousseau was carried over into Cynicism; the notoriously scandalous was left unsaid. Kant discovered the basic truth of Cynicism through Rousseau, namely that happiness is increased rather by the decrease than by the increase of needs. "The Cynic sect says the highest good is a thing of nature, not art. For Diogenes the means of happiness were negative. He said that human nature is satisfied with little, for, when in accordance with nature, human beings do not have needs. Thus a human being does not experience the lack of means and enjoys his happiness precisely in the light of this lack. There is a lot of truth in Diogenes, for nature's supply of means and talents increases our needs. For the more means we have at our disposal, the more needs arise, and the human inclination toward greater satisfaction increases steadily; therefore the mind is restless at all times. Rousseau, the subtle Diogenes, also insists that our will is good by nature; it is only we who succumb to corruption, and that nature gave us everything; it is only we who create ever-new needs. He also thinks that the education of children should be merely negative." [22]

Soon the comparison with Diogenes became a commonplace among Rousseau's contemporaries. Rousseau himself, however, only rarely referred to the Cynic. The identification or comparison with Diogenes was barely of any importance in his case—contrary, for example, to Wieland or Diderot. The proto-

20. M. Forschner, *Rousseau* (Freiburg 1977) 7.
21. J. Starobinski, "Diderot's Satire 'Rameau's Neffe,'" in *Das Rettende in der Gefahr: Kunstgriffe der Aufklärung,* trans. H. Günther (Frankfurt 1990), 308.
22. Paul Menzer, ed., *Eine Vorlesung Kants über Ethik* (Berlin 1924) 8f.

Cynic was mentioned only one single time in the two literary works that gave Rousseau the reputation of being a new Diogenes: in the second *Discours* he is mentioned, together with Cato, as the example of an untimely man. Diogenes and Cato belonged to a past—that is, better—age. That is the reason "why Diogenes did not find a single man, namely because he wanted to meet men from a time long past among his contemporaries." [23]

It is surprising that he who was *the* new Diogenes in the eyes of his contemporaries would avoid the comparison with Diogenes. As a matter of fact, Rousseau had several reasons to avoid this comparison: the virtue he stressed so emphatically in his early writings is Spartan and Roman, but not philosophical. For philosophy as learnedness is partly responsible for the decay of morals. In the preface to *Narcisse,* written between the first and the second *Discours,* Rousseau counted Diogenes among the founders of paradoxical philosophical systems, which cause more evil than good, because the motifs of their creators are vanity and the craze for originality. Not virtue but their own reputation is the actual purpose of these teachers, who go to any length for it. "The first philosophers gained a great reputation for teaching men to carry out their duties and the principles of virtue. But soon these teachings had become universal, and others felt the need to distinguish themselves by going opposite ways. Here lies the origin of the paradoxical systems of Leucippus, Diogenes, Pyrrho, Protagoras, Lucretius." [24]

The paragon of virtue is not a philosopher but Cato; he is the "greatest man." (Later Rousseau was going to put Jesus above Socrates.) From the fact that Diogenes is mentioned together with Cato, it does not follow that he must be considered an equally positive model. When the Diogenes who searched for a human being is mentioned, the stress is on the critical aspect: virtuous men no longer exist. That Diogenes is himself a virtuous man is not said, and Rousseau did not insist on it. Time and again, however, he said it of Cato.

After the success of the first *Discours,* Rousseau changed his demeanor conspicuously and adopted the behavior of a Cynic: "Up to that point he was a man of compliments, courteous, well mannered, sweet as honey in his demeanor, and through the use of mannered idioms he became almost tiresome. Suddenly, however, he cloaked himself in the coat of the Cynic and fell into the other extreme, which stood in stark contrast to the nature of his character. But while he hurled around his sarcasms, he was always considerate enough to make exceptions as far as the people who lived with him were concerned. He also knew well how to combine his harsh and Cynic tone with his previous

23. Jean-Jacques Rousseau, *Schriften,* ed. H. Ritter (Munich 1978), 1.263. The combination of the two notorious judges of morals, Diogenes and Cato, was not new; in the eighteenth century, there was an anonymous publication *Le Caton et Diogène françois* and a quarrel about the misuse of the names of Diogenes and Cato. Cf. Herding (above, n. 8) 238 n. 22.

24. Rousseau (above, n. 23) 1.154.

refinements and artful compliments. This he did particularly when he was deal-ing with women." [25] One should not distrust this description because it stems from Diderot's closest friend, Grimm, and was made after the break between Diderot's circle and Rousseau had already occurred. Rousseau himself con-firmed the description in a paragraph of the *Confessions.* There he interprets his own Cynicism as the precautionary mechanism of a shy person who is helpless in his world. Because he was afraid to breach the etiquette of the big world of which he now was a part, time and again because of his clumsiness he assumed the role of a despiser of convention: "For shyness I became a Cynic and mocker, and I pretended to scorn deeply the good manners I had been unable to acquire." [26] A few pages later, when describing the premiere of his musical comedy *The Village Prophet* (1752), Rousseau gave the most beau-tiful examples of his personal Cynicism and its function. The hidden meaning of this description lies in the demonstration that, when all is said and done, he was *no* Cynic. He himself time and again unraveled the Cynic pattern he wove.

To this event, where the king was present as well, he showed up in the outfit of a Cynic, unshaven and with an unkempt wig. This was supposed to raise his courage, as he admitted. This Cynicism was preventive: in his outer appearance Rousseau tried out the ridiculousness that, he feared, would befall him through the failure of his play. "One will find me ridiculous and inconsiderate," he said to himself. "Well, who cares? I must try to accept ridicule and disapproval calmly, particularly since they are not justified in any way." [27] Against the feared failure he armed himself with Cynicism—but not against the success that really ensued and broke through the Cynic armor of his sentimental soul: Rousseau was moved to tears.

That was not yet all: that very evening he was told that the king wanted to receive him the following day; the prospect of a pension from the king was held out to him. Rousseau did not show up; the pension was lost. Was this Cynic courage before the thrones of kings, as exemplified in the Diogenes anecdotes? Rousseau himself went against this pattern relentlessly—as one is almost in-clined to say—by giving reasons for his absence. These reasons were totally un-Cynical: he did not sleep all night long, because he feared that he would be stricken with his ailment, enuresis, precisely in the presence of the king. A true Cynic would not have been unnerved by this; he might have even turned the urgency into a gesture of contempt. The second reason is Rousseau's "accursed shyness." The thought that he might not find the appropriate words before the king caused him to panic: "What would I become in such a moment, observed by the whole court, if, because of the excitement, I let one of my usual boorish

25. Frédéric-Melchior Baron de Grimm, quoted after J. Popper-Lynkeus, *Voltaire,* 3d ed. (Vi-enna 1925), 296.
26. Jean-Jacques Rousseau, *Bekenntnisse,* 3d ed., trans. E. Hardt (Frankfurt 1955), 468.
27. Ibid. 480f.

remarks come over my lips? This danger put me in such fear, such horror, that I decided not to expose myself to it at any cost and no matter what would result from it." [28]

Rousseau—this he made clear in these disclosures about himself—was essentially not a callous Cynic, but exactly the opposite. Cynicism was foreign to his nature; whenever he adopted Cynicism or pretended to be a Cynic, it was out of necessity and not of virtue. It was the others who made him a Cynic, the public, even his friends: "As far as Diderot is concerned, I have no clue how it happened that all the conversations with him always led to the point where I became more satirical and biting than was my nature." [29] Once he left the city and retired to the Hermitage, he immediately shed this Cynicism that had been forced upon him. The Cynic is a product of city life. The change "happened as soon as I had left Paris and my outrage about the vices of this big city was not renewed time and again by its sight. When I did not see people any longer, I ceased despising them; when I did not see evil people any longer, I ceased hating them." [30] Far away from the people, in the loneliness of nature, Rousseau regained his essence, his nature. Cynicism is not natural, but artificial. Rousseau became good again. His friends, especially the social Diderot, did not understand this; herein lay the reason for the break. First they made fun of the hermit, only to take offense eventually. "Only the evil man is alone," wrote Diderot in the appendix of the *Natural Son,* which he sent to Rousseau. Rousseau immediately related this sentence to himself—the break occurred.

Rousseau's Cynicism was not a basic conviction or position, but a temporary reaction—and an image that others had made of him. That he avoided the comparison with Diogenes might have been due to the fact that—and especially the way that—others had compared the two. He had not chosen the role of Diogenes freely; rather, he had been pushed into this role, and it had been ascribed to him by others. That is how he saw it in the justification of his life, *Rousseau Judges Jean-Jacques.* Did Jean-Jacques really have to do the low work of copying notes, Rousseau asked, in order to earn his living? Or was it only a pose? Did he simulate simplicity and poverty "in order, as their masters claimed, to play Epictetus and Diogenes?" [31]

In this passage, Rousseau did not reveal what overtones the comparison between himself and Diogenes usually had, and the connection with the honorable Epictetus concealed these overtones. Nevertheless, Kant talked with great respect—and Wieland with some—of Rousseau the Diogenes. In the preface to his *Diogenes,* Wieland cited Rousseau as a timely example of the fact that a wise man like Diogenes might be considered a foolish eccentric by

28. Ibid. 483.
29. Ibid. 516 note.
30. Ibid. 532.
31. Rousseau (above, n. 23) 2.450.

his contemporaries: "One would have little knowledge of the world, if one did not know that a few peculiar traits and deviations from the ordinary forms of moral behavior are sufficient to misrepresent even the most outstanding man. We have an excellent illustration of this proposition in the example of the famous Jean-Jacques Rousseau of Geneva (a man who probably is not even half as strange as he seems)." [32] This insight did not prevent Wieland, in the following essays on Rousseau, from declaring Rousseau's "follies" about early humankind ridiculous and mocking them.

Wieland's mockery is harmless and mild when compared to the sarcasm, scorn, and contempt others expressed in the comparison between Rousseau and Diogenes. Here I can present only a few examples, starting with another relatively mild variant. In 1762, Frederick the Great of Prussia granted asylum to Rousseau in Neuchâtel. In a letter to Lord George Keith, the governor of Neuchâtel, Frederick expressed his support for the asylum seeker, but at the same time used the opportunity to formulate his rejection of Rousseau's cultural critique and his principal philosophical opposition to Rousseau: "Frankly speaking, my opinions are as opposed to his as the finite to the infinite." [33] Frederick, too, rejected exaggerated sumptuousness, but without condemning enjoyment: "One must be capable of dispensing with everything and yet not forgo anything." This "true philosophy" he found in Locke, Lucretius, and Marcus Aurelius. To the contrary, according to the king, some modern philosophers proclaimed only paradoxes and violated common sense because of their craving for originality; Rousseau was one of them.

Frederick's ideal was above all Marcus Aurelius, the Roman emperor and Stoic. A Stoic as monarch: that was possible; but not a Cynic. Like Alexander the Great, Frederick once asked himself the question what he should have become had he not become king. The answer was that he would have become a private man and a philosopher, but not the philosopher Alexander had wished to be: "Alexander the Great, who truly knew glory, envied the unselfishness and temperance of Diogenes, that insolent Cynic, whom I certainly would not have chosen as a model." [34]

But Rousseau had chosen him as his model and thus became ridiculous: "I believe that Rousseau missed his calling. He clearly had what it takes to become a famous hermit, a Desert Father impressive because of his moral rigor and his self-castigation, or a stylite. He would have performed miracles, would have been canonized, and would have increased the catalogue of martyrs even more. Nowadays, however, he is seen only as a philosophical eccentric who

32. *Wieland's Werke* (above, n. 6) 24.12.

33. *Briefe Friedrichs des Großen,* ed. M. Hein, trans. F. von Oppeln-Bronikowski and E. König (Berlin 1914), 2.105.

34. Ibid. 169.

tries to revive the sect of Diogenes after two millennia. It does not pay to eat grass and make enemies of all contemporary philosophers." [35]

A few years later, when Voltaire asked Frederick the Great about his opinion of Rousseau, the king repeated his rejection of the philosopher as well as his generous liberality toward the man: "You ask me what I think about Rousseau of Geneva. I think he is unhappy and pitiable. I like neither his paradoxes nor his Cynical tone. . . . One must respect those persecuted by fate; only depraved souls would harm them." [36]

Was this also an admonition to the addressee of the letter to soften his attacks on Rousseau—in spite of all the sympathy for his rejection of Rousseau's Cynical tone? Voltaire must have been upset by that tone, since, after all, Rousseau used it to attack him personally. Already two years before Frederick's letter, Voltaire had started to react with severity against those attacks.

The king and the rich, well-educated castle owner and lover of the theater agreed in their aversion to the Cynicism of Rousseau's cultural critique. It is not improbable that Frederick's comparison of Rousseau and Diogenes was inspired by Voltaire, who kept repeating, varying, and intensifying this comparison in his letters. Rousseau "put himself into a tub that he takes to be Diogenes', and he thinks that there he has the right to act the Cynic. He shouts at passersby: Admire my rags." This is the relatively harmless, basic version of the comparison. Already harsher and more scornful: Rousseau is Diogenes' ape or Diogenes' bastard. Even harsher: he is Diogenes' dog's bastard. The harshest: "If Diogenes' dog and Erostrata's bitch reproduced, the puppy would be Jean-Jacques."

There was a constant tendency to depict Rousseau not so much as Diogenes himself, but rather as a presumptuous, false, and depraved Diogenes: he is a Diogenes without a lantern—that is, without the insignia of the Enlightenment! And finally, Voltaire loaded the comparison with his contempt for the character Rousseau. He is not only a false Diogenes but also a false person, who poisons every friendship. Rousseau descends in direct line from the union between the dog of Diogenes and the viper of discord. He is not only a fool, and in addition to that a bothersome fool, but also a malicious fool; he hides the mind of a scoundrel under the coat of Diogenes. [37] As Diogenes, in Plato's eyes, was a Socrates gone mad, so Rousseau, in Voltaire's eyes, was a foolish and false Diogenes.

35. Ibid. 105.

36. *Voltaires Briefwechsel mit Friedrich dem Großen und Katharina II.*, trans. W. Mönch (Berlin 1944), 200.

37. For documentation see H. Gouhier, *Rousseau et Voltaire: Portraits dans deux miroirs* (Paris 1983) 472 s.v. *Diogène;* Starobinski (above, n. 21) 308f.; J. Orieux, *Das Leben des Voltaire,* trans. J. Kirschner (Frankfurt 1978), 733f.

On the other hand, Voltaire himself—like almost all representatives of the Enlightenment—occasionally assumed the role of Diogenes. "You fought against the crazy Jean-Jacques with rational arguments," he wrote to d'Alembert, "but I follow him whose only answer to arguments was to march in the opposite direction. Jean-Jacques proves that the theater is impossible in Geneva, but I build one." [38] Voltaire was careful to withhold that the philosopher whom he was imitating in this statement was Diogenes, who used this gesture to refute Zeno's proof against movement. After all, Voltaire had consistently called him whom *he* refuted Diogenes.

The confusion became even more complete, because the third member of the triad, d'Alembert, was a Diogenes as well—the same d'Alembert to whom Voltaire addressed his letter and to whom Rousseau had previously addressed his Cynical attack on the theater, because in his *Encyclopédie* d'Alembert had advised the citizens of Geneva to build a theater. "Diogenism" was ever present in the Enlightenment. D'Alembert had a well-known preference for the Cynic, in whom he recognized the ideal of independence. "Every age," he wrote, "and ours in particular needs its Diogenes; however, the difficulty is to find those men who have the courage to be Diogenes and those who have the courage to bear the consequences." [39] This appeal found its resonance in the book *Le Diogène de d'Alembert* by Pierre Le Guai de Premontval.

Even in the eyes of his friends, d'Alembert was a Diogenes. When he turned down an invitation to the Russian court, Grimm commented: "Is this man made to live side by side with kings? —He is a Diogenes, whom one must leave in his tub." [40] Frederick the Great capped this by making d'Alembert into that true man for whom Diogenes had searched in vain. When the philosopher took his leave of the king of Prussia in 1763, the king wrote him a farewell note: "I'm sorry to see the time of your departure approach! Never shall I forget the bliss of having seen a true philosopher. I was happier than Diogenes, for I found the man for whom he had been searching in vain for so long." [41] In order to honor d'Alembert, the king even resorted to comparing himself with Diogenes, whom he did not otherwise like. However, he could accept the comparison only insofar as he saw himself in a more favorable position than that insolent Cynic.

Let us return to Voltaire. He certainly was no Cynic in the sense of a Cyni-

---

38. Quoted by Orieux, ibid. 654. The refutation in action as paradigmatically demonstrated by Diogenes—Bayle had quoted this anecdote in the article "Diogenes"—was copied by many; Diderot and Frederick the Great referred to it as well. Rousseau cited the anecdote as an illustration of the expressive capacity of nonverbal language, which in his view had more powerful and immediate expressive qualities than spoken language: "Essay über den Ursprung der Sprachen, worin auch über Melodie und musikalische Nachahmung gesprochen wird," in Jean-Jacques Rousseau, *Musik und Sprache: Ausgewählte Schriften,* ed. P. Gülke (Leipzig 1989), 101.

39. Quoted by Starobinski (above, n. 21) 298 note.

40. Quoted by Starobinski, ibid. 298.

41. *Briefe Friedrichs des Großen* (above, n. 33) 2.131.

cism that despises culture, the sciences, and the arts and reduces human needs to the natural minimum. On the contrary, to him such an attitude seemed ridiculous and paradoxical, and constituted an attack on his mode of living. Nevertheless, something connected him, too, with Cynicism: it was the biting sarcasm of which he was capable and that he particularly turned against religion in its unenlightened form. In this respect, he bears comparison with Lucian, who was also both a cynic and satirist of Cynics. By taking possession of this Cynic heritage, which was to become a vital part of modern cynicism, Voltaire became a cynic. The religious Counter-Enlightenment did revile him as a cynic. In the image that Joseph de Maistre drew of him with extreme vindictiveness, he appeared as a perverted Cynic in the classical sense and cynic in the modern sense at the same time. The image of the dirty, ugly, and wicked Cynic merged with that of the cynic. In this context, Voltaire's cynicism became physiologically tangible; it was written across his face: "Look at this base forehead, which never blushed out of shame, these two extinct craters in which debauchery and hatred still seem to boil. This mouth—I may be saying something evil, but that is not my fault—this horrible snout reaching from one ear to the other, and these lips, pressed together like a spring of steel by sneering wickedness, ready at any moment to attack with derision and calumny." This is the description of Voltaire's death mask. His cynicism appeared as wickedly perverted Cynicism. De Maistre scorned Voltaire as a perverted Cynic, as Voltaire scorned Rousseau as a false Diogenes. Contempt and hatred exaggerated in the extreme are evidenced in both polemics alike. "Other Cynics managed to astonish Virtue; Voltaire astonished Vice. He throws himself into filth and wallows in it, in order to soak himself in it. He drives his imagination to the point of hellish enthusiasm, which infuses all its powers in him in order to lead him to the outermost boundaries of evil." [42]

We have followed the modern reception of Diogenes and Cynicism in three steps: the comparison of the Enlightenment's representative with Diogenes, the Enlightenment's use of the name Diogenes as an insult against the fools and renegades of the Enlightenment, and finally the slandering of the Enlightenment's representatives as cynics by the Counter-Enlightenment.

With this third step, the reactionary view of the Enlightenment's representative as cynic, I prejudged the matter. That the representative of the Enlightenment became the cynic was not only due to the malicious view of the Counter-Enlightenment, but was the fear of the reflective Enlightenment philosopher himself. This point leads me to Diderot and the third aspect of the

---

42. *Abendstunden zu St. Petersburg oder Gespräche über das Walten der göttlichen Vorsicht in zeitlichen Dingen,* trans. M. Lieber (Frankfurt 1824), 234, 236. Cf. Flaubert's definition of cynicism as the "irony of vice," in *Briefe,* trans. H. Scheffel (Stuttgart 1964), 199.

Enlightenment's reception of Cynicism, namely the Cynical self-endangering of the Enlightenment and the degeneration of the Enlightenment into cynicism. Diderot occupied a special position in the history of the reception of Cynicism, because he not only received and practiced the modern moment of Cynicism—that is, cynicism—but he also reflected upon it. As a consequence of the general interest in the topic of Cynicism and cynicism, Diderot's position toward Cynicism and cynicism has been analyzed repeatedly in recent times.[43] In this context, Starobinski and Groh came to the conclusion that Diderot should be regarded as not so much a Diogenes as, rather, a Menippus of the Enlightenment: his affinity with Cynicism was not an affinity with the Cynic mode of living, but rather with Menippean satire. Relying on exact observations, Starobinski put forward the thesis that, in Diderot, Rousseau's presence underlies the discussion of Diogenes and the Cynics.

Like Starobinski, Groh called into question the Cynic or Diogenes Diderot. I find their reasoning unpersuasive. Diderot supposedly rejected Cynicism for systematic reasons, because the Cynic was not a social being, whereas Diderot valued the social aspect highly. But Diogenes is not Timon. Rousseau, as explained above, knew better. Furthermore, the argument goes, the role of Diogenes was already occupied by Rousseau in the discourse of the Enlightenment. But Rousseau laid claim to this role to a much lesser degree than other philosophers of the Enlightenment. The fact that he was scorned as a Diogenes, and a false one at that, did not prevent other Enlightenment representatives from comparing themselves with Diogenes—not even Diderot.

Such a comparison, as we have seen time and again, need not have implied all aspects of Cynicism. No doubt Diderot was not a dogmatic Cynic. He did not live according to the Cynic's minimum satisfaction of needs and thus was not a faithful student of Diogenes in this respect; but rather, like Wieland, he branched out to Aristippus and hedonism. Diderot recognized and regretted this disloyalty in humorous words: "Ah, Diogenes, if you could see your student in the splendid coat of Aristippus, how you would laugh at him! And as far as you are concerned, Aristippus, this splendid coat has been bought at the price of many a base act. What a difference is there between this spoiled, servile, and lax existence and the free and constant life of the Cynic in his rags! And I—I have left the tub, where I used to be my own master, only to enter into the service of a tyrant." [44]

For Diderot, as for d'Alembert and Wieland, Diogenes represented the ideal of autonomy, the free and self-reliant life. Naturally, Diderot knew about his

43. Besides Starobinski's work, I know of H. Harth, "Der Aufklärer und sein Schatten: Zynismus im 'Neveu de Rameau,'" in *Denis Diderot 1713–1784*, ed. T. Heydenreich (Erlangen 1984), 95–105; R. Groh, "Diderot—Ein Menippeer der Aufklärung," in *Denis Diderot oder die Ambivalenz der Aufklärung*, ed. D. Harth and M. Raether (Würzburg 1987), 45–62.

44. *Gründe, meinem alten Hausrock nachzutrauern.* I quote the translation by H.M. Enzensberger in *Die Zeit* of 1 December 1989.

own inadequacy and the insufficiency of his age when measured by this ideal. He did not live in a tub, but in an attic at best, and he did not behave toward the Russian czarina as Diogenes had done toward Alexander. In modern times, it was difficult but not impossible to be a Diogenes in the classical style. For education and morals barely permitted such strength of character any longer: "Who would still dare to stand up against ridicule and contempt these days? In our world, Diogenes would live in an attic and not in a tub. In no European country would he play as important a role as he played in Athens. Maybe he would have been able to preserve the independent and unflinching soul that nature gave him, but by no means would he have answered any of our rulers as he answered Alexander: Stand out of my light!" [45] But even when modern reality no longer permitted a Diogenes-like existence in its original rigor, the ideal of an autonomous and free personality remained, and Diogenes continued to serve as its shining example.

For Diderot, Diogenes represented yet another exemplary aspect: candid impudence. Diderot occasionally liked to adopt the Cynic style also, particularly in the scandalous form of sexual impudence. To many a contemporary he was a Cynic precisely because of this. For him, impudence was not an essential obstacle to virtue. The Cynics, he wrote in the article on them in the *Encyclopédie,* were "indecorous but very virtuous." That shamefacedness was not necessarily a philosophical virtue and that the love of truth could also require the courage of shamelessness had already been maintained by Plato's Socrates in the *Gorgias.* He demonstrated it in a way that caused the indignation even of Callicles, the most shameless of Socrates' three opponents. Testing of truth and penetrating to truth through prejudices and convention might in certain cases require a violation of the sense of shame. And he who wants to participate in the business of testing the truth must, according to Socrates, possess not only insight and benevolence, but also frankness or freedom of speech, *parrhēsia.* Precisely this *parrhēsia* was to become one of the more typical characteristics of Cynicism. When asked what was the most beautiful thing among human beings, Diogenes answered, *Parrhēsia.*[46] The *parrhēsia* of Old Comedy and the philosophical *parrhēsia* of the Socratic dialogue lived on in the Cynicism of Diogenes and in the Cynical satire.

This connection in the history of literature was depicted by the emperor Marcus Aurelius in a sketch about the development from tragedy to comedy: "After tragedy, comedy was introduced. Comedy demonstrated a didactic freedom of speech and purposefully recalled modesty precisely through its open language. To this purpose, Diogenes picked up these things as well" (*Med.* 11.6). It is likely that Diderot knew this passage, the importance of which has

45. "Essay über die Herrschaft der Kaiser Claudius und Nero sowie über das Leben und die Schriften Senecas," in *Philosophische Schriften,* trans. T. Lücke (Berlin 1961), 2.257.
46. D.L. 6.69.

not been recognized sufficiently by the more recent scholarship on Cynicism. For his favorite author, Shaftesbury, quoted it and drew a parallel in the history of philosophy to the development of the drama as described by Marcus Aurelius: as comedy emerged in reaction to tragedy, the comical philosophy of Diogenes and the Cynics came into being in reaction to the sublime philosophy of Socrates and Plato. A little farther on, Shaftesbury explains that Homer was the source of all poetic forms; similarly, all the different styles of philosophy derived from Socrates. Plato, who was of noble birth and possessed a soaring spirit, chose the sublime part. "He of mean birth and poorest circumstances," Antisthenes, "whose constitution as well as condition inclined him most to the way we call satiric, took the reproving part, which in his better-humoured and more agreeable successor," Diogenes, "turned into the comic kind, and went upon the model of that ancient comedy which was then prevalent." [47] That Diderot did know these remarks can also be assumed because, like Shaftesbury, he drew distinctions between Antisthenes and Diogenes according to their tempers in his article "Cyniques." Antisthenes' virtue was peevish and caused his ill humor and sarcasm. Diogenes, on the contrary, possessed a natural serenity.[48]

The Cynicism of Diogenes not only represented a philosophical and moral ideal for Diderot, but also a humorous or satirical possibility, a style of comical philosophy, to use Shaftesbury's term. Diderot used this possibility particularly in *Rameau's Nephew*, his second *Satire*, in order to think through a problem that is intertwined with Cynicism as well as modern cynicism: the problem of contempt and contemptibility. Because of this, *Rameau's Nephew* became the fundamental book of modern cynicism.[49]

The Cynic of antiquity was the prototype of contempt in a twofold sense of the word, namely in its active as well as its passive meaning. He was a genius at expressing contempt, and, at the same time, he was the paragon of everything contemptible. "He was especially strong when it came to expressing his contempt for others," one reads about Diogenes.[50] The Cynical defacing of the currency, the revaluation of existing values, consisted primarily in the Cynic's paradigmatic actions that demonstrate his refusal to recognize *nomos* (law) and conventional morality. The Cynic neither broke the law—as the anecdote about his defacing the currency implied—nor undermined convention through theoretical criticism. Instead, he ridiculed those who represented the accepted sys-

---

47. *Soliloquy; or, Advice to an Author.* I quote this passage after D. O'Gorman, who sees in it the main paradigm for the two characters in *Rameau's Nephew: Diderot the Satirist* (Toronto 1971) 200.

48. The Cynic of this article, whose image fits Rousseau's, is rather Antisthenes than Diogenes; Diderot connects Cato, Rousseau's ideal of virtue, with Antisthenes. One should keep in mind that the article was written in 1754, before the final break with Rousseau.

49. Thus the *Wörterbuch der philosophischen Begriffe*, ed. J. Hoffmeister (Hamburg 1955), 2d ed., s.v. *Zynismus*.

50. D.L. 6.24.

tem of values and acted as role models, people of high rank who were highly regarded by society. By destroying the foundation of all respect, he became contemptible himself, and thus ridiculousness and contemptibility were part of his calling; they became the mark of his independence from accepted opinion and public esteem.

The Cynic, who deliberately rejected recognition by others, was the most despised of men. But he was *not* a man of pain. This addition is important. The Cynic was laughed at because of his contemptibility; but he was, as Diogenes said about himself, not beaten down by laughter.[51] Cynicism became the exercise and eventually the art of swallowing contempt and being unperturbed by it. To pretend consciously to be contemptible could—from a psychological point of view—be a defense against unwanted contempt and an act of self-determination. As we have seen, Rousseau interpreted his own early Cynicism as preventive.

It is only consistent with his own philosophy that the Cynic has to devalue and despise Cynic independence once that has itself become an accepted and respected value. Cynicism relies on a dialectic that, if not controlled, ultimately forces the Cynic to mock even the ideal of independence and thus to give up his own self. This marks the way to the parasitical Cynic as we know him from Lucian's satires.

The type of the parasitical Cynic nearly leads us to the protagonist of Diderot's second *Satire*. In the beginning of the dialogue, Rameau's nephew identifies himself explicitly with Diogenes, as his partner, the first-person narrator, is going to do in the end. Besides this explicit reference to the Cynic and the controversy about the Cynic at the end of the dialogue, the dialogue's closeness to Cynicism becomes apparent in a series of Cynic expressions, metaphors, images, and commonplaces, particularly in the nephew's diction. There is the frivolous and shameless talk about sexual matters, which to contemporaries seemed Cynical above all. Furthermore, there are the open advocacy of the satisfaction of creaturely needs, the animal metaphors, the commonplace of the fool and of folly, the perspective of perversion and reversal. Rameau's nephew is the mad Rameau (*Rameau le fou*) as much as Diogenes is the mad Socrates.

Thus *Rameau's Nephew* is a dialogue on and entirely in keeping with Cynicism. With the figure of the nephew, the contemptuous style of Cynicism is clearly foregrounded. To this understanding of Cynicism the first-person narrator juxtaposes the ideal Cynicism of his understanding of Diogenes, but he can barely stand his ground against the nephew's dominance.

Whatever else Diderot's second *Satire* is, it is first and foremost a work of contempt and about contemptibility. The contempt is directed against the enemies of the Enlightenment and of the philosophers as well as their social relations. But Diderot does not express this contempt directly from the point of

51. D.L. 6.54.

view of superior morals and respectability. His literary method consists of making the contempt express itself from the perspective of amoral baseness and in the medium of personified contemptibility, the medium of the nephew. The nephew represents the baseness and contemptibility of this culture perfectly. He is distinguished from society, however, insofar as he has consciously chosen contemptibility and openly reflects on it. This makes him philosophically interesting. Unlike the others, the nephew does not feign decency; rather he expresses and declares his allegiance to baseness. Thus he enlightens the state of society. He is also a representative of the Enlightenment. "This is indeed the most striking difference between my man and most other human beings who surround us. He admitted to his vices—vices that the others have as well. But he was no hypocrite. He provoked neither more nor less repugnance than the others. He was only more open and more consistent and sometimes more profound in his depravity." [52]

As paradoxical as it may sound, the nephew has an ethos of contemptibility. He lives his contemptible existence consciously, openly, and actively. He is in agreement with this existence. Eclipsed by his famous uncle, he cannot accept that he is no genius. He is no genius of art, no genius of morals, not even a genius of crime. At best he may achieve the caricature of a genius or the genius of caricature and imitation—of pantomime. Even his baseness is determined by the ill-fated will to genius: if not in art or another respected field, he wants to be ingenious at least in this area; he is a genius of contemptibility.

This contemptibility reaches its peak in the way the nephew comments on the crime against the Jews of Avignon. He is not a criminal himself. He does not have the energy for the truly enormous crime, the crime against humanity, but he admires crime. This marks the difference between the criminal and the cynic: the latter commits the crime only in his thoughts; he views it theoretically and enjoys it aesthetically. His is an attitude of theoretical and aesthetic distance. This attitude toward crime, the constancy of his depravity, the openness and shamelessness with which he presents himself and unveils not only his own depravity, but also the corruption of the social circles of which he partakes as a parasite—all this turns the nephew into a cynic in the modern sense of the word.

In a letter to Schiller dated December 21, 1804, Goethe wrote that Diderot's satire was a bomb that exploded right in the middle of French literature. What would he have said had he known O'Gorman's thesis that this bomb was not primarily directed against a second-rate writer like Palissot but rather against Rousseau? Using numerous references, O'Gorman tries to prove that the nephew is modeled after Rousseau in many cynical details, and he comes to the conclusion that "*Le Neveu de Rameau* is the fruit of fifteen years spent with

---

52. "Rameaus Neffe," trans. R. Rütten, in Denis Diderot, *Sämtliche Romane und Erzählungen* (Munich 1979) 2.84.

Jean-Jacques and not of an afternoon spent in the company of Jean-François Rameau." [53] In order not to go beyond the scope of this essay, I cannot discuss this thesis any further at this point. Many references are indeed striking. O'Gorman's arguments cannot be simply dismissed if one compares the predominant tenor of contempt in *Rameau's Nephew* with the tone of utter disdain in the *Essay on the Life of Seneca* (1779), to Diderot's suppositions about Rousseau and suspected revelations in the *Confessions*. However, O'Gorman makes it perfectly clear that the nephew is a literary character and not just a copy of a real model, not even of Rousseau.

O'Gorman is less careful when he identifies the first-person narrator with Diderot. Contrary to this line of argument, I am more convinced by the traditional thesis that Diderot does not identify himself fully with any figure of the dialogue and ascribes some of his own traits even to the nephew. The nephew's cynicism constitutes the antithesis to a one-sided moralizing that could become bothersome. Diderot himself did succumb to this danger. Cynicism was the necessary antidote, as it also was the antidote to sentimental and whining tendencies: "All of Diderot was dualistic. In his expression he was *sentimental* in one moment and *cynical* the next. . . . His Cynicism could be regarded as a reaction of his reason against the abundance of sentiment. It reconstituted the whole man in him and kept him from drowning in sentimentality." [54] Certainly, this psychological view does not exhaust Diderot's cynicism, and even less so the cynicism displayed in *Rameau's Nephew*. But it throws light on one noteworthy aspect.

"The loss of our prejudices compensates for the loss of our innocence," the nephew says at one point. This is one of those thoughts that elevate him above the level of an unreflecting parasite and give his persona a philosophical dimension that irritates and fascinates the first-person narrator. To undo all prejudices was the aim of the Enlightenment. In Rameau's nephew the Enlightenment encounters the other side of its ideal. Through him the Enlightenment perceives the nightmare that undermines its moral optimism. The nightmare makes clear that the totally enlightened person who has been freed of all prejudices is not the embodiment of the pure ideal of humanity like Wieland's beautiful Diogenes, but a disillusioned, callous, and filthy cynic à la Rameau. By means of cynical laughter that borders on madness the nephew reasserts himself, thus ending the dialogue. Could this laughter possibly be the final stage of the Enlightenment? The dialogue leaves us with this unnerving question.

—————•◆•—————

This question was posed again by Nietzsche in his parable of the madman. After Diderot, Nietzsche represented the most important stage in the history of

53. O'Gorman (above, n. 47) 216 n. 4.
54. K. Rosenkranz, *Diderots Leben und Werke* vol. 2 (Leipzig 1866) 387.

the reception of Cynicism that eventually led to the modern concept of cynicism. This is the history of the transformation from Cynicism to cynicism. That Nietzsche still used the one word *Cynismus* and did not distinguish between *Kynismus* and *Zynismus* demonstrates the unity of this history until the end of the nineteenth century.

Nietzsche's reception of Cynicism is historical—but not only historical. In his reflections, Nietzsche directed his interest beyond the merely historical question and inquired what possibilities Cynicism could offer beyond its historical uniqueness and past: possible modes of living; moral possibilities, particularly the problematization and critique of morals; possibilities of shedding light on morals; possibilities of an enlightened personal style critical of morals; rhetorical-literary and polemical possibilities. Eventually he adopted all these possibilities of Cynicism, and finally he emphatically declared his allegiance to "Cynicism." In the self-assessment of *Ecce Homo,* he said about his books that they occasionally did reach "the highest one can reach on earth: Cynicism." Furthermore, in a letter to Georg Brandes, he announced *Ecce Homo* as a "Cynicism that will become world-historical." To these self-interpretive statements one could add the apodictic sentence that opens the preface of the *Will to Power:* "Great things require that one be silent about them or talk about them on a grand scale: on a grand scale means cynically and with innocence." [55]

Nietzsche's earliest occupation with Cynicism was philological. It was no small feat for Nietzsche to have captured and appreciated the literary side of Cynicism in its uniqueness. The professional historiographers of philosophy have usually neglected this aspect. In a letter written on the occasion of his application for a professorship in philology at Basel, Nietzsche thematized the Cynics' influence on Greek literature. He ascribed to them the invention of a new style that did not conform to the rule of purity and uniformity of style: "They dared to treat the form as an *adiaphoron* [a matter of indifference] and to mix the styles; they translated Socrates as it were into a literary genre complete with the satyr shell and the god inside. Thus they became the humorists of antiquity." [56]

This aspect of Cynicism enters into *The Birth of Tragedy:* the Cynic writers topped the mixture of styles in the Platonic dialogues with even more extreme skewbald coloring and thus continued what had begun with the naive Cynicism of their teacher Socrates, namely the destruction of tragedy.[57]

---

55. *Nietzsche's Werke* (Leipzig 1905–) 15.54; letter of 20 November 1888, in Friedrich Nietzsche, *Gesammelte Briefe* (Berlin 1900ff.) 3.321; *Werke* 15.137. G. Colli's and M. Montinari's critical edition gives a second version besides the one quoted: "Great things require that one be silent about them or talk about them on a grand scale: on a grand scale means with innocence—cynically" (8.3.335; cf. 271). The aphorism was written in the spring or summer of 1888. All of these statements thus were made in the year 1888.

56. *Werke* (above, n. 55) 19 (*Philologica* 3) 387.

57. Ibid. 1.98f.

The comparison between Plato and the Cynics on the basis of a criticism of their styles returned in Nietzsche's late work *Twilight of the Idols:* "Plato, as it seems to me, mixes all forms of style and thus is the first *décadent* of style: he has something on his conscience similar to the Cynics who invented the *satura Menippea.*"[58]

Since Nietzsche was not only a philologist and critic of style, but was himself a highly ambitious stylist, the question of what such statements meant in the context of his own stylistic ambitions is inescapable. In any case, they should not disguise the fact that he never realized a uniform style, but rather tried out and mixed different styles. That grave tone with which he started his career as a writer in *The Birth of Tragedy* he did not keep. Later, he explicitly distanced himself from it. Now, he himself used literary means and forms typical of the "humorists of antiquity": polemics, satire, irony, parody; his preference for the short form of the anecdote falls under this category as well.

An example of literary Cynicism as understood by Nietzsche can be found at the end of *The Gay Science.* "Incipit Tragoedia" is the title of the last aphorism of the fourth (originally the last) book. This aphorism introduces Zarathustra: the notion of the superman is about to become serious. The "extreme seriousness" commences, "the tragedy *begins*"; thus ends the second-to-last aphorism of the added fifth book. It is followed only by an epilogue—the comedy: in it, the "most malicious, and most briskly impish laughter" breaks loose. In an appendix, the "Songs of Prince Vogelfrei" follow. These are for the most part parodic poems, the first of which, *To Goethe,* parodies the closing verses of the paradigmatic German tragedy, the "chorus mysticus" of *Faust II.* After *The Birth of Tragedy,* the purely tragic no longer occurred at all, and tragedy not without parody. Thus Nietzsche announced himself and his future works in the preface to *The Gay Science,* when he wrote " 'Incipit tragoedia' is written at the end of this doubtfully unobjectionable book: be on your guard! Something of exemplary naughtiness and malice announces itself: *incipit parodia,* there is no doubt."[59]

The convergence between Nietzsche and the "humorists of antiquity" becomes even more obvious if one compares corresponding descriptions of the Cynics with Nietzsche's self-descriptions. In a draft of the letter mentioned above, "philosophy in the garb of a buffoon" was Nietzsche's translation of the classical image that said of the Cynic Bion that he had dressed philosophy in the colorful garment of a courtesan. "Buffoon" and "scientific satyr" are the names of the Cynic in an aphorism that I will discuss in further detail below. These are names that Nietzsche took in connection to himself, particularly during his late period—from which also stem the quoted panegyrics on his own Cynicism—and in part already during the mental breakdown: "I do not want

58. Ibid. 8.167f.
59. Ibid. 5.4f.

to be a saint; I would prefer to be a buffoon"; "perhaps I am a buffoon"; "to the most serious things I add a little tail of buffoonery"; "since I am condemned to entertain the next eternity with bad jokes. . . ."[60] Franz Overbeck described Nietzsche as he had met him immediately after the breakdown: "Overall the statements about the profession he ascribed to himself—to be the buffoon of the new eternities—were predominant."[61]

From the beginning, Nietzsche put his reflections on Cynicism in the context of his main topics and central problems, and vice versa: the discussions of these topics and problems included Cynicism. One example is the main topic Nietzsche took over from his philosophical teacher, Schopenhauer: pessimism. In a list of projects from the end of the time of his studies in Leipzig, the title "Pessimism in Antiquity" was recorded and supplemented by "or, The Reclamations [*Rettungen*] of the Cynics" in parentheses.[62]

What does this supplement mean? It means primarily, How should the genitive "of the Cynics" be understood? As an objective genitive? Or as a subjective genitive? Did Nietzsche intend a reclamation of the Cynics in the sense of a rehabilitation of their bad reputation in the historiography of philosophy, precisely like a certain F. Hersche, who had just written a rehabilitation of Diogenes of Sinope?[63]

Presumably something else was intended; the reference was to the salvations the Cynic mobilizes against pessimism and its consequences. This presumption is suggested by a series of statements in which, through Schopenhauer's lens, the essence of Cynicism is seen in the tension between pessimism and eudaemonism. Like hardly any other philosopher, the Cynic knows about the suffering of life; in that he is a pessimist. But Cynic pessimism does not lead to a negation of life—quite the contrary. To avoid the suffering of life, but to affirm life itself: this is the sense of Cynicism as Nietzsche interpreted it when he closely read an anecdote in the chapter "Ways of Dying" in his lectures on Greek literature. In it, Antisthenes, plagued by pain and very ill, asks

60. Ibid. 15.116; letter of 4 May 1888, to Georg Brandes, *Gesammelte Briefe* (above, n. 55) 3.306; letter of 5 or 6 January 1889 to Jacob Burckhardt, in *Werke*, ed. Schlechta, 3.1351.

61. Letter of 15 January 1889 to Peter Gast (i.e., Köselitz). Quoted after C. A. Bernoulli, *Franz Overbeck und Friedrich Nietzsche* vol. 2 (Jena 1908) 234. On this topic, cf. Walter Bröcker, "Nietzsches Narrentum," in *Nietzsche-Studien* 1 (1972) 138–46. Bröcker is primarily interested in Nietzsche's concept of truth. He wants to demonstrate its inconsistency. Folly appears mainly as a suspension of truth. Bröcker has no understanding for the rhetorical-literary function of folly as a mask and the perspective representation. By no means does he exhaust this topic. Besides, he does not even touch upon Nietzsche's reception of the figure of the Cynic or the problem of cynicism. K. Jaspers at least recognized a connection here: "Nowhere does Nietzsche seem more contradictory than in questions of the fool as mask. With meaningful ambiguity, jester, buffoon, clown, cynic occur time and again in his works equally as contrasts to himself and as identical with himself" (*Nietzsche: Einführung in das Verständnis seines Philosophierens* [Berlin 1908] 404).

62. *Werke und Briefe*, ed. H. J. Mette and K. Schlechta (Munich 1937), 4.119.

63. "Diogenes von Sinope: Eine Ehrenrettung," in *Zwei Charakterbilder aus dem classischen Altertum* (Lucerne 1865).

who would liberate him from his suffering; Diogenes shows him a dagger. Antisthenes replies: "I said from suffering, not from life." "A very profound statement," comments Nietzsche; "one cannot get the better of the love of life by means of a dagger. Yet that is the real suffering. It is obvious that the Cynic clings to life more than the other philosophers: 'the shortest way to happiness' is nothing but the love of life in itself and complete needlessness with reference to all other goods." [64]

Cynicism is "the shortest way to happiness." In antiquity, Cynicism was considered the shortcut to virtue; the reformulation of this formula Nietzsche took from Schopenhauer.[65] Cynicism is the most consistent eudaemonism, if one views happiness from the point of view of its importance for the self-assertion of life: man is in need of happiness in order not to become weary of life. To be able to forget is part of happiness, as Nietzsche stated at the beginning of the second *Untimely Meditation*. Happiness is purest in the animal's or the child's existence, which is free of recollection and expectation and is utterly absorbed by the moment. To the Cynic, the animal's and the child's existence becomes a model for his attempt to reduce all needs to the natural minimum. Thus he achieves the closest philosophical approximation to ideal happiness: "If it is happiness, the striving for new happiness, that keeps the living being in life, then perhaps no other philosopher is more correct than the Cynic: for the happiness of the animal as the most perfect Cynic is living proof for the claim of Cynicism." [66]

The Cynic "comes closer to the domestic animal," Nietzsche wrote in an aphorism in which he compared the Cynics and the Epicureans.[67] From Schopenhauer he took the explanation that the Cynic's starting point is the insight into "the connection between the increased and stronger suffering of the more cultivated human being and the abundance of needs." On the basis of this pessimistic insight, the Cynic withdraws from the requirements of culture and sets out for an animalistic level. However, is the animal really the most perfect Cynic? Nietzsche pointed out two essential elements of Cynicism that place the Cynic once again well beyond the animals' world of emotions: the Cynic gains satisfaction from his conscious self-positioning in contrast to society and from his use of abuse. Because of the joy Cynicism gains from provocation and abuse, it is not just a negative eudaemonism that views happiness solely as the avoidance of suffering.

Nietzsche dedicated an entire *Reflection* to the contrast with the environment and to provocation, which constitute the source of Cynical happiness. The Cynic's happiness is derived from other philosophers' anger about him: "In the

64. *Werke* (above, n. 55) 18 (*Philologica* 2) 196.
65. *Die Welt als Wille und Vorstellung* 2.16, in *Werke in zehn Bänden* (Zurich 1977) 3.80.
66. *Werke* (above, n. 55) 1.285.
67. *Menschliches, Allzumenschliches* 1.275, in *Werke* (above, n. 55) 2.255f.

time when philosophy used to be a matter of public contest—in third-century Greece—there were quite a few philosophers who were made happy by the ulterior motive that others who lived and tortured themselves according to other principles would have to be angry at their happiness; they thought that they refuted the others most effectively by means of their happiness, and for that purpose they considered it sufficient always to seem happy. Thus, however, they had to *become* happy in the long run! This was the fate of—for example—the Cynics." [68] From such provocation, cynicism as well as Cynicism derives its pleasure; thus, Cynics as well as cynics fix their eyes on society. Hegel wrote that Diogenes was determined by "the opinion against which his manner acted." [69]

That abuse or scorn can be enjoyable, and *how* enjoyable they can be, Nietzsche had learned from Schopenhauer, the genius of scorn among philosophers. And from this viewpoint he compared Schopenhauer with the Cynics. In a late insight about the philosophical idol of his youth, Nietzsche came to the conclusion that Schopenhauer was not at all the pessimist he seemed to be in his theory. But he would have become a pessimist were it not for the pleasure he derived from his polemics. From polemics he derived that happiness without which his life would have become unbearable: "Otherwise Schopenhauer would *not* have stayed here; you may bet on that: he would have run away. But his opponents kept him in place; time and again his opponents seduced him into existence. As for the Cynics of antiquity, his anger was his comfort, his recreation, his remuneration, his *remedium* against repulsion, his happiness." [70]

An aphorism from the unpublished works of the 1880s sums up his reflections on the specific Cynic connection between pessimism and eudaemonism: "Life's worthlessness was recognized in Cynicism, and yet it was not yet turned against life. No: there, many small overcomings and a loose tongue *satisfy!*" [71]

For Nietzsche himself happiness was neither the highest aim of life nor the principle of morals. In reference to the post-Socratic philosophers, he even talked of an "ugly pretension to happiness" that could not be found in the Presocratics, the philosophers of the "tragic age of Greece." [72] Furthermore, he made a satirical, scornful comment on the Cynics' cost-free happiness in a verse entitled "From Diogenes' Tub": "Pressing need is cheap; without a price is happiness: / Therefore I do not sit on gold, but I sit on my ass." [73] But Nietzsche himself occasionally practiced Cynicism and the Cynic reduction to the minimum necessary for life as a strategy of survival and a self-assertion against

68. *Morgenröthe* 367, in *Werke* (above, n. 55) 4.272.
69. *Rechtsphilosophie* §195, in *Sämmtliche Werke* (Stuttgart 1938) 7.276.
70. *Zur Genealogie der Moral*, in *Werke* (above, n. 55) 7.411.
71. *Werke* (above, n. 55) 13.103f.
72. Ibid. 10.221.
73. Ibid. 8.363.

suffering. "Indeed, a minimum of life, an unchaining from all coarser desires, an independence in the middle of all kinds of outer nuisances; a bit of Cynicism perhaps, a bit of 'tub'"": thus he retrospectively characterizes the state and frame of mind in which he wrote the second volume of *Human, All Too Human,* a time of struggles with his disease and of war "as I fought it back then with myself against the pessimism that results from weariness of life." [74]

However, Cynicism did not gain its highest importance in and for Nietzsche as a positive moral philosophy, as instruction for happiness or precepts for life, but as a certain paradigm of the criticism of morals and of an enlightenment critical of morals. Nietzsche discovered Cynicism as a position beyond good and evil, as a didactic play of the free spirit. Particularly from this point of view, the rejuvenation of Cynicism and the transformation into cynicism were to take place.

The reinterpretation of the "shortest way to happiness" into a shortcut to knowledge—namely the knowledge of human nature—can be found in an aphorism in *Beyond Good and Evil* in the section "The Free Spirit." [75] The aphorism offers a piece of black moralizing: Nietzsche expresses the repulsion the chosen man feels in the encounters with the average man, with the masses, the many, the most. In ancient moral philosophy, such contempt for human beings was represented mainly by two figures: Timon, the prototype of misanthropy, and the proto-Cynic Diogenes. While the misanthropist was driven into solitude by his loathing for man, the Cynic remained within society in order to enlighten people about their depravity and to show them the natural way of life free of culture.

Nietzsche had a deep understanding for the chosen man's desire for solitude and isolation from those he holds in contempt. But the philosopher is not supposed to give in to this urge; he would cut himself off from the object of his knowledge: "The study of *average* man, long, serious, and to this end a lot of disguise, overcoming of oneself, intimacy, keeping bad company . . . all this amounts to a necessary piece of the life history of any philosopher, perhaps the least agreeable, the most malodorous, and the most disappointing piece." Under happy circumstances, this long way of unpleasant experiences can become shorter for him who is in search of knowledge—that is, if he encounters people who can actually shorten and facilitate his task: "I mean the so-called Cynics, people who recognize the animal, the baseness, the 'rule' in itself, and yet still have that degree of intelligence and gumption that forces them to talk about themselves and people like them *in front of witnesses*—occasionally they even wallow in books as in their own dirt."

74. Ibid. 3.10. Cf. also the sister's euphemistic description: "There is no doubt that, at that time, my brother tried a little bit to imitate Diogenes in the tub; he wanted to find out with how little a philosopher could do" (Elisabeth Förster-Nietzsche, *Der einsame Nietzsche* [Leipzig 1925] 81).

75. *Werke* (above, n. 55) 7.44–46.

The Cynic recognizes the animal nature in himself, and he bears witness to this authentic nature of man. At this point, Nietzsche perceived the Cynic reduction to animalistic nature no longer as a moral technique but as a standpoint of enlightenment. The Cynic reveals that the nature of man is covered by shame and morality; thus he is more honest than moral man: "Cynicism is the only form in which common souls come close to honesty; and the higher man must prick up his ears at every Cynicism—whether coarse or refined—and congratulate himself, whenever a buffoon without shame or a scientific satyr speaks out in his presence." [76]

We encountered such a shameless buffoon in the person of Rameau's nephew, and Nietzsche's description of the Cynic reads as if it had been derived from this figure: "And where one only speaks without bitterness and rather harmlessly of man as of a belly with two needs and a head with one; everywhere where somebody sees and looks for and *wants* to see only hunger, sexual lust, and vanity, as if they were the actual and only motive of human actions; in a word, where one talks 'badly' about man—and not even *wickedly*—there a lover of knowledge should listen diligently and carefully; he should listen wherever one talks without indignation. For a man who feels indignant and anyone who tears to pieces and mangles himself (or, as a substitute, the world, or God, or society) may, from a moral point of view, stand higher than the laughing and self-satisfied satyr, but from every other point of view he is the more typical, more indifferent, and didactically less interesting case. And nobody *lies* as often as one who feels indignant."

Cynicism—and this now is the specifically modern meaning of the word—comes into being when man leaves behind animal nature, or, in Nietzsche's words, when he goes beyond the animals' world of emotions, and does not reach morality, but assumes a consciousness free of morals. Cynicism is the conscious and demonstrative rejection of a required moral attitude. The moral attitude is pushed aside and replaced, for example, by a comical attitude: at that point cynical humor comes into being. The proto-Cynic is the buffoon without shame. However, cynicism also emerges where morals are replaced by mere sagacity or a scientific attitude, where "the genius is attached to such an indiscreet he-goat and monkey" and where "the scientific head is placed on the body of a monkey, and an exquisite and exceptional understanding is placed on a common soul—especially among doctors and physiologists of morality this is no rare occurrence."

That Nietzsche ascribed Cynicism to the common souls is probably, like many other elements of this aphorism, a reminiscence of antique Cynicism, more specifically of the fact that many of its representatives were slaves or of

---

76. [Translator's Note] This translation is from R. J. Hollingdale's *Beyond Good and Evil* (Harmondsworth 1973); all other translations are my own.

low birth. In his thoughts about Cynic literature, Nietzsche took careful note of this sociological aspect. Later he abandoned the reduction of Cynicism to common souls. But already in *Beyond Good and Evil* (§26), he pointed out Abbé Galiani as an example of a Cynic of genius. Nietzsche referred to him again in another passage of *Beyond Good and Evil,* this time as an example of a noble and resigned Cynicism: "There are free, insolent spirits who want to conceal and deny that they are broken, proud, incurable hearts (Hamlet's Cynicism; the case of Galiani); and occasionally folly itself is the mask for an unfortunate all-too-certain knowledge." [77]

In *Human, All Too Human,* under the title "The Modern Diogenes," Nietzsche had already posed the question: "Before one searches for man, one must have found a lantern. —Will it have to be the *Cynic's* lantern?"[78] The extensively quoted aphorism from *Beyond Good and Evil* (§26) gives an unmistakable answer.

The Cynic's folly as a "mask for an unfortunate all-too-certain knowledge" is also an allusion to Nietzsche himself. For when he wrote these words, he had proclaimed his own unfortunate all-too-certain knowledge in the guise of this mask: the knowledge of God's death in the story of the madman.[79] In a grandiose gesture, intensifying the Cynic's critique of morals into an enlightened critique of religion, Nietzsche made the popular anecdote of Diogenes with the lantern into the literary frame and expression of one of his central thoughts.

The anecdote was quoted for the first time in a theological context by the Church Father Tertullian, who was inspired by the lantern motif because of the metaphor of light that could be easily derived from it. When comparing the two "barbaric" compatriots Diogenes and Marcion in a striking fashion, the eloquent apologist preferred the Cynic over the heretic: "For even the dog Diogenes wanted to find a man and therefore carried a lamp in broad daylight; after the light of his faith expired, Marcion lost God, whom he had found." [80] If Nietzsche knew this passage, the metaphor of the light of faith must have seemed as paradoxical to him as Tertullian's *Credo, quia absurdum est,* which he derided: *Credo, quia absurdus sum.*[81] For him light, and the torch in particular, was metaphorically linked to the Enlightenment.

For Nietzsche, too, the anecdote was connected to the loss of God, but not in a manner that would complement or rather surpass the philosophical light of reason with a light of faith that would make it possible to find God. Rather, the lantern became the ironic metaphor of the pointless search for God: "Have you not heard of that madman who lighted a lantern in broad daylight, ran to the

77. *Werke* (above, n. 55) 7.259.
78. Ibid. 3.205.
79. *Die fröhliche Wissenschaft,* in *Werke* (above, n. 55) 5.163f.
80. *Adversus Marcionem,* ed. E. Evans (Oxford 1972), 4.
81. Cf. *Werke* (above, n. 55) 2.405; 4.7, 286, 417.

marketplace, and kept shouting: 'I am looking for God! I am looking for God!'?"

Even the description of this enlightening figure as a madman can be traced back to the Cynic tradition. For it was typical of the Cynic, particularly as depicted by Diogenes Laertius, that on the one hand he caused laughter by means of his humor and satire, but on the other hand caused consternation and was declared mad because of his paradoxical, exalted, and shameless behavior. Nietzsche made his ironic-satirical enlightener undergo the same treatment: he is laughed at. The people around him answer with irony, and when the madman becomes serious, they react with consternation. Nietzsche surpassed the original story, because his character, unlike its prototype, does not take revenge in the sense of he who laughs last laughs best. Because of the seriousness of his message of God's death and its consequences, the madman cannot maintain his initial irony. He is frustrated by his audience's lack of understanding and really becomes mad; or, to be more precise, he flees from the lack of understanding into the eclipse of understanding: "and occasionally folly itself is the mask for an unfortunate all-too-certain knowledge." Nietzsche added one motif to the adopted frame of the Diogenes anecdote: the destruction of the lantern. "At that point, the madman grew silent and looked at his audience again, and his audience was silent as well and looked at him with consternation. Eventually, he threw his lantern to the ground so that it broke into pieces and expired."

In the story "The Madman," irony, satire, and an almost grave earnestness intermingle in the face of the meaning of God's death for man. Accordingly, the style is at the same time parody and sermon. Besides the frequent citation of the figure of the Cynic, which amounts to a leitmotif, the parodic citation of Christian revelation and death rites also is part of its ironic satire: "It is said that on that very day the madman entered several churches and began to sing his *Requiem Aeternam Deo.* After he was ushered out and taken to task, he is said to have answered only this: 'What else are the churches, if they are not the vaults and tombs of God?' "

In Nietzsche's own life the fate of his madman came to pass in a frightening fashion. This raises the question of whether Nietzsche's failure was also due to Cynicism. In the time before his mental breakdown, he ostentatiously and forcibly stylized his own work and in particular his fight against Christianity and Christian morals into Cynicism. There is a disturbing letter that makes clear with how much energy Nietzsche tried to mobilize Cynicism against morals, finally even within his own emotional life. This document is disturbing, because in retrospect it seems like a prophecy of a scene from the mental collapse, and because in this context it makes visible the violence and the overstrain of Nietzsche's effort. Thus Nietzsche pushed himself into a kind of moral schizophrenia. "Yesterday I invented an image of, in Diderot's phrase, a *moralité larmoyante.* Winter landscape. An old wagoner who with an expression of the most brutal Cynicism, harder even than the winter all around, is peeing

against his own horse. The horse, this poor flayed creature, looks around, gratefully, *very* gratefully—" [82] Is this image itself an expression of Cynicism, or
of *moralité larmoyante?* Or of Cynicism as self-affirmation against one's own
moralité larmoyante?

Diderot had formed this moral schizophrenia into literature in *Rameau's
Nephew* and thus had kept it at arm's length. Nietzsche was broken by it. Less
than nine months later, in the winter of 1888–89, his fantastic vision became
reality. He ṣaw how at the cab stand in front of his door an old cart horse was
abused by the coachman. Weeping, he fell around the "flayed creature's" neck.
Later, this scene was to be interpreted by his acquaintances as the first sign of
the beginning madness.[83]

Nietzsche's Neo-Cynicism is one of the models for the most spectacular
reception and literary actualization of Cynicism in recent times. Peter Sloterdijk's *Critique of Cynical Reason* (1983) has been the biggest best-seller of any
philosophical book in Germany since 1945. Sloterdijk also employs Cynicism—as well as the concept of cynicism—in the service of a critique of the
Enlightenment and reason. The book's title is a conscious allusion to Kant's
critique of reason. But Sloterdijk is indebted not so much to Kant as he is to
the more skeptical theory of reason and view of the Enlightenment as it was
formulated—following Schopenhauer and Nietzsche—by Horkheimer and
Adorno from the 1940s onward. Critical theory dominated the intellectual discussion in West Germany during the late 1960s and the 1970s, and it had an
enormous influence on the student movement of those years. Besides his light-
handed and often virtuoso writing style, Sloterdijk's success is essentially
based on his continuity with critical theory, while he at the same time avoids
the dead end into which this theory was driven because it rejected any perspective that would have permitted a practical solution to the dilemma of the dialectic of Enlightenment and instrumental reason. Sloterdijk's solution is Cynicism.
With this bid he meets halfway those tendencies that succeeded the (ultimately
unsuccessful) phase of the political realization of critical theory. These tendencies include the retirement from the public sphere, the ecological movement,
the new sensuality and body consciousness, feminism, and even a sectarian
movement like the Bhagwan's. Sloterdijk's book is a true mirror of the educational development [*Bildungsgang*] of the generation of the student movement.
This explains its enormous resonance; in it, a generation recognized itself.

Sloterdijk breaks up the connection (with regard to the history of the concept) between the reception of Cynicism and the modern concept of cynicism,

82. Letter of 13 May 1888 to R. von Seydlitz, in *Gesammelte Briefe* (above, n. 55) 1.445.
83. Cf. Otto Flake, *Nietzsche: Rückblick auf eine Philosophie,* 2d ed. (Baden-Baden 1947),
168f.

by diametrically juxtaposing Cynicism and cynicism. "Modern cynicism is *enlightened false consciousness.* It is the modernized unhappy consciousness on which the Enlightenment worked successfully and at the same time in vain. This consciousness has learned the Enlightenment's lesson, but it has not realized it, nor was it able to realize it. In comfortable circumstances and at the same time miserable, this consciousness is no longer affected by any critique of ideology; its falseness is already reflectively safeguarded." [84] The most successful passages of the book are constituted by the phenomenology of different types of cynicism and the typology of the cynic. Less convincing are the systematic frame of the juxtaposition of cynicism and Cynicism and the declaration that Cynicism is the only alternative to the universal cynicism of the present.

The Cynics' method consists in the rejection of formal argument. Instead of theoretical discourse, the Cynic prefers nonverbal and bodily means of expression. In Cynicism, the lower organs revolt against the head and the heavy intellectuality of traditional philosophy.

Sloterdijk argues that the essential difference between Cynicism and cynicism consists in their respective relation to power: Cynicism is the rebelliousness, insolence, and criticism of those who do not participate in power and therefore are not corrupted by it. Such Cynicism is legitimate as the critique of power per se. Contrary to this, cynicism is in an eminent sense the cynicism of masters, critique that went over to the enemy; precisely this makes cynicism suspect and robs it of its moral justification. Whereas Cynicism frees, cynicism oppresses. In this handy and comprehensible dichotomy, Cynicism becomes an attractive bid for identification: the Cynic is insolent and audacious, but not spiteful; he is critical, but not obstinate; he is calm, but not indolent; he is reflective, but not broken or even schizoid. The Cynical expressions of misanthropy or contempt are harsh realism. For the cynic, the opposite is true throughout. Thus, cynicism becomes the object of unequivocally negative criticism. The question arises how a figure like the nephew in Diderot's satire would fit into this binary opposition. Sloterdijk, who unfortunately hardly deals with this figure and Diderot's works in general, summarily categorizes him as a Cynic without another thought. Had he dealt with *Rameau's Nephew* more intensively, this assessment—as well as the simple juxtaposition of Cynicism and cynicism—would have seemed problematic to him.

To anyone who knows the history of Cynicism's effects and reception, the separation of cynicism and Cynicism seems like the continuation of the attempt to distinguish an authentic and original Cynicism from a false and degenerate one, a Cynicism worthy of respect from one worthy of rejection, a good Cynicism from a bad and evil one. This attempt is coextensive with the history of

---

84. Sloterdijk (above, n. 5) 37f.

Cynicism itself. It seems to me that Cynicism itself does not provide any measure for such a distinction. A critique of Cynicism and cynicism seems to depend on an evaluation according to external principles. In the end, the critique of cynicism moves within the boundaries of universal and basic moral assumptions and their concretizations, which form the center of what most recently has been called a "high-culture ethics" and is primarily the heritage of Platonism, Christianity, and the Enlightenment.

Picturing Diogenes

Diskin Clay

The School of Greece

One imagines an ancient villa or a Vatican stanza with a gallery filled with statues of the ancient philosophers—an indoor and sheltered School of Greece. Along its four walls and standing in its intercolumnar spaces are arranged philosophers grouped by schools and chronology. They are in marble, bronze, and terra cotta; freestanding and seated; cast as small and portable figurines; painted on the walls; depicted in mosaics on the floor; engraved on jewels; stamped on coins and medallions in cabinets. A *Sebasteion* to the goddess Philosophia and her ancient votaries. Such a gallery or *musée imaginaire* is the ideal only imperfectly realized in La Stanza dei Filosofi of the Capitoline Museum in Rome and in La Villa dei Papiri in Herculaneum.[1] There were also the attempts to assemble collections of statues of philosophers in the so-called Villa of Brutus near Tivoli and the exedra with its eleven sages and poets in the Serapeum of Ptolemy I in Memphis.[2] The private collections including the

I thank here my colleagues Mary T. Boatwright, who has helped me greatly with my illustrations; Lawrence Richardson, Jr., who has guided me through the Roman and Parisian sections of this new terrain and taught me to focus on what I see; and Louise Rice, who has helped me with Raphael and Poussin. Thanks too to Donna Hall, who has supervised this project from its beginning with a vigilant eye, and to the staff of the Hanes Art Library of the University of North Carolina, Chapel Hill.

1. The object of an important study by D. Pandermalis, "Zur Programm der Statuensammlung in der Villa dei Papiri," *MDAI(A)* 83 (1971) 173–209; and the catalogue of Maria Rita Wojcik, *La Villa dei Papiri ad Ercolano: Contributo alla reconstruzione della ideologia della nobilitas tardoreppublicana* (Rome 1986).

2. Published by Charles Picard in Jean Philippe Lauer and Charles Picard, *Les statues ptolémaïques du Serapeion de Memphis* (Paris 1955) 38–47, 48–172. The one attempt to assemble all

busts of famous figures from antiquity are the original and organizing principle of books like G. B. Bellori's *Veterum Philosophorum Imagines* (Rome 1685) and its distinguished predecessors—Achilles Statius's *Inlustrium Virorum Expressi Vultus* (Rome 1569) and Fulvius Ursinus's *Imagines* (Rome 1569), the first mostly illustrated from Stazio's private collection of antiquities.[3] And these collections of prints from the sixteenth and seventeenth centuries are the exemplar of photographic museums such as Karl Schefold's *Bildnisse der antiken Dichter, Redner, und Denker* (Basel 1943), G. M. A. Richter's *The Portraits of the Greeks* (London 1965), and Lucia A. Scatozza Höricht's *Il volto dei filosofi antichi* (Naples 1986).[4]

One of the most striking features of the gallery, published as a printed collection of images, is the fascination exercised by the face of the philosopher, and most often we only have the bust of an ancient philosopher—*vultus, il volto.* Cicero, in one of his most boastful moments, claimed that Latin was a more expressive language than Greek because it possessed the term *vultus,* which means not only the face (*prosōpon*) but the significant expression worn by a face.[5] When Pliny the Elder speaks of the passion of knowing what a figure from the past was really like, he obviously meant what he or she looked like (*NH* 35.9–10). And it is not surprising that Cicero, as a Roman, should make this claim for the expressivity of the Roman *vultus,* for Roman portraiture was unlike the Greek in its fixation on the *imago*—that is, the expressive wax mask of the ancestors religiously kept and displayed with pride in the houses of the Roman aristocracy.[6] These death masks of solemn, powerful, and fixed faces

---

the evidence for antique collections of statues of philosophers and poets is Thuri Lorenz, *Gallerien von griechischen Philosophen- und Dichterbildnissen der Römern* (Mainz 1965).

3. For Fulvio Orsini (1529–1600), librarian of the Palazzo Farnese, and the subtle theft of his *Imagines* by André Thevet (1516–92), there is now the revealing study of Eugene Dwyer, "André Thevet and Fulvio Orsini: The Beginnings of the Modern Tradition of Classical Portrait Iconography in France," *The Art Bulletin* 75.3 (1993) 467–80. This is not the place for a review of the Roman and European collections of *viri illustres,* but one can note for Rome the drawings of contemporary collections of ancient statuary by Maarten Van Heemskerck (active in Rome around 1535), ed. Christian Hülsen and Hermann Egger, *Die römischen Skizzenbücher von Marten Van Heemskerck,* 2 vols. Berlin 1913–16; repr. Soest Holland 1975); Ulisses Aldroandi, *Le statue di Roma,* in Lucio Mauro, *Le antichità della città di Roma* (Venice 1562) 115–315 (repr. Hildesheim 1975); S. Howard, "An Antiquarian Handlist and the Beginnings of the Pio-Clementino," *Eighteenth-Century Studies* 7 (1973) 40–61; G. Hülsen, "Hermeninschriften," *MDAI(R)* 16 (1901) 128–208; W. Liebenwein, "Die Villa Albani und die Geschichte der Kunstsammlung," in *Forschungen zur Villa Albani* (Berlin 1982) 463–505; for the collectors, Phyllis Pray Bober and Ruth Rubenstein, *Renaissance Artist and Antique Sculpture* (Oxford 1986) app. 2, pp. 471–80; and farther afield there is the survey of F. Poulsen, *Greek and Roman Portraits in English Country Houses* (Oxford 1923).

4. For full references, see the appendix to this essay.

5. Cicero, *De Legibus* 1.9.27.

6. The privilege was reserved for Romans who had attained curule office and was the indigenous source of Roman portraiture. These wax masks were stored in cupboards (*armoria*) and displayed on ledges in the atria of Roman houses and were removed and publicly displayed at the death of a member of the household of curule rank; cf. Polybius 6.55; Pliny, *NH* 35.6–23; Erich Bethe, *Ähnenbild und Familiengeschichte bei Römern und Griechischen* (Munich 1935) 1–31.

(*vultus*) would not find a place in the galleries of an imaginary School of Greece. They belong to the atria of the aristocratic houses of Rome and the funeral processions of great Roman families.[7]

The Truncated Cynic

As likenesses and icons, the vast majority of ancient philosophers survive only as portrait busts in ancient displays familiar from the aristocratic Villa dei Papiri in Herculaneum (and now from the Museo Nazionale of Naples) and the long, stately rows of busts surmounting pillars in the galleries of the Vatican Museums. But the Cynics are not very sociable in museums, although they depended absolutely on the audiences of their contemporary societies. We find Cynics in both Herculaneum (and now in Naples) and in the Vatican too, along with other philosophers. But in the case of the Cynic, the portrait bust is an unsatisfactory solution to the problem of representing either an individual Cynic or the Cynic type. The Cynics presented problems to the ancient artists who depicted them that have been passed on to collectors and museum directors.

It is, of course, possible to collect portrait busts of the Cynics and display them in a row along with busts of the other ancient philosophers. They can be identified at their base: *ANTISTHENĒS* (Antisthenes) of the Vatican would be the first of the series (II, 1);[8] *DIOGENĒS SINŌPEUS* (Diogenes of Sinope) follows (III, 1).[9] The obvious problem with this solution is what has been described as the Cynic uniform. Disheveled hair, an uncropped and untended beard, a savage expression can all be represented in portrait heads, and they are strikingly present in what has been identified as the head of a Cynic philosopher from the wreck off Porticello in Reggio di Calabria (V, 1). But their staffs and wallets cannot be represented in the truncated medium of the portrait head, and only the fold of a *tribōn* can be represented on the shoulder of a bust.

A gallery displaying a series of distinctively Cynic but detached and individual busts assimilates the Cynics and literally places them on the level of all other ancient philosophers. And this is how the visitor of the Museo Nazionale

7. These masks must have served as originals for the kind of portrait busts held by the Barbarini Togatus in the Conservatori Museum, Rome. The statue with the two busts of ancestors is conveniently illustrated in *The Oxford History of Classical Art,* ed. John Boardman (Oxford 1993), fig. 238 (p. 244).

8. My numbers refer to the photographic sources for the representations of the Cynics discussed in the appendix to this essay.

9. Both these busts are now in the Vatican Museums in Rome. Busts and not full figures of the *uomini illustri* were the objects of early collections. For Diogenes, see Beatrice Palma Venetucci, *Uomini illustri dell'antichità* 1.1, *Pirro Ligorio e le erme tiburtine* (Rome 1992) 27–29; and for the antiquarian dispute over the Puteanus bust (Epicurus or Diogenes) see Bernard Frischer, *The Sculpted Word: Epicureanism and Philosophical Recruitment in Ancient Greece* (Berkeley and Los Angeles 1982) 158–66.

Figure 1.   "Crates," Museo Nazionale,
Naples. (Photo: Fratelli Alinari)

in Naples confronts "Crates" (IV, 1; Fig. 1). The bust of this figure, with no
indication of clothing, stands on a pedestal that places him on a level with the
other philosophers displayed in the room. His mouth is turned down; his eyes
gaze out into a distance past any viewer. In his lower face and downturned
mouth he bears a certain resemblance to one type of Socrates (Type B), but he
does not have Socrates' uplifted gaze of rapture and discovery (I, 1; Fig. 2).[10]
He is merely a bust. In the Villa dei Papiri and associated with its library, the
portrait bust of Diogenes stood in a like relation to the other philosophical
heads displayed there. But he is out of place in the context of a library. So far

10. Lucia A. Scatozza Höricht, *Il volto dei filosofi antichi* (Naples 1986; hereafter *Il volto*)
fig. 48 (p. 130). The two types are exhibited on facing pages in G. M. A. Richter, *The Portraits of
the Greeks,* abr. and rev. R. R. R. Smith (Ithaca 1984; hereafter *POG²*), 160–61. Both are now in
the Museo Nazionale, Naples (inv. 6129, Type A; inv. 6415, Type B). Some thirty examples of
Type B survive: G. M. A. Richter, *The Portraits of the Greeks* (London 1965; hereafter *POG*)
1.112–16. In the treatment of his mustache, which gives the impression of a downturned mouth,
"Crates" bears a resemblance not only to the Socrates of the Museo delle Terme, but to the portrait
bust identified as Crates by Jirí Frel, *Greek Portraits in the J. Paul Getty Museum* (Malibu 1981)
no. 44 (p. 94).

Figure 2.   Socrates, Musei Capitolini,
Rome. (Photo: Art Resource)

as we can tell, the Cynics were not popular in the decor of libraries, for the
obvious reason that they would disturb the noble contemplation of the reader.[11]

Some other philosophers require gestures, which serve as emblematic identifications. Zeno needs an outstretched hand or clenched fist to illustrate his
doctrine of the degrees of comprehension.[12] But a portrait bust of a Cynic philosopher is only slightly more revealing than the pedestal that supported him.
Interestingly, there are no double herms of Cynic philosophers surviving. It
seems they could be paired neither with another Cynic nor with a philosopher
from another related school.[13]

The Whole Cynic

The fullest icons of the Cynic as a type are verbal. They come from the
second century A.D., and are confirmed in their details by Diogenes Laertius in

11. This is apparent from Lorenz's survey (above, n. 2), which includes the library at Pergamum, the Villa dei Papiri, the Library of Apollo on the Palatine, and the Library of Pantaenus in
Athens.

12. There is no statue of Zeno exhibiting this famous gesture (for which see Cicero, *Academica* 2.145 = *SVF* I no. 66), but Cicero's description of a statue of Chrysippus in the Ceramicus
with an outstretched hand (*De Finibus* 1.2.39) is the basis for the reconstruction of the right hand
of the seated statue of Chrysippus in the Louvre (*Il volto* [above, n. 10] fig. 82 [p. 196]).

13. A survey in Jean Marcadé, "Hermes Doubles," *BCH* 76 (1952) 596–624.

the third. In his essay *How to Tell a Flatterer from a Friend,* Plutarch allows us to distinguish the philosopher from the normal human being intent on the pleasures of life and living in conformity to society. For Plutarch's flatterer the transformation to the role of the philosopher is simply effected: "If he is after a studious young academic, he changes tack, surrounds himself with books, and lets his beard grow down to his feet; arrayed in the requisite threadbare cloak and indifferent to the world, he spouts mathematics and Platonic right-angled triangles." [14]

The transformation from the philosopher is also easily effected. It takes time to grow long hair and a long beard, but no time to buy a coarse, worn cloak, a wallet, and a walking stick, and practice a fierce look of confrontation. A *tribōn,* worn during the day and folded at night for bedding; a wallet to carry one's earthly possessions and provisions; sometimes a begging cup, or, in the case of Diogenes of Sinope, a drinking cup; a walking stick that proclaimed the Cynic as a traveler and a stranger, in any city, yet at home in the world—these were the significant emblems of the Cynic's autarky, autonomy, and contempt for convention. Antisthenes disputed with Diogenes of Sinope the title of inventor of this Cynic stage costume, although Socrates and one Diodorus of Aspendus also had some claims to the originality that led to centuries of conformity.[15]

The whole Cynic is most dramatically represented in literature by Lucian in *On the Death of Peregrinus.* In this description, by an author who had no equal in his depiction of the mime of philosophy as enacted in the second century A.D., we find Peregrinus returned to his native Parium to defend himself against a charge of parricide. He has exchanged the role of Christian in Palestine for the part of the Cynic philosopher—which is to say, the philosopher—in Parium on the Hellespont: "His hair was already long. He had dressed himself in a soiled cloak and suspended a satchel from his shoulder, and he held a walking stick. He came well prepared for the role of protagonist in this solemn farce" (*Peregr.* 15).[16] According to Lucian, Peregrinus's fellow citizens in Parium dedicated a statue to him after his spectacular self-immolation at the Olympic Games of 165 A.D., as did the people of Elis (ibid. 44). These statues too have

14. *Moralia* 52c, transl. Robin Waterfield, *Plutarch: Essays* (London 1992) 68.

15. The claims of Antisthenes, Diogenes, and Diodorus are stated in D.L. 6.13, 22. Socrates is noticed wearing a worn cloak (*tribōn*): Plato, *Symposium* 219b, *Protagoras* 335d; cf. Epictetus, *Diatr.* 3.1.24. The folded *tribōn* and wallet are ambiguous as signs: they are signs of homelessness and autonomy as well as cosmopolitanism; the walking stick is a sign of the life of the traveler who belongs to no city at all. This seems to explain Diogenes' reluctance to carry his walking stick in Athens (D.L. 6.23). The Cynic of Lucian's *Cynicus* 1 is described as having long hair, a long beard, bare torso, and bare feet—all visible signs of his ἀπάνθρωπος βίος.

16. I treat the costumes for the mime of philosophy in the Second Sophistic in "Lucian of Samosata: Four Philosophical Lives," *ANRW* 36.5 (Berlin 1992) 3414–20. Gabriele Giannantoni sets out the testimonia for the Cynic costume as inaugurated by Diogenes of Sinope in *Socratis et Socraticorum Reliquiae* (Naples 1990) 4.499–505. One should add to this list the description of the philosopher typical of the age who marches in the procession of Isis in Apuleius, *Metamorphosis* 11.9.

Figure 3.   Crates and Hipparchia, Museo delle Terme, Rome. (Photo: Fratelli Alinari)

been melted down, but the sculptors who had the commission of rendering a likeness of Peregrinus had a model in the well-established Cynic type.

The finest and fullest visual representation of the whole Cynic is a painting from the garden of the Villa Farnesina showing two itinerant figures (IV, 2; Fig. 3). These have convincingly been identified as Crates and Hipparchia.[17] The literary descriptions of Crates are disappointing initially; they tell us only that he was ugly (D.L. 6.91) and that in paintings he was depicted barefoot in the barefoot company of Diogenes (Philostr. *Ep.* 18 [22]). In this wall painting, Crates is shown with a long beard and disheveled hair; in his right hand he carries a walking stick, and from the position of his right leg it seems that he is about to set off. In his left hand he grips the thong of a satchel. A skin is draped over his left shoulder, and he is wearing a short, thick cloak. The fact that he is wearing sandals confirms the artist's suggestion that we have caught him as he is about to start on a journey. But he is detained. His head has turned to recog-

17. Irene Bragantini and Mariette de Vos, *Le decorazioni della villa romana della Farnesina* 2.1, *Le pitture* (Rome 1982). The elements of the identification are laid out by Heinrich Fuhrmann, "Krates und Hipparcheia," *MDAI(R)* 40 (1940) 86–91, who cites the lines describing the pair from Menander's *Twin Sisters* (D.L. 6.93).

nize the presence of a conservatively dressed young woman, who is reaching out to him with her right arm.

The scene is a page out of Diogenes Laertius and his source. As the most memorable episode of Crates' life is captured by Diogenes, Crates confronts the noble and wealthy young woman who has fallen in love with him and his talk. The parents of Hipparchia have tried to prevent a disgraceful elopement, but, in the presence of the woman who is in love with him, Crates stands up and deposits all his belongings at her feet, saying: "Here is your bridegroom; these are his possessions. Look on these and make up your mind. You will never be my companion unless you can share my way of life." "And," Diogenes writes, "the girl made her choice" (D.L. 6.96–97). One detail of the painting now becomes significant. Hipparchia is delicately balancing a box on her head with an uplifted left hand. This box makes it clear that Hipparchia has come to Crates as his bride, for it is a box to hold the bride's possessions as she comes to the groom in a wedding procession; such a box is well exampled by the wedding vase of Beazley's Washing Painter.[18] If the implied narrative of the painting from the garden of the Farnesina were continued in another frame, Hipparchia would have left her wedding chest behind her, to be seen in public with Crates and even to attend dinner parties with him.

Crates had the nickname Door Opener (*Thurepanoiktēs*), and the houses whose doors he entered welcomed him with the sign Entrance of the Good Spirit (*Eisodos Agathou Daimonos:* D.L. 6.91; Jul. *Or.* 6, p. 201 Bidez). In this, he was the model of Lucian's genial Cynic Demonax (*Demon.* 63). The Cynics were especially welcome in the houses and villas of the Roman aristocracy, and, like the fashionable old fishermen and peasant women, they entered many doors closed to the lower, disruptive, and threatening classes of Roman society. But they made their entry into these great houses as works of art. In the case of the Roman wall painting showing Crates and Hipparchia at the moment of Hipparchia's decision, these remarkable Cynics from the first generation of the Cynic movement opened the doors to one of the most important houses in Rome—that of Agrippa.

The Cynic Engaged

Some ancient artists understood what moderns have not. Daumier offers one example of the modern understanding; Raphael another. Daumier has at least three versions of the Cynic. One is his rendition of the encounter between a

---

18. Beazley, *ARV*² 1126.1, shown in G.M.A. Richter and L.F. Hall, *Red-Figured Athenian Vases* 2 (New York 1936) pl. 146. Further examples in Fuhrmann (above, n. 17) 88 n. 1; and now the abundant and fine illustrations in John H. Oakley and Rebecca H. Sinos, *The Wedding in Ancient Athens* (Madison 1993) figs. 23, 29, 34, 36, 38. For illustrations of the chests carried in the wedding procession, see figs. 75, 76, 93, 105, 125, 126.

Figure 4.   Honoré Daumier, *Le cynique* (*Propriétaires et locataires*). (Photo: Jenny Strauss Clay)

fatuous Alexander and a savvy and irritated Diogenes, whose torso is obscured by the shadow cast by the standing figure of Alexander. Diogenes is puffing agreeably on a pipe. His lantern is placed at his side, as is his walking stick with a blade fixed to its head. His eyes are open a slit, and he looks away from the armed and plumed figure who stands over him. With his left hand he en-counters Alexander's leg. In this *dessin* Daumier has produced the image of the disengagement of the Cynic from his society. Then there is Daumier's other and parallel scene from *Histoire ancienne:* Diogenes with his vendor's pack, carrying his walking stick with a blade at its head and a lantern. He turns to the viewer with his *Oeil lent-terne,* and the citizens of his ancient city study him from a distance. In one of his other lithographs (Fig. 4), Daumier limns the Cynic who was his contemporary. This Cynic is not the only Cynic in this drawing, but he addresses no other human being as he pronounces his verdict on his involuntary fate: "Il est un peu dur d'être obligé de loger dans un ton-neau quand on n'est pas né pour être cynique" (It's tough to have to live in a barrel when you're not born for the life of a Cynic). There are in fact two other barrel dwellers in this scene. The speaking Cynic lives his life of desolation and isolation. Unlike Diogenes of Sinope, who took temporary lodgings in a great storage jar (pithos) in the Metröon of Athens, Daumier's Cynic is disen-gaged. He contemplates the walls of his barrel. His head is in profile as he emerges from his barrel, quite unlike the Diogenes who emerges from a tondo barrel to confront the viewer face-to-face in the Cologne mosaic (III, 2).

In Raphael's *La scuola di Atene,* on a wall in the Stanza della Segnatura of the Vatican, we discover another solitary Cynic philosopher, Diogenes of Sinope (Fig. 5). He is sprawled out on the second of the three steps leading up to a platform surmounted by the two central figures that dominate the scene. A well-dressed figure mounts the stairs and passes Diogenes with a dismissive gesture of his left hand. Plato and Aristotle, who dominate the scene above, are identified by titles of the books they are carrying in their left hands—*Timeo* and *Etica.* The title of the *Timaeus* is vertical; of the *Ethics,* horizontal. Plato's right hand is lifted, and with an extended finger he points upward; Aristotle has turned to look at Plato and stretches his right hand forcefully toward the viewer. The Cynic is clothed only in a loose cloak that leaves his legs and upper chest exposed; he is barefoot, and the only figure on the wall who offers so much of his body exposed. His hair and beard are full and uncared for. His right arm is propped on a garment that is evidently a *tribōn.* Nearly disguised by the *tribōn* is a drinking cup. He is reading intently from a papyrus roll he holds out to the light in his lowered left hand, supremely indifferent to the distinguished philosophers who collect in groups about him and the young man who has just passed him. His isolation is indicated by the distance that separates him from the other figures on the wall. The only other solitary figure is Raphael's Heraclitus, whose dress is modern and who sits alone at the base of the staircase in an attitude of melancholy meditation.[19]

It is by an accident and a fallacy of duration that in some ancient representations the Cynics have become disengaged from their human contexts and social antagonisms, as the full works of art in which they were once displayed have become fragmented. Perhaps the best and most regrettable example of this fragmentation is the Villa Albani relief of the confrontation between Alexander

---

19. There is no difficulty in this identification. Diogenes is the first figure identified by Giorgio Vasari in his appreciation of *La scuola di Atene* in his *Le vite de' più eccelenti pittori, scultori e architettori* (first published in 1550): "Here are depicted all the sages of the world. Diogenes with his cup is lying on the steps rapt in his own thoughts, a well imagined figure, much to be commended both for the beauty of the form and the characteristic negligence of the garments" (Vasari, *Lives of the Artists,* abr. and ed. Betty Burroughs [New York 1946] 222). There is an intriguing confirmation of this identification in Poussin's *Diogenes in a Landscape* (Louvre; 1648). Poussin's Diogenes is a younger version of Raphael's. Diogenes is standing at a riverbank with a distant city in the background. Crouched before him, a boy is drinking water from the river with a cupped hand. Diogenes' drinking cup has fallen to the ground, and Diogenes is fixed in contemplation of the figure of the drinking boy. The story is from D.L. 6.37; photo in Anthony Blunt, *Nicolas Poussin* 2 (New York 1967) pl. 188. Interestingly for the history of taste, this depiction of Diogenes' abandoning a last unnecessary possession was commissioned by a Swiss banker based in Paris (Blunt 1.215). Interestingly, too, Poussin studied Raphael's Stanza della Segnatura while in Rome (1624–30), and his Prado *Parnassus* is the product of this study (Blunt vol. 2 pl. 18). Anton Heinrich Springer's collation of the identifications of the figures in *La scuola di Atene* shows that the identification of the isolated, seated figure with Diogenes has not been challenged since Vasari made it (*Raffaels Schule von Athen* [Vienna 1883] opp. p. xxxiv).

Figure 5.   Diogenes in Raphael, *La scuola di Atene,* Stanza della Segnatura, Vatican.
(Photo: Art Resource)

Figure 6. Diogenes and Alexander (restored), Villa Albani, Rome. (Photo: Fratelli Alinari)

the Great and Diogenes. In *Il volto dei filosofi antichi* we can admire a photograph of a marble panel executed in low relief of this famous encounter between philosopher and conqueror (III, 3; Fig. 6).[20] The scene is perfect. It is set just outside the walls of a city dominated by a temple on its acropolis. A youthful and beardless Alexander in the dress of a soldier stands facing Diogenes in

20. By one tradition, the encounter between Diogenes and Alexander occurred not in Athens and the Metröon but in the Corinthian suburb of Cranium: cf. Cicero, *TD* 5.32.92; Plutarch, *Alexander* 14; D.L. 6.23. The tradition that Diogenes lodged in a pithos in the Metröon of Athens comes from D.L. 6.38 (cf. n. 29 below). These distinct traditions meld in Juvenal, *Sat.* 14.308–14; Seneca, *Ep.* 90.14; and Lucian, *Hist. Conscr.* 2.364; and in the Villa Albani relief. There is a close parallel to the iconography of the Villa Albani relief in a sarcophagus relief of the late second century A.D. with Muses and on one end Diogenes in his pithos, now in the J. Paul Getty Museum in Malibu. Diogenes is shown with his head turned slightly to the left; he is wrapped in a cloak, and he holds a staff in his right hand and a papyrus roll in his left. As in the Villa Albani relief, his pack hangs out of the bottom of the pithos. A companionable dog is positioned on the upper left shoulder of the pithos. See Frel (above, n. 10) no. 47 (p. 98).

an attitude of calm self-command. Diogenes reacts violently in his intrusive presence; his indignation is expressed by a scowl of deep annoyance. Diogenes emerges from a cracked pithos from which his staff protrudes. This great storage jar is surmounted by a mangy dog who is occupied attacking fleas with an annoyance matched by that of Diogenes at the sight of Alexander. Another emblem of Diogenes' Cynic mode of life is the wallet that just hangs out at the bottom of his pithos.[21]

One half of this confrontation is a reconstruction executed in the eighteenth century. The entire right side of this dramatic framed panel is restored. Only a hand survives from the figure confronting Diogenes, and Diogenes has lost his head and right forearm, and only the tip of his stick survives. This fragment (78.5 cm H × 70 cm w) was discovered on the Testaccio in Rome in 1726. It once belonged to the Stosch Collection, and it could be viewed in the Villa Albani, along with a small freestanding statue of Diogenes (III, 4; Fig. 9).[22] We know of its condition before restoration from a drawing by Ghezzi in the codex Ottobonianus latinus 3109 in the Vatican Library (III, 3; Fig. 7).

This scene and its unkind fate have a parallel in another representation of a philosopher once confronting figures of power in his society. The west wall of Room H of the Villa of Fannius Synistor at Boscoreale is now in Naples in the Museo Nazionale; the east wall, in the Metropolitan Museum of Art in New York. The standing philosopher is separated from the two female allegorical figures he contemplates from a distance, but the trompe-l'œil column casting its shadow on the panel to the right also connects the scenes in the entablature it carries. The three painted walls of Room H, a dining room, were reconstructed as a whole in 1979 for the exposition at the Villa Hügel in Essen (V, 2; Fig. 8).

The standing figure is surely a philosopher. He has been variously identified; Franz Studniczka identified him as Menedemus of Eretria, but he has also been identified as Zeno of Citium, Epicurus, and Aratus.[23] I lean to the identification of this enigmatic figure as Diogenes of Sinope.[24] If Klaus Fittschen and Martin Robertson are right in identifying the two female figures who stare bale-

---

21. The pithos as frame for Diogenes figures in other representations. There is the medallion enclosing Diogenes (and other philosophers) in the Cologne mosaic (K. Schefold, *Die Bildnisse der antiken Dichter, Redner, und Denker* (Basel 1943) 154–55; Richter, *POG* [above, n. 10] 2.185 and fig. 1066); and, other than the carnelians in the Thorvaldsen Museum, Copenhagen, and in Saint Petersburg (Richter, *POG* 2.185), there is the pithos frame in the gem published in *Museo Vittoriano overo Raccolta di varj monumenti antichi esistenti nello studio di D. Ferdinando Vittoria in Roma* (Rome 1708). I owe this reference to Claire Lyons of The Getty Center for the History of Art and the Humanities.

22. Itself heavily restored: *Il volto* (above, n. 10) fig. 47 (p. 128)

23. In his "Imagines Illustrium," *JDAI* 38–39 (1923–24) 80–82.

24. An identification that is made possible by the identification of the two female figures as Macedonia and Asia. It has been suggested to me by Lawrence Richardson, Jr., and is congenial to the argument of this essay.

Figure 7.   Diogenes and Alexander before restoration, codex Ottobonianus latinus 3109, f. 113. (Photo: Biblioteca Apostolica Vaticana)

Figure 8.   Diogenes(?) contemplating two allegorical figures, from the Villa of Fannius Synistor, Boscoreale. (Photo: From Gilbert Picard, *Roman Painting* [London 1970] pl. 33 [p. 53])

fully at one another as Macedonia (the higher seated figure holding a spear) and Asia (the lower seated figure wearing a Phrygian cap, sometimes described as a Persian tiara), Diogenes, the mocker of Alexander and empire, seems a possible identification. The telling feature in the iconography of this panel is the gold shield with the Macedonian star of eight radii now familiar from the gold chest discovered in the royal tombs of Vergina.[25] Diogenes (if Diogenes he is) leans on a gnarled and bent stick that he holds in his right hand. His staff is the figurative counterpart to the long spear held in both hands by Macedonia to his right. He is draped in a voluminous cloak. He is wearing sandals. His beard is long, uncombed, with highlights of gray; his hair is long and receding, revealing a prominent forehead. His nose is angular and pronounced. On the ring finger of his left hand he is wearing a ring with a red stone incised with

25. D. Robertson first made the identification of the two female figures as Macedonia and Asia, "The Boscoreale Figure-Paintings," *JRS* 45 (1955) 58–67; and Klaus Fittschen has reviewed his case and endorsed the identification: "Zum Figurenfries der Villa von Boscoreale," in *Neue Forschungen im Pompeji und den anderen vom Vesuvausbruch 79 n.Chr. verschütten Städten* (Recklinghausen 1975) 93–100 and figs. 70, 71. Fittschen helpfully offers a conspectus of the five main lines of interpretation of the figures of the west wall on p. 100.

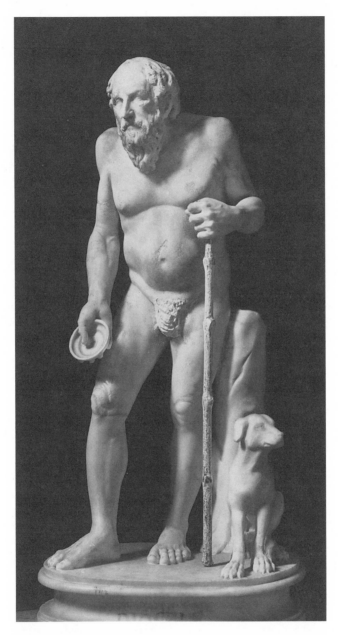

Figure 9.   Diogenes as a beggar, divided (perhaps) between the
Museo Nazionale, Naples, and The Metropolitan Museum of Art,
New York. (Photo: Museo Nazionale, Naples; Fratelli Alinari)

the letter E.[26] His intense eyes are fixed on the two female figures separated from him by the trompe-l'œil painted column (V, 2; Fig. 8).[27] Diogenes' gaze is not a hostile gaze; he contemplates serenely and from a distance the hostile gaze locking a seated and superior Macedonia and a seated and inferior Asia. He is distant from and superior to both.

The Viewer Engaged

The literary reports of the Cynic philosopher bear a distinctive feature: they display the Cynic as he engaged and indeed tormented the prominent and not so prominent members of his society—the society whose social currency he had rejected in order to issue his own.[28] Or, as in the case of the Diogenes (if it is he) depicted on the wall of the Villa of Fannius Synistor in Boscoreale, he is content only to observe. But engagement is the sign of the Cynic, as is the dog. In the atypical case of Diogenes, we find him engaged by Alexander, who has disturbed him with an inopportune question. In the case of most other Cynics, it is the Cynic who is on the attack: Diogenes on Plato; Demetrius on the young reader of Euripides' *Bacchae;* Peregrinus Proteus on Herodes Atticus; Demonax on the procession of worthies recorded on the pages of Lucian's *Demonax.*[29] This confrontational and antagonistic character of the ancient Cynics poses one last challenge to the artist who would depict them: an engagement with his viewer—which is to say, with the owner of the work of art produced by the artist and with the guests he has invited to his house. These viewers attract the stern and sometimes hostile gaze of the Cynic, and, in the case of

26. Fittschen (n. 25 above) 96 n. 29 accepts the fact that the letter incised on the ring is E, but sees it as emblematic not of Epicurus but of the Delphic E and the equivalence of E with εἶ (Know Thyself) of the Delphic Oracle. For this, see Plutarch, *Moralia* 20.293a–d.

27. Conveniently illustrated in Maxwell L. Anderson, "Pompeian Frescos in the Metropolitan Museum of Art," *The Metropolitan Museum of Art Bulletin,* 1987/88, 26–27; and in Fittschen (n. 25 above).

28. παραχαράττειν τὸ νόμισμα (defacing the currency) is applied to the project of Diogenes of Sinope, whose own father was accused of adulterating the coinage of Sinope (D.L. 6.20).

29. Diogenes and Alexander: n. 20 above; and Léonce Pacquet, *Les cyniques grecs: Fragments et témoignages,* 2d ed. (Ottawa 1988), nos. 34, 35. Diogenes and Plato: D.L. 6.25, 26, 27; Alice Reginos Swift, *Platonica: The Anecdotes Concerning the Life and Writings of Plato,* Columbia Studies in the Classical Tradition 3 (Leiden 1970), 111–18; Demetrius, *Against the Uncultured* 19; Margarethe Billerbeck, *Der Kyniker Demetrius: Ein Beitrag zur Geschichte der Frühkaiserzeitlichen Popularphilosophie,* Philosophia Antiqua 36 (Leiden 1979), 51. Peregrinus and Herodes: Lucian, *Peregrinus* 19; Philostratus, *Lives of the Sophists* 2.1.33.563. Peregrinus and a dull Roman who was present at his conversations: Aulus Gellius, *Nights in Attica* 8.3. Lucian constructs his account of the career of Demonax as a series of confrontations on which he threads biting and humiliating ripostes. As I argue in my study of Lucian's *Demonax* (above, n. 16: 3425–29), Demonax is Lucian's own genial invention; thus Lucian gives us not only a rendering of the Cynic type but the typical anecdotal biography of the Cynic. In two recent studies of the ancient Cynics the historical reality of Demonax has been accepted (as it was already by Eunapius of Sardis): Paquet, *op. cit.* 227–34; Marie-Odile Goulet-Cazé, *L'ascèse cynique: Un commentaire de Diogène Laërce VI 70–71* (Paris 1986) 234.

a statue and two small statuettes of Cynics, the viewer is implied in the work of art.

For the wealthy consumer of ancient works of art, there were ways of living comfortably with other ancient philosophers. They could stand as portrait busts on herms decorously positioned along the walls of a library (as they were in the Villa dei Papiri and the library at Pergamum) or they could be collected and displayed in a suburban villa to advertise the culture of the owner (as they were in the Villa of Brutus near Tivoli).[30] They could be admired as they were organized in mosaics on the floor of a great room, as in Cologne and Baalbek.[31] They could keep their owners company in the form of small, portable bronzes, as they did in the Villa dei Papiri. Perhaps the most ingenious project to accommodate philosophers and poets comfortably to the viewer was the stone benches or exedra constructed in the Ptolemaic Serapeum in Memphis.[32] Here the visitor could sit and communicate with the eleven figures of poets and philosophers positioned between the benches forming the half-circle of the exedra.

In some Roman houses the arrangement for accommodating freestanding statues of some Cynics was not as comfortable to the viewer as was the exedra of the Serapeum of Memphis. The statuettes of Diogenes now in the Villa Albani and the Metropolitan Museum of Art in New York (III, 4; Fig. 9) were possibly once a single statue.[33] What is missing in the one is preserved in the other, but nonetheless they have lost too many limbs and attributes for us to be confident in the work of their modern restorers. The less severely truncated figure of the Villa Albani has been restored to show a standing and somewhat bent Diogenes, supporting himself on a staff held in his left hand; he is supported too by a tree against which a modern dog leans as well. This is as far as reconstruction was undertaken in the eighteenth century, and this is what is recorded by Winckelmann in the plate for his *Monumenti antichi inediti*.[34] Since that time, Diogenes' offensive nudity has been plastered over, his staff shortened, and a beggar's cup inserted into his extended left hand. This restoration, if not the original, was inspired by the description in Diogenes Laertius's *Lives of the Philosophers* (6.23): "Once, when he had become ill, he supported himself on a staff, not within the city, but on the road, where he carried it along with his satchel." Instead of a satchel, Diogenes of the Villa

30. For this villa, excavated in 1744, see Richter, *POG* (above, n. 10) 1.83; Lorenz (above, n. 2) 20–26.

31. Richter, *POG* (above, n. 10) 1.81, nos. 3, 4, figs. 351–59; Schefold (above, n. 21) 155, nos. 4, 5 (for the Cologne mosaic).

32. Lauer and Picard (*locc. citt.* above, n. 2); Richter, *POG* (above, n. 10) 1.82, figs. 318–20.

33. The relation between the two is clearly set out in Richter, ibid. 2.183. The closest parallel is the unpublished statuette of Diogenes as a beggar from the Afyon Museum (Turkey). There is a photograph of this in Frel (above, n. 10) fig. 105 (p. 96).

34. Vol. 2 (Rome 1767) pl. 172; reprinted as *Studien zur deutschen Kunstgeschichte* 345, 346 (Baden-Baden 1967); shown in Richter, *POG* (above, n. 10) 2.183. Winckelmann describes the statuette on 1.229–30.

Figure 10.   Standing Cynic, Musei Capitolini, Rome.
(Photo: Art Resource)

Albani has been given a beggar's cup and represented as a *Bittelphilosoph*. There is a striking anecdote in Diogenes Laertius where Diogenes is described as a beggar. He once begged from a statue. When asked why, he replied, "I want to get used to failure." When he begged from living humans, he would say: "If you have given, give again. If you have not, begin now" (D.L. 6.49).[35]

Another freestanding statue of a Cynic is in the Capitoline Museums in Rome (V, 3; Fig. 10).[36] This Cynic does not carry a beggar's cup or a staff; he is wearing sandals and has a cloak—and not a *tribōn*—wrapped around him, covering his knees and revealing the muscular chest of an older man. His hair and beard are uncared for, and he is supported by a civilized column, not a tree trunk. His eyes are tightly focused on the viewer. The papyrus roll he grips in his right hand (restored), which extends downward and not outward, suggests that he is not merely a reader but a writer. If a writer, his attitude suggests that what he has to say to his viewer—and reader—is as sour and biting as the expression he wears on his face. The details by which this philosopher is rendered encourage an identification with Menippus of Gadara. (Velázquez's wry, dissolute, and knowing Menippus, designed apparently for La Torre de la Parada and now in the Prado Museum, Madrid, stands with a collection of books at his feet.)[37] Menippus's attitude resembles that of a small bronze statuette of a Cynic ("Hermarchus") surmounting a bronze column capital in the Metropolitan Museum of Art in New York.[38] "Hermarchus" is draped in a voluminous himation, and wears a beard. It seems that this figure might have once held a lantern in his right hand. Like his fellow Cynic in the Capitoline Museums, he is diminutive: 26.3 cm H (54.1 cm H with plinth). The height of Diogenes in the Villa Albani is only 54.6 cm with plinth. As they stood in the public rooms of the wealthy amateurs of art and philosophy—and of the unconventional in philosophy—in the great houses and villas of Rome and Italy, the Cynics that accosted the members of these households and their visitors were so small that the engagement of the Cynic was much diminished and the man of taste immune from the violence of their attack. And we are reminded that the wealthy sometimes invited the Cynics to dinner, as, in another age,

35. The first passage in Diogenes Laertius does not present Diogenes as a beggar, and it is silent on any companionable or emblematic dog; but Diogenes' life as a mendicant is also mentioned by Plutarch, *Moralia* 632e, 449d.

36. Schefold (above, n. 21) 123, 124, no. 1.

37. Menippus and his companion Aesop are well illustrated in Jonathan Brown, *Velázquez: Painter and Courtier* (New Haven 1986) figs. 189, 191 (pp. 165–66). Erwin W. Palm offers a philosophical context for the pair in his "Diego Velázquez: *Aesop* und *Menipp*," in *Lebende Antike: Symposium für Hans-Joachim Zimmermann*, ed. H. Miller and H.-J. Zimmermann (Berlin 1967), 207–17.

38. Schefold (above, n. 21) 124, no. 4. This might be the sole ancient example of Diogenes holding a lamp. He (or the philosopher represented) has the index finger of his right hand extended, perhaps to hold a miniature lamp. He stands on a lamp stand in the form of an Ionic capital and is severely miniaturized. The bronze is said to be from Ostia. (Metropolitan Museum of Art, Rogers Fund 1910, 10.231.1.)

Baron d'Holbach invited Jean-Jacques Rousseau to his hotel, dressed as Rousseau was in the eighteenth-century equivalent of a *tribōn*.[39] But more often the Cynics were invited into the houses of the great in Rome and Italy when they were long dead. And now, when the wealthy who displayed the Cynic philosophers in their great rooms are themselves long dead, we are confronted by only their poor guests.

Appendix: Sources for the Ancient Representations of Cynic Philosophers Discussed

ABBREVIATIONS: *Monumenti inediti* = Johann Joachim Winckelmann, *Monumenti antichi inediti*, 2 vols. (Rome 1767); *Bildnisse* = Karl Schefold, *Die Bildnisse der antiken Dichter, Redner, und Denker* (Basel 1943); *POG* = G. M. A. Richter, *The Portraits of the Greeks*, 3 vols. (London 1965), with *Supplement* (London 1972); *POG*² = ead., *The Portraits of the Greeks,* abr. and rev. R. R. R. Smith (Ithaca 1984); *Il volto* = Lucia A. Scatozza Höricht, *Il volto dei filosofi antichi* (Naples 1986).

I   SOCRATES: 1 (Fig. 2) Herm, Musei Capitolini, Rome: *POG* 1.112, no. 6, figs. 487–89.

II   ANTISTHENES: 1 Inscribed bust, Salla delle Muse, Vatican: *Bildnisse* 86–87; *POG* 1.180, no. 1, figs. 1037–39; *POG*² 88; *Il volto* fig. 45 (p. 124).

III   DIOGENES OF SINOPE: 1 Base of herm with feet; sumounted with a bust of Thales: Sala delle Muse, Vatican, *POG* 2.182, no. 1, fig. 1062.

2 Represented in a mosaic in Cologne: *Bildnisse* 155, no. 9; *POG* 1.81, 2.185h; *POG*² 115, fig. 76.

3 (Figs. 6, 7) Relief from the Villa Albani: *Monumenti inediti* vol. 2 pl. 174; *POG* 2.184a, fig. 1067; *Il volto* fig. 46 (p. 127); Lucia Guerrini, *Marmi antichi nei disegni di Pier Leone Ghezzi* (Vatican City 1971) no. 32 (p. 19).

4 (Fig. 9) Standing statue of Diogenes as a beggar, Villa Albani, Rome, and The Metropolitan Museum of Art, New York: *Monumenti inediti* vol. 2 pl. 172; *Bildnisse* 147, no. 4 (p. 146); *POG* 2.182–83, fig. 1057; *POG*² 114–15; *Il volto* fig. 47 (p. 128); G. M. A. Richter, *Catalogue of Greek Sculptures in the Metropolitan Museum of Art* (Cambridge, Mass., 1954) no. 191 (p. 100).

For Diogenes(?) of the west wall of Room H of the Villa of Fannius Synistor, see V, 2.

---

39. "A nobleman was expected to dress like a nobleman, a bourgeois like a bourgeois, but a philosopher—at any rate a recognized philosopher—could dress as he pleased": Maurice Cranston, *Jean-Jacques: The Early Life and Work of Jean-Jacques Rousseau, 1712–1754* (Chicago 1991) 257.

IV CRATES (AND HIPPARCHIA): 1 (Fig. 1) Bust, Museo Nazionale, Naples: Bildnisse 89, no. 1 (p. 88); *POG* 1.186; *Il volto* fig. 48 (p. 130).

2 (Fig. 3) Wall painting from the garden of the Villa Farnesina, Museo delle Terme, Rome: *POG* 2.186; *Il volto* fig. 49 (p. 131).

V OTHERS AND DISPUTED IDENTIFICATIONS: 1 Cynic(?) from the Reggio di Calabria shipwreck: *Il volto* fig. 53 (p. 136).

2 (Fig. 8) Diogenes(?) wall painting from the west wall of Room H of the Villa of Fannius Synistor, Boscoreale: *POG* 2.244; *Il volto* fig. 42 (p. 117); Fittschen (above n. 25) figs. 70, 71.

3 (Fig. 10) Statue of a Cynic, Musei Capitolini, Rome: *Bildnisse* 122; *Il volto* fig. 51 (p. 134).

Appendix A

A Comprehensive Catalogue
of Known Cynic Philosophers

M.-O. Goulet-Cazé

As there has never been a systematic and exhaustive index compiled of this group of philosophers, it is difficult to get any idea of the size of the Cynic movement. This is why it has seemed to me useful to give a short index of the known Cynics. The sole aim of the short notes that accompany each name is to allow the identification of that person. They usually include a chronological indication and the reference of the *Realencyclopädie der classischen Alter-tumswissenschaft* (abbreviated *RE* below), the *Prosopography of the Later Roman Empire* (*PLRE*), the *Prosopographia Imperii Romani,* 2d ed. (*PIR*²), or the *Dictionnaire des philosophes antiques* (*DPhA*) vols. 1 and 2 (Paris 1989, 1994), where one exists. In order to avoid confusion, the entries have been arranged into eight groups:

    I.   Cynics whose historical authenticity is confirmed (83).

   II.   Anonymous Cynics (14).

  III.   Persons whose link with Cynicism is uncertain (10).

  IV.   Cynics of the pseudepigraphical *Cynic Epistles* (31).

   V.   Cynics, almost certainly fictitious, who appear in literature (13).

  VI.   A Cynic by mistake (1).

 VII.   People who were not Cynics but were known as "dogs" (4).

VIII.   Titles in which the word "dog" appears.

Many thanks are due to Helena Caine-Suarez, who translated a large part of this index, and to the Librairie Philosophique J. Vrin (Paris), which kindly granted permission to publish this revised version of the "Répertoire des philosophes cyniques connus" previously edited in my *L'ascèse cynique: Un commentaire de Diogène Laërce VI 70–71* (Paris 1986) 231–48.

I. Cynics Whose Historical Authenticity Is Confirmed

AGATHOBULUS OF ALEXANDRIA (*RE* 1). Second century A.D. An Alexandrian Cynic who practiced a rigorous asceticism, he was the master of Demonax (Lucian, *Demonax* 3); we know that Peregrinus visited him in Egypt (*On the Death of Peregrinus* 17). In Jerome's *Chronicle* (p. 198.1–3 Helm), he is one of the *philosophi insignes* known of in 119 A.D., along with Plutarch of Chaeronea, Sextus, and Oenomaus. Dudley, *A History of Cynicism* 175 n. 3, suggests that he could be "the famous sophist of Rhodes" under whose guidance Demetrius of Sunium practiced Cynic asceticism at Alexandria. Cf. *RE* 1.1 (1893) col. 745 (von Arnim); *DPhA* A 36.

ANAXIMENES OF LAMPSACUS (*RE* 3). Fourth century B.C. A rhetor, represented by the *Suda* s.v. (A 1989) as being a pupil of Diogenes the Dog and of Zoilus of Amphipolis. However, the two anecdotes reported by Diogenes Laertius 6.57 that bring Diogenes and Anaximenes together are far from proving that the rhetor really was the pupil of the philosopher. Cf. *RE* 1.2 (1894) cols. 2086–98 (Brzoska); *DPhA* A 167.

ANDROSTHENES OF AEGINA (*RE* 10). Fourth century B.C. The son of Onesicritus of Aegina. Like his father and his brother Philiscus, he was a pupil of Diogenes the Dog. Cf. *RE* 1.2 (1894) col. 2173 (Natorp); *DPhA* A 182.

ANTIOCHUS OF CILICIA called "the Renegade" (*RE* 64). Second and third centuries A.D. Dio Cassius, epitome of Book 78 (19), followed by the *Suda* (A 2695), says that "at first he had pretended to be a philosopher of the Cynic school" and that during the war against the Parthians he cheered up the soldiers, who were dispirited by reason of the excessive cold, by throwing himself into the snow and rolling in it. This led to his being rewarded with money and honors from Severus as well as from Caracalla, but he nonetheless deserted to the Parthian king. Cf. *RE* 1.2 (1894) col. 2494 (von Arnim); *PIR*² A 743; *DPhA* A 201.

ANTISTHENES (*RE* 10). Ca. 445–336 B.C. The son of an Athenian called Antisthenes and a Thracian woman; he studied rhetoric under Gorgias and became a rhetor in his turn. After this he attached himself to Socrates and was one of those pupils present at his death. Tradition holds him to be the master of Diogenes, which poses a certain number of chronological problems. He is also by some accounts the founder of Cynicism (cf. D.L. 6.13, 15). Antisthenes dispensed his teaching at the gymnasium of the Cynosarges (which was exclusively for *nothoi,* the offspring of illegitimate unions), whence, according to some (D.L. 6.13), the name "Cynicism." He himself was known as *haplokuōn* (ibid.)—"simple dog" or "natural dog." His prolific literary output, in the domains of both rhetoric and philosophy, created widespread interest. Cf. *RE* 1.2 (1894) cols. 2538–45 (Natorp); *DPhA* A 211.

ASCLEPIADES (*RE* 19). Second half of the fourth century A.D. A Cynic philosopher who visited the emperor Julian at Antioch in 362. His carelessness was responsible for the outbreak of a fire in the temple of Apollo at Daphne (Amm. Marc. 22.13.3). Cf. *RE* 2.2 (1896) col. 1625 (Seeck); *PLRE* I (4); *DPhA* A 443.

AVIDIENUS. First century B.C. Mentioned by Horace, *Satires* 2.2.55–62, but otherwise unknown. Horace introduces him thus: "Avidienus, to whom the nickname 'Dog' is so rightly attached, was characterized by the sordidness of his life." Cf. *RE* 2.2 (1896) col. 2378 (Klebs); *DPhA* A 514.

BESAS. Fourth century A.D. A Cynic who had visited the tomb of Ramses IV in the mountain of Thebes. No. 1381 in J. Baillet, *Inscriptions grecques et latines des tombeaux des rois ou Syringes,* Mémoires Publiés par les Membres de l'Institut Français d'Archéologie Orientale 42 (Cairo 1926). Cf. *DPhA* B 28.

BETION. Third century B.C. An associate of Bion of Borysthenes (D.L. 4.54). Cf *DPhA* B 30.

BION OF BORYSTHENES (*RE* 10). Ca. 335–245. The son of a freedman who was a dealer in salt fish; his mother was originally a prostitute; he was sold with his family after his father cheated on his taxes. He was bought by a rhetor and received an education in rhetoric. On the death of his master he went to Athens, where he was able to benefit from a wide general philosophical education: first at the Academy under Xenocrates and Crates, then with the Cynics, the Cyrenaics (as a disciple of Theodorus the Atheist), and finally the Peripatetics as a follower of Theophrastus. D.L. 2.77 assigns some *diatribai* to him, and this has given rise to the idea that he might have been the originator of the literary form of the diatribe. Cf. *RE* 3.1 (1897) cols. 483–85 (von Arnim); *DPhA* B 32.

CANTHARUS. Second century A.D. A figure in Lucian's *Fugitivi;* friend of the Cynic Peregrinus Proteus. Cantharus (Κάνθαρος) is a nickname meaning "Scarab." His real name is unknown. Cf. *DPhA* C 37a.

CARNEADES. First century A.D. Only Eunapius's *Lives of the Philosophers and Sophists* 2.1.5 attests to his existence. Eunapius represents Carneades as a contemporary of Apollonius of Tyana and one of the remarkable representatives of Cynicism, alongside "Musonius, Demetrius, Menippus and many others." Cf. *DPhA* C 40.

CERCIDAS OF MEGALOPOLIS (*RE* 2). Ca. 290–220 B.C. A politician and friend of Aratus of Sicyon; he was a legislator, a Cynic poet, author of iambic and meliambic verses and possibly of a moral anthology. Cf. *RE* 11.1 (1921) cols. 294–308 (Gerhard-Kroll); *DPhA* C 83.

CHYTRON. Fourth century A.D. A Cynic known to the emperor Julian (*Or.* 7.18.224d). Should he be identified with Demetrius of Alexandria, known as

"Cythras," as was suggested by O. Seeck, *RE* 4.2 (1901) col. 2804? There is no argument to support this. Cf. *RE* 3.2 (1899) col. 2532 (von Arnim); *PLRE* 1; *DPhA* C 122.

CLEANTHES OF ASSOS (*RE* 2). Ca. 331–231 B.C. A Stoic philosopher, he was both pupil and successor to Zeno. Nonnus described him as a Cynic, *In Invect. 1 adversus Iukianum (Or. 4) Historia* 35, col. 1004. The *Suda* K 1711 depicts him as "a disciple of Crates, then of Zeno, whose successor he became." His nickname, "the Second Heracles," with its Cynic overtones, should also be noted. Cf. *RE* 11.1 (1921) cols. 558–74 (von Arnim); *RE* Suppl. 12 (1970) cols. 1705–9 (Dörrie); *DPhA* C 138.

CLEOMENES (*RE* 12). Fourth and third centuries B.C. He was a pupil not, as is generally supposed, of Metrocles but of Crates of Thebes, if the end of the chapter on Metrocles in D.L. 6.95, which gives a list of disciples, is, as I suggest, to be taken as referring to Crates rather than Metrocles (the introductory words *mathētai d' autou* are taken again from 6.93). To support this hypothesis, I would point out that 6.98 returns to the biography of Crates, dealing with his literary output and his death. Cleomenes was the master of Timarchus of Alexandria and Echecles of Ephesus. He wrote a *Paedagogicus,* in which he chiefly recounts how Diogenes upbraided the foolishness of the disciples who wished to buy him back after he had been sold as a slave to Xeniades of Corinth. Cf. *RE* 11.1 (1921) col. 712 (von Arnim); *DPhA* C 163.

CLEOMENES OF CONSTANTINOPLE (*RE* 11). Fourth century A.D. Libanius writes about him in his letters (nos. 399, 432, 446 Foerster). He was a Cynic and friend of Andronicus, who was living at Constantinople in 355. Cf *RE* 11.1 (1921) col. 712 (Seeck); *DPhA* C 164.

CRATES OF THEBES (*RE* 6). Ca. 360–280 B.C. He was the brother of the Megarian philosopher Pasicles, the husband of Hipparchia of Maronea, and the pupil of Diogenes. However, Hippobotus maintained that he was the pupil of Bryson the Achaean (D.L. 6.85) rather than of Diogenes. He came to Cynicism after watching a tragedy that featured the character of Telephus carrying a miserable little basket and looking thoroughly wretched (D.L. 6.87). His literary works include tragedies, elegies, parodies, a poem in hexameters entitled *Pēra* (Knapsack), a *Hymn to Simplicity, Letters,* and a *Praise of the Lentil.* Metrocles, Zeno, Cleanthes, Hipparchia, and Monimus were all his disciples, as well as Cleomenes, Theombrotus, and Menippus. Cf. *RE* 11.2 (1922) cols. 1625–31 (Stenzel); *DPhA* C 205.

CRESCENS (*RE* 3). His existence is attested (*agnoscitur*) in 154 A.D. by Eusebius (Jerome, *Chronicle,* p. 203.13–18 Helm). He lived in Rome under the Antonines, attacked the Christians, and was responsible for the martyrdom of Justin in 165. Cf. *RE* 4.2 (1901) col. 1707 (von Arnim); *DPhA* C 211.

DEMETRIUS. No. 319 in J. Baillet, *Inscriptions grecques et latines des tombeaux des rois ou Syringes,* Mémoires Publiés par les Membres de l'Institut Français d'Archéologie Orientale 42 (Cairo 1926). But his reading of the graffito (κύων Δημήτριος) has now been corrected by G. Seure and E. Bernand, who read ἀχέων Δημήτριος. Cf. *DPhA* D 44.

DEMETRIUS OF ALEXANDRIA (*RE* 88). Ca. 300 B.C. Disciple of Theombrotus (D.L. 6.95). Cf. *RE* 4.2 (1901) col. 2842 (von Arnim); *DPhA* D 46.

DEMETRIUS OF CORINTH (*RE* 91). First century A.D. A friend of Seneca and Thrasea Paetus, he taught at Rome under Caligula, Nero, and Vespasian, but apparently wrote nothing. Curiously enough, in 70 he took the defense of P. Egnatius Celer against Musonius Rufus (Tacitus, *Histories* 4.40). Vespasian exiled him in 71 along with all the other philosophers (Dio Cassius, epitome of Book 65 [13.2]). Should he be identified with Demetrius of Sunium, known by Lucian, *Toxaris* 27–34? Dudley (*A History of Cynicism* 175 n. 3) and M. Billerbeck (*DPhA* D 56) reject this suggestion, with some arguments. (See next entry.) But on the other hand, the Demetrius depicted in an anecdote set in Corinth, *Adversus Indoctum* 19, is most probably Seneca's friend. The same could be said for Demetrius the Cynic who (in Lucian, *De Saltatione* 63) objects to dancing, since the episode is situated at the time of the emperor Nero. It is also generally accepted that the Demetrius represented by Philostratus as a disciple of Apollonius of Tyana and as the master of Menippus of Lycia is to be identified with the philosopher friend of Seneca, even if the information found in *The Life of Apollonius of Tyana* is of dubious historical value. It should also be noted that one of Apollonius's letters (*Ep.* 111 Hercher = 77e Penella) was addressed to Demetrius the Cynic, except in one manuscript of the fifteenth century that has "Demetrius of Sunium." Cf. *DPhA* D 43.

DEMETRIUS OF SUNIUM. Second century A.D.? Lucian, *Toxaris* 27, mentions a Demetrius of Sunium who practiced Cynic asceticism under the guidance of "the famous sophist of Rhodes," perhaps Agathobulus of Alexandria (cf. *DPhA* A 36). Dudley, *A History of Cynicism* 175 n. 3, underlines the fact that Demetrius is a most common name, that nothing proves that Demetrius of Corinth ever went to Egypt, and that: "We know of no 'famous' Cynic, Rhodian or otherwise, from whom the first-century Demetrius could have learned the philosophy. The most satisfactory inference is that Demetrius of Sunium is not the same person as the friend of Seneca, but lived considerably later and was the pupil of Agathoboulos." Cf. *DPhA* D 56.

DEMONAX OF CYPRUS (*RE* 1). Ca. 70–170 A.D. Primarily known through the biography that Lucian wrote of him. He was born at Cyprus and spent his life at Athens. Epictetus, Timocrates of Heraclea, Agathobulus, and Demetrius were his masters, and Lucian his student. He apparently practiced a gentler form of Cynicism, which permitted him to venerate Socrates, admire Diogenes, and love Aristippus (*Demonax* 62). He left no written work. He allowed himself to starve to death and was given a state funeral by Athens. Cf. *RE* 5.1 (1903) cols. 143–44 (von Arnim); *DPhA* D 74.

DIDYMUS, nicknamed PLANETIADES (*RE* 5). First century A.D. One of the interlocutors of Plutarch's *De Defectu Oraculorum* (7.412f–413d). Cf. *RE* 5.1 (1903) col. 444 (von Arnim); *DPhA* D 103.

DIITREPHES. A figure in Parmeniscus's *Symposium of the Cynics,* quoted by Cynulcus in Athenaeus's *Deipnosophists* 4.156f. He could be one of the six "dogs" who partake in the symposium under the lead of Carneius of Megara. Cf. *DPhA* D 107.

DIO CHRYSOSTOM (*RE* 18). Ca. 40–after 112 A.D. Born in Prusa (Bithynia), this sophist started off as an adversary of philosophy but then became a student of Musonius Rufus. He was banished by Domitian from both Bithynia and Italy in 82. For several years he led the life of a wandering preacher and took on the appearance of a Cynic philosopher, with a cloak, long hair, beard, and wallet. This way of life came to an end when he was rehabilitated by Nerva. But in the years that followed he took to the road again and went from town to town giving speeches as a popular philosopher. He later became a notable in Bithynia and meddled in his own town's affairs, which caused him to become unpopular with many of his fellow citizens and to be put on trial in 111/112. Among the many discourses he composed, *Or.* 4, 6, and 8–10 are particularly important for Cynicism. Cf. *RE* 5.1 (1903) cols. 848–77 (W. Schmid); *PIR*² D 93; *DPhA* D 166.

DIOCLES. Nos. 1542, 1611, 1721, 1735 in J. Baillet, *Inscriptions grecques et latines des tombeaux des rois ou Syringes,* Mémoires Publiés par les Membres de l'Institut Français d'Archéologie Orientale 42 (Cairo 1926). This Cynic philosopher left his signature in four places on the walls of the tomb of Ramses VI. Cf. *DPhA* D 111a (Addenda).

DIOGENES OF SINOPE (*RE* 44). Fourth century B.C. His father was the banker Hicesias (called "Hicetas" in Diogenes' pseudepigraphical *Epistle* 30). According to tradition he left Sinope after defacing the currency and went to Athens, where he attached himself to Antisthenes. This involves chronological problems. During a sea voyage, he was taken prisoner by pirates and sold to Xeniades of Corinth, with whom he supposedly lived until he died in 323 B.C., on the same day as Alexander the Great. This is what is claimed by Demetrius in his work *On Men of the Same Name* (D.L. 6.79), though in the life of Diogenes it is often difficult to separate legend and historical fact. His disciples were Onesicritus of Aegina, Onesicritus's two sons Androsthenes and Philiscus, Monimus of Syracuse, Menander *Drumos,* Hegesias of Sinope *Kloios,* Crates of Thebes, Phocion "the Good," and Stilpo the Megarian. The reports of his literary activity differ. According to D.L. 6.80, Sosicrates in Book 1 of his *Successions of the Philosophers* and Satyrus in Book 4 of his *Lives* allege that he left nothing in writing. Satyrus says that the tragedies are by his disciple Philiscus of Aegina. Diogenes Laertius nonetheless gives two lists of writings: the first contains thirteen titles of dialogues, some letters, and seven tragedies; the second, from Sotion, consists of twelve titles of dialogues (of which eight are not included in the first series) as well as some *chreiai* and letters (D.L. 6.80). Cf. *RE* 5.1 (1903) cols. 765–73 (Natorp); *DPhA* D 147.

DIOGENES THE SOPHIST (*RE* 25). First century A.D. In 75, he made his way into the packed theater at Rome hurling various insults about Titus and Berenice, who acted like Titus's wife and evidently hoped to marry him. Diogenes was flogged (Dio Cassius, epitome of Book 65 [15.5]). Cf. *RE* 5.1 (1903) col. 736 (Stein); *PIR*² D 97; *DPhA* D 151.

DOMITIUS. No. 1825 in J. Baillet, *Inscriptions grecques et latines des tombeaux des rois ou Syringes,* Mémoires Publiés par les Membres de l'Institut Français d'Archéologie Orientale 42 (Cairo 1926). Cf. *DPhA* D 218.

ECHECLES OF EPHESUS (*RE* 2). Fourth and third centuries B.C. A disciple of Cleomenes and Theombrotus, he was the master of Menedemus of Lampsacus (D.L. 6.95). Cf. *RE* 5.2 (1905) col. 1909 (Natorp).

FAVONIUS (*RE* 1). First century A.D. Aedile in 52 and praetor in 49, this politician was a follower of Cato Uticensis, whose *parrhēsia* he imitated (Plutarch, *Caesar* 41.3; *Pompey,* 60.7–8). Brutus qualified him as *haplokuna* and *pseudokuna* (id. *Brutus* 34.7). Cf. *RE* 6.2 (1909) cols. 2074–77 (Münzer).

GORGIAS. We find two anonymous lines in the *Greek Anthology* 7.134 that read: "Here I, the head of the Cynic Gorgias, have found rest. / But I no longer spit or sniff."

HEGESIANAX (*RE* 3). According to Photius, *Bibl.* cod. 167, p. 114b24 Bekker, he is one of the ten Cynics mentioned in the second part of Stobaeus's lost *Prooemium.* Cf. *RE* 7.2 (1912) col. 2606 (von Arnim).

HEGESIAS OF SINOPE, nicknamed KLOIOS (Dog Collar). A disciple of Diogenes the Dog (D.L. 6.84). Natorp suggested that his nickname could stem from his devotion to the Dog. Cf. *RE* 7.2 (1912) col. 2607 (Natorp).

HERACLIUS (*RE* 12, 16). A Cynic who lived at the time of the emperor Julian, who wrote against him his seventh discourse: Πρὸς Ἡράκλειον Κυνικὸν περὶ τοῦ Πῶς Κυνιστέον, *Against the Cynic Heraclius on How to Live as a Cynic* (cf. Eunapius, *Chronicle* fr. 18.3 Müller). Eunapius (ibid. fr. 31) reports Heraclius's words to Procopius, a relative of Julian, who wished to usurp the emperor's title. Cf. *RE* 8.1 (1912) col. 503 (Seeck and von Arnim [these two articles are doublets]).

HERAS (*RE* 3). Like Diogenes the Sophist (q.v.), in 75, during the reign of Vespasian, he got into the theater of Rome. But whereas Diogenes had been flogged for his insults, Heras, who had expected the same punishment for his Cynic raillery against Titus and Berenice, was beheaded (Dio Cassius, epitome of Book 65 [15.5]). Cf. *RE* 8.1 (1912) col. 529 (von Arnim); *PIR*² H 91.

HERMODOTUS. First century A.D. He is mentioned in an epigram by Lucilius (*Greek Anthology* 11.154).

HIPPARCHIA OF MARONEA (*RE* 1). Fourth and third centuries B.C. From a wealthy family, she was the sister of the Cynic Metrocles and wanted to marry Crates of Thebes, even threatening to commit suicide unless she should be given in marriage to him. D.L. 6.96–98 does not mention any written work by her, but the *Suda* I 517 says she wrote some *Philosophical Subjects* (Φιλοσό-φους Ὑποθέσεις), *Epikheirēmata,* and some *Questions* (Προτάσεις) to Theodorus the Atheist. Cf. *RE* 8.2 (1913) col. 1662 (von Arnim).

HONORATUS (*RE* 10). Second century A.D. This Cynic philosophized dressed in a bearskin (*arktos*). This is why Demonax (Lucian, *Demonax* 19) called him Arcesilaus (*Arkesilaos*) rather than Honoratus. Cf. *RE* 8.2 (1913) col. 2276 (von Arnim); *PIR*² H 195.

HORUS. Fourth century A.D. An Egyptian, son of Valens, and brother of Phanes. A boxer, in 364 he was a victor at the Olympic Games at Antioch (Libanius, *Ep.* 1278, 1279). He also appears as one of the interlocutors of Macrobius's *Saturnalia.* Cf. *RE* 8.2 (1913) col. 2489 (Seeck); *PLRE* 1.

IPHICLES (*RE* 2, 3). Fourth century A.D. A companion of the emperor Julian at the time when he was being educated by Mardonius. Julian remembered him as having "dirty hair, a half-dressed look, and a miserable old cloak over his shoulders in the middle of winter" (*Or.* 9.16.198a). He is probably the Iphicles mentioned by Libanius in a letter to Themistius in 356/357 (*Ep.* 508) and also the one sent against his will in 375 by the Epirotes to the emperor Valentinian at Carnuntum at the demand of Probus, then the praetorian prefect. Instead of regaling the emperor with an account of the merits of Probus, Iphicles, who was renowned for his force of character, openly denounced all his misdeeds (Amm. Marc. 30.5.8–10). Cf. *RE* 9.2 (1916) cols. 2018–19 (von Arnim and Seeck [these two articles are doublets]); *PLRE* 1.

ISIDORUS (*RE* 9). First century B.C. He publicly made fun of Nero, who punished him with exile from Rome and Italy (Suetonius, *Nero* 39.5–6). Cf. *RE* 9.2 (1916) col. 2062 (Stein); *PIR*² I 55.

MAXIMUS HERO OF ALEXANDRIA (*RE* 109). Fourth century A.D. A Christian Cynic who fought against the Arian Lucius after the death of Athanasius. While he was still a friend of Gregory of Nazianzius, who had delivered a flattering speech about him (*Or.* 25), he won the confidence of the bishop Peter II and got himself secretly consecrated bishop of Constantinople. This led to the rupture with Gregory and the various hostile references in the latter's *Carmina* and *Epistles*. Maximus's consecration was pronounced uncanonical at the ecumenical council of Constantinople in 381. R. Weijenborg, in "Is Evagrius Ponticus the Author of the Longer Recension of the Ignatian Letters?" *Antonianum* 44 (1969) 339–47, unconvincingly proposes the identification of Maximus Hero, Evagrius of Antioch, and Evagrius Ponticus. Cf. *RE* Suppl. 5 (1931) col. 676 (Ensslin).

MELEAGER OF GADARA (*RE* 7). Ca. 135–50; *fl.* 96 B.C. A Cynic poet who lived at Tyre, then at Cos. He composed satires in the style of Menippus: the Χάριτες (Graces), a work that contained a Λεκίθου καὶ Φακῆς Σύγκρισις (Comparison of Pease Porridge with Lentil Soup: Athenaeus, *Deipnosophists* 4.157b), a *Symposium* (ibid. 11.502c), and some epigrams, of predominately esoteric content, around 130 of which have survived. He inserted them into the *Garland* of ancient epigrams, which he composed in 70. Cf. *RE* 15.1 (1931) cols. 481–88 (Geffcken).

MENANDER, nicknamed DRUMOS (Oakwood) (*RE* 17). Fourth century B.C. A disciple of Diogenes the Dog and an admirer of Homer (D.L. 6.84). Cf. *RE* 15.1 (1931) col. 764 (von Fritz).

MENEDEMUS OF LAMPSACUS (*RE* 11). Third century B.C. A disciple of the Epicurean Colotes of Lampsacus, then of the Cynic Echecles of Ephesus, who was in turn a disciple of Cleomenes and Theombrotus. A polemic broke out between Colotes and Menedemus, notably on the subject of poetry and ethics. Part of this polemic has been preserved in the Herculaneum papyri. It is possible, as has been suggested for instance by Crönert and Mejer, that the section devoted to Menedemus in D.L. 6.102 is based upon a confusion with Menippus. Cf. *RE* 15.1 (1931) cols. 794–95 (von Fritz).

MENESTRATUS (*RE* 7). First century A.D. An epigram by Lucilius represents him as being a Cynic (*Greek Anthology* 11.153). Should he be identified with a Menestratus mentioned by Lucilius in another epigram (ibid. 11.104)? In *RE* 15.1 (1931) col. 856 von Fritz does not refer to the epigram 11.153.

MENIPPUS OF GADARA (*RE* 10). *Fl.* first half of the third century B.C. A Phoenician slave in the service of Baton, a citizen of Pontus (D.L. 6.99), whence the qualifier "Sinopeus" given to him by D.L. 6.95. He then obtained his freedom, either begging or practicing usury (his nickname was *Hēmērodaneistēs* [Lender at Daily Rates], and he was a speculator in marine insurance), but this tradition "is probably apocryphal, resting as it does on the always dubious authority of Hermippus" (Dudley, *A History of Cynicism* 70). He was a disciple of Crates of Thebes (D.L. 6.95). He eventually lost all his money in a plot and hanged himself in despair. D.L. 6.101 says that his works comprised thirteen books, for which he gives the titles of six. Among these is the *Necyia,* which was to exert a large influence on Lucian. Diogenes Laertius also reminds us that, according to some, Dionysius and Zopyrus of Colophon are the true authors of Menippus's work. Athenaeus cites a *Symposium (Deipnosophists* 14.629f) and an *Arcesilaus* (14.664e) of his, and D.L. 6.29 makes use of his *Sale of Diogenes.* Menippus influenced Meleager of Gadara, Varro's *Saturae Menippeae,* and Seneca's *Apocolocyntosis* as well as Petronius, Lucian, and, later, Martianus Capella and Boethius. Cf. *RE* 15.1 (1931) cols. 888–93 (Helm).

MENIPPUS OF LYCIA. First century A.D. Eunapius in his *Lives of Philosophers and Sophists* 2.1.5 claims Menippus of Lycia is one of the notable representatives of Cynicism, along with Musonius, Demetrius, and Carneades. Philostratus in his *Life of Apollonius of Tyana* 4.25 shows Menippus of Lycia as a disciple of Demetrius of Corinth, but adds that Menippus and many others were converted by Demetrius to Apollonius. With Damis Menippus passed letters from Apollonius to Musonius, who was then in prison (ibid. 46). This Menippus was twenty-five years old and resembled a fine and gentlemanly athlete (ibid. 25). Philostratus (ibid. 38) sets him alongside Apollonius among those who opposed Nero and tells how he became besotted with a lamia until Apollonius woke him to reality.

METROCLES OF MARONEA. Third century B.C. The brother of Hipparchia, wife of Crates of Thebes. He became a disciple first of Theophrastus, then of Xenocrates, finally of Crates (Teles, *Diatribe* 4A). According to Hecaton of Rhodes he burned all his own writings, but others say that it was only the notes he took in Theophrastus's school that he burned (D.L. 6.95). He evidently specialized in the *chreia,* a short anecdote or apophthegm that can be learned by heart and recalled in the difficult moments of life. The disciples seemingly ascribed to him at the end of D.L. 6.95 are more probably disciples of Crates. He died when very old by holding his breath. It should be noted that Stilpo wrote a dialogue entitled *Metrocles* (fr. 190 Döring). Cf *RE* 15.2 (1932) cols. 1483–84 (von Fritz).

MONIMUS OF SYRACUSE (*RE* 10). Fourth century B.C. While the slave of a Corinthian banker he heard of Diogenes through Xeniades, Diogenes' master. In order to be able to leave his own master and become a disciple of Diogenes, he started throwing all the money out a window. He also made the acquaintance of Crates of Thebes (D.L. 6.82). He left Παίγνια σπουδῇ λεληθυίᾳ μεμιγμένα (Trifles blended with covert earnestness)—and accordingly is considered to be one of the original seriocomic (*spoudogeloios*) writers—and two books Περὶ Ὁρμῶν (On Impulses) and an *Exhortation to Philosophy.* According to Sextus Empiricus (*Adversus Mathematicos* 7.48, 87–88; 8.5), Monimus the

Dog is connected with Xeniades of Corinth. Actually the Xeniades of Corinth in question is not the master of Diogenes but a philosopher of the first half of the fifth century B.C., who claimed that no criterion of truth really exists and that every impression and opinion are false (*Outlines of Pyrrhonism* 2.18, *Adversus Mathematicos* 7.53). In linking the ideas of Monimus the Dog with those of this Xeniades, Sextus is probably mistaking one Xeniades for the other. Cf. *RE* 16.1 (1933) cols. 126–27 (von Fritz).

MUSONIUS RUFUS (*RE* 1). First century A.D. A Stoic philosopher influenced by Cynicism. Eunapius in his *Lives of Philosophers and Sophists* 2.1.5 sets him alongside Demetrius, Menippus, and Carneades as one of the notable representatives of Cynicism. In reality, Eunapius is drawing on Philostratus's *Life of Apollonius of Tyana,* which speaks of a Musonius of Babylon, whose character is probably based on that of Musonius Rufus. (See Musonius of Babylon, Section V below.) In the scholia to Lucian, *De Peregrini Morte* 18, p. 221 Rabe, Musonius is again given the title "Cynic," this time along with Dio and Epictetus. It seems, however, that characterization as Cynic here does not imply adherence to a particular school but only signifies that these three philosophers practiced the *parrhēsia* characteristic of the Cynics. CF *RE* 16.1 (1933) cols. 893–97 (von Fritz).

OENOMAUS OF GADARA (*RE* 5). Second century A.D. A contemporary of Hadrian, he was the author of numerous works cited in the *Suda* Οι 123: Περὶ Κυνισμοῦ (On Cynicism), Πολιτεία (Republic), Περὶ τῆς καθ' "Ομηρον Φιλοσοφίας (On the Philosophy According to Homer), Περὶ Κράτητος καὶ Διογένους καὶ τῶν Λοιπῶν (On Crates and Diogenes and the Rest). According to Julian he wrote tragedies (*Or.* 7.6.210d–211a), a work called Ἡ τοῦ Κυνὸς Αὐτοφωνία (The Very Voice of the Dog) and a Κατὰ τῶν Χρηστηρίων (Against the Oracles). This last work can most probably be identified with the Γοητῶν Φωρά (The Charlatans Exposed), fragments of which were preserved in Eusebius's *Praeparatio Evangelica*. In this work, Oenomaus attacked Stoic determinism and derided oracles. Julian criticized his works severely. Cf *RE* 17.2 (1937) cols. 2249–51 (Mette).

ONESICRITUS OF ASTYPALAEA. 380/375–305/300. A disciple of Diogenes of Sinope (Plutarch, *De Alexandri Magni Fortuna aut Virtute* 10.331e, *Life of Alexander* 65.701c). Attempts have been made, erroneously, to identify him with Onesicritus of Aegina, who with his two sons was also a disciple of Diogenes the Dog. (Cf. D.L. 6.84: "Some say he is an Aeginetan, but Demetrius of Magnesia says he is a native from Astypalaea.") He joined the expedition of Alexander and was the pilot of the king's ship on a voyage up the Hydaspes and the Indus. He was sent by the king as interpreter to the Indian gymnosophists of Taxila. In 324, Alexander presented him with a golden wreath. He wrote a work about Alexander called Πῶς 'Αλέξανδρος "Ηχθη (How Alexander Was Educated), drawing his diction from Xenophon's *Cyropaedia.* The reliability of this work was contested even in ancient times, but it was perhaps a source for Arrian of Nicomedia's *Anabasis.* Strasburger contests the identification of Onesicritus of Astypalaea with Onesicritus of Aegina. He supports his argument by noting that D.L. 6.75 introduces Onesicritus of Aegina as though he were unknown (*Onēsikriton tina* [a certain Onesicritus] of Aegina) and by suggesting that if the historian had two sons who were disciples of Diogenes before he went off with Alexander, he must have been somewhat old to take on the functions entrusted to him during the expedition. Cf. *RE* 18.1 (1939) cols. 460–67 (Strasburger).

ONESICRITUS OF AEGINA. Fourth century B.C. D.L. 6.75 mentions "a certain Onesicritus of Aegina" who sent his sons Androsthenes and Philiscus, one after the other, to Diogenes and then, since they did not return, went to the philosopher himself and was so impressed that he remained with him as a disciple. Cf. *RE* 18.1 (1939) col. 461 (Strasburger).

OURANIOS KUNIKOS. No. 562 in J. Baillet, *Inscriptions grecques et latines des tombeaux des rois ou Syringes,* Mémoires Publiés par les membres de l'Institut Français d'Archéologie Orientale 42 (Cairo 1926). Should we imagine that a Cynic took as his name an expression usually applied to Diogenes? For in the *Meliambi* of Cercidas of Megapolis, Diogenes is referred to as "the offspring of Zeus" and "truly *ouranios kuōn*" (D.L. 6.76). In an epigram in the *Greek Anthology* (11.158) Antipater of Thessalonica also recalls that Diogenes was a heavenly dog, and the philosopher himself, in an apocryphal letter to his father, Hicetas [*sic: Ep.* 7], states: "They call me a heavenly dog [κύων ὁ οὐρανοῦ], not an earthly one."

PANCRATES (1) (*RE* 6). Second century A.D. A Cynic who lived at the time of Hadrian and Antoninus Pius. Philostratus, *Lives of the Sophists* 1.23, recounts how one day Lollianus of Ephesus, who held the chair of rhetoric at Athens as well as the office of hoplite general, was nearly stoned to death in the bread sellers' quarter of the city. Pancrates, who later professed philosophy at the Isthmus, came forward before the Athenians and said, "Lollianus does not sell bread [ἀρτοπώλης] but words [λογοπώλης]," which so diverted the Athenians that they dropped the stones that were in their hands. Nothing suggests an identification with the Pancrates mentioned by Alciphron, *Ep.* 3.55, p. 86 Hercher (see Pancrates [2], Section IV below). Cf. *RE* 18.3 (1949) col. 619 (von Fritz).

PANISCUS. No. 172 in Baillet, *Inscriptions grecques et latines des tombeaux des rois ou Syringes,* Mémoires Publiés par les Membres de l'Institut Français d'Archéologie Orientale 42 (Cairo 1926). Baillet's reading is [Pani]skos.

PARMENISCUS (*RE* 2). Dates unknown. He was the author of a *Symposium of the Cynics* dedicated to one Molpis, a large chunk of which was quoted by

Athenaeus (*Deipnosophists* 4.156c–157d). Meleager of Gadara is represented in it as the *progonos* of the Cynics at the banquet, which therefore could not have taken place earlier than the end of the first century B.C. Cf. *RE* 18.3 (1949) col. 619 (von Fritz).

PASICLES OF THEBES (*RE* 6). Fourth century B.C. The brother of Crates of Thebes, he was, according to the *Suda* s.v. Στίλπων (Σ 1114), a student of his own brother (wherefore he is listed here). He is actually better known as a Megarian philosopher who was, according to the *Suda* (ibid)., the follower of Dioclides, himself a pupil of Euclides. However, Diogenes Laertius (6.89) describes him as a student of Euclides, but it is possible that Εὐκλείδου there has been confused with Διοκλείδου. The *Suda* makes him out to have been the master of Stilpo. Cf. *RE* 18.4 (1949) col. 2061 (von Fritz).

PEREGRINUS (*RE* 16), nicknamed PROTEUS (*RE* 3). Ca. 100–165 A.D. Born at Parium in Mysia. Our knowledge of him comes almost entirely from Lucian's *On the Death of Peregrinus.* He was suspected of murdering his father and fleeing with his goods for Palestine, where he came into contact with some Christians. While associated with the Christians, he was thrown into prison. He then went back to Parium and became a Cynic, but soon he resumed his travels. Breaking with the Christians, he went to Egypt and studied under the Cynic philosopher Agathobulus, under whom Demonax also studied. He then became a wandering preacher and went to Rome and then back to Greece. Gellius heard him at Athens. Peregrinus met Herodes Atticus, Demonax, and Lucian himself. His suicide by immolation at the Olympic Games of 165 was both theatrical and pathetic but was meant to illustrate Cynic contempt for death and suffering. The rhetor Menander, *Peri Epideikt.* 2.1, quotes an Ἐγκώμιον Πενίας [ἢ τοῦ] Πρωτέως τοῦ Κυνός, which we can suppose refers to Peregrinus (cf. M. Narcy, *DPhA* 1 s.v. "Alcidamas d'Élée," p. 108); on the other hand, the *Suda* Φ 422 attributes a Πρωτεὺς Κύων ἢ Σοφιστής to the first Philostratus. Either there could actually be two separate works, Πρωτεύς and Κύων ἢ Σοφιστής, as W. Aly suggests—in which case *Prōteus* would refer to the god of the sea and the second part would be a title in the style of Lucian—or else we have to admit that Peregrinus is intended in the title. Cf. *RE* 19.1 (1937) cols. 656–63 (von Fritz); *RE* 23.1 (1957) col. 975 (Aly).

PHILISCUS OF AEGINA (*RE* 6.) Fourth century B.C. Brother of Androsthenes and son of Onesicritus of Aegina (D.L. 6.75), he was a pupil of Diogenes of Sinope. If Satyrus is to be believed, the seven tragedies attributed to Diogenes are actually his work (D.L. 6.73, 80). Curiously enough, among the works of Diogenes, Sotion does list a *Philiscus* (D.L. 6.80). According to Hermippus, quoted in the *Suda* Φ 359, he was a pupil of Stilpo. The *Suda* adds that he taught Alexander the Great to read and that he wrote dialogues, one of which was a *Codrus*. Actually it would be chronologically difficult for him to have been the pupil of Stilpo and the master of Alexander. In his chapter on *philoponia* (3.29.40), Stobaeus reports something said by one Philiscus, who could well have been a disciple of Diogenes, to judge by the content of the remark. Finally, it should be noted that Philiscus of Aegina probably had nothing to do with the shoemaker Philiscus who addresses Crates in a fragment of Teles (4B: *On Poverty and Wealth*). Cf. *RE* 23.1 (1957) col. 975 (Aly).

PHOCION, nicknamed CHRESTOS (the Good). Fourth century B.C. This important Athenian general and statesman is represented by D.L. 6.76 and the *Suda* Φ 362 as being a disciple of Diogenes.

POLYZELUS (*RE* 5). According to Photius, *Bibl.* cod. 167, p. 114b25 Bekker, one of the ten Cynics mentioned in the second part of Stobaeus's lost *Prooemium.* Cf. *RE* 21.2 (1952) col. 1865 (Ziegler).

(PO)SOCHARES. *See* Sochares.

SALOUSTIOS (*RE* 39). Fifth century A.D. This Syrian-born philosopher is above all known through Damascius's *Life of Isidorus.* He studied law and received an education in rhetoric at Emesa from the sophist Eunoeus. Having decided to adopt the sophist's life, he went to Athens and from there to Alexandria in the company of the Neoplatonic philosopher Isidorus. There he frequented the schools of rhetoric. In spite of his Neoplatonic connections, it was to Cynic philosophy that he devoted himself, practicing rigorous ascetic austerity. He maintained that for men to philosophize is not simply difficult but impossible and managed to divert Athenodorus, a member of the circle of Proclus, away from philosophy. He also quarreled with Proclus himself. He stayed for some time with the Dalmatian prince Marcellinus. Cf. *RE* 1A2 (1920) cols. 1967–70 (Praechter); *PLRE* 2 (7).

SECUNDUS THE SILENT PHILOSOPHER. Beginning of the second century A.D. Known only through an anonymous legendary *vita.* Upon the death of his mother, for which he was responsible, he imposed a vow of silence on himself and was therefore represented as a Pythagorean. Nevertheless, it is said that at the end of his studies he went back to his own land, "displaying the asceticism of the dog, carrying staff and wallet and letting his hair and beard grow long." The emperor Hadrian tried in vain to get him to break his vow of silence, though he did agree to answer twenty questions from the emperor on philosophical subjects. These questions are preserved along with the anonymous *vita.* We might ask if Secundus is to be identified with the Athenian rhetor of the same name, who was known as "the Kingpin," master of Herodes Atticus, mentioned by Philostratus (*Lives of the Sophists* 1.26). In *RE* 2A1 (1921) col. 922, Fluss dedicates a short article to Secundus of Athens, the first-century philosopher, without touching on the problem; but in *RE* Suppl. 8 (1956) s.v. "Zweite Sophistik," col. 767, R. Gerth identifies the two figures as one, without giving any justification.

SERENIANUS (*RE* 1). Fourth century A.D. Julian in *Or.* 7.18, 224d, introduces him as a contemporary. Cf. *RE* 2A2 (1923) col. 1674 (von Arnim); *PLRE* 1 (1).

SOCHARES. "Sochares" is the correct form of the name according to Meineke's proposed correction (and not "Posochares" with ms. P of the *Greek Anthology* and the *Suda* s.v. Βλαύτη). This Cynic is known only from two epigrams by Leonidas of Tarentum (third century B.C.) in the *Greek Anthology* (6.293, 298). See S. Follet, "Les cyniques dans la poésie épigrammatique à l'époque impériale" in *Le cynisme ancien et ses prolongements,* ed. M.-O. Goulet-Cazé and R. Goulet (Paris 1993), 372–74.

SOTADES OF MARONEA (*RE* 2). Third century B.C. An iambic poet and the inventor of the *versus Sotadeus,* a minor ionic meter. The *Suda* (Σ 871) has preserved the title of several of his works. Among these, note should be taken of a *Necyia,* the theme of which is typically Cynic. It is certain that a Cynic atmosphere is to be found in his works, dominated by *parrhēsia* and *anaideia.* Cf. *RE* 3A1 (1927) cols. 1207–9 (Aly).

SPHODRIAS (*RE* 2). The author of an *Art of Love* as recorded by Athenaeus, *Deipnosophists* 4.162b–c. Otherwise unknown. Athenaeus mentions him along with Archestratus of Gela, author of a *Gastrology,* Protagorides, author of some *Recitations of Love,* and Persaeus, author of *Convivial Dialogues.* Cf. *RE* 3A2 (1929) cols. 1750–57 (Hobein).

STILPO OF MEGARA. Ca. 360–280. Stilpo is described as both a Cynic and, principally, as an adherent of the Megarian school, which he led after Ichthyas. According to D.L. 6.76 (= fr. 149 Döring), he was a student of Diogenes of Sinope; according to Heraclides Lembus (D.L. 2.113 = fr. 147 Döring), he was a student of Thrasymachus of Corinth, himself a disciple of Ichthyas; and according to the *Suda* (Σ 1114), he was a student of Euclides—which is chronologically impossible—and of Pasicles of Thebes, the brother of Crates the Cynic. Crates himself is supposed to have been his disciple. This account is a rather complex one: Stilpo is a disciple of Pasicles; Pasicles is a disciple of his own brother, Crates; Crates is a disciple of Stilpo. It should also be noted that the Stoic Zeno was a student of Stilpo (D.L. 7.2), as was Philiscus of Aegina (*Suda* Φ 359, giving the opinion of Hermippus). If it is chronologically unlikely that Stilpo was both a disciple of Euclides and of Pasicles, himself a third-generation Megarian, it is quite plausible that he was a disciple of Diogenes and that Crates was his pupil. However, on this hypothesis, ought we to conclude that Crates left Diogenes to follow Stilpo? As far as his literary work is concerned, Diogenes Laertius shows evidence of two differing traditions. In his prologue (1.16) he places Stilpo among those who, "according to some," wrote nothing. In 2.120, he goes on to list the titles of nine dialogues supposedly composed by him. One of these titles, *Metrocles* (D.L. 2.120), shows Stilpo's adherence to Cynicism. A quotation from this text has survived (fr. 190

Döring). This same Cynic, Metrocles, appears in an anecdote in Stilpo's company (Plutarch, *De Tranquillitate Animi* 6.468a; fr. 154 Döring). Fragments 3 and 7 of the *Diatribes* of Teles, a teacher of Cynic obedience, report some of the philosopher's sayings. Cf. *RE* 3A2 (1929) cols. 2525–33 (Praechter); *RE* Suppl. 5 (1931) col. 721 s.v. "Megariker" (von Fritz).

TELES (*RE* 2). *Fl.* middle of the third century B.C. A teacher of philosophy attached to the Cynic school. Seven extracts from his diatribes, borrowed from the epitome of one Theodorus, have been preserved by Stobaeus. They are the oldest remaining evidence of the Cynic-Stoic diatribe. Teles mentions various Cynic philosophers: Diogenes, Crates, Metrocles, Stilpo, and his preferred role model, Bion of Borysthenes. Cf. *RE* 5A1 (1934) cols. 375–81 (Anneliese Modrze).

THEAGENES OF PATRAS (*RE* 11). Second century A.D. Originally from Patras, he was a disciple of Peregrinus and excessive in praise of his master, particularly on the subject of his suicide by fire; he compares Peregrinus to the gymnosophists in India. Lucian heard him deliver a eulogy of Peregrinus at Elis, and in *On the Death of Peregrinus* Lucian is scathing toward Theagenes and his brand of Cynicism. Galen (*Methodi Medendi* 13.15, 10.909–10 Kühn) recalls how he taught publicly in the Forum of Trajan at Rome every day, and says that he died when he was given inappropriate treatment for inflammation of the liver by the doctor Attalus, a pupil of Soranus. But in spite of this, should the Cynic be identified with the philosopher Theagenes who, according to Lucian (*Cataplus* 6), committed suicide for love of "the courtesan from Megara"? J. Bernays, *Lucian und die Kyniker* (Berlin 1879) p. 90 n. 7, rejects the idea. Cf. *RE* 5A2 (1934) cols. 1348–49 (Anneliese Modrze).

THEOMBROTUS (*RE* 1). Fourth and third centuries B.C. A disciple of Crates at the same time as Cleomenes (q.v. above) and Metrocles. His disciples were Demetrius of Alexandria and Echecles of Ephesus. Echecles was likewise a disciple of Cleomenes. Cf. *RE* 5A2 (1934) cols. 2033–34 (Anneliese Modrze).

THEOMNESTUS (*RE* 12). According to Photius, *Bibl.* cod. 167, p. 114b25 Bekker, he was one of the ten Cynics mentioned in the second part of Stobaeus's lost *Prooemium.* Cf. *RE* 5A2 (1934) col. 2036 (Anneliese Modrze).

THRASYLLUS (*RE* 6). Fourth century B.C. A Cynic who lived at the time of Antigonus Monophthalmus (ca. 382–301). Plutarch (*Regum et Imperatorum Apophthegmata, Antigonus* 15.182e; cf. *De Vitioso Pudore* 7.531f, where he mentions a Cynic, but not by name) and Seneca (*De Beneficiis* 2.17.1) both report an anecdote that brings together Alexander's successor Antigonus Monophthalmus and the Cynic Thrasyllus. Thrasyllus asks the king for a drachma and receives the answer that the sum is unworthy of a king, whereupon he asks for a talent and is then told that the sum is unworthy of a Cynic. Cf. *RE* 6A1 (1936) col. 581 (Anneliese Modrze).

TIMARCHUS OF ALEXANDRIA (*RE* 9). Second half of the third century B.C. According to D.L. 6.95, Timarchus, like Echecles of Ephesus, was a disciple of Cleomenes. Should he be identified (as suggested by Beckby in his edition of the *Greek Anthology*) with Timarchus son of Pausanias, of the tribe Ptolemaïs, who is mentioned in an epigram by Callimachus (7.520)? Cf. *RE* 6A1 (1936) col. 1238 (Nestle).

VARRO, Marcus Terentius (*RE* 84). 116–27 B.C. Among other works, he wrote *Saturae Menippeae*. It is probably because of this imitation of Menippus that Tertullian (*Apologeticus* 14.9) calls him *Romanus Cynicus*. Cf. *RE* Suppl. 6 (1935) cols. 1172–1277 (Dahlmann).

XANTHIPPUS. According to Photius, *Bibl.* cod. 167, p. 114b25 Bekker, he was one of the ten Cynics mentioned in the second part of Stobaeus' lost *Prooemium*.

XENIADES OF CORINTH (*RE* 2). Fourth century B.C. Sailing for Aegina, Diogenes the Dog was captured by pirates led by Scirpalus, then taken to Crete and sold (D.L. 6.74). When the herald asked him what he could do, Diogenes replied, "Govern men." Xeniades purchased him and took him to Corinth, where he put him in charge of his children and his household (D.L. 6.74). Monimus acquired his passionate admiration for Diogenes when he heard Xeniades praising the philosopher's goodness in word and deed (D.L. 6.82). But what historical truth can be assigned to Xeniades' role in the biography of Diogenes? Should we believe that the philosopher spent the rest of his life in Xeniades' house, or that, as other anecdotes suggest, he lived as a free man, in his tub in Corinth in the summer and at Athens in the winter? The episode involving Monimus in D.L. 6.82 indicates that there may be a certain core of truth to the story, around which a number of fabrications then formed. At any rate, the theme of the sale of Diogenes was reused by Menippus in his *Sale of Diogenes* (D.L. 6.29), by Eubulus in his work of the same name (D.L. 6.30), and by Cleomenes in his *Paidagōgikos* (D.L. 6.75). Cf. *RE* 9A2 (1967) cols. 1439–40 (von Fritz).

ZENO OF CITIUM (*RE* 2). Ca. 335–263. Before going on to found Stoicism, Zeno was a follower of Crates of Thebes (D.L. 7.2). His first work, the *Republic*, "written on the tail of the Dog" (D.L. 7.4), seems to have betrayed considerable Cynic influence. He was the disciple of other philosophers: Stilpo, from whom Crates tried to deflect him; the Academics Xenocrates and Polemo (D.L. 7.2); and the Megarian Diodorus Cronus (D.L. 7.25). Cf. *RE* 10A (1972) cols. 83–121 (von Fritz).

II. Anonymous Cynics

1. Fourth century B.C. Athenaeus, *Deipnosophists* 9.366b–c. Antiphanes, poet of the Middle Comedy (fourth century B.C.), quotes some lines of an

anonymous Cynic in his play *The Wallet*. (This person could, therefore, equally well have been classified among the fictitious Cynics.)

2. Fourth and third centuries B.C. Gregory of Nazianzus, *Carmina* 1, *Poemata Theologica* 2, *Poemata Moralia* 10: *De Virtute* 250–58; *PG* 37 col.698. The author alludes to one of the ἀρχαίων κυνῶν who approached an unidentified king and asked him for food. The king bestowed a talent of gold on the Cynic, who accepted. In full view of the king, he then turned round and bought a loaf of bread, paying the entire talent for it. As he did so, he commented: "It was this bread I wanted, not smoke [τῦφος]. You can't eat that."

3. Fourth and third centuries B.C. D.L. 7.17. A Cynic asked Zeno for oil and was refused. As the man went away, Zeno bade him consider which of them was the more impudent.

4. First century B.C. and first century A.D. Antipater of Thessalonica (*Greek Anthology* 11.158) mocks a Cynic who, he says, usurps the attributes of Diogenes.

5. First century A.D. Martial, *Epigrams* 4.53. An old Cynic with dirty hair and beard, dressed in filthy clothes and carrying a staff and wallet, is often to be found in the sanctuary of the temple of Minerva and at the threshold of the temple of Augustus, where he begs for food.

6. First century A.D. A philosopher who seems to be a Cynic is attacked by Lucilius (*Greek Anthology* 11.155).

7. First century A.D. Lucilius (*Greek Anthology* 11.410) criticizes a Cynic gourmet whose refined tastes belie his fine words.

8. Second century A.D. Lucian, *Demonax* 48. Demonax sees a Cynic with cloak and wallet, but with a bar (ὕπερον) for a staff. The Cynic creates an uproar and says that he is the follower of Antisthenes, Crates, and Diogenes. Demonax says: "Don't lie! You are really a disciple of Barson ['Υπερείδου]."

9. Second century A.D. Lucian, *Demonax* 50. A Cynic mounted on a stone called the proconsul a catamite. In anger, the proconsul ordered the Cynic to be beaten or sent into exile. Demonax intervened and begged him to pardon the man, for he was only practicing traditional *parrhēsia* (free speech). The proconsul gave in, but asked how he should punish the man if he ever dared to do such a thing again; Demonax replied: "Have him depilated."

10. Second century A.D. Artemidorus, Ὀνειροκριτικά 4.33, p. 267.6–14 Pack. A Cynic quarrels with the philosopher Alexander (possibly Alexander of Seleucia, the secretary of Marcus Aurelius) and hits him over the head with his staff.

11. Second century A.D. *Act. Mart. Apoll.* 33, p. 98.22–23 Musurillo. At the trial of the martyr Apollonius Sacceas in the years 180–85, a Cynic was present along with other sages.

12. Fourth century A.D. Julian, *Ep.* 26.414d (to Maximus the Philosopher). The emperor tells the Neoplatonic philosopher Maximus of Ephesus, his former teacher, that he encountered a Cynic with cloak and staff near Besançon. From a distance, he took him first for Maximus, then for his messenger.

13. Fourth century A.D. Julian *Or.* 9.180d, recalls a Cynic who accuses Diogenes of vainglory and complains about his having eaten a raw octopus. This Cynic himself, however, as Julian observes, refuses to bathe in cold water although he is in the prime of his life.

14. Fourth century A.D. David, *Prolegomena Philosophiae* 11, quotes the words of an "already half-dried up [ἡμίξηρος]" Cynic to Julian.

III. Persons Whose Link with Cynicism Is Uncertain

DEMETRIUS OF ALEXANDRIA, nicknamed CYTHRAS (*RE* 63). Fourth century A.D. He was already a very old man when a trial was instigated against him under Constantius II at Scythopolis in the year 359, on the charge that he was pagan and offered sacrifices. He was interrogated and tortured but stood his ground. He was acquitted and allowed to return to his home town of Alexandria (Ammianus Marcellinus 19.12.12). The identification, suggested by Seeck, of Cythras with Chytron (Section I above), has no other foundation than the similarity of their names. Cf. *DPhA* D 47a.

DIODORUS OF ASPENDUS (*RE* 40). Fourth century B.C. A Pythagorean philosopher who was close to Cynicism in his lifestyle and appearance: he had a beard and long hair, went barefoot, and was dirty. He was a contemporary of Archestratus of Gela and of the musician Stratonicus (Athenaeus, *Deipnosophists* 4.163d–f). According to Sosicrates in Book 3 of the *Successions,* he was the first person to double his cloak, which was to become a common practice among the Cynics. However, Diocles of Magnesia and Neanthes of Cyzicus maintain that this custom owes its origin to Antisthenes (D.L. 6.13). Cf. *RE* 5.1 (1903) col. 705 (Wellmann).

EUBULUS. Third century B.C. The author of a *Sale of Diogenes,* which appears to have been a kind of educational novel. A long excerpt of it is quoted by Diogenes Laertius (6.30–31). Should *Euboulos* be corrected to *Euboulides,* and Eubulus identified with Eubulides, as was suggested by Ménage (= Long's *app. crit.* to D.L. 6.30)?

EUBULIDES. Third century B.C. According to the *On Diogenes* of this author, it was Diogenes himself and not his father who defaced the currency, and both had to go into exile (D.L. 6.20 = fr. 67[?] Döring). Should he be identified with the Eubulus of 6.30–31 (cf. preceding entry), with the Eubulides mentioned by D.L. 2.42 (= fr. 66 Döring), who reports that Socrates at his trial offered to pay a fee of one hundred drachmas, or with the Megarian philosopher Eubulides of Miletus? This last suggestion is rejected by Natorp in *RE* 6.1 (1907) col. 870, s.v. "Eubulides" (8). See K. Döring, *Die Megariker* (Amsterdam 1972) 114.

HERMIAS OF CURIUM (*RE* 10). In Athenaeus, *Deipnosophists* 13.563d–e, the Cynic Myrtilus quotes five lines from Hermias's *Iamboi* in which he attacks

Stoic hypocrisy in a meter and with a bitterness reminiscent of the Cynics. Cf. *RE* 8.1 (1912) col. 732 (Maas).

HOSTILIANUS (*RE* 1). First century A.D. One of the philosophers expelled from Rome by Vespasian in 74. He was sent to the islands along with Demetrius the Cynic (Dio Cassius, epitome of Book 65.13.2). But is he a Cynic or a Stoic? If the latter, should he be identified with the Stoic philosopher C. Tutilius Hostilianus? Cf. *RE* 8.2 (1913) col. 2501 (Stein); *PIR²* H 222.

NILUS. Fourth century A.D. The emperor Julian, who also called him Dionysius, railed against him in a letter that he wrote at Antioch (*Ep.* 82). This aristocrat had refused the office offered him by Julian. Trying to justify himself and get back into Julian's good graces, he had him sent a text in which he developed his own apology and begged the emperor to accept his services. The latter replied in an open letter in which he reproached Nilus for his presumptuousness and impertinence. In a letter that seems to date from the end of 362, Libanius (*Ep.* 758; see also *Or.* 18.198) invokes this misfortune of Nilus as though it was a recent occurrence. For R. Asmus ("Zur Kritik und Erklärung von Julian. Ep. 59 ed. Hertl.," *Philologus* 71 [1912] 376–89) Nilus was one of the group of Cynics resented by Julian. But J. Geffcken (*Kaiser Julianus* [Leipzig 1914] 158–59) refutes this hypothesis. At any rate, it is clear that Julian recognized him as a philosopher to whose *parrhēsia* and extreme self-sufficiency he objected, along with his extravagant behavior and immoderate language. Cf. *PLRE* 1 (2).

SOSTRATUS HERACLES (*RE* 6a). Second century A.D. This Sostratus is known from *Demonax* 1 ("the Boeotian Sostratus, whom the Greeks called Heracles and believed to be that very hero"), where Lucian claims to have devoted a work to him, which is unfortunately lost. He lived in the open on Mount Parnassus and built roads and bridges. Should we take him for a Cynic, as Dudley (*A History of Cynicism* 182) and Weber ("De Dione Chrysostomo Cynicorum Sectatore," *Leipziger Studien zur Classischen Philologie* 10 [1887] 237) have done? J. F. Kindstrand ("Sostratus-Hercules-Agathion: The Rise of a Legend," *Annales Societatis Litterarum Humaniorum Regiae Upsaliensis,* 1979–80, 50–79) reserves judgment, saying it is difficult to consider Sostratus a member of a particular school even if Lucian interprets his character along Cynic lines and sees him rather as a champion of a practical philosophy. Kindstrand asks above all if Lucian's Sostratus should be identified with the Heracles-Agathion described by Herodes Atticus (in Philostratus's *Lives of the Sophists* 2.1.7) as having "bushy eyebrows that met as though they were but one," "an impulsive temperament," "an aquiline nose," "a solidly built neck," being "clothed in wolf skins," and contending against wild animals, and with the Sostratus of Plutarch (*Quaestiones Convivales* 4.1.660e). In the end, he decides that they can be so identified. Cf. *RE* Suppl. 8 (1956) col. 782 (Johanna Schmidt).

THEOXENUS. Fourth century B.C.? Lucian, *Scytha* 8, reports that Anacharsis was the only barbarian to have been initiated into the Mysteries of Eleusis, "if Theoxenus is to be believed, who also gives this information on this subject." This is found again in the fourth-century sophist Himerius (*Or.* 29 Colonna). Drawing on this testimony, A. Colonna (*Scripta Minora* [Brescia 1981] 127–29) suggests that Theoxenus might be a Cynic philosopher of the middle or end of the fourth century B.C. who wrote a book on Anacharsis, which may have been used by Lucian and later by Himerius. He also mentions a scholion on Theocritus 1.3–4 (p. 32.1 C. Wendel) that reads, "Theoxenus says that Pan is a heavenly god."

ZOILUS OF AMPHIPOLIS, nicknamed HOMEROMASTIX (*RE* 14). Fourth century B.C. An adversary of Isocrates and critic of Homer. If Aelian is to be believed (*Varia Historia* 11.10), he was given the nickname *kuōn rhētorikos* because of his Cynic garb and his aggressiveness. According to the *Suda* Z 130, he was a rhetor and a philosopher. Dionysius of Halicarnassus (*Epistula ad Pompeium Geminum* 1.16) recalls that Zoilus and his disciples criticized the doctrines of Plato. It is also known that he was a disciple of Polycrates (Ael. ibid.) and the master of Anaximenes of Lampsacus (*Suda* A 1989). But the historians nonetheless diverge on whether or not he was a Cynic philosopher. Cf. *RE* Suppl. 15 (1978) cols. 1531–54 (Gärtner).

IV. Cynics of the Pseudepigraphical *Cynic Epistles*

In this section, we will only list those recipients of letters by Cynics who are otherwise unknown. Thus philosophers like Plato, Antisthenes, Crates, Hipparchia, Metrocles, Monimus, and Zeno, political figures such as Dionysius, Perdiccas, Alexander, and Antipater, as well as people we know for certain were not Cynics, Hicetas (*sic*), the father of Diogenes, or his mother, Olympias, are not indicated.

Recipients of the *Cynic Epistles*

The Diogenes Epistles

AGESILAUS, *Ep.* 22	HIPPON, *Ep.* 25
AMYNANDER, *Ep.* 21	LACYDES, *Ep.* 23; cf. *Ep.* 37
ANAXILAUS, *Ep.* 19	MELESIPPE, *Ep.* 42
ANNICERIS, *Ep.* 27	MELESIPPUS, *Epp.* 20, 41
ANTALCIDES, *Ep.* 17	PHAENYLUS, *Ep.* 31
APOLEXIS, *Epp.* 13, 16, 18	PHANOMACHUS, *Ep.* 33
ARUECAS, *Ep.* 49	RHESUS, *Ep.* 48
CHARMIDAS, *Ep.* 50	SOPOLIS, *Ep.* 35
EPIMENIDES, *Ep.* 51	TIMOMACHUS, *Ep.* 36
EUGNESIUS, *Ep.* 8	

The Crates Epistles

APER, *Ep.* 35	LYSIS, *Ep.* 10
DINOMACHUS, *Ep.* 36	MNASO, *Ep.* 9
EUMOLPUS, *Ep.* 13	ORION, *Ep.* 12
GANYMEDES, *Ep.* 23	PATROCLES, *Ep.* 19
HERMAISCUS, *Ep.* 4	

Cynics Mentioned in the *Cynic Epistles*

PANCRATES (2). Alciphron's *Ep.* 3.55.5 (from Autocletus to Hetoemaristus) narrates a symposium offered by Scamonides for his daughter's birthday. Many philosophers from different schools were present, among them the Cynic Pancrates, described with the outfit and the shamelessness typical of his school. Von Fritz suggests that in this letter, which copies Lucian's *Symposium,* Alciphron replaced Lucian's names with others, which nonetheless have their origins with Lucian in some way. Thus it is that the Cynic Alcidamas in Lucian παγκρατιάζει with Satyrion, whence the name Pancrates in Alciphron. But J. Schwartz ("Onomastique des philosophes chez Lucien de Samosate et Alciphron," *Antiquité Classique* 51 [1982] 263) thinks that the name comes from Lucian's *Philopseudes,* where there is an Egyptian magician called Pancrates. Whatever the truth of the matter, it is more or less certain that the Pancrates of Alciphron has nothing to do with Pancrates the Cynic philosopher mentioned by Philostratus (see Section I, Pancrates [1]).

PHRYNICHUS OF LARISSA. Diogenes' *Ep.* 48 presents him as Diogenes' disciple (ἀκουστὴς ἡμῶν).

THE SON OF PHILOMETOR. In Alciphron's *Ep.* 3.40 (from Philometor to Philisus) Philometor complains that his son went into town to sell some wood and barley and then decided to live like a Cynic he met there rather than return to the fields.

NOTE: It should also be pointed out that four letters of Theophylact Simocatta (seventh century; *Epp.* 19 [*to Chryses*], 43 [*to Demonicus*], 46 [*to Aristarchus*], 76 [*to Sotion*]) are presented as having being sent by one Diogenes. Is this the Cynic philosopher? We cannot be certain, but it seems highly probable.

V. Cynics, Almost Certainly Fictitious, Who Appear in Literature

In addition to the characters whose names are found in the *Cynic Epistles* and may well be fictitious, I think it worth mentioning a number of Cynics who appear in literary works (for instance, those of Lucian and Athenaeus) but who are more likely to be fictitious than to be historical.

AGATHOCLES. This Cynic was probably fictitiously named in a rhetorical handbook of which fragments have been preserved in *PMilVogliano,* edited by

G. Bastianini in *Corpus dei papiri filosofici greci e latini* part I, vol. I * (Florence 1989) 92–93.

ALCIDAMAS. A character in Lucian's *Symposium* who demonstrates Cynic shamelessness.

CARNEIUS OF MEGARA. Parmeniscus alludes to this character in his *Symposium of the Cynics,* quoted by Cynulcus in Athenaeus, *Deipnosophists* 4.156c–e. The leader of a group of six "dogs," Carneius attended a dinner given by Cebes of Cyzicus during the festival of Dionysus at Athens. Cf. *DPhA* C 45.

CEBES OF CYZICUS. It is likely that he was a Cynic (cf. preceding entry). Nothing enables us to identify him as the author of the *Pinax of Cebes.* Cf. *RE* 11.1 (1921) col. 103 s.v. "Kebes (2)" (von Arnim). Cf. *DPhA* C 61.

CRATO. The interlocutor of Lycinus in Lucian's *On Dance.* Lycinus alludes to him as a dog with sharp teeth (*Salt.* 4). As Demetrius the Cynic was initially hostile to dancing but was won over by the demonstration of a famous dancer, so Crato was against this art to begin with, but allowed himself to be won round by Lycinus's arguments. Cf. *DPhA* C 209.

CYNISCUS. He appears in two dialogues by Lucian: *The Downward Journey or the Tyrant 7,* where he is said to have died after eating a raw octopus, and *Zeus Refuted,* where he is the interlocutor of Zeus. Cf. *DPhA* C 230.

CYNULCUS. *See* Theodorus.

HEROPHILUS. (*RE* 3). Third century B.C. In Lucian's *Icaromenippus* 16, Menippus claims to have seen this Cynic asleep in a brothel. Cf. *RE* 8.1 (1912) col. 1104 (von Arnim).

HYPERIDES. In Lucian's *Demonax* 48, Demonax says to a Cynic carrying a bar (ὕπερον) and claiming to be a disciple of Antisthenes, Crates, and Diogenes (cf. above, Section II no. 8) that he is more like a disciple of Barson (Ὑπερείδου). It is not known if this name was invented for the joke or if it corresponds to some real person, for example, Hyperides the rhetor.

MUSONIUS OF BABYLON. This character is mentioned several times by Philostratus as exchanging letters with Apollonius of Tyana through the intermediaries Menippus and Damis. He was thrown into prison by Nero, and in Lucian's dialogue *Nero or the Digging of the Isthmus* he debates with the Cynic Demetrius. According to von Fritz, anecdotes originally told of Musonius Rufus became associated with the figure of Musonius of Babylon. Cf. *RE* 16.1 (1933) col. 887 (von Fritz).

MYRTILUS (*RE* 7). One of the interlocutors of Athenaeus's *Deipnosophists,* professing Cynic views and attacking the Stoics. He was the son of a Thessalian shoemaker. Ulpian refers to him as a *didaskalos* (*Deipn.* 9.386e), and elsewhere in the *Deipnosophists* he is again called a *grammatikos* (13.610c). Cf. *RE* 16.1 (1933) col. 1166 (Hanslik).

NICION called DOG FLY. A courtesan in Parmeniscus's *Symposium of the Cynics* (cf. Athen. *Deipn.* 4.157a). She quotes Meleager of Gadara's Χάριτες and "Antisthenes the Socratic."

THEODORUS. Introduced by Athenaeus in *Deipnosophists* 15. Democritus the Nicomedian calls him Theodorus at 15.669e and declares it to be his real name, but at 15.692b he is called Theodorus Cynulcus, ("Conductor of Dogs"). At the banquet, he is shown as the principal opponent of Ulpian of Tyre.

THESMOPOLIS. A Stoic philosopher who appears in Lucian's *On Salaried Posts in Great Houses* 33–34. He was in the household of a rich woman who one day asked him to take care of her dog during a journey, as it was due to have a litter, and make sure it wanted for nothing. Pressed, he ended by accepting. On the journey, the dog wet him, barked, licked his beard, and even had her puppies in his clothes. A profligate sitting next to him in the carriage later made fun of him at a dinner, saying: "As to Thesmopolis, all I can say is that our Stoic has finally gone to the dogs [i.e., had become a Cynic]."

VI. A Cynic by Mistake

NABAL. By association with Hebrew *kéléb* (dog), the Septuagint in 1 Kings (= 1 Samuel) 25.3 mistranslates the word *kālibbī,* used of Nabal, as *kunikos;* but the word means "Calebite," "of the tribe of Caleb." But we don't know if the word *kunikos* in the Septuagint means "Cynic" in the technical sense. The translation could mean that Nabal behaved like a dog. In any case, the readers of the Greek Bible understood *kunikos* as meaning that Nabal was a Cynic. This is why Flavius Josephus (*Jewish Antiquities* 6.296) says that Nabal was "rough and rude, for he lived according to Cynic asceticism."

VII. People Who Were Not Cynics but Were Known as "Dogs"

ARISTIPPUS OF CYRENE (*RE* 8). D.L. 2.66 says that Diogenes called Aristippus a royal dog because he made the most of the pleasure that was within his reach without bothering unduly about any that was not. Cf. *RE* 2.1 (1895) cols. 902–6 (Natorp).

ARISTOGITON (*RE* 2). In the first oration *Against Aristogiton* attributed to Demosthenes (*Or.* 25.40), this fourth-century-B.C. Athenian orator was called "dog of the people." Accordingly the *Suda* A 3912 says he received the nickname "dog" for his impudence. Cf. *RE* 2.1 (1895) cols. 931–2 (Thalheim).

MENEDEMUS OF ERETRIA (*RE* 9). 339/337–247 B.C. According to D.L. 2.140, the inhabitants of Eretria were suspicious of him at first, calling him a dog and a humbug; but later he was greatly admired, and they entrusted him with the government of the state.

THERSITES. In Lucian, *Demonax* 61, Demonax sings the praises of the Homeric Thersites (*Il.* 2.212–77), calling him a mob orator of the Cynic type.

VIII. Titles in Which the Word "Dog" Appears

The word "dog" appears in the titles of various works of literature. Unfortunately, most of the time it is impossible to know in what sense.

Athenaeus 6.247e mentions a line from a comedy entitled *Kunēgetai* ("Conductors of Dogs"?) by Anaxandrides, a poet of the Middle Comedy.

Athenaeus 7.280c and 13.570f and 587e–f quotes several lines of a *Kunagis Cynagis* ("Conductress of Dogs"?) by Philetaerus, a poet of the Middle Comedy.

D.L. 8.89 (= Eudoxus, fr. 374 Lasserre): Eratosthenes says in *Against Baton* that Eudoxus (fourth century B.C.) also composed *Dialogues of Dogs*.

Suda Φ 422 (4.734.11–17 Adler): "The first Philostratus, the son of Verus and father of the second Philostratus, was himself a sophist, practicing at Athens in the time of Nero. He wrote . . . *The Dog or the Sophist*[?]." On this title, see the entry for Peregrinus Proteus above in Section I.

Suda E 3023 (2.411.27 Adler): "Hermagoras of Amphipolis, philosopher and disciple of Persaeus [third century B.C.]." He wrote dialogues, among them a *Misokuōn*.

Appendix B

Who Was the First Dog?

M.-O. Goulet-Cazé

Who was the first Dog? Opinions are divided between Antisthenes—a follower of Socrates whose claim is based on a tradition of ancient sources, the only defect of which is that they are late (Epictetus, Dio Chrysostom, Aelian, Diogenes Laertius, Stobaeus, and the Suda)—and Diogenes of Sinope, whose claim is supported by modern scholarship.[1] All the arguments recently assembled by G. Giannantoni support the idea that Cynicism originates with Diogenes;[2] some of these arguments are developed by Long in his contribution to this volume. Giannantoni's and Long's arguments seem convincing.[3]

Nevertheless, we would here like to add to the case an element that, to our knowledge, no one has yet pointed out, one that may perhaps cause us to question the now dominant hypothesis that Cynicism effectively originated with Diogenes. In his *Rhetoric* Aristotle says, "Cephisodotus used to call triremes

1. E. Dupréel, *La légende socratique et les sources de Platon* (Brussels, 1922); K. von Fritz, *Quellenuntersuchungen zu Leben und Philosophie des Diogenes von Sinope,* Philologus Suppl. 18.2 (Leipzig 1926); D.R. Dudley, *A History of Cynicism from Diogenes to the Sixth Century A.D.* (London 1937; repr. New York 1974, Chicago 1993).

2. G. Giannantoni, *Socratis et Socraticorum Reliquiae* (Naples 1990) 4.226–33, n. 24, "Antistene: La presunta fondazione della scuola cinica"; *id.,* "Antistene fondatore della scuola cinica?" in M.-O. Goulet-Cazé and R. Goulet, eds., *Le cynisme ancien et ses prolongements: Actes du Colloque international du C.N.R.S.* (Paris 1993) 15–34; see also H. Bannert, "Numismatisches zu Biographie und Lehre des Hundes Diogenes," *Litterae Numismaticae Vindobonenses* 1 (1979) 49–53; for a different point of view, K. Döring, "Diogenes und Antisthenes," in G. Giannantoni et al., *La tradizione socratica* (Naples 1995) 125–50.

3. See also M.-O. Goulet-Cazé, "Le livre VI de Diogène Laërce: Analyse de sa structure et réflexions méthodologiques," *ANRW* 2.36.6 (Berlin 1992) 3880–4048, especially the excursus (pp. 3951–70) entitled "Le *bios* d'Antisthène," in which our analysis of Diogenes Laertius's chapter on the life of Antisthenes tends to confirm the hypothesis that Antisthenes' studies under Diogenes were invented after the fact in order to provide a Socratic affiliation for the Stoa.

'colored windmills,' and the Dog used to call taverns [*ta kapēleia*] 'the mess tables [*ta phiditia*] of Attica.' " [4] Scholars have perhaps been a bit too quick to affirm that the "Dog" in question could not be anyone other than Diogenes.[5] The point is of capital importance, for if it could be demonstrated that it is in fact Antisthenes who is meant, then we would have proof from the fourth century that it was Antisthenes and not Diogenes who was first known as "the Dog."

This passage calls for a few remarks. Aristotle never mentions Diogenes; this would thus be the only place where he alludes to our philosopher. He does, however, mention Antisthenes on five occasions, one of which occurs precisely in Book 3 of the *Rhetoric*. This second passage deserves to be quoted, for, curiously enough, it also mentions the fourth-century orator Cephisodotus: "Thus Antisthenes compared Cephisodotus, who was thin, to incense, because he caused pleasure as he consumed himself." [6]

Is it not at least probable that Aristotle, speaking a few pages apart of Cephisodotus and Antisthenes on the one hand and of Cephisodotus and the Dog on the other, is referring both times to the same person? Another detail—secondary, to be sure, but not negligible—might seem to support this hypothesis. The "Dog" evoked by Aristotle makes a comparison concerning the taverns of Attica; now, in Athenaeus's *Deipnosophists,* we read the following: "Antisthenes says in the treatise *On Physiognomy* 'For those female tavern-keepers [*hai kapēlides*] must feed their little pigs whether they will or no.' " [7]

The interest of this apparently obscene fragment resides in the fact that it allows us to affirm that Antisthenes spoke about taverns—which was precisely the topic dealt with by "the Dog" of the *Rhetoric*—in a work whose full title, as preserved for us by Diogenes Laertius (6.15), was *On the Sophists: A Treatise on Physiognomy* (*Peri tōn Sophistōn Phusiognōmonikos*). We might thus have, in Aristotle's testimony, a new fragment of Antisthenes' treatise on physiognomy. All these details, added to the fact that Antisthenes' nickname was *Haplokuōn* ("Simple Dog"? "Pure Dog"? "Natural Dog"?),[8] invite us to see in "the Dog" of the *Rhetoric* not Diogenes but Antisthenes.

These remarks suggest that in Athens, by the middle of the fourth century B.C., when a philosopher like Aristotle spoke of the "Dog," his readers would understand that he was alluding to Antisthenes. Unfortunately, this doesn't settle the problem of Diogenes' attending Antisthenes' lectures, nor the question of who the original instigator of the Cynic movement was.

---

4. Aristotle, *Rhetoric* 3.10.1411a24–25 (= V B 184 Giannantoni). The meaning of the passage is obscure; cf. A. Wartelle in his Budé edition of the *Rhetoric* (vol. 3 [Paris 1973] 116 n. 13).

5. So Dudley (above n. 1) 23; Wartelle (above, n. 4) 66 n. 1; Giannantoni (above, n. 2) 4.491, n. 47, "Diogene: L'epiteto 'cane.' "

6. Aristotle, *Rhetoric* 3.4.1407a10.

7. Athenaeus, *Deipnosophists* 14.656f (= V A 62 G.), after C.B. Gulick's translation in the Loeb Classical Library (vol. 7 [London 1941] 21).

8. Cf. D.L. 6.13. On the meaning of this nickname applied by Brutus in the first century B.C. to the politician Favonius, a disciple of Cato of Utica (Plutarch, *Brutus* 34.7), see M.-O. Goulet-Cazé, "Le cynisme à l'époque impériale," *ANRW* 2.36.4 (Berlin 1990) 2723–24.

Contributors

MARGARETHE BILLERBECK studied classics in Basel, Berlin, and Oxford; she currently holds the German-language Chair of Classical Languages and Literatures at the University of Fribourg (Switzerland). Her main areas of research include Greek and Roman popular philosophy, especially Cynicism, and imperial Latin poetry as well as ancient lexicography. She is the author of *Epiktet: Vom Kynismus* (Leiden 1978), and *Der Kyniker Demetrius* (Leiden 1979), and the editor of *Die Kyniker in der modernen Forschung* (Amsterdam 1991). Her book *Senecas Tragödien: Sprachliche und stilistische Untersuchungen* (1988) will soon be followed by a detailed commentary on Seneca's *Hercules Furens*. Together with B. K. Braswell she is preparing a new critical edition of Stephanus of Byzantium, *Ethnika*.

R. BRACHT BRANHAM, coeditor of this volume, is Associate Professor of Classics and Comparative Literature at Emory University. He is the author of *Unruly Eloquence: Lucian and the Comedy of Traditions* (Cambridge, Mass., 1989), awarded the Wilson Prize by Harvard University Press. He is also editor and translator (with Daniel Kinney) of Petronius's *Satyrica* (Berkeley and Los Angeles 1996). His current projects include a collection of articles entitled *Bahktin and the Classics* and a comparative study of the origins of fiction in the West.

DISKIN CLAY is Professor of Classical Studies at Duke University. His publications have been in Greek literature and philosophy and include *Sophocles: Oedipus the King* (with Stephen Berg; Oxford 1978), *Lucretius and Epicurus* (Ithaca 1983), *John Locke: Questions concerning the Law of Nature* (with Jenny Strauss Clay and Robert Horwitz; Ithaca 1990), and the monographs *The Philosophical Inscription of Diogenes of Oenoanda* and *Lucian of Samosata: Four Philosophical Lives* for *Aufstieg und Niedergang der Römischen Welt* (Berlin 1990, 1992). He has just completed a book on Plato for the Hermes Guides series for Yale University Press.

MARIE-ODILE GOULET-CAZÉ, coeditor of this volume, is Director of Research at the Centre National de la Recherche Scientifique, Paris, and head of the research team Histoire des Doctrines de la Fin de l'Antiquité et du Haut Moyen-Age—L'Année Philologique (U.P.R. 76). Her main field of study is ancient philosophy. She is the author of *L'ascèse cynique* (Paris 1986) and the editor of *Le cynisme ancien et ses prolongements, Actes du Colloque international du C.N.R.S.* (Paris 1993). With other members of U.P.R. 76, she published *Porphyry, La vie de Plotin*, 2 vols. (Paris 1982, 1992). She is also contributing to a new collective translation of Diogenes Laertius.

MIRIAM GRIFFIN is the Tutorial Fellow in Ancient History at Somerville College, Oxford, and in charge of ancient history at Trinity College, Oxford. She is the author of *Seneca, a Philosopher in Politics* (Oxford 1976; reissued with Postscript, 1992), of *Nero, the End of a Dynasty* (London 1984), and (with E. M. Atkins) of *Cicero: On Duties* (Cambridge 1991). She is also coeditor with Jonathan Barnes of *Philosophia Togata* (Oxford 1989) and of its forthcoming sequel *Plato and Aristotle at Rome*. She is currently working on a commentary on Seneca's *De Beneficiis*.

DANIEL KINNEY is Associate Professor of English and Director of the Comparative Literature Program at the University of Virginia. He has written several studies of medieval and Renaissance engagements with classical culture and won prizes for editions and translations of Latin writings by Sir Thomas More and Abraham Cowley. With R. Bracht Branham he has also translated Petronius's *Satyrica* (Berkeley and Los Angeles 1996).

DEREK KRUEGER is Assistant Professor of Religious Studies at the University of North Carolina at Greensboro. He is the author of *Symeon the Holy Fool: Leontius's Life and the Late Antique City* (Berkeley and Los Angeles 1996). He is currently at work on a study of theology, narrative, and aesthetics in early Byzantine saints' lives.

A. A. LONG is Professor of Classics and Irving Stone Professor of Literature at the University of California at Berkeley. He is the author of *Language and Thought in Sophocles* (1968), *Hellenistic Philosophy* (2d ed. 1986), *Stoic Studies* (1996); coauthor (with D. N. Sedley) of *The Hellenistic Philosophers* (1987), and (with G. Bastianini) of *Hierocles* (1992); and editor of *Problems in Stoicism* (1971), (with J. Dillon) of *The Question of Eclecticism* (1988), and (with A. Bulloch et al.) of *Images and Ideologies* (1993).

R. P. MARTIN is Professor of Classics at Princeton University. He is the author of *Healing, Sacrifice, and Battle* (Innsbruck 1983), *The Language of Heroes: Speech and Performance in the Iliad* (Ithaca 1989), and articles on Greek poetry, myth, and folklore. He is currently completing a book on Telemachus, *The Trickster's Son: The Generation of the Odyssey.*

S. MATTON is Researcher in the History of Philosophy at the Centre National de la Recherche Scientifique, Paris. He is the founder and director of *Chrysopoeia*, a journal devoted to the history of alchemy. In addition to many articles, he produced a critical edition of the *De Pulchro* and the *Opuscula Inedita* of F. Cattani da Diacceto [1466–1522] (Pisa 1986); he is also editor with Professor J.-C. Margolin of *Alchimie et philosophie à la Renaissance* (Paris 1993).

JOHN L. MOLES is Reader in Classics at the University of Durham (England). He is the author of *Plutarch: Cicero* (Warminster 1989) and of numerous articles on Plutarch, Dio Chrysostom, Cynicism, and ancient historiography and biography. He is currently working on an edition of Plutarch's *Life of Brutus*.

HEINRICH NIEHUES-PRÖBSTING is Professor of Philosophy in Erfurt. His main interests are the philosophy of rhetoric, aesthetics, the history of philosophy, cynicism in the ancient and the modern sense, phenomenology, and Platonism. His publications include *Der Kynismus des Diogenes und der Begriff des Zynismus* (2d ed. Frankfurt a.M. 1988), *Überredung zur Einsicht: Der Zusammenhang von Philosophie und Rhetorik bei Platon und in der Phänomenologie* (Frankfurt a.M. 1987), "Ästhetik und Rhetorik in der *Geburt der Tragödie*" in *Nietzsche oder 'Die Sprache ist Rhetorik'* (Munich 1994), and "Das Ende der Rhetorik und der Anfang der Geisteswissenschaften" in *Mesotes: Zeitschrift für philosophischen Ost-West-Dialog* 1 (1994).

J. I. PORTER is Associate Professor of Classics and Comparative Literature at the University of Michigan. He is the author of *Nietzsche's Atoms* (Stanford, forthcoming) and of articles on classical and modern literature and literary theory. He is currently completing *The Material Sublime,* a book on noncanonical poetics in classical antiquity.

JOEL C. RELIHAN is Chair of the Department of Classics at Wheaton College and the author of *Ancient Menippean Satire* (Baltimore 1993). He is currently finishing a book on Boethius and beginning work on a new translation of *The Consolation of Philosophy.*

JAMES ROMM is Assistant Professor of Classics at Bard College. His article in this volume is adapted from his book *The Edges of the Earth in Ancient Thought: Geography, Exploration and Fiction* (Princeton 1992). Currently he is working on a study of Herodotus.

Selected and Annotated Bibliography

The editors have based this bibliography on an earlier version by A.A. Long.

Works on the Ancient Cynics

Until recently there was no authoritative collection of the evidence on the early Cynics. That gap has now been filled by G. Giannantoni in his monumental *Socratis et Socraticorum Reliquiae,* 4 vols. (Naples 1990), parts of which Giannantoni had previously published under the title *Socraticorum Reliquiae* (Naples 1986). Volume 2 of Giannantoni's 1990 work includes the fragments and testimonia for Antisthenes, Diogenes, Crates, and minor Cynics; and extensive notes on these texts are included in volume 4. (For Crates, there is also the edition of E. Diehl, *Anthologia Lyrica Graeca* 1 [Leipzig 1958]; and for Teles, the edition of O. Hense, *Teletis Reliquiae* [Freiburg 1889]; Spanish translation and commentary by P.P. Fuentes González, *Las diatribas de Teles : estudio introductorio y comentario de los textos conservados,* tesis doctoral, Universidad de Granada, 1990. For text and translation of the pseudo-Cynic letters, see A.J. Malherbe, *The Cynic Epistles* (Missoula 1977) and E. Müseler, *Die Kynikerbriefe,* 2 vols. (Paderborn 1994). A.G. Gerhard (*Phoinix von Kolophon* [Leipzig 1909]) and J.F. Kindstrand (*Bion of Borysthenes* [Uppsala 1976]) should be consulted on the language and literary influence of Cynicism in the early Hellenistic period; for a brief summary, see A.A. Long, *Cambridge History of Classical Literature,* vol. 1, *Greece* (Cambridge 1985) 637–39, 852–54.

On Antisthenes, Fernanda Decleva Caizzi's collection and notes, *Antisthenis Fragmenta* (Milan 1966), remains extremely useful, as does her general study "Antistene," *Studi Urbinati* 1 (1964) 25–76. There is nothing comparable in English, though W.K.C. Guthrie's scattered remarks in *A History of Greek Philosophy,* part 1, vol. 3 (Cambridge 1969), are sensible so far as they go. And we now have a French translation and comprehensive dossier for the declamations attributed to Antisthenes: see M.-O.

Goulet-Cazé, *Sophiēs Maiētores, "Chercheurs de Sagesse", Hommage à Jean Pepin,* Collection des Études Augustiniennes, Serie Antiquité 131 (Paris 1992), 5–36.
For a pioneering study of the sources of early Cynicism, see K. von Fritz, *Quellen-untersuchunen zur Leben und Philosophie des Diogenes von Sinope,* Philologus Suppl. 18 (Leipzig 1926); but essential reading on the doxographical tradition underlying Diogenes Laertius's treatment of the Cynic Diogenes now includes J. Mansfeld, "Diogenes Laertius on Stoic Philosophy," *Elenchos* 7 (1986) 296–382, esp. 317–51 (reprinted with the original pagination in his *Studies in the Historiography of Greek Philosophy* [Assen 1990]); D. Hahm, "Diogenes Laertius VII: On the Stoics," *ANRW* 2.36.6 (Berlin 1992) esp. 4082–4105; and M.-O. Goulet-Cazé, "Le livre VI de Diogène Laërce: Analyse de sa structure et réflexions méthodologiques," *ANRW* 2.36.6 (Berlin 1992), 3880–4048.
The best general introduction to the Cynic tradition in English is still D. R. Dudley, *A History of Cynicism from Diogenes to the Sixth Century* A.D. (London 1937). R. Höistad, *Cynic Hero and Cynic King* (Uppsala 1948), is still worth reading but is vitiated by its rejection of the anecdotal tradition. (Höistad's views are briefly summarized in his article "Cynicism" in P. H. Wiener, ed., *The Dictionary of the History of Ideas* [New York 1973]). F. Sayre, *The Greek Cynics* (Baltimore 1949), is often eccentric, but does survey much of the ancient evidence in English. For a much more sophisticated treatment than that offered by these scholars, see H. Niehues-Pröbsting, *Der Kynismus des Diogenes und der Begriff des Kynismus* (Munich 1979). This book—probably the best account of the whole tradition, ancient and modern, in one volume—is particularly informative on the modern reception of Cynicism, especially that of Nietzsche. For an excellent survey of the ancient Cynics, see F. Decleva Caizzi, "I cinici," in *Dizionario degli scrittori greci e latini* (1988) 503–11. The central idea of Diogenes' ethics are lucidly discussed by M.-O. Goulet-Cazé in a work broader in scope than its title suggests: *L'ascèse cynique: Un commentaire de Diogène Laërce VI 70–71* (Paris 1986). For a valuable study of Onesicritus, which includes a well-balanced account of Diogenes, see T. S. Brown, *Onesicritus* (Berkeley and Los Angeles 1949). For a comprehensive survey of Cynicism in the Roman empire, see M.-O. Goulet-Cazé, "Le cynisme à l'époque impériale," *ANRW* 2.36.4 (Berlin 1990), 2720–2833. M. Billerbeck, ed., *Die Kyniker in der modernen Forschung* (Amsterdam 1991), provides a useful selection of influential articles and an excellent general bibliography, which is now supplemented by L.E. Navia, *The Philosophy of Cynicism: An Annotated Bibliography* (London, 1995). For a valuable collection of current work on the Cynics, see *Le cynisme ancien et ses prolongements: Actes du Colloque international du C.N.R.S.,* ed. M.-O. Goulet-Cazé and R. Goulet (Paris 1993).
For the idea of the *spoudogeloios* (seriocomic), which comes up so often in these pages, see R. Bracht Branham, *Unruly Eloquence: Lucian and the Comedy of Traditions* (Cambridge, Mass., 1989), especially chapter 1; and K. Döring, " 'Spielereien, mit verdecktem Ernst vermischt': Unterhaltsame Formen literarischer Wissenvermittlung bei Diogenes von Sinope und den frühen Kynikern," in *Vermittlung und Tradierung von Wissen in der griechischen Kultur,* ed. W. Kullmann and J. Althof (Tübingen 1993), 337–52.
For Stoic use of Cynicism, see J. M. Rist, *Stoic Philosophy* (Cambridge 1969); A. M. Ioppolo, *Aristone di Chio e lo stoicismo antico* (Naples 1980); and M. Schofield, *The Stoic Idea of the City* (Cambridge 1991), especially the appendixes.
For English translations of our major sources, see s.v. "Cynics" in the *Routledge Encyclopedia of Philosophy* (forthcoming).

Works on the Reception of Cynicism

For the reception of Cynicism (in addition to the works cited in n. 60 to the Introduction) see the works listed below.

Bakhtin, M. *The Dialogic Imagination.* Trans. C. Emerson and M. Holquist. Austin 1981.
———. *Problems of Dostoevsky's Poetics.* Trans. C. Emerson. Minneapolis 1984.
———. *Rabelais and His World.* Trans. H. Iswolsky. Bloomington 1984.
Blanchard, W.S. *Scholars' Bedlam: Menippean Satire in the Renaissance.* Lewisburg, Pa. 1995.
Downing, F.G. *Cynics and Christian Origins.* Edinburgh 1992.
Flynn, T. "Foucault as Parrhesiast: His Last Course at the Collège de France (1984)." In *Final Foucault,* ed. J. Bernauer and D. Rasmussen. Cambridge, Mass., 1988.
Gutas, D. "Sayings by Diogenes Preserved in Arabic." In *Le cynisme ancien et ses prolongements,* see M.-O. Goulet-Cazé and R. Goulet, 475–519. Paris 1993.
Krueger, D. *Symeon the Holy Fool: Leontius's "Life" and the Late Antique City.* Berkeley and Los Angeles 1995.
Marshall, P. *Demanding the Impossible: A History of Anarchism.* London 1992.
Onfray, M. *Cynismes: Portrait du philosophie en chien.* Paris 1990.
Relihan, J.C. *Ancient Menippean Satire.* Baltimore 1992.
Sloterdijk, P. *Critique of Cynical Reason.* Trans. M. Eldred. Minneapolis 1987.

Index Locorum

Diogenes Sinopensis

Index Nominum

Compositor:	G&S Typesetters, Inc.
Text:	10/12 Times Roman
Display:	Bodoni
Printer:	Thomson-Shore, Inc.
Binder:	Thomson-Shore, Inc.
Indices:	Catherine Joubaud